"Little by little, with a raft of new insights, and a clear and empathetic eye, Nicholas Stargardt's remarkable new book transforms our view of something we thought we already understood: the German population's evolving attitudes during the war. For the first time, the wartime chronology of German sentiment, of popular hopes and fears, realism and fantasy, becomes truly visible. A powerful and compelling account."—Mark Roseman, Professor of History, Indiana University

"Why did most Germans, reluctant to enter a second world war in 1939, ultimately unify behind an effort that by 1943 seemed doomed to failure? Weaving together first-person testimonies drawn from diaries, memoirs and letters, Nicholas Stargardt provides insightful, illuminating, complex and convincing answers in this big book. Seven decades and a mountain of monographs later, I wouldn't have thought there'd be much more to say about WWII. Stargardt has proven me wrong."—Robert Moeller, Professor of History, University of California, Irvine

"Forcing reflection on many different levels, Nicholas Stargardt's book pierces through the tangles of both propaganda and moralism to offer a searching and compulsively readable account of a conflict that was understood from within as a German, not just a Nazi, war. Stargardt negotiates the considerable risks of writing from inside German experiences of this brutally destructive war with subtlety, humanity and wisdom. This is a rich and deeply impressive lesson in ethical understanding without sacrifice of historical distance or critical judgment."
—Jane Caplan, Emeritus Fellow, St Antony's College, Oxford

THE GERMAN WAR

THE GERMAN WAR

A Nation Under Arms, 1939–1945

CITIZENS AND SOLDIERS

Nicholas Stargardt

BASIC BOOKS
A Member of the Perseus Books Group
New York

Books published by Basic Books are available at special discounts for bulk purchases in the United States by corporations, institutions, and other organizations. For more information, please contact the Special Markets Department at the Perseus Books Group, 2300 Chestnut Street, Suite 200, Philadelphia, PA 19103, or call (800) 810-4145, ext. 5000, or e-mail special.markets@perseusbooks.com.

A catalog record for this book is available from the Library of Congress.
Library of Congress Catalog Number: 2015945013
ISBN: 978-0-465-01899-4 (HC)
ISBN: 978-0-465-07397-9 (EB)

First published in Great Britain in 2015 by The Bodley Head

10 9 8 7

Contents

Maps

under British occupation from April 1940

to Iceland

Faroe Islands

Atlantic Ocean

NORWAY
June 1940

Oslo○

Stavanger○

Skagerrak

SWEDE

Kattegat

North Sea

DENMARK
April 1940

Copenhagen○

Malm.

○Kiel

○Belfast

Wilhelmshaven○

○Hamburg

○Bremen

Amsterdam○

NETHERLANDS

Hanover○

Berlin□

○Dublin

IRELAND

GREAT BRITAIN

London○

Rotterdam○

May 1940

GERMANY

○Leip.

Calais○

Brussels○

○Cologne

Le Havre○

BELGIUM

Brest○

Paris○

○Frankfurt

Pra

June 1940

Nuremberg○

○Stuttgart

Munich○

Austr

Atlantic Ocean

FRANCE

Vichy○

○Berne

SWITZERLAND

Lyon○

Vichy-France
(June 1940)

○Milan

Tries

○Turin

Venice

○Toulouse

○Genoa

San Marino○

SPAIN

0   100   200   300 km

Marseilles○

Mediterranean Sea

Corsica

ITALY

The first year of the war (Sep. 1939 – Aug. 1940)

Legend:
- German advance in the west and in Norway, 1940
- Germany, its allies and occupied territories
- Occupied territories, April/June 1940
- German-Soviet line of partition, Oct. 1940
- Territories occupied by the Soviet Union, 1939–40
- Occupied by Italy, 1939
- Annexed by Hungary, 1938–40
- Borders of 1938

FINLAND

Karelian Isthmus March 1940

Lake Ladoga

Helsinki

Leningrad

Narva

Novgorod

Tallinn

Estonia

Stockholm

Pskov

Riga

Latvia

August 1940

Baltic Sea

Lithuania

Vilno Region Lithuanian from 28 Oct. 1939

Memel

Kaunas

Vilnius

Minsk

Königsberg

Belorussia

Danzig

East Prussia

SOVIET UNION

Białystok occupied in 1939

Pinsk

Kharkov

Posen

Warsaw

Brest

Lublin

Kiev

Zhitomir

General Government

Rowne

Dniepropetrovsk

Breslau

Ukraine

Cracow

Lwów

Vinnitsa

otectorate f Bohemia-Moravia

SLOVAKIA
Germany's ally from 24 Nov. 1940

1939

Chernivtsi

Kherson

ienna

1938

Kishinev

Odessa

Crimea

Budapest

Hungarian from Aug. 1940

Bessarabia Juni 1940

Cluj

Sevastopol

Yalta

HUNGARY
Germany's ally from 20 Nov. 1940

ROMANIA
Germany's ally from 23 Nov. 1940

lovenia

iume

Croatia

Bucharest

Black Sea

Belgrade

Bulgarian from Aug. 1940

Varna

YUGOSLAVIA

Serbia

Sarajevo

BULGARIA

Burgas

Sofia

Istanbul

TURKEY

Adriatic Sea

Skopje

The invasion
of the Soviet Union
June–December 1941

Soviet counter-offensive
6 December 1941 to end of March 1942

FINLAND
Lake Ladoga
Helsinki
Vyborg
Leningrad
Baltic Sea
Tallinn
Lake Peipus
Novgorod
SOVIET UNION
Demyansk
Riga
Kalinin
Memel
Daugavpils
Polotsk
Rzhev
Moscow
Vyaz'ma
Kolomna
Königsberg
Kaunas
Vitebsk
Tula
Mikhailov
Vilnius
Smolensk
Minsk
Mogilev
Białystok
Bryansk
Orel
Yelets
Brest-Litovsk
Pinsk
Gomel
Voronezh
Warsaw
Pripet Marshes
Kursk
Lublin
Konotop
Belgorod
Lwów
Kiev
Kharkov
Izyum
Dniepropetrovsk
Rostov

0   100   200   300 km

Kalinin
30
20
WESTERN FRONT
ZHUKOV
Rzhev
9th ARMY
Strauß
16
Moscow
Melitopol
4th ARMY
Hoepner
Borodino
5
Sea of Asov
Vyaz'ma
33
Podolsk
Crimea
Kerch
Yartsevo
43
Kolomna
Novorossiysk
49
Kashira
10
4th ARMY
Kluge
Kaluga
50
Tula
Roslavl
Mikhailov
Black Sea
Belyov
2nd ARMY
Guderian
Bryansk
Mzensk
61
Orel

➜ Soviet offensive
◼ retaken by Feb. 1942

0   50 100 150 km

➜ Soviet offensive
◼ retaken by Soviet forces (end of 1941 to end of March 1942)

Concentration camps in Europe (1937–1943)

- ■ Main concentrations camps (with year of building)
- ◆ Death camps (built 1941–2)
- ⬤ Euthanasia centres
- ● Places of mass murder
- ▲ Main ghettos
- ○ Cities
- –·–·– International borders
- ············ Lines of partition 1939–41

SWEDEN

DENMARK

North
Sea

○ Copenhagen

Neuengamme ■   ○ Rostock

Westerbork ▲   ■ Esterwegen   ○ Hamburg
                                      Ravensbrück ○ Stettin
NETHERLANDS   ○ Bremen   ■ 1936
Amsterdam ○   ■ Bergen-Belsen
                                1936 ■ Sachsenhausen
                   ○ Hanover   ○ Berlin
's-Hertogenbosch ■ 1943 Mittelbau-Dora ■   1939   ○ Pose
Calais ○   1943 Magde-   ⬤ Brandenburg
          Malines ▲   burg   Gro
   ○ Brussels   ■ Sachsenburg   Rose
BELGIUM   ○ Cologne 1937 ■ ⬤ Bernburg Sonnen- ■ 1
         1941 ⬤ Hadamar Buchenwald 1939 ○ Leipzig stein
                                  Weimar ○ Dresden ○ 1939 Br
Compiègne   GERMANY   Theresienstadt ▲■
▲   Eichberg ⬤ ○ Frankfurt   1939/41
   ▲ Drancy   ○ Luxembourg   ○ Prague
Paris ○   Metz ○   Flossenbürg ■
                                1938   CZECHO
      ○ Strasbourg Stuttgart Nuremberg ○
Natzweiler ■   ○ Grafeneck
                        1939 ⬤   1941
                     Dachau   ○ Linz ■ Mauthau
                     ■ 1933   ○ Vienna
          ○ Basle Munich ○   1939 ⬤
          ○ Berne Eglfing-Haar ⬤ ○ Schloß Hartheim
FRANCE   SWITZERLAND   ○ Salzburg
Lyon ○   ○ Innsbruck   AUSTRIA

                              ▲ Bolzano
                                        Loborgrad D
                              Laibach ○ 1941 ■
         ○ Turin ▲○ Milan   Zagreb ○
                              Trieste ○ Jasenovac
                         ○ Venice Fiume ○ 1941 S
Genoa ○   ▲ Fossoli   Jadovno ○ Grad
                    ○ Bologna   1941
                  ITALY   Kausc
Marseilles ○ Nice ○   ⎇ Adriatic
         ○ Florence   Sea

0   50   100   150 km

LATVIA

1941 Kaiserwald
Riga ○ ○ Rumbuli
Jungernhof ○ △ 1941
1942

Memel ○

LITHUANIA

Vitebsk ○
Smolensk ○
△

Kaunas
□ △
○

Königsberg ○

1941
Vilnius △ ○ ○ Ponar
Minsk ○ △

Belorussia

Stutthof □
1939
East Prussia

Maly Trostinets ● 1942

SOVIET UNION

Gomel ○

Białystok △

POLAND

Pripet

1942 ◆
Treblinka

lmno △ ■
1941
Warsaw
1943
Radom ○ △

Babi Yar ○ ○ Kiev
1941

Drobitsky Yar
○ ○ 1941
Kharkov

Łódź △

1943 ◆
Sobibór
1942

Zhitomir ●

Majdanek △ ◆
Częstochowa ◆ ○ Lublin

Kielce
snowiec ○ △ △ △ ○ Nisko
Płaszów ■ △ Bełżec
schwitz △ ○ Tarno 1941 △ ○ Janowska
1940 Cracow Lwów 1941
Pezemys

Ukraine

Bar ■
1941

SLOVAKIA

slava ○

Budapest ○

HUNGARY

Balanovka ■
1942
Edineţ ■ 1941

Czernowitz/
Chernivtsi ○

Kishinev ○

Bessarabia

Odessa ○

Klausenburg ○

Transylvania

Kronstadt ○

Timişoara ○

ROMANIA

akovo ■
1941
Tašmajdan ■ △ Zemun
1941 □
Belgrade
△ □ Sajmište
Šabac 1941

Bucharest ○

Wallachia

Constanţa ○

Danube

Black Sea

Sarajevo ○
snia
Serbia

YUGOSLAVIA

Niš ○

BULGARIA

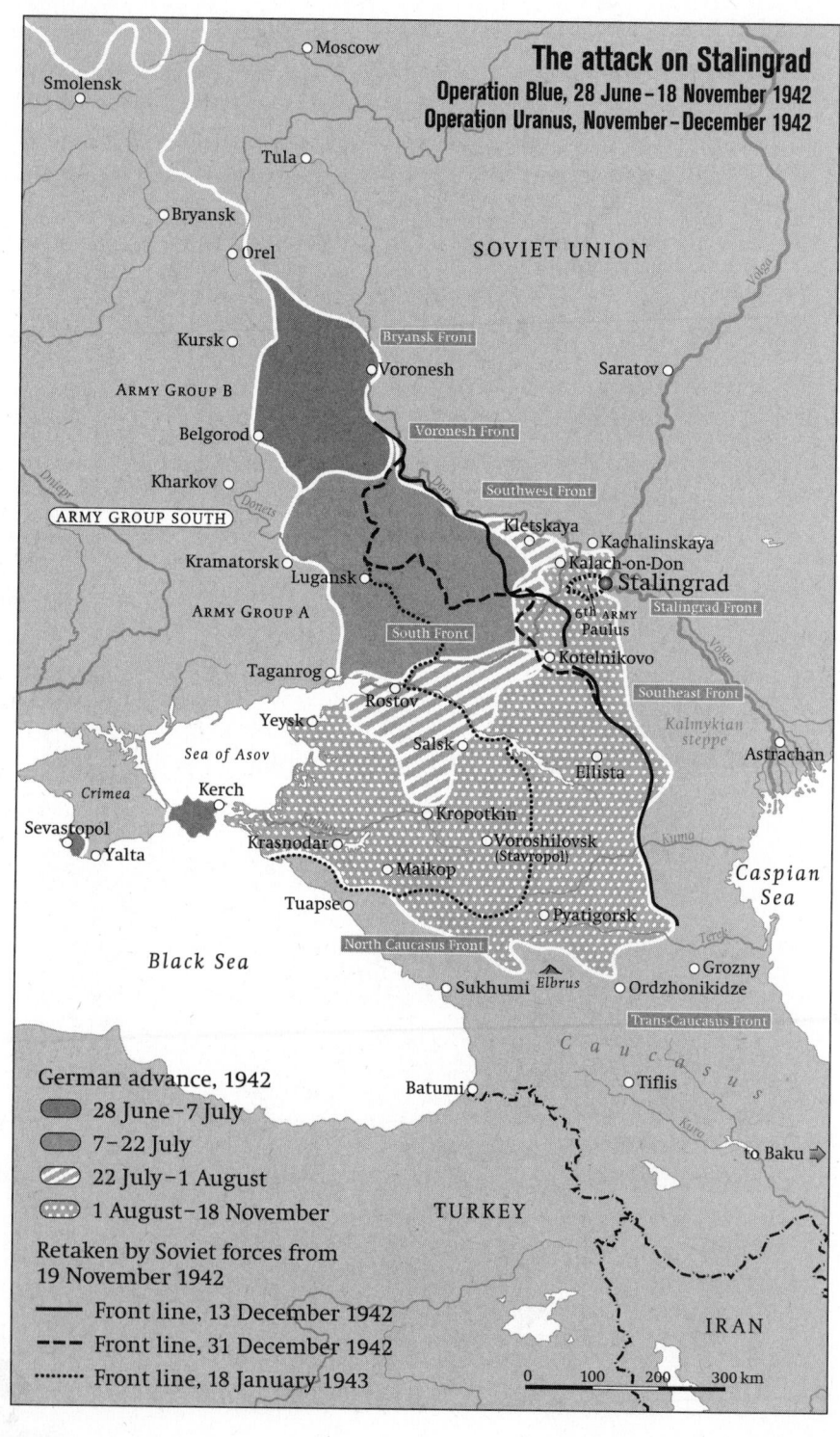

The attack on Stalingrad
Operation Blue, 28 June – 18 November 1942
Operation Uranus, November – December 1942

German advance, 1942
28 June – 7 July
7 – 22 July
22 July – 1 August
1 August – 18 November

Retaken by Soviet forces from
19 November 1942

—— Front line, 13 December 1942
--- Front line, 31 December 1942
······ Front line, 18 January 1943

0   100   200   300 km

Bombing and evacuation (until 30 Sep. 1944)

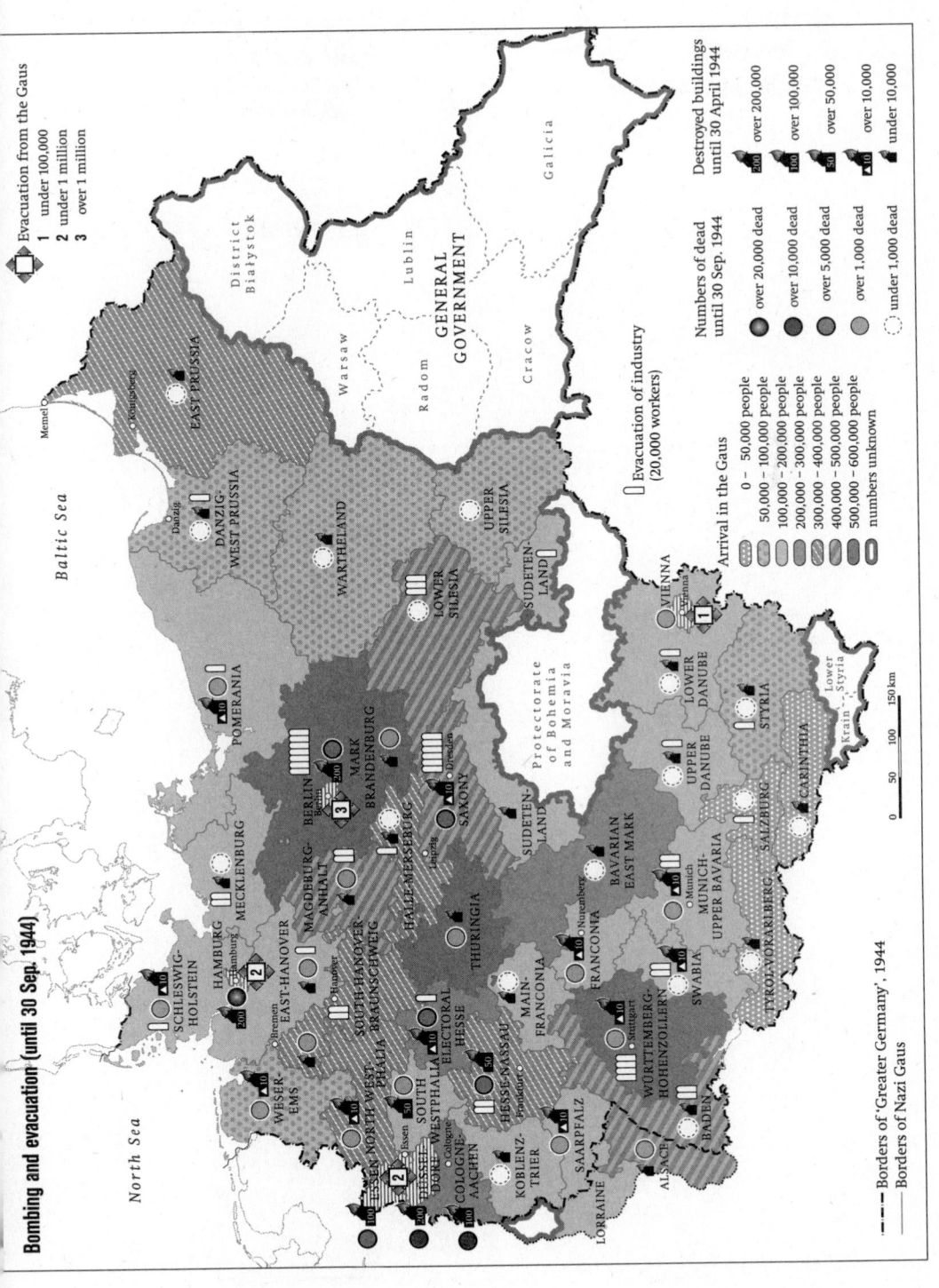

Evacuation from the Gaus
1 under 100,000
2 under 1 million
3 over 1 million

Evacuation of industry (20,000 workers)

Arrival in the Gaus
0 – 50,000 people
50,000 – 100,000 people
100,000 – 200,000 people
200,000 – 300,000 people
300,000 – 400,000 people
400,000 – 500,000 people
500,000 – 600,000 people
numbers unknown

Numbers of dead until 30 Sep. 1944
over 20,000 dead
over 10,000 dead
over 5,000 dead
over 1,000 dead
under 1,000 dead

Destroyed buildings until 30 April 1944
200 over 200,000
100 over 100,000
50 over 50,000
10 over 10,000
under 10,000

--- Borders of 'Greater Germany', 1944
— Borders of Nazi Gaus

North Sea
Baltic Sea

SCHLESWIG-HOLSTEIN
HAMBURG
MECKLENBURG
POMERANIA
WESER-EMS
EAST-HANOVER
SOUTH-HANOVER BRAUNSCHWEIG
MAGDEBURG-ANHALT
MARK BRANDENBURG
BERLIN
Berlin
Dresden
HALLE-MERSEBURG
SAXONY
Leipzig
THURINGIA
ESSEN
DÜSSELDORF
SOUTH WESTPHALIA
NORTH WESTPHALIA
Cologne
COLOGNE
AACHEN
KOBLENZ-TRIER
ELECTORAL HESSE
HESSE-NASSAU
Frankfurt
MAIN-FRANCONIA
SAARPFALZ
LORRAINE
ALSACE
BADEN
WÜRTTEMBERG-HOHENZOLLERN
Stuttgart
SWABIA
FRANCONIA
Nuremberg
BAVARIAN EAST MARK
MUNICH-UPPER BAVARIA
Munich
TYROL-VORARLBERG
SALZBURG
UPPER DANUBE
LOWER DANUBE
VIENNA
Vienna
STYRIA
CARINTHIA
Lower Styria
Krain

Memel
Königsberg
EAST PRUSSIA
Danzig
DANZIG-WEST PRUSSIA
WARTHELAND
LOWER SILESIA
UPPER SILESIA
SUDETEN-LAND
Protectorate of Bohemia and Moravia

District Białystok
Warsaw
Lublin
Radom
GENERAL GOVERNMENT
Cracow
Galicia

Bremen
Hamburg

0   50   100   150 km

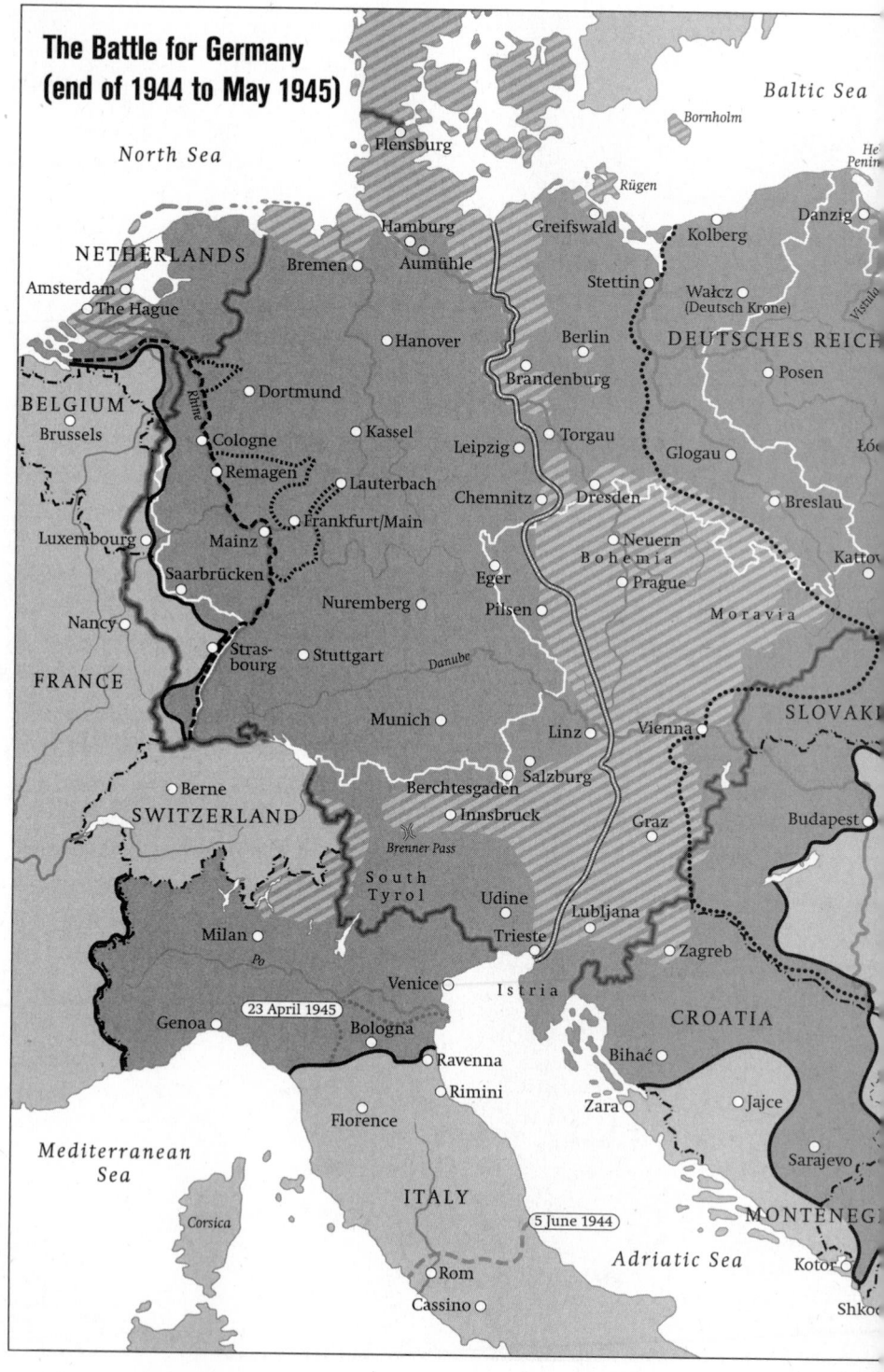

**The Battle for Germany
(end of 1944 to May 1945)**

North Sea

Baltic Sea

Bornholm

Rügen

*He
Penin*

Flensburg

Hamburg
Aumühle

Greifswald

Kolberg

Danzig

NETHERLANDS

Bremen

Stettin

Wałcz
(Deutsch Krone)

Vistula

Amsterdam
The Hague

Hanover

Berlin

DEUTSCHES REICH

Posen

BELGIUM

Dortmund

Brandenburg

Brussels

Cologne

Kassel

Leipzig

Torgau

Glogau

Łó

Rhine

Remagen

Lauterbach

Chemnitz

Dresden

Breslau

Luxembourg

Mainz

Frankfurt/Main

Neuern

Bohemia

Kattov

Saarbrücken

Eger

Prague

Nancy

Nuremberg

Pilsen

Moravia

Strasbourg

Stuttgart

Danube

FRANCE

Munich

Linz

Vienna

SLOVAKI

Berne

SWITZERLAND

Salzburg

Berchtesgaden

Innsbruck

Graz

Budapest

Brenner Pass

*South
Tyrol*

Udine

Lubljana

Milan

Trieste

Zagreb

Po

Venice

Istria

CROATIA

Genoa

23 April 1945

Bologna

Bihać

Ravenna

Rimini

Zara

Jajce

Florence

*Mediterranean
Sea*

Corsica

ITALY

5 June 1944

Adriatic Sea

Sarajevo

MONTENEG

Kotor

Rom

Cassino

Shko

Legend:

- Territory held by Germany on 16 Dec. 1944
- Front line on 16 Dec. 1944
- Front line on 7 March 1945
- Front line on 28 March 1945
- Front line on 16 April 1945
- Demarcation line between Soviet troops and Western Allies after 12 May 1945
- Territory held by German troops at the beginning of May 1945
- 'Greater Germany'
- Borders of Germany and Danzig in 1937

Memel

REICH COMMISSARIAT EAST

Königsberg

Kaunas

Vilnius

East Prussia

Minsk

Białystok

Warsaw

Siedlce

Brest-Litovsk

SOVIET UNION

Lublin

Lutsk

Rovno

Kiev

Zhitomir

General Government

Berdichev

cracow

Lwów

Vinnitsa

REICH COMMISSARIAT UKRAINE

Uman

Uzhhorod (Ungvar)

Cernauti

Dniester

Prut

Dniepr

HUNGARY

Debrecen

Iaşi

Cluj (Klausenburg)

Kishinev

Odessa

Crimea

Arad

Sibiu

Izmail (Ismail)

Sevastopol

ROMANIA

Ploieşti

Belgrade

Bukarest

Constanţa

Craiova

Danube

SERBIA

Black Sea

Nisch

Varna

Sofia

Burgas

BULGARIA

Skopje

TURKEY (neutral)

List of Illustrations

Irene Reitz and Ernst Guicking (*estate of Irene and Ernst Guicking, reproduced courtesy of Bernhild Breithaupt*).

Wilm and Helmut Hosenfeld (*estate of Wilm Hosenfeld, reproduced courtesy of Detlev Hosenfeld*).

August and Karl-Christoph Töpperwien (*estate of August Töpperwien, reproduced courtesy of Lorenz Töpperwien*).

Kazimiera Mika with her sister, killed by a German plane (*Julien Bryan/United States Holocaust Memorial Museum #50897*).

View from the nose of a Heinkel He III P bomber (*Bundesarchiv Bild 183-S52911*).

Frieda and Josef Rimpl's wedding (*Jehovas Zeugen in Deutschland*).

Ernst Guicking in France (*estate of Irene and Ernst Guicking, reproduced courtesy of Bernhild Breithaupt*).

Practising air raid defence in Berlin, 1939 (*Bildagentur der Stiftung Preußischer Kulturbesitz 30013762*).

Liselotte Purper with her Rolleiflex (*Bildagentur der Stiftung Preußischer Kulturbesitz 20014683*)

Jews crossing from one part of the Łódź ghetto to another (*Deutsches Historisches Museum, Orgel-Köhne 4762/12*).

Girls from Hagen on the Baltic coast (*courtesy of Gerhard Sollbach*).

Female anti-aircraft personnel repairing a search light (*Bundesarchiv Bild 101I-674-7798-04*).

Commemorating the dead of the Hamburg firestorm (*Staatsarchiv Hamburg*).

Flight from East Prussia across the Frische Nehrung, January / February 1945 (*Bildagentur der Stiftung Preußischer Kulturbesitz 00012112*).

Dead concentration camp prisoners on a train, April 1945 (*United States Holocaust Memorial Museum 06531*).

Teenage soldiers surrender at Veckerhagen (*Bundesarchiv Bild 146-1971-053-21*).

Eva and Victor Klemperer outside their home in Dölzschen in Saxony, c.1940 (*DDP Images*).

Red Army Lieutenant Vladimir Gelfand and Berlin girlfriend (*courtesy of Vitaly Gelfand*).

Berliners swimming near the remains of the Zoo bunker, 1945 (*Bundesarchiv Bild 146-1982-028-14*).

Black market in Berlin (*Deutsches Historisches Museum, GG 72/20*).

Missing children poster (*Bildagentur der Stiftung Preußischer Kulturbesitz 30008096*).

Cellar dwelling in Hamburg, July 1947 (*reproduced from Victor Gollancz, In Darkest Germany, 1947*).

Rehabilitation of a war amputee (*Deutsches Historisches Museum, Orgel-Köhne 11269/4*).

Preface

This book completes a period of just over twenty years in which I have tried to understand the experience of those who lived in Germany and under German occupation during the Second World War. It is also a book I did not originally intend to write. In 2005, I promised myself and anyone else who would listen that having just completed *Witnesses of War: Children's Lives under the Nazis*, I would not be writing anything more on children, the Holocaust or Nazi Germany. This book began as a short essay about what Germans were fighting for, as something that I felt needed to be said before I could move on, and started to take shape as something far bigger during a sabbatical year spent at the Free University in Berlin in 2006–7.

There are some clear continuities between the two books, most obviously my interest in exploring the subjective dimensions of social history, using the contemporary record to work out how people judged and understood events while they were unfolding around them and before they knew the eventual outcome. There are also some clear differences. In *Witnesses of War*, I wanted above all to treat children as social actors in their own right; I also set out to juxtapose the irreconcilable perspectives of children divided by war and racist persecution into victors and vanquished. *The German War* presents a different problem: how to uncover the fears and hopes of the society from which the victors and perpetrators came in order to understand how Germans justified this war to themselves. To focus on this question I have tried to develop both a sense of breadth and of depth: breadth by using 'macro' snapshots of opinion, drawing on what eavesdropping reporters for the regime picked up from public conversations or military censors from sampling the mail bags; depth by following a select cast of individuals, drawn from a wide range of backgrounds, over a considerable period of time, exploring how their personal hopes and plans were entwined with their changing experience of the war. Doing this has made the voices of the victims less prominent than in *Witnesses of War* but they are never absent: without their contrasting perspective, we would not know how differently – and often solipsistically – Germans framed their understanding of the war.

One of the key ingredients of this book are the collections of letters between lovers, close friends, parents and children, and married couples. Many historians have used these kinds of sources, but often to different effect. For example, the Bibliothek für Zeitgeschichte in Stuttgart has a famous collection of some 25,000 letters assembled by Reinhold Sterz. Unfortunately, the letters were catalogued by time and not by author, so that they provide a snap-shot of subjective opinions at particular moments of the war, without it being possible to test how firmly the letter writers held these opinions over any length of time. What guided my selection was the opposite principle: I wanted to read collections of letters in which both sides of the correspondence are preserved and which continued for several years at least, so that it would be possible to see how the personal relationships between the correspondents – their principal purpose in writing at all – developed and altered over the course of the war. This allows us to reconstruct more carefully the private prisms through which individuals viewed major events. It is the kind of research which historians of the First World War have been developing since the 1990s and I have learned a great deal from Christa Hämmerle about how to do this.

I was particularly fortunate in having access to the private archive assembled by Walter Kempowski while he was still alive, and well remember the generous welcome which Walter and Hildegard Kempowski gave me to their home in Natum: the archive itself is now held at the Akademie der Künste in Berlin. At the Deutsches Tagebucharchiv in Emmendingen, Gerhard Seitz was very helpful, as was Irina Renz at the Bibliothek für Zeitgeschichte in Stuttgart. In Berlin, Andreas Michaelis at the Deutsches Historisches Museum, Veit Didczuneit and Thomas Jander at the Feldpostarchiv of the Museum für Kommunikation and the Bundesarchiv all provided invaluable source materials, as did Christiane Botzet at the Bundesarchiv-Militärarchiv in Freiburg. Klaus Baum and Konrad Schulz from the archive of the Jehovas Zeugen in Deutschland at Selters-Taunus provided copies of the last letters which Jehovah's Witnesses wrote before their execution for refusing to perform military service, and Alexander von Plato at the Institut für Geschichte und Biographie in Lüdenscheid introduced me to the large collection from the early 1950s of schoolchildren's recollections of the war in the Wilhelm Roessler-Archiv. I am grateful too to Li Gerhalter and Günter Müller for mat-erial from the Dokumentation lebensgeschichtliche Aufzeichungen and the Sammlung Frauennachlässe, both at the University of Vienna. I owe a special debt to Jacques Schuhmacher for his indefatigible willingness to help in every way he could at many stages of this research. It was supported financially by the Alexander von Humboldt Foundation and the Leverhulme Trust and I am grateful to both.

The intellectual debts I have accumulated over such a long period are too large and numerous to do justice to. During the year 2006–7 in Berlin, Jürgen Kocka was a wonderful host and many other people made my time in Germany memorable and fruitful. Many friends and colleagues have encouraged me along the way, shared their ideas and findings, giving me a very vivid sense of history as a collective endeavour. Among my wonderful colleagues in Oxford at the History Faculty and Magdalen College, I am particularly grateful to Paul Betts, Laurence Brockliss, Jane Caplan, Martin Conway, Robert Gildea, Ruth Harris, Matt Houlbrook, Jane Humphries, John Nightingale, Sian Pooley and Chris Wickham.

At the Bodley Head I have been privileged to work with Jörg Hensgen, Will Sulkin and, following Will's retirement, Stuart Williams. With her extraordinary energy and acuity, Lara Heimert brought me into the world of Basic Books. Their commitment to publishing books they believe in is incredibly affirming and, time and again, has provided just the kind of assurance I needed. Lara and Jörg acted as twin editors, without ever stepping on each other's toes or mine, with Jörg's taking on the painstaking task of editing page by page. They have been wonderful to work with and I am deeply grateful to all four of them. Clare Alexander and Sally Riley at Aitken-Alexander have remained a pair of fairy godmothers sharing their wisdom and encouraging me throughout. I have been very fortunate.

Without the great intellectual generosity and support of many friends, there probably would have been no book at all. Paul Betts,

Tom Brodie, Stefan Ludwig Hoffmann, Ian Kershaw, Mark Roseman, Jacques Schuhmacher, Jon Waterlow and Bernd Weisbrod all interrupted their own work to read the whole manuscript for me. I am grateful to each of them for making invaluable suggestions, sharing their own research and saving me from making, at least some, historical howlers. Ruth Harris and Lyndal Roper read the whole thing twice and so have both left an indelible imprint on it. At every stage of this project, Lyndal has discussed the key ideas as I was trying to formulate them. I cannot thank her enough.

Nicholas Stargardt
Oxford, 3 June 2015

Dramatis Personae
(in order of appearance)

Ernst Guicking, farmer's son from Hesse, professional soldier, infantryman; and **Irene Reitz**, a florist from Lauterbach, Hesse; they marry during the war.

Wilm Hosenfeld, Catholic, First World War veteran and village schoolteacher in Thalau in Hesse, serves in the German garrison in Warsaw; and his wife **Annemie**, a trained singer and Protestant convert to Catholicism; they have five children.

Jochen Klepper, a writer from Nikolassee, Berlin; married to Johanna, a Jewish convert to Protestantism, with two step-daughters.

Liselotte Purper, photo-journalist from Berlin; and **Kurt Orgel**, jurist from Hamburg, artillery officer; they marry during the war.

Victor Klemperer, Jewish convert to Protestantism, First World War veteran and academic; and his wife **Eva**, a former concert pianist.

August Töpperwien, First World War veteran and Gymnasium teacher from Solingen, officer in charge of prisoners of war; and his wife **Margarete**.

Fritz Probst, a carpenter from Thuringia, building battalion; and his wife **Hildegard**; they have three young children.

Helmut Paulus, doctor's son from Pforzheim and eldest of four teenage children, infantryman.

Hans Albring and **Eugen Altrogge**, from Gelsenkirchen-Buer near Münster, friends and members of Catholic youth movement, signals and infantryman.

Wilhelm Moldenhauer, shopkeeper from Nordstemmen near Hanover, radio operator.

Marianne Strauss, Jewish kindergarten teacher from Essen.

Ursula von Kardorff, journalist from Berlin.

Peter Stölten from Zehlendorf in Berlin, despatch rider and tank commander.

Lisa de Boor, journalist from Marburg; married to Wolf, with three grown-up children: Monika, Anton and Hans.

Willy Reese, trainee bank clerk from Duisburg, infantryman.

Maria Kundera, railway worker at Michelbeuern near Vienna; and **Hans H.**, railwayman's son, paratrooper.

Introduction

The Second World War was a German war like no other. The Nazi regime turned the conflict which it had started into the most horrific war in European history, resorting to genocidal methods well before building the first gas chambers in occupied Poland. The Third Reich was also unique in enacting its own 'total defeat' in 1945, in the process expending and exhausting all the moral and physical reserves of German society. Even the Japanese did not fight to the gates of the Imperial Palace in Tokyo as the Germans fought for the Reich Chancellery in Berlin. To wage a war on this scale the Nazis had to harness levels of social mobilisation and personal commitment which went far deeper than anything they had tried to achieve in the pre-war period. Yet, seventy years on – despite whole libraries of books about the war's origins, course and atrocities – we still do not know what Germans thought they were fighting for or how they managed to continue their war until the bitter end. This book is about how the German people experienced and sustained this war.[1]

Instead of shrinking in significance with the gradual passing of the generations who lived through it, the Second World War has grown in the public imagination. Nowhere more so than in Germany, where the last fifteen years have seen a deluge of films, documentaries, exhibitions and books. Yet both scholarly and popular representations tend towards a fundamentally split view of the conflict, casting Germans as either victims or perpetrators. Over the last decade, the victim narrative has been most prominent, as interviewers have concentrated on unearthing the buried memories of civilians who experienced the fire-bombing of German cities by the RAF and the USAAF, the epic flight ahead of the Red Army and the killing and rape which so often followed. Many of the elderly Germans retelling their most painful memories simply wanted to be heard and to leave a record behind. The media turned the wartime suffering of German civilians into a present-day preoccupation, focusing on sleep deprivation, anxiety attacks and recurring nightmares. Groups of self-designated 'war children' formed and everywhere commentators reached for terms like 'trauma' and 'collective trauma', in a kind of catch-all formula to describe these experiences. Yet talking about trauma tends to emphasise the passivity and innocence of the victims, and it has a strong moral resonance: in the 1980s and 1990s the notion of 'collective trauma' was deployed to encompass the memories of Holocaust survivors, with the promise of 'empowering' the victims by according them political recognition.[2]

Only on the political margin occupied by the extreme Right, which marches each February to commemorate the fire-bombing of Dresden in 1945 with banners proclaiming 'Bombing-Holocaust', does anyone equate the suffering of German civilians with that of the victims of Nazi extermination policies. And even this kind of provocative act is far removed from the unreconstructed nationalism sponsored in 1950s West Germany, where German soldiers were commemorated for the heroism of their 'sacrifice', while any German 'atrocities' were blamed on a handful of intransigent Nazis, in particular the SS. That convenient Cold War excuse of the 'good' Wehrmacht and the 'bad' SS – which helped underpin the rearmament of West Germany as a full member of NATO in the mid-1950s – became unsustainable by the mid-1990s, thanks in no small part to the travelling exhibition of 'Crimes of the Wehrmacht', which showed the photographs of public hangings and mass shootings taken by ordinary soldiers. The public display of private images that soldiers had carried in their uniform pockets alongside photos of their children and wives evoked powerful responses, especially in places such as Austria or former East Germany which had largely avoided open discussion of such issues until the 1990s. But there were counter-reactions too, and as the focus turned to German women and children as victims of British and American bombing or Soviet rape, some commentators feared a return to the kind of competition over national suffering which had been prevalent in the 1950s.[3]

Instead, the two emotionally powerful narratives of the war have maintained their parallel trajectories. Despite the shared moral awareness evident in the decision to place a massive Holocaust memorial at the centre of contemporary Berlin, a profound divide persists in talking about this period: Germans remain either victims or perpetrators. As I followed the public soul-searching in Germany which accompanied the 60th anniversary of the end of the Second World War in 2005, I realised that the contemporary need to draw the right didactic lessons from this past had led scholars as well as the media to neglect one of the essential tasks of historical enquiry – first and above all, to understand the past. Crucially historians have not been asking how Germans talked and thought about their roles at the time. To what extent, for example, did they discuss the fact that they were fighting for a regime that was committing genocide? And how did the conclusions they reached alter their view of the war as a whole?

One might assume that no such conversation could have taken place in a police state during wartime. In fact, in the summer and autumn of 1943, Germans began to talk openly in public about the murder of the Jews, equating it with the Allied bombing of German civilians. In Hamburg it was noted 'that the common people, the middle classes, and the rest of the population make repeated remarks in intimate circles and also in larger gatherings that the attacks count as retaliation for our treatment of the Jews'. In Schweinfurt in Bavaria, people were saying exactly the same thing: 'the terror attacks are a consequence of the measures carried out against the Jews'. After the USAAF's second raid on the town in October 1943, people complained openly 'that if we hadn't treated the Jews so badly, we wouldn't have to suffer so from the terror attacks'. By this point, such views were reported to the authorities in Berlin not just from all major German cities but even from quiet backwaters which had little or no direct experience of the bombing.[4]

When I first learned this, I was astonished. I already knew that Germans' common post-war claim to have known and done nothing was a convenient subterfuge. Existing scholarship showed that plenty of information circulated in wartime Germany about the genocide. But, like other historians, I had assumed that most of this information was communicated discreetly to close friends and family, passing beyond the closed circles of intimacy only as anonymous rumour. How could the Holocaust have become a matter of public conversation? Moreover, these discussions were monitored and analysed by the same secret police authorities who had been organising the deportation and murder of the Jews for the previous two years. Even more bizarrely, a couple of months *after* these reports came in, the head of the police and SS, Heinrich Himmler, could still insist to the leaders of the Third Reich that extermination of European Jewry was a responsibility to be shared only with them and that 'we will take the secret with us to our graves'. How then had this supposed secret been broached? For the last twenty-five years, the Holocaust has come to occupy a central position in how we think about the Nazi period and the Second World War. But that is still a relatively recent development, and does not tell us how Germans thought about their own role in it at the time.[5]

On 18 November 1943, Captain Dr August Töpperwien noted in his diary that he had 'heard *dreadful*, apparently accurate details about how we have exterminated the Jews (from infants to the aged) in Lithuania!' He had recorded rumours of massacres before, as early as 1939 and 1940, but not on this scale. This time, Töpperwien strove to put the terrible facts into some kind of moral order, asking himself who could legitimately be killed in war. He extended the list from enemy soldiers and partisans operating behind German lines to limited collective reprisals against the civilians who abetted them, but still he felt forced to admit that what was being done to the Jews was of an entirely different order: 'We are not just destroying the Jews fighting against us, we literally want to exterminate this people as such!'[6]

A pious Protestant and conservative schoolmaster, August Töpperwien had harboured doubts from the outset about the sheer brutality of Hitler's war. He appears to personify that state of moral and political alienation from Nazism which found its expression, not in any outward show of resistance, but in a degree of nonconformity and 'inner' withdrawal from the regime's exhortations and demands. But did such a safe spiritual haven exist? Are all expressions of doubts in family letters and personal diaries signs of inner opposition, rather than merely airing the writer's own uncertainties and dilemmas? In fact, August Töpperwien would continue to serve loyally until the last days of the war. Having made his momentous acknowledgement that 'we literally want to exterminate this people as such', he fell silent. He could not square this admission with his own belief in Germany's civilising mission in the east and its defence of Europe against Bolshevism.

Töpperwien did not return to the murder of the Jews again until March 1945, when he finally began to grasp – for the first time – that Germany was facing complete and unavoidable defeat: 'A mankind that wages war like this has become godless. The Russian barbarities in the German east – the terror attacks of the British and Americans – our struggle against the Jews (sterilisation of healthy women, shooting everyone from infants to old women, gassing of Jewish transport trains)!' If Germany's impending defeat appeared to him now a kind of divine punishment for what it had done to the Jews, then Töpperwien was also clear that this act was no worse than what the Allies were doing to Germans.[7]

Back in the summer and autumn of 1943 what impelled civilians on the home front, from Hamburg to Schweinfurt, to talk so openly about German responsibility for the murder of the Jews was a different kind of impending doom. Between 25 July and 2 August 1943, the city of Hamburg was bombed, unleashing a firestorm of huge proportions. Half the city was devastated and 34,000 people killed. To many Germans it felt like the Apocalypse. Because of the demonstrable threat to the major cities, the SS Security Service (the SD) reported, all 'feeling of security' had collapsed across Germany 'with great suddenness', replaced by 'blind rage'. On the first day of the firestorm, 25 July, another event had occurred further afield. The Italian dictator Benito Mussolini was toppled, after twenty-one years in power, in a bloodless coup. Germans quickly linked the two events. For the next five weeks, people were reported to be talking openly in public about the possibility of following the Italian example and replacing the Nazi regime with a military dictatorship as offering 'the best', or possibly even 'the last', way of reaching a 'separate peace' with the Western Allies. For the Nazi leadership these reports seemed to point to the collapse of civilian morale and a replay of the capitulation and revolution of November 1918. In fact the moment of crisis was short-lived. By early September 1943 it was over, as the regime threw resources into civil defence and organised mass evacuation from the cities. The Wehrmacht's military position also stabilised with the occupation of most of Italy, and the Gestapo finally imposed a selective crackdown on such 'defeatist' talk. As in Töpperwien's private ruminations, so these public discussions of German responsibility for the murder of the Jews were prompted by feelings of profound moral and physical unease, as the unrelenting onslaught of the RAF's Bomber Command spread a sense of vulnerability far beyond the bombed cities themselves. The significance of the temporary political crisis triggered by the bombing of Hamburg was that it brought these fears to the surface: future crises would evoke the same patterns of public discussion, in which Germans mixed anxieties about their culpability with a sense of their own victimhood.[8]

For German Jews the unfolding Holocaust inevitably shaped their understanding of the war. But other Germans perceived everything from the opposite direction: the war was their primary concern, against which they developed their understanding of the genocide. These were very different perspectives on the same events, conditioned by deep inequalities of power and choice and refracted in profoundly different hopes and fears. This problem has shaped the way I have approached writing the history of wartime Germany. Where other historians have highlighted the machinery of mass murder, and discussed why or how the Holocaust happened, I find myself more concerned with how German society received and assimilated this knowledge as accomplished fact. How did it affect Germans to gradually realise that they were fighting a genocidal war? Or to put it the other way around, how did the war shape their perception of genocide?

July and August 1943 were clearly a moment of profound crisis in wartime Germany, when people from Hamburg to Bavaria explained the unlimited Allied attacks on civilians as retaliation for 'what we did to the Jews'. Such talk about Allied punishment or 'Jewish retaliation' confirmed that the endless Nazi propaganda – especially in the first six months of 1943 – which depicted the air raids as 'Jewish terror bombing' was generally accepted by the population. But these reflections entailed a strangely self-accusatory twist, which appalled Goebbels and other Nazi leaders. It seemed that people wished to undo this mutually destructive cycle, now that German cities were being obliterated. But the 'measures carried out against the Jews', as the SD reporters euphemistically called them, already lay in the past: the Europe-wide deportation of the Jews had taken place the previous year. The Hamburg firestorm confronted Germans with a new kind of absolute war as the threat of aerial destruction escaped all limits.

The Manichaean metaphors of 'either/or', 'to be or not to be', 'everything or nothing', 'victory or destruction' had a long rhetorical history in Germany. They had constituted Hitler's central ideas since Germany's defeat in 1918, and had been staples of First World War propaganda since the Kaiser made his 'Declaration to the German People' on 6 August 1914. But this apocalyptic outlook was not what made Hitler's rule popular in the 1930s or even in the first years of war. What changed in the latter half of the Second World War was that German society became far more receptive to these ways of thinking. The turn in German fortunes changed extremist rhetoric into sound common sense. In the wake of Allied 'terror bombing', the fundamental existential threat, 'To be or not to be' acquired a disturbing literalness. What fuelled the sense of crisis in the summer of 1943 was a widespread fear that Germans could not escape the consequences of a ruthless racial war of their own making. In overcoming that moment of crisis, people not only had to scrap their earlier expectations and prognoses about the course of the war: they also shed traditional moral inhibitions, overstepping existing notions of decency and shame. Germans did not have to be Nazis to fight for Hitler, but they would discover that it was impossible to remain untouched by the ruthlessness of the war and the apocalyptic mentality it created.[9]

This capacity of wartime crises to transform or radicalise social values profoundly affects how we think about the relationship between the Nazi regime and German society. For the last thirty years, most historians have assumed that crises such as followed the Hamburg firestorm or occurred a few months earlier after the loss of the 6th Army at Stalingrad tipped German society into irrevocable defeatism: increasingly alienated from all that the regime stood for, the majority of the population was only kept going by Nazi terror. In fact, there is no direct index during the middle of the war between falling consent and increasing repression: death sentences handed down by the courts jumped dramatically from 1,292 in 1941 to 4,457 in 1942 – well before the defeat at Stalingrad. German judges were responding not to mounting opposition and discontent from below but to pressure from above, especially from Hitler, to deal with repeat offenders, usually petty criminals, far more harshly. This was also a system of racial justice, in which Poles and Czechs forced to work in Germany accounted for a disporportionate number of those killed. It was not until the autumn of 1944, with the Allied armies

on the German frontiers, that 'ordinary Germans' were subjected
to a rising wave of repression, but by far the worst excesses of terror
were confined to the final weeks of fighting in March, April and the
first week of May 1945. Even during this last spasm of mass violence,
terror did not atomise and silence German society: on the contrary,
many German citizens continued to feel that as loyal patriots they
were entitled to criticise Nazi failures in public. In their own minds,
their commitment continued to count for a great deal until the very
end of the war.[10]

The long-lasting consensus that Germans became defeatists rests
on a piece of common sense: historians equate the regime's successes
with consent and its failures with criticism and opposition. This align-
ment almost certainly holds good in times of peace – but not for the
conditions of a world war. It cannot explain what actually happened.
How did Germans manage to continue fighting from 1943 until 1945,
years during which they had to surmount rising devastation and losses
on their side? *The German War* offers a very different understanding
of the effects that wartime defeats and crises had on German society.
Terror undoubtedly played its part at particular moments, but it never
provided the only – or the most important – reason for going on.
Neither Nazism nor the war itself could be rejected, because Germans
envisaged their own defeat in existential terms. The worse their war
went, the more obviously 'defensive' it became. Far from leading to
collapse, successive crises acted as catalysts of radical transformation,
as Germans tried to master the situation and rethink what they could
expect. Major disasters like Stalingrad and Hamburg did indeed lead
to a catastrophic fall in the regime's popularity, but they did not in
themselves call patriotic commitment into question. The strains of
war showed in a whole range of resentments and conflicts within
German society, many of which the regime was called upon to mediate
and mitigate. However unpopular the war became, it still remained
legitimate – more so than Nazism itself. Germany's mid-war crises
resulted not in defeatism but in a hardening of social attitudes. It is
these more complex, dynamic and disturbing elements in German
responses to war with which I am concerned in this book.

*

When mobilisation orders were issued on 26 August 1939 Germans had no idea of what lay ahead. But that did not prevent most from taking a bleak view of war. They knew what lay behind them: 1.8 million military dead in the last war; the 'turnip winter' of 1917; the Spanish flu of 1918; and the faces of children famished because the Royal Navy maintained its blockade into 1919 in order to compel the new German government to sign a humiliating 'dictated' peace agreement. German politics of the 1920s and '30s was dominated by attempts to escape the strictures of the Versailles treaty, but even Hitler's greatest foreign policy triumphs such as at the Munich summit of 1938 were overshadowed by popular fear of war. The first lesson of 1914–18 was not to repeat it. When war and rationing came, both were greeted with profound gloom. In the first winter, city-dwellers compared shortages of food, clothing and, above all, heating coal with the winters of 1916 and 1917, grumbling about chronic shortages. It did not augur particularly well for Germans' capacity to 'hold out', as the SD repeatedly warned the Nazi leadership in its weekly reports on the 'public mood'.

For the Nazis, the first months of the war raised crucial questions about the stability of the rule they had established since coming to power in 1933. On the surface, they had enjoyed a runaway success in the pre-war years. Driven by a variety of motives, ranging from opportunism to conformity or conviction, Party membership rose from 850,000 at the end of 1932 to 5.5 million on the eve of war. By that time, the National Socialist Women's League had 2.3 million members and the Hitler Youth and League of German Girls 8.7 million, and they all ran ideological training courses, from evening get-togethers to week-long summer camps. The successors of the working-class welfare and trade union organisations, the National Socialist People's Welfare and the German Labour Front, boasted 14 and 22 million members respectively. Even more impressively, the majority of staff were volunteers. Overall by 1939, two-thirds of the population signed up to at least one of the Party's mass organisations.[11]

This success had been built on a bitterly divisive legacy of coercion and consent. In 1933, the Nazis set out to complete the work of their street-fighting years and obliterate the political Left. With the active assistance of police, army, even fire brigades, SA and SS men sealed off 'Red' housing estates, conducted house-to-house searches, intimidating and beating the occupants, and they arrested local activists and functionaries. The formal banning of the left-wing parties followed in the wake of these repeated raids: the Communists in March, the trade unions in May and the Social Democrats finally in June 1933. In May, 50,000 oppositionists were already in concentration camps, most of them Communists and Social Democrats. By the summer of 1934, when terror against the Left had run its course, perhaps as many as 200,000 men and women had been churned through this new apparatus of Nazi terror. Public punishment in the camps, alongside a whole repertoire of humiliating, pointless drills, was designed to enforce conformity and break the prisoners' will. The real success of this programme of 're-education' came with the mass release of cowed and chastened prisoners back to their families and communities: by the summer of 1935, when fewer than 4,000 prisoners were still in the camps, the 'other Germany' which the Left had represented had been destroyed politically.[12]

When Germany mobilised in August 1939, the Gestapo took the precaution of re-arresting former Social Democratic politicians. What was harder to gauge was the regime's success in eradicating the working-class subculture which had sustained left-wing politics since the 1860s. Certainly, pockets of it remained under the new aegis. Before 1933, football had been dominated by the workers' sports clubs, which counted 700,000 members, and by the 240,000-strong Catholic clubs. Although the German Labour Front rapidly absorbed them and the Nazis reorganised the whole structure of the football leagues, making them far more competitive and exciting, they could not really control the fans. In November 1940, a friendly match in Vienna ended in a full-scale riot, with local fans storming the pitch after the final whistle and throwing stones at the visiting players before they could get away. The windows of their bus were smashed and even the car belonging to the Gauleiter of Vienna was wrecked. Although the Security Police saw this as primarily a political demonstration, they were almost certainly mistaken. In fact both clubs had a traditional, fiercely loyal and formerly 'Red', working-class base; and the match itself, billed as a 'friendly', was seen by all the supporters of Vienna's local clubs as an opportunity to take revenge for Admira's humiliating 9–0 loss to Schalke in the 1939 German cup final – a loss which fans inevitably credited not to the Ruhr team's incredible string of successes but to biased refereeing in Berlin. The riot was as much about a set of male loyalties to neighbourhood and city as it was an Austrian protest against the influx of arrogant 'Prussians' into Vienna after the *Anschluss* of March 1938.[13]

Such residues of working-class identity had little potency. The world that Social Democrats had painstakingly built up through mutual aid, choral societies, gymnasts' clubs, burial societies, kindergartens and cycling clubs had either been corralled into Nazi organisations or had been suppressed. In July 1936, the exiled Social Democrats bemoaned the collapse of the tradition of collective identity they represented, admitting that 'the [workers'] interest in their fate as a class has to a large degree disappeared completely. It has been replaced by the most petty-minded individual and family egotism.' When the Left re-formed after the war, its vote recovered quickly but it proved incapable of recreating the dense organisational subculture and sense of identity it had possessed before 1933. The SD and Gestapo could not of course know how successful their combination of coercion and inclusion had been when war broke out, and they would continue to monitor the threat of working-class action.[14]

The Nazis could be far more secure in their support from the middle classes – farmers, self-employed businessmen, skilled craftsmen, educated professionals and managers. Protestants welcomed the Nazis' 'national revolution' with an enthusiasm and hope for spiritual revival comparable only to the fervour with which they had endorsed war in 1914. They united in rejecting the 'godless' modernism of Weimar, which they associated with the 'ideas of 1789', pacifism, democrats, Jews and those who embraced defeat. This was a broad alliance, which was already being forged by Protestant pastors and theologians in the 1920s and whose talk of creating a new 'national community' appealed powerfully across the political spectrum. Former Liberals, Conservatives, members of the Catholic Centre Party, even former Social Democratic voters, could all remember having espoused the idea of a 'national community' during the First World War and the Weimar years – before it became a key Nazi slogan. Even conservative Jewish nationalists, like the historians Hans Rothfels and Ernst Kantorowicz, wanted to embrace this 'national revolution' and found adjustment hard when they were forced into emigration because of their 'non-Aryan' origins.[15]

Such non-Nazis put national repentance for the failure of 1918 at the centre of what their fellow citizens had to accomplish on the road to 'national salvation'. Many of the arguments which served the Nazis well were supplied by others, such as the young theologian and former military chaplain Paul Althaus. He had denounced pacifism as early as 1919 and argued that Germans needed to prove themselves worthy of God's renewed trust by standing up against Versailles. Mixing the subtlety of theological argument with militant nationalism, Althaus became a formidable and increasingly central propagandist for conservative Lutheranism and for the view that the Germans were God's chosen people. But they would have to redeem themselves if they were to prove worthy of His trust. More radical Nazis might try – unsuccessfully – to wean Germans off religion, but they enthusiastically endorsed such calls for the spiritual rebirth of their nation. Moreover, other – more universalist and pacifist – points of view, such as the ideas championed by Paul Tillich, had already been sidelined and denigrated by non-Nazi theologians such as Althaus.[16]

When they came to power, the Nazis decided against large-scale social engineering, aiming first at a revolution of feeling. After their takeover, they choreographed the popular theatre of paramilitary formations, flags, boots and uniforms, and torchlit mass parades. Nazi ambitions reached into the inner sanctum of bourgeois culture, the municipal theatre, where it challenged the nineteenth-century classical repertoire with agitprop plays about the *Freikorps* resistance to the French occupation of the Ruhr in the 1920s. They reached beyond the physical confines of the theatre itself in 1933–34 by organising the *Thingspiele*, a new kind of morality play staged in the open air with huge *tableaux vivants* and massed casts of up to 17,000 participants which attracted audiences of up to 60,000. Many of these huge spectacles sought to make Germans relive and exorcise their defeat in the First World War. In Richard Euringer's *German Passion*, the fallen soldiers of the First World War literally rose up to march in battalion strength across the stage, their white, ghostly faces gleaming under their steel helmets, and spoke to the longing for unity and regeneration.[17]

By 1935, the vogue for *Thingspiele* had run its course, as had the Nazi agitprop productions in the municipal theatres. Goebbels faced a rebellion of season-ticket holders who started cancelling their subscriptions. He promptly changed tack, sacked the new Nazi theatre directors and replaced them with competent traditionalists. What these overwhelmingly middle-class audiences wanted and got were the classics: in November 1933, the 10th anniversary of the Munich Beer Hall Putsch was celebrated with Nazi plays; ten years later, by Mozart operas. Despite this retreat on content, Goebbels continued to channel huge resources into theatres – more money in fact than he spent on propaganda itself.[18]

There was a risk that the Nazis' very success in ending the dire poverty and insecurity of the Great Depression had provided powerful yet superficial reasons for supporting the Third Reich. Key Party and state agencies also worried that their success might prove to be relatively ephemeral: they had grave difficulties judging whether or not they were succeeding in inculcating core Nazi values and beliefs. Under the umbrella of the 'national community', there were debates over economic redistribution and social policy, about 'life reform' and pedagogy, and even about whether women could wear trousers rather than skirts. Hitler was careful never to make 'papal' pronouncements in public; and the Party's chief ideologue, Alfred Rosenberg, who did issue statements of dogma, was widely discredited for his virulent anti-Christian positions and clearly lacked political power within the new regime.[19]

On the eve of war most Germans belonged to both an established Christian denomination and a Nazi Party organisation; far more of them – 94 per cent – remained members of a Catholic or Protestant church than the two-thirds who belonged to Nazi organisations. The churches were the most important independent civic institutions in Germany, and a number of obdurate priests and pastors were sent to concentration camps for criticising Nazi actions from the pulpit. In July 1937, the most outspoken pastor in Berlin, Martin Niemöller, was arrested by the Gestapo. He would spend the rest of the Third Reich in the camps. In April 1945, the young Protestant theologian Dietrich Bonhoeffer was hanged at Flossenbürg concentration camp. Both men would become powerful symbols of civil courage in the face of Nazi oppression, but this was a much later development: Bonhoeffer repre-sented a liberal, humanitarian theology which had been sidelined and gone into exile with Paul Tillich. Neither the ideas nor Bonhoeffer as a symbolic figure would re-emerge in post-war West Germany until the late 1950s and early 1960s. Niemöller was altogether different. He was not a liberal democrat but an anti-Semitic, conservative nationalist, a submarine captain in the First World War who had served in the *Freikorps* in 1919–20 before retraining as a clergyman. He had also actively supported Hitler at elections from 1924 to 1933. When war broke out in 1939, Niemöller would write from Sachsenhausen to Admiral Raeder, the Commander of the Navy, volunteering to serve his country again. Niemöller's dissent in the 1930s was more religious than political and the type of Christianity he stood for was struggling for its place within German Protestantism.[20]

Having enthusiastically supported the Nazis' 'national revolution' in 1933, Protestants soon split in three directions. Many pastors joined the German Christian Movement, which wanted to deepen the spiritual renewal into a liturgical and theological one – banning the Old Testament and expurgating the New of Jewish influence, and excluding Jewish converts from Protestant ministry. Traditionalists who wanted to safeguard their scripture and liturgy and defend the Church from state interference formed themselves first into the Pastors' Emergency League and then, in May 1934, into the Confessing Church. This split has been widely misunderstood and misrepresented as one waged between liberals and Nazis for the soul of the Church. It was not: although Karl Barth, the main author of the Barmen Confession, remained critical of the dictatorship and returned to Switzerland, he was not widely read even by pastors who belonged to the Confessing Church; Barth was not a Lutheran, like most German Protestants, but a Calvinist. Many pastors on both sides of this divide – including Niemöller – subscribed to the same key nationalist, authoritarian and socially unifying political values, and this gave scope for a third group of non-aligned Lutheran theologians around Paul Althaus to wield huge influence. He did not join the Nazi Party, but he did greet Hitler's accession to the Chancellorship as a 'miracle and gift of God'. Although Althaus never participated in ritual burning of books by banned authors, he justified them. In the wake of the November 1938 pogrom against Germany's Jews he pointed out that, since God guided history, their recent sufferings testified to the Jews' guilt.[21]

The world of German Catholicism was divided too, but by generation. Catholic bishops were men aged 60–80, a generation older than the major Protestant theologians and the Nazi leaders. Most bishops had been ordained in the decades before the First World War and trained in a fiercely conservative neo-Aristotelian theology, consistent in its logic and abstract in its choice of language. They blamed 'modernity' for the ills of liberalism, socialism, communism and atheism. The gulf between the elderly bishops and younger clergy and laity also made for tensions within the Church, both over the form of communication and the substance of policy. Where the bishops tended to take a very insular, conservative view of social reform, many younger Catholics saw the 'national revolution' of 1933 as an opportunity to become more engaged in helping to shape German society. The war would amplify this generational divide between conservatives and reformers.[22]

The Nazis exerted pressure too, banning the Catholic youth movement, trying to secularise education further and seeking to bring the Caritas network of psychiatric asylums into line with the new law on compulsory sterilisation. In 1938, Nazi activists removed crucifixes from schools in Bavaria during the summer holidays, thoroughly antagonising rural and small-town Bavarians who blamed known radicals like the SS, the local Gauleiter and the Party's ideologist-in-chief, Alfred Rosenberg. But Catholics did not tar the whole movement with the same brush and many remained active members of Nazi organisations, looking for support from other more sympathetic leaders such as Hermann Göring. Hitler himself censored his own views on religion so successfully that the Archbishop of Munich, Cardinal Faulhaber, and the primate of the German Church, Cardinal Bertram of Breslau, both remained convinced that the Führer was a deeply religious man. Their shared national commitments would bring the Catholic Church and the Nazi regime into what recent historians have called an uneasy 'antagonistic co-operation' during the war.[23]

Deprived of clear spiritual leadership, individual Catholics and Protestants were left to resolve their problems of conscience in the privacy of diaries and letters, in the process providing the historian with an invaluable moral register for some of the more liberal and humane members of the 'national community'.[24]

★

When war broke out in September 1939, it was deeply unpopular in Germany. Yet there was no great soul-searching about why it had occurred. Whereas in Britain and France it was self-evident that Hitler was waging a war of conquest by launching an unprovoked attack on Poland, it was equally obvious to most Germans that they were caught up in a war of national defence, forced upon them by Allied machinations and Polish aggression. Such views have for so long been banished from serious historical research, eking out a fringe existence in websites pandering to neo-Nazi opinions, that it seems strange to a contemporary audience that they should have been earnestly and honestly held at the time by so many Germans who were not dyed-in-the-wool Nazis. How could they confuse a deliberate and brutal war of colonial conquest with a war of national defence? How could they see themselves as beleaguered patriots, rather than as warriors for Hitler's master race?

The First World War served as a yardstick not only for measuring shortages and hardship on the home front. It also fundamentally conditioned how people understood the causes of this second war within a generation. On 3 September 1939, it was Britain and France that declared war on Germany, just as Russia had mobilised first in 1914 and then invaded East Prussia. In August 1914 war came after a long process of 'encirclement' by hostile foreign powers, purportedly orchestrated by Britain to safeguard its own world empire and cut Germany down to size. The same reasoning, expressed in many of the selfsame phrases, resurfaced in 1939, as Germans noted the progress of the Polish crisis in their diaries. Again, British imperialist ambitions were the root cause of everything and Britain's bellicosity was underlined by its government's brusque rejection of Hitler's repeated peace offers after the conquest of Poland and again, in 1940, after the fall of France. The view that this was a defensive war was not simply spawned by Nazi propaganda. Many who remained critical of the Nazis regarded the war in this way too. Everyone in Germany saw the Second World War through the lens of the First, whether or not they had lived through it. At least Germans were initially spared the nightmare of the kind of two-front war they had faced in 1914, thanks to the last-minute non-aggression pact with Soviet Russia. But by Christmas 1941, Germany was once more at war with Britain, Russia and America – just as it had been in 1917.

The cult of the 'front generation' and the literature of the First World War – whether critical like Erich Maria Remarque's *All Quiet on the Western Front* or celebratory like Ernst Jünger's *Storm of Steel* – shaped an impression that the generation of 1914–18 was unique. Above all, it had been cut off from the generation of their fathers, who had grown up knowing only peace. Whether or not it really was a conflict between fathers and sons, the First World War came to be seen as such. This was not true of the Second. The sense of being caught up in a terrible cycle of repeated wars fought over the same issues fostered a sense of fraternal 'comradeship' across the generations. When Helmut Paulus was sent to the eastern front in 1941, his father, a GP and reserve officer from the previous war, began writing to him as a 'comrade'. As Helmut's unit advanced through Romania and into southern Ukraine, they found themselves in the same locations as German troops had occupied in the previous war, and his parents were not slow to find neighbours and acquaintances back in Pforzheim who could describe the terrain or unfold old war maps to work out where their sons must be fighting. Men, proud to have withstood their 'baptism of fire' in the trenches, compared artillery barrages with the ten-month battle of Verdun in 1916, equating its legendary destructive force with the ultimate test. German commanders too cast their fears in terms of that war, haunted as they closed on Moscow in November 1941 by the danger of a repetition of the sudden, unexpected change in fortunes they had experienced at the Marne, when they were within reach of Paris, twenty-seven years earlier.

What bound fathers and sons together was more than shared experience. It was a sense of intergenerational responsibility. The sons had to achieve what their fathers had failed to do. They had to break the cycle of repetition, which condemned each generation to fight in Russia. Whereas left-wing and liberal thinkers saw history in linear, progressive terms, many conservatives believed that it was circular and repetitive, like the life cycle. The dire predictions of the decline of Western culture, epitomised by Oswald Spengler's *Decline of the West*, had been overturned by the 'national rebirth' in 1933, but the cyclical, naturalising metaphors had remained. The German war in the Soviet Union turned metaphor into reality, the abstract threat of destructive repetition into an immediate and existential struggle. The immense brutality of the German war in the east only heighted the sense that Germany finally had to break this cycle – or else it would be condemning the next generation to repeat the slaughter.

This had been a concern from the outset. When soldiers waited for the fighting to start in the west in autumn 1939, some reflected that 'It's better to clear the decks now, then it's to be hoped we won't have to be involved in a war again.' German schoolchildren had been taught for generations that France was the 'hereditary enemy' but in a visceral, emotional sense it was Russia that really mattered. From 1890 even the oppositional Social Democrats had pledged that if ever Germany was attacked by Tsarist Russia, they would defend the country against the barbarians from the east. In August 1914, the Russian invasion of East Prussia triggered a wave of highly exaggerated horror stories in the German press and the little-known Prussian general who defeated them, Paul von Hindenburg, became an enduring national hero. In 1941, it was not difficult to persuade the population that the new war in Russia had to be fought to a finish so that the next generation would not have to go through it again. From the veterans of the eastern front from 1914–17 to young soldiers just out of school and teenagers still at home, families identified the war, not with the Nazi regime, but with their own intergenerational familial responsibilities. It was the strongest foundation for their patriotism.[25]

Such utter and complete commitment to serve was only thinkable because it was never unlimited and unbounded. It had a temporal dimension. As one soldier reassured his wife in February 1940, 'Next year we'll make up for everything, yes?' Two years later, another was vowing 'to catch up on everything later which we're missing out on now'. Their dreams of a post-war life formed the focus of hope, the personal version of what victory – or, increasingly, simply avoiding defeat – meant to them. However justified and necessary, the war years were lost time; real time would only begin afterwards; one man spoke for many when he promised his wife, 'Then our life will actually begin.' Just before Christmas 1944, a young tank commander on the eastern front wrote to his fiancée in Berlin complaining about his thwarted ambitions to become an artist and expressing his fear that the war would not break the endless cycle of conflict: 'After this war will soon come, perhaps in twenty years, another, which is already faintly discernible today', he warned her, adding that 'the life of this generation seems to me to be measured by catastrophes'.[26]

For families and individuals the war proved to be unutterably long. They were touched by the great events but the millions of family

letters carried each day by the field post chronicled domestic stratagems to cope with the excessive demands of war and plotted the
incremental, unconscious adjustments each side had to make. In their
need to reassure each other, many couples concealed how difficult
their relationships were becoming and how much they had changed
was only revealed when they were reunited after the war. In the early
post-war years, the divorce rate soared. This book is about the long
war. It charts the transformations of German society and the subtle
but often irreversible ways in which individuals adapted to a war they
felt increasingly they could not control. It traces the changing expectations, oscillating hopes and fears of individuals through the events
which shaped them. Their lives provide both an emotional measure
of experience and a moral barometer for a society set on a self-
destructive path.

PART ONE

DEFENDING THE ATTACK

I

Unwelcome War

'Don't wait for me. There is no more leave,' the young soldier scribbled in haste to his girlfriend. 'I've got to go straight to the barracks and load vehicles. It's the mobilisation alarm.' He just had time to drop off his personal effects at the home of Irene's aunt in the Liebigstrasse. But it was the weekend and the young florist had already left for her parents' home. Unable to say goodbye to her, he managed to scrawl their address on the envelope, 'To Fräulein Irene Reitz, Lauterbach, Bahnhofstrasse 105'. A young professional soldier, who had signed on as a corporal two years before, Ernst Guicking was one of the first men to be sent off, joining the 163rd Infantry Regiment in Eschwege.[1]

The next day, 26 August 1939, Germany officially mobilised. Wilm Hosenfeld, the village schoolmaster at Thalau, reported to a girls' high school on the other side of the valley in Fulda. Like many schools across Germany, it became a military assembly point that day, and Hosenfeld resumed his First World War rank of sergeant major. Many of the men in his company of infantry reservists were also veterans of the last war and, as he doled out their weapons and equipment, he judged their mood to be 'serious but determined'. They were, he thought, all convinced 'that it won't come to war'.[2]

In Flensburg, a young fireman took the tram to the Junkerhohlweg barracks where he was appointed 'equipment sergeant' and issued with a bicycle. The 26th Infantry Regiment marched off to the railway station at eleven that night. Despite the late hour, the streets of Flensburg were thronged with people who had come to see them off. In the 12th Company, Gerhard M. had no idea where they were bound. He found a space under a bench in their cattle truck and, once the train finally got moving, he slept 'the sleep of the just'.[3]

In the leafy Nikolassee suburb of Berlin, Jochen Klepper felt himself sliding into a state of nervous exhaustion. Hoping against hope that war would be averted, he saw things too bleakly to fall for the optimistic rumours repeated to him by everyone from the block warden to his newspaper editor. Klepper's general fear of war focused on the future facing his Jewish wife, Johanna, and 17-year-old stepdaughter, Renate. When a letter arrived from Croydon, it was from Johanna's elder daughter, Brigitte, who had emigrated to England at the start of the year: she told them that the evacuation of London was already under way. Over the coming months, Klepper would blame himself for talking Johanna and Renate out of leaving with Brigitte. He found some consolation: the tone of the German press and radio was less shrill than during the Czechoslovakian crisis the previous year. They also dropped their usual references to 'war-mongering Jewry' since Germany had signed the Non-Aggression Pact with the Soviet Union on 23 August.[4]

★

Throughout the spring and summer of 1939, the German government had complained about violence against the German minority in Poland. The neutral, 'free city' of Danzig played a central role as the crisis developed. With its largely German population but cut off from the rest of the Reich, in Danzig all the anomalies and resentments of the post-First World War settlement were concentrated, and the Nazi Party Gauleiter, Albert Forster, was given careful instructions throughout the summer on how to increase tensions without letting the conflict explode. Focusing on the Polish ability to choke off the city's food supply through its control of the customs post, he kept the issue in the headlines. Events escalated dramatically on 30 August, when Joachim von Ribbentrop, the German Foreign Minister, abruptly called the British Ambassador to a sudden, late-night meeting, in order to relay his government's 'final offer' to resolve the crisis. The ambassador, Sir Nevile Henderson, did not receive a written copy of the German demands before being sent off to London. The Polish embassy and government were not presented with them at all. Hitler's terms, which required that new plebiscites should be held on the future of the Polish Corridor and of the former German territories in western

Poland, would have reignited the ethno-nationalist civil war that had raged there after the First World War. Acceding to Hitler's demands would have broken Poland up and made it completely indefensible.[5]

Danzig was the second international crisis in a year. The previous summer had been dominated by Hitler's championship of the Sudeten Germans, who accounted for a third of the population of Czechoslovakia. War had been averted by an agreement brokered at Munich, without any input from Czechoslovakia or the Soviet Union, in September 1938, but the crisis had forced the British and French to rearm. Within six months, Hitler broke his solemn promise that the Sudetenland would be his 'last territorial demand', sending the Wehrmacht across the new Czech border and turning the Czech lands into a 'Reich Protectorate'. Even dovish British Conservatives could not ignore this breach, though the Bank of England did perform a final service to the Reich by sending the Czech gold reserves back from London. In Britain and France, the occupation of Prague on 15 March 1939 underlined the futility of Munich.[6]

Within Germany the same events were read quite differently. In Austria, especially, the idea of the new 'Reich Protectorate of Bohemia and Moravia' augured well, with its sense of restoring the old Habsburg Crown lands to their rightful place under German control. Elsewhere in Germany, where this heritage meant little, opinions were more divided. In the coal-mining belt of the Ruhr, with its Polish and Czech immigrant population, some expressed sympathy for the Czechs. During the 1938 crisis, virtually the entire country, including the political and military elites, had been convinced that Germany could not win a war. So great was this reported 'war psychosis' that when agreement was reached at Munich, the propagandists' triumphalism was quite swamped by the public outpouring of relief: Goebbels had to remind newpapers to celebrate Germany's success. Hitler had raged in frustration that he had been 'cheated of his war', but in this he was alone even amongst the Nazi elite.[7]

By the summer of 1939, the public mood had changed. In 1938, huge crowds had cheered Chamberlain at Munich, seeing him as the peace-bringer. A year later, the British prime minister had become a figure of fun, personifying the decay and impotence of the Western democracies. At 70, he was a full twenty years older than the Führer, and German children mimicked his walk and, above all, his patrician umbrella. Ernst Guicking's girlfriend, Irene Reitz, followed popular usage and called Chamberlain's government the 'Umbrella govern-ment'. The occupation of Prague in March 1939, like Hitler's entry into Vienna a year earlier, appeared to be another bloodless triumph, confirming that the French and British were unlikely to act.[8]

Hitler had succeeded in portraying himself as the champion of an injured and besieged German minority, mobilising reservoirs of resent-ment at the loss of territories in the post-1918 settlement. To many Germans, from former Social Democrats and ex-voters for the Catholic Centre Party to Protestant conservatives, the post-war Polish state was another excrescence of the Versailles Diktat, a peace treaty which the German delegation was forced to sign without ever having the chance of negotiating its terms. The clandestine reporters in Germany for the exiled Social Democrats had no doubt that Hitler was pushing at an open door when it came to Poland: 'An action against Poland would be welcomed by the overwhelming mass of the German people. The Poles are enormously hated among the masses for what they did at the end of the War.' They concluded that even amongst their own old working-class supporters, people believed 'that if Hitler strikes out against the Poles, he will have a majority of the population behind him'. Above all, propaganda blamed the intransigence of the Poles on Britain and its policy of preventing Germany's resurgence through 'encirclement'. Already in the early summer, a Social Democratic reporter noted, 'The agitation against England is so strong at this time that I am convinced that, but for the official "Heil Hitler" greeting, people would surely greet each other as they did in the World War with "God punish England".' Hitler was slowly recreating the broad patriotic coalition which had reached across German society in 1914, from the moderate Social Democratic Left to conservative nationalists: the parties themselves may have been suppressed, but the Nazi regime knew that their subcultures remained and it was not slow to plug into them.[9]

In August 1939, the German government set the wheels in motion for a rapid and limited war of conquest. On 15 August, military commanders were given orders to prepare for an invasion of Poland. Briefing the top brass at his Alpine retreat on 22 August – the day Ribbentrop flew to Moscow to agree terms with Stalin and Molotov – Hitler maintained that the British and French would not resort to arms. The German–Soviet Pact, with its secret protocol to divide

Poland between the two powers, was greeted with relief by Hitler's deeply anti-communist generals, because it effectively removed the threat of a two-front war. It now looked as if action could be confined to the Polish theatre with a short, victorious campaign, which would re-establish Germany's military credentials. According to its own internal assessments, the government still needed several years to arm for what Hitler saw as the 'inevitable' confrontation with Britain and France.[10]

On 31 August at 9 p.m., German radio cleared its schedules and broadcast the Führer's sixteen-point proposal to solve the crisis. Hitler confessed later in the hearing of his diplomatic translator, Dr Paul Schmidt, that the broadcast provided 'a pretext, especially for the German people, to show them that I have done everything to preserve peace'. The world still watched Ambassador Henderson's frantic shuttle diplomacy between London and Berlin. Behind the scenes Hitler made sure that Göring and Mussolini, the principal mediators with Britain and France in the Sudeten crisis, played no part, fearing 'that at the last moment some swine or other will yet submit to me a plan for mediation'.[11]

At 10 a.m. on Friday 1 September, Jochen and Johanna Klepper listened to Hitler's speech on the radio. 'Last night regular Polish soldiers fired on our territory for the first time,' the Führer told the hastily convened Reichstag, announcing that 'Since 5.45 a.m.' – actually 4.45 a.m. – 'the fire has been returned.' To cheering deputies, Hitler added that he would 'put on the field-grey uniform and not take it off till the war was over'. It was not a declaration of war – Poland was never honoured with one. Rather, it was a justification of self-defence to the German nation. The phrase 'returning fire' entered the official lexicon.[12]

In order to provide evidence of Polish 'provocation', the SS and police apparatus run by Reinhard Heydrich enlisted the help of local ethnic Germans who were given bombs with timers and a list of 223 ethnic German newspapers, schools, theatres, monuments and Protestant churches to show that they were the victims of Polish attacks. Unfortunately for them, Polish policemen managed to foil many of the attacks and only twenty-three targets were destroyed. To persuade the British not to fulfil their military undertaking to come to Poland's aid, Heydrich was also instructed to manufacture 'border incidents', elaborating a plan to confuse and lure Polish troops across the border at Hohenlinden. It could not be enacted because the Wehrmacht itself destroyed the Polish border station there. Instead, on the night of 31 August, an SS commando unit clad in Polish uniforms attacked the German radio station at Gleiwitz and a Polish member of the unit then read a communiqué in Polish and German, ending with the words 'Long live Poland!' He was then shot by his SS comrades and his body left behind as evidence. The Gleiwitz station lay 5 kilometres inside the German border, making it hard to explain how a Polish unit had penetrated so far through German lines without detection. To make things worse, the transmitter was too weak for Heydrich to pick up the broadcast in Berlin. As a pretext for war, it was flimsy and could not have convinced an international audience or even the Wehrmacht war crimes investigators sent to these scenes. Only a national audience, already primed, would recognise Germany as the injured party.[13]

*

The 1st of September 1939 found the teacher Wilm Hosenfeld still in the girls' school in Fulda where his unit had assembled. He used the lull to write a letter to his elder son Helmut, who had just started doing his six months of Reich Labour Service on a farm: 'now the die is cast. The terrible uncertainty is over. We know what we face. In the east the storm is rising.' Hosenfeld believed that war could have been avoided: 'The Führer's proposals were acceptable, modest and would serve to preserve the peace.'[14]

Coming from a family of devout Catholics and rural craftsmen, Hosenfeld had been 19 when he was called up in 1914, and served at the front until he was severely wounded in 1917. In the 1920s, he had revelled in the free comradeship of the youth movement, the *Wandervögel*. This and his love of organised sport prompted him to join the Nazi storm troopers and represent their 'modern' values in a traditional village like Thalau. Attending the Nuremberg Party rallies in 1936 and 1938 imbued Hosenfeld with a powerful sense of mystical unity with the German nation. An educational progressive, who rejected the kind of rote learning with the cane favoured by traditional Catholic educators, he remained profoundly religious and, by 1938, was alarmed at the attacks on religion by radicals within the Nazi movement. Wilm Hosenfeld was a man of deep and conflicting commitments.

As he continued his letter to his son that fateful Friday 1 September, to Hosenfeld it felt like the summer of 1914 all over again. Now, as then, war was being forced on Germany and the real cause was British 'encirclement'; he was convinced that any other regime would have ended up 'in conflict with E[ngland]'. 'Today fate again reigns over us,' he wrote. 'The leaders are only characters in a higher hand and must do what He wills. All domestic ideological political differences have to step back, and everyone has to be a German, to take a stand for his people.' His letter echoed the Kaiser's words of twenty-five years before, that he saw 'no parties, only Germans'.[15]

Jochen Klepper agreed. As anti-Nazi, piously Protestant and Prussian as Hosenfeld was Nazi, Catholic and Hessian, Klepper expected nothing good from this new war. 'All the sufferings of the Germans in Poland which provide the grounds for war,' he reasoned, 'will be dealt out to the Jews in Germany in exact measure.' With painfully vivid memories of the anti-Jewish pogrom of a mere ten months earlier, he feared for his Jewish wife and stepdaughter. A month after it, Jochen had had Johanna baptised and their marriage consecrated in church to try and protect her. He had chosen the brand-new Martin Luther Memorial Church in Mariendorf, with its portraits and busts of Luther, Hindenburg and Hitler in the antechapel. The 800 terracotta tiles in the nave alternated Nazi and Christian motifs, while a Hitler Youth, a storm trooper and a soldier jointly supported the pulpit. Klepper had found fame in 1937 by writing a novel which celebrated the founder of the Hohenzollern dynasty, King Frederick William I: holding up the Calvinist rectitude of the Prussian dynasty as a model, the novel was made required reading in the officer corps and annoyed many Nazis. It gave Klepper an entrée into conservative circles, now willing to overlook his 'unfortunate' Jewish marriage, and afforded him a degree of protection. In spite of his ominous forebodings, Klepper was completely convinced by the justice of the German claims to Danzig and of the need for a link through the Polish Corridor: 'The German East is too important for us not to need to understand what is now being decided there.' As Jochen and Johanna waited on events, they felt trapped by their own sense of loyalty: 'We cannot wish for the fall of the Third Reich out of bitterness as many do. That is quite impossible. In this hour of external threat we cannot hope for a rebellion or a coup.'[16]

On 1 September 1939, there were no patriotic marches and no mass rallies like those of August 1914. Instead, the streets remained eerily quiet. Reservists reported to their call-up points; civilians remained businesslike and subdued. The *Deutsche Allgemeine Zeitung* felt compelled to comment that everyone was preoccupied with 'what will happen in the coming hours and days'. In his Nikolassee suburb, Jochen Klepper read the article and wondered, 'how can a people cope with a war without any enthusiasm whatever, so downcast?!' The population seemed to be collectively holding its breath, waiting for the British and French response to the German 'counter-attack' on Poland. Many reasoned – in much the same way as Hitler did himself – that the Western powers were not likely to go to war over Danzig, having given way over the Sudetenland. Nevertheless, the fear that the disasters of the First World War were about to be repeated was palpable.[17]

Towards the end of that day, the air raid sirens sounded in Berlin, where the young press photographer Liselotte Purper was nailing blackout paper to the window frames of her flat. Banging their windows and doors shut, she and her neighbours rushed downstairs to the cellar of their apartment block, a dank hole which smelled of potatoes. They waited together, many with tear-stained faces, a young mother holding her three-week-old baby. Liselotte was frightened by the sirens, she wrote to her boyfriend Kurt, their wail 'arousing deep-seated childhood terrors'. Her Spanish neighbour, impeccably attired in his elegant coat and hat, staggered slightly, his nose and mouth completely covered with a wet towel in case of a gas attack. Soon after, the all-clear sounded. Liselotte later heard that Polish planes had penetrated 15 kilometres into German airspace. As the whole apartment block prepared for air raids in earnest, she reflected on how her life had changed in so few days: all the men she knew had been called up for front-line service. The 27-year-old decided to volunteer for the Red Cross.[18]

Out in the suburbs, Jochen Klepper had heard the air raid alarm too, and went to bed expecting the bombers to come during the night, but he slept soundly, exhausted by fears for Johanna's and Renate's safety. He thought his wife 'once more looks as bad as in

November' after the pogrom. As they clung to each other for support and waited to be separated, his stepdaughter Renate was being 'particularly gentle'. In Dresden, the scholar of eighteenth-century French literature Victor Klemperer knew that he would not be called up: he was already 58, and the 1935 race laws also excluded the First World War veteran from this duty of citizenship. As a Jew, he expected in the first week of the war to be shot or sent to a concentration camp. Instead, he noted with surprise that the rash of 'Jew-baiting' in the press quickly subsided. When two friendly policemen came to search the apartment, they asked the Klemperers solicitously, 'And why aren't you abroad yet?'[19]

After travelling for a week from Flensburg, the 26th Infantry Regiment finally crossed the German–Polish border at 5 a.m. on 3 September. By early afternoon they passed through the first abandoned villages, saw the many mined bridges and struggled through the dry, yellow sand. Trucks became bogged down, horses tired from hauling the carts, and Gerhard M. had to carry his bike for long stretches. Cycle messenger was an accidentally appropriate job for the 25-year-old fireman whose parents ran a bike shop in Flensburg. It was the first Sunday of the war.[20]

Gerhard M. and his Flensburg comrades crossed the old, pre-1914, German–Russian border in Poland on 5 September and Gerhard experienced a strong sense of entering a different, un-German world. He was struck by the poverty and misery of the Polish civilians fleeing towards them, their bedding, bicycles and small children all piled on the small farm-carts pulled by a single horse, the ubiquitous *Panjewagen*. On the outskirts of Kalisz, they came under fire for the first time, took cover, and returned it with rifles and a machine gun. It took their artillery piece to knock out the Polish machine gun in an old factory and set the whole building alight. Gerhard saw German soldiers herd a dozen Polish civilians out of a house – 'damned snipers', he noted in his diary. He did not see what happened to them, as he turned his full attention to levering the boards off the door of an abandoned chocolate shop. Gerhard chortled in his diary how they 'cleared the shop on credit', before marching on into the night.[21]

In Solingen, Dr August Töpperwien was dozing in his back garden on the afternoon of 3 September when the subdued voices of his wife and a neighbour roused him. The British government had declared war. At 5 p.m., the French government followed suit. A senior high-school teacher with the pensionable rank of a civil servant, Töpperwien was conscious of his civic responsibilities and rushed to the local military offices to volunteer, only to be sent home again. To German Protestants like him, a new war immediately evoked memories of the national calamity of 1918. There was more than politics at stake. Germans had needed to be redeemed from the sin of revolution and self-inflicted defeat. Casting around for something to say to his first religious studies class of the war, Töpperwien turned for inspiration to the writings of the theologian Emanuel Hirsch and chose as his theme the words embossed on German soldiers' brass belt buckles: 'Gott mit uns' – 'With God on our side'.[22]

The official gazette of the Protestant Church immediately rallied: 'So we unite in this hour with our people in our plea for the Führer and the Reich, for the entire Wehrmacht and for all who perform their duty for the Fatherland at home.' The Bishop of Hanover offered a prayer to God: 'Bless the Führer. Strengthen all those who stand in the service of our people, in the Wehrmacht, on land, water and in the air, and in all tasks which the Fatherland sets.' Bishop Meiser, who had endured house arrest in 1934 for rejecting Nazi attempts to dragoon Bavarian Protestants into a single Reich Church, reminded pastors in Bavaria that the war gave them the opportunity to work for the German nation's spiritual renewal, for 'a new encounter between our people and its God so that the hidden blessing of this time for our people is not lost'.[23]

The response of Catholic bishops was less enthusiastic than in 1914. Then the Archbishop of Cologne had asked God to 'Bless the German armed forces. Lead us to victory', and spoken the same language of spiritual renewal of the nation as his Protestant colleagues. Now, the Archbishopric of Cologne published administrative instructions to its parishes and a series of prayers for wartime. A few bishops went further, like the 'brown' Bishop of Freiburg, Conrad Gröber, and the conservative aristocrat Clemens August von Galen of Münster, who called on the lower clergy to join the war effort not just as priests but also 'as German men'. But their voices were rare. Catholic prelates were generally wary of attaching the great hopes for spiritual rebirth to this war which they had invested in its predecessor. Instead, they interpreted the war as a punishment for the secular materialism of modern society. As irreconcilable foes of godless Bolshevism, the

Catholic Church was also dismayed by the pact with Stalin, fearing it would spark a new church–state conflict at home.[24]

Ernst Guicking was part of the skeleton army sent to guard Germany's western border from the French, while the bulk of the Wehrmacht's combat divisions were fighting in Poland. On 5 September he wrote his first letter to Irene since being deployed. After the flurry of activity, he had time to notice how ripe the grapes were on the vines – 'Otherwise there's not much to report.' Irene's first letter was already on its way to him, written as soon as the postal embargo, imposed while the troops were moving to the front, was lifted. 'Let's hope you all return home again healthy and happy as victorious soldiers,' she told Ernst. Admitting that 'I think so often of the horrors of a war', the young florist rallied them both: 'Let's not invite trouble . . . when your head is bursting, then let's both think of the happy hours and that it will be still more lovely when you can remain with me for ever.' The young lovers remained focused on two families, her work in the greenhouses and his life in his military unit, but that did nothing to lessen their sense of foreboding. War had come; and, like many others, Irene concluded that the British 'would have it so'. The 3rd of September 1939, when Britain and France declared war on Germany, entered all German calendars and diaries printed during the next six years as the start of the war. As for 1 September, it featured as no more than a 'counter-attack' on Poland.[25]

Like most of their fellow countrymen, Irene Reitz and Ernst Guicking, August Töpperwien and Jochen Klepper, Liselotte Purper and Wilm Hosenfeld wished that war could be avoided. Irene and Ernst had no overt political opinions. Klepper, Hosenfeld and Töpperwien were repelled by elements within the Nazi movement, especially its anti-religious wing. Most Germans may have believed as they did that the invasion of Poland was justified, but few felt it was worth war with Britain and France. One report from Upper Franconia had offered a pithy precis of opinion during the summer: 'The answer to the question of how the problem "Danzig and the Corridor" is to be solved is still the same among the general public: incorporation in the Reich? Yes. Through war? No.'[26]

Such views would not have surprised Hitler, who knew that his own bellicose instincts far outstripped those of the nation he ruled. In a moment of euphoric candour, he had told an audience of leading

German journalists that he knew that the five-month Sudeten crisis had terrified their 'chicken-hearted nation'. He even confided that 'circumstances have compelled me to speak for decades almost solely of peace', adding that 'only through continued emphasis on the German desire for peace and intentions for peace was it possible for me . . . to provide the German people with the armaments which were always necessary as the basis for the next step'. That had been in November 1938. In July 1939, the annual Nuremberg Party rally had been announced for 2–11 September as the 'Reich Party Rally of Peace'. In late August, following German mobilisation, it was abruptly cancelled, as the Nazi leader had intended it would be. Sending Ambassador Henderson off to London in a last-minute masquerade of shuttle diplomacy was the final piece in the choreography of Hitler's performance as a frustrated peacemaker. This may no longer have convinced many abroad, but it did carry domestic opinion. In early September, when Wilm Hosenfeld, August Töpperwien, Irene Reitz and Jochen Klepper concluded that 'The English would have it so', they were indicting the British not just for failing to force Poland to accept Germany's 'reasonable' terms, but also for maintaining the 'encirclement' which aimed to keep their nation in its post-1918 thrall. As Germans closed ranks, they convinced themselves that war had been forced upon them.[27]

*

The 30th Infantry Division, including the 26th Infantry Regiment from Flensburg, reached the river Warthe on 7 September, crossing over the bailey bridge the German engineers had built, and passing through the abandoned Polish fortifications. They met armed resistance first from villagers, defending their homes. Gerhard M. watched his comrades leading off twenty young men, who he believed were 'cowardly snipers'. 'Burning houses, weeping women, howling children. A picture of despair. But,' Gerhard reminded himself in his diary, 'the Polish people didn't want it better.' From a primitive peasant hut, a woman fired a machine gun. Gerhard's unit surrounded the house and set it alight. When she tried to escape, 'We prevented her, hard as it was . . . Her cries rang in my ears for a long time.' The Germans had to walk down the middle of the street, so great was the heat of the houses burning along both sides. As night fell, they saw that the eastern horizon was red with the blaze of other villages. Gerhard's chief concern was staying on his bike. Its wheels kept sinking into the sandy soil of the path, pitching him on to his face in the darkness. But the young fireman from Flensburg was also aware that he had become an arsonist.[28]

On the night of 9 September, the 30th Infantry Division was attacked by Polish cavalry. Gerhard M.'s company was still in the rear of the division when panic rippled through the ranks. Over the next two days, the 8th Army, under General Johannes Blaskowitz, was pushed back 20 kilometres to the south, off its direct line of march on Warsaw. As they retreated, they set fire to houses from which they believed shots had come. 'Soon burning houses lined our path, and from the flames resounded the cries of those who had hidden inside and were no longer able to save themselves,' Gerhard M. noted. 'The cattle lowed in fear, a dog howled till it was burned up, but the worst was the screaming of the people. It was cruel. But they shot and so deserved death.' He admitted that both officers and men were extremely 'nervous'.[29]

The next day he found himself in his first regular battle, part of a thin line of German infantry lying on their stomachs in shallow holes they had hastily scooped out of the ground. Shielding an artillery position behind them, they waited for the brown dots of the Polish infantry to inch closer. Increasingly nervous, they were told to hold their fire until the enemy was only 300 metres away. Aiming, firing and reloading his rifle, Gerhard M. described his movements as 'mechanical as on the barracks' square'. Still the Germans were forced back, taking heavy casualties. Of the 140 men in his company, only Gerhard M. and six others rejoined the rest of their battalion in a wood. The next day they were relieved, the 30th Infantry Division's shattered line shored up by two others and a slow-moving column of tanks.[30]

Gerhard M. had taken part in the major battle of the campaign. When the Germans invaded on 1 September, the Wehrmacht found the Polish Army still in the midst of mobilisation. It was committed to defending the country's borders – an impossible task, given that the Germans were attacking from three sides: from East Prussia in the north, across Slovakian territory in the south, and along a broad front in the west stretching from Silesia to Pomerania. Taking Hitler's demands at face value, the Poles had believed that the Wehrmacht was trying to recapture the old Prussian–Polish borderlands between East and West Prussia. In fact, the German attack largely bypassed them and concentrated on two major thrusts, from the north and south, towards Warsaw. Advancing from Breslau, units of the 8th Army had occupied the major textile city of Łódź on 7 September. The next day, the 4th Panzer Division reached the outskirts of Warsaw.[31]

Meanwhile, the two Polish armies which had been trapped in the Polish Corridor managed to retreat from the borderlands and form a formidable force under General Tadeusz Kutrzeba. Stuck between German forces holding the north bank of the Vistula and those on the south bank of the Bzura river, Kutrzeba seized his one advantage. The Germans had lost contact with his forces and did not know that he was poised to strike the exposed lines of the 30th Infantry Division, stretched over a 30-kilometre defensive line while the rest of Blaskowitz's 8th Army continued its march towards Warsaw. It was this thin line that Gerhard M. and his comrades found themselves defending on 10 September. The German command was forced to call off the 4th Panzer Division's assault on Warsaw and bring it back, redirecting the main force of the German 10th Army and the reserves of Army Group South to shore up their weak lines. By 12 September, the initial Polish attack had petered out. Kutrzeba began to withdraw his Poznań Army to defend Warsaw, while the Pomorze Army soon found itself encircled, bombarded by German artillery and Heinkel 111 bombers which set the woods protecting the Polish troops ablaze.

While the battle of the Bzura was still raging, the Polish government and military command fell back towards the Romanian border. Their plan to withdraw into the interior was rendered hopeless when the Red Army invaded Poland from the east, on 17 September, finally fulfilling its secret pact with Germany. With nowhere left to retreat to, President Mościcki decided to establish a government-in-exile in Paris, and crossed the border into neutral Romania. The Polish survivors of the battle of the Bzura surrendered two days later. The battle had bought the Poles time to strengthen the defences of Warsaw. Abandoned by the government, the capital held out, despite massive German air raids, until 28 September.

Further west, the very speed of the German advance seemed to have left daily life untouched. Accompanied by a non-commissioned officer and six men, Wilm Hosenfeld drove into Pabianice, 10 kilometres south-west of Łódź, looking for quarters for his company. Covered in dust from the unsealed roads, the men jumped out of the car and doused themselves under the pump in a courtyard. What really caught the attention of the children looking on was Hosenfeld getting out his toothbrush. He gave 10 pfennig to the boy who had pumped the water and the Germans wandered off to buy chocolate ice cream from a stand in the park. The next day Hosenfeld went shopping. There was little war damage; just crowds of refugees from the border regions, their thin horses pulling overloaded carts. Many of the women and children tramped barefoot in the dust, carrying heavy bundles, pulling handcarts and pushing prams.[32]

Hosenfeld and his company were detailed to guard the large prisoner-of-war camp which had been set up in one of the town's textile mills. Each day, thousands of prisoners arrived. Ethnic Germans, who had served in the Polish Army, were immediately released and sent home. Jewish soldiers were singled out too. 'The rough treatment outrages me,' Hosenfeld wrote, but he noted too how the Polish prisoners watched it 'with relish', telling anyone who would listen how the Jews had exploited them. Finding no rich Jews in the town, Hosenfeld concluded that since 'the rich J[ews] have left anyway, the poor Jews have to pay the price'. Pabianice's Jews were quickly set to work shovelling the earth back into the defensive trenches which had been dug during the previous weeks. Back in the camp, Hosenfeld admired the Polish officers' impromptu evensong and choral singing and the German Catholic automatically removed his service cap. With 10,000 prisoners crammed into the textile works, food became desperately scarce and the men restive from hunger and overcrowding. Hosenfeld was ordered to make the camp secure, guarding it with barbed wire, watch towers and machine guns.[33]

The Polish campaign achieved a swift and decisive victory. In September 1939, the German military discovered how to wage a new kind of 'total' war, strafing and dive-bombing refugee columns, bombing cities without restriction and carrying out mass reprisals against prisoners of war and civilians, with little or no normative restraint. Speaking to his senior military commanders on 22 August, Hitler had had no compunction in advising them that they were to wage a racial war. His main points are preserved in graphic diary notes: 'In the foreground the destruction of Poland. Aim is not reaching a particular line, but getting rid of the living reserves . . . Close the heart against sympathy. Brutal action. 80 million [German] people must have their rights. Their existence must be secured. The stronger has the right. Greatest harshness.'[34]

Ordinary soldiers like Gerhard M. could not know what was said at Hitler's mountain retreat in Berchtesgaden. But it was clear to them that all means served the purpose of rapidly and completely destroying the enemy's forces. From the outset, there was a veritable flood of reports of 'snipers', 'guerrillas', 'bands' and other civilian 'irregulars' operating in the German rear. There was also an ominous lack of details, and the German military police units charged with investigating them generally found the allegations groundless. One army group admitted that in their first encounter with the enemy, 'the troops easily see spectres and lose their nerve'; for the inexperienced German soldiers, 'air attacks, a hostile population and irregulars are all bound to increase' this tendency.[35]

A week after the invasion began, the respected Berlin daily, the *Deutsche Allgemeine Zeitung*, published a long article on the international laws of war, confirming that 'Germany has the right to take hard but effective measures. In doing so it would be acting within the recognised boundaries of international law.' Often no more than a few shots fired by Polish soldiers trying to defend a hamlet proved sufficient for the highly strung German troops to take drastic reprisals against the civilian population, as Gerhard M. was candid enough to record. These spontaneous responses were ratified by orders from above. On 10 September, General Fedor von Bock issued an order to Army Group North: 'If there is shooting from a village behind the front and if it proves impossible to identify the house from which the shots came, then the whole village is to be burned to the ground.' Other commanders followed suit. It was no more than what Gerhard M. and his comrades were already doing. During the four weeks of fighting and the further four weeks of German military administration in Poland, between 16,000 and 27,000 Poles were executed and 531 towns and villages torched. By the time the generals handed over to civilian administrators on 26 October 1939, they were worrying about how to maintain military discipline over their troops and admitting that their men suffered from a 'psychosis' about irregulars. Such fears had not developed in a void. From their derogatory references to 'Polacks' to the expectation that they would be shot at from behind, the German armies had been ideologically primed to fight a culturally inferior and cowardly opponent.[36]

In Pabianice, Hosenfeld noted that the ethnic Germans 'have a terrible rage against the Poles'. He was increasingly shocked by what he read and heard during the second half of September. All had been well, so Hosenfeld understood, till the beginning of the year and then it had changed, with the onset of anti-German agitation. 'I have already spoken with so many, you always hear the same thing,' Hosenfeld wrote to his elder son, Helmut, on 30 September. Trying to gauge human nature, he added: 'Since seeing the roughness of our own soldiers with my own eyes, I believe in the bestial behaviour of the Poles who were irresponsibly incited.' Whatever the Germans were capable of, he assumed the Poles would have exceeded.[37]

It was much worse in the disputed western Polish border regions, like the former Prussian province of the Posen. In the town of Kępno/Kempen, the reservist Konrad Jarausch listened to the tales of ethnic German refugees when he sat down to eat at the German hotel. They told how they had been marched in pairs through Thorn to Łowicz, their wrists tied to each other. Stragglers had been shot. In Łowicz, 5,000 of them were herded into the church square and they could see the machine guns which had been set up to execute them, when German troops liberated them in the nick of time. Despite their bedraggled state, the refugees impressed Jarausch. The thoughtful high-school teacher at a Gymnasium in Magdeburg had 'never been greeted with a Hitler salute with such shining eyes'. Not a Nazi but a conservative, Protestant nationalist, Jarausch regarded the gesture as their embrace of 'everything which aligns itself with Germandom'. More ominously, the refugees all blamed the atrocities on 'the Papists and Jews'.[38]

During the summer, the Army High Command had agreed that a special task force, or *Einsatzgruppe*, led by the SS Security Service, the SD, should be attached to each of the five invading armies in order to 'repress all hostile elements' in the rear. Two further *Einsatzgruppen* were soon added. Fielding no more than 2,700 men, they were far too few and lacked the local knowledge to cope with the tasks they were given: they were rapidly supplemented by 100,000 local ethnic Germans eager to volunteer for service. Even before the battle of the Bzura ended, these local German militias were rampaging through the Polish Corridor in and around Bromberg.[39]

They were not just looking for 'revenge' for the events of the previous weeks and months, but were intent on finishing off the business of the immediate post-war years. In 1919–21, rival militias had fought each other to determine the outcome of ethno-national plebiscites in the border areas of the 'successor states' to the old multinational empires: here US President Woodrow Wilson's principle of 'the right of nations to self-determination' had given ample scope for terror and civil war. When the overwhelmingly German town of Konitz, for example, was allotted to Poland after the First World War, all civic and religious institutions in the town had split along national and ethnic lines. Throughout this formerly West Prussian region, religion acted as a proxy for nationality, with Protestants seen as Germans and Catholics as Poles. Although the Jewish communities in West Prussia declared their unshakeable allegiances to 'Germandom' as early as 1919, decrying 'Polish arbitrariness and intolerance' as the greater threat, their loyalty did not save them two decades later. When German militiamen entered Konitz in 1939, they immediately turned on their Polish Catholic and Jewish neighbours. On 26 September, they shot forty people. The next day a Polish priest was killed, and the day after that the killing extended to the 208 psychiatric patients at the Konitz hospital. By January 1940, with the assistance of the Wehrmacht and the Gestapo, the local militias had killed 900 Poles and Jews from Konitz and its surrounding villages.[40]

When they were unable to find any more Polish men, some militiamen hunted down Polish women and children instead. Many were out for private vengeance. Others aped the 'pacification methods' practised by the German military. In Bromberg, Boy Scouts who had acted as runners for the Polish Army were lined up against a wall and shot alongside the priest who wanted to give them the last rites. Many of the local militia commanders turned the basements and courtyards of their improvised prisons into torture chambers where prisoners were whipped, had nails driven into their backs and their eyes gouged out with bayonets.[41]

It was like the 'wild' concentration camps which local Nazis, SA

and SS units had established in Germany in 1933 – but with one difference: in Germany, that wave of violence had been contained, and
most prisoners were released by the summer of 1934. In occupied
Poland, as 'German order' was established, the terror increased further.
Hitler was set on preventing the Polish ruling class from re-establishing
an independent nation state. Heinrich Himmler, the head of the SS,
and his deputy, Reinhard Heydrich, grasped their opportunity to
organise the 'action against the intelligentsia' – the liquidation of the
Polish elites. Key targets were teachers, priests, academics, officers
and officials, landowners, politicians and journalists. All became liable
to arrest, summary execution or deportation to concentration camps,
where further mass executions were carried out. Pursuing their own
ideological common sense, militias and *Einsatzkommandos* routinely
included Jews as well as psychiatric patients in their 'actions' without
seeking further clarification.[42]

The largest massacres were conducted by ethnic German militias,
often acting under SD and Gestapo command, in former West Prussian
towns. Six thousand were shot in the woods around Piasnica / Neustadt,
7,000 in Szpedawsk (Preußisch-Stargard), and at Kocborowo 1,692
asylum patients were killed. On the Gruppa parade ground 6,500 Poles
and Jews from Graudenz were shot while 3,000 were killed in
Lszkówko. In Mniszek, 10,000–12,000 Poles and Jews from the Schwetz
area were shot in gravel pits. Some 3,000 Jews and Poles were killed
on the airstrip at Fordon and in the sand dunes of Miedzyn by Gestapo,
SS and militiamen. In the woodland of Rusinowo (Kreis Rippin) the
militia shot 4,200 people, and by 15 November members of the militia
and the Wehrmacht had executed 8,000 people in the forest near
Karlshof. In the absence of complete figures, some order of magnitude
is suggested by the fact that these major 'actions', in each of which
more than a thousand people were killed, alone accounted for over
65,000 deaths. Of these, 20,000–30,000 people were killed by local
German militias. The overall death toll of the first months of German
occupation must be far higher still. Already, these massacres set a new
precedent even in the bloodstained annals of Hitler's regime. They
would serve as a starting point for the future campaigns in the east.[43]

Many of the shootings were staged out of the public eye, in forests
and on airbases, but others attracted numerous spectators. During the
evening of Saturday 7 October, the soldiers stationed in Schwetz were

talking about the shootings which had been carried out that day and were scheduled to continue at the Jewish cemetery the next morning. On Sunday, Corporal Paul Kluge got there early, taking up a position close to the trench. As so often, it was the sight of the first group of victims that left the most enduring impression. A woman with three children got off the bus which had brought the prisoners to the Jewish cemetery and walked the 30 metres to the trench. Carrying her youngest child in her arms, she was made to climb down into it. She then lifted one of the other children in, while an SS man picked up the remaining little boy and passed him down to her. The woman then had to get her children to lie down on their stomachs next to her. Kluge stayed on, managing to get near enough to the four-man firing squad to look right down into the trench and observe how the men held their rifles about 20 centimetres from the back of the neck of their victims. Afterwards, he was asked to shovel earth over the corpses. He unhesitatingly obliged.[44]

Unable to watch children being killed, some of the soldiers walked away, but returned in time to see the shooting of the Polish men who arrived in a second bus. Paul Roschinski, a non-commissioned officer, noticed that some spectators got so close to the trench that their uniforms were sprinkled with the 'flesh, brain and sand' that flew out of it. Many of the soldiers who witnessed such events across Poland took rolls of photographs, which they sent home to be developed and printed. In this way, a visual record passed through the hands of parents, wives and photographic assistants before being returned to the 'execution tourists' in Poland. In most places, the Wehrmacht co-operated with the police and the SS, sometimes providing personnel for the firing squads.[45]

For some witnesses, these executions violated a moral boundary. The chief doctor to the 4th Army was so outraged that he compiled a dossier of eyewitness statements, which he addressed directly to 'the Commander-in-Chief of the Wehrmacht and the Führer of the German people Adolf Hitler'. His report was doomed for the archives, but the head of the military occupation in Poland, General Johannes Blaskowitz, also made it an issue. A devout Lutheran, Blaskowitz was so appalled by the reports reaching him that he repeatedly lobbied Walther von Brauchitsch, his Commander-in-Chief, and wrote to Hitler to protest about the behaviour of the SS, police and administration, underscoring the corrosive effects of such killings on military morale. Hitler dismissed his protests, declaring that 'one cannot wage war with Salvation Army methods'. Blaskowitz persisted, warning in February 1940 that the more brutal the occupation, the more German troops it would tie down. Indeed, the Wehrmacht could never reduce its occupation force below 500,000 men. After five months of badgering, Hitler eventually replaced Blaskowitz, but he did not retire him permanently.[46]

With a thousand priests among the victims of SS terror, the exiled primate of Poland, Cardinal Hlond, published a damning indictment of the German occupation in London. The Vatican tried to intervene through diplomatic channels, only to be told that the Concordat with the Church did not apply to the new territories; the State Secretary at the Foreign Ministry, Ernst von Weizsäcker, simply refused to acknowledge the Vatican's protest about the treatment of Polish clergy. Although the German Catholic Church made some effort to minister to Polish prisoners of war, no German bishop raised his voice to join Cardinal Hlond's condemnation of the murder of Polish Catholic priests.[47]

As a Catholic, Wilm Hosenfeld found himself having to follow his own moral compass. He had been horrified by the pogrom against the Jews in November 1938, and he quickly realised that the scale of violence against the Poles was out of all proportion to the tales of woe he had heard from the local German population. 'It's not about retaliation,' he wrote to his wife on 10 November 1939; 'it looks more like imitating the Russians and trying to exterminate the intelligentsia.' He had no idea how accurate his guess was. 'Who would have thought it of a regime with a deadly hatred of Bolshevism,' he continued. 'How gladly I became a soldier, but today I'd like to tear the [field-] grey uniform into pieces.' Was he there to hold 'the shield . . . behind which these crimes against humanity can happen?' During these first months in Poland, Hosenfeld intervened personally a couple of times to have Poles released from German custody, and, as a result, befriended their families. During the years that followed, Hosenfeld would keep in touch and even bring his wife from Thalau to stay with his Polish friends, disregarding all the norms of communal apartheid typical of German occupation.[48]

Hosenfeld's Catholic faith served as an important bridge across the chasm between occupied and occupier. Unable to express his sense of shock and abhorrence openly, let alone to alter the course of events, he had to force his emotional response inwards where it grew into a gnawing and profound sense of shame. His letters to his wife became a private confessional. 'We still have these letters,' Hosenfeld wrote to Annemie on 10 November, closing his most unhappy letter of the war so far. 'I am going to sleep now. If I could weep, I'd like to do it in your arms, and that would be such a sweet comfort.' The longer the war lasted, the more isolated he would become. Hosenfeld still believed that the Germans had a right to occupy Poland, sharing in the conventional notions of the 'right of the higher culture'; it was his sense of moral restraint and humanitarian conviction that was becoming increasingly rare.[49]

To another devout Catholic soldier, it all looked quite different. Even after the Poles had been defeated and cowed, Heinrich Böll looked into their faces and saw lurking 'behind the melancholy of their eyes, hatred and real fanaticism'. The eighth child of a Catholic carpenter in Cologne, Böll had just started studying literature at university and trying his hand at writing when war broke out. A generation younger than Hosenfeld, he had been called up that summer. 'If there was no more military here, within three weeks not a single ethnic German would survive. One sees quite clearly in their eyes that this people is predestined for revolution,' the 21-year-old wrote home from Bromberg. They needed a strong German hand, and he needed his mother to send him the latest cure-all to stay alert and on his guard – Pervitin, a methamphetamine whose use the Reich Health Leader tried to limit without much success.[50]

Böll's reflections were more typical of soldiers' views than Hosenfeld's and the German media had done its best to make sure that Poles would be viewed with suspicion. In mid-August, it had reported on mass deportations of Germans from the borderlands to 'concentration camps' in the Polish interior, with the outbreak of war precipitating a string of massacres in which ethnic German women and children were the principal victims. The weekly cinema news, the *Wochenschau*, carried graphic reports of these events and portrayed captured Polish soldiers and civilian 'irregulars' as criminally degenerate 'subhumans', who had been ordered to exterminate the German minority. The Wehrmacht Office for the Investigation of War Crimes was sent in to find evidence of a deliberate, top-down, Polish attempt at genocide.[51]

The German Foreign Office had been busy for months prior to the war, gathering the evidence that would justify the invasion. In the event, the upsurge of spontaneous ethnic violence in the borderlands in the first week of war provided real evidence, which could be magnified and manipulated to serve German needs. In November 1939 the Foreign Office rushed out a book with hundreds of pages of testimony and over a hundred documentary photographs. Carefully selected to create a powerful emotional narrative, it included intimate images of grieving wives and mothers, weeping quietly in their homes or beside carts laden with the dead; forensic photos of women who had been dismembered, or killed in positions suggestive of rape; children whose heads had been smashed in; corpses, like the First World War veteran with his full-length prosthetic leg still attached and his face obliterated beyond all recognition, laid out naked on the mortuary slab. One particularly grisly photo showed a woman giving birth at the moment she and her newborn baby were murdered, the umbilical cord still visibly connecting them. The Foreign Office publication was intended to justify Germany's occupation of Poland and to influence neutral, especially American, opinion. A second German edition followed in February 1940, and an English edition was published in May.[52]

The violence was real enough, especially in northern Posen around Bromberg/Bydgoszcz, where many ethnic Germans were killed, mainly by retreating Polish soldiers who believed that they had been shot at from the houses of Germans or who searched them for Nazi flags and symbols. Some of the dynamics at work here had been seen in the initial violence visited on Polish villages by German troops, but this time on a lesser scale: despite German propaganda claims to be countering a centrally planned attempt at deportation and genocide by the Polish state, even the Wehrmacht War Crimes Investigators found only evidence of spontaneous and uncoordinated violence, with some Polish military units even warning ethnic Germans about the mood of the troops following them.

There was also one major difference between the two German editions of the Foreign Office's *Documents on Polish Cruelty*: in November 1939, the number of German victims was put at 5,800, a figure still broadly accepted by scholars. In February 1940, it increased tenfold, possibly at Hitler's behest. Goebbels ordered newspapers to underline the new findings, and a fresh wave of press coverage drove the point home with headlines like '58,000 VICTIMS OF POLISH TERROR' and '20 YEARS OF POLISH RULE OF MURDER'. On the home front, the publication was criticised only for minimising the 'justified' German retaliatory measures against the Poles. Whether or not people fully believed that the Polish state had ordered the deliberate extermination of the German minority, they certainly did not forget these events. Indeed, in spring 1943, when Goebbels tried to mobilise public opinion – for the one and only time – in sympathy with the Poles, in order to showcase the far greater threat of Soviet terror, he had to contend with the popular memories of 1939. People pointed to the 'fact' that 60,000 Germans had been killed by Poles and asked why they merited German sympathy, even against killers from the Soviet secret police, the NKVD. The Propaganda Ministry could not remake public sympathies at will.[53]

Such arguments appropriated victimhood, justifying all subsequent German actions. They worked not by denying German violence but by making it, comparatively, insignificant. Only the numbers of German dead mattered, because only German rights mattered; and they had to be multiplied ten times in order to carry the right moral weight. The first two German documentary films of the war, *The Campaign in Poland* and *Baptism of Fire*, both opened with the threat of mass murder of ethnic Germans. The feelings evoked by existential threat and rescue also lent themselves to feature films, and the first of these appeared in 1940 with the fitting title *Enemies*. When Polish workers kill the German owner of a sawmill in the summer of 1939, the film's stars, Brigitte Horney and Willy Birgel, rescue his children and join other German refugees on their way to safety across the borders of the Reich. Directed by the renowned émigré Russian film-maker Viktor Tourjansky, the film cast Horney as the heroine rescuing her fellow ethnic Germans from their murderous enemies. The plot-line and the role of the German heroine were reprised the following year, in the bigger-budget film *Homecoming*. Here a group of Germans, hiding in a barn and listening secretly to Hitler's speech of 1 September 1939, are discovered by Poles and locked up in a partially submerged cellar. Expecting to be liquidated at any moment, they are saved by the passion and bravery of the young Nazi teacher, Paula Wessely, who leads them across the border – this time the Russian–German demarcation line. Against her emotional final monologue, the film ends with a shot of her blending into the refugee trek to be greeted by a giant image of Hitler at the border post. In keeping with Nazi aesthetics the film elevated the existential threat to the ethnic Germans into a quasi-religious experience. As they recognise the imminence of their own martyrdom, their readiness for sacrifice transforms them and, it was hoped, the watching audience. The film received standing ovations when it opened in the Reich. In contrast to the passive female and child victims portrayed by the documentation of the Foreign Ministry, here were German heroines capable of providing moral leadership. They were spiritual not physical combatants, unlike the depraved Polish women irregulars, whom Gerhard M. and his comrades had burned alive.[54]

The Lutheran churches expressed the prevalent sense of Prusso-German nationalism. In an official exchange of greetings with the Evangelical Consistory in Poland, the Protestant Church of the Old Prussian Union welcomed its co-religionists back into the national fold, acknowledging that 'The events of these weeks legitimise the twenty-year struggle in which the Evangelical Consistory of the now liberated parishes of Poland and West Prussia has waged.' Whatever had happened during and after the short military campaign was more than justified. As the text that the churches' *Gazette* carried for Harvest Festivals of Thanksgiving read, 'We thank Him that age-old German territory was permitted to return to the Fatherland and that our German brothers are free once more . . . We thank Him that decades of injustice have been broken through the gift of His mercy and the way opened for a new ordering of the nations, for a peace of honour and justice.'[55]

Poland itself rapidly became a non-topic in Germany. By mid-October 1939, a mere two weeks after Hitler had reviewed his victorious troops in Warsaw and only a week after the church bells had stopped ringing in celebration, an undercover reporter for the exiled German Social Democrats could find 'hardly a single person who still spoke of the "victory" over Poland'. Now that the dispute over Poland had been settled with the country's dismemberment, hopes revived that peaceful relations with the Western powers could be restored.[56]

On 6 October, Hitler addressed the Reichstag. The CBS reporter in

Berlin, William Shirer, noticed that it was 'a lovely fall day, cold and sunny, which seemed to contribute to everybody's good feelings'. Underscoring his pacific intentions, Hitler insisted again that he had no territorial claims on Britain and France and once more offered to make peace with the Western powers. He even offered to create a rump Polish state. As usual, Hitler blamed 'a certain international Jewish capitalism and journalism' for the warmongering, leaving it to the good sense of the British to avoid the death and destruction which would follow if they chose to continue the war. In any event, he insisted, Germany would never surrender: 'A November 1918 will never be repeated in German history.'[57]

Seated with the rest of the press in the gallery of the former opera house, Shirer had a sense of déjà vu. Hitler's words, he noted,

> were almost identical with those I've heard him offer from the same rostrum after every conquest he has made since the march into the Rhineland in 1936 . . . And though they were the fifth at least, and just like the others and just as sincerely spoken, most Germans I've talked to since seem aghast if you suggest that perhaps the outside world will put no more trust in them than they have learned by bitter experience to put in the others.

The German press made the most of it, the banner headlines of the Party's daily paper, the *Völkischer Beobachter*, screaming, 'GERMANY'S WILL FOR PEACE – NO WAR AIMS AGAINST FRANCE AND ENGLAND – NO MORE REVISION CLAIMS EXCEPT FOR COLONIES – REDUCTION OF ARMAMENTS – CO-OPERATION WITH ALL NATIONS OF EUROPE – PROPOSAL FOR A CONFERENCE'. Perhaps, Shirer remarked wearily, 'If the Nazis were sincere they might have spoken this sweet language before the "counter-attack" was launched.'[58]

On Monday 9 October, troops returning to Vienna from Poland were greeted with the news that the British government had resigned and the war was over. The next morning excited civilians shouted the wonderful news to the troop trains as they passed through the outskirts of Berlin: 'You can go home, the war's over!' As the news spread in the capital, people ran out into the streets and squares to celebrate. Students rushed from the lecture halls and held spontaneous meetings. At the weekly farmers' market in the Berlin neighbourhood of Prenzlauer Berg, new customers refused to add their names to the official lists, convinced that rationing would soon cease. On the stock exchange, the news drove up the price of government bonds. The rumour spread nationwide, questioned and reconfirmed by officials at the German telephone and telegraph exchanges, down the line in Bratislava (Pressburg), Reichenberg, Rumburg, Idar-Oberstein, Baden-Baden and Graz, as late as 10.30 a.m. on 10 October. So great was the popular desire for peace that it took a radio announcement to bring the speculation to an end.[59]

Britain and France immediately rejected the German 'peace offer', prompting German children to sing a new ditty in the street: 'Oh Chamberlain, oh Chamberlain, whatever will become of you?' to the tune of the Christmas carol, 'O Tannenbaum, O Tannenbaum'. A parody of the Lord's Prayer also spread across the country, which gave voice to the sense of national frustration – and disappointment: 'Father Chamberlain, who is in London / May your name be cursed / May your kingdom vanish.' The main achievement of Hitler's initiative was to continue the pretence of speaking peace in order to usher the German people further down the path of war. Yet the rumours of an armistice revealed, according to the SD, 'how strong is the general public's *wish for peace*'. Soothsayers and fortune tellers continued to do a brisk trade. In Bavaria, it was said that the popular stigmatic Therese Neumann from Konnersreuth had prophesied an early end to the war.[60]

Despite the victory over Poland, the real war had not yet begun. By pinning all the responsibility on the British, the Nazi regime was reminding its population that they faced a tough opponent in the British. Morever, the French Army was still larger and better equipped than the German forces, and the line of French fortifications in the south had been turned into the formidable Maginot Line. No one could see how Germany could ever defeat France and Britain, and the failure of diplomatic overtures in late August and again in early October deepened the sense of national gloom. Convinced that Germany would not be ready to launch an offensive in the west for at least two years, on 17 September the Army High Command issued a directive to prepare for a static, defensive war. When Hitler abruptly reversed this order ten days later, telling his generals in a face-to-face meeting that Germany was to launch an offensive that very autumn, even the ultra-loyal Nazi General, Walther von Reichenau, considered his leader's plans 'nothing short of criminal'. Hermann Göring, effectively the second most powerful man in the Reich, redoubled his efforts to find a diplomatic solution at the same time as he was directing the Luftwaffe's bombing campaign against Polish cities. On 10 October, Hitler pressured his military leaders by advocating a campaign through Belgium. Confronted with such concrete proposals, the Chief of the General Staff, Franz Halder, had little choice but to work them up into what even he later described as an 'unimaginitive rehash of the Schlieffen Plan' of 1914.[61]

In the atmosphere of despair, the head of military counter-intelligence, Admiral Canaris, and his deputy, Hans Oster, renewed their plotting to oust Hitler. In their search for a military figurehead they tried to recruit Halder and sounded out the commanders of the three army groups on the western front, Gerd von Rundstedt, Fedor von Bock and Ritter von Leeb. None believed that the attack plans through Belgium would work; but none saw any alternative to staying at their posts and doing their duty. While Canaris and Oster went on looking for a general willing to play politics, Hitler continued to control the military through the head of the Wehrmacht High Command office, General Wilhelm Keitel, the Wehrmacht Operations Staff, headed by Alfred Jodl and his deputy Walter Warlimont, and Brauchitsch, the Commander-in-Chief of the Army. But there was little appetite for the attack they were about to launch. To most commanders' relief, on 7 November the German offensive was postponed because of bad weather, the first of twenty-nine cancellations that winter.

*

The run-up to Christmas was the peak of the theatre season, and on 9 December 1939 Gustaf Gründgens unveiled a new production at the State Theatre on the Gendarmenmarkt. With beautiful, night-time sets based on paintings and engravings of Paris during the French Revolution, *Danton's Death* was a lavish production. The theatre's new, revolving stage expedited its twenty-five scene changes, and it followed the theatre's pre-Nazi tradition of combining the whole cast, lighting, sets and sounds into a single ensemble. The subject matter of revolutionary terror was so subversive that Georg Büchner's play had waited until 1902 for its German premiere – sixty-seven years after it was written – and the last major production in Berlin had been directed by the now exiled Max Reinhardt in 1916. Gründgens ranked alongside

Heinrich George at the Schiller Theatre and Heinz Hilpert at the German Theatre as one of the brilliant actor-managers Goebbels and Göring had hired to run the Berlin theatres, determined that the Reich capital should outshine Vienna. They frequently proved wayward in their choice of repertoire or production, but though Goebbels had his officials chivvy and chide, cajole and plead with them, in the end he let the actor-managers run their own theatres. The very subject of the play challenged Goebbels's boast in 1933 that with the Nazi seizure of power 'the year 1789 has been expunged from the records of history'. The Nazi Party paper, *Der Angriff*, was so appalled that it asked whether such a flawed play was 'worth so much effort'.[62]

Gründgens avoided any propagandistic interpretation and directed the two principals, Danton and Robespierre, as tragic figures, the one rousing himself from melancholic passivity to rail against his enemies, the other quietly consumed by the fire of true belief burning within him. Danton, played by Gustav Knuth, brought the house down with his speech to the Revolutionary Tribunal, turning from defendant to accuser as he foretold dictatorship, terror and war – 'You want bread and they throw you heads.' But the production impressed the *Deutsche Allgemeine Zeitung*'s reviewer, Bruno Werner, above all for its almost lyrical restraint and for the quiet space it gave to the female roles, no more so than in the final scene in which an Ophelia-voiced Marianne Hoppe keened for her executed husband, Camille Desmoulins, rocking herself to and fro on the wooden steps to the guillotine behind her, singing:

> Dear cradle, who lulled my Camille to sleep, smothering him
>   beneath your roses
> Death-bell, who sang him to his grave with your sweet tongue.
> Hundreds of thousands are all
> The uncounted who under the blade fall.[63]

With the audience facing the spectacle of the guillotine and the impending slaughter of an entire generation in terror and revolutionary war, the final curtain fell. Before the standing ovations began, there was a long and shocked silence.[64]

2

Closing Ranks

In September 1939, August Töpperwien was impressed by the 'machine-like precision' with which the country went on to a war footing. In fact, many of the measures he marvelled at depended on a great deal of improvisation. Töpperwien's wife Gretel went off to the Solingen shops to buy extra plates and spoons to help feed the evacuees from the Saarland. To clear the western border region with France of civilians, special trains were laid on for those without transport. They were met at the stations by teenage girls and boys from the League of German Girls (BDM), and Hitler Youth, served soup at makeshift railway canteens by the National Socialist People's Welfare and accommodated in school buildings which had just served as military assembly points. The success of the operation depended on goodwill.[1]

Farmers trekked eastwards out of the Saar region. Their carts piled high with bedding and leading their horses and livestock, they brought chaos to the streets and prompted a spontaneous outpouring of solidarity. In the Hessian village of Altenburschla, Ernst Guicking's father welcomed a mother and her four young children into their farmhouse. With Ernst himself stationed on the Saarland front, his family farm saw this as a direct kind of exchange: 'We are happy to do everything we can, if only you can return to us soon. Let God grant that.' But his tolerance, if not his patriotism, had clear limits. When the evacuees finally returned home two months later, it came none too soon for the old man: 'In the long run we couldn't have kept them here. Just think of how dreadful the beds looked. We couldn't cope because they were very unclean.' While the hosts were blaming the evacuees for infesting villages with lice, the Catholic Church was complaining that there was no place for devout Saarlanders to worship in Protestant Thuringia. By early November the Security Police estimated that up to 80 per cent of the evacuees were so unhappy with their reception that they had either tried to make their own arrangements or turned around and gone home again.[2]

Compared to the dislocations which were still to come, the Saarland evacuation was small-scale and, if not forgotten, at least soon overlaid by other experiences of war. Yet the dynamics at work were also a fore-taste of what was to come. There was a genuine upsurge of patriotic goodwill, which helped mobilise teenage volunteers, like the BDM girls who turned out at railway stations in the night to provide hot drinks, and which enabled individual hosts to open their doors to bedraggled and needy strangers. This was exactly the kind of patriotism the Nazis had aimed to foster before the war through Hot Pot Sundays where middle-class professionals and managers ate from the same pot of stew along with their workers, or by taking youth groups to different parts of the Reich so as to overcome regional antagonisms and prejudices. Bolstered by references to the German 'national community' formed in the crucible of the previous war, such spontaneous national solidarity was seen as a kind of test of the nation's ability to meet this new challenge through purposeful and united action.[3]

It was a test that German society never really passed. There was no lack of patriotic commitment or understanding of the justice of the German cause. The flaw lay in the very notion that a few ritual gestures could turn a highly differentiated and often conflictual modern society into a cosy pre-modern 'community' that had only ever existed in romantic imaginings of a lost 'golden age' before industrialisation. The longer the war lasted, the more the central state, the Party and its mass organisations, local authorities and the churches would have to do in order to offset this shortfall in national solidarity.

★

The regime knew that both military victory and its own political survival depended on how successfully and equitably it fed the German popula-tion. In the First World War, food distribution had been a disaster, with rampant price inflation and an even more exorbitant black market reducing the urban working class to near-famine conditions. The Royal Navy's blockade, the provisioning crisis and the 'turnip winter' of 1916–17 had paved the way for the revolution of November 1918. In the Ruhr by 1916, children's growth was markedly stunted. By 1917 and 1918, the death rate of civilians living in Berlin had outstripped that of soldiers conscripted from the city; it had been highest amongst teenage girls and young women, as tuberculosis swept through the unheated tenement blocks that housed the urban working class. This, the authorities were determined, would not occur again. Hitler in particular remained apprehensive about what level of hardship the German people would endure, and the SD's reports duly found that the 'mood of the population' was influenced by food supplies more than anything else.[4]

Food rationing was introduced on 27 August 1939, the day after Germany mobilised its armed forces. 'For a couple of days my stomach has been troubling me, especially now that we have to save on food,' Irene Reitz reluctantly reported to her boyfriend Ernst Guicking, conscious that civilians were not meant to give soldiers reason to worry. Watching everyone else foraging for flour, sugar and fat in the first weeks of the war, she had not worried, confining her own efforts to going to a stationer's and buying 'silk paper in all colours. You know, to be able to wrap presents prettily in the future. Wasn't that a good idea?' In late September it all changed, when one of her co-workers in the flower-growing business in Giessen was called up: he had always brought in extra bread and sausage for her lunch from his village. 'I miss him a lot now, especially the sandwiches,' Irene admitted.[5]

Fearing a run on the shops, the sale of linen, footwear and clothing was prohibited except for those with an official chit. But as the public piled into the understaffed rationing offices, the bureaucrats had no way of checking if the claimants needed the items they were asking for. Though they had to sign a declaration consenting to having their households inspected, it is doubtful how far this deterred civilians gripped by fear of a goods famine. 'Anyone with two pairs of shoes doesn't receive a new chit to buy a new pair,' Irene reported to Ernst. 'So of course everyone writes that he only has one pair. Thank God that I've not needed to go there yet. You can easily queue for two hours.' Meanwhile, the SD reported, shopkeepers did not know whether to demand chits for gloves or not, and whether only for leather pairs or also for cloth ones. It took two months to overhaul the system and introduce clothing cards which gave most people 100 points for the coming year, backdated to 1 September. Socks and stockings took 5 points, for example – but no more than five could be bought in a year – pyjamas took 30 and a coat or suit 60 points.[6]

Dependent on imports for half of its leather, shoe production went into immediate crisis and there was no more leather for resoling shoes; across the country, customers were being told they would have to wait six to eight weeks even for repairs using synthetic soles. However, German consumers had effectively been living in a war economy for the previous six years. Even the return to full employment had not lifted real wages to the level attained prior to the crash of 1929, with household income only rising as more family members found jobs. Years of rearmament, consuming an unheard-of 20 per cent of domestic production in peacetime, curbed the output of clothing, furniture, cars and housewares. Autarchic economic policies, bent on preserving precious foreign currency reserves, restricted imported items like real coffee, turning it into a precious luxury even before 1939. In order to conserve wool and reduce cotton imports, spun rayon was used as a substitute, especially in winter coats, even though it tended to remain stretched after becoming wet and had very poor insulating properties.[7]

War depressed the standard of living further, driving civilian consumption down 11 per cent during the first year. The national diet became more monotonous, revolving around bread, potatoes and preserves. Beer became thin, sausage was padded out with other ingredients. When the French pulled back from the territory along the Rhine near Kehl, which they had briefly occupied during the Polish campaign, Ernst Guicking grabbed the supplies they abandoned. He was able to send a packet of real coffee back to Irene and her aunt in Giessen. They were delighted to have a break from the synthetic brew known colloquially as 'Horst Wessel coffee' because – like the eponymous Nazi martyr of the Party anthem – 'the beans only marched with them in spirit'.[8]

Meat shortages were altogether more serious. Germany depended on the import of animal feeds from North America, now cut by the British naval blockade. The cost of feed led to culls in the German swine herd in early autumn. Unlike in Britain, in Germany many industrial workers had traditionally supplemented their wages by tending allotments and keeping rabbits or even a pig, a common practice particularly amongst coal miners. More town-dwellers of all classes now started to cultivate vegetables and keep hens or rabbits, but keeping pigs became less popular, not just because of the high cost of feed but also because such 'self-providers' were not entitled to meat rations. Lack of refrigeration was blamed for problems in transporting milk, eggs and meat across the country, with Berlin soon suffering from milk shortfalls. In western Germany the cattle herds were so depleted that only 35–40 per cent of the meat quotas could be handed out, while there was a temporary abundance in the south, with one old Social Democrat marvelling at his butcher's ability to offer 'sides of bacon without ration stamps'.[9]

By issuing food ration cards for periods of four weeks, the Food Ministry maintained maximum flexibility: potatoes could easily be replaced with bread or, less popularly, with rice, if supplies dried up. Because the food stamps could not be carried over to the next month, no mountain of back-claims could accumulate. On the other hand, these short-term horizons and fluctuations rapidly turned food into an obses-sion, where real and imagined shortages exercised an influence far beyond their actual scale. People of all walks of life, one Social Democratic reporter noted wryly, 'speak far more about provisioning than about politics. Each person is entirely taken up with how to get his ration. How can I get something extra?' On Sundays local trains were full of people – including teenagers in Hitler Youth uniform – all leaving the towns to go foraging for foodstuffs in the countryside, much as in the previous war. As a general fear of wartime inflation once again took hold in Germany, people rushed to turn their cash into anything that could be traded later on: luxury items such as furs, porcelain and furni-ture, which remained unrationed, were swiftly sold out.[10]

By October 1939, many believed that the country would not be able to hold out as long as in the last war 'because there's already nothing left to eat'. Only the soldiers, everyone agreed, had enough. Resentment of the privileged lifestyle of Nazi officials was aired in bitter parody. In Cologne, Josef Grohé became the butt of many jokes, and in early October, a picture of the Gauleiter with his rounded jowls was cut out of the pages of the local paper and pinned up on the blackboard of a factory. Underneath, someone had scrawled:

> One people, one leader, one nation
> Before the law all are equal
> Grohé is starving unstintingly
> For the national comrades quite a model.

Four Gestapo officials came to investigate but could not find the culprit. By early November, some local Nazi Party officials were so afraid of being called cowards and shirkers that they asked to serve at the front.[11]

Social discontent fed off the discrepancy between promise and reality. The rationing system strove to balance merit – as measured through work – and social need in allocating food, which led to an elaborate hierarchy of entitlement. The most stark divide was race. At the outbreak of war, 185,000 registered Jews remained in the Reich, perhaps 40 per cent of the Jewish population of 1933. After the November 1938 pogrom most of the young had emigrated, leaving an ageing and increasingly destitute community, concentrated mainly in the cities, especially Berlin and Frankfurt. They were prevented from buying underwear, shoes and clothing, even for their growing teenage children. Although initially their food rations remained pegged on the same level as everyone else's – a fact the Kleppers found very reassuring – their cards were speckled with red 'J's for 'Jude', reminding neighbours, shoppers and sales assistants alike to enforce the host of new regulations stipulating where Jews could shop and which foodstuffs they were prohibited from purchasing. Different local authorities set their own shopping curfews to prevent Jews from inconveniencing German shoppers. As Polish prisoners of war and civilian workers were brought to work in German industry, their entitlements were also set below those of their German co-workers.[12]

Even for 'Aryan national comrades', there was no simple, one-size-fits-all allocation, as there was in Britain, a country haunted by its own legacy of unfair and incompetent rationing in the First World War. Instead, Germany started out with three basic categories, covering 'normal consumers', 'heavy workers' and 'very heavy workers'. There were supplements for those doing shift- and night-work. Supplements were added for young children, for children aged 6–18, for pregnant women and nursing mothers, as well as for the sick. By April 1945, they had extended into sixteen different categories; in cities of more than 10,000 inhabitants even dogs were allotted offal according to a system grading their usefulness.

The system was based on nutritional research. A 1937 study of 350 workers' families had established an average benchmark of 2,750 calories per person per day. Further research and lobbying led to much subsequent tweaking. There were warnings from Berlin that shortages of protein and fats might lead to infertility in adolescent girls, thereby undermining the regime's pro-natalist policies. Women turned these policies to their own advantage, warning that the difficulties they had in feeding their children might dissuade them from having more. The head of the National Socialist People's Welfare, Erich Hilgenfeldt, successfully pressed for the introduction of 'family support' payments to help poorer families fund the food rations they were entitled to draw. In practice, however, 'family support' remained very modest, intended to help poorer Germans survive without upsetting the 'natural order' of meritocratic social selection. This was a system of state regulation, designed to meet social needs without ever appearing too socialist or egalitarian.[13]

Inevitably, Germans soon became aware of unfairnesses in this system. With a daily allocation of 4,200 calories, industrial workers doing 'very heavy labour' received the most. Exempt from conscription because they were deemed 'irreplaceable', they were skilled men whom the coal industry and large armaments factories did not want to lose. The firms were able to count on the support of the German Labour Front and the local Gauleiter, and so had little difficulty when pushing for their workers to be classified in the top band. White-collar workers in offices, retail and commerce lacked the kind of leverage exercised by those in the military-industrial sector and generally received the standard 2,400 calories a day allotted to the 'normal consumer', as did middle-class professionals. Researchers for the German Labour Front warned as early as September 1939 that rationing would raise consumption for one half of the population and lower it for the other. There was also a shift in resources from older to younger adults: comparing data from December 1937 and February 1942, a study of 1,774 adult workers found that male workers aged 55–60 and women in the 60–65 group lost weight, whereas men aged 20–30 and women aged 20–35 all gained it. The material prosperity of the young would be paralleled in a loosening of social and familial controls over them.[14]

Another study came to the surprising conclusion that the greatest loss of weight among 6,500 male industrial workers was to be found amongst those classified as doing heavy or very heavy labour – the very groups awarded the highest rations. Apparently, the men pooled their ration supplements for their families. In an effort to reverse such trends, factory managers were encouraged to introduce works canteens to make sure that their workers ate a hot meal at lunch. But because the canteens demanded food stamps which could be saved for the family, take-up was low. Only the special 'Hermann-Göring sandwiches', doled out during exceptionally long shifts, proved popular because they generally remained off-ration. By the end of 1941, the Ministry of Food suspected that many pits were returning false log-books of miners' working hours in order to justify providing them.[15]

On 4 September 1939, a draconian War Economy Decree introduced compulsory Sunday working, froze wages, cut overtime rates and increased taxes. The police presence in factories had to be stepped up immediately. Even before the war broke out, the authorities had been facing a wave of working-class discontent at long working hours. The armaments boom had led to a shortage of labour, making for an over-worked and increasingly restless workforce. Coal production had dropped, causing cuts of deliveries to the railways as well as to domestic heating in January 1939. While Nazi surveillance of the shop floor repressed any form of collective action, by the summer of 1939 labour discipline in the heartland of heavy industry in the Ruhr was described as 'catastrophic'. Workers responded to the new wartime decree by intensifying the kinds of low-level resistance which had already proved effective before the war. Absenteeism – especially on Mondays – rose, as did sickness and refusal to work overtime. The SD urged the regime to make concessions and it did, reversing the wage cuts and restoring bonus payments for overtime and working on Sundays.[16]

Winter came early and hard in November 1939, and rail transport promptly collapsed. Overstretched by having to support the campaign in Poland, the evacuation from the Saar and a war economy, the German railways lacked the rolling stock to move coal from the pitheads of the Ruhr. That month the Coal Syndicate of the Rhine and Westphalia was forced to stockpile 1.2 million tonnes of coal. The resulting coal shortage proved so serious that, even in towns near to the Ruhr, firms had to go on to short-time working or start their Christmas break early. Across Germany, people had to wear outdoor clothing at home. Schools – which had only just reopened after serving as military assembly points, after accommodating evacuees and storing the harvest – promptly closed again because they could not be heated. In some cities, crowds gathered outside coal yards and the police had to prevent delivery trucks from being stormed. When the waterways froze in early January, coal barges could not make deliveries in Berlin. With temperatures plummeting to −15°C, the American journalist William Shirer was moved to pity as he watched 'people carrying a sack of coal home in a baby-carriage or on their shoulders . . . Everyone is grumbling. Nothing like continual cold to lower your morale.'[17]

As the crisis deepened, local officials began raiding coal trains that passed through their areas, to provide for their populations. The mayor of Glogau, for instance, authorised the unloading of wagons whose 'axles had over-heated'. Furious at such selfishness, the Deputy Führer Rudolf Hess reminded local Party officials that the rationing system depended on all parts of the country carrying the same burdens. And, by and large, they did. Partly because of the measures instituted before the war in order to rearm, state control of pricing and distribution was far stronger than in the previous war. In the coming years, rationing and especially food distribution would regularly be criticised for being too centralised, inflexible and insensitive to local circumstances – let alone regional culinary traditions – but those criticisms also represented a victory of sorts. Despite crises, local particularism did not overwhelm the rationing system, at least not until early 1945.[18]

Subsequent winters would produce more coal shortages and 'coal holidays' for schoolchildren, but, as people's expectations adjusted, these would not have the same significance. The first coal crisis of the war reawakened social memories and resentments from the previous war, gripping both state authorities and society at large with the fear of history repeating itself. In the old heartlands of the German labour movement, in cities such as Dortmund, Düsseldorf, Dresden, Bielefeld and Plauen, communist slogans, like 'Red Front' and 'Down with Hitler', started to appear again. Marxist leaflets – some of them, thanks to the pact with Stalin, Trotskyite in orientation – were found in workplaces or stuffed into letterboxes. In Vienna and Linz, there were reports of renewed propaganda for Austrian independence and the restoration of the Habsburgs. But it was not in Germany and Austria that political discontent spilled out on to the street. That happened in Prague, where a major demonstration took place outside the Gestapo headquarters on 28 October 1939. Elsewhere in the 'Reich Protectorate' of Bohemia and

and intellectuals held silent protests and vigils. They
y a regime determined to impose order on its non-
Among German and Austrian 'national comrades',
humour and graffiti did not translate into political
alist émigrés who had hoped for a revolution during
ears of Nazi dictatorship had to admit in late October

1939 that revolt was unlikely, concluding instead: 'Only if famine takes hold and has worn their nerves down, and, above all, if the Western powers succeed in gaining successes in the West and in occupying large portions of German territory, may the time for a revolution begin to ripen.'[19]

*

Following the precedent of the previous war the police and welfare authorities were primed for a crisis of juvenile delinquency. By the start of November 1939, the SD was already convinced that 'clearly the most difficult problem' for law and order in Germany was the appearance of 'wayward youths'. Young people of both sexes were flocking to reopened dance halls. In small towns and the countryside, they were drinking and smoking to excess in the taverns and playing cards as if these were ordinary times. In Cologne, 'more and more young female persons' were reportedly gathering in front of and inside the main railway station, in order to meet soldiers 'and in a manner which left no doubt about the eventual point . . . Of ten girls found with men, none of whom was registered with the vice squad, five had a sexual disease.'[20]

The first signs of 'wayward youth' likely to attract the attention of the police, local youth boards and welfare officials were truancy and loitering at street corners. Among girls, this was automatically equated with promiscuity, prostitution and venereal disease; among boys, with theft and an inexorable descent into 'habitual' crime. There was nothing uniquely Nazi about these highly resilient – and gendered – motifs of the sexually 'prematurely mature' adolescent girl and the thieving teenage boy, joy-riding on stolen bicycles. The same categories of 'wayward' behaviour were being used across North America, Western Europe and Australia from the late nineteenth century until well into the 1950s, building a broad consensus that 'difficult' children needed to be placed in institutions to save them and society at large from a vicious circle of moral depravity.[21]

Despite wartime constraints on social spending, the number of children and teenagers sent to reformatories kept rising. By 1941, the number reached 100,000, probably their full capacity, thereby restricting how many young people could be sent to 'educative' institutions. Who would be left alone and who would be taken into care remained a lottery, with the odds stacked against the traditional clientele of welfare officials, the children of the urban poor. Most had committed no crime; they were sent for 'preventive' purposes, or simply because they were seen as a danger to the community.[22]

The former Benedictine monastery at Breitenau served as one of Hesse's harsher reformatories. Set in the rolling countryside of northern Hesse near a bend in the river Fulda, its tall baroque buildings, steeply pitched roofs and enclosed inner courtyard were naturally imposing and forbidding. It was where children and teenagers who had run away from other, more open institutions were sent. On arrival, they went through a similar routine to adult prisoners and workhouse inmates with whom they shared the building – the beggars, vagrants, unemployed and criminals who were given a spell in a workhouse at the end of their prison term to help 'educate' them to a life of morality, discipline and hard work before being readmitted to the 'national community'. Stripped of their clothes and possessions, the children and teenagers were clad in simple browny-grey sackcloth. The working day for everyone was at least eleven to twelve hours. Lateness for work, running away and other infractions were punished by unofficial beatings or, worse, by an officially regulated spell of solitary confinement in the punishment cells or extensions to their sentence.[23]

Among their number were several girls who had themselves been the victims of sexual abuse. Fourteen-year-old Ronald and his 13-year-old sister Ingeborg were sent for 'corrective education' after it became clear that he and his friends had been forcing her to have sex with them over an eighteen-month period. 'Ronald and Ingeborg', the judgment read, 'are already seriously wayward. The father is in the armed forces, the mother has to work. It is therefore not possible to combat the depravity of the children in their parental home and so correctional education must be instituted.'[24]

Fifteen-year-old Anni N. was sent to Breitenau after giving birth to an illegitimate child in July 1940. She confided to the local woman social worker how her stepfather had come into her bed in the middle of the night and forced himself on her while her mother was asleep in the same room. The male police officials who dealt with her case did not believe her, and the Youth Welfare Board concluded that 'she does not stay in any employment, she lies and she leads a dissolute life'.[25]

Anni's case was only too typical: she had to be taken out of school and off the streets. It was not about helping the victims of sexual abuse but, rather, about protecting their peers from being drawn into the same 'degenerative' spiral. Nazi policy worked within an existing set of ideas. Religious conservatives and liberal reformers, jurists and psychologists were all disinclined to accept the testimony of children in sex abuse cases, turning the 'mendacious' child into the problem.

In February 1942, the governor of Breitenau advised the Youth Welfare Board in Apolda against placing Anni N. in outside employment too soon: 'Normally with such girls at least a one-year stint is necessary so that she has a certain fear of being sent here, for only this [fear] can still make her into a useful member of the national community.' On 1 June 1942 Anni died of tuberculosis. She was not alone. Waltraud Pfeil died within a month of being sent back to Breitenau after attempting to run away to Kassel in the summer of 1942. A few months later, Ruth Felsmann died after serving a two-week spell in solitary confinement. In August 1944, the local hospital in Melsungen found that Lieselotte Schmitz's weight had dropped from 62 to 38 kilos. Like Anni, she had contracted tuberculosis in Breitenau and died soon after. The fact that teenage girls died as a result of their treatment there testified to an erosion of institutional checks on disciplinary measures typical of the Nazi state. However much the German government worried about the corrosive effect food shortages would have on German civilian morale, the war ended any effective restriction on starving those youngsters who had been taken out of the 'national community' and placed in closed institutions.[26]

Release from corrective education came slowly, via probationary work placements, generally on outlying farms. It was an education in the ethos of hard work, steady behaviour and obedience. In any dispute the farmers and their wives were swift to remind the children and teenagers of their reformatory pasts and to enlist official threats to re-incarcerate them. Girls' love affairs with soldiers led to tests for venereal disease; boys failing to feed the cows on a Sunday afternoon prompted official warnings for sabotaging the war effort. The stigma of the reformatory clung to them. After being put into care at the age of 12, Lieselotte S. tried to justify herself six years later to a mother she hardly knew:

I was a child at the time I left you and now I'm already grown-up and you don't know what kind of person I am . . . Forget everything I did to you. I want to make it all up to you. I hereby promise you that I'll change my ways out of love for you.[27]

Isolated and – rightly – afraid that society was on the side of the experts and administrators, Lieselotte was not at all sure the general social contempt stopped at her own family. For girls like her, the road back into the 'national community' depended on diligence, perseverance and not stepping out of line. It was also a reminder to others that belonging had to be earned.

★

Throughout Germany, children found that they suddenly enjoyed greater freedom and teenagers were asked to take on more responsibility for watching over younger siblings. As men were called up, women became single parents and struggled with erratic school hours, queued for items in short supply and waited at local government offices. In most families, women also faced growing economic pressure to work. Women took over running family businesses and returned to the classrooms to replace male teachers of military age. Working-class women took up jobs in armaments factories and labour suddenly became scarce in traditional – and badly paid – sectors of female employment, such as agriculture and domestic service.[28]

Absent fathers could sense that their role as the all-powerful head of the family was diminished with distance. Within a fortnight of the invasion of Poland, the Thuringian cabinetmaker Fritz Probst was exhorting his teenage son, Karl-Heinz, 'Do your duty too as a German boy is meant to. Work and help where you can and don't just think of playing now. Think of our soldiers standing before the enemy . . . Then you too can say later: "I contributed to saving our Germany of today from destruction."'[29] Like so many other fathers, Probst knew that he had no direct control over his older son, and his latent conflict with Karl-Heinz soon burst out into the open. Three months into the war, Probst chided him,

Karl-Heinz! You should be a bit ashamed to be so rude to your mother at a time like this. Didn't I tell you once, I think it was a year ago just before Christmas when Mummy was at the shops, how you must treat your mother? I hope you haven't forgotten it. And you gave your word

of honour that you would always be proper. Have you broken your word?
Well, please reply *soon* to this.[30]

Probst advised his wife that 'a strict upbringing is good for character-
building'.[31] A self-employed cabinetmaker, he had joined an engineering
corps specialising in bridge construction behind the western front. On
19 September, he had been able to write home with some pride: they
had just completed their first bridge – 415 metres long and 10 metres
wide. He did not know when or how it would be used.

For most Germans the war remained distant. The campaign in
Poland had been replaced with months of stalemate in the west. The
U-boat campaign against the Royal Naval blockade was the only
action to report. In 1914 a news-hungry public had stormed the kiosks,
buying up special editions. September 1939 saw the greatest spike in
demand for radio receivers, with sales rocketing by 75 per cent
compared to a year before, bringing total ownership of private sets
up to 13,435,301. Listening to the news became more important than
ever, though the lack of action made people worry that the government was keeping bad news from them, especially losses of air and
submarine crews. According to the SD, the dearth of information
prompted people to complain that they were 'politically mature
enough to deal with negative events and developments'.[32]

The Sunday radio programme the *Voice of the Front* exhorted civilians to be worthy of the men defending them: 'The nation must draw
together in the struggle and form a community of fate, which is tied
together for life and for death . . . Look at the soldier, how firmly he
grasps his rifle, how sternly he looks across the trench . . . the same
attitude should be that of every man and woman at home.' The
counterpoint to such idealised images of Germans at war was to be
found in the deceit and immorality, injustice and cruelty of Germany's
enemies, led by Jewish warmongers – in England by the Secretary of
State for War, Leslie Hore-Belisha, in France by Léon Blum and
Georges Mandel – who put their Jewish bellicosity above their own
nation's peaceful interests. As the sharp-eyed émigrés who monitored
the daily output of German radio for the BBC put it, 'Total war
becomes a struggle between total morality and total immorality. The
result is that the German radio is one of the most moralistic systems
of communication in the world.' By stressing sacrifice on the home

front and educating the German people in hatred, in the very first months of the war German radio worked up the themes that would inform its reporting through the weary years to come.[33]

The emotional counterpoint to such morally demanding broadcasts was light entertainment. One of Goebbels's first injunctions to the German radio executives, back in 1933, had been: 'The primary rule is: just don't be boring. I prioritize this above *everything* else. Whatever you do, do not broadcast tedium, do not present the desired attitude on a silver platter, do not think that one can best serve the national government by playing thunderous military marches every evening.' If the real danger facing a modern dictatorship was that it would quickly lose touch with 'modern sensibilities', then the director of radio programming, Eugen Hadamovsky, broke with the cultural elitism of Weimar to pave the way for lighter populist fare. In March 1936, serious 'opus music' lost its prime evening slot of 8–10 p.m., in favour of a catch-all schedule of lighter concerts, variety shows and dance music. A 1939 survey of listeners' preferences showed that the new *variété* format worked across all the different sections of German society; even professionals and intellectuals preferred this popular fare to classical concerts.[34]

On 1 October 1939 a new prime-time radio show was launched, the *Request Concert for the Wehrmacht*, which rapidly established itself as *the* programme. In the first broadcast, the actor Gustaf Gründgens promised German soldiers that they would feel 'the homeland's loyalty' across space and time. It was equally effective on the home front. As Irene Reitz wrote eagerly to Ernst Guicking, 'Each time when a request concert is announced, I'm there of course . . . I don't think I missed anything. I sit so close to the loudspeaker, as if I wanted to crawl inside it . . . I'm longing for the next concert. But it may take a little bit longer because the dear wireless has just mountains of mail to answer.'[35]

They did indeed: 23,117 requests poured in for the second show and the mailbags were soon too big for the number of individual letters to be counted. Presented by Heinz Goedecke – who like many other popular radio personalities had made his name as a sports commentator – it combined light music and personal requests with dedications, using a format which mixed marching music and popular *Schlager*, love ballads, classical overtures, operatic arias and children's lullabies, short readings and poems, all performed in front of a live studio audience. The programme began with a bugle fanfare and Hitler's favourite march, the *Badenweiler*, it closed with a list of the day's contributors – all of whom performed gratis. Over the years, Goebbels flattered or bullied many major stars of stage and screen into contributing, including Hans Albers, Willy Birgel, Zarah Leander, Gustav Gründgens, Werner Krauss, Katharina Söderbaum, Jenny Jugo, Hans Söhnker, Grethe Weiser, Paul Hörbiger, Willy Fritsch, Heinz Rühmann and Marika Rökk. The *Request Concert* was allotted three hours on Wednesday evenings in addition to its prime Sunday slot.[36] The dedications brought together couples separated by war in a shared moment of public intimacy. Irene Reitz tried to describe to Ernst Guicking the emotions coursing through her as she listened:

> My eyes filled with tears. Especially when the Request Concert starts and you hear [the letter being read out] that Daddy should come back, should come soon, very soon . . . And for every greeting two marks have to be donated to the Winter Relief Fund. Who doesn't give gladly now? I haven't ever sacrificed so much before as now. You finally really know what you're giving for.[37]

On 29 October 1939, Irene Reitz snatched a moment midway through the broadcast to write quickly and tell Ernst that she was listening, still hoping to catch a dedication from him. She had a particular reason to feel close. That Sunday she had finally told her parents that she and Ernst wanted to become engaged. It had all gone far more smoothly than she had dared to expect. 'My parents have already been thinking about it much earlier than us. Now I could box my own ears,' she told him, thinking back over the weeks of stomach aches, procrastination and forceful letters from Ernst urging her to act. 'Why didn't I speak earlier? Why did I have these damned inhibitions? I could have had such an easy time of it.' Irene and Ernst wanted to get engaged during the Christmas holiday. It was the time he was most likely to be granted leave, even if the war had not ended yet. Ernst kept pushing and the engagement party soon turned into the wedding itself. Irene's mother reminded them that she and Irene's father had married in the First World War, and advised them to wait and have children once the hardships of war were past. She knew what she was talking about: like Ernst himself, Irene had been born in wartime.[38]

The only objection to the couple's plans for a modern, secular wedding in the registry office came from Ernst's sister, Anna, who penned a gentle plea to Irene pointing out that a church wedding was 'the norm for us in the village'. But even on the family farm in Protestant Altenburschla, with its solid black-and-white half-timbered houses, she left it up to 'each person to follow his free will'. Rather than make do with the new wartime, stainless-steel wedding rings on offer, Ernst found a jeweller in the Saarland where he was stationed who could still supply a gold ring for Irene. They were married on Saturday, 23 December 1939, just before everything closed for Christmas. Two weeks later, Ernst returned to his unit.[39]

After all the excitement, the newly-weds settled back into their routine of letter-writing, sharing her parents' worries as they fretted about the time it was taking for the marriage certificate to arrive: without it, they could not begin to plan their future home, because the local authorities would not issue chits for household linen. Both wished for an early end to the war, looked forward to Ernst's next leave, and Irene went back to listening to the *Request Concert*.

Later that year, art would imitate art in the first blockbuster feature film of the war. Entitled simply *The Request Concert*, it had the show's compère, Heinz Goedecke, play himself, with the programme serving to reunite two lovers brought together in Berlin by the 1936 Olympics and separated soon afterwards by the hero's military duty. As an air force pilot, he has to leave on a secret mission with the Condor Legion in the Spanish Civil War without a word of farewell. On his return, he discovers that his beloved, Inge, has moved and he cannot find her. Eventually, by now serving in the present war, he sends a message to the *Request Concert* asking that the Olympic anthem be played for her. Hearing it, Inge writes back, her love for him undiminished by the long silence, separation, or indeed by the advances of another suitor.[40]

Between 20 and 25 million people went to see the film, the highest box office for any German movie until then. The radio show was even more successful. Up to half the country tuned in to listen. By the time the programme was dropped in May 1941, after some seventy-five concerts, the names of 52,797 soldiers and units had been read out, 9,297 fathers had been told of the births of their children, and 15,477,374.62 marks collected for the Winter Relief Fund. Even the downbeat SD was thrilled, enthusing in April 1940 that the programme had 'awakened the experience of the National Community in thousands'.[41]

This was the lodestone the Nazis sought: a single moment of emotional unity in which all individual egotism dissolved into all-powerful national feeling. But in its focus on the private threads of intimate relationships held together by the airwaves, the radio show and the *Request Concert* film recognised that the personal relationships of love and family were central to patriotic loyalty. In mobilising love, the Nazis were going for the most powerful but also most unpredictable of human emotions.[42]

By early October 1939, Fritz Probst had resigned himself to a longer war. A convinced Nazi, the Thuringian cabinetmaker was no militarist. Rather, he shared in the general view that the war had been forced upon Germany by the machinations of the Western powers. 'It's better to clear the decks now,' he wrote to his wife Hildegard; 'then it's to be hoped we won't have to be involved in a war again.'[43]

There was no room here for the bellicose tradition of 1914 which had lauded the manly, character-building benefits of war as a positive virtue. Such ideas might still inform Hitler's private view of war but he did not say so in public, and they found little expression in the letters of the middle-aged family men in 1939. However convinced they were of the war's necessity, for them it was simply lost time. 'Hopefully the time will come, sooner or later, when I am with you again,' Probst wrote to his wife. 'Then you will be recompensed for all that you have to bear, then it will be springtime in our happy marriage once more.' Like others in 1939, Probst was painfully aware that the failure of the previous generation was being visited on this one. Above all, he drew inspiration from the prospect of what would happen were that failure to be repeated and were the cycle of war to be handed on to the next generation. As he wrote home, 'for what we sacrifice now our children will not need to do when they grow up'. The sense of quiet familial resolve to see it through was palpable. In the same letter in which this rather diffident man confessed to his wife from his chilly billet in the Saarland that it would be 'nice if I could come to you in the warm bed', he also affirmed, 'I believe in Adolf Hitler and a victory of the German people.'[44]

3

Extreme Measures

At 6.10 a.m. on 24 October 1939, Karl Kühnel was led from his cell in Berlin-Plötzensee prison into a large, bright room, strapped to a plank and guillotined. 'When this letter reaches you,' he had written to his wife Rose the previous day, 'I am a prisoner no longer. Instead, my earthly life is already finished. I already said farewell to you once . . . Do not lose heart, and harbour no rancour against anyone. It doesn't help. Now forge your own good fortune.' The 42-year-old carpenter from the Erzgebirge had already served in the previous war, suffering from the thought that his machine gun might 'tear a father from his children who had done me no harm. I tried,' he explained, 'to kill my conscience with counter-arguments and gradually succeeded to some extent.' He had volunteered this personal explanation in a letter to his local recruiting office on 1 January 1937: 'It is not possible to act against my conscience and so not possible to take up a weapon against a person and do him harm.' It was a step from which Kühnel would not retreat.[1]

On 14 December 1939 Josef Rimpl wrote to his wife and children on the eve of his execution, reminding them that no one was without fault but: 'I can claim with a good conscience that I am no criminal and not a murderer and robber. It is better, if it is the will of the Lord, to suffer for good than for evil.' Rupert Sauseng, a 43-year-old worker from Eisenach, prayed that his wife would 'trust in Him, who alone can give comfort and strength and mercy, that you and [our] child can withstand the heaviest trial through His strength'. Karl Endstrasser wrote to his wife in Graz telling her to sell his tools and quoting from 1 Corinthians: 'for we are made a spectacle unto the world, and to angels, and to men'. Like Kühnel, all three men were beheaded just after 6 a.m. the next day. They were all Jehovah's Witnesses and refused to swear oaths to Hitler or perform military service.[2]

As soon as military conscription had been reintroduced in Germany in 1935, the sporadic persecution of Jehovah's Witnesses became more serious and systematic. Some were picked up and interrogated for stuffing letterboxes with anti-Nazi leaflets. The SD set up a special desk to deal with them, just as it had done for Freemasons. In the concentration camps, Jehovah's Witnesses were unique amongst religious prisoners for being separated out from the 'politicals' and given their own marker, a purple triangle. Uniquely too amongst camp prisoners, many had the power to reverse their fate: all they had to do was to accept their call-up papers and enter the Wehrmacht.

August Dickmann was the first Jehovah's Witness in the Sachsenhausen concentration camp to be sent his draft papers – forwarded by his wife from home. He was summoned to the political department of the camp and given his military pass to sign. He refused, was beaten and put in solitary confinement while the camp commandant asked Himmler for permission to make an example of him. On 15 September 1939, all 8,500 prisoners were kept back after evening roll call in order to watch the firing squad do its work. The final *coup de grâce* was performed by Rudolf Höss, the future commandant of Auschwitz. As a final exemplary measure, four Jehovah's Witnesses were kept back from the rest of the prisoners and ordered to lay Dickmann out in his coffin, while they were warned what lay in store for them. August Dickmann's brother, Heinrich, was made to nail down the lid. The next day, a small item appeared in the German press, announcing Dickmann's execution 'for refusal to fulfil his duty as a soldier'. Dickmann, it was announced, 'was a "Jehovah's Witness"; he was a fanatical follower of the international sect of the Earnest Bible Students'. He was the first conscientious objector to be executed, and the sentence was publicised, as so often in Nazi Germany, because it served an educative, exemplary purpose.[3]

Conscientious objection normally came under military jurisdiction, on the grounds that it was the issue of call-up papers, not their ratification by the recipient, that spelled the beginning of military service. It was so grave and rare an offence that it was heard by the highest military court, the Reich Military Tribunal in Berlin-Charlottenburg, whose senior judge was Admiral Bastian. Since the military mutinies of November 1918 had started in the naval base at Kiel, the naval officer corps went to great lengths to re-establish its credentials as a bastion of counter-revolution. As one judge from the navy boasted, 'In determining the punishment I take into account whether the defendant could be considered a revolutionary type or not. I make sure that 1918 will not be repeated. I exterminate revolutionary types.' Military judges saw the rise of desertion, pacifism and a failure of nerve as the symptoms of defeat. 'As is well known, the increase in desertion in 1918 can be traced back primarily to the fact that our court martials dealt with weak-willed soldiers and those of diminished capacity in a faulty manner, namely, far too leniently,' as one judgment of the Wehrmacht's military bench read.[4]

The military judges were interpreting the 'Special Penal Regulations during War' which came into effect on the day of German mobilisation, 26 August 1939. Drafted by lawyers in the early years of the regime, these stipulated death as the standard penalty for 'demoralising the armed forces'. The key regulation was Article 48 of the pre-war Military Penal Code, and the legal commentators had targeted especially 'members of sectarian groups and pacifists'. The court duly affirmed that the duty to obey took precedence over 'the duty to follow one's conscience'. Further articles covered refusal to swear the oath of personal loyalty to the Führer required of every new recruit and classed any subsequent failure to carry out military duties as 'desertion'. Some judges even offered Jehovah's Witnesses the opportunity to perform military service in a non-combat role, an opportunity which they generally rejected. Those who recanted could expect a suspended prison sentence and loss of civil rights (held over for the duration of the war), and in the meantime they were sent to a punishment battalion, deployed in mine-clearance and other dangerous duties on the front line. Children were put into care and the family businesses and homes forcibly sold to put pressure on those who proved obdurate. In some cases, relatives who were not co-believers were allowed to visit the prison at Berlin-Plötzensee and plead with the objector to change his mind. Stays of execution and extended spells in the condemned cells near the guillotine increased the pressure.[5]

The night before he was scheduled to die at Brandenburg-Görden prison, Bernhard Grimm received a visit from the prison chaplain, Dr Werner Jentsch. Afterwards, in the stillness of the night, the 19-year-old wrote his farewell letter to his mother and brother, telling them about 'a Protestant Pastor who visited me [and] referred to the Old Testament as a history book of the Jews and the exegesis of Revelation as a very dangerous story and put the Day of Judgement off into the unknown future'. Grimm had previously signalled his willingness to serve as a medical orderly or in another non-combat role but this had been refused by the court. Having just withstood this final theological temptation to recant, he assured them, 'My dearest ones, we can only be grateful that everything is so far advanced . . . After the first small terror, which is only to be expected, at my asking and trusting in Him our heavenly Father took me still more firmly by the hand.' When Jentsch returned in the morning to accompany Bernhard Grimm to the guillotine, he was greatly impressed by the young man's resolve.[6]

During the first year of the war, 112 German soldiers were executed, nearly all of them for conscientious objection, with Jehovah's Witnesses accounting for the great majority. Like other millenarian sects before them, they believed that they were living in the 'final days' and that the Last Judgement was nigh. The Jehovah's Witnesses were joined by small numbers of Reform Adventists and Christadelphians, one of whom, Albert Merz, was executed. But such was the pressure to participate that other 'peace churches' like the Quakers and Seventh Day Adventists negotiated non-combat roles for their members within the military, while the German Mennonites turned their back on their Anabaptist tradition and announced in 1936 that their youths were 'enthusiastically ready' to do military service. Reared on a diet of religious nationalism and anti-Semitism, many Seventh-Day Adventists joined them on the front line. The thin ranks of those who were willing to face execution for their pacifist beliefs were joined by a single Austrian Catholic priest, Franz Reinisch, who, in his turn, inspired the farmer Franz Jägerstätter to reject military service; and, in the whole Reich, there was just one Protestant conscientious objector, Hermann Stöhr. Pariahs within their own churches, not one of them received any support from their bishops. Werner Jentsch, the German Christian prison chaplain who had accompanied Grimm to the scaffold, wrote a short theological tract setting out the arguments he had used to try and persuade the young man to recant, which the Military Tribunals agreed to distribute for use by other chaplains dealing with such cases.[7]

When considering such instances of unshakeable faith, military judges wondered whether they were in fact dealing with madness. A plea of diminished responsibility was a theoretical possibility, given that the authorities were themselves ready to equate 'people who refuse military service for religious reasons' with 'peace-talkers and freedom-crazy enthusiasts' and classify them as 'unrealistic and peculiar psychopaths'. The answer to this judicial question had been supplied soon after conscription was reintroduced in 1935 in a psychiatric study of eleven Jehovah's Witnesses conducted at Breslau University under the direction of Professor Johannes Lange. It concluded that they were not deranged but merely cowards or attention-seekers who ought to be handled in the same way as others who refused to carry out military service. The psychiatrists did, however, acknowledge at a 1936 professional conference that a small minority were guided by 'sincere faith' and courted martyrdom.[8]

At the end of November 1939, the Chief of the Wehrmacht High Command, Wilhelm Keitel, took the matter up with Hitler personally, who confirmed that, 'if it is not possible to destroy the will of the man who refuses military service, the sentence has to be carried out'. Individual religious convictions could not be allowed to trump the greater good of the national community, even if publicising these cases did not seem to be having the desired exemplary effect. By the end of 1939, they were beginning to look like 'propaganda for the opponents', as Friedrich Fromm, the commander of the Replacement Army, warned. By early 1940, Jehovah's Witnesses were themselves secretly circulating printed copies of farewell letters from the condemned to inspire further resistance amongst their brethren. Keitel ordered the military courts to cease publicising the sentences, although a further 118 conscientious objectors were executed during the following five years.[9]

Health professionals also signalled their keenness to combat the wider 'loss of nerve', the 'victory' of cowards and neurotics in the armed forces and of hysterical women on the home front, which they too believed had led to the defeat of 1918. In 1936, a section for Military Psychiatry and Psychology was added to the Military Medical Academy and Otto Wuth was appointed Chief Psychiatrist to the Army Medical Corps. Military psychiatrists were determined to prevent another epidemic of 'war shakers' by refusing to allow temporary battle shock to be inflated into a 'neurosis'. And they pointed to the salutary effect in 1926 of ceasing to pay military pensions on neuro-psychiatric discharges from the army: the 'shell-shock cases with shaking, paralysis, mutism, Ganser syndrome and so on' had allegedly disappeared 'almost entirely'.[10]

In September 1939, Friedrich Panse was called up and immediately assigned to the Military Psychiatry section at Ensen, on the east bank of the Rhine. Having served in the last year of the First World War,

Panse had gone on to study medicine and then trained under the famous psychiatrist and director of the Berlin Charité, Karl Bonhoeffer. Panse had qualified as a doctor, but harboured academic ambitions and, with his higher doctorate still to write, he set out to make his career under the Third Reich, joining the SS, the Party and a string of its professional associations. He and his patron at the University of Bonn, Kurt Pohlisch, worked enthusiastically for the new Hereditary Health courts, setting up a pioneering databank on the families of those designated 'hereditarily ill'. They wrote expert reports, assessing cases for compulsory sterilisation, and lectured to colleagues on the subject. Authorities like Karl Bonhoeffer participated too, at least enough to give a seal of approval to the energetic efforts of the younger generation. Hungry for recognition, Panse was still waiting to be appointed to a full academic chair when war broke out.[11]

In the first month of the war, Wuth, Panse and their colleagues helped the Wehrmacht distinguish between those 'who *cannot*' and 'those who *do not* want' to serve. Expecting the Polish campaign to bring a rush of cases of 'classical war neuroses', similar to those of the previous war, they found that the campaign had produced digestive problems rather than shakes. They were not interested in the widespread allegations by officers of 'nervousness' among German soldiers which had led to massive reprisals against Polish civilians. Instead, two professional conferences in January and February 1940 revealed their energetic attempts to draw sharp lines between those with genuine 'psychosomatic disturbances' and malingering 'psychopaths' who they recommended should be sent to concentration camps. The army responded by establishing three special units for such misfits. The point, as Otto Wuth explained, was to 'teach them to be men'. The military itself tended to be more sympathetic to the 'misfits' than the psychiatrists were. Significantly, it was the Wehrmacht High Command which decided to curb the neurologists, refusing to allow such extreme treatments as electric shock therapy, which had been tried for shell shock in the previous war, without patient consent.[12]

★

If there was a 'psychosis' at work here, it was amongst Germany's military and civilian elites. The ferocity and speed of their onslaught against such tiny and powerless groups of pacifists and 'war neurotics' in 1939 speaks of a desperation not just to avoid repeating the mistakes of the previous war, but somehow to expunge that experience. Theirs was a kind of premature excess of violence, and the intellectuals who prepared its way were at least as often non-Nazis as Nazis. Already in 1919, the young theologian and former military chaplain Paul Althaus was denouncing pacifism and arguing for the need for Germans to prove themselves worthy of God's grace by overcoming their defeat: 'A great people which does not stand with resolute will and all its force behind its historic rights . . . surrenders its historic rights and simply deserves the violent peace which has put it in chains. That is the hard but healthy and manly justice of history.' Propagating the fear that Germans risked being abandoned by God gave religious power to conservative and radical nationalist interpretations of November 1918 as a 'stab in the back'. Other Lutherans before him had argued that the Germans had replaced the Jews as the 'Chosen People', but Althaus gave it a contemporary relevance. In his own 'theology of creation', he insisted that Christian universalism could only be lived out through separate nations, each imbued with its own character and identity and required to learn God's plans for it through its historical struggles. Nationalism was not just natural; it was a sacred duty. Unlike Calvinist predestination, this German Lutheran variant repeatedly emphasised the moral risk of failure. Mixing the subtlety of theological argument with the militant language of radical nationalism honed in his First World War sermons, Althaus soon became a formidable and central figure in the Luther revival of the 1920s, alongside Werner Elert and Emanuel Hirsch, taking a prestigious chair in theology at Erlangen in 1925 and becoming President of the Luther Society a year later, an honorific post he would occupy for the next forty years. In this version of Protestant providentialism, Germans had become God's chosen people, but they would have to redeem themselves if they were to prove worthy of His trust.[13]

Such ideas were common currency amongst the educated classes. By 5 September 1939, August Töpperwien had already registered that 'Adolf Hitler's struggle against Poland and England will be ruthlessly total: total commitment of all means in his power, total degradation of the enemy. How brave and how profound is Luther's teaching on the two kingdoms', the Solingen teacher comforted himself. That distinction between earthly and heavenly precepts allowed the pious Protestant to accept that it was impossible to act in the world without sinning and yet to go on seeking moral orientation in the war, mainly by reference to the theology of Althaus and Hirsch. Töpperwien remained a loyal reader of *Eckhart*, a journal close to the Confessing Church and highly critical of the Nazi German Christian movement, taking in an eclectic spread of German writers from anti-Nazi dissidents like Hans Carossa and Edzard Schaper to conservatives like Paul Ernst and racists such as Heinrich Zillich. From the outset his doubts over the Führer's actions made him ask himself whether Hitler was sent by God or sent to try God, but he did not doubt his right to lead or Germans' need to stand fast. Holding out against the 'spirit of November 1918' featured as a measure of their own salvation. To fail for a second time would prove that Germany was not God's chosen nation.[14]

This national Protestant version of German redemption was just one variant in an anti-liberal and anti-democratic culture which strove to overcome *the* German disaster of 1918. With their fear that history would follow a cyclical path, conservatives believed that they had to intervene drastically to avoid repeated failure. In the early 1920s, German culture had been awash with predictions of post-war decay, decline and degeneration, epitomised by Oswald Spengler's *Decline of the West*. These dire predictions had been overturned by the 'national rebirth' in 1933, and many Catholic and Protestant intellectuals continued to hope that the Nazis' 'national revolution' would lead to a spiritual revival even after their first flush of enthusiasm had been tempered by disappointments with the Nazi Party, if not with Hitler himself. Yet their key ideas – especially their rejection of Weimar democracy, liberalism, pacifism, socialism, the Jews and those who had accepted defeat – did not change. The outbreak of a new war brought everything they had thought about 1918 back into focus, testing their belief in Germany's redemption to the core. This generalised urge to avoid the mistakes of the previous war helps to explain why the Reich's professional elites were so prepared to engage in lethal violence from the very outset. It also explains the fact that the most extreme measures were not always the work of the most obviously radical and Nazi agencies.[15]

The Nazi police state had more than enough power to maintain the dictatorship. As soon as Germany mobilised for war, the list of forbidden activities lengthened, from telling jokes that undermined the morale of the armed forces to failing to work on Sundays: soon over forty offences were punishable by death. German society was full of people who broke Nazi regulations in small ways and upheld them in large ones, thereby helping to shape a 'national community' constructed on violence, merit and exclusion. It proved impossible to silence critical voices when it came to inequities in rationing, but people generally silenced themselves when it came to the principal targets of Nazi repression. This was both a complex, conflictual society and one where nationalism had already seeped into the pre-political practices of everyday life, shaping what people observed and felt worthy of note.

The problem for the regime was not its control over the means of coercion but, rather, how selectively to deploy them. It had used mass terror in 1933 to destroy the old labour movement and again, in June 1934, against the leadership of the storm troopers. After that, the regime had deliberately scaled back the concentration camps, and when they began to grow again in 1938 they were filled with Jews, and later Czechs and Poles. For the social majority, terror had become something directed at others, at foreigners or 'asocial outsiders' such as communists and male homosexuals.[16]

By the end of January 1940, Franz Gürtner, the Minister of Justice, counted eighteen extrajudicial executions by the Gestapo since the war began and complained that the civil courts were being bypassed. In fact, this relatively small number of interventions often stemmed directly from Hitler's reading of the sensationalist crime reporting in the *Völkischer Beobachter*. In October 1939, he was outraged to learn about a petty thief in Munich who had been sentenced to ten years in prison for stealing a woman's purse during the evening blackout. Even though the purse only contained a few marks and no violence had been used, Hitler demanded that the man be executed to set an example. This sent a clear signal back to German judges. A few weeks later, the Berlin Special Court sentenced another man to death who had taken advantage of the blackout to steal a woman's purse in order to demonstrate 'that the solid wall of the inner front cannot be worn down by sub-humanity'. What made petty crime seem so abhorrent was its apparently ineradicable character. Repeat offenders soon found themselves being sent to concentration camps like Mauthausen, where they were treated far worse than serious and violent criminals. Just as the SS's execution of the Jehovah's Witness August Dickmann potentially threatened the jurisdiction of the military courts, so civilian judges were quick to defend their domain from encroachment by the arbitrary actions of the police: such turf wars themselves encouraged different agencies to compete in enacting harsher sentences.[17]

On the eve of war, the Gestapo re-arrested former Social Democratic parliamentarians and other political suspects. Despite this ratcheting up of violence in autumn 1939, the Gestapo was very careful to maintain a two-speed police state. It was one thing to strike against identified 'enemies', such as Communists, Freemasons, Jews and Jehovah's Witnesses, who could expect to be sent before a special court or straight to a concentration camp if they were denounced for telling 'defeatist' jokes or trading on the black market. But relatively few people were punished for telling political jokes about the regime's leaders. For ordinary 'national comrades' a warning was usually enough. Unlike Stalin's regime, which was willing to wage war on the majority of its population in order to push through its social revolution, Hitler's dictatorship continued to calibrate its violence so that the majority of Germans did not feel it. Pragmatism as well as ideology drove this distinction: the Gestapo had never had a large staff and depended to a large extent on public compliance and denunciations to assist it in spotting transgressors. The war quickly reduced their manpower further: in Cologne, the Gestapo went from ninety-nine officers in 1939 to sixty-nine by 1942; it was a similar story elsewhere.[18]

One of the most contentious of the new prohibitions was listening to enemy radio. Labels pasted on all new sets warned that listening to foreign broadcasts was a 'crime against national security', but the ban was unenforceable. Despite its obsession with propaganda and image, the Nazi dictatorship enjoyed far less control over information than had Imperial Germany. Whereas newsprint could be censored and border controls enforced so that, as late as the summer of 1918, the German home front had remained ignorant of the military catastrophe unfolding on the western front, nothing could prevent people from changing wavebands. As long as they took due precautions, what people chose to listen to in private remained – in practice – their own concern. For the most part, they took care to preserve appearances, keeping the volume low, changing the dial back again to German stations afterwards, perhaps listening to neutral rather than enemy broadcasts – Swiss or Swedish radio rather than the BBC – even getting one of the children to look out for neighbours hovering on the landing outside the front door. In Prague, the SD had heard, the Czechs had started using headphones so that their neighbours could not overhear and denounce them. The ban proved predictably unpopular in Germany, where it was described as 'infantilising' and an 'insult and humiliation'. The SD reported a strong strain of 'loyal criticism', with people complaining noisily that 'a good National Socialist can hear these [foreign] broadcasts with equanimity, for they really can't affect him; on the contrary they only strengthen his hostility and commitment to the struggles against the enemy powers'. Many people were confused: did it cover all foreign broadcasters or were they still allowed to tune in to neutral stations, such as the jazz programmes of Radio Luxembourg, ever popular with the young? As usual when confronted by a truly unpopular measure, numerous people were overheard expressing disbelief that the Führer could have permitted such a thing.[19]

In a tacit admission of how things stood, German radio regularly offered its own commentaries to mock and refute the claims of the British or French broadcasts. With their thirst for information, people also picked up the millions of leaflets which the RAF dropped that winter, although they did not necessarily believe what they read. In Essen, Carola Reissner was outraged. 'They are apparently trying to inflame the population,' she wrote to her relatives, adding forcefully, 'these are obviously Jewish ploys.' The suspicion came naturally, for she had heard for years how the Jews had manipulated and tricked their way to power and influence in Germany. German radio nicknamed Churchill 'the Lord of Lies', when not simply rubbishing him as 'W.C.' Playing the popular First World War song 'For We Are Marching Against Eng-e-land' at the end of news bulletins proved so successful that it became one of the signature tunes of German broadcasting.[20]

The new ban on foreign radio could only be enforced selectively. On 18 November 1939, a young officer from the Koblenz Gestapo was sent out to investigate a complaint about illegal radio-listening in a small town on the western side of the Rhine. The accused, Arnulf V., was alleged to listen to the German service broadcast by Radio Strasbourg every evening. To make things worse, he had been a leading local Social Democrat in the Weimar years and was also said to have made disparaging comments about both the accuracy of German news and the Führer himself. Arnulf was arrested, brought to Koblenz and interrogated until he admitted that he had listened to the French station several times. He was held in Gestapo custody for three weeks while further investigations took place, including a search of his home which netted his radio and some old Social Democratic materials. The local Nazi Party organisation confirmed that like many former socialists he attended few Party functions and contributed little to their charitable drives. He also quarrelled frequently with his wife. On the other hand, his employers gave him a good reference and he was a decorated First World War veteran who had been wounded four times. These last two facts decided the case when it finally came to court ten months later, in September 1940, and the judges acquitted him on all counts. The other factor which eventually weighed in Arnulf V.'s favour was that he had been denounced by his brother-in-law out of personal spite following a major family row. The Gestapo was used to safeguarding itself from being made use of in this way and in a similar case it urged the special court to dismiss allegations lodged by a quarrelsome former business associate, even though the accused had once been a Communist. By 1943, a mere 3,450 people had been punished for listening to foreign radio.[21]

As Gestapo officers became bogged down in questioning neighbours, relatives and employers to ascertain whether a former Communist or Social Democrat was an 'enemy' who needed to be surgically removed from the 'body of nation' or really a decent 'national comrade' who had fallen into the wrong company in the 1920s, they were creating a coercive practice which was both arbitrary and strangely consistent: arbitrary, because very different penalties were imposed on different people for the same offences; consistent, because the civil and military judges and the Gestapo all tried to form a judgment based on the 'character' of the offender rather than simply on the offence itself. Changes to the Criminal Code introduced between December 1939 and February 1941 signalled a clear shift away from the crime to the criminal: it referred no longer to murder, sexual crime or recidivism but, rather, to 'the murderer', 'the sexual offender' and 'the habitual criminal'.[22]

No one could accuse the Nazis of being soft on crime. When the German Reich went to war, the country had 108,000 prisoners in state institutions, and another 21,000 in concentration camps. By the end of the war, the prison population would double and the number of concentration camp inmates would rise to 714,211. Dire as these statistics are, at the outbreak of the war, Germany stood comparison with Switzerland, Finland and the United States in the proportion of prisoners in the population, occupying the punitive end of the international spectrum of law enforcement, with England, France, Belgium and the Netherlands locking away far fewer of their citizens. Compared to Nazi terror in Poland, with its methods of mass executions, collective reprisals and wholesale expulsions, Nazi policy at home remained selective and worked on the basis of individual case files. Until at least 1943, the 'normal' system of state prisons and state and charitable reformatories held more offenders than specifically Nazi agencies, such as the concentration camps run by the SS, the overwhelming majority of whose inmates came from Germany's racial enemies, principally Polish and later Soviet prisoners.[23]

Within the Reich itself, the most radical and violent action prompted by the outbreak of the war occurred in a hidden backwater. This was the murder of psychiatric patients in Germany's asylums. Like the execution of conscientious objectors, it began as soon as war broke out and would continue until the very end: by May 1945, it would claim at least 216,400 victims' lives, outstripping even the number of German Jews who were killed by the regime. The principal actors were not specifically Nazi institutions like Himmler's Reich Security Main Office, which had taken charge of racial policy in Poland. Instead, the operation was conducted by medical doctors and bureaucrats working in the normal health and provincial administrations.[24]

The so-called 'euthanasia action' began with the children. On 18 August 1939, the Reich Committee for the Registration of Serious Hereditary and Congenital Illnesses made it compulsory for doctors to report all newborn children suffering from idiocy, Down's syndrome, microcephaly, hydrocephaly, spastic paralysis or missing limbs. The registration forms were initially forwarded to three medical experts. As a result of this pilot study, about 5,000 children were killed, and soon thirty psychiatric asylums had established their own so-called 'children's units' where they killed children through a mixture of drugs and starvation.[25]

A second, secret, centralised programme was established to comb through the files of adult patients in the asylums under the direction of Philipp Bouhler, head of the Chancellery of the Führer, and Hitler's physician, Dr Karl Brandt. Code-named 'T-4' after the address of its headquarters at Tiergartenstrasse 4, Berlin, the programme set out to find a quota of 70,000 patients deemed 'unworthy of life'. The crucial test was whether the patients were ever likely to contribute to society through work. A positive medical judgement, registered by a '+' sign, meant death; letting them live was registered as a negative, marked by a '−' sign. As the programme got under way and grew in scale, more clinicians were needed to evaluate the case files. In early 1940, Friedrich Panse and Kurt Pohlisch, who were already advising the Wehrmacht about 'war neuroses', were invited to a confidential conference in Berlin, where they were inducted into this secret programme and asked to join its growing panel of medical experts. They both complied.[26]

Some evaluators were more squeamish than others. By the end of January 1941, Panse and Pohlisch would find themselves dropped as T-4 referees, probably because they had returned too few 'positive' recommendations. A number of other prominent psychiatrists continued to fulfil the dual role of military psychiatrist and expert referee for the medical killing programme on top of their academic and clinical day jobs, men like Carl Schneider, director of the Neurological Clinic at the Univeristy of Heidelberg, Friedrich Mauz, his peer at the University of Königsberg, or the illustrious child psychiatrist Werner Villinger, who had introduced psychotherapy into Hamburg's youth welfare programme in the 1920s, only to become a convinced Nazi and firm advocate of forcibly sterilising juvenile delinquents.[27]

In January 1940, after attending a demonstration of gassing at the former hard labour penitentiary at Brandenburg, the experts and T-4 bureaucrats knew they had a method for killing at least twenty patients at a time. Before the month's end, patients from asylums across the Reich were channelled through a system of holding sanatoria to Brandenburg and Grafeneck in the Swabian Alps and Hartheim near Linz to be killed. As operations were wound down at Brandenburg in September, another centre was constructed at Bernburg. At Professor Paul Nitsche's Sonnenstein asylum at Pirna near Dresden, the patients had already been subjected to a cost-cutting 'hunger diet' since the start of 1939, a regimen copied in other Saxon asylums. By May 1940, Nitsche joined the staff running the central T-4 operation full-time.

Whereas the execution of conscientious objectors was public knowledge and covered by military law, killing the disabled was neither announced nor covered by a legal decree, although key figures involved in it clearly lobbied for one. Eventually, Bouhler and Brandt extracted two lines in Hitler's hand sanctioning a 'mercy death'. Even though the meaning of that confidential document remained ambiguous, the dictator would never again take the risk of putting his name to further documents permitting secret killing. The process of selecting patients and even arranging for the killing often fell to the medical directors of psychiatric asylums like Friedrich Mennecke, urged on by senior provincial bureaucrats such as Fritz Bernotat in Hesse-Nassau. Many were Nazis, but they had the scope to take their own initiatives and their guiding ideas were not of uniquely Nazi origin. Rather, they took their cue from the 1920 tract *Permission for the Destruction of Life Unworthy of Life* by Karl Binding and Alfred Hoche, which had radically redefined 'mercy killing' from a matter of individual choice to escape a painful terminal illness to a legitimate means for society to dispose of 'useless ballast existences'.

The repeated financial crises of provincial and national government during the 1920s – and especially following the Wall Street crash of 1929 – only steeped German bureaucrats more deeply in this culture of cost-cutting and harsh choices about resource allocation. In their eyes, petty criminals became 'psychopaths' and vagrants and the long-term unemployed were classified as 'asocials' and, most irredeemably, 'community aliens'. The Nazi regime encouraged such tendencies, fostering an administrative culture where police, the courts, youth and social welfare boards, the SS, prison governors and reformatory directors could all see themselves as engaged in a common project of national discipline. This was not difficult, because so many of these middle-class, politically conservative men had drawn the same lessons from the breakdown of order at the end of the last war. The country had simply not fought it ruthlessly enough.[28]

What the Nazi regime did was to provide the impetus, institutional cover and secrecy that enabled the implementation of ideas which had never won over a majority within the medical and welfare lobbies, let alone mainstream public opinion. From the first, the medical killing was conducted on the assumption that the German public would not approve of such measures, and that at least sections of religious opinion would oppose them. Considerable effort was expended on keeping the families of their victims away, mainly by manipulating normal bureaucratic procedures, such as inserting delays in informing families about each of the stages by which patients were transferred

via a network of intermediary asylums to a killing institution like
Hartheim or Grafeneck until it was too late. Some asylums, like the
Kalmenhof in the Hessian town of Idstein, routinely used the excuse
of military priorities on the railways to forbid visits.[29]

The sheer numbers led doctors to be careless in logging false causes
of death as they sought to preserve the programme's secrecy. Some
relatives were told that patients had died of appendicitis when they
had had the organ removed long before. Even sending paper urns of
ashes to families had its pitfalls. When relatives found a woman's
hairpins in the urn for a man or received an urn for a son whom they
had removed from an asylum two weeks before, they began to ask
questions. In the immediate vicinity of asylums like Grafeneck in
the Swabian Alps, the gassing was no secret at all. In Swabia, where the
Confessing Church was strong, the provincial Church Council and the
Inner Mission, which ran Protestant psychiatric asylums, joined together
and channelled local protests to the regime. In early July 1940, a member
of the Church Council, Reinhold Sautter, wrote to Gauleiter Wilhelm
Murr's office, while Bishop Theophil Wurm took the matter up with
the Minister for Church Affairs, Hanns Kerrl, the Interior Minister,
Wilhelm Frick, and finally, on 25 July, wrote to Hans Lammers, head
of the Reich Chancellery. All these interventions were couched in
terms of loyal criticism, warning that the action was undermining
popular belief in the ideal of the 'national community' and the Nazi
Party's own commitment to care for all and support a 'positive
Christianity'. Although copies of these letters of petition continued
to circulate in private, the clerics contained their protests within these
confidential channels and studiously avoided any open breach with
the regime. The number of petitions to the Gauleiter was so great
that even Murr passed on his reservations to Berlin.[30]

In September 1940, pastor Ludwig Schlaich, the director of the asylum
at Stetten, received notice that another 150 patients would be collected
from his asylum. He wrote to Goebbels, Murr, the Minister of Justice,
Franz Gürtner, and Lammers, questioning the ethics and legality of the
programme. When Frick sent a curt reply, telling him to co-operate,
Schlaich took the unprecedented step of contacting the relatives of his
patients, telling them to come to the asylum before it was too late to save
their loved ones: many came to say heart-rending farewells, leaving highly
agitated patients behind. Of the 441 patients at Stetten who were put on

successive transport lists, a mere 16 were saved by their relatives. Few families took this opportunity, even, Schlaich ruefully noted, amongst those with sufficient means to care for someone with a disability at home. Some other Protestant asylum directors in Württemberg followed Schlaich's example and informed relatives that they could no longer guarantee their patients' safety.

The civic courage displayed by Schlaich remained highly unusual. Beyond Württemberg, the asylums run by the Inner Mission made no effort to warn families. Instead they fell into line with greater or lesser enthusiasm behind the President of their Central Committee, Pastor Constantin Frick. An ardent advocate of 'euthanasia', he was in a position to force recalcitrant directors of Protestant asylums to fall into line. Usually, threatening them with the ruinous loss of state-funded patients was enough; in other cases, they were replaced. Many actively assisted in the programme. Some of the asylums run by the Catholic charity Caritas followed suit, despite official Catholic opposition to both contraception and euthanasia.[31]

It was easier to silence than to persuade the theologians. Paul Althaus had spoken out briefly against the radical 'racial hygienists' in July 1933, and – despite his general view that in all other things the individual was subordinate to the needs of the national community – in this one key instance he insisted that 'God is the creator and master of life.' Within the month he was instructed by the Bavarian Ministry of the Interior not to discuss issues connected with 'race hygiene' again. Althaus held his peace, although he had personal reasons to remain concerned: his disabled daughter lived in the Bethel asylum, which actively participated in the 'euthanasia' programme.[32]

Once the killing was under way, it proved impossible to prevent knowledge spreading and opposition mounting in the immediate vicinity of the asylums. As a result of the Swabian protests, killing operations were transferred during January to March 1941 to Hadamar on the Lahn from Grafeneck but not before 9,839 people had been gassed there. At Hadamar too the crematoria chimneys gave off thick plumes of smoke, which confirmed the loose talk of the labourers responsible for disposing of the bodies, and soon local children were greeting the grey buses as they drove patients through Hadamar with the chant, 'Here come the murder boxes'. Elsewhere news leaked out more slowly, mainly through private channels of communication in the public health system and via the churches. But, if they lived far from the asylums, did not belong to the well-connected professions, and were unable to visit often because of wartime travel restrictions, many relatives remained ignorant of what was unfolding. News spread unevenly, starved – during the first eighteen months of medical killing – of the oxygen of public discussion.[33]

★

The German war began with massive targeted violence. In occupied Poland, it aimed to make the destruction of the Polish nation permanent by removing those who could provide 'national leadership'; and it prepared parts of the country for German colonial settlement. Within Germany's pre-war borders, state violence targeted small and socially marginal groups which might undermine the war effort – Freemasons, Communists and Jehovah's Witnesses – and it swept away those whose 'idiocy' drew on resources urgently needed elsewhere. All of these were pre-emptive, ground-clearing operations, dealing with an anticipated threat or difficulty rather than a serious challenge which had already manifested itself. Many were not the work of new, Nazi institutions: they were carried out by existing professional elites who formulated the general rationale of what they were doing in their own fashion. In one way or another, they were expunging the ignominy of November 1918, that betrayal of Germany's armed forces by communists, women and Jews. Given this mindset, the most surprising omission from the list of 'internal enemies' identified for liquidation in 1939 was Germany's remaining Jewish community.

War immediately provoked fears of a new pogrom. Instead, Jochen Klepper and Victor Klemperer were astonished to find that the media quickly toned its anti-Semitic rhetoric down, perhaps as a gesture towards its new Soviet ally. Then, at 9.20 p.m. on 8 November, a bomb went off without warning in the Munich beer cellar where the 'old fighters' of the Nazi movement were gathered for the annual celebration of their putsch attempt of 1923. Hitler had left to catch the train back to Berlin a mere ten minutes before the bomb exploded in the pillar behind the podium where he had stood, killing eight people and injuring sixty-four others. As news of the assassination attempt spread the next day, many employers called special workplace meetings and extra assemblies were held at schools where the children gave thanks for the Führer's providential escape by singing the Lutheran hymn 'Now Let All Give Thanks to God'. People spoke bitterly about those they presumed to be responsible for the attack – 'the English and the Jews' – and expected retaliation against both.[34]

Official response to this attempt on the life of the Führer was muted, especially compared to the Beer Hall reunion of November 1938. Then, Goebbels had exploited the death of a minor German diplomat at the hands of a Polish Jew in Paris to launch a nationwide pogrom in which Nazi storm troopers, SS men and in some places even boys and girls had dragged Jews from their homes, beating and clubbing them, looting their shops and setting synagogues ablaze, while the fire brigade stood by to make sure that no adjacent buildings caught fire. Then ninety-one Jews had been killed outright, by the official count, and 25,000 men were bundled off to concentration camps where hundreds of them were murdered.[35]

Now, in November 1939, two British agents were arrested on the Dutch border and the media contented itself with pointing the finger of blame – wrongly, as it turned out – at the British and Jewish warmongers. But there was no fresh pogrom. Instead of the fierce onslaught that Victor Klemperer and Jochen Klepper awaited with trepidation, the ageing community of Jews who had been unable or unwilling to emigrate was subjected to a deluge of minor regulations. Between the pogrom of 9 November 1938 and the outbreak of war, 229 anti-Jewish decrees had been issued. Between September 1939 and the autumn of 1941, agencies worked out a particular anti-Jewish variant to every new measure governing the German home front and published another 525 decrees constraining the daily lives of Jews. They were prevented from buying underwear, shoes and clothing, even for their growing teenage children. Radios and record players had to be surrendered. By the Nazis' own measure of things, this was an extraordinarily restrained response to the one group it held principally guilty for both wars. Given Hitler's linkage of anti-Semitic policy to international relations, it suggested that he still hoped to come to terms with Britain and France.[36]

PART TWO

MASTERS OF EUROPE

4

Breaking Out

From first light on 10 May 1940, there was no chance of sleep for Paulheinz Wantzen. The pillow would not block out the continuous roar of aero-engines. When the newspaperman got up, he could see the bombers and fighters climbing above the roofs in a tight spiral from Münster's two airfields. As soon as Wantzen reached his office, he turned on the radio and heard the news. The phone rang at the same moment – the Propaganda Ministry with instructions to print a special edition. Wantzen hardly managed to write the editorial comment, because the phone kept ringing. Every civic authority in Münster was trying to find out what was happening. How far had German troops got? Were they facing resistance? Was it true that Italy had entered the war? The SD phoned and told him that the military orders for the attack had gone out so late the previous evening that the police had to round up soldiers from the cinemas, theatres and pubs. Then the first plane returned carrying three German dead and eight wounded from the assault on the Dutch airfield of Ypenburg near Rotterdam. At 11 a.m., press guidelines arrived from the Propaganda Ministry, announcing that 'Holland and Belgium are the new objectives for attack by the Western powers. English and French troops have marched into Holland and Belgium. We are hitting back.' The Allied aim was 'to advance against the Ruhr'. In the afternoon, the SD rang back to ask Wantzen 'about the mood of the population': it clearly hoped that the journalist had his ear to the ground.[1]

German radio broadcast the first military bulletin that evening, announcing the start of the general German offensive in the west and the news that the Führer had set off for the front. When he left his hectic office, Wantzen entered another world. 'Münster's street scene', he observed that evening, 'was unchanged, everything was calm and peaceful', only the higher demand at the newspaper kiosks telling of the events taking place. He fully expected Münster to be bombed that night: 'If the English don't accomplish that,' he opined, 'then they have already lost the war.'[2]

The bombers did not come, but on 10 May some sixty bombs were dropped on the small Badenese city of Freiburg. It was the first time a German civilian target had been hit. Most of the bombs fell near the railway station. The German communiqué blamed the action on 'three Allied planes [which] dropped bombs in the middle of Freiburg, killing twenty-four civilians', and threatened that 'from now on, every enemy bombing of German civilians will be answered by five times as many German planes bombing English and French cities'. The following day, it was announced that thirteen of the victims were children, killed while playing in the municipal playground. The death toll had risen to fifty-seven. The media kept the Freiburg bombing in the news. When people heard that the planes were French, the SD immediately registered the response as 'general outrage . . . and in the final instance feelings of hatred against France'. The incident of 10 May was endlessly invoked as the 'Children's murder at Freiburg'. In fact, the planes were German bombers, which had lost their way in heavy cloud and struck the wrong target, mistaking Freiburg for Dijon. The media did issue a correction later, though not one which admitted German culpability: the French planes became British ones. They were to blame for starting the war against children.[3]

The young doctor's son Helmut Paulus was in the middle of a training exercise with fixed bayonets when the news broke. Many of his comrades came from the Badenese Rhineland, or even had family in Freiburg, and were deeply affected. One man who was generally known for his even temper and optimistic outlook 'couldn't cope any more and suddenly started to weep in the middle of the exercise', Paulus wrote home. The drill was cut short that day, so that the men had time to collect themselves. It was just as well, because the bayonet of one his comrades went straight through its leather cover before sliding off Helmut's steel helmet and lightly scratching his throat. It was the daily claustrophobia of wearing gas masks which made them fear the worst for their families at home. Helmut was not alone in his belief that the British would drop poison gas. Throughout

Germany, it was one of the most widely shared fears about aerial warfare. In Pforzheim, his parents cancelled their planned trip to Vienna and his father installed air raid windows in the cellars and kept them shut 'till these grave days are past'.[4]

Most people's anxieties dwelt on the events unfolding at the front. 'Now the long-feared event has happened. The battle in the west has begun,' Wilm Hosenfeld wrote home from Węgrów in occupied Poland. He had woken that day at 4 a.m., filled with a sense of gratitude at being alive. Later he had taken his new captain for a ride on horseback to see the Jewish quarter, where Hosenfeld was in the habit of throwing sweets to the hordes of ragged children. However alienated the brutality of German actions in Poland made him feel, Hosenfeld had become completely involved: 'It's now a battle of life and death,' he continued to Annemie. 'I can't rid myself of thoughts about the events taking place in the west. They weigh on my soul like a nightmare.'[5]

Hurriedly collecting reports from across the Reich, the SD reported how surprised the population was by the sudden invasion of Holland and Belgium and admitted that the general mood quickly changed 'into *deep seriousness*'. The Führer's proclamation 'that the hour of decision has come has made the population realise that the battles beginning in the west will demand the greatest sacrifices. If a deep seriousness and concern for their family members in the field is palpable among mothers and wives, the *fundamental attitude* in the population is *firm and confident*.' All regional reports confirmed that people were 'inwardly convinced of the necessity of this grave step and of the sacrifices it will require'.[6]

The German attack had begun with the infiltration of troops into Luxembourg during the night. Just before dawn on 10 May, the full-scale invasion of Belgium and the Netherlands began. Although the Netherlands had remained neutral in the previous war, in all other respects it looked as if the Wehrmacht was repeating a variant of the 1914 Schlieffen Plan, by attacking France through the Low Countries. Everyone knew that there could be no guarantee of repeating the swift advance across Belgium of August and September 1914, as the Belgians had done much to fortify their eastern border in the interwar years. Massive reinforced concrete forts now protected their three lines of canals and river defences, with the Albert Canal and Fort Eben

Emael at their centre. It was here that the German invasion began, with the silent arrival of ten gliders on the flat roof of the fort complex at dawn; the eleventh, carrying the young lieutenant in command of the operation, blew off course, but the eighty paratroopers had been well rehearsed and carried on until he rejoined them. Scaling the fort's hydraulically controlled gun turrets, they used hollow charges, a new weapon, to disable them. Firing flame-throwers into the openings of the concrete casements, they flushed out the confused defenders. By the end of that day, the fort and the two key bridges it controlled at Veldwezelt and Vroenhoven were in German hands and the way into central Belgium lay open for the tanks of the German 6th Army. When the news was broadcast on Saturday 11 May, it had an immediate effect on morale at home.[7]

In the evening, the Belgian Command withdrew its forces behind the Dyle Line, its third and final line of defence, stretching from Antwerp to Namur. Its weak point was the wide and open countryside at Gembloux, between Wavre and Namur, perfect terrain for tanks and devoid of prepared or entrenched positions. It was into this gap that the French now sent their own mechanised and motorised divisions along with their strongest formation, the 1st Army. On 12 May, General Erich Hoepner's Panzer Corps crashed into General René Prioux's Cavalry Corps at Hannut. The 176 SOMUA and 239 Hotchkiss tanks wrought carnage on the German armour, most of them the lightly armed and armoured Mark I and II machines, which had already fared badly in Poland. They could not damage the French medium battlefield tanks, and Hoepner had too few medium tanks with sufficient firepower. On the following day he attacked again, pinpointing his effort to break through the long and thin French tank line. Without radio in their vehicles, the French could not manoeuvre rapidly and had no choice but to pull back when the Germans broke through, leaving the technically inferior German corps in command of the field, a gain which allowed them to retrieve and repair a hundred of their broken machines. It was the first large-scale tank battle.[8]

From an Allied point of view, the battle of Hannut had served its purpose by slowing the German advance and giving the massed infantry divisions of the French 1st Army time to reach the Dyle Line. Anticipating just such a rerun of the 1914 invasion as seemed to be under way, this was where the French Commander-in-Chief, Maurice

Gamelin, had always intended to hold the Germans. Because of the fall of Fort Eben Emael and the Dutch evacuation northwards into 'Fortress Holland', the German advance had been much swifter, and the Allies had had a mere five days rather than the planned three weeks to deploy into Belgium. But by committing most of his modern mechanised units, Gamelin had also achieved the first aim of his campaign and entrenched his best forces along the Dyle. It was also exactly where the Germans wanted them to go.[9]

Twenty-nine German divisions had attacked through the southern Netherlands and central Belgium to the Dyle. Meanwhile, another forty-five were advancing through the hills of Luxembourg and southern Belgium towards the French border and the river Meuse. It was a surprising and highly risky move, as 41,000 German vehicles tried to drive up the four narrow, winding access roads into the hilly, densely wooded Ardennes. Stretching back to the far side of the Rhine and presenting a near-stationary target for French and British bombers, the German columns could have been destroyed before they ever got going. The Chief of the General Staff, Franz Halder, and other German generals, had opposed this plan because it seemed too reckless. But the French failed to send aircraft there, despite confidential warnings from the Swiss of major German troop movements in the area: most Allied air squadrons were already suffering heavy losses in the air battles in the north. At the head of the slowly uncoiling traffic jam were seven panzer divisions: an independent strike force of 1,222 tanks and 378 support vehicles, carrying motorised infantry, anti-tank and anti-aircraft batteries, under the command of Generals Heinz Guderian, Georg-Hans Reinhardt and Hermann Hoth.[10]

The weak French forces that encountered the Germans in the Ardennes on 10 and 11 May pulled back to the far bank of the river Meuse, which was held by the French 2nd Army. Gamelin's deputy, General Georges, ordered French reserve divisions there on 11 May, the day before the first German units reached the river. The French generals thought that they had time to bring up infantry and tanks, because they estimated it would take the Germans until about 20 May to build up sufficient artillery and infantry to force the river crossings. This was in fact exactly the same as Halder's planned schedule.

On 13 May, Luftwaffe bombers carried out 3,940 sorties, carpet-bombing the French positions, while two squadrons of Stukas flew a further 300 strafing and dive-bombing missions. The Luftwaffe had already earned its sobriquet as 'flying artillery' in Poland, where it had perfected the battlefield and ground attack roles it had pioneered in the Spanish Civil War. Göring delivered at the Meuse eight hours of continuous bombing, unprecedented in its ferocity and unmatched by the Luftwaffe even later in the war. They were unable to destroy French gun emplacements and bunkers, but they did break French morale.[11] Throughout that afternoon, the German motorised infantry attached to Guderian's 19th Panzer Corps and the elite Grossdeutschland infantry regiment tried to force their way across the river. Manning 103 pillboxes, the French front line held on and pinned the Germans down. In the late afternoon assault engineers from the Grossdeutschland regiment penetrated the one part of the bank where a bend in the river prevented the pillboxes from covering it with flanking fire. By midnight, the Germans had crossed the Meuse in three places, although at Monthermé they only held a tiny strip of 1.5 kilometres, and their bridgeheads at Sedan and Dinant remained highly vulnerable too.

Where the Germans had attacked precipitously, taking heavy casualties to bring their rubber assault boats across the river, the French stuck to their tactical doctrine of 'methodical battle', waiting until they had brought up more armour and artillery reinforcements before counterattacking Guderian's Sedan bridgehead at dawn on 14 May. Where the German position had been precarious the previous evening, they had managed to bring sufficient tanks of their own across during the night to weather the French tanks' assault and then destroy them. Disregarding orders, the French infantry began to retreat. Panic spread to the neighbouring 71st Infantry Division, with troops fleeing even before the battle reached them. Throughout the day French and British bombers attempted to destroy the German pontoon bridges. Flying in small groups of ten to twenty planes they sustained high casualties without hitting their targets. They lacked the dive-bombing precision of the German Stukas or the carpet-bombing tactics the medium bombers had displayed the day before. According to Halder's dispositions, after winning their bridgeheads, the panzer corps were to dig in and safeguard them, while the mass of the German infantry divisions crossed the Meuse. This would leave the German armies free to prepare for a classic battle of encirclement or, if the Allied armies turned back from Belgium to meet them, for an open encounter in which the Germans would have the advantage of pressing from two sides. When Guderian asked to enlarge his bridgehead by 20 kilometres, both Kleist and Rundstedt stuck to plan and ordered him to stay within 8 kilometres.[12]

That day brought no fewer than four Special Announcements to the German home front, lessening the mood of collective anxiety: 'Now wide sections of the population are of the opinion that there is a "lightning campaign" in the west', the SD reported, noting the confidence that 'the Luftwaffe has succeeded in securing its predominance in the air from the outset'. After fearing a repetition of the static war of 1914–18, the German people were fascinated by the paratroopers' capture of Eben Emael, the 'strongest fort', they were told, in all of Europe.[13]

The next day, 15 May, Guderian and the commander of the 7th Panzer Division, Erwin Rommel, disobeyed their direct orders and broke out of their bridgeheads at Sedan and Dinant. Instead of turning south and attacking the Maginot Line from the rear, as the French expected, they headed west and north-west. Rommel's column encountered the French 1st Reserve Tank Division with its fearsome heavy Char-B tanks. Most of the French vehicles were refuelling at the time and in the fighting the Germans succeeded in disabling 100 tanks, destroying the far superior French division. The two German commanders pushed on. Guderian covered the 80 kilometres to Marle and Rommel 100 kilometres, crossing the river Sambre at Le Cateau. The next two days, 17 and 18 May, were spent eating, sleeping, refuelling and repairing their battered vehicles, while units of motorised infantry were rushed forward to catch up with the isolated panzer divisions.[14]

Backed up by close air support from the 8th Air Fleet, the tank divisions showed that they could operate as an independent strike force. With his background in logistics and communications in the First World War, Guderian valued good radio links within the panzer divisions and now benefited from excellent land–air connections. When forward liaison officers radioed for air support, the Stukas responded quickly, sometimes within ten minutes, breaking up fortified positions, disrupting the enemy rear and protecting the tanks from flanking attacks. In fact, the tank divisions took a route so far to the west of the main body of the Allied armies that they managed by and large to avoid contact. It was a move which astonished both the German and French General

Staffs. The tremendous, almost unopposed, speed of forces working jointly gave the infantrymen following behind a delirious sense of unchecked momentum. The sleep-deprived troops were kept going with 35 million tablets of Pervitin and Isophan. When military supplies ran low, men wrote home asking their families to buy the amphetamines over the counter. On the evening of 20 May, a jubilant reconnaissance unit from the 2nd Panzer Division reached Noyelles-sur-Mer and looked out over the Somme estuary at the English Channel.[15]

Since the start of fighting ten days earlier, many Germans had not switched off their radios. Despite early shifts, the SD reported, people were waiting up to hear the final Wehrmacht bulletin at midnight. The news that German forces had 'broken through to the Channel and completed the encirclement of large enemy armies raised the tension in the population to a maximum and released renewed excitement everywhere'. Speculation was already rife that France would soon fall and that the invasion of Britain would follow, 'with the frequently expressed wish that this time England should experience war in its own land'. The military commentaries provided by the Propaganda Ministry official Hans Fritzsche proved so popular that the SD billed them as the perfect antidote to listening to enemy radio. Göring chose this moment to reveal to the press that the Führer had planned the whole campaign, down to the detail of individual actions. Only enemy bombing of western German cities continued to cause alarm, and, increasingly, provoke demands for retaliation.[16]

Ernst Guicking was on leave when the western offensive began, and it took twelve days for him to catch up with his regiment in Luxembourg. 'Yesterday still in the mud in the shell fire of the Maginot Line and the marshy holes of Luxembourg and this morning we are on the flank of the French,' he wrote to Irene on 28 May. After missing the start of the campaign, he was delighted to be part of it: 'Irene, that fills us with special pride.' As for the mortar fire, Ernst adapted the popular sailor's song, 'That Can't Shake a Squaddie'. He and his comrades went swimming morning and evening, but made the local women taste their drinking water first because they feared poisoned wells. For preference they quenched their thirst on wine. On Sunday 2 June, they marched 35 kilometres before making camp. A 200-litre barrel of wine got tent room. A cow was slaughtered and hung from a tree to be carved. The locals, Ernst reported, just kept repeating

'*Bon Alleman[d]*'. You don't hear anything else. They also can't say anything else. And to their question, 'where to?', we answer, 'to Paris', to '*Monsieur Daladier*'. Then they run off and cry, '*Oh la France, Grand Malheur, Grand Malheur*'. We could kill ourselves laughing. Irene, I tell you, a campaign could not be finer than this.

Indeed, 'the land where dreams come true is nothing to compare with it'. As for the fighting itself, he was glad to have 'passed the baptism of fire wonderfully well'. The constant drone of what he estimated to be 1,500 German planes flying low overhead gave him a headache, but much of the campaign had become a spectator sport. 'We look like pigs. But God couldn't have sent us a better war. Thousands of prisoners.'[17]

The young high-school graduate Hans Albring began the campaign in the west with a yearning to see the great French cathedrals. Girding himself morally like Christ before 'this terrible Passion, which our soldiers but especially the French are suffering', with the help of a dictionary he read Racine and Paul Claudel in his trench. A fervent Catholic from the Münsterland, Hans confided to his closest friend, Eugen Altrogge, that there were so few military chaplains that he feared being 'without any opportunity for confession and communion'. He wondered too why the French hated the Germans so much. 'The blacks are particularly bad,' he confided. 'They hang in the trees and are good shots.' Each day swamped Albring with irreconcilable impressions. One moment they were baking potato cakes and drinking old Bordeaux, rejoicing over the sheer quantities of real coffee; the next they came upon a field full of rotting animals lying on their backs, 'legs in the air like wooden rocking horses'. Along the road they saw 'a crowd of blacks lying on the way, gruesomely mangled' – almost certainly, French colonial soldiers from Senegal – and 'everywhere [there are] crosses with steel helmets on fresh graves'. He begged his friend not to breathe a word of any of this to his family, who believed him safe in the rear. After a shell had burst 200 metres away, Hans broached the personal question of all wars with Eugen: 'If I . . . and not you, look after my books and pictures. The letters should be burned.'[18]

Eugen reassured his friend. 'I believe in your good star – may nothing befall you,' he replied. 'We need each other still for the future . . . *Pax Domini sit semper tecum* [May the peace of the Lord be always with you].' Meanwhile Eugen's military service saw him posted to Vienna, where he chafed at being so far from the fighting, condemned to spend his evenings going to the opera. Up in the gods, he quickly got to know the other faces and paid a mere 75 pfennig to see Lehár and Puccini ('easy to listen to'). Like most of his fellow countrymen he preferred Verdi to Wagner, finding his 'great feeling and his resounding melodies which display power and delicacy far more congenial'. Above all, Mozart's *Don Giovanni* enraptured him, especially the final descent into hell. It moved him so much that the young would-be artist kept thinking about how he could draw 'a dance between death and the demons'. While Hans was on campaign, Eugen was more than half at peace.[19]

Fritz Probst followed the front through Belgium by bus, rebuilding the bridges blown up by the retreating Belgians and French. Whereas Hans Albring took pains to conceal the dangers he was running from his family, the 33-year-old boasted to his wife Hildegard that 'we are near the front and belong to the fighting troops'. His anxiety to avoid the stigma of serving in the rear trumped his concern to reassure her about his safety. Occasionally, they would come upon a village which had changed hands unscathed, but wherever the French had fought, the Stukas had evidently left nothing intact.[20]

While battle was still raging in France and Belgium, German radio journalists and cameramen brought the sights and sounds of the conflict to home audiences. Three successive newsreels accompanied the French campaign, and they doubled in length to forty minutes. Embedded in the fighting units, German cameramen had unparalleled access to the front; and also re-enacted key scenes for the camera. People marvelled at the risks reporters ran in order to bring them images of combat, gasping and shouting as they beheld the scenes of destruction. Crafted to give viewers the sense of being eyewitnesses to events, the cameras often looked up into German soldiers' faces from slightly below, throwing their angular, battle-hardened features into relief. With added sound effects and dramatic musical accompaniment – often adaptations of classical pieces by the house composer Franz R. Friedl – the newsreels aimed to draw in and overwhelm the viewer. This was no ordinary cinema news, but a total visual, acoustic and emotional experience, the mounting tension heightened and channelled by the voiceover: 'New German tanks ready for attack, ready for a mighty push forward. These tanks carry with them the new romance of fighting. They are what the knights were in the Middle Ages. They are as mobile as cavalry was in the last war.' Many cinemas 'simply could not cope with the crush of patrons', the *Film-Kurier* noted, with some theatres offering up to ten shows per day. The lights were turned on again after the newsreel, instituting an interval to give audiences a chance to calm down, talk to each other. Many people left before the supposed main feature, not wanting to ruin what they had just seen by a 'shallow feature film'.[21]

On 24 May, with Calais already under siege, Hitler and Rundstedt agreed to halt the tanks, allowing them to make urgent repairs so that they could be turned against the French armies in the south, and leaving the Luftwaffe to deal with the Allied divisions trudging over the canal-crossed terrain towards Dunkirk. Having enjoyed air supremacy for much of the previous ten days, at this point the Luftwaffe unexpectedly failed. It succeeded in bombing the beaches, sinking many ships, including nine destroyers, and in limiting Allied operations to night-time, but proved unable to prevent the evacuation of 338,000 British and French troops. Flying from its bases in southern England, the RAF played a major part in challenging German air power, making over 4,822 sorties between 26 May and 4 June. For the first time, German losses in the air were considerably greater than Allied ones.[22]

Travelling in a truck and a signals van, Hans Albring had far more leisure to write than the infantryman Ernst Guicking. With ambitions to become an artist, he tried to sketch word pictures for his rapidly shifting impressions – the old man at the farm gazing in bitter silence through puckered eyelids, the captured officer by the roadside, looking at the victorious Germans 'confidently and coldly, quite composed with a terrible, extreme calm'. In Poitiers, the beauty of the frescoes in the ancient Baptistery won him over, and he grieved at the loss of so many stained-glass windows. The plump, well-fed women seemed to come straight out of a Van Eyck canvas. From the grunting pigs in the sties where he slept to the prodigious quantities of butter, cheese, meat, home-made preserves, snow-white bread and deep-red wine, as heavy as oil, the cornucopia of France amazed him. Delighted to find a copy of Hölderlin's 'Song before Battle', he took refuge in the Romantic poet's verse. As for the fighting itself, he could only describe what the faces of his comrades looked like afterwards:

'Cheerfulness failed them, no one spoke or laughed any more.' They were dull and 'witless'. Like so many soldiers, Albring had words for everything except battle.[23]

Sixty-five French divisions had been thrown into a new line behind the Somme and Aisne rivers, which connected the Maginot Line to the coast. On 5 June, the Germans attacked, rapidly breaking through at numerous points along the Somme and pushing the entire front back towards the Seine. The French government fled on 10 June, declaring Paris an open city. Four days later German troops entered the capital. On 15 June, infantry divisions of the German 7th Army attacked across the Rhine, capturing the cities of Colmar and Strasbourg. The third newsreel of the campaign dwelt on the German infantry and artillery, ensuring that each of the branches of service received its due. Audiences warmed to the glimpses of the everyday routines of ordinary soldiers. Irene Guicking hoped to spot Ernst. Seeing so many faces 'laughing into the camera, in each soldier I saw you and was content'. If the Führer were to raise a women's regiment, she mused, she would not hesitate to join.[24]

On 18 June, the French Army began blowing up the bridges over the Loire, and a new government under Marshal Pétain requested an armistice. As negotiations began, the Germans pushed on. Ernst Guicking and Fritz Probst both found their units heading south towards Dijon. Probst complained about the French prisoners idling away in their camps while he and his comrades rebuilt what they had destroyed: 'Is that really right?' he wrote to Hildegard. Quite suddenly, they entered a landscape untouched by war. Quartered in a chocolate factory, Probst and his comrades were prevented by orders against looting from sending any confectionery home, but not from gorging themselves.[25]

In Poland, Wilm Hosenfeld felt he missed out on the war. At 45, Hosenfeld was a full generation older than the young trainee officers in his unit. He was a veteran of the previous war and the father of five children. Their eldest son, Helmut, had just been called for his army medical and his parents were apprehensive: Wilm tried to assure his wife that the war would be over before Helmut could serve, whilst writing to his son: 'Better if you stayed where you are; I am glad to be a soldier in your stead. In any case, Mother is sacrificing herself enough for all of us.' This was not likely to dampen Helmut's eager idealism, and Wilm tried to warn him that war was like any natural disaster, 'or some other catastrophe', and that God sent wars to the world because the 'people belong to a large extent to the Devil'. Drawing on Catholic teaching, he concluded 'that the innocent have to suffer as well is the secret of suffering on behalf of others which Jesus took upon himself'. Wilm admitted to his wife that he would have preferred a posting to the west, but he hastened to assure Annemie that 'my life doesn't belong to me and my sense of adventure . . . [I am] cooled by thinking of you and the children.' Although family duty trumped glory, he could not quite quash his craving for the kind of heroic victory which had eluded his generation in 1918.[26]

The younger generation was even more frustrated. In the third month of his military training in Brünn, Helmut Paulus realised that he and his comrades had been born 'too late after all'. Despite having tried to volunteer back in August 1939, he had missed the war. Certain that Britain would give up, his months of training now seemed a waste. Restless for some kind of war-related service, teenagers besieged the offices of the Reich Labour Service to find out when they would be called up to serve in it. By now the Armaments Inspectorates reported that even workers in sought-after occupations exempt from conscription were impatient to join up.[27]

Shortly after the fall of Paris, another newsreel astonished audiences with its depiction of the battle for Dunkirk shot from from the cockpit of a Stuka. Audiences dived with the plane towards the British transport ships below. It was a cinematic technique already used in the coverage of the Polish campaign, but when the dive-bombers' vertiginous speed was set to a soundtrack of their engines with rising background music it became gut-wrenchingly involving. Night-time shots of burning oil tanks and railway junctions bombed by day provided images of precision bombing. Since the start of the war, Goebbels had struggled to convince the Germans that the English were cowardly and treacherous: Dunkirk now provided a welcome opportunity to make the accusations stick. The 'Tommies', who had danced in nightclubs behind the lines in France, the Netherlands and Belgium, had simply abandoned their allies at the first sign of attack. While distraught-looking French prisoners testified to the true impact of German arms, the calm, self-satisfied expressions of British prisoners suggested that they had given up all too easily.[28]

Across Germany, audiences recoiled in horror and disgust from the French West African troops they saw on screen: 'The French and English let such animals loose on us – the Devil take them!' and 'That's an infamy for a civilised nation which debases England and France for ever!' were typical exclamations. In Reichenberg, women confessed they felt paralysed with fear by the 'coloured' faces, and could breathe again only when German soldiers reappeared on screen. In many cinemas, according to the SD, audiences shouted: 'Shoot these black beasts immediately after taking them prisoner.' Fritz Probst agreed, warning his wife that 'no one would have survived if this rabble had reached Germany'. What went unreported, except in private letters such as Hans Albring's, was that several thousand Senegalese soldiers were butchered as they tried to surrender or when already in captivity. In Poland, acts of mutilation and sniping from trees had been attributed both to Polish civilians and soldiers. In France, only black troops were singled out in this way, and were maltreated, tortured and killed. Alongside acts of reprisal, the Germans were compensating too for the much-cultivated memory of French occupation of the Rhineland in 1923, in which the sexual exploitation of German women by black colonial troops featured prominently. Even in this generally 'clean' campaign in the west, the German Army thus committed racial atrocities.[29]

On 22 June, the French surrendered. Hitler insisted on an exact replay of the armistice of November 1918, and the next newsreel culminated with the acceptance of German terms in the same railway carriage in the forest clearing at Compiègne. Afterwards, in a classic compensatory gesture, the carriage was brought to Berlin and exhibited at the foot of the steps to the Museum of Antiquities. There could be no clearer symbol that the outcome of the previous war had finally been reversed. As the extent of the victory became clear, people rushed out into the streets and squares to hold impromptu celebrations, though air raid warnings forced many inside again, where they listened to the radio announcements in their cellars. When Hitler ordered bells to be rung for a week and flags to be flown for ten days, the SD had no trouble describing how, after the 'stormy excitement of the last weeks', the national mood 'gave way to a celebratory mood of quiet, proud joy and thanksgiving for the Führer and the Wehrmacht'.[30]

Throughout the 1920s, German schoolchildren had been taught to see France as 'the hereditary enemy'. Now, like a mythological monster, it lay vanquished. All the luck and improvisation that had gone into the victory were swiftly corralled into a doctrine of invincible mobile warfare, with Wilhelm Keitel leading the praise for Hitler as 'the greatest warlord of all time'. To every cinema the *Wochenschau* news brought the images of the perfectly dressed ranks of soldiers marching out from the shadow of the Arc de Triomphe into the bright sunlight. But it was Hitler who stole the show, his appearance greeted across the Reich by thunderous applause and shouts of 'Heil!' Then, in reverential silence, the audiences settled down to watch him sit down with his generals. People worried about his personal safety, as they saw him driving past columns of prisoners near the front line. But when he got into his car and smiled, audiences collectively released their breath. Forgetting that Britain was not yet defeated and forgetting – briefly – their normal gripes about shortages and the venality of the 'big shots', their euphoria focused on *him*. Even the proverbially dour Swabians acknowledged 'wholly, joyfully, and thankfully the superhuman greatness of the Führer and his work'. After conquering Poland, few Germans had felt like celebrating. But now clamour for new photos of the Führer was accompanied by doting discussion of his expressions. Tough, working-class districts which had seen much street fighting between Nazi storm troopers and communists in the early 1930s finally succumbed.[31]

Still waiting to be called up from his high school in Solingen, August Töpperwien had greeted the campaign in the west with the assumption that 'We all have to recognise that real historical decisions are being made here, executed by Adolf Hitler! Here it is not "good" and "evil" but "historically powerful" and "historically powerless" that count.' If this vogue for reading Nietzsche as a philosopher of power placed the war 'beyond good and evil', Töpperwien discounted his own moral qualms at the terrible air power unleashed against French civilians by telling himself that a 'nation can only consent to our destructive aerial warfare which has brought forth a *Nietzsche*' (his emphasis). Addressing the conference of Bavarian Protestant pastors, Bishop Meiser declared that

the hot breath of history strikes us in the face. Without doubt we cannot measure the greatness of the world event of today . . . a new world is arising out of the primal depths of being. Our German people stands at the centre of this event. It is the core strength from which a new, transfiguring will spreads over the whole earth.[32]

Victory was sweet because it seemed astonishingly easy. Arriving at the Loire, a Swabian soldier was amazed. 'Where is the enemy?' he asked. 'On the right a couple of men disappeared into the bushes. But of the enemy nothing is to be seen. Where are the poilus?' The Wehrmacht published this private letter in a commemorative volume, helping to embed the experience in popular memory. Hitler had delivered the German people from a conflict on the scale of the world war that had cost Germany nearly two million military dead. In Berlin, by 1917, the military death toll had been overtaken by the civilian one, as hunger, cold and illness wrought havoc on the city. Unlike the 'phoney war' in Britain and the '*drôle de guerre*' in France, Germans experienced the seven long months of foreboding from September till mid-May not as a *Sitzkrieg* so much as, in the words of the SD, 'a war of nerves'. When the dreaded battles in the west finally began, the first news of bulletins had confirmed a universal sense of replay of the battles in Flanders and of impending carnage. Instead, at the end of June 1940 Ernst Guicking found himself in Toulon, eating

first pork leg, then roast calf, sausage with vegetables and to finish a wonderful dessert. Apricots with cherries. To go with it two bottles of red wine. And the whole lot cost the impossible price of nine francs. That's 75 German pfennig. Yes, yes, you're right. We're living like 'God in France'.[33]

In the summer of 1940, the Wehrmacht reported 26,500 dead in the French campaign. The statistics were a slight underestimate and would be revised upwards, but even so there was no comparison with the 2,055,000 killed in the last war: the country had lost 61,500 men in the conquest of Poland, Denmark, Norway, the Netherlands, Belgium, Luxembourg and France. The final newsreel of the campaign in the west showed Hitler paying silent homage in front of a small group of German war graves before accepting the French surrender at Compiègne. Now it was time to end the conflict with Britain too and restore the peace the whole population craved.[34]

On 18 July 1940, the 218th Infantry Division returned home to Berlin.

Crowds up to twenty rows deep lined the new East–West Axis, with enterprising onlookers clambering on to trees, lamp posts and statues along the route to get a better view. The crowds threw confetti and flowers at the troops, while the military bands played. After marching through the Brandenburg Gate to the Pariser Platz, the division was welcomed by the city's Gauleiter, Joseph Goebbels. He reminded the holiday crowd that the last time troops had marched through the Gate was on 16 December 1918, when the returning Prussian Guard regiments were met by 'gangsters and strikers': 'Not this time!' he shouted.[35]

The following evening, Hitler addressed the Reichstag in the Kroll Opera House. Wreaths were laid on six seats for the deputies who had been killed in action. The American journalist William Shirer, sitting once again in the gallery, had never seen so much gold braid and military uniforms. The press wondered if Hitler would announce 'a new *Blitzkrieg* – this time against Britain – or an offer of peace'. After Hermann Göring heaved himself into the Speaker's chair and the audience hushed, Hitler spoke for over two hours about the course of the war and the military campaign. With an outstretched salute, he promoted twelve generals to the rank of field marshal; they sprang to attention and saluted back. Since Göring already held that title, Hitler created the new rank of 'Reich Marshal' for him. Shirer considered this speech to be one of Hitler's most outstanding performances. There was no note of hysteria, the American journalist observed; indeed the Führer's voice was pitched slightly deeper than usual, the movement of his hands and body almost as expressive as his words. 'The Hitler we saw in the Reichstag tonight', Shirer noted down a few hours later, 'was the conqueror, and conscious of it, and yet so wonderful an actor, so magnificent a handler of the German mind, that he mixed superbly the full confidence of the conqueror with the humbleness which always goes down so well with the masses when they know a man is on top.'

At the very end, Hitler 'stretched out his hand' to offer peace: 'In this hour I feel it my duty before my own conscience to appeal once more to reason and common sense. I can see no reason why this war must go on.' The auditorium remained tense and expectant as Hitler struck a tone more of sorrow than of anger. 'I am grieved to think of the sacrifices it will claim. I should like to avert them, also for my own people.' He reminded his audience of his peace offer the previous

October and regretted that 'in spite of all my efforts I have not succeeded in becoming friends with England'. The BBC broadcast Halifax's official rejection of Hitler's new peace initiative three days later.[36]

The Führer may have misjudged the British government, but not the mood in Germany. With the magnanimity of the true conqueror, Hitler had given Britain the chance to end the conflict – and all the responsibility for prolonging it. Even before the British government's formal rejection, some German people wondered whether their government's offer to the 'real warmonger and guilty party in this war' had been too generous. It was not just the unpolitical Irene and Ernst Guicking who expected the Führer 'not to be merciful'. Even Wilm Hosenfeld set his religious compassion to one side when he wrote to his wife, 'The war can now only be decided with brutal force. The English want it so.' This man, who had felt so ashamed of the violence he witnessed in Poland, was certain now: 'No, one doesn't need to feel sorry for them. Hitler offered them the hand of peace often enough.'[37]

★

Five days before Hitler's Reichstag speech, on 14 July, Churchill had pledged to the world that Britain would fight on alone. On 3 July, the Royal Navy had sunk the French fleet anchored off the Tunisian coast, to prevent it falling into German hands, an act Churchill described as a 'sad duty'. To the new government at Vichy, whose control over the French Navy was assured by the terms of the Armistice, the unprovoked assault amounted to a treacherous attack by its recent ally. This was also the image of Britain which German propaganda had been cultivating all summer: on 4 July, the German News Bureau released excerpts of captured documents detailing Allied plans to bomb Soviet oilfields from the Middle East, an operation intended to disrupt the Soviet supply of oil to Germany, but which the News Bureau could portray as a deceitful Allied attempt to widen the war.[38]

On 1 September 1939, the American President Roosevelt had appealed to all European powers to undertake not to conduct air raids against civilians or 'open' cities. Hitler and Chamberlain assented on the same day, with the British and French governments issuing a joint declaration that they would not be the first to resort to such action.

The British could now point to the Luftwaffe's bombing of Warsaw and Rotterdam as the fundamental breach, while German propaganda claimed that these cities had been militarily defended: until they were surrendered as 'open' cities like Paris, they remained legitimate military targets. For the German public, however, the 'Children's murder at Freiburg' of 10 May 1940 marked the point when the British had unilaterally broken the undertaking to spare civilian population centres. As Hitler told his dinner guests two years later, 'It was the English who started air attacks . . . The German is always restrained by moral scruples, which mean nothing to the English; to the latter such an attitude is merely a sign of weakness and stupidity.' This 'fact' was kept alive in the court of international public opinion, figuring prominently in a 1943 publication of the Foreign Ministry addressed to the neutral countries, its *8th White-Book: Documents on England's Sole Guilt for the Bombing War against the Civilian Population.*[39]

Freiburg may have been a convenient fiction, but on the night of 11 May 1940, the RAF launched its first air raid on Germany, against Mönchengladbach in the Ruhr. In the weeks following France's capitulation, the RAF stepped up its night attacks, sending over hundreds of bombers at a time. The more significant raids, like that of the night of 23–24 June on Dortmund, left one dead and six wounded and in Düsseldorf seven people were killed and seven wounded. RAF targeting was so inaccurate, however, that by July farmhouses and villages were being hit. Both the regularity and the aimlessness of the bombing forced German civil defence volunteers to tighten air raid precautions across the towns and cities of north-western Germany. In Hamburg, the 'chief complaint', Shirer found, 'was not the damage caused but the fact that the British raids robbed them of their sleep', as every false alarm drove the city's entire population from their beds. The clamour for retaliation grew.[40]

At rallies, Nazi speakers dropped hints of powerful new weapons, sparking a rash of rumours about an invasion of Britain. Gliders, like those used to such effect against Norway and Belgium, were to land paratroops, while countless new tanks and naval vessels were said to be ready. There was talk of a force of 2,000 Stukas and huge new bombs; of jet aircraft capable of flying at 1,000 kilometres an hour; of death rays and something even the SD did not seem to understand and just quoted verbatim, '"the deployment of liquid air with electron dust", causing unheard-of explosive force and spread of heat'. As the weeks rolled by bringing no news of military action, astrologers again did a brisk trade. Political rumours ran riot too. Lloyd George and the Duke of Windsor (the former Edward VIII) were said to be in Berlin; George VI had abdicated and Churchill fled. Some geopolitically minded citizens wondered aloud whether Germany had an economic interest in preserving the British Empire. Indeed, Hitler asked the same question and worried that its dismemberment would benefit not Germany, but 'foreign great powers'.[41]

Even after his 'peace offer' was rejected, Hitler hesitated over his final decision. He had ordered his commanders to prepare operational plans for the 'war against England' in early July, but it was not until 1 August that he finally issued a directive to the Luftwaffe to start the 'England attack'. The day before he had ordered the General Staff to begin planning for a military campaign against the Soviet Union, on the grounds that it remained Britain's last potential ally on the Continent. That Hitler was already thinking about conquering the Soviet Union in preference to invading Britain indicates both his cautious appraisal of Germany's chances of challenging the power of the Royal Navy from the air, and his long-cherished desire to force the British to become German partners. During July and early August, the Luftwaffe ringed the North Sea and Channel coasts from Norway to western France with new bases; and it tried to win temporary control over the Channel, successfully attacking British convoys until the Admiralty was forced to halt their passage. In Berlin, construction crews began erecting review stands on the Pariser Platz in preparation for another victory parade. This time they were decorated with large wooden eagles, which were given a lick of gold paint. Thanks to the terrible English summer weather, 'Eagle Day', as the attack was code-named, could not be launched until 13 August.[42]

For the first three weeks the Luftwaffe attacked the airfields of RAF Fighter Command. On 18 August, it was the turn of Biggin Hill in Kent: returning German pilots reported seeing the airfield in a sea of flames, runways destroyed, buildings ruined and no sign of enemy aircraft or anti-aircraft fire. They concluded that the base was 'completely destroyed . . . wiped out of existence'. They were astonished by the ease with which they were winning the battle. 'Young men,' a returning pilot explained excitedly to the ground crew, 'that was nothing at all: we had imagined a quite different defence.' By 19 August, the Luftwaffe claimed to have shot down 624 British planes, with the loss of 174 of their own. That night, as the German air force expanded its bombing of the aircraft industry, it began to target the outer London suburbs of Wimbledon and Croydon. On 24–25 August, it was Harrow and Hayes, Uxbridge, Lewisham and Croydon, and on 28–29 August, Hendon, Southgate, Wembley and Mill Hill, but also the inner London boroughs of St Pancras, Finchley and the Old Kent Road. Hitler had forbidden the bombing of London, but mission creep took its toll on a capital ringed with military bases and industrial plants.[43]

Although it was much easier for the Luftwaffe to reach Britain from their new Continental bases than it was for the RAF to strike at Germany, Churchill ordered an immediate response to the first accidental raid on London. On the night of 25–26 August, twenty-two Hampden and Wellington bombers struck Berlin. It was a pinprick raid, causing slight damage, but it defied the promise issued to the home front by Hermann Göring. At the outbreak of the war, he had gone on the radio to pledge that if a single plane reached the Ruhr, then his name was 'not Göring but Meier'. Now they had penetrated all the way to the Reich capital. Playing on the Reich Marshal's famous fondness for the chase, wits soon starting calling the air raid sirens in Berlin and the Ruhr 'Meier's hunting-horn', or simply referred to him pithily as 'Hermann Meier'. A second minor raid on Berlin followed on 29–30 August, killing ten and injuring twenty-one people. The psychological and strategic consequences were enormous. Berliners were shocked that British planes could penetrate so deeply into German airspace; Hitler also.[44]

He seized the first opportunity to address the nation, speaking to a young female audience of nurses and social workers assembled to launch the Party's Winter Relief Fund on 4 September. 'I waited three months without answering the British night bombing in the hope they would stop this mischief,' Hitler told the packed Berlin Sportpalast. 'But Herr Churchill saw this as a sign of our weakness. You will understand that we are now answering, night for night and on an increasing scale. And when the British air force drops two or three or four thousand kilograms of bombs, then we will in one night drop 150, 180, 230, 300, 400,000, a million kilograms.' Pausing to let the wild applause die down, Hitler continued, 'When they declare that they will increase their attacks on our cities, then we will erase their cities from the earth.' William Shirer was there, and recorded that 'the young nurses and social workers were quite beside themselves and applauded frenetically'. Suffering from a heavy cold, the American found the screaming audience very trying, but was still impressed by the way Hitler 'squeezed every ounce of humour and sarcasm out of his voice' promising, 'We will put an end to the work of these night pirates, so help us God. The day will come when one of us two breaks and it will not be National Socialist Germany.' Two hours later, the speech was broadcast. The pledge to 'erase' British cities would be long remembered.[45]

Even Hitler's overt threat was couched in what had become the accustomed, defensive, retaliatory terms with which each step of the war had been justified. A few days earlier, Shirer had recorded a conversation with his cleaner, a woman from a working-class family, married, he surmised, to an ex-communist or socialist. 'Why do they do it?' she asked. 'Because you bomb London,' Shirer replied. 'Yes, but we hit military objectives, while the British they bomb our homes.' 'Maybe,' Shirer interjected, 'you bomb their homes too.' 'Our papers say not,' she argued. 'Why didn't the British accept the Führer's offer?'[46]

On the evening of 7 September, a fanfare introduced a fresh special announcement: 'for the first time the city and port of London' had been attacked 'as a reprisal' for RAF raids. In fulfilment of the Führer's threat, 3,000 planes had 'set their course for London'. 'Chasing through the night sky like comets', they had left behind 'one great cloud of smoke [which] tonight stretches from the middle of London to the mouth of the Thames'. The military bulletin did not forget to state that the Luftwaffe was waging 'fair and chivalrous warfare', restricted to 'military objectives'. The next day all the papers carried the same headline: 'BIG ATTACK ON LONDON AS REPRISAL'. Although only 348 bombers, protected by 617 fighters, had attacked the British capital, returning pilots broadly confirmed these reports, having seen 'thick black clouds of smoke, which grew like giant mushrooms' from 50–60 kilometres away. Dropping large oil bombs as well as high explosive bombs, they ignited major fires in the East End docks. The RAF had barely troubled them.[47]

On the night of 10 September, the British bombed the centre of

Berlin again, hitting the American embassy and Goebbels's nearby garden: Shirer noted that it was 'the severest bombing yet', but it was still minor compared to what the Luftwaffe was doing. When the BBC mistakenly claimed that the nearby Potsdamer station had been hit, Shirer was not surprised to be told by 'at least three Germans' that 'they felt a little disillusioned at the British radio's lack of veracity'. Even the respectable *Börsen Zeitung* insisted that 'While the attack of the German air force is made on purely military objectives – this fact is recognised by both the British press and radio – the RAF knows nothing better to do than continually to attack non-military objectives in Germany.'[48]

From September 1940, huge resources were devoted to civil defence, especially to building massive ferroconcrete bunkers for the urban population of northern and north-western Germany. Many rose slowly above ground: great, rectangular, windowless fortresses. The Berlin towers were erected in three parks. The first opened in April 1941 in the Tiergarten near the Zoo, its four-metre-thick walls surmounted by flat roofs and smaller, square corner towers which served as the platforms for the anti-aircraft guns, radar equipment and searchlights. A second was completed at Friedrichshain in October 1941, and a third at Humboldthain the following April. Each could accommodate 10,000 people. They were not only places of protection; the towers also became symbols of the national 'will to hold out'. Similar massive fortresses were built in the Hamburg neighbourhoods of St Pauli and Wilhelmsburg. At Hamm in the Ruhr, six bunker towers were inserted into the ring of the town walls, projecting the image of a medieval fortified town. In Dortmund, the local planners equipped the tunnels that had been sunk 15 metres below the city for an underground railway system in 1937. They now offered shelter to 20,000. Hanover also opted for tunnels. Essen, the capital of the Krupp armament empire, was equipped with serious anti-aircraft artillery and a bunker-building programme began which would make it one of the best-defended cities in Germany. The public bunkers could only ever accommodate a minority of the urban population – no more than 10 per cent of Berliners, for example – but their psychological importance and utility are hard to overestimate. Most citizens relied on the basements of their apartment blocks, where windows and doors were replaced with steel, blast-proof ones. For those with the money, space and contacts, the building of private shelters in their gardens also continued apace.[49]

*

The regime had been so confident in the Luftwaffe's ability to defend German airspace that it had made no plans to evacuate children. While London children boarded trains at Liverpool Street as early as September 1939, most German children remained at home. When evacuation finally began, it remained voluntary and families were reluctant to send their children away. On 10 July 1940, the first special train left Münster, but volunteers from the Nazi Women's Organisation had to go from door to door browbeating parents in order to fill the 200 places.[50]

On 27 September 1940, Martin Bormann, Hitler's Party Secretary, notified higher Party and state officials that a newly 'extended' programme of 'sending children to the countryside' was now under way, the *Kinderlandverschickung* or, as it was universally called, the KLV. The name had comforting connotations of the summer camps for workers' children from the big cities which had been pioneered by church and Social Democratic welfare organisations before and after the First World War – and which the Nazis had taken over and continued throughout the 1930s. Bormann forbade the use of the fear-inspiring term 'evacuation', and did everything in his power to reinforce the fiction of an an 'extension' of limited, recuperative spells in the countryside away from the 'areas threatened by air attack'.[51]

Hitler entrusted Baldur von Schirach with the task of drawing up the guidelines and organising the KLV. As the former leader of the Hitler Youth before he became Gauleiter of Vienna, Schirach hoped to elbow aside the schools and the Ministry of Education to implement his own educational programme. He wanted the single-sex homes, or 'camps', for 10- to 14-year-olds to serve as a showcase. By redeploying youth hostels and requisitioning hotels, convents, monasteries and children's homes, Schirach's staff rapidly assembled a stock of 3,855 buildings with places for 200,000–260,000 children. The National Socialist People's Welfare organised special trains, paid for the children's health care, and even arranged for local families to do their laundry. The Hitler Youth had never freed itself completely from parental and teacherly constraint and would not succeed in doing so now, but Schirach conceived his scheme as a permanent element of youth education designed to last into the post-war era and greatly enhance the Hitler Youth's influence. Fearing just such a development, priests in the largely Catholic Rhineland waged a low-level – and not very successful – campaign against parental take-up.[52]

To the frustration of local Nazi officials, consent remained a parental prerogative. By insisting on this, Hitler reined in the anti-clerical wing of the Party and forced functionaries to win public backing. Ironically, for a regime so bent on reassuring its citizens, the evacuation scheme's success depended on parents' fear for their children's lives. In Berlin and Hamburg 189,543 children were evacuated in the first two months of the national scheme, by which point rumours in Dresden were describing Berlin as a devastated city. As the scheme was extended to the vulnerable cities of north-western Germany and parents desperately sought to save their children from the danger of a direct hit, numbers continued to rise, reaching some 320,000 by 20 February 1941, 413,000 by the end of March and 619,000 by late June.[53]

At the outset organisation was haphazard, with children sleeping on loose straw while bunks were being built in their dormitories, but there was no shortage of enthusiastic improvisation. On 28 January 1941, Anneliese A. wrote home from Silesia to tell her parents that she had arrived safely at a convent, where the nuns catered for them. They had been busy preparing their beds but her parents needed to send her extra bed linen. Two days later, she wrote that she was skiing to school and settling in well, sharing a dormitory with two of her best friends. Ten-year-old Gisela Henn left Cologne for an East Prussian farm in September 1940. It was her first time away from home and she had to adjust quickly. By the time she was sent on another six-month placement in Saxony the following April, she was expected to feed the ducks and help out with the summer harvest. It was a success and her mother remained in contact with the Saxon farmer's wife. A third and happy placement in a KLV home was organised through Gisela's school.[54]

Social workers from the National Socialist People's Welfare supervised the placements and did their best to move children who were unhappy to other families, while the Hitler Youth organised group activities, such as the evening programme of group discussions and singalongs, team sports and route marches. This sense of collective belonging may have helped combat homesickness and isolation, but it also exacerbated clashes between different classes, regions and cultures. Ruhr boys who jeered at the 'cultural trash of the east' made themselves thoroughly unpopular in the villages of Pomerania and East Prussia. In the countryside, these new arrivals from from the industrial cities stood out and were automatically blamed for any acts of theft or vandalism.[55]

More popular than the insular world of the Prussian eastern marches, with their flat expanses of *Junker* great estates, were southern Germany and the Czech lands, where the evacuation programme re-stimulated a tourist infrastructure that had been stagnating since 1939. Even in the more convivial world of south-west German family farms, however, first impressions could be jarring. When a group of boys from the Ruhr arrived in Megesheim in February 1941, they were lined up in front of the village school while the farmers' wives inspected them. Ten-year-old Rudolf Lenz, the last to be picked, described the whole episode as a 'slave market'. The city boys looked puny, and he learned later that the local farmers had been promised strong and healthy boys to fill the shortfall of agricultural labour. Brought up as a Protestant in a fairly secular area, he had never encountered anything like the Catholicism of a Swabian village, where his foster mother knelt down in the fields when the church bell rang for midday and evening prayers. But at 10, he adjusted easily, enjoyed helping with the harvest, and his parents had trouble understanding his strong Swabian accent when they saw him at the end of the summer.[56]

Another special train left Essen on 27 April 1941, taking teenage girls to the Moravian town of Kremsier. Welcomed at the station by local members of the League of German Girls and the Hitler Youth, they marched to the requisitioned convent that became their new home. Some of the nuns had been kept on to cater for the girls. It was the kind of set-up that Schirach and his team set out to create. The new intake quickly learned the communal routines of bed-making, tidying their lockers and dormitories, as well as appearing on time and correctly dressed for the morning assembly, when the flag was raised. It was like a boarding school without corporal punishment. True to their motto that 'Youth leads youth', order was maintained by the BDM leader, and to foster a sense of comradeship, penalties were meted out to the whole group – holding back the post for three days, and, on the worst occasion, an 8-kilometre march, executed in utter silence. But the BDM leader, an older teenager herself, let the girls tease her and also borrow her radio so that they could dance on every birthday.[57]

One of the older girls from Essen, 15-year-old Ilse Pfofe, found their 'propaganda marches' especially empowering; she felt that they were helping to stamp a German and secular culture on the predominantly Czech and Catholic town. They marched on Palm Sunday to disrupt the church procession and again for a sports festival on 29 June, where they were led by a military band. Afterwards, Ilse noted happily that the 'Czechs are bursting with rage'. Left to their own devices, the girls started sunbathing in their gym slips and swimming costumes and doing exercises in the French park, where they could be admired by the young men in the German garrison. At the end of one such summer day, Ilse reckoned she had been photographed forty times. However innocent their cinema dates, she already felt far more grown up than when she had left Essen.[58]

★

After the opening mass raid of 7 September 1940, London was bombed on 9, 11 and 14 September during the day and on every single one of the next fifty-seven nights. The head of German radio, Eugen Hadamovsky, wangled his way on to one of the first night raids, providing listeners with a first-hand account:

> Beneath us, we saw the red blazing metropolis of England, the centre of plutocrats and slaveholders, the capital of World-Enemy No. 1. We saw the fires of destruction. Clouds of smoke and pillars of fire looked like the flow of lava from a titanic volcano . . . London is wrapped in flames . . . Unheard by us, without respite, the most dreadful scenes must be occurring down here, beneath our machines . . . Anti-aircraft shells explode around us. Suddenly a searchlight appears in our vicinity. Heavens! It has caught us, it keeps us. We are blinded and cannot see. A sudden move of the pilot, the machine rushes downwards, into the depths. Saved, and he has refound the darkness.[59]

The Wehrmacht bulletins continued to present the raids on London and other 'non-military' objectives as retaliation for the 'night pirates' of the RAF. News bulletins often started with accounts of RAF bombing of churches, graveyards and schools in Germany, before turning to the Luftwaffe. Each day the radio brought news of the 'worst' attack, the 'longest' alarm, the 'heaviest' bombardment, the 'heaviest attack of all times'. 'Increasing' was the word most often heard on German radio. 'The air war over England increases day by day and hour by hour. It is like a howling crescendo.'[60]

The German public knew that this was a different kind of campaign from conquering enemy territory. National papers like the *Völkischer Beobachter* printed maps which illustrated the targets of the previous night's raids, or, more rarely, aerial photos of the bombed airfields to satisfy demands for more detailed information. The local press could not satisfy the public's thirst for this kind of information, and so readers turned increasingly to national titles. The newsreels relayed images of long-range guns firing across the Channel at Dover, squadrons flying over the English coast and action by Stukas and bombers, but without film it had to pad out its forty minutes with footage of circus performances, horse racing, football and, of course, the Führer.[61]

In this war of attrition, both sides lived by numbers. From July to September, Luftwaffe fighters claimed to have shot down 3,198 British planes, while the RAF asserted it had downed 2,698 German ones. From the outset, the British and German communiqués disputed each other's figures, with German radio insisting on 15 August that since the reliability of the German news 'has so far never disappointed, naturally the German, not the English, reports of recent air battles are believed in the world'. At the end of August, ordinary people trying to keep tally realised that German losses were higher than in the battle for France. Still, they seemed sustainable. By mid-September, however, doubt grew after a radio talk given by Air Force General Erich Quade, whose sober tone contrasted with the more upbeat reports of the war reporters embedded in the Luftwaffe. The SD noted that people were perturbed that the numbers Quade cited no longer matched their own running tallies: 'If England only possessed the number of planes named by Quade at the start of the war, then, adding up all the numbers of hits, it can't have a single plane left today, or else British aircraft production is achieving something quite

extraordinary.' They were surprised too to hear the general praise the
Spitfire, having become accustomed to reports that it was no match
for the Messerschmitt 109.[62]

In the absence of hard fact, rumours abounded. There was talk of
French and Japanese declarations of war on Britain, and news of Italian
air squadrons being brought to Berlin, all feeding the hope that the
long-awaited invasion of England was imminent. While Germans
continued to trust the eyewitness reports of the bombing of Britain,
they increasingly questioned their media's reporting from the home
front. They queried whether the RAF deliberately targeted hospitals
and schools, or had simply missed nearby military targets. Had the
British really meant to bomb the US embassy in Berlin? As the weeks
dragged on, people listened increasingly to foreign radio. As one wit
put it, 'They lie and we are lying also.'[63]

The air war put German propaganda to the test. Goebbels himself
believed that the superiority of British propaganda in the previous
war had significantly contributed to the 'stab in the back' of 1918.
Anglophilia had been widespread in the 1920s and '30s, encouraged
by, amongst others, the Nazis themselves. A barrage of films, books,
newspaper articles and radio features now set out to correct such
views, lambasting the British class system and the evils it had inflicted
on the Boers, the Irish and the English working class. From February
1940, 6,000 student volunteers helped the Propaganda Ministry by
combing the libraries and amassing data on British unemployment,
health insurance, working-class slums and malnutrition amongst
schoolchildren. The BBC would eventually enlist George Orwell for
its wartime broadcasts to India, but German propaganda immediately
reprinted his damning indictment of working-class poverty. A glossy
coffee-table publication like *The Doomed Island* juxtaposed the two
Englands, contrasting photos of the East End and the Jarrow hunger
marchers with shots of toffs at Royal Ascot and Henley Royal Regatta.
The Nazi regime claimed it was fighting the same 'plutocracy' that
had ruined Weimar Germany and was stifling social progress in Britain.
Against the 'empty' formal freedoms of liberal Britain, Germany had
guaranteed the greatest freedom of all: social freedom from want. It
had overcome the poverty and hunger of the Depression years, solved
unemployment and abolished free-market capitalism. England still
needed to be liberated from a decadent, aristocratic class system, into

which the Jewish city huckster had insinuated himself. There were frequent calls for the bombing not to spare the 'plutocratic neighbourhoods' of London's West End. Germany's 'blood brothers' across the North Sea needed to be helped to liberate themselves – from poverty, hunger, injustice and domination by an alien race.[64]

Despite German outrage at British intransigence and its 'cowardly', 'terroristic' way of waging war, a powerful strain of Anglophilia remained. The idea of a Jewish 'plutocracy' at work in London allowed the Nazi regime to maintain a clear distinction between fighting the British government and hating the British people. In Münster the journalist Paulheinz Wantzen noted that 'Our policy aims at dividing people and government'. This very Anglophile Anglophobia emphasised things that Germans already believed, without undermining their admiration of British 'character-building' and other achievements. Above all, the student researchers provided ready quotations of eminent 'British authors criticising Britain' – from Thomas Carlyle, John Ruskin, Aldous Huxley and H.G. Wells to George Orwell and, above all, George Bernard Shaw. Jonathan Swift's A Modest Proposal was reprinted and cited to underline the callousness of the English ruling class in the face of famine in Ireland. Anglophone critics of domestic and colonial injustice served to unmask the altruism of Britain's imperial 'burden', as Shaw had done with ironic wit in his preface to The Man of Destiny. By relying on British critics, Goebbels's propagandists claimed a degree of objectivity as well as the high moral ground, while allowing Germans to go on admiring and assimilating British culture.

In 1940, personnel of one Berlin flak battery divided their time between watching out for RAF bombers while on duty and performing A Midsummer Night's Dream while off duty. During the 1930s Shakespeare had been performed more frequently in Germany than in Britain. Hitler, who once remarked that 'in no other country is Shakespeare performed as badly as in England', intervened personally to have the enemy dramatist unbanned after the outbreak of war. The director of the German Theatre in Berlin, Heinz Hilpert, responded to the bombing of Britain by planning to put on no fewer than three plays by Shaw and another three by Shakespeare in a single season.[65]

With its world empire, Britain remained the power that the Nazi leadership wanted Germany to become. Attacking the 'hypocrisy' and 'cant' of British claims to be defending 'humanity' generated a peculiar kind of Nazi anti-imperialism. It mobilised a righteous sense of outrage; nowhere more so than in the epic film *Ohm Krüger*, the story of the Boer War from the Afrikaner perspective. Released in April 1941, as the bombing of London and the British ports continued, the film was one of the greatest box office hits. Told in flashback by Paul Krüger who recalled the events of 1899, the film portrayed Cecil Rhodes's merciless drive for gold and profit in southern Africa. It culminated in scenes in a British concentration camp that held Boer women and children. When one of their hunted husbands is caught speaking to his wife through the barbed wire, the brutal commandant – bearing a striking resemblance to Winston Churchill – forces all the women and children in the camp to watch the man being hanged, and responds to the mounting tumult by ordering his troops to open fire. It was the only massacre in a concentration camp ever to be shown in Nazi Germany. As they were meant to, viewers unhesitatingly identified with the Boer victims. In the final hush, audiences could hear the great actor Emil Jannings deliver Krüger's plea: 'But the day of retaliation will come. I don't know when . . . We were only a small, weak nation. Greater and stronger nations . . . will smite England's soil. God will be with him. Then the way will be free for a better life.'[66]

If the Luftwaffe's bombing led to 'eight million going mad' in London, Hitler mused on 14 September, it would force Britain out of the war and make an invasion unnecessary. Two days later, Göring ordered the Luftwaffe to focus on night-time bombing, and on the 17th Hitler shelved his plans for the invasion indefinitely. The public was not told. Instead, on 18 September, the radio commentator Hans Fritzsche warned in his 'front reports' that London had to choose 'between the fate of Warsaw and Paris' – between being blasted from the skies or declaring itself an 'open' city and surrendering. By this point, publication of neutral Swedish and American eyewitness accounts of the Blitz helped to boost the morale of the German air crews and home front alike. When Goebbels read them, he was elated by their 'really apocalyptic' descriptions, and other readers too hoped they proved that the onslaught was working. At the same time, after a month of bombing, the SD picked up a new, grudging admiration at the 'toughness of the English and especially the residents of London': no one else had withstood the Luftwaffe this long.[67]

Through October and November the air raids increased in scale, and by late November the Propaganda Minister wondered in his diary, 'When will Churchill capitulate?' Within a fortnight, the SD reported widespread rumours that Britain was on the brink of revolution. The longer the British held out, however, the more it impressed German opinion. By mid-January 1941, reports of bleak social conditions in Britain were 'meeting with a critical reaction'. The SD surveyed Germans' growing disillusion with their own propaganda, noting typical comments such as 'the people of Britain surely did not feel that they were languishing under a plutocratic regime'. Increasingly, people shrugged off tales of British inequality with the comment, 'Well, it's no different here.' Neither capitulation nor revolution looked likely across the North Sea.[68]

By early May 1941, Göring was trying to reassure German bomber squadrons that they had inflicted 'enormous damage to the point of complete destruction' on British armaments production. British wartime surveys exaggerated in the other direction, speaking of a 5 per cent fall in output, but failing to take account of the huge shift in resources to civil defence. By the time the air offensive ended in June 1941, some 700,000 British men and women were employed full-time and a further 1.5 million part-time in air and civil defence; and the British civilian death toll had reached 43,384. On the German side, the continual sorties took their toll on air crews. In November 1940, German neurologists had found their first real evidence of the kind of 'war neuroses' they had been looking for since the beginning of the war, and recommended that air crews should be given spells of leave at home, in winter sports spas or in Paris and Brussels to relieve the stress. Psychiatric cases were treated at a hotel on the Breton coast.

On 10 May, exactly a year after the start of the campaign in the west, 505 planes raided London, dropping 718 tonnes of high explosive and damaging the Houses of Parliament. It was the last major night raid. By now, the operational strength of the Luftwaffe's bombing arm was down to 70 per cent of its capacity in May 1940. As the bombing of Britain tailed off, the media switched its attention to the U-boats' war on the Atlantic convoys. Propagandists toned down their taunts about 'English cowardice', lying, 'Jewish' influence and 'plutocracy'. There was no point in reminding the German public of their confident expectations of the previous autumn.[69]

On 27 September 1940, Paulheinz Wantzen counted the hundredth alarm in Münster. The main effect of the air raids was cumulative tiredness. For the whole of 1940, the city listed just eight fatalities. Hamburg reported nineteen and Wilhelmshaven four. Carola Reissner reported in November 1940 that the bombing had not caused enough damage to put a single plant in Essen out of commission. The national count at the end of 1940 was 975 dead. Neither side made its death statistics public.[70]

Germans quietly adjusted. By end of 1940 bomb damage in Berlin had become a tourist attraction, to be photographed before it disappeared. Liselotte Purper was on a night train to the Netherlands, dreaming that she was back at school, when the sirens went. She did not even wake up till the all-clear sounded. Carola Reissner also stopped getting out of bed for air raid alarms in Essen. As the Christmas holidays passed uneventfully in Münster, Paulheinz Wantzen thought that 'in general people are reckoning with a long war, without being particularly worried or bothered about it. In its current phase the war is hardly noticeable.'[71]

5

Winners and Losers

In the summer of 1940, while all of Germany rejoiced over the Wehrmacht's triumph in the west, Robert Schmuhl pined in East Prussia. Sent to the other end of the country, he missed the busy routine of his Hamburg bakery and the comradeship he had enjoyed during his military training. The farmer he was billeted on was unfriendly and made it quite clear that he did not need Robert to guard the twenty-five French prisoners working for him. Robert might be safe, but if this was all his war amounted to, then he would cut a sorry figure after it was all over, with no tales of battle to tell. He could at least write to his wife, Mia, but it was such a new habit that she took to correcting his grammar and spelling. Perhaps just because he was so untutored, he quickly discovered a rare intimacy in letters. 'Dearest mouse,' he wrote a few weeks into his posting,

> I've got a proposal for you: from now on we'll write in each letter about one of the many nice love experiences we've shared. I think that'd be nice wouldn't it? What do you think? I am looking forward to the first love story from you. Then I'll answer straight away and write about one of the many love experiences too. So dearest mouse, you start and make me happy.[1]

Realising his wife might be reluctant to begin, in his next letter Robert decided to set an example himself. He recalled a trip they had taken to the North Sea coast where they had stayed in a little hotel seven years earlier. 'Snuggling up very close together, full of hot love,' he went on,

> quite soon the little giver of joy was standing before his favourite door, but we had to be very careful, because of the sound of steps in the

corridor and we didn't want to draw attention to it. After I had stroked the clit of the little pussy a couple of times with my giver of joy, someone came along the corridor again. In the meantime our excitement had reached boiling point and I carefully stuck the little one in the pussy. When we had rocked back and forth quite carefully a couple of times making the bed creak, I again heard steps in the corridor, but I kept the little one in the pussy and at the same instant noticed that my little mouse was shaking with joy. And at the same time the little pussy twitched around me, the wonderful feeling of the spasm bringing me to a peak of excitement and we both came together. Full of happiness over this wonderful feeling we looked into each other's shining eyes and pressed our bodies together.[2]

Robert's letter did the trick. Mia rewarded him for 'much, much happiness' and wrote back about a trip to the beach where 'we enjoyed the happiness of love again and again'. Though she was still too bashful to regale him with the details, as they continued to write to each other two to three times a week during these months of enforced separation, Mia's confidence grew. She began to adopt Robert's private language for sex and overcame her own inhibitions about writing it down. By 1 October, she was reminding him of a quiet Sunday afternoon when they had gone to bed after lunch, 'and you quite carefully pulled my pants down and stroked the little one first with your finger and drove it crazy with your b.[ringer of] j.[oy].' As both their confidence and frustration grew, Robert broached another taboo: 'Sometimes, my dearest mouse, I just can't hold out any longer. I miss you so much. Then I imagine one of our beautiful love moments and sometimes succeed in relieving myself.' It took longer to overcome Mia's inhibitions this time and Robert wrote again a few weeks later, gently inducting his wife into the art of female masturbation. 'It can't make so much difference,' he suggested, 'if you stroke the little clit gently with your finger as I have so often and made you come, or is it a big difference?'[3]

By encouraging each other to finding a way of articulating their feelings and desires, by taking out their own sexual memories and intimate names and placing them on the page, Robert and Mia discovered a directness and candour which was highly unusual in wartime Germany. There was of course a tradition of both pornography and moral campaigns against it in Germany, but the way their letters developed suggests that they had to find their own private language, with Mia taking over the words that Robert had used. All couples faced the same problem of reassuring themselves and each other that the loss of sex had changed nothing between them. Sexual longing was universal. But most bundled their desires into conventional packaging, sending each other hugs and kisses, and imagining holding hands.[4]

Many of the letters travelling between 'home' and 'front' were anodyne and conveyed little sense of what husbands and wives were living through, but that was often the point: to show that everything was still intact, that nothing had changed. Sex was most visible as a photographic negative – as anxious jealousies conjured up by absence. Men and women were too constrained to write about sex but they wrote often and without restraint about their terror of sexual infidelity. Dieter D. was only too typical in suspecting his wife as soon as the stream of letters dried up: 'Are you cross with me or do you have something against me, Herta? Or aren't you well enough to write to me? You haven't forgotten me, or do you now have another lover? . . . Do I have to hear again that you're hanging around in the evening with other men?' Every gap in the mail was put down, not to problems with the military postal service, but to infidelity.[5]

In March 1941, to his great relief, Robert was transferred from East Prussia to northern France. At last, after the months of isolation, he was among comrades. Instead of his useless guard duties, he was busy baking bread for the troops. Robert's euphoria was palpable. He began to write to Mia about the 'comradely get-togethers', visits to the bars, and, under her suspicious questioning, admitted to having accompanied others to the brothels in Lille, but – he insisted – only to look at what went on there. Despite his protests that 'love isn't a business', Mia was left in some uncertainty about what had actually transpired. Robert had already told her that virtually all the men who did not have French girlfriends 'help themselves out. You should just hear the conversations here the day before leaving for Paris: it's all about one particular thing.'[6]

Robert and Mia were exceptional in discussing this most ubiquitous of German soldiers' activities. Brothels tracked the march of the conquerors across Europe. When German troops arrived in Nantes in 1940, they were filmed waving at the children on the Place Royale and then headed straight for the brothels, shooting down the doors. The Wehrmacht moved to establish separate brothels for their troops and their officers. This was one of the many areas of agreement between the German and French authorities, as they concurred in managing a nineteenth-century system of licensed, controlled prostitution, with 'closed houses' and compulsory medical checks in order to mitigate the danger of sexually transmitted diseases. For the conservative Vichy authorities, the real danger was unregulated prostitution, and the police carried out periodic sweeps of their towns. Sanctions against covert prostitution became harsher, and from autumn 1941 women were liable to incarceration in the camps at La Lande and Jargeau. French officials had difficulty separating prostitution from women drinking, flirting in bars and receiving gifts. The complex culture of casual sex that developed both around the German bases and in towns where they lodged privately would have been hard to police, even if the French authorities had had the powers to arrest German soldiers. Although the German Field Command also wanted to control the risk of disease from 'debauched' French women, it reacted badly to any French efforts to check its own men's sexual adventures with housemaids, cleaners, laundry women, waitresses, bar staff, hairdressers, landladies, bathhouse attendants, shorthand secretaries, shopkeepers and other acquaintances.[7]

In the Catholic and largely conservative Loire region, the thriving port districts of Nantes and St-Nazaire provided a drinking and partying Mecca. In Nantes, the young of all classes flocked to the small cafés on the Quai de la Fosse where musicians played. On Saturday and Sunday evenings, as the drink flowed and the men circled the women, the freewheeling atmosphere could easily flip into drunken brawls. One particularly bad night in September 1941 left two German soldiers wounded, prompting investigations by both the German and French police. The incident may have been more serious than usual, but the French police commissioner concluded philosophically, 'Incidents often happen in these places because of the mingling of males and females and above all because of the abuse of alcohol.' 'Cohabitation' of occupiers and occupied remained largely peaceable.[8]

The German occupiers were young, generous and newly wealthy – 'They were the best-looking men I have ever seen,' avowed one woman from Touraine. And they were settling down in a country from which 1.5 million Frenchmen had just been removed. In August 1940, a waitress at the Hôtel des Bains in Morlaix on Brittany's Finistère coast noticed a new arrival. Like many of the other Germans who came to eat in the restaurant, Walter was quartered in the hotel. Gradually, their chance conversations grew longer, with the help of his dictionary, and they fell in love. It was Aline's first love affair, and, as she told a French historian sixty-three years later, she could not pass the building where the hotel had been without remembering that time: 'There at the Hôtel des Bains is where I lost my virginity.' The relationship lasted. For her 23rd birthday, in January 1942, a florist delivered twenty-three red roses from Walter. Aline could scarcely believe it. Since she lived with her parents, it was also his way of announcing that his intentions were honourable. When they went out in public, Walter took care to dress in civilian suits rather than his uniform – a respectable couple, who looked stouter and older than their years. Interviewed at the age of 84, Aline insisted, 'I didn't do it because he was a German but because I loved him. Full stop. There is no frontier to love.'[9]

But there was a stigma. Women deemed guilty of 'horizontal collaboration' would find themselves amongst the principal targets of local violence during the Libération. Those, like Aline, who had formed durable relationships and entertained Germans in the privacy of their homes, rather than casually meeting them in public places, faced particular condemnation and attracted a moral opprobrium from which most male collaborators, including those in positions of economic and political influence, were spared. This conviction that women's bodies belonged first to the nation and only then to themselves encapsulated a certain kind of patriotism that was shared by the male-led resistance movements across Europe. It was shared too by conservative elites seeking to accommodate the Germans, and – when it came to German women back in the Reich – also by German authorities. Scorned and condemned by their neighbours after the end of the war, the women themselves retreated into silence and isolation. It was an act of trust and courage for Aline to uncover her memories of a long-censored love.[10]

In Denmark too, the presence of German soldiers made itself felt. Unlike defeated France, the German occupation was conducted under the guise of protecting the country's neutrality and so young Danish men had not been incarcerated as prisoners of war. Nonetheless the young

Danish fishermen in the west coast port of Esbjerg found themselves competing on an unequal playing field with the 3,000–4,000 German troops who joined the local population of 32,000. By early August 1940, the local police chief warned that there was general outrage among the town's young men at the 'German fraternisation with the young Danish women in town and the way this fraternisation takes place'. Unlike young Danes, the Germans had a lot of free time. Military drill aside, the life of occupying troops was one of profound idleness, with abundant opportunities for courtship, friendships and hobbies which they would have had difficulty pursuing in civilian life. When a group of Danish girls was interviewed shortly after the war, the most significant reason they gave for preferring Germans over Danes was that they had better, more courtly manners. A small number thought they were better lovers, showing, as one put it, 'consideration for the soul of the woman concerned'. In line with the German attempt to exercise a model occupation in Denmark, local German commanders made a determined effort to hold their troops in check, issuing strict guidelines against accosting women on the street, for instance, and punishing rape severely.[11]

Like their colleagues in youth welfare offices in Germany, the Danes projected their general frustration with the increased sexual freedom of young women on to the one group they were authorised to control – teenagers. Determined to prevent an epidemic of venereal disease, moral corruption and prostitution, the police and welfare officials concentrated on picking up girls in parks, air raid shelters and near German military bases. In August 1940, one 14-year-old told police questioning her that it was unfair of them to pick up her and her friend and that she went with soldiers 'because that's what all girls did, now they thought it was fun, so why shouldn't they?' The pull of being taken to cafés, bars and restaurants became the stuff of peer-group envy and boasting about real or imagined exploits at school. One 13-year-old girl regaled her classmates with a tale of being locked in a room and given ice cream by the Germans. As fantasies of foreign abundance added to the allure of the conqueror, many young people were eager to kick over the traces which had constrained them in peacetime.[12]

Whereas the German occupiers did nothing to discourage sexual relationships in western Europe – indeed, in Norway, they were actively encouraged on racial grounds – the occupation of Poland began with prohibitions on contact with Poles, which were modelled on the

Nuremberg race laws of 1935 forbidding all manner of relationships with Jews. Especially in the first months of the occupation, Germans openly flouted the bans, taking Polish women past the signs 'Only for Germans' which had been placed on the doors to bars and restaurants, and interpreting the ban as applying principally to Polish men. Although enforcement in some places became stricter by 1940, there was little to prevent any number of fleeting affairs between the 400,000 troops stationed in the annexed territories or the further 500,000 in the General Government. In ethnically mixed areas like Silesia and Posen which in the past had been ruled by Austria or Prussia, many Poles also spoke German and were willing to apply for registration as ethnic Germans in the new nationality lists, so easing subsequent applications to marry.

Moreover, those who were entrusted with enforcing the new ordinances – the 60,000 members of the German police and SS – were also counted alongside postal and railway officials amongst those who stayed longest and were most prone to put down roots. Despite the opprobrium heaped by both German officialdom and the Polish resistance on close and enduring relationships, among the many Germans found living openly with Polish girlfriends in their quarters were a considerable number of Gestapo and SS officers. In the Lublin office of the SD, Alouis Fischotter fell in love with one of the secretaries, Uszula B., and after lengthy personal negotiations with Himmler obtained his permission to marry and make their child legitimate. When Franz Maiwald, the head of the Gestapo in Zakopane, was killed by the Polish resistance in February 1944, his Polish lover, Maria T., wept openly at his graveside.[13]

*

For Ernst Guicking, it was France's abundance that promised to rescue the newly-weds from the strictures of wartime rationing at home. In early August 1940, he was proud to send Irene a parcel of red and blue silk for her and some cloth to have a suit made for himself. Then came a knitted waistcoat, trousers, and 4 metres of the brown fabric for French uniforms: he advised her to have it dyed before having it made into overcoats. A comrade going on leave agreed to take this bulky package home. As Ernst requested Irene's size in bras, blouses and panties, he had to find new comrades willing to bring his parcels home, and he had to ask her to send him more money for further purchases. Irene was grateful for both the attention and the garments but, with her practical eye, suggested swapping the silk for woollen cloth.[14]

None of this was easy for an ordinary infantryman. Drivers could send enormous numbers of parcels home by using their transport to consign them to the military post from different bases. A member of a flak battery in the Netherlands was able to ship back a valuable Philips radio by using their motor vehicles. Those with connections to the quartermaster's department or the Staff section in Paris managed to bring home Persian carpets and fine china. A young actor at the German theatre in Prague wrote home to take orders for furniture and antiques, describing how one of his colleagues had set himself up as a dealer. This lively traffic was further aided by the abolition of the customs border between the Reich and the Protectorate of Bohemia and Moravia on 1 October 1940, which, according to one eyewitness, saw German officers' luggage bulging with Czech 'furs, watches, medicines, shoes, in quite unimaginable quantities'.[15]

Through the autumn, Ernst Guicking was only allowed to receive remittances of up to 50 marks a month, but for Christmas the limit was raised to 200 so he went on a further shopping spree, buying for the whole extended family. From a cash-poor family of farmers, Guicking let the money run through his fingers, asking Irene to send him more frequent sums, intent on a triumphant return at Christmas. At the same time, he had been encouraging Irene to take the lead in furnishing their home. Teasing her that he would spend the most time where he was most comfortable, he suggested she pay especial attention to their bed. Irene was entranced by the modern designs, and Ernst urged her to order only the very best, even if it meant asking to borrow 1,000 marks from her parents. But with long waiting lists for furniture and household goods, gratification had to be deferred. The population may have wanted to enjoy Continental peace, but the German economy remained on a war footing.[16]

Ernst Guicking's spendthrift side was a natural response to years of suppressed demand in which Germans had saved because there was relatively little to buy. When Germany went to war, 20 per cent of economic production was allocated to armament and this had rapidly increased to over a third of GDP. Suppressed domestic demand led to high rates of savings. Through regulatory controls these private savings accounts were themselves silently redeployed by the government to finance the war effort, thus avoiding a repeat of the public appeals to buy war bonds which had been such a feature of the First World War.[17]

From the point of view of the German consumer, 1940 spelled a sudden bonanza, made possible by the fact that the Reichsmark was deliberately overvalued in each country the Wehrmacht occupied. For Germans, local prices were cheap and as families made good on what they could not buy at home, they started to strip consumer goods out of even the Dutch ports, still stocked with goods from before the occupation: in the Netherlands each soldier was permitted to receive 1,000 marks a month. In Belgium, German finance officials calculated that in the first year of the occupation 34 million marks was sent to soldiers stationed there. In October 1940, Hermann Göring made himself the champion of the German soldier – and consumer – by ordering that all restrictions be lifted on Germans buying 'furs, jewellery, carpets, silks and luxury goods', on the grounds that the victorious occupying troops should have the same opportunities as the local civilian population. Whilst controls remained firmly in place for sending parcels from Germany, Göring insisted that the military postal service should transport an unlimited number of parcels of up to 1 kilo in weight to the Fatherland. Within a year, the number of parcels being sent home from France had gone up fivefold to reach 3.1 million per month. Above all, Göring ordered that soldiers were to be permitted to bring home as much as they could carry themselves without interference from customs. Long discussions ensued about whether soldiers should be forbidden from strapping their excess luggage on to a carrying harness in case it prevented them from saluting their superiors. In any case, whatever restrictions were imposed on luggage were routinely disregarded. At the Gare de l'Est in Paris, hordes of German soldiers swarmed across the station concourse, staggering under inordinate amounts of luggage, bound for home.[18]

Apart from cash payments, the most common form of currency used were Reich Credit Notes. Although it was illegal for private individuals to use them, there were so many in circulation that a young soldier like Heinrich Böll had little difficulty arranging for his family to send him quantities of these Credit Notes. The reports filed by customs officials lift a small corner of the curtain behind which much larger and more ambitious trading operations were taking shape. In 1940–41, for instance, a group of employees from the railway postal service were discovered to be sending their empty postal wagon from Nuremberg as far as Metz, where they handed it over to their French colleagues along with tens of thousands of marks' worth of Reich Credit Notes. Each week, the wagon returned from Paris filled with 'scarce goods like coffee, tea, cocoa, chocolate, brandy, champagne, wine, spirits, clothes, stockings, etc.' The Nuremberg employees sold on most of the goods to other postal workers, setting off a small chain of black-market activities.[19]

Coffee remained a particular favourite. In the 1930s the import and sale of coffee beans had been sharply restricted in Germany in order to safeguard the country's scarce foreign currency reserves. Coffee substitutes had never gone down well with German consumers, and so it came as little surprise that when Heinrich Böll reached Rotterdam the first thing he bought was a half-pound of coffee, which had survived the incendiary bombing of the docks. Throughout the summer of 1940, he wrote home about his regular 'coffee hunts', interspersed with his 'butter travels'. By September, the young soldier noticed that the shops were being emptied of stock and, although the Germans were paying for everything, it felt more like 'stripping a corpse'. The German bank commissioner in the Netherlands agreed, warning that hoovering up goods would inevitably lead to inflation and entail 'damaging political consequences for the rate of exchange'.[20]

*

The generation of Germans that grew up in the 1920s and '30s had been taught to detest France but to admire and emulate French culture. If their *Blitzkrieg* victory purged their fear of French martial virtue, their cultural curiosity and respect remained intact. Hans Albring snatched all his free time in Poitiers to change into civvies and visit the local churches. His favourite was the thirteenth-century church of Saint-Radegonde with its red and brown frescoes of Lazarus rising from the dead and Daniel in the lions' den. In spite of the summer heat and sore feet from climbing up and down the 218 steps from the barracks to the town and back again, he kept returning to the Baptistery with its altar, said to be the oldest in the whole of France. He sent postcards of them to his friend Eugen Altrogge, to give him a sense of what he was missing, and he even commissioned a local photographer to produce a large-format print of the fresco depicting the mounted Emperor Constantine. With some of his comrades Albring attended High Mass in the cathedral of St Pierre, where he was particularly moved by the Jubilate. As the choirboys' treble voices resonated through the full height of the great building, Hans had an extraordinary sense of being lifted into the light of grace. He also noticed the deadly glances cast at him and the other Germans by the whole choir and congregation, and had the sense of being pursued by parochial hatred.[21]

Albring's next posting was to Rouen, where he celebrated his promotion to sergeant and increase in salary by buying several rare books with valuable woodcuts. Leafing through the bookseller's stock of prints and antiquarian books, Hans spent hours in happy conversation with the Frenchman whose views he found 'very sensitive and understated. I notice how everything he says is well-founded and profound, registered with all his senses.' Eventually, the young soldier popped the question of whether the French hated the Germans. 'No,' the bookseller replied, 'and if they do, it is like a child's tantrum.' But, surely, Albring insisted, the ruined buildings of Rouen must provoke the 'desire for revenge'? No, came the reply. What the French want is 'to be left to get on with their work; to be left with their constitution and form of government'. This was as far as Albring could delve. Their conversation veered back to the safe topic of his passion for collecting prints of the old Italian and modern French masters. Before long Hans had put together a parcel of over 700 prints and woodcuts – salvaged from an early-seventeenth-century book – to send back to Gelsenkirchen with a comrade who was going home on leave. He was already planning how he could recoup part of the cost by selling some of these, no doubt to fund future purchases.[22]

Full of the hyper-aestheticism of boys just out of grammar school, Hans Albring and Eugen Altrogge were both on a kind of cultural pilgrimage. Eugen waxed lyrical about the interplay of Romanesque and Gothic styles he found in Austria, the one so solid and grounded, the other, it seemed to him, restless and expressing the 'Faust-like' strivings of men. Hans agreed, far less impressed by the exterior architecture of the Romanesque cathedrals of Poitiers and Rouen. Only Chartres matched his craving for soaring spires: he was so excited when their truck drove through the city in the middle of the night that he rummaged in his pack so that he could compare the reproduction of a drawing with the real cathedral, its twin towers appearing 'far more slender and far higher' in the moonlight. His was a particularly German gaze, informed by the late-Gothic spires of Cologne and Strasbourg, which was why the older Romanesque towers of Rouen and Poitiers seemed disappointingly squat by comparison. This was the verticality, the striving to reach the heavens, which had so overwhelmed the young Goethe when he first saw Strasbourg's west facade and made him single it out as the epitome of 'German architecture'.[23]

Like Goethe, the young photographer Liselotte Purper thought the cathedral looked best as the slanting evening light fell on its west end. While the houses hemming in the square 'slowly sank into shadow', she jotted in her travel diary, all the Gothic ornaments of the arches, towers and statues were revealed. She had a special reason to visit Strasbourg in September 1940. In 1919, when she was not yet seven, her parents had been expelled from the city along with other 'Reich Germans'. It was her first visit back and, as she tramped the winding streets with her parents' old map, she felt the pull of the 'very special magic' of the half-timbered houses with their brightly painted wooden shutters. Criss-crossing the bridges over the canal and walking under the plane trees and chestnuts along the bank of the river Ill, she felt she had finally come home. Strasbourg, Colmar and the villages of Alsace were welcomed back into the Reich after this 1940 victory, becoming part of a joint Gau with Baden. Special exhibitions celebrated their folk traditions and contribution to German culture. Whenever the Alsatians seemed slow to embrace their new patriotic duties, the Nazi authorities responded with further educational measures, explaining their true national identity to them once again. The Jews, meanwhile, were summarily expelled.[24]

Liselotte's next stop was the Hotel Wartheland in Wielún. She came at the start of October 1940 to photograph the work of colonisation going on in these other newly 'recovered' territories in the east. In the Wartheland, the task was more demanding than in Alsace, and Liselotte immediately noticed the large numbers of Jews. She considered them 'a traffic hazard', because they were forced to walk on the street rather than the pavement. Later that month, Jews in this new Gau were ordered to doff their caps in the presence of any German in uniform and some officials started promenading with riding crops and dog whips to enforce the new code. The previous December, the SS Resettlement Office had begun expelling the Jews, clearing the western – formerly Prussian – part of the Wartheland entirely, but winter coal shortages curtailed this operation. In the most important city in the eastern Wartheland, Łódź, the Jews were herded into a provisional ghetto instead, making this the first ghetto within the Reich's borders.[25]

Liselotte Purper made a trip to Litzmannstadt – as Łódź had been renamed, in honour of the German general who conquered it in 1915 – and took photographs of Jews for her own private collection. The ghetto became a popular subject and similar photos of 'Germany's sixth largest city' taken by another female photo-journalist, Erika Schmachtenberger, were published in the *Münchner Illustrierte*. One of Hitler's personal photographers, Hugo Jaeger, rushed to take colour slides of the Jews in the Kutno ghetto, creating a mixture of 'ethno-graphic' pictures of dishevelled shanty-dwellers and full-length portraits of beautiful young women. But, in October 1940, Liselotte Purper's commission in the Wartheland was a different one.[26]

The new Gau became a model of colonial resettlement, or 're-Germanisation'. Eventually, 619,000 Polish citizens were 'resettled' into the rump Polish territory of the 'General Government' ruled by Hans Frank in order to make way for Germans. The great majority – some 435,000 – came from the Wartheland, where the new Gauleiter, Arthur Greiser, enthusiastically shared Himmler's vision of radical colonial settlement. In the winter of 1939–40, the deportees were often forced on to the trains without adequate food, water or clothing. Because many were Jews, the SS and police chief of the Lublin district, Odilo Globočnik, proposed in February 1940 that their journeys should be deliberately slowed down and they 'should be allowed to starve'. When the train doors were pulled open at Cracow, Dębica and Sandomierz, station staff discovered entire goods wagons in which children and their mothers had frozen to death.[27]

Liselotte Purper was there to document and celebrate the other side of this resettlement action, the incoming Germans. The final partition lines agreed with the Soviets in October 1939 included stipu-lations for the orderly transfer of German minorities. They came from Volhynia in eastern Poland, where many could not speak German, and they came from the Baltic states, where 60,000 ethnic Germans were uprooted, ending a history of proud independence stretching back 700 years. Faced with the prospect of Soviet occupation, they agreed to be sent 'home into the Reich', as the German government called it: Liselotte thought they complained too much and were insufficiently grateful. She was more impressed by the simple farming folk from the Polish–Ukrainian borderlands of Volhynia and Galicia: 'The happiness at our visit shone in all their faces.' Despite having spent months festering in temporary German camps, while they waited for homes, farms and businesses to be cleared for them, they struck her as truly grateful. All they wanted, she thought, was to start tilling their own land 'so that they can give the German people bread'.[28]

In November 1940, Liselotte travelled on to document the resettlement of ethnic Romanian Germans from Bessarabia, Bukovina and Dobruja. Joining the SS Resettlement Commission, Liselotte visited their villages near the Black Sea port of Constantia, with their tidy whitewashed houses, talking to families about their expectations as they packed their belongings. She accompanied them on the Danube steamer through the gorge and cataracts of the Iron Gates. But she did not socialise with them. Instead, the fear of catching fleas from the 'still not disinfected' settlers features prominently in her diary, and she became obsessed with hygiene, keeping a scorecard for the record catch of fleas on board ship: it stood at twenty in ten minutes. These minor difficulties made her feel, at the end of the journey, like a 'shining victor' returned from the battlefield. Both her private diary and her professional photography depict the settlers as grateful but passive recipients of the well-organised charity of Germans from the 'old' Reich.

In Belgrade, Liselotte was joined by her close friend, Margot Monnier. 'Hada', as Liselotte invariably called her in a play on her maiden name, enjoyed their expeditions so much that she often acted as Liselotte's photographic assistant, although she actually occupied a position as head of the photographic section of the German Women's Organisation – and as the younger sister of Eugen Hadamovsky, the head of German radio – where she could act as Liselotte's patron. The two young women knew how to have fun, finding time to take a side trip to go shopping in Budapest. In Belgrade, the head of the local SS Resettlement Commission turned out to be an old family friend, who took Liselotte on a tour of the city's nightlife. These two elegant and witty young women had the knack of persuading men to help them, whether it was passes from the Romanians, assistance from a German railway conductor with smuggling their purchases back into the Reich, or asking chivalrous, if rather dull, SS officers to accompany them on a night-time excursion to the castle in Budapest. After enjoying the company of the Austrian captain and officers on the steamer, they took the train to Vienna, where Liselotte and Hada ceremonially drowned the 'last flea'.[29]

In the Wartheland, 28-year-old Liselotte had been hugely impressed by the female student volunteers from Germany and the girls helping the settlers as part of their compulsory Reich Labour Service. It was they who winkled out Poles returning to their former farms and sent them packing. The 18-year-old girls on Labour Service were frequently deployed in equal numbers alongside SS men in the resettlement actions. Some of them would go to the railway stations to welcome the German settlers, others would assist the SS in evicting Poles and then supervise Polish women who were forced to clean up and leave their homes spick and span for the new owners. Describing her deployment for an audience back home, a student volunteer reflected on her own reaction to watching the SS herd Polish villagers into a shed during one such eviction:

> Sympathy with these creatures? – No, at most I felt quietly appalled that such people exist, people who are in their very being so infinitely alien and incomprehensible to us that there is no way to reach them. For the first time in our lives people whose life or death is a matter of indifference.[30]

For Poles, the only way to secure their property rights was to be classified as 'Germans' on the new 'National List' which was being compiled in the annexed territories. Being registered as German also automatically entitled families to higher levels of rations, better education and improved employment prospects. Left to enact this programme of 'Re-Germanisation' in their own manner, other regions did not all follow Greiser's hard line by handing over racial screening to the SS, preferring to maintain the skilled workforce crucial to the industrial heartland of Upper Silesia. Here virtually the entire population was reclassified as German. Eastern Pomerania did likewise, while in Danzig–West Prussia, the scene of the greatest violence against Poles by ethnic German militias in 1939, most of the population were classified as either German or as possessing the 'necessary qualities to become full members of the German national community'. It would all depend on how they performed. As in Alsace, one of the new tests for men was service in the Wehrmacht.[31]

For Poles who did not manage to be reclassified into one of these categories, the lessons in subservience came thick and fast. Whatever the variations from Gau to Gau and between the annexed territories and the General Government, the objective remained the same. A string of German decrees banned Polish schools from teaching all the subjects which were regarded as central to shaping a sense of patriotism: sport, geography, history and national literature. In the Wartheland even instruction in Polish was prohibited; yet schools were also forbidden to teach German grammar properly, lest 'Poles should succeed in passing themselves off as Germans'. After most Polish teachers and priests had been executed or expelled, the authorities in the Wartheland turned large classes, which met for only a couple of hours a day, over to the wives of German farmers and non-commissioned officers, who drilled the Polish children in 'cleanliness and order, in respectful conduct and obedience to the Germans'.[32]

The enormous numbers of Poles forcibly 'resettled' to the General Government – a 'native reservation', as Hitler dubbed it – were surpassed by the numbers of Poles shipped to Germany. To start with, 300,000 Polish prisoners of war were sent to help bring in the harvest in 1939; and there was no initial shortage of civilian volunteers, as Poles looked for employment under German occupation. By the end of May 1940 there were over 850,000 foreign workers in Germany, nearly two-thirds of whom were employed in agriculture, which had a long tradition of drawing on seasonal migrant Polish labour. For a regime which focused on national – and racial – purity, there was much greater reluctance to see Poles working and living in German cities, even though the armaments industry was so desperately short of labour that many factories depended on the Wehrmacht releasing skilled workers after the French campaign in order to keep going.[33]

In Nazi eyes, the whole 'home front' was a female, domestic space, into which threatening foreign men were now intruding. This sexualised and gendered concept drew on the nineteenth-century ideal of separate male and female spheres, in which work, politics and public life had been affairs of men while women concentrated on creating a Biedermeier idyll of family and home. This notional divide had already broken down during the First World War when women had taken over men's jobs in engineering and armaments production, driven trams and become nurses for the Red Cross. Despite the Nazis' espousal of patriarchal ideals, the same pattern of female involvement had immediately emerged even more strongly in this war. The number of female students at university had never been higher, and more women were entering the professions than ever before. But instead of giving up on the notion of separate male and female destinies, the Nazis merely redefined them. The traditional 'female sphere' of the home was thus enlarged to include the whole of the home front, while men's activities 'out there' no longer referred to associational life or work but to guarding the borders of the Fatherland. This dramatic extension of the female sphere to include almost every social and economic activity from which women had previously been excluded only made sense because there was still one thing they were not meant to be part of: the military. In fact, women had served in the police before the war and, alongside the 400,000 nurses drafted into the Red Cross, another 500,000 women were recruited by the Wehrmacht itself, most to work for its telephone and postal services after attending a two- to three-month training course at Giessen.[34]

The idea of women actually bearing arms, however, remained anathema and had already legitimised the most extreme counter-measures on the part of German soldiers during the Polish campaign. Male honour became entirely bound up with military service, comradeship and calmness under fire; so much so that 'war neurotics', cowards and deserters were seen as neither honourable nor real men. Female honour continued to be measured in terms of chastity and sexual virtue. The Reich Ministry of Justice issued guidelines in 1943 which merely repeated the basic axiom that 'German women who engage in sexual relations with prisoners of war have betrayed the front, done gross injury to their nation's honour, and damaged the reputation of German womanhood abroad'. In these very different ways, the bodies of individual men and women were seen as carrying the honour of the German people.[35]

The moral guardian of national honour became the Nazi Party, with the head of the Office of Racial Policy asserting in August 1940 that

There can be little doubt that racial policy considerations demand that we combat with all available means the extraordinary threat of contamination and pollution this concentration of foreign workers poses . . . to our Germanic lineage. This alien population was until recently our most bitter enemy, and inwardly remains so today, and we can and may not stand idly by while they invade the vital essence of our people, impregnate women of German blood, and corrupt our youth.

In particular, the Gestapo and SD liked to think of themselves as occupying the place vacated by absent husbands, fathers, brothers and fiancés. In the face of the influx of foreign workers, the Gestapo upheld a blanket injunction against 'forbidden contact', investigating specific offences such as 'personal, intimate / friendly relations', 'friendly or sociable behaviour towards Poles' and 'giving to Poles'. All of this made sense to officials steeped in notions of a 'slippery slope' towards 'degenerate' behaviour. Just as playing truant from school would lead boys to a life of theft and petty crime and girls to promiscuity, venereal disease and prostitution, so all social contact with Poles would inevitably end in bed. In this pessimistic view, police intervention was necessary, even in cases of mild transgression, to avoid greater disorder.[36]

From June 1940 onwards, the Gestapo began to hang Polish men in public for 'forbidden contact'. In early July, in Ingeleben near Helmstedt a Polish prisoner of war, who had been remanded to the military prison for sexual intercourse with a German woman, was handed over to the Gestapo and 'hanged from a tree as a warning to others'. On 26 July, Stanislau Smyl was hanged on the order of the Reich Security Main Office in Berlin, even though the local Gestapo office in Paderborn advised against it on mental grounds. He had apparently approached a married woman in the street, made 'strange sounds' and displayed his penis. On 24 August, the Gestapo took a 17-year-old Polish worker from the court prison in Gotha and hanged him by the roadside. Fifty Poles were forced to witness the execution, alongside a large crowd of Germans who had come along to watch. He was accused of having had intercourse with a German prostitute, and his body was left hanging for twenty-four hours.[37]

These public and degrading forms of capital punishment were designed to deter others. Although the Nazi state in principle penetrated as far down as the ranks of concierges, porters and schoolchildren, it lacked the active manpower to do more than demonstrate the risks of 'forbidden relations'. The Gestapo might enjoy its omnipresent, omniscient and omnipotent reputation but its totalitarian aspirations were curtailed by staff shortages, which became worse during the war. Just as when policing contact between Jewish men and 'Aryan' women before the war, so now the Gestapo depended on inquisitive neighbours denouncing those who broke the norms of the 'national community'. By turning to terrifying, exemplary public executions, the political police were also admitting that they were far too weak to enforce the norms of the Nazi racial order universally. For the entire war, the Gestapo generated a mere 165 case files on 'forbidden relations' in Düsseldorf, 150 in the Palatinate, and another 146 cases in Lower Franconia.[38]

There was a populist side to these new rituals of public punishment. As early as March 1940, the Jena higher court complained that it had become normal in Thuringia to shave the head of a woman accused of 'forbidden relations', hang a placard on her proclaiming her crime and parade her through the village, even before she was charged. On 15 November 1940, people crowded into the town square of Eisenach to mock a German woman and her Polish lover, tied back to back to a post on a small platform. Above her shaven head, the placard proclaimed, 'I let myself go with a Pole'; his read, 'I am a race-defiler'. Mothers brought their young children to the front or lifted them up so that they could see too.[39]

Often there were calls for the woman to be forced to attend the execution of her lover, or even for her to suffer the same fate. Sometimes she was held to be the 'seducer'; at others, people pointed out that she should have known better. As the kerbside judgement of a case in Regensburg would have it, 'the larger part of the city population actually apportioned the greater guilt to the German girl'. For, it was said, 'the Polish man was simply satisfying his sexual need, while the German girl, from whom more could be expected than the Pole, had damaged the honour of the nation'. In this view, the woman bore greater responsibility because she represented the 'higher culture'. While the authorities slipped between notions of 'honour', 'race' and 'culture' and hesitated over how far to trump the rights of husbands, the details of its citizens' sex lives were presented as local news stories.

In the case of married women, the husband – usually absent on military service – would be asked if he forgave his wife: if he did, then she might be given a lighter sentence or even be released.[40]

Re-erecting the pillory and gallows in public inevitably created problems. In Straubing, people complained that the gallows was set up too close to a youth-training camp for girls. In Lichtenfels district, it was said to ruin a 'beautiful' hill. The Nazis clearly intended to mobilise communities by reconnecting them with early-modern rituals of spectacular punishment but the cultural tradition had been broken and social responses were mixed.[41]

The new vogue for public executions was most successful in Thuringia. Even the SD was disturbed by the scale of popular enthusiasm when 800–1,000 spectators flocked to watch the mass hanging of twenty Poles in Hildburghausen – and that was not counting the 600–700 women and children whom the police prevented from attending. But this was a region conspicuous for its early conversion to National Socialism and where Protestant pastors had embraced the German Christian movement wholesale: there were no institutions here which encouraged any other view of things.[42]

Elsewhere, especially in Catholic areas, things were not so straightforward. Instead of creating social unity, the new scapegoating might provoke dissent. German women were not slow to voice their resentment at the sexual double standard. Spectators to a woman being paraded in the streets of Bramberg near Ebern in early 1941 for having taken a French lover 'ventured to ask', the SD noted, 'whether the same would be done to a man who had an affair with a French woman while in France'. Most women in the crowd, even Party members, joined in the criticism and someone was heard shouting that 'Thumbscrew and torture chambers are all that is needed: then we shall be fully back in the Middle Ages.' Meanwhile, some of the men in the crowd retaliated, calling for 'a beating' to be added to the woman's punishment.[43]

One reason for the humanitarian revulsion against the new rituals in Catholic areas was that the Poles and French were treated as co-religionists. In Kempen-Niederrhein near Düsseldorf the Gestapo ascribed the fairly hostile response to the hanging of a Pole to the influence of the Church and its rejection of such forms of public execution. The Rhineland and Ruhr had also absorbed many Polish migrants since the industrial revolution. In Schweinfurt the local Gestapo decided to move the execution of two Poles, one of whom had made a 15-year-old girl pregnant, to a concentration camp, so as to avoid the 'great agitation' that 'would have resulted among the Catholic population'. In October 1941, Hitler banned the public shaming rituals and punishments, though not the public execution of foreigners. But by this time he was dealing with a humanitarian outcry of a different kind altogether, in which the country's Catholic bishops played a leading role.[44]

★

On 9 March 1941, Konrad von Preysing, the Catholic Bishop of Berlin, used the celebration of Pius XII's enthronement to remind his congregation at St Hedwig's Cathedral that the Pope had 'reaffirmed the doctrine of the Church, according to which there is no justification and no excuse for the killing of the sick or of the abnormal on any economic or eugenic grounds'. It was the first public repudiation of the Nazis' secret 'euthanasia' programme. Both Protestant and Catholic bishops had been well informed of its progress, because directors of Church-run psychiatric asylums had found themselves on the front line, some fervent adherents, others deeply critical. But for the last year and a half the annual Conference of Catholic Bishops at Fulda continued to follow the lead of Cardinal Bertram and send mildly phrased and private letters asking the government if the rumours could be true. In the summer of 1941, however, legitimate petition gave way to more radical public confrontation. On 3 August, the Bishop of Münster, Clemens August, Count von Galen, used his pulpit in the Lamberti church to preach publicly against euthanasia. Whereas Preysing had merely reaffirmed the Church's opposition to killing the infirm in abstract and general terms, Galen mounted an impassioned attack:

Fellow Christians! . . . for some months we have been hearing reports that, on the orders of Berlin, patients from mental asylums who have been ill for a long time, and may appear incurable, are being compulsorily removed. Then, after a short time, the relatives are regularly informed that the corpse has been burned and the ashes can be delivered. There is a general suspicion, verging on certainty, that these numerous unexpected deaths of mentally ill people do not occur of themselves but are deliberately brought about, that the doctrine is being followed, according to which one may destroy so-called 'worthless life', that is kill innocent people, if one considers that their lives are of no further value for the nation and the state.

Detailing the first transport of patients from the Marienthal asylum near Münster, Galen read out the letter he had sent the local police president warning of the intended murders and citing his duty as a citizen, under Article 139 of the Criminal Code, to inform the authorities of 'the intention to commit a crime against life'. Galen then turned to the central ethical issue at stake, warning what would happen to the old, the frail, and wounded war veterans 'if you establish and apply the principle that you can kill "unproductive" human beings'. Galen's sermon made a significant local impression. It was read out in diocesan churches in the Münsterland and circulated widely in clerical circles in Cologne.[45]

Many of the rumours about medical killing originated in the decentralised, provincial health bureaucracy itself: administrators had to sanction payments for patients in state care and so were able to follow the flow of money towards the killing centres; they also picked up and passed on information from colleagues. This knowledge, some of it detailed, some fragmentary, had circulated in private until Galen decided to use the Church's independence to give it a public platform. His sermon, with its demagogic directness, flung down an open challenge.[46]

The reflex reaction of the Minister for Church Affairs, Hanns Kerrl, the Party Secretary, Martin Bormann, and the local Gauleiter, Alfred Meyer, was that Galen should be repressed. Was it better to put him on trial and execute him for treason as a public example, quietly arrest him and send him to a concentration camp, or merely prohibit him from preaching? Local Party activists and functionaries in the Münsterland were outraged, denouncing Galen as a British agent. Goebbels and Hitler were equally incensed by this public attack but, as lapsed Catholics themselves, were also far more aware of the dangers of a hasty response: 'If any action were taken against the bishop,' Goebbels apparently said, 'the population of Münster, and for that matter the whole of Westphalia, could be written off for the duration of the war.' Hitler agreed that inaction was the wisest course too, although he privately vowed to have Galen's head once the war was won.[47]

Through the late summer and autumn of 1941, the Catholic bishops continued to exert pressure. Antonius Hilfrich, Bishop of Limburg, was kept well informed by the clergy at Hadamar, a mere 8 kilometres away, and he joined the Archbishop of Cologne and the Bishop of Paderborn in writing collectively to the Ministers of the Interior, Justice and Church Affairs at the end of August: 'We consider ourselves obliged to take a public stand against it [medical killing] for the education and enlightenment of the Catholic people, so that our people are not confused about the basis of true morality.' Three days later, Bishop Bornewasser of Trier followed Galen's example and preached a sermon in his cathedral against the killing of patients. He returned to the theme a fortnight later, on 14 September, asking, rhetorically, whether paragraph 211 of the Criminal Code was still being enforced in Germany. Galen himself wrote to the clergy in Oldenburg to have his sermon read out there, and in October and November the RAF dropped leaflets with excerpts from it. Bishop Albert Stohr of Mainz used the festival of Christ the King at the end of October to preach to a packed cathedral. On the eve of All Souls, Preysing returned to the theme at St Hedwig's Cathedral in Berlin, denouncing the big-budget feature film *I Accuse* as a crude piece of propaganda, and drawing a direct link between the box-office hit of the summer and the killing of psychiatric patients.[48]

The film, directed by Wolfgang Liebeneiner, dealt with the assisted suicide of a woman who was dying slowly and painfully from multiple sclerosis. The audience found itself alternately placed in the position of the doctor trying to find a cure for her and the jurors in court judging his decision to help her die with dignity. Goebbels had reviewed and rejected all the drafts for crude propaganda films on the subject, settling for this 'soft sell' approach. His choice of medium showed that the Propaganda Minister did not think the German people 'unsentimental' enough to be told the truth about 'euthanasia'; they would have to be prepared for it gently. The professional elites involved in the programme saw themselves as simply extending an extreme utilitarianism to the right to life: readiness to work had long been the key criterion influencing judgements on 'asocials', 'wayward' teen-agers, the 'work-shy' and other recipients of the attention of welfare authorities and police. But, however great the stigma associated with mental or physical disability, German society was not ready to impose the same sanctions on those who could not work as on those who would not. There was all the world of difference between the lazy and the disabled. Galen's most potent example was the threat that gravely wounded soldiers might be put to death. When his sermon was read out in the local church at Appelhülsen on 11 August 1941 the women in the congregation began to weep aloud, believing that their sons at the front were now threatened with 'euthanasia'.[49]

I Accuse came out just before Galen preached his devastating sermon, and it reached a national audience. By January 1945, 15.3 million people had gone to see it, but not all necessarily connected the intimate drama revolving around the dilemma of a patient's choice with the wholesale killing actually under way in the wards of Germany's asylums. Where people did make the connection, particu-larly in the Münsterland and Passau, the film flopped. But the fact that it was otherwise very successful indicates that Germany was not fully focused on the reality of medical killing. Both knowledge and protests remained patchy.[50]

In some places the Security Service did observe a severe collapse of confidence in the public health authorities, especially in Swabia, with 'many national comrades refusing to take part in the X-ray tests, because they feared that they would be disposed of (euthanasia) as "unproductive" people following the scaremongering sermons of the Bishops of Münster and Trier'. Among Protestants, too, there was considerable disquiet and Galen's sermon was admired by some members of the Confessing Church. Bishop Theophil Wurm of Württemberg had lodged private protests in July 1940 with the minis-ters of Church Affairs and the Interior as well as with Lammers, the head of the Reich Chancellery, but no Protestant objected in public. Moreover, apart from one or two cases where Protestant and Catholic directors of psychiatric asylums tipped each other off about imminent visits by 'T-4' commissions, the rival Christian confessions did not draw closer together in the face of this challenge.[51]

In August 1941, Hitler ordered a halt to T-4 killing of adult asylum patients. Yet the Church protests continued because the order could not be made public: after all, the programme of murder itself was a state secret. Prelates had their own reasons for keeping up pressure on the issue at this time. Their principal concern in the summer of 1941 was to defend Church houses and lands. As Alsace and Luxembourg joined the western Polish provinces as areas annexed to the Reich, the government decided that the provisions of the 1933 Concordat with the Church did not apply to these territories. The Gestapo and Party bosses lost no time in falling on the spoils, and during 1940 and 1941 over 300 monasteries and other religious lands and buildings were expropriated. As the practice spread back to the 'Old Reich', it provoked strong local protests. In Württemberg, the monasteries at Untermarchtal and Kellenried and their lands were seized. In Bavaria, where seven more foundations were closed, farmers armed with pitchforks turned out to defend the Benedictine Abbey at Münsterschwarzach, whose church had only just been completed. Such direct action remained the exception. Galen decided to speak out when the expropriation of Church property reached his own diocese. In Lüdinghausen, a convent was turned into a state boarding school and ten of the nuns were forced to stay on as cooks, cleaners and laundresses while the others were expelled. The Münster Jesuits were forced to move diocese, and finally monastic property in the town itself was seized in July.[52]

Galen's great sermon of 3 August in which he preached against medical killing was the third of three attacking radical Nazi policies: the first two, on 13 and 20 July, were wholly taken up with defending the religious orders from the despoliation of their houses by a secular authority which had abandoned any pretence of obeying the rule of law. Referring to the 161 members of religious orders serving 'as German soldiers in the field, some of them in the front lines', he decried the fact that their 'Heimat is being taken away from them, the convent that is their home is destroyed – ruthlessly and without any justification'. Other bishops openly linked these attacks on the Church with the massacre of the innocent in Germany's asylums.[53]

That summer, the conflict between Church and Party ran out of control in Bavaria, almost entirely thanks to the efforts of Adolf Wagner, the Bavarian Minister for Education and Gauleiter of Munich and Upper Bavaria. Here the state takeover of Church lands and buildings disturbed an intense, local sense of sacred landscape and inherited order. Next Catholic journals, nurseries and, above all, education became targets for secularisation. Things came to a head when Wagner issued a decree that crucifixes and Christian pictures be removed from schools during the summer holidays. For hardliners like Wagner, it was time to complete the unfinished business of driving the Church out of education. Although Hitler had forbidden the Party from taking measures against the Protestant or Catholic churches for the war's duration, Wagner could take some comfort from a circular sent by Bormann in June 1941, encouraging the Gauleiter to break the power of the Church. Despite warnings about the unpopularity of the measure from different branches of government as well as ordinary Party members, during the summer and early autumn 389 primary schools in Upper Bavaria lost their crucifixes.[54]

As opposition mounted, Wagner was forced to rescind the order on 28 August, but in many places local and district Party leaders decided to continue as a matter of prestige and conviction, which led to a series of confrontations with angry crowds in small towns and villages. In the Upper Palatinate town of Velburg, they pushed into the house of the mayor after Sunday Mass on 21 September, holding him down when he reached for his pistol. His wife then handed over the keys to the school so that the protesters could put back the crucifixes. Elsewhere, moderate Party members and local officials frequently added their names to petitions, joined demonstrations and sent in their own reports of events to higher authority. In many towns and villages, mothers organised school strikes or collected money to buy new crucifixes; in a number of cases, they were symbolically installed in the classrooms by soldiers on leave after they had attended a memorial Mass for their dead comrades.[55]

For Michael Faulhaber, the Cardinal Archbishop of Munich and Freising, the Bavarian crucifix struggle was a perfect opportunity to regain lost ground. In his pastoral letter of 17 August 1941, he contrasted the removal of the crosses from the schools with those planted on the graves of the military dead. Four weeks later, on 14 September, the letter was due to be read again in churches on the Feast Day of the Elevation of the Holy Cross. The threat was enough. Wagner instructed the Education Ministry to climb down and fifty-nine priests who had been arrested for participating in the protests were released. Hitler also intervened, warning Wagner, hitherto one of his most trusted Gauleiters, that he would put him in Dachau if he ever did anything so stupid again. In the months that followed, Wagner lost ground to his political rivals in Bavaria, and in June 1942 he suffered a major stroke; he died two years later. The Nazi radicals within the Party or the SS did not dare initiate an open conflict with the Church again during the war.

Amongst Catholics in the Rhineland and Ruhr, the conflict provoked divided responses. On 2 August, the day before Galen's momentous sermon on euthanasia, fly-posters went up in Werl, south of Hamm, demanding to know, 'Why are the German Bolsheviks not being fought? Do our soldiers at the front know nothing of them?' and calling for 'Catholics [to] remain united!' Wives of active Party members complained at the barrage of criticism they endured when they went into shops and businesses. Many saw it as a rehearsal for a full-scale, post-war showdown between the Party and the Church. In mid-September, a comrade passed on a copy of the sermon delivered by the Bishop of Trier to Hans Albring. Like many Catholics, he was moved to compare the threat at home with the satanic foe abroad. After the Church's previous silence, the bishop's call had the impact of a 'letter from the Apostles', Albring assured his friend, Eugen Altrogge: 'Believe me, you can't remain silent about such things any more . . . What these barbarians want to destroy is not just the Church but the spirit of Christianity and German history and culture in general.'[56]

Both at home and at the front, there was also a significant strand of Catholic opinion which opposed the bishops. Even in the rural district of Tecklenburg in Westphalia, Gestapo informants reported that anti-clerical Catholics considered it 'quite right' that monks and nuns 'should finally be brought into the labour process'. 'Today,' they opined, 'it is the duty of every German to fight and work for victory.' In the far more secular population of the big cities, Galen was criticised for undermining the unity of the home front, with people asking 'was it necessary during the war?' Accusations of betrayal multiplied as the bishops continued their protests through the autumn of 1941, especially after the RAF started dropping thousands of copies of Galen's sermon over Germany. One Hadamar resident was sent to Ravensbrück concentration camp for six months for possessing a copy. When she returned home, she found that she had not only lost her job but that the townspeople shunned her. A number of Catholic soldiers even compared their bishops' 'treasonous' action to a renewed 'stab in the back'. In a letter to their parish priest on 1 September, three soldiers raged that 'with your damned smear campaign, you are trying to shatter that home front just like in 1918'. One devout Catholic and Nazi soldier was horrified to pick up a rumour that a monastery in Bochum had hidden a radio to communicate with the British, but he did not think it unlikely. Others declared that they would have nothing more to do with a Church leadership so stubbornly reactionary and unwilling to commit fully to the war effort.[57]

The bishops' public protests against the killing of psychiatric patients in 1941 served to broaden a conflict in which they felt that vital Church interests were at stake. They succeeded in returning crucifixes to the schools of Upper Bavaria during September and October. But they did not regain their lost lands and monastic buildings, although Hitler did ban further sequestrations of Church property. Neither side had anything to gain from the confrontation, and the bishops also set about scaling down their protests. Even at the height of the struggle, Galen's criticism of local Party leaders and the local Gestapo never extended to national leaders. Indeed, all three of his sermons of protest in July and August 1941 closed with prayers for the Führer. The bishops slowly returned to Cardinal Bertram's tried and tested method of staying within the bounds and sending to members of the regime private letters of protest against specific violations of the Concordat. Neither Galen nor his Paderborn colleague, Lorenz Jäger, would make medical killing a public issue again.[58]

Even more psychiatric patients were killed in Germany after August 1941 than in the 'T-4' action. The murder of children did not stop at all; it was simply decentralised further. The killing of adults resumed after a year-long pause: 87,400 patients fell victim from 1942 to 1945, more than the 70,000 who were gassed in the first phase from 1939 to 1941. Almost as many patients again died of starvation in asylums which did not specialise in killing, bringing the total number of deaths to over 216,000. This time more effort was made to hide the evidence. But news did reach the Church leaders through priests working in Catholic asylums. By November 1942, the Catholic Church possessed incontrovertible evidence that medical killing had restarted. Its Fulda Bishops' Conference determined not to take a stand in public again: instead, the Catholic asylums were simply discouraged from co-operating in the action. Even Bishop Galen, informed by a priest that the killing of the mentally ill had resumed, carefully avoided

breaking the public truce and contented himself with a private letter
of enquiry, addressed not to any of the national leaders but to the
head of the provincial administration. He did not receive a reply and
let the matter drop.[59]

In August 1942, a new team was assembled at Hadamar under the
abrasive chief administrator Alfons Klein, and his gentle-mannered chief
doctor, the 66-year-old Dr Adolf Wahlmann. Over 90 per cent of patients
sent to Hadamar between August 1942 and March 1945 died, accounting
for at least 4,400 deaths. On arrival at Hadamar, adult patients were
immediately divided into those who could and those who could not
work. Those unable to work received stinging nettle soup three times
a week until they died of starvation. Each morning, Wahlmann met
with Klein to compile the list of patients to be killed. The nursing staff
then usually administered the lethal doses of Trional or Veronal in tablet
form in the evening. Those still alive the next morning were injected
with morphine–scopolamine. In order not to dismay the locals by the
telltale plume of smoke billowing out of the crematorium chimney, the
bodies were buried in a new cemetery behind the asylum. If relatives
attended the funeral, there was a brief service with a coffin; if not, the
bodies were consigned, naked, to mass graves.

Much of the information about the first phase of 'euthanasia' had
leaked out of the medical and social welfare bureaucracy itself. In
particular, as payments for medical care followed the patients from one
psychiatric asylum to another, the money trail revealed their final destination. In the second phase, from 1942 onwards, a new payments office was
inserted as a buffer so that the provincial administration which paid for
a patient's care could no longer see this trail. An unintended consequence
of this new layer of secrecy within the bureaucracy was to undermine
one of the principal purposes of medical murder: instead of ploughing
the money saved on patient care back into the war effort, it had to be
retained within the provincial administration in order to safeguard the
secret of its origins. Unspent surpluses accumulated in the coffers of
provincial administrations where patients were killed. In Hesse-Nassau,
murder at Hadamar released millions of marks for building funds and
other forms of civic expenditure, from war memorials to the Nassau
provincial library and the Rhine-Main provincial orchestra.[60]

Despite all these precautions, revelations emerged. In October 1942,
two months after Hadamar restarted, the Senior President of the

Rhine Province wrote to Adolf Wahlmann to ask why so many of their patients had died so soon after arriving in his asylum. Although he held back from explaining how the patients had died, the chief doctor's reply was anything but a denial:

> I cannot square it with my National Socialist outlook to devote medical resources, be they medicinal or any other kind, to prolonging the life of these individuals who have completely fallen out of human society, most of all in the current time of our struggle for existence, in which each bed is needed for the most valued of our people.[61]

The number of Germans murdered in the psychiatric asylums exceeded that of any other group of domestic victims of Nazi persecution. They had relatives spread throughout German society and, for a brief period, it looked as if the Catholic Church was willing to use its standing as the most powerful civic institution to champion their cause. But without such institutional backing, families faced major obstacles. An administrative paperchase made it even more difficult for families to reach the asylums before their relatives died, with deliberate delays in sending telegrams warning of serious illness, and forward-dating of the deaths. Instead of receiving paper urns with ashes, in the post-1942 phase of killing, families had the right – if they could afford the costs – to have the bodies collected by firms of undertakers for private burial. The firms themselves soon complained about the rough, unfinished coffins and the state of the naked corpses. But, as the Church fell silent, the hundreds of thousands of Germans affected by medical killing were isolated. Many lived far away from the asylums where their relatives were killed and may have remained unaware of what had really happened. Many too felt isolated in their communities, embarrassed by the stigma of carrying a 'degenerative illness' within their families.

Others struggled to care for a relative with utterly inadequate support and came to rely on the asylums as partners in care; as places of temporary respite. Ria was 5 when her mother left home for the first time. From 1925 onwards, Maria M. spent brief spells in Heidelberg Psychiatric Clinic and the asylum at Wiesloch for what was diagnosed as 'schizophrenia'. In 1929, Ria's father died. His sister, Sophie, stepped into the breach to care for his 9-year-old daughter and widow. Sophie also came to rely on the Wiesloch asylum as a partner she could rely on, and the next time, Maria stayed there for five years. In 1941, after a long, stable period at home, she again started hearing voices and suffering from insomnia. Ria told the admitting doctor that her mother's symptoms were the result of the noise of all the building works in Mannheim, to construct air raid shelters. Soon Ria and her aunt were writing separately to the asylum director, the one lobbying to have her mother released, the other to persuade him that her sister-in-law should remain there. In 1942, Ria succeeded in bringing her mother home again, but within six weeks Maria M. had a sudden violent episode in which she smashed the windows and a kitchen cabinet and her daughter had to return her yet again to Wiesloch. On 6 June 1944, Ria received a letter from the asylum at Hadamar to say that her mother had been transferred there, but that 'owing to the difficult conditions of travel', visits would only be permitted in 'especially pressing' cases. Shortly afterwards, on 13 July, Ria received a telegram from Hadamar informing her that her mother had contracted pleurisy. The death notice followed two days later. On 18 July Ria travelled to Hadamar to collect her mother's wedding ring, savings account book and clothes.[62]

That was not the end of the matter, however. A month later, Ria wrote to Hadamar's chief doctor, Adolf Wahlmann, to ask his advice on hereditary illness. Having become a mother herself, she wanted to know whether her mother's schizophrenia could be inherited by her own son, 'and if so', she asked, 'whether it would not be better for me to allow myself, and later on my son, to be sterilised, so as to smother the genetic trait in its cell'. Wahlmann took the time to reassure the unhappy young mother by return of post. Pointing out that, as long as there was no history of the illness on her husband's side, the fact that she had grown up without evincing any symptoms suggested that the illness would not reappear in the next generation. Ria's extraordinary letter to Wahlmann highlights a pattern discernible in many other cases. Under the strain of coping with a difficult and dependent relative, Ria and her aunt had each seen the asylum as a stable and trustworthy partner, occasionally to be lobbied as they argued with each other over their ability to care for Maria at home. They were hardly in a position to question, let alone rally opposition against, what was happening in Hadamar on their own. With neighbourhood sympathy never free of stigma, theirs were private tragedies, the cause of shame as well as grief.[63]

PART THREE

THE SHADOW OF 1812

6

German Crusade

As darkness fell on 22 June 1941, the men sheltering in the small wood checked their equipment one more time, while engineers pumped up the inflatable assault craft for the crossing. Marking the Romanian–Soviet border, the river Prut was a fairly wide but slow-flowing tributary of the lower Moldovian stretch of the Danube. Helmut Paulus embarked in one of the first boats of the 305th Infantry Regiment and, as their regimental commander waved to them, he was reminded of Roman gladiators and their greeting, 'Those who are about to die salute you'. Then pandemonium broke out. A nervous non-commissioned officer fired his sub-machine gun into the side of one of the inflatables, and the occupants of another panicked and capsized their boat. The heavy machine gun and ammunition boxes sank to the bottom. The men had to wade through chest-high water to other boats. From their left came the rattle of machine guns, but nothing hit them. Other German units had crossed further upstream and were flushing the Russians out of Skuleni, the Bessarabian village on the opposite bank.[1]

As the Red Army units pulled back and the Germans advanced, Helmut's infantry company reached a hilltop where they dug in. From daybreak, waves of Soviet planes strafed them every three to four hours, trying to dislodge the German bridgehead. Two days later, Helmut was still there, cowering in a tank trap they had dug, waiting for the Russian armoured divisions to resume their counter-assault. 'One has feelings which are indescribable,' he jotted in his notebook. He had envied the men who conquered France in 1940 while he was still doing basic training. Now, enduring his own 'baptism of fire', the 19-year-old was terrified. Apart from their company commander, a veteran of the First World War, none of them had seen battle. They clung to their bridgehead until 1 July, weathering the Soviet counter-attacks. Having been trained to operate in small primary groups, the men could count on those loyalties above all others. Finally, after nine days, their 198th Infantry Division broke out and Helmut's company found itself leading an attack on Finduri. It cost them thirty-seven men.[2]

Helmut and his comrades were part of the 11th Army. Fighting alongside Romanian troops, they formed the most southerly wing of the 3.5-million-strong force invading the Soviet Union. Commanded by Gerd von Rundstedt, Army Group South's objective was the conquest of Ukraine, the breadbasket of the Soviet Union. Hitler also coveted Soviet oil, and the route to the wells in the Caucasus lay via Ukraine's Black Sea coastline. Meanwhile, Army Groups North and Centre were to strike at the nerve centres of Leningrad and Moscow. Hitler had issued his first orders for the invasion of the Soviet Union nearly eleven months earlier, on 31 July 1940, the same day that he had given the green light to bombing Britain. For Hitler the two campaigns remained closely linked. As the 'England attack' failed, he convinced himself that blockading Britain and eliminating her Soviet ally would create another means to bring Britain to the negotiating table. But the German dictator's strategic choices also fulfilled a long-cherished desire to destroy 'Jewish Bolshevism' and conquer colonial 'living space' in the east, goals Hitler had openly proclaimed in *Mein Kampf*.

There was another important link between the two campaigns. By continuing to mount major bombing raids against Britain into June 1941, the Luftwaffe succeeded in disguising the movement of most of its forces to the east. Ivan Maisky, the Soviet ambassador to London, was certainly fooled, as was Stalin. So, too, were most Germans. To start with, Helmut Paulus had mistaken the river crossing for an exercise. At daybreak on Sunday, 22 June 1941, just after the invasion of the Soviet Union had begun, Hitler's proclamation to the troops was read out. At 5.30 a.m. Goebbels read a similar announcement over German radio, dictated by Hitler the previous day. Its tone was patient and forbearing. 'Burdened by grave worries, condemned for months to silence, finally the hour has come in which I can speak openly,' Hitler began before setting out the history of British attempts to encircle Germany, most recently with Soviet help. He admitted that the alliance with Stalin had been a necessary expedient to break British attempts to force Germany into another two-front war. Despite all the signs of Soviet aggression against Finland, Yugoslavia and, most recently, Romania, the Führer had held back, but now action could no longer be delayed:

> Today, some 160 Russian divisions stand on our border. For weeks, continual infringements of this border have been taking place . . . Russian pilots have made a sport of simply overflying it to demonstrate that they feel they are already masters of this region. On the night of 17–18 June, Russian patrols once more crossed into the Reich and were only driven back after a prolonged firefight.
>
> With that the hour has come in which it is necessary to go into action against this conspiracy of the Jewish-Anglo-Saxon warmongers and Jewish power-holders of the Bolshevik Centre in Moscow . . .
>
> The task of this front [from Arctic Finland to the Black Sea] is thus no longer the defence of individual countries but the security of Europe and so the salvation of all. I have today decided to place the fate and future of the German Reich and of our people once more in the hands of our soldiers.
>
> May the Lord God help us in this struggle![3]

In a café in the centre of Dresden, Victor and Eva Klemperer were trying to assess the local mood when a woman handed them the special edition of the paper with the words, 'Our Führer! He has had to bear it all alone, so as not to trouble his people!' Their waiter, who had been a prisoner in Russia in the previous war, was confident, pronouncing, 'The war will come to an end quickly now.' Another couple and a drunk commercial traveller at their table joined in, the traveller telling anti-Nazi jokes that greatly alarmed Klemperer but, as he noted sadly that evening, 'it was all told in high spirits and full of confidence in victory'. At the Toll House there was dancing. The next day, the former professor of Romance Languages would begin an eight-day spell in police prison for having left a corner of his study window without blackout material four months earlier.[4]

On holiday in Bad Reichenhall, Helmut Paulus's mother Erna came down from her hotel room to hear Goebbels on the radio. 'It was like being hit on the head,' she wrote to her son. 'We had heard for a long time about the troop build-ups in the east and yet were surprised by the fact . . . My first thought was of you, of course.' As a mother, she was not enthusiastic, but there was no panic. She and Helmut's sister Irmgard stayed on for the remaining four days of their holiday in the pretty spa town at the foot of the Bavarian Alps. Irmgard had hired a bike to ride to nearby Berchtesgaden and, evading the barbed-wire security fence, had managed to see the guest house, though not Hitler's residence. A month later, Helmut's father persisted in taking the other children on a trip to Italy, for which the family had saved for ages. While they travelled from the Brenner Pass down to Mount Vesuvius and back, Helmut's mother oversaw the renovation of her husband's medical surgery in their house in Pforzheim. However grave their anxieties for their elder son, they slotted the war into their existing summer plans.[5]

On Monday 23 June, the Security Service noted how 'complete surprise' had been the first reaction everywhere. No one had expected war with Stalin to break out at this particular time. Indeed, there had been widespread rumours of a new agreement between the two powers and even of a forthcoming visit by Stalin to Berlin. But, remarkably swiftly, people adjusted to the reality. By the first afternoon and evening the conviction was being expressed in many reports that the 'Reich government could not have done otherwise than to answer Russia's "treacherous conduct" with military force'. Some raised the spectre of a longer war, pointing out that the campaign in the east could help buy Britain time and might also herald America's entry into the war. Women, in particular, worried aloud about the cost in German lives and about the subjection of prisoners of war to the Soviets' 'Asiatic methods'. However, Finland's remarkable success against Soviet troops in the recent Winter War encouraged expect-ations that victory should be won within three months. The more people talked, the more relieved they were that 'the Führer had recog-nised the true intentions of Russia and also of England'. Indeed, like the woman who passed the paper to Victor Klemperer in the Dresden café, people expressed their 'sympathy for the Führer, for having to remain silent to his people for so long'. The Münster newspaperman Paulheinz Wantzen heard that many women wept, not because they feared failure, but at the price of victory measured in the lengthy separations that military operations and subsequent occupation would impose on families. Faced with the prospect of finally taking on Germany's real enemy, Wantzen wished he could fight. The most widespread anxiety was that German rations would be cut, in order to feed the huge numbers of Russian prisoners of war bound to fall into German hands as the Bolshevik colossus crumbled.[6]

It had not been possible to assemble armies of 3.5 million men totally in secret. The build-up had prompted speculation about mounting tensions between the two allies, with conflicting stories circulating in Münster of a peace conference in Berlin, a Soviet invasion of Germany, a German invasion of Russia and enormous concessions by Stalin. Paulheinz Wantzen was well placed to notice the small but significant transfers of personnel eastwards, most notably the local head of the SD, Karl Jäger, who was sent on an *Einsatzkommando* course to train with sub-machine guns before heading out to Danzig. Since the Pact with the Soviet Union remained in place until 22 June, there had been no matching propaganda build-up. Thirty million leaflets and 200,000 pamphlets intended for the eastern front were printed and stored in the Propaganda Ministry, but to maintain abso-lute security, the printers and packers were locked in with them until the invasion was under way.[7]

Despite the lack of psychological preparation, Hitler's announcement of a 'preventive war' sparked an enormous response.[8] His reference to border incursions may have been a simple replay of the pretexts used against Poland in 1939, but it also spoke to deeper German fears and memories. In 1914, Russian mobilisation had been enough to persuade even the anti-militarist German Social Democratic Party to vote for war credits and declare a 'social truce' for the war's duration. When Russian armies invaded East Prussia, lurid tales of 'semi-barbarians, who scorch, murder, loot, who shoot Samaritans, who vandalise medical stations, and spare neither women nor the injured' had filled all the German papers, including the main Social Democratic daily, *Vorwärts*. When the Russian 2nd Army was totally defeated on 29 August 1914 near Tannenberg, the German commander, the elderly and relatively untalented Paul von Hindenburg, became an instant and enduring hero. In 1941, the Red Army had mobilised too, but made no provisions to launch an attack. Instead, its divisions remained on the defensive, strung along the frontier, easy prey for German encirclement. Despite the lack of any evidence of Soviet plans to attack Germany, it was a claim that found ready credence on the German home front.[9]

In mobilising the deep-seated fear of 'Bolshevism', the Nazis were appealing to the same broad coalition of German public opinion as had come together to repel 'Russian barbarism' in 1914. From former Social Democratic voters to conservative nationalists, this was a matter of profound – and axiomatic – importance. In 1939, many Catholic bishops had given a low-key endorsement of the war against Britain and France, fearing that the Ribbentrop–Molotov Pact might herald an upsurge in anti-clericalism at home. That had not happened until the summer of 1941. Now, despite their ongoing domestic conflict with radical Nazis, the bishops gave full-blooded support to the attack on the Soviet Union, blessing it as a 'crusade' against 'Godless Bolshevism'. For Bishop Galen of Münster, it was German Catholics who represented the true patriots standing by the Führer, and he went on to emphasise – to the rage of the Security Service – that their struggle against Nazi materialism and atheism at home – 'behind the backs of our victorious soldiers' – was the same as the German crusade against Bolshevism abroad. The new war would prevent 'Moscow's attempt to impose its Bolshevik false teaching and rule by force over Germany and Europe'. Now, he and the other bishops could lead prayers, calling on God to lead their soldiers to victory. By the end of the summer, the conflict with the Party had died down and the Bishop of Münster issued a powerful pastoral letter on 14 September, endorsing the war against 'Judaeo-Bolshevism'. Quoting Hitler directly, Galen insisted that the war was defensive in character and that 'for decades the Jewish-Bolshevik rulers from Moscow have been trying to set not just Germany but the whole of Europe in flames'. Among 'national comrades', no political camp had a monopoly on good Nazi-speak that summer, as the mutually suspicious claimants to the soul of the German 'national community' learned to co-operate once more. Anti-Bolshevism encompassed them all.[10]

On 28 June 1941, the first images of the war were disseminated in a rapidly compiled and oddly edited newsreel. It began with the German football cup final between Schalke and Rapid Vienna, followed by several minor diplomatic events, before turning to images of Stukas and heavy artillery attacking British positions in North Africa. Then audiences sat in dead silence while Goebbels read Hitler's declaration, breaking into stormy applause as he ended and German troops took a frontier post. Tension mounted as viewers waited to see their first images of the enemy. When a ragged column of prisoners finally marched across the screen, people shouted, 'Savages', 'Sub-humans', 'Convicts'. Outraged women complained that their menfolk had to 'fight against such "animals"'.[11]

On 30 June, German war crimes investigators converged on Lwów, or Lemberg, the old Habsburg name that Germans used. Accompanied by a military doctor, two military judges toured the Soviet prisons, as did a separate unit of the Secret Field Police. As in Poland, they were seeking to document atrocities committed against German prisoners of war. Though it was not part of their brief, they also compiled evidence of mass executions and torture carried out by the Soviet secret police, the NKVD, on its own citizens. In the city prison they found one corpse lying in a courtyard, four more in one cellar room with a further twenty to thirty piled on top of each other in another room. In the NKVD prison, one of the judges noted three mass graves covered with sand in a courtyard and a further pile of corpses inside the building: one woman had had her breast cut off. In the military prison three photographers from the Reich Propaganda Ministry took pictures of piles of bodies reaching to the ceiling. Most had died from a shot through the back of the neck, a form of execution regarded as the hallmark of 'Jewish-Bolshevik terror'. On this first day in the city, the investigators found no German victims, but they did discover a number of Jews, whose murder they ascribed to their being Zionists, political enemies of the Jewish-Communist regime.[12] That same day, a German soldier wrote home to his wife from Lwów:

> Here we have really come as liberators from an unbearable yoke. I have seen images in the GPU [former NKVD] cellars which I cannot and will not describe to you in your condition. 3,000 to 5,000 lie in the prisons, butchered in the most bestial fashion . . . How I have sometimes thought the depictions of Bolshevik Russia or at that time Red Spain were exaggerated, a primitive appeal to sensationalism. Today I know better . . . They wanted to let these Jewish-Asiatic hordes loose on our old land of culture.[13]

Goebbels lost no time in sending in twenty journalists and radio reporters to cover the Soviet atrocities. By 5 July the *Völkischer Beobachter* was proclaiming Lemberg the epitome of 'Jewish-Bolshevik' rule. By 8 July, it could announce that 'the German soldier brings back the human rights that Moscow sought to suffocate in blood'. Not to be outdone, the *Deutsche Allgemeine Zeitung* reminded its readers about Jewish ritual murder. Although the victims were not German, the cruelty of the NKVD proved, as Robert Ley, leader of the German Labour Front, put it in a banner headline, that 'Germany was meant to be exterminated'. Ley was also the first to remind Germans of Hitler's warning of 30 January 1939, when he had prophesied that a new world war would lead, not to the destruction of the Germans, but to the destruction of the Jews.[14]

In Lwów itself, German soldiers photographed the atrocity sites themselves and also the lynch-justice that followed, as lines of local Jews were forced to run the gauntlet of local Ukrainian nationalists through the prison gates and were beaten, as one of them noted in his diary, with 'whips, planks, fists'. The second newsreel from the Soviet campaign included a fleeting scene of Jews beaten to death in Riga by Latvians with clubs. According to the SD, German cinema audiences greeted this popular revenge on the Jews with 'encouraging exclamations'. Just as the German media had dropped all mention of Polish border incursions in 1939 once it had evidence of Polish atrocities at Bromberg, so Hitler's flimsy claim that Soviet troops had violated German territory was quietly shelved now, in favour of the graphic evidence from Lwów.[15]

*

His teeth chattering in a chilly and damp log cabin in early July, Hans Albring fondly remembered the cultural treasures of France. He had no doubt that he had been sent to a barbaric land where 'Europe ends'. Writing to his friend Eugen Altrogge, now posted to Paris, Albring contrasted the cultured 'Occident' with the impenetrable 'natural world' he could see from his signals van: 'pine forests stretching into the distance and few huts. Nature.' The young Catholic was also appalled by the crassness of the Marxist pamphlets discovered in a Communist Party building, and he fumed against Bolshevik atheism, the destruction of the Catholic churches and vandalisation of the Orthodox ones. He recalled the putrefying stench in the Soviet prison and the photos they had found of those murdered there. As for the Jewish women who peeled their potatoes, he wrote to Eugen, 'a caricature couldn't add much'.[16]

He also found much to admire – the peasant women in their bright dresses and white headscarves, who welcomed him at the door of their wooden churches and gave him bunches of wild flowers. Fascinated by the old icons that now came out of their hiding places, he was impressed too by the priests with their flowing white beards and the chanting of the Orthodox rite. When the Germans held a service of their own, the peasants came along, bringing their icons and weeping openly at their liberation. As Albring wrote to his friend, 'here everyone knew what this simple military holy communion meant to each Russian after twenty-four years of suffering'. By contrast, as they marched through the first villages where 'Hebraic German' was spoken, Albring recoiled from such 'nests', using the term the Nazis had coined for the breeding grounds of 'Jewish Bolshevism'. However much he might distrust what Nazi propaganda said about the Catholic Church at home, he did not question its view of the Soviet Union. Like his bishop in Münster, Albring was fully committed to the crusade against 'Jewish Bolshevism'. [17]

Participating in this crusade profoundly changed Albring's sensibilities. A new phase in his war began in late August when he watched as a German unit executed partisans near a small watermill. They were led up, one by one, shot in the back of the neck and kicked into a ditch. While a Russian shovelled calcium chloride over one body, the next was already being led forward. Albring got close enough to see the exit wound in the head. 'It is a hard but just end,' he explained to Eugen, with a shadow of self-justificatory doubt: 'if you know what led up to it and however much one may dispute the method, which,' he added with a cultivated shrug, 'bears the *signa temporis*', the 'sign of the times'. Albring was just as fascinated as the Germans who had watched similar executions in Poland in 1939. 'You have to see everything, in order to know everything and to reckon with everything,' he wrote. He did not question the justice or racial politics of the actions, nor did he wonder who these people were. What fascinated him was something else, the mystery – and power – involved in snuffing out life: 'What is that which we hang on to and which is snuffed out and gone in a fraction of a second?'[18]

In the vanguard of Army Group Centre, Fritz Farnbacher witnessed another kind of war. On 20 July, the alarm came through at 2 a.m. and he took charge of an artillery battery, providing covering fire for the infantrymen ahead of him. As day broke, it became clear that it had been a false alarm. 'You could get annoyed about something like this,' he noted in his diary; 'but I do understand the riflemen well.' Regularly targeted by 'pinpoint accurate' mortar fire, 'the men are gradually becoming more jumpy'. A lieutenant on the staff of the 103rd Tank Artillery Regiment, the 26-year-old Farnbacher had simply done what he had been trained to do. Both the artillery and infantrymen were part of the elite 4th Panzer Division, and had just captured the small Belorussian town of Cherikov. As the sun rose on a glorious summer's day, the young pietist remembered it was Sunday and sang the 36th Psalm to himself: 'Your loving kindness, O Lord, extends to the heavens, / Your faithfulness reaches to the skies.'[19]

Intermittent fighting began again and Farnbacher's battery lost its telephone line to headquarters. Jumping into a despatch rider's sidecar, Farnbacher reported to Major Hoffmann at the regimental command post. They were interrupted by the arrival of a group of Red Army deserters, all clutching leaflets dropped by the Luftwaffe promising them good treatment. One was said to be a commissar and a Jew. 'It's decided to shoot the Jew. According to higher orders, commissars are to be shot,' Farnbacher jotted down.[20] With his reputation for bravery and wearing his Knight's Cross, Major Hoffmann cut quite a figure. He decided to interrogate the man to discover where all the other commissars in Cherikov had hidden, and had a messenger fetch his 'Jew-comforter' – a stout stick, decorated with various runes and Soviet stars. Forced to stand by with the rest of the staff, Farnbacher fixed his eyes on the the red star nailed to the stick, watching as it became covered in blood while the major beat the prisoner over the head. Eventually, Hoffmann had the Jew led away to where five German soldiers had been freshly buried. At each grave, the major beat the prisoner again with his stick, before finally sending him off to be shot. For Farnbacher, it was a 'most unpleasant' way to end his Sunday.[21]

Farnbacher's distaste at the example set by a highly decorated superior officer was moral and religious. But he was not absolutely opposed to it. On 2 July, after they had held the bridge over the Berezina, Farnbacher and his best friend in the regiment went to see where their battle dead lay. An infantry staff sergeant told them how the wounded had been butchered by the Soviets in a 'bestial manner', stabbed with bayonets and their skulls smashed in. 'One really may not show false leniency there,' Farnbacher concluded. He did not add in his diary that his regiment executed a hundred 'irregulars' in retaliation. Six weeks later, Farnbacher was astonished by the bitter Soviet defence of a village, the enemy refusing to come out of their bunkers, trenches and foxholes even after the fighting had ended. Some who did raise their hands in surrender threw hand grenades between the feet of their captors. 'You can well comprehend if the squaddies simply bump off the next Russians they catch,' Farnbacher reasoned. While some of the men shot the Russians who would not surrender, others set every house in the village ablaze.[22]

As one unit after another adapted to this kind of war, German soldiers chronicled in letters and diaries the new norms they learned on the eastern front: for mutilated German dead, no prisoners were taken; for snipers, reprisals of a hundred to one; gallows erected in every village. As Hans Albring tried to describe to his friend Eugen Altrogge what he witnessed, he helplessly sought some points of artistic and religious reference:

Just to be alive still seems like a gift of God and I don't just want to give thanks with words if we survive this man- and life-eating ogre Russia with all our limbs and senses intact. The sight of bestially mutilated corpses which wear the same uniform as you cuts into your whole mental map of where you are. But also the staring faces of the hanged. The pits full of the shot – pictures darker than the darkest of Goya – oh, Eugen, you can never forget it, even if you want to. And in such proximity it takes away our sense of being carefree and . . . gives us something instead of the harried creature, of the pitiful, impoverished man. Our path here is strewn with some kind of self-portraits, whether they have lost their lives or are still living, you find yourself in them. It is just like those who sit by the path in the Gospels, plagued by this and that, until the Saviour comes. I have not yet found a poem that encompasses what is happening here – much must remain forever unsaid, saved up for the hour when it is handed down to people without mediation.[23]

Nothing had prepared him for this. By January 1942, Albring would write about the Jews as 'these people who are doomed to die'. He was close enough to the Army's Security Divisions, German police and SS *Einsatzgruppen* to have had other opportunities to witness the mass executions being conducted in the rear of Army Group Centre's advance, but he mentioned just one further incident to Eugen. On 21 March 1942, by now serving in the front line, he would note that '[t]he corpses which used to be thrown without order on to a heap have been sorted out as well as possible and lime has already been scattered over the half a thousand Jews who were shot'. As if antici-pating Eugen's shock at this cursory reference, he added hastily, 'This isn't the place to go into detail about what happened here.' Hans Albring would not write about these mass executions again. His path to self-censorship took over nine months of campaigning.[24]

But there was no typical learning curve. Wilhelm Moldenhauer, a radio operator with Army Group South, was also not predisposed to think well of the Jews. The owner of a successful general store in a village outside Hanover, Moldenhauer seemed to be just another comfortable member of the provincial middle class who had joined the storm troopers in 1937 and went on subscribing to his local paper on the eastern front. His political views showed in his choice of anti-Semitic phrases. Like Helmut Paulus, his campaign had begun in Romania, where he had watched with satisfaction the embarkation of Romanian Jews at the port of Constanta. On entering Ukraine, he typically attributed the poverty and oppression he encountered to Jewish and Bolshevik rule: 'here', he wrote home, 'the functionaries and Jews did a lot of work with their propaganda'. Yet, as his radio truck criss-crossed places where Jews were massacred in the late summer and autumn of 1941, Moldenhauer soon stopped referring in his letters to what he saw. He had a more personal reason for silence than Hans Albring: Wilhelm was descended from converted Jews on his mother's side of the family. Whereas he had eagerly photographed the 'camera-shy' Jews he encountered in Poland and Romania, now he turned his Leica to charting his travelogue across the empty steppes.[25]

In contrast to these men, there were many 'execution tourists' in the Wehrmacht, snapping away at the public hangings of Jews and partisans. The reserve policeman Hermann Gieschen, a shopkeeper in Bremen in his civilian life, realised that his battalion would face a difficult task, imagining that it would be 'a bit like in Poland'. He managed to buy a cine-projector in Riga, hoping that the film of his battalion's tour of duty in Latvia and Russia would 'later become a document and be of great interest for our children'. On 7 August 1941, he wrote to his wife, Hanna, about the actions of his unit: the previous night, '150 Jews from this place were shot, men, women and children, all bumped off. The Jews are being completely exterminated.' He quickly added, 'Please don't think about it, that's how it has to be. And don't tell R. about it, leave it for later!' Not yet telling their son about such 'actions' became a characteristic refrain in the letters that followed.[26]

As his unit followed the advance of Army Group North on Leningrad, Gieschen left the bustling towns of Latvia for the forests of northern Russia, 'not a maintained forest, but primeval forests, [full of] undergrowth, thickets, disordered, untended and terrifying'. Remembering a family acquaintance in Hamburg with communist leanings, he wrote, 'Tell Z., he should come and look at Russia. Anyone who still has a grain of communism in his soul will be cured of it here, utterly.' They marched ten Russian prisoners ahead of them to take the brunt of any mines along the forest trails, but the middle-aged reserve policemen found the going exhausting. It was easier to search villages for partisans – even though Gieschen quickly learned that it was rare to catch them there. In fact, they could only locate the partisans by using informers.

To make them talk, they tied their prisoners to poles and left them standing without food or water all night just outside the company cookhouse. One prisoner, whose eye had been shot out in the firefight with the German patrol, succumbed to the torture and led the police company to the village harbouring partisans. But the German captain was too incompetent to surround it fully and Hermann watched as a dozen partisans legged it to the relative safety of the forest. After entering the village, the German policemen began to nail up posters announcing that they had come not as conquerors but as liberators: 'He who plunders will be shot' seemed to reassure the villagers and one woman began to cook a large pot of eggs for the whole company, while others brought out flasks of milk and pickled cucumbers. Despite the reassuring placards, the captain went through the houses, helping himself to a box gramophone – 'I've been looking for one of them for ages' – and making off with a bolt of cloth. Hermann Gieschen worried that this crass contrast with the promise on the posters cast their leadership in a poor light, but he was still proud of their mission and assumed that they would go on being welcomed as liberators because 'the people were so intimidated and exploited by the Communists and Jews and commissars that they are happy to be rid of the scoundrels and really do see us as their liberators'.[27]

Soon after crossing into Russia, Gieschen had reported that a 'gun-woman' had been handed over to them, 'a person of twenty, dark and forbidding, in uniform and high boots . . . Dreadful that women give way to such things.' He was fairly confident, he wrote home, that his comrades would shoot her: one of them, a former hairdresser, had become 'an expert in killing'. They kept a photo of the woman. As a communist perversion of natural female domesticity, women in the Red Army seemed to epitomise the cruel, untamed woman of the Steppes and fascinated Germans. As early as July, the newsreel panned rows of Russian prisoners to pick out a Russian woman huddled on the ground, 'a Bolshevik gun-woman in uniform', as the voice-over emphasised. It was she, rather than any of the other prisoners, even those whose 'Asiatic' features had been singled out, whom German cinema audiences discussed animatedly afterwards. The common verdict was that 'such types should not be allowed to live'.[28]

Hermann Gieschen was not a cruel or sadistic man. In fact, he was rather squeamish and managed to avoid witnessing an execution for the first four months of his campaign, even though he passed on to Hanna details he learned from his comrades. Aware of his own short-comings, he wrote admiringly to his wife about one of the men who played the 'revolver-toting hero' by shooting three civilians in front of the whole company. When he finally watched an execution, he was struck by how the victims stood, tall and unbending like trees. 'It was all very quick,' he wrote. 'We watched the show and then went back to work, as if nothing had happened,' he wrote, adding a customary justification: 'Partisans are enemies and blackguards and must vanish.' Four weeks later, he had acclimatised enough to photograph the execution of eight partisans.[29]

Men like Gieschen who wrote with approval about the murder of the Jews, quoting Nazi slogans in their family letters, appear to have constituted a small minority. Studies of German soldiers' letters have found that mention of Jews was either absent or peripheral, with

Jewish ghettos, forced labour and confiscation of property mentioned only in passing. In his letters home, Helmut Paulus did not mention such events at all. The only reference to Jews in over 1,000 surviving letters sent by Helmut to his cultivated medical family in Pforzheim came during the first week of the campaign, when he noted that his regiment had set up headquarters in a Jewish cemetery on 28 June 1941. His subsequent silence seems too complete to be casual.[30]

Such silence did not prevent knowledge of what was going on in the east seeping back to Germany. Instead, it marked out the moral limits of what husbands should tell wives; or if, like Hermann Gieschen, they did tell them, then what wives were meant to keep from the children. Such familial censorship worked differently from the relatively light-touch military censorship, which sampled divisional mailbags, occasionally blacking out passages of letters and sending in monthly reports on military morale, all of which helped commanders to issue moral guidelines on what their men should tell those on the home front. Still, news leaked back via men on leave, gossip, and film sent home for processing. Soldiers, officers, even police officials travelling across Germany, often talked rather frankly to strangers they met on trains. That summer, a description of mass shootings even found its way into a volume of soldiers' letters published by the Propaganda Ministry.[31]

On the eastern front itself, soldiers adapted to mass killing in various ways. Individual moral and psychological make-up and the dynamics within their small units were filtered through different levels of exposure, experience and involvement. These varied greatly, especially between the front and the rear. Front-line mechanised units, like Fritz Farnbacher's, witnessed the selective killing of political commissars and Jewish prisoners and the torching of villages. These were fleeting events, before the units moved on. Those like Helmut Paulus, Wilhelm Moldenhauer and Hans Albring, who followed the vanguard or were stationed in the rear, saw much more. On the eve of the invasion General Gotthard Heinrici, a devout Lutheran in command of the 43rd Army Corps, made his own sense of the orders from on high authorising the execution of 'Jewish Commissars', by reasoning that the front would be protected by a 'preventive terror' waged in the rear. It was here, behind the lines, that the real orgy of mass killing unfolded.[32]

When the 221st Security Division occupied Białystok on the morning of 27 June 1941, the streets were silent and deserted. After drinking heavily, the 500 men in the 309th Police Battalion fired indiscriminately through windows, before driving hundreds of Jewish men into the synagogue and setting it alight in an act of arson which destroyed much of the city centre. Some Wehrmacht officers intervened to curtail the wanton violence, and the divisional commander, General Johann Pflugbeil was seriously annoyed when the officer in charge of the police battalion was too drunk to report for duty. But Pflugbeil made his own sympathies clear. When a group of Jewish men threw themselves to the ground in front of him and begged for his protection, a policeman unbuttoned his trousers and urinated on them. General Pflugbeil simply walked away. Afterwards, he tried to gloss over the resulting massacre of 2,000 Jews in his report and awarded decorations to some of the police.[33]

Racial violence often also had a sexual dimension. On 29 June, German forces entered Riga, the Latvian capital, and an eye witness reported that the officers of a regiment from Baden-Württemberg immediately set up a drinking den to which they 'forced several dozen Jewish girls to come, to undress fully, to dance and to sing. Many of the unfortunate women were', he continued, 'raped, then led out into the courtyard and shot.' Freed from the strict controls enforced in occupied western Europe, soldiers on the eastern front could – and did – perpetrate extreme sexual violence with impunity.[34]

Paulheinz Wantzen's contact in the Münster SD, Karl Jäger, had indeed been seconded, as the journalist had surmised in June 1941. When Jäger reached Gumbinnen in East Prussia, he joined the SS *Einsatzgruppe* A, operating under the overall command of SS-Brigadeführer Dr Franz Walter Stahlecker. Jäger took charge of one of its five *Einsatzkommandos* and followed Army Group North into the Lithuanian city of Kaunas on 25 June. Here local nationalists orchestrated their own massacres with German encouragement, punishing the Jews for their country's occupation by the Red Army. On the first night alone, more than 1,500 Jews were killed in the streets and several synagogues burned. Local women witnessing the pogrom held their children up high or climbed on to chairs and boxes so that they could see better, and German troops crowded in to take photographs. From 2 July, the SD took over security police duties from the Wehrmacht and the Lithuanian nationalists, many of whom they enrolled as armed auxiliary police. Because of the speed of the German advance, the *Einsatzgruppen* had to patrol huge swathes of territory and so each group split up, leaving its smaller *Kommandos* to operate more or less independently. Karl Jäger, a former maker of musical instruments, kept a precise log of their tour of duty, starting with the execution of 463 Jews in one of the circle of military forts surrounding Kaunas. By the end of July, their 'total carried forward' on Jäger's list came to 3,834.[35]

In late August, Himmler increased the number of men allotted to the *Einsatzgruppen*, especially those operating in Belorussia and Ukraine in the rear of Army Groups Centre and South, who were dealing with much larger Jewish populations spread over much greater distances than in Lithuania. They copied the procedures of Stahlecker's *Einsatzgruppe* A and, instead of targeting only Jewish men of military age, started killing Jewish women and children as well. But it was also becoming clear that the men might be needed for labour, and Karl Jäger had been compelled by strong protests from the German civil administration and the Wehrmacht to spare the 34,500 Jewish workers and their families who remained in Kaunas, Šiauliai and Vilnius, although he still recommended their sterilisation. On 1 December 1941, Jäger filed his final report on his *Einsatzkommando*'s activities, commenting on the difficulties of organising so many daily operations, often involving a round trip of 160–200 kilometres from Kaunas. He and his men had also cleared out the local prisons, releasing those held on 'spurious charges' or to settle local scores. Teenage girls who had applied to join the Communist Youth in order to get work were set free by the Germans, whereas the Communist officials were given 'ten to forty lashes with the whip' before being shot. Jäger concluded triumphantly, 'Today I can confirm that our objective, to solve the Jewish problem in Lithuania, has been achieved by EK 3.' His men had executed 137,346 'Jews, Jewesses and Jewish children'.[36]

Despite the logistical difficulties posed by the terrain, in other respects things generally went smoothly. In particular, there was less friction between army officers and the SS than in Poland, and tensions arose only when army personnel intervened. On 20 August, men of the 295th Infantry Division discovered some eighty or ninety Jewish children on the first floor of a house in the Ukrainian town of Belaia Tserkov, lying and sitting on the floor in their own faeces. The soldiers were shocked and turned to their military chaplains for help. Having learned that their parents had already been executed, Lt-Col. Helmuth Groscurth, the division's General Staff officer, tried to save the children, setting a cordon of troops to prevent the SS and Ukrainian militiamen from taking them away. Groscurth was an unusual officer. Through the winter of 1939–40, he had been one of the key liaison men at Army General Staff headquarters in Zossen, helping Admiral Canaris and Colonel Hans Oster to persuade Franz Halder to lead a military coup against Hitler. As part of his effort to recruit dissidents among the military elite, Groscurth had collected evidence of SS atrocities in Poland. At that time, no other senior general had followed Johannes Blaskowitz, the military commander in Poland, and dared to protest to Hitler.[37]

At Belaia Tserkov, Groscurth could only take his case as far as the commander of the 6th Army, and he had to couch his argument against shooting the Jewish children in terms acceptable to his superiors. Thus, he argued, it would have been more humane to have killed the children at the same time as their parents: having failed to do so, the children should be cared for. At 6th Army Headquarters, Field Marshal von Reichenau angrily quashed Groscurth's plea, and two days later the SS and their Ukrainian militiamen shot the children.[38]

On 10 October, Reichenau clarified matters by issuing a general order to all his troops to co-operate fully in exterminating the Jews:

There is still a lot of uncertainty regarding the behaviour of the troops towards the Bolshevist system . . . The main aim of the campaign against the Jewish-Bolshevist system is the complete destruction of its forces and the extermination of the Asiatic influence in the sphere of European culture. As a result, the troops have to take on tasks which go beyond the conventional purely military ones. In the eastern sphere the soldier is not simply a fighter according to the rules of war, but the supporter of a ruthless racial [völkisch] ideology and the avenger of all the bestialities which have been inflicted on the German nation and those ethnic groups related to it.

For this reason soldiers must show full understanding of the necessity for the severe atonement being required of the Jewish subhumans. It also has the further purpose of nipping in the bud uprisings in the rear of the Wehrmacht which experience shows are invariably instigated by Jews . . .

Only in this way will we fulfil our historic duty of liberating the German people once and for all from the Asiatic-Jewish threat.[39]

Reichenau was one of the most Nazi of German generals. He had joined the Party back in 1932, when it had still been illegal for members of the German armed forces to do so. He endeared himself so much to Hitler that he occasionally alarmed the more traditional top brass, including his immediate superior Gerd von Rundstedt. Not on this occasion: within two days, Rundstedt issued Reichenau's order to the whole of Army Group South. Hitler was delighted with Reichenau's 'excellent' formulation, and, on 28 October, the Army High Command instructed all other army leaders to issue similar orders; by mid-November, it reached units of Army Groups Centre and North.[40]

★

In the first eighteen days of the invasion, Fedor von Bock's Army Group Centre advanced 500 kilometres, reaching the gap between the Dvina and Dniepr rivers and between Vitebsk and Orsha. Just behind this front line lay the city of Smolensk. On 10 July, Bock's troops launched their assault, two panzer groups leading the encirclement of Smolensk against the fierce resistance of the five Soviet armies protecting it. Instead of pulling back as the German pincers began to close around the city, fresh Red Army troops poured in, giving impetus to continual counter-attacks. It took until 27 July for the Germans to close the pocket and the fighting continued for a further five weeks before the remaining 300,000 Soviet troops surrendered. It was a major victory: the Red Army lost at least 1,300 tanks, the Germans less than 200. With Guderian's tanks in control of the Yelna crossing of the Desna river, at the end of July the main highway to Moscow lay open.[41]

The victory closed the first phase of the German campaign, beyond which no detailed plans had been made. The Wehrmacht was two weeks ahead of Napoleon, whose Grande Armée had taken Smolensk on 18 August 1812. From the Commander-in-Chief of the Army, Walther von Brauchitsch, and Chief of the General Staff, Franz Halder, down to the front-line commanders like Bock, Guderian and Hoth, the generals wanted to follow the example of the French emperor and push on to Moscow as swiftly as possible. Brought up on the lessons of Napoleonic warfare theorised by the great nineteenth-century strategist Carl von Clausewitz, they adhered to his notion of the 'decisive battle', in which the enemy's forces could be concentrated and destroyed. Nothing seemed more likely to produce this than an assault on the Soviet capital. Hitler had never singled out Moscow as the main objective of the campaign, however, and spent a week arguing with Halder over what to do next, pitting economic against military logic. The Nazi leader wanted to turn the armoured divisions south-wards and capture Ukraine, whose grain was vital to Germany's food security. Ukraine also held the gateway to the Caucasian oilfields. Oil and grain would turn the Reich into an autarkic superpower, enabling Germany to reflate the western European industries and withstand a long war of attrition with Britain and even the United States.[42]

On 18 August, to Halder's and Bock's dismay, Hitler decided for Ukraine and against Moscow, ordering Guderian's panzer group to swing southwards. Halder later blamed the outcome of the war on this decision, but never did the Chief of the General Staff ask himself whether the military's mantra about a single 'decisive' battle was the correct strategy for victory in a war on this scale. In fact, Hitler's unorthodox – and unexpected – directive led to some of the Germans' most decisive victories in the war.[43]

The August days were hot, but the nights were already turning chilly. During the night of 20 August, Robert R. dreamed that he was with his wife at home in Eichstätt. The pious couple were at a memorial service for the fallen in the cathedral. He drew her attention to the graves – 'Look, there are so many of them!' Then he knelt down before the altar, until someone snarled at him to move on. But in the altercation he lost sight of Maria and saw, instead, that a post office had been set up in the cathedral and people were frantically sorting the soldiers' mail. While he looked for Maria in the packed congregation, people asked him whether it was true that he had died too. 'No,' he replied, 'I'm alive!' He went to kneel in the front pew – 'which I take to be reserved for me' – and found himself thinking, 'Oh, now I won't see Maria any more.' It was then that Robert's comrades nudged him awake to prepare for an attack on the small town of Pochep. Full of premonitions of his own death, Robert kept thinking about what had prompted this dream, putting it down to the mail that had been delivered to them in their forward positions earlier that evening. Unable to read Maria's letters in the darkness, he had kept on looking at the photo of their 2-year-old son Rainer she had sent him, till he had fallen asleep.[44]

While the German artillery barrage on Pochep began, hitting a flock of geese in a village on the outskirts, Robert read his wife's letters in the trench in the rapidly brightening dawn. Waiting in his trench all day, he had just started to write to Maria when the order to attack finally came. Dusk was already falling as they approached the village, but the tension kept rising: 'we're thinking, once we're at the edge of the village, direct fire will start, which always has such a terrible effect'. Luckily, darkness fell swiftly, concealing their arrival along the drainage ditches into which they stumbled. Munching apples as they advanced, the soldiers reached a potato field and dug themselves in. When a Red Army soldier suddenly approached 'doubled over', one of Robert's comrades opened fire. Robert and his lieutenant immediately jumped out of their trench and ran forwards, making for a kitchen garden, where an old man started pleading for his life. While Robert tried to comfort him, the old man began kissing his hands and embracing his knees. Finally reassured, he took Robert to where his daughters and sons were hiding in a foxhole in the garden. 'They come out, weeping from fear and relief, quite small children in their arms. It's a misery,' Robert wrote in his diary the next day. 'I tell them, they can quietly go into the house, no one will set it alight.' A couple of houses had caught fire during the fighting, probably from the artillery rounds.

Pushing on into Pochep alone and unarmed, Robert began to feel apprehensive, uncertain whether the village was still being defended. Meeting whole families carrying their beds and other possessions into the streets, he tried to reassure them that no one would burn down their homes. He felt overwhelmed and ashamed by their gratitude as they rushed forward to kiss his hands. A woman led him to a courtyard where a table and chairs had been set out, and made him sit down and share milk, bread, lard and butter with her family. She sent food back to his comrades in the potato field and children brought the men water to drink. The battle over, the German panzers moved on. Lying under the stars, replaying the day's events, Robert wept and fell asleep. Writing home to Maria the next day, he admitted that many villages were less lucky, caught in the crossfire of the Soviet and

German artillery. The skirmish for Pochep was the start of the advance of Guderian's panzers from the north, and Robert R. was serving in one of the leading motorised infantry regiments.[45]

A week later, as the column halted in the rain for the night, men from the 3rd Company mistook some of Robert's comrades for Russians as they sat talking and laughing in a village house and threw a grenade inside. One man was killed outright, another so badly wounded that the platoon leader shot him, and a 10-year-old Russian girl lost an eye. As the motorised infantry moved on, the rocking of the vehicle sent Robert to sleep. Again he dreamed of Maria: this time they were walking in the countryside. A swarm of Red Air Force planes came, but Maria did not recognise them and he did not want to alarm her. He was wearing his uniform, and so tried to hide in some bushes, where he was discovered and grabbed by the back of the neck. 'Officers question me and order me to be taken away. I ask to say goodbye to Maria and am allowed to. I hug Maria and lift her off the ground and we weep bitterly,' he jotted in his diary. Robert woke up when the truck stopped, its way blocked by a bomb crater and dead horses. In the woodland to the left, near wrecked vehicles and corpses, he saw women's clothing. He also found a waterproof bag, which he took to keep his things dry, still ruminating about the fears he had expressed in his dream.[46]

Robert R. hated the war, and his diary carefully chronicled what he wanted to explain to Maria when he was home again. It was here, rather than in his letters, that he described the shooting of prisoners and how his comrades set fire to houses: this was for 'later, when we are together again'. But the more he detested the war, the more he convinced himself that this time it must be fought to a conclusion: he had to prevent his 2-year-old son from becoming the third generation that had to fight in Russia. 'No, that must never happen, that Raini should ever have to come here where I am now!' Robert wrote to his wife. 'No! No! Rather that I came again, rather that I go through all hells once again and die there. This finest lad, whose picture I carry with me now, whose golden locks have sucked up so much sun. I thank you for giving him to me.' Above all, he assured Maria that he was protected by their 'transcendent love, which shares in all the love of the whole world'. For a man like Robert R., therefore, the horrible conduct of the war both unsettled him and intensified his commitment. Such a war must never come home to Germany, and it had to be won decisively. Soldiers and their families identified the war, not with the Nazi regime, but with their own inter-generational responsibilities. It proved the strongest foundation for their patriotism.[47]

The 2nd Panzer Group continued to advance south into Ukraine. As long as the Wehrmacht had been heading for Moscow, the huge westward bulge of the Soviet south-western front had pinned the Germans back on three sides, threatening to become a springboard for an attack northward into the rear of Army Group Centre. Instead, by swinging south from their most advanced positions on the Moscow highway, it was the German tanks which were now poised to slice through the rear of the Soviet armies. Pushing up from the south, Kleist's 1st Panzer Group met Guderian's thrust from the north at Lokhvytsia on 14 September, encircling the entire Soviet south-western front. At 4.30 a.m., Wilhelm Moldenhauer found a moment to write an excited letter to his wife about 'A new great success, which is still not being spoken of yet for understandable reasons'. He followed military protocol and did not divulge where he was, but did tell her that all through the day and night he could hear 'how our trucks and now and then heavy tracked vehicles rumble over the bad cobbles of these streets'. In high spirits, he and two comrades went in search of a statue of Lenin and then held mock revolutionary speeches in a bookshop.[48]

Three days later, as Moldenhauer's unit advanced further into Ukraine, he was welcomed into one of the cleanest houses he had yet seen, where he was given milk and shared the family's meal of baked potatoes, cabbage and meat. After he returned from duty at 8 p.m., his hostess welcomed him back with more milk and pork fat; in return, he produced a bottle of vodka. For the next two hours, while the entire family sat around the large table, he took a good look at the living room, to describe it later to his wife, its table lit by a petroleum lamp, the gilded icons glinting in their glass cases against the whitewashed walls. Moldenhauer felt that the welcome was utterly genuine. 'And perhaps for that very reason,' he wrote home to his wife Erika on 17 September, 'because communism directed its strong, warmongering propaganda against Germany and because they suffered so much under Soviet and Jewish rule. And now the Germans are there and the people can convince themselves again and again that the Germans are nice decent chaps. That demolishes all the enemy propaganda at one blow.'[49]

As the Soviet south-western front tried to break out of its encirclement, the German armoured divisions that had closed the eastern side of the pocket came under intense pressure. On 22 September, Lieutenant Fritz Farnbacher was in the forward observation post of his 103rd Tank Artillery Regiment, when he heard the first shouts of 'The tanks are coming!' One of the heavy Soviet tanks immediately scored a hit on a German troop carrier. Hiding in little hollows and pressing their faces into the soil, the Germans hoped that the tanks would not see them. If it had not been so dangerous, Farnbacher would have laughed as he watched them playing hide-and-seek with the steel monsters. He was astonished by the speed with which the Soviet tanks could turn, and surprised that the 37mm German anti-tank guns made no impact on their armour plate. When a tank suddenly headed straight for the ditch where Farnbacher was lying, its looming mass blotted out the daylight. He lay there hoping that it would roll harmlessly across the top, but one of its tracks slipped into the trench, threatening to squash him. Crawling frantically to his right, Farnbacher just managed to get clear. The track missed his left foot by 2 centimetres, its steel links ripping the hem of his greatcoat. The small engagement cost his unit eighty-nine dead and wounded. The division lost five field howitzers, three anti-tank guns, two infantry guns, three heavy machine guns and two troop carriers, alongside ammunition boxes and other equipment. The survival of Farnbacher's gun battery owed most to the Germans' tactical ability to compensate for inadequate equipment through the use of radio communications and combined arms. It was the united power of field artillery and the Luftwaffe which drove off the tanks.[50]

By the time Farnbacher wrote up his diary, he was already moulding the narrative to fit his romantic preconceptions of war, dwelling on the dying words of a comrade who had asked their commander, 'Captain, if I return, and I hope that's very soon, can I remain a soldier?' To which the officer ostensibly replied, 'My boy, but of course, you remain a soldier!' As Farnbacher imbued the young man's death with the heroism and comradeship he himself had hoped to find in the war, he created one of those minor battlefield legends which soldiers lived by.[51]

On 18 September, Kiev fell. On entering the city the 296th Infantry

Division found its inhabitants impoverished, undernourished and apathetic. As Wilhem Moldenhauer put it, after seeing a 3-year-old child with 'an unnatural appearance' and terribly thin legs lying on a bed, he was reminded of 'our propaganda posters about the conditions in the Soviet Union'. Watching a column of 9,000 Red Army prisoners file past on 20 September, Moldenhauer struggled to grasp the scale of their victory: 'The column of the defeated had no end. That an army thrown together from this mish-mash of peoples can defend itself so toughly is astonishing. It also clearly only worked under the knout of the commissars.' In total, over 660,000 Soviet soldiers surrendered in Ukraine. It was the greatest German victory of the war so far. But the most pressing question everyone asked was, 'Are we staying here for the winter or not?'[52]

On 23 September, Fritz Probst arrived in Kiev with his engineering corps and, over the next month, they rebuilt the great bridge over the Dniepr which the Red Army had blown up. A father of three, Probst had been called up along with other reservists in their early thirties at the end of August 1939, and had already served two years. In 1940 and 1941 he had followed the front, rather than taking part in the battles, managing to send raisins home from his most recent posting in Greece. His first impressions of the Soviet Union were not hopeful. The retreating Red Army had created a wasteland. 'I have already seen terrible images of destruction,' he wrote to his family, 'and can only tell you, you should thank the Führer that he has liberated us from this danger.' A few days later, he returned to the theme:

> What we're doing is a great sacrifice, but we're doing it gladly, because if this war were waged in the Fatherland, well, then it'd have been much worse . . . If these beasts had come to Germany, then it'd have been a much greater misfortune for us. We just have to put up with it and perhaps the victorious end is closer than we think.

While the words and sentiments of this self-employed carpenter and convinced Nazi from Görmar, a small town in staunchly Protestant Thuringia, differed sharply from the humane and sentimental Catholic teacher Robert R., both men were nonetheless convinced that this was a defensive, 'preventive war'. And they both hoped that one final push would finish the campaign.[53]

Within days of the German entry into Kiev, the fires started. With their long timer delays, the mines planted by the retreating Red Army and NKVD created havoc and set fire to entire neighbourhoods. In the 296th Infantry Division, Lieutenant Reinert raged against the Bolshevik 'beasts' and observed how the ordinary Kievans, 'their eyes filled with fear of their own countrymen', were turning to the German soldiers for protection. To Reinert it was clear who was to blame. 'The police drive the instigators of this sub-humanity together: the Jews,' he noted. 'Revolting types pass the car, faces you'd want to trample on with your boots, Jews, who hid till now in their cellar dwellings and now have been driven into the daylight by the raids.' He believed that the prime movers were long gone: 'These aren't the Jewish wire-pullers who give the orders – they vanished in time – it's their willing tools, the vermin of this city.' In fact, the Wehrmacht knew about the Soviet fuses with thirty-five-day timers and had issued instructions to the troops the day before they entered Kiev to expect booby traps throughout the city. But they also believed that the Bolshevik dictatorship was Jewish rule, and so they did not protest about the mass round-ups of Jewish men. Shootings of Jews began in Kiev on 27 September.[54]

By this time, Lieutenant Reinert, along with most of the 296th Infantry Division, had already left the city, but some of the men relayed the news. 'There have been fires for eight days already, all done by the Jews,' one wrote on 28 September. 'For that the Jews aged between 14 and 60 years old have been shot, and the wives of the Jews are still being shot, otherwise there's no end to it.' The Jews of Kiev were taken to Babi Yar, a ravine just 4 kilometres outside the city, where the SS *Sonderkommando* 4a and two police battalions shot 33,771 Jews over the next two days. Carried out with the approval of the commander of the 6th Army, Walther von Reichenau, Babi Yar was the greatest single massacre of Jews on the eastern front. Johannes Hähle, a war photographer with the 6th Army, got there in time to photograph the SS searching through the piles of clothing abandoned in the ravine. He sent the roll of Agfa colour film home to his wife.[55]

Within a month, the ravine was also being used to carry out collective reprisals against the non-Jewish population of the city. A hundred people were shot on 22 October, 300 people on 2 November, and 400 on 29 November. The reprisals were not for attacks on Germans, but for acts of 'sabotage': explosions, fires at a city market and cutting German phone lines. Ukrainian engineers and factory workers were astonished by the Germans' lack of interest in getting industrial production up and running in the city. Workers in the mining and metalworking plants took the initiative themselves, recovering machines and parts which they had hidden in wells and ponds to save them from Soviet evacuation measures. Apart from a handful of strategic enterprises, such as manganese mining at Nikopol, the Germans did little to organise industry. It was not part of their plan.[56]

Ten days after the capture of Kiev, on 30 September 1941, the Economy Inspectorate South banned the supply of food to the Ukrainian capital. Experts had calculated that the food stocks of the city would be exhausted by this date. The city's pre-war population of 850,000 had already been halved, thanks to Red Army recruitment, the Soviet evacuation of civilians and the German massacre of the Jews. Ukrainian and German policemen now set up checkpoints on the roads and the bridges, stopping cars, carts and pedestrians, confiscating food and barring peasants from entering the city. Kievans who fought their way to the head of the bakery queues were rewarded with bread made from millet. Dubbed a 'brick' for its clay-like texture by some, 'emery' for its yellow shine by others, the bread fell apart into hard crumbs, which were difficult to digest and tasted bitter because barley, chestnuts and lupins had been added to the dough. Its quality continued to decline. By November, the city had gone 'dead' during the day, with a few Germans and policemen in the streets, alongside motionless beggars with amputated or swollen limbs. A Ukrainian teacher jotted in her diary on Boxing Day 1941,

> The Germans are celebrating. They all walk full and content, all have lights on their Christmas trees. But we all move about like shadows, there is total famine. People are buying food by the cup and boil a watery soup, which they eat without bread, because bread is given out only two times per week, 200 grams. And this diet is the best-case scenario. Those who have things exchange them in the countryside, but those who have nothing swell up from hunger, they are already dying. Many people have typhus.[57]

The German blockade fulfilled the terms of the 'Hunger Plan' devised by the State Secretary at the Ministry for Food and Agriculture,

Herbert Backe, back in December 1940 when planning for the Soviet campaign had begun. In order to feed the Wehrmacht and the home front, he envisaged a division of Soviet territory into 'forested' north and 'agricultural' south, and into town and countryside. The northern 'forested area' and all the cities would be left to starve, so that the enormous surpluses produced by the southern, rich 'black lands' of Ukraine would feed the Reich. On 2 May 1941, seven weeks before the invasion started, the plan was formally adopted, officials assuming that 'umpteen million people will doubtless starve, if what we need is taken out of the country'. By the time Ukraine was in German hands in the autumn, the Gauleiter of Thuringia and Reich Plenipotentiary for Labour Mobilisation, Fritz Sauckel, had been told repeatedly that 'at least ten to twenty million of these people' would starve to death in the coming winter. Backe's own estimates were that 20–30 million 'Slavs' would die. The 'Hunger Plan' became a central element of German military planning for Barbarossa.[58]

Blockading Kiev fulfilled a second objective: Hitler's desire to 'wipe' the major Soviet cities 'off the face of the earth'. The Führer had ordered the Wehrmacht at the start of the Ukrainian operation 'to destroy the city by incendiary bombs and gunfire as soon as the supply positions allow' or, in Halder's laconic note of 18 August, 'Reduce to rubble'. The Luftwaffe, entrusted with part of that task, did not have enough bombs, a missed opportunity which Hitler would recall bitterly a year later as another of Göring's failures. Halder had already noted that Leningrad and Moscow were not to be permitted to capitulate either.[59]

In the north, the German advance was even swifter than in the south, leaving Leningrad, the cradle of the Russian Revolution and the Soviet Union's second city, highly exposed. On 30 August, the last rail link to Leningrad was cut at Mga. On 8 September, the Schlisselburg fortress fell. Built where the river Neva flows out of Lake Ladoga, it was the key to the city's communications and industrial power supplies. Leningrad was now completely encircled by land, and the only route in or out of the city lay across Lake Ladoga itself. That same day, the Luftwaffe began massed raids on Leningrad's food depots. Professor Wilhelm Ziegelmayer, the expert on nutrition advising the Wehrmacht High Command, noted in his diary on 10 September 1941 that 'We will not burden ourselves with future demands for the surrender of Leningrad. It must be destroyed by a scientifically based method.' At this time, the Quartermaster's department of the 18th Army asked for guidance about whether they were expected to use military supplies to feed the city – if it surrendered. The answer from the Quartermaster-General of the Wehrmacht, Eduard Wagner, was a categorical no: 'Every train bringing provisions from the homeland cuts foodstuffs there. It is better that our relatives have something to eat and that the Russians starve.' Wagner had already written to his wife that 'the next thing will have to be to leave the people in [St] Petersburg to stew. What are we to do with a city of 3.2 million, which would just be a burden on our provisioning purse?' He had ended with one of Hitler's favourite expressions when justifying murderous conclusions: 'There is no room for sentimentality here.'

As Goebbels began to prepare 'an effective excuse' which he could use to influence international opinion once the 'cruel fate of the city' became evident, he was delighted that the Bolsheviks were insisting on defending Leningrad to the 'last man'. By mid-September, however, the German High Command worried about the danger of epidemics spreading from the city to their own lines and about the psychological strain on German infantrymen who might have to 'shoot at women and children trying to escape' from the city. To make sure this did not happen, Field Marshal Ritter von Leeb, the commander of Army Group North, ordered the artillery to mow down any civilians breaking out of the city while they were still too far away to upset German infantrymen on the front line.[60]

During the week from 21 September, the decision was confirmed and reiterated that Leningrad was to be 'razed to the ground. If this creates a situation which produces calls for surrender, they will be refused. In this war, we are not interested in preserving even a part of the population of this large city.' Capitalising on this ruthlessness, the Reich Security Main Office set about drafting its own 'General Plan for the East' in which it predicted that the future region of 'Ingermanland' on the Soviet Baltic coast would be a sparsely populated, agricultural area of German and Finnish settlement, with a population which had fallen from 3.2 million to just 200,000. The missing 3 million people in this plan for the post-war future were the Leningraders. The original authors of the 'Hunger Plan', Herbert Backe and his colleague Hans-Joachim Riecke, would publish their rationales too so that German professionals could acclimatise themselves to the times.[61]

By the end of September 1941, a 250-gram bread ration was introduced for dependants in the city. The Luftwaffe had bombed Leningrad twenty-three times and the artillery had fired over 5,000 shells in its daily barrages. German artillerymen were starting to joke that they were 'feeding the city' by reducing the number of civilian mouths. By mid-November, Army Group North's war diary noted the first successful attempt by artillery to prevent civilians from approaching their lines, although German generals continued to worry that 'false' compassion might get the better of their men. Commanders began to ask for the first time about the consequences of genocidal warfare on their soldiers. If they proved capable of shooting down unarmed civilians, would it lead to a 'loss of inner balance'? Would their troops 'no longer be scared of committing such acts even after the war was over'? Where, they were asking, would the brutalisation end?[62]

★

Even before the encirclement of the Red Army in Ukraine was complete and Leningrad fully under siege, Halder, Brauchitsch and Hitler turned their attention back to Moscow. Astounded by their easy victory in Ukraine, they could not imagine that the Red Army still possessed major forces. Halder as much as Hitler stoked expectations, proposing that Army Group South could reach Stalingrad and the Maikop oilfields before winter, and that Army Group Centre could reach Moscow with reduced air support and fewer panzers. Like Leningrad, the capital was to be encircled and cut off. At one point, Hitler imagined that Moscow could simply be made to disappear, preferably under cleansing flood waters.[63]

On 2 October 1941, the troops heard a second proclamation from the Führer, announcing that Moscow was the final goal of the campaign. Despite his anxiety that the war might last into the winter, Wilhelm Moldenhauer was thrilled when he heard the broadcast of Hitler's solemn call to arms for the decisive battle against Bolshevism. The public moment was also an intimate one, as he imagined his wife listening to the proclamation on the radio 'and that with each word, maybe your thoughts were also with me'. Fritz Farnbacher and the 4th Panzer Division had started out already, the freezing fog chilling them to the bone but concealing their movements. On the first day, they covered 130 kilometres and, four days later, on the afternoon of 3 October, they reached Orel. As they advanced over open terrain towards the city, the motorised infantry manoeuvred their light vehicles around the tanks, using them as cover against the Soviet aeroplanes they could see taking off from the airfield nearby. They had seen nothing of the Luftwaffe for days. The infantrymen had to jump off their vehicles and take cover under the tanks over thirty times before they reached the outskirts of Orel. When the first tanks entered the streets, the trams were still running. One tram driver even rang his bell, taking the tank for one of their own. As it swung its gun turret towards the tram, the street emptied.[64]

Just as at Smolensk and in Ukraine, the German tanks led the encirclement. From Orel, the 2nd Panzer Group swiftly completed the encirclement of Bryansk. To the west, the 3rd and 4th Panzer Groups had closed Vyaz'ma in a double pincer grip. By 7 October, virtually the whole of the remaining Soviet forces on the western front were trapped in this double pocket, leaving the road to Moscow open for the Germans. At Führer headquarters, Jodl saw it as the most decisive day of the campaign and compared it to the swift Prussian victory over Austria in 1866. Two days later, Hitler's personal spokesman, Otto Dietrich, called a special press conference to tell the world that nothing but 'empty space' now stood between the German armies and Moscow. Goebbels was dismayed, both by the premature triumphalism and his own inability to control Dietrich. But he did not rein the press in. 'The great hour has struck!' and 'The military end of the Bolsheviks', the *Völkischer Beobachter* proclaimed. Bookshops displayed Russian grammars for future occupation officials and cinemas advertised a forthcoming documentary, *The Germans Enter Moscow*.[65]

It was not just hyperbole. There were now a mere 90,000 Red Army men defending the capital against the advance of the million-strong forces of Army Group Centre. The magnitude of the German victory was even greater than in Ukraine: the Wehrmacht captured 673,000 prisoners and 1,300 tanks. Taking the two victories together, within a period of five weeks, 1,447,000 Red Army soldiers had surrendered to the Germans. The German General Staff and the High Command had given no thought to what to do with so many prisoners, even though their whole plan of campaign depended on the rapid collapse of the Red Army. Hitler and his closest advisors had no interest in them at all, except – possibly – as a labour supply, but in the autumn of 1941 such ideas were not a priority. The problem was simply left to the department for prisoners of war and the rear service areas to solve with whatever resources they could find.[66]

In the aftermath of the Vyaz'ma and Bryansk battles, the 2nd Army's 580th Rear Army Area Command set up feeding centres and shipped its prisoners back, by 'deploying all usable trucks and carts, assigning peasant leaders and prisoners of war' to the task. At the beginning of October, it moved forward its 203rd transit camp for prisoners – a 'Dulag' in the contracted military terminology – to Kritchev, where a sawmill and cement factory were converted into barracks for 10,000 prisoners. Instead, 20,000 arrived in a single night, while another 11,000 were marched further back to the rear. By 19 October, the camp held over 30,000 Red Army soldiers. Most of them were simply left out in the open, until entrenching spades could be borrowed from neighbouring German units to dig holes in the ground which could be covered with branches and soil. Although the camp was next to the railway line and had access to water, supplying it ranked very low on the list of military priorities.

The officer in charge of the kitchens was a well-meaning veteran of the First World War. Too old for front-line service, Konrad Jarausch eloquently described the unfolding disaster in his letters home. The cooking was done in old fuel drums and there were few utensils. Many Red Army prisoners had had to hold out their military caps as substitute mess tins, catching perhaps half of the thin soup they were served. At its peak after the Bryansk battle, Konrad Jarausch had to feed 16,000–18,000 men a day in his subsection of Dulag 203. There were five Germans to run the administration and kitchen as well as eight guards, he explained to his friend, Werner Hass, 'And so you can imagine that there had to be beatings and shootings . . . just to create order in the surroundings of the kitchen'. As departures for the huge camps further west started to outstrip new arrivals, numbers dropped to 6,000 and Jarausch wrote with a sense of relief to his wife, 'I haven't had to play the policeman quite so much and didn't need to beat anyone down to the ground with the rubber truncheon or to have anyone shot down. Nonetheless there was enough that was appalling.' Despite the obstacles, he and the other older officers who 'still have some old-fashioned humanity' managed to distribute food twice a day – despite the resistance of the camp inspectorate.[67]

Jarausch gathered a group of prisoner functionaries around him who ran the kitchens and benefited from their privileged access to food. Jarausch distributed cigarettes to them, and in return these prisoners of war looked after him, providing him with soup thickened with milk or cream twice a day and up to four eggs, even when these became rare. He knew that he was also profiting from the foraging expeditions of his more 'ruthless' comrades, who requisitioned food from local villages. But there was no danger from partisan raids, because, he assured his wife, 'it's quiet. The SS is making a terribly clean sweep.' A gentle, religious studies teacher and anti-Nazi from Magdeburg, Konrad Jarausch was more curious than hostile to his Russian prisoners. Equipped with a Russian primer, he began learning the language, finding an educated prisoner to teach him.[68]

In early November, an SS *Einsatzkommando* arrived to comb the camp for Jewish prisoners of war and civilians. Some were shot in the cellar of the cement factory. Jarausch only hinted at such events in his letters home. When his Russian teacher turned out to be a 'half-Jew', he did not tell his wife, Charlotte, what happened to the man, but he had explained that he had seen 'Jews barefoot in the snow' and that 'some hard things, which I could not prevent, have left very bitter impressions. On that, by word of mouth.' Two days later, he wrote more enthusiastically, this time about his new teacher, a Muscovite and, like Jarausch himself, a schoolmaster in his forties. As the man read a Turgenev story aloud, Jarausch felt 'as if I were touching the soul of this country, the way it perceives and knows itself'. Like Hans Albring, Jarausch was simultaneously moved by Russian culture and certain that he was dealing with people who were 'half children'. Seeing how terribly they had suffered under the Bolshevik tyranny, he felt it was his duty to spread the Gospel amongst them. Writing to fellow members of the Martin Luther Association, Jarausch explained, 'I would like to believe that the Russian people which clung so loyally to its Christ, still has much to say to us Christians in the coming years, once the spell [of Bolshevism] has been broken.'[69]

No matter how much the war's brutality disturbed him, Jarausch could not disown the German cause. On 14 November he wrote to Charlotte, telling her that they had found a fresh case of cannibalism. Of the 2,000 prisoners in the cement factory, 25 were dying each day. For the civilians, 'above all the Jews' who had nothing but their shirts to wear in the frost, 'then it is really the most merciful thing, if they are led into the forest and done in there, according to the technical term'. He confessed that 'you could be thrown into doubt about the sense of the whole thing, if you didn't hear continually from the Russians what they suffered under Bolshevism'. It might, Jarausch admitted to his wife, be 'more murder than war', but, then, he just had to do his 'bit of duty'.[70]

From Orel, Fritz Farnbacher and the 4th Panzer Division headed towards Tula, the key to Moscow's southern defences, which the Wehrmacht had to overcome in order to encircle the capital. In the autumn weeks, the Soviets had fortified in depth the direct approach to Moscow along the western highway. Beyond the two existing Mozhaisk defensive lines, a triple ring of trenches had been dug in front of the city, with bunkers and strongpoints, each protected by minefields, making a frontal assault no longer viable. In any case, the Germans had no intention of launching a direct assault: here, too, the High Command planned for a final battle of encirclement. Operating from the northern and southern wings of Army Group Centre, the panzer groups would envelop Moscow, meeting at a junction east of the capital and hopefully trapping inside the remnants of the Red Army and the Soviet leadership.

With its population of 272,000, Tula, 150 kilometres south of Moscow, was an old armaments centre that lay in the middle of the Moscow lignite fields. Unless the Germans could take over the city's railway junction and the airfield, Guderian could not risk sending his forces further east to surround Moscow: his 2nd Panzer Group may have just been upgraded to a Panzer Army but its lines were already extended and vulnerable. Entrusted with spearheading the assault on the Soviet capital from the south, Guderian struck a typically bravura note with his officers: 'Tula? Short, hard battles – long trip – blond girl'.[71]

But the 2nd Panzer Army and its constituent parts, such as the 24th Panzer Corps and the 4th Panzer Division, were not the same units as had taken Orel without interrupting their line of march. Fritz Farnbacher saw his first snow on the night of 6–7 October. It turned to rain and the unsealed roads, baked hard by the summer, turned into a quagmire – 'a liquid, bottomless swamp, black pastry mixed by thousands and thousands of boots, wheels, caterpillars', as the Soviet journalist Vasily Grossman described it. Across Army Group Centre's entire 500-kilometre front line, tanks and artillery pieces, trucks, half-tracks and horse-drawn carts were all sinking into the mire. By 15 October, the staff of Army Group Centre were registering that 'the psychologically critical moment of the campaign has arrived'. In one week, the 6th Panzer Division had gone from 200 tanks to 60 operational vehicles. The 20th Panzer Division was down from 283 machines two weeks earlier to 43 semi-wrecks; and the 4th Panzer Division possessed a mere 38 tanks. It took a week to get the 4th Panzer Division under way, its commander warning that 'the uninterrupted efforts and hard battles . . . have not passed over the officers and men without leaving a trace' and that any attack would only 'succeed with heavy and bloody losses', if at all. It was more than the weather that slowed down the German advance. Since the beginning of October, the Luftwaffe had hardly been sighted, while the Red Air Force struck ever more effectively against the nearly stationary German targets. The closer the Germans came to Moscow, the stronger the Soviet defence became. Still, on 29 October the 4th Panzer Division advanced to within 4 kilometres of Tula, before getting stuck once more in the mud of the highway. The Wehrmacht's confidential report for the next day recounted how units from the 4th Panzer Division and the Grossdeutschland regiment entered a wood south of Tula, where they fought on foot against Soviet tanks.[72]

In 1812, Napoleon's Grande Armée had lost most of its men and horses not in its disastrous winter retreat, but earlier, during their victorious summer advance. So too in 1941, the Germans suffered the greatest number of casualties while advancing, losing 41,048 men in the last week of June, 172,214 in July, 196,592 in August and 141,144 in September. It was even worse in the German panzer divisions. By the end of July, the 35th Panzer Regiment, the armoured core of the 4th Panzer Division, retained only 49 of its original complement of 177 tanks. Guderian had to ask Hitler personally to send spare parts for his 2nd Panzer Group. The motorised infantrymen who fought on foot, scattered in the open between the tanks in any attack, were particularly exposed: by August their numbers were down by 50–70 per cent.[73]

The speed of the German advance became self-defeating. As the supply lines grew longer, the quartermaster-generals were confronted with impossible choices. The Germans did not possess enough rolling stock and locomotives to supply the eastern front. They had captured so few undamaged Soviet broad-gauge wagons and locomotives that they had to invest more heavily than they had expected in converting lines to standard-gauge rails, a slow business which grew in scale with the German advance. Moving goods from their depots along the railway also proved increasingly difficult, thanks to the loss of motor vehicles and horses. By mid-November, 425,000 of the 500,000 vehicles with which the German Army had begun the campaign had broken down and there were too few repair facilities to fix them. Horses, which provided most of the draught power, began to fall ill and die in their tens of thousands. The main highway from Smolensk to Moscow was a dual carriageway for most of its length, but the retreating Red Army had laid multiple landmines on long-running timers. Each day, craters 30 metres wide and 10 metres deep were torn in the road. The situation became so bad that much of the 5th Infantry Division was turned over to mending the road instead of being sent to France to recuperate.[74]

As the temperature dropped at the end of autumn, the Wehrmacht recovered some mobility over the frozen ground. But the cold brought new problems. When the snows came in mid-November, only half the men in the 4th Panzer Division had greatcoats, and only a third possessed woollen blankets. More men were now being invalided out with frostbite and other illnesses than with wounds, though both numbers were rising. In late July and early August, orders for winter equipment had been issued, but only for the fifty-eight divisions slated to stay and occupy the Soviet Union after the German victory. In the desperate juggling of transport priorities on the rails and roads, most of the winter clothing remained stockpiled at the railheads in Poland. Even postal deliveries, regarded as a vital to morale, were held back, as Army Group Centre concentrated on supplying the front line with munitions and petrol.[75]

According to the military censors for the 2nd Army, the 'fighting spirit' remained 'unbroken' and 'confident' through most of October, despite the difficult weather. 'The contents of the letters in the past month was shaped by the great successes of the encirclement battles of Bryansk and Vyaz'ma and the advance on Moscow. Each man sees the end of the campaign against the Bolsheviks within touching distance and with it the longed for return to the Reich', they reported. In fact, according to a smaller, in-depth survey of the letters of twenty-five correspondents, expectations of imminent victory were higher in October than they had been in June, July and August. In this month, even adversity appeared to confirm that victory was in the offing: one man complained about the poor food, but noted that supplies were always bad when 'something major is under way'.[76]

In Army Group South things were much worse. As Helmut Paulus wrote to his parents the day after they reached Stalino in the Donetsk region, 'Our feet have had it from the 2,000 kilometres which we have covered since July. You can't stand for five minutes without getting pain in the feet and calf muscles. It's not just like that for me but all comrades.' Without any fat for his boots, he could not stop the leather from cracking and the stitching from coming apart. To cover the 500 kilometres from Dnepropetrovsk to Stalino, they had sometimes marched for twenty hours, struggling through the mud and darkness. On 17 October, the 17th Army and Kleist's redesignated Panzer Army reached the river Mius, taking Taganrog, but the rains and mud halted them there. By early November the Paulus family in Pforzheim reported hopeful rumours that troops who had fought since the start of the campaign would be rotated away from the front and exchanged with those who had been in France. Helmut replied that soldiers' conversations always revolved around 'food, post, leave. Everyone is dreaming day and night of leave.' He promised to eat only pretzels and Danish pastries, and on no account any Russian 'black bread', when he got leave. But he knew too that, as an unmarried man, his own chances of leave were nil.[77]

At the other end of the eastern front, Albert Joos and his comrades were entrenched near the coastline of the Gulf of Finland. A farmer's son who had left school at 13, Joos had begun his diary when he was called up on 28 August 1939. He wanted to chronicle his war 'as a brave person [ready] to give and do everything for the beloved home-land'. After the rigours of agricultural labour, he had coped well with basic training, welcoming the way that the Reich Labour Service and the army had liberated him from the closed and authoritarian world of the village fathers. Almost as soon as Joos had joined Army Group North in mid-October 1941, he had witnessed 'two commissars' being hanged for having blown up a transport train. They stood on the back of a car, the nooses were slung around their necks and the car pulled away. 'What most shocked me', Joos noted, 'was the behaviour of the children, who not only played around the hanged men, but actually went up to them. So, that's Russia.'[78]

After this introduction to the eastern front, Joos's company was sent to take over shallow trenches from an exhausted East Prussian regiment, 20 kilometres west of Strelna. Here they were to shield the German heavy artillery so it could bombard the Soviet naval base at Kronstadt. For three days and nights, Joos and his comrades dug themselves into the hard ground, excavating 60 cubic metres of soil to construct a trench. 'Like herrings', they squeezed inside, fitted it with four bunk beds, built in their own stove, and even found a small glass door to block out the wind. The nearby woodland was full of snipers and Joos's close friend was shot through the mouth and killed. Amid heavy artillery fire and repeated Soviet infantry attacks, the company kept moving, but each time it was harder to dig in and they had to break up the 'stone-hard, frozen ground with hand-grenades'.[79]

Meanwhile, the road to Moscow remained shut. A frontal assault on Tula was driven back after bitter fighting. The 4th Panzer Division was left with only twenty-five tanks and insufficient transport vehicles. Without protective emplacements and with little or no shelter, the ranks of both officers and men were thinning fast through illness. 'To save German blood', the 2nd Panzer Army instructed its divisions to use Soviet prisoners to clear the minefields surrounding the city. Its dwindling stock of heavy weaponry meant that the division's own casualty numbers rose sharply too. Geyr von Schweppenburg, the commander of the 24th Panzer Corps, had to tell Guderian 'that the capacity of the troops and materiel is exhausted'. The official war diary of the 2nd Panzer Army went even further, reporting the first doubts amongst the troops: 'The troops are exhausted, emaciated from the cold and effort. They want to know finally now what is supposed to happen.'[80]

On 1 November, Fritz Farnbacher had been shocked by the sight of a badly wounded Russian lying on the edge of the highway, writhing in wordless agony. 'No one has any time for him; as an enemy, it is terrible to be wounded!' the young lieutenant had concluded. On 20 November it was his closest friend, Peter Siegert, who was hit. Back in the summer, the two had become inseparable. Now, as he sat cradling his dying friend, he could think of nothing but their mothers:

'Everything was empty, everything around me so pointless.' At 2 p.m. Siegert died and Farnbacher felt that 'a piece of [himself]' was left behind too – just like in Uhland's song, 'Ich hatt' einen Kameraden'.[81]

Having failed to capture Tula, the 4th Panzer Division occupied the lignite mining town of Stalinogorsk to the south-east. The divisional command treated the local civilians with hatred and contempt, dubbing them the 'nastiest workers' nest encountered in the Soviet Union'. For the first time, the division took over the functions of an occupying force. The troops no longer differentiated between Red Army units cut off from retreat, untrained local militiamen, civilians and partisans. They quickly came to rely on 'police methods' to secure intelligence, and adopted the tactics of the 'dirty war' of denunciations, interrogations and beatings. A foreman was found to be training the population in shooting and fieldcraft. Another man was discovered with explosives: he had been tasked with blowing up the mine; his wife and son were said to be accomplices. As in Kiev, the Germans did not distinguish between workers who wanted to collaborate in order to survive and dangerous 'Reds'.[82]

Robert R. was ordered to torch the village of Mikhailovka in reprisal for the shooting of four German soldiers. 'The whole village?' he had asked his superior. 'Why?' came the sardonic reply. 'Is it large? Then it's worth the effort at least.' As his unit's personnel carrier reached the machine-tractor station outside the village, Robert had to set up a machine gun before the women and children obeyed the order to leave. They walked into the freezing gloom with no possessions. 'I shouted without feeling and felt like weeping,' Robert noted in his diary, but he avoided executing anyone. Dismissing his machine-gunner, he told the villagers in his broken Russian to report on any further partisan activity or risk even greater reprisals. Thanking him for sparing their lives, they watched the flames springing into the night sky as another German detachment set the village itself alight.[83]

At this critical juncture, when the elite mobile divisions of Army Group Centre were starting to do the tasks normally carried out by the Wehrmacht's security and rear area divisions who worked closely with the police battalions and the SS *Einsatzgruppen*, Reichenau's order of 10 October reached them. The commander of the 4th Panzer Division urged his men to 'become essentially still harder in the struggle against the Bolshevik-Jewish threat'. Driving back to their quarters from a briefing session for company commanders on 17 November, Fritz

Farnbacher learned from his captain that the 'key point is ruthless action and crack down against the Russians'. As the young pietist squirmed inside, he tried to find some kind of inner distance from what he had heard: 'What was laid out in several hours of discussion is not in itself fundamentally German', he concluded. Meanwhile, the division issued new and clear 'Watch-words for the day':

> 21.11.41: Carrier and inciter of the Bolshevik idea is the Jew.
>
> German soldier, always consider, where Jews still live, there is no security behind the front. Jewish civilians and partisans do not belong in the prisoner-of-war camps, they are to be shot . . .
>
> 25.11.41: The population must be more fearful in its bones of German measures than of the terror of roaming Bolshevik remnants and partisans. For Bolshevik subhumans, there is no mercy, not for women and children either. Partisans and accomplices to the next tree![84]

In the following weeks, such mottos justified burning villages, killing inhabitants who resisted or seemed suspect, or driving them out into the freezing snow and forests. German soldiers now acted on their own initiative and began killing Jews and shooting Soviet prisoners rather than taking them to distant reception points. Judging how to respond to civilian threats was no longer the prerogative of senior officers, and the log of official executions dwindled. As this central element of military discipline disappeared, the genocidal war of the rear finally caught up with the front line. There was no shortage of prosaic reasons for killing civilians, let alone the Red Army soldiers who had remained at large in the forests. The further the Germans advanced and the thinner and more isolated their lines became, the more they feared the partisans. Their anxieties were justified. By late December, partisan units were able to retake villages and towns, even from Schweppenburg's elite 24th Panzer Corps.[85]

Often German 'pacification' measures had more to do with soldiers' sense of isolation and vulnerability than with any real threat from partisans or civilians. Fritz Farnbacher still chronicled instances where 'suspicious' civilians were killed, but he was becoming harder to shock. He decided his men should return to villages where they had requisitioned food before, rather than forage further afield and risk landmines, even if it meant 'taking their last cow away!' As the Germans shivered and huddled together in their thin grey lines against the vastness of the white landscape, the snow effaced landmarks and even removed the distinction between land and sky, both lost in a blend of grey and white.[86]

While the Reichenau order spread through the German Army on the eastern front, the verbal assault on the Jews also reached a new height. Hitler opened the rhetorical floodgates himself on 2 October, with his Proclamation to the soldiers on the eastern front to take Moscow, declaring that their key foes were 'Jews and only Jews!' The next day, he repeated the point to the home front in a speech at the Berlin Sportpalast. On 8 November, the anniversary of the Beer Hall Putsch, Hitler lectured his audience about how he had 'come to know these Jews as world arsonists'. The 'entire national intelligentsia' of Russia 'had been slaughtered and a mindless, forcibly proletarianised sub-humanity left behind over which an enormous organisation of Jewish commissars – that is in reality slave-holders – rules'. Hitler hammered his point home: 'This struggle is now, my old Party comrades, really a struggle not just for Germany but for the whole of Europe, a struggle to be or not to be!'[87] The turn to apocalyptic rhetoric was unmistakable as Germany took on the mantle of a pan-European crusade against 'Judaeo-Bolshevism'. Goebbels devoted his regular article in the weekly *Das Reich* on 16 November 1941 to telling his readers that 'The Jews are guilty'. He also reminded them of the Führer's 'prophecy' of 1939 that the Jews would perish if they started another European war:

We are now witnessing the fulfilment of this prophecy; the fate befalling the Jews is harsh, but it is more than deserved. Pity or regret is completely out of place in this case. In triggering this war, world Jewry completely miscalculated the forces it could muster. It is now gradually being engulfed by the same extermination process that it had intended for us and that it would have allowed to happen without any scruples, had it had the power to do so. But now it undergoes destruction according to its own law: 'An eye for an eye, a tooth for a tooth!'[88]

*

Poorly shod, poorly clothed and poorly fed, the 4th Panzer Division was still meant to attack. The frontal assault on Tula having failed,

Guderian tried to keep the momentum going, bypassing the town to the south-east and pressing on towards Kolomna and the eastern outskirts of Moscow. On 24 November, the 2nd Panzer Army took Venev and Mikhailov, and moved on Kashira, a town which the Red Army could not afford to lose because it supplied Tula's power. Here, on 30 November, in a lull in the fighting outside this town east of Moscow, Robert R. took time out to write to Maria. Two days earlier their vehicle had broken down and had to be pushed through the snow in the midst of an artillery bombardment. Robert jotted down briefly what happened when a shell fragment hit one of his comrades: 'R. Anton is hit, ripping his chest open. He dies. Before marching off G. has to paint a sign for the graves quickly. No wreath, no steel helmet.' Robert's thoughts were dwelling ever more on death. Only his young son helped anchor him to the hope that 'so much has been promised for the future and He who promised it to us does not lie.' After helping to burn down the village of Mikhailovka, Robert had fallen prey to a new bitterness and self-doubt. A fortnight later, he had been sent back to Mtsensk to recuperate and given light guard duty at a prisoner-of-war camp. The sick and starving prisoners he saw there left Robert unable to eat for most of the three days of his posting.[89]

Robert spared Maria from sharing in these experiences but he did tell her about his state of mind:

> I've very seldom wept. Weeping is no way out as long as you are in the thick of things. Only when I'm back with you again, resting and getting over it, will we have to weep a great deal and it will also help you to understand your husband . . . 'Sympathy' here is pointless, if it replaces help and action. What is growing is a feeling of human poverty and the guilt of mankind, which has its roots in each individual. A deep shame is growing. Sometimes I am even ashamed to be loved.[90]

What he feared most now was his own moral disintegration, the 'inner decay in place of the external one'. His sole remedy remained 'love and the secret [of the] family'. It was to be his final letter. As the Germans were slowly driven back, Robert R. was severely wounded on 4 December. His comrades carried him for 7 kilometres, but were unable to save him. They found a fitting spot to bury him near the entrance to a Soviet school. The four school exercise books in which Robert had kept his diary were brought home to his wife Maria by one of his comrades.[91]

The Germans redoubled their effort to take Tula, this time by encirclement. But, as an officer in the 4th Panzer Division's 12th Rifle Regiment complained, the men were 'underfed, overtired, badly clothed', their fighting power 'frighteningly slight'. Fritz Farnbacher realised that his comrades in the division's artillery were exhausted too. They prayed that the Red Army was even weaker than they were, a hope shared by divisional command. On 2 December, the 24th Panzer Corps at last managed to cut the Tula–Moscow road and, the next day, they severed the last rail link between Tula and Serpukhov. At temperatures of −32 ⁰C, General Gotthard Heinrici's 43rd Army Corps was desperately fighting its way through to them from the west. But the Germans could not bridge a final 9-kilometre gap to complete the encirclement. On 5 December, Guderian halted the attacks and persuaded the commander of Army Group Centre, Fedor von Bock, to let him call off the offensive. He relinquished his headquarters at Tolstoy's old house at Yasnaya Polyana, leaving seventy German dead buried in the park near the writer's grave, and four Russians hanging in the village square.[92]

7

The First Defeat

At 2 a.m. on 6 December 1941, Soviet artillery and mortars began shelling the lines of the 12th Rifle Regiment of the 4th Panzer Division. It was the night of St Nicholas when parents leave presents in their children's shoes in Germany. On the Russian front, the temperature had dropped to −40°C. When the guns fell silent again, Smilo Freiherr von Lüttwitz sank back into the sleep of an exhausted regimental commander. At 3.30 a.m. he was woken again by the sound of his own side's heavy gun firing back. He sent an adjutant out and discovered that two Red Army battalions had silently infiltrated a long ditch into the middle of the village. Their approach was involuntarily quiet: it was so cold that neither side's rifles and machine guns would fire. Lüttwitz's men were saved only because they had set up one machine gun under the overhang of a roof, which kept it warm enough to work. With it they managed to drive the attackers back.[1]

The leading sections of the German vanguard immediately registered that their fortunes had changed for the worse. Stranded in the snows where their attack on the Tula–Moscow road had stalled, the beleaguered panzer divisions and the 43rd Army Corps were the most exposed to the Soviet counter-attack which began that night. It took longer for this realisation to percolate through to the rest of the German vanguard. On 6 December Lieutenant Hans Reinert's main worry was trying to stay awake in his stuffy staff hut as he busied himself with the 296th Infantry Division's operational plans. He did not register that anything had changed until the following night, when he was woken again and again by urgent phone calls. Staring bleary-eyed at the massed waves of attacking infantry, Reinert found it hard to fathom how Soviet commanders could be so profligate with their men's lives. Nor could he grasp where these new masses of troops had come from: 'It's like a river. You can divert it, but then more fresh water flows down it.' He found the purpose of the attack equally baffling:

And it's not a battle for a continuous front. It's a battle for settlements. There's nothing between them! . . . We keep asking ourselves why the Russians make these pointless attacks, repeatedly at the same positions which we have now closed up around, so that nothing can escape us any more. What are they trying to achieve? Yes, maybe they'll get some settlements, [but] so what?

The divisional staff calculated that this one engagement alone cost the Red Army at least 2,000 men.[2]

It was not only Hans Reinert and Smilo von Lüttwitz who were taken by surprise by the Red Army's enormous counter-offensive. As late as 4 December, the staff of Army Group Centre as a whole had been confident that, with their own offensive tailing off, they were about to see a long winter lull. According to their intelligence, the Red Army could not 'launch a counter-offensive with the forces currently available'. They could not have been more wrong. In mid-October, a mere 90,000 men had defended Moscow. Six weeks later, the Soviets had raised whole new armies from scratch and moved experienced troops from the Far East, so that the capital was now defended by over a million men, equipped with 8,000 guns and mortars, 720 tanks and 1,370 aircraft. Buoyed by their successes – and still more by the biblical scale of Soviet losses in the autumn battles – the Germans continued to underestimate the strength and striking power of their enemy. From the Chief of the General Staff, Franz Halder, and the commander of Army Group Centre, Fedor von Bock, down to brigade and regimental commanders such as Eberbach and Lüttwitz, and on to junior officers like Fritz Farnbacher and Hans Reinert, the entire German chain of command remained convinced of their own superiority. They clung to the comforting belief that the Red Army remained on the point of collapse despite all the mounting evidence to the contrary. This was a delusion born of a habit of victory, which gave an extraordinary unity of perspective to German soldiers on the eastern front. Events over the following months would shatter the supreme confidence with which they had set off to conquer Moscow, but the illusions they had about their own capacity to go on fighting and winning against the odds would survive.[3]

The German encirclement of Moscow had frozen to a halt in mid-execution, the front lines shaped like a great, lopsided crescent, 600 kilometres from end to end. The horns of the assault, led by the tank divisions, were the first targets of attack, and as they recoiled they exposed the main body of the German 4th and 9th Armies which held the middle of the front on both sides of the Moscow highway. For much of December, January and February, the whole of Army Group Centre would be threatened with destruction. The northern horn of the German attack had closed to within 30 kilometres of the Kremlin, the crews of Georg-Hans Reinhardt's 3rd Panzer Group briefly winning the crucial bridgehead over the Moscow–Volga canal, the last physical barrier before the northern suburbs of the city. It was here that elite Red Army troops, drawn from the Siberian, Far Eastern and Central Asian divisions, launched their counter-attack on 6 December. Within a day, Reinhardt was reporting that his best troops were 'no longer . . . operational' and that it was 'impossible to seal off enemy penetrations or even launch counter-thrusts'. With Soviet tanks suddenly appearing in their rear, the Germans succumbed to a *Panzer-Schreck* of their own. The official diary of the panzer group which two weeks earlier had looked poised to take Moscow betrayed something of its present straits: 'Many individual soldiers can be seen here and there with a horse-sleigh or leading a cow . . . The men themselves look indifferent . . . Practically nobody is contemplating repulsing the many enemy air raids. Soldiers killed by bombs are simply left lying there.'[4]

It was even worse around Tula and Kashira in the south. For Eberbach's crack 5th Panzer Brigade of the 4th Panzer Division, the situation quickly became 'critical', as they were forced to retreat before the Soviet counter-attack. Vehicles would not start and had to be abandoned, alongside much of the equipment they had carried. Compared to the 40–50 kilometres a day they had covered during the advance, they were now down to a mere 6.5 kilometres. The dreadful slowness of all movement only added to the retreating Germans' mounting sense of terror and foreboding. The highway from Tula to Orel had become an icy piste, covered in places by drifting snow. Burning ever more scarce fuel just to keep going, the tanks repeatedly had to be dug out of the drifts. With withering irony and tender concern, Fritz Farnbacher surveyed his command:

> You really can't tell what a thrilling business it is each time till the funeral procession gets moving . . . My proud 'family' today looks like: at the front, the boss's car with its front-wheel drive; the differential for the rear-drive croaked yesterday; I fear we may not get over the hills, it's spluttering a bit, but it goes.

And so it went, each precious vehicle patched up in a different way, the leaf springs distorted under the loads, the oil feed leaking, the first aid trailer hooked up to the truck with the field kitchen. 'That's my proud bunch,' Farnbacher concluded.[5]

Things were no better for the 296th Infantry Division, as they were forced to give way before the attacks of the Red Army. While the divisional diary laconically noted the 'Difficult passage . . . in the gullies east of Odoev', Lieutenant Reinert left a more vivid account: 'In icy north wind. Waiting in the dark night till they can get down. Each vehicle can follow at 200-metre intervals, the men holding them back with ropes to stop them from sliding down the icy piste into the gullies.' With carthorses slipping down on their rear haunches into the deep ditches, and the carts and cars after them, men had to keep clambering back up again to lower the next vehicle down. The guns were worst, too heavy to hold. Those that slipped out of control still had to be hauled back out of the way. It took all night for the underfed, inadequately clothed and terrified men to clear the passage, the painful slowness of all movement adding to the cold and fear. On 22 December, Reinert noted, 'Well, the order: Back! We are completely morally done in. I can't describe what we feel in these minutes. It's too enormous. We could howl aloud . . .' By New Year's Day, he was reporting that 'The men suddenly can't march any further, they fall down and die on the spot or freeze to death on the transport to the next shelter. It is a cruel time.' Of the 1,000 casualties suffered by the 296th Infantry Division in December, 351 had frostbite.[6]

In a sombre survey of the state of morale right across its forces, Army Group Centre concluded on 19 December that it had reached crisis point:

The setbacks can be attributed to the physical and mental state of our troops, which has sunk far below the limits of efficiency, fear of being taken prisoner by the Russians, decimated fighting strengths, a shortage of fuel, the strained supply situation, and the poor state of the horses. On top of this, there is a feeling of defencelessness against the heavy Russian tanks . . . This enables the Russians, employing increasingly astounding masses of men despite sometimes extraordinary losses in dead and wounded, to trickle through our own thin lines as a result of the divisions' exceedingly long sectors of the front.

Describing the Soviet breakthroughs into the German rear, which were causing 'chaos', the army group admitted that it could no longer make its own soldiers counter-attack. Under such circumstances, the poorly equipped and scarcely trained new Soviet armies could score very real victories.[7]

As the two armoured horns of Army Group Centre crumpled, the bulk of the German forces facing Moscow came under sustained – and near fatal – attack. From the last week of December until mid-January, the Red Army tore holes in the German lines, threatening to break up and destroy the entire army group. A breach in the southern sector along the Oka left German troops holding Sukhinichi completely surrounded. Taking back Mosalsk, Zhizdra and Kirov, two Soviet armies opened up a huge semicircle, separating the 2nd Panzer Army from the German 4th Army and creating space for four Soviet armies to advance on Iukhnov and the vital Smolensk–Moscow Highway. In the north, it was just as bad. The Soviet 29th Army smashed its way through the German 4th Army Corps at Staritsa on 29–30 December, and advanced on Rzhev, whose low ridge held the key to the German position. Within three days, the Soviet 39th Army succeeded in breaking through west of Rzhev and swung southwards towards Sychevka. Beyond Sychevka lay Vyaz'ma and the Smolensk–Moscow Highway. It looked as if the Soviet counter-attack was now poised to exploit these gaps in order to execute the kind of huge encirclement which the Germans had used to such effect during the summer and autumn battles. On 12 January, the Red Army opened up a second major gap in the north, at Volokolamsk.[8]

To the south, things were even worse. Instead of supporting the desperately under-resourced attack on Tula, the 2nd Army had been ordered further south-east to occupy the approaches to the Upper Don, the General Staff's post-Moscow objective. The Soviet counter-attack now found the 2nd Army stranded in the snowy wastes near Efremov, completely isolated from both its neighbours, the 2nd Panzer Army and Army Group South. By 8 December, the Red Army tore a 30-kilometre hole in the German lines, encircling three infantry divisions. By 14 December, Field Marshal Bock anticipated that the 134th Infantry Division might just get through but not the shattered remnants of the 45th; in fact, the commander of the 134th had shot himself the day before. The official diary of the 45th Infantry Division reported 'ghostly night marches':

> Occasionally the thick ice-cold snowstorm abated and some visibility returned. Everywhere in the east was lit up by huge fires. Parts of the route are covered over and only to be found with the help of locals . . . The whole day, the storm whipped up the fine, powder snow without ceasing and drove it into eyes and faces, till it felt like being in a painful hailstorm . . . It was easy for him [the enemy] to bring his shock troops up to our lines under cover of the snow clouds, so that they were only seen at the last moment.[9]

Here retreat became a panic-ridden flight, with vehicles, horses, heavy weapons, field kitchens, tools, sacks of flour and spare parts simply abandoned. In order to restore discipline, the commander of the 2nd Army, General Rudolf Schmidt, ordered 'individuals who make defeatist remarks to be singled out and shot as an example'. For the men of the 45th, raised in Linz, comradeship born out of the fear of being left behind helped to keep their narrow columns of dark-clad figures together and moving through the blizzard of white. With no idea where the German lines lay, they depended on local guides, who were often shot afterwards to prevent them revealing their route to their pursuers. Without horses or motor transport, the Germans were forced to drag their wounded on sledges. Between 5 and 17 December, their dead amounted to 233 men, with another 232 missing; but they brought back another 567 wounded. In the end, German planes found them, and, like a variation of 'Hansel and Gretel', dropped leaflets to guide their line of march. On 17 December, after eleven days of retreating, as the winter sun was setting, the column met a single German, the liaison officer for the 56th Infantry Division. Having finally reached the safety of their own lines, the divisional command made a swift assessment: 'Battle-worthiness of the troops zero, because totally exhausted.'[10]

A week later, on 25 December, the divisional doctor concluded that many soldiers were suffering from 'nervous exhaustion'. Their clothing had been wet through, their boots poor and worn through for months. He estimated that some 70 per cent of the men were suffering from frostbite, 40 per cent from diarrhoea and vomiting, and all were utterly lice-ridden. Yet, despite their losses and complete encirclement, they had not been destroyed. This narrow difference still separated them from the fate of Napoleon's Grande Armée. Throughout that winter, while they waited for replacements to reach them from France and Austria, the men from the 45th Infantry Division remained in the front line.

Everywhere, the crisis prompted thoughts of defeat. General Gotthard Heinrici, who had led the infantry attack on the Tula highway, wrote home ten days into the Soviet counter-offensive, predicting that 'we can't recover from the blow, for so much is done for'. Fritz Farnbacher could not stop thinking about 'Napoleon's Russian experiences'. He was not alone in seeing the shadow of 1812.[11]

*

In the rear, a fresh crisis was engulfing Dulag 203, one of the many transit camps for prisoners of war. Despite Konrad Jarausch's best efforts to dole out food three times a day, he had to admit by 4 January 1942 that he was failing. Prisoner numbers in his section of the camp had risen to 3,000 again and, after months of stripping the surrounding countryside bare, the requisitioning parties were coming back empty-handed. By now typhus fever had also broken out in the camp. On 8 January 1942, he complained to his wife that he had to use his fists so often to keep order when food arrived that his right hand had become swollen. The situation was worse than ever.

'Hundreds move in the camp around us who are dying of famine,' he confessed to her. 'Each distribution of food is a tragedy. The cravings become ever greater till complete exhaustion and indifference set in.' Even if more provisions arrived in the next few days, it would be too late. Two days later, he reckoned twenty prisoners were dying a day. One Russian prisoner told him, 'Hitler promised us bread and good treatment and now, after we voluntarily gave ourselves up, we are all dying.'[12]

The tragedy being played out in Dulag 203 was a microcosm of a human disaster which, for the time being, overshadowed even the *Einsatzgruppen* killings of the Jews. The winter retreat exacerbated the crisis of providing for the 3.2 million Soviet prisoners of war, and epidemics swept through the camps. When the Nazi regime realised in November that it badly needed to deploy prisoners of war to make up for labour shortages in Germany, very few of them were found to be fit enough to be sent to the Reich. On 13 January, Jarausch thanked his wife for all her letters. 'The love which speaks from them warms me and fills me with thanks,' he assured her. 'Now, take care, you and the child.' He did not tell her that he too had contracted typhus and was writing from the field hospital at Roslavl. A fortnight later, Konrad Jarausch was dead. By that time, at least two million Soviet prisoners had perished in German custody.[13]

It was not easy to reverse the annihilatory principles on which the German campaign had been planned. On the contrary, the winter retreat bound the German Army in the East (*Ostheer*) together in a common culture marked by mass slaughter. In the summer, the orders from the High Command to execute political commissars and Jewish communists had been interpreted in widely divergent ways, with some divisions screening out all their Jewish prisoners and others not. In October, the Reichenau order was promulgated in Army Group South. It took a further month to reach the other two army groups, coinciding with the final, faltering stages of the German advance, when elite tank divisions took on policing villages to the rear. As they now adopted the same methods of interrogation, pacification and terror practised by the German security divisions behind the lines, they entered a new phase of the war, where decisions on the life and death of Red Army prisoners and civilians were made on the spot without recourse to higher authority.

The retreat quickened this process, reshaping the entire outlook and self-understanding of the eastern front.

Faced with an existential threat, the retreating Germans tried to slow down the Soviet counter-offensive by all and any means. As it began its withdrawal from the Tula area on 7 December 1941, the 103rd Tank Artillery Regiment destroyed anything that could be of use to the enemy. 'Anishino is burning. Every single house is set alight once the troops have left,' Fritz Farnbacher noted. 'I don't set alight the one we stayed in; instead, others do it. The commander too isn't in favour. But it has to be done, just to slow the Russians a bit. We also aren't allowed to ask if the civilian population starves, freezes or dies in some other way.' Retreating troops torched villages and towns, blew up bridges and railway lines and wrecked industrial and power plants. With temperatures regularly down to −30 °C and −40 °C, the soldiers shed their last remaining moral scruples and drove the entire civilian population out of their villages. It bought the Wehrmacht a small time buffer over the pursuing Red Army, but no more. Weeks before Hitler ordered the German Army in the East, on 21 December, to pursue a 'scorched earth' policy it had already become common practice. As Farnbacher tried to square events with his Protestant conscience he sought consolation in the thought that

> I still haven't fired a single shot, neither with a cannon, a pistol nor a rifle or machine gun, I haven't slaughtered a single chicken or goose, still not set fire to a house, still not given the order to shoot a single Russian, and still not been present at an execution; how strange, almost unbelievable that sounds! But I am so grateful for it. There has been enough murdering, burning, destruction in this most ill-fated of all wars!

But he did not question the military logic of the orders, given 'just to slow the Russians down a bit'. By 17 December, he wondered as he wrote up his diary in the evening and looked across the hut at their hosts, 'whether their roof will be burned over their heads all too soon'.[14]

The Germans mastered their existential crisis by perpetrating extreme violence. It made no difference which part of the Reich the units were recruited from or whether their civilian environment had been hostile to or supportive of National Socialism. Drawn from the Ruhr working class and with an equal mix of Protestants and Catholics, the 253rd Infantry Division went through the same transformation as more Nazified divisions drawn from the countryside. The retreat fomented a potent mixture of rage and fear: rage at having to destroy their own vehicles, guns and heavy equipment and give up territory they had fought hard for; shock at the Soviets' ability to handle the winter conditions so much better than themselves; terror at their own lack of secure lines to which to retreat. Neither side was taking prisoners any longer. Farnbacher envisaged that when the Soviets saw 'the burnt villages and the soldiers shot on the roadside' they would take no Germans alive. On 30 December, he was met with 'almost bestial' guffaws when he asked a group of German engineers what information they had gained from the thirty Russian prisoners they were supposed to bring to the collection point. He was shocked by the way they admitted to killing them 'as a matter of course'. While part of him was outraged, realising how much the men had changed from five months earlier, another part felt compelled to jot down a justification: 'Just no mercy for these vultures and beasts!'[15]

Farnbacher realised that he himself had become 'hard and ruthless'. With its double connotations of 'hardness' and 'toughness', *Härte* had long been a male, military virtue in Germany. Hitler Youths were taught to strive for it, and soldiers sought to master it during their months of basic training and first 'baptisms' of fire. During the final, difficult weeks of the retreat from Moscow, the 4th Panzer Division's chief doctor noted with approval how the men had learned to be 'hard on themselves'. The word was now acquiring something of the meaning Hitler gave it in closed briefing sessions, when he used 'hard' as a metaphor for genocidal measures. Hinting at the process of self-brutalisation, 'hard' and 'harsh' increasingly complemented the sacralising language of heroic self-sacrifice used in both official and private accounts.[16]

Near the coast of the Gulf of Finland, Albert Joos chronicled a similar process of 'hardening', as he and his comrades weathered the winter war of position. With little protection as the temperature fell to −30 °C in the second half of December, Joos had begun to suffer terrible headaches. All month they continued building out their positions at night and enduring machine-gun and mortar attacks during the day. As was his wont, Albert Joos spent New Year reviewing not just the last year, but his 'whole past life' in order to perceive 'the Lord's unlimited power and providence out of this . . . confusion of life'. He affirmed his 'unshakeable faith in the Lord and with it the trust that He will also direct things for my best in this year. With this trust I will remain upright in this year too and master my life with a sense of duty.' His patriotic fervour may have been more Catholic than National Socialist, but his sense of personal duty was at least as keen.[17]

In January, things got worse. Soviet artillery began firing shrapnel at their trenches and, as the temperature plummeted to −40 °C, the gunners aimed at the German field kitchens, depriving the soldiers of warm food. Their own sentries had to be relieved every hour because of the extreme cold and when Joos, now an acting sergeant, went on his rounds his earmuffs froze to his skin. They had to use hand grenades to excavate the frozen soil. After each snowstorm, as drifts filled the German trenches, the Red Army men attacked in massed waves, only to be mown down by the German machine guns. Without access to a priest or religious services, the farmer's son confessed to his diary in order 'to keep a balance of my life, to consider what is right and wrong and to keep perspective'. Fumbling in the cold to get the words down, Albert Joos concluded, 'Very rarely are people subjected in their lives to such brutalisation [*Verrohung*] and forced to live in such primitive conditions as in the trenches.' He did not exclude himself from this process. Trench warfare had also schooled him to focus narrowly on survival and killing: 'the continual lying in wait for the enemy, in order to do him in at any opportunity, that lets one become properly harsh [*roh*].' Existential fear now turned Nazi propaganda about Jewish-Bolshevism, treacherous civilians and dangerous partisans into common sense. However nagging the lingering scruples of individuals, who recognised with distaste how 'hard', 'harsh', 'brutal' and 'coarse' they themselves had become, the collective self-transformation of the eastern front was complete.[18]

Hans Albring survived the winter months in the small town of Velizh, in the rear of Army Group Centre. Coming under attack in late January 1942, here the Germans held out for eight weeks in fearful conditions. Unwashed, lice-ridden and hungry, Hans emerged from the ordeal convinced that 'comparison with the Apocalypse is not

On the eve: Irene Reitz and Ernst Guicking.

Fathers and sons:
August and Karl-Christoph Töpperwien.

Fathers and sons:
Wilm and Helmut Hosenfeld.

The Polish view: 10-year-old Kazimiera Mika finds her older sister, killed by a German plane while digging potatoes in Warsaw.

The German view, from the nose of a Heinkel He 111 P bomber.

Frieda and Josef Rimpl's wedding: he was executed for conscientious objection in December 1939.

Ernst Guicking reading *Das Reich* in France.

Top: Practising air raid defence:
Berlin, 1939.

Left: Liselotte Purper
with her Rolleiflex.

Right: Jews crossing from one part of the Łódź ghetto to another.

Below: 'Repatriation': ethnic Germans from Romania boarding a Danube steamer.

Café in Cracow.

Café in Paris.

German soldiers visit a synagogue converted into a brothel in Brest, France.

Enforcing racial separation at home: a German woman and her Polish lover tied to a pillory in Eisenach, 15 November 1940.

Fritz Probst (extreme right), Christmas 1939.

Kurt Orgel (second from right), January 1945.

too far-fetched'. But he was able to tell his friend Eugen Altrogge on 21 March that 'what I have gained in experience is greater than what I lost'. By mid-April, two weeks after the Red Army had finally stopped its attacks, Hans seized eagerly on a letter from one of his Catholic mentors in Münster, quoting it at length to Eugen, in support of the view he had formed: '"And, who knows, perhaps this is the meta-physical meaning of the war, that a new and true image of humanity is arising in us, after we have followed a false, and increasingly distorting, image of humanity for so many hundreds of years."'[19]

★

On 17 February 1942, Corporal Anton Brandhuber slipped away from his battalion at Aleksandrovka, while it was being marched towards the German front line. A veteran of the campaigns of 1939 and 1940, Brandhuber had found himself amongst hastily despatched replace-ments from Lower Austria, in which raw recruits rubbed shoulders with experienced soldiers like himself. Their train took them as far as Orel. From there, they marched for three days through −40°C degree blizzards. Periodically bombed by the Red Air Force, the men had been kept moving by their pistol-toting officers. They were on their way to shore up the depleted lines of the 45th Infantry Division, the division from Linz which had narrowly escaped the encirclement of the 2nd Army in December. Scanning the faces of the troops they met returning from the front to see what awaited him, Brandhuber saw only 'drained, over-tired and distrustful and miserable' men. At halts, they spoke of their winter retreat and of the enormous amounts of equipment they had had to abandon.[20]

Perhaps his experience of the campaigns against Poland and France had given Anton Brandhuber a heightened sense of present danger. He set off from Aleksandrovka alone, and when he had walked back 15 kilometres along the road they had come, he buried his rifle along with his gas mask and cartridge case under the snow and ate his bread. Still in his uniform, but now without most of his equipment, Brandhuber managed to hitch a ride from a passing car to the next railway junction, where he made his way to sidings. Mingling with the lightly wounded, he climbed on to a train which took him via Orel to Gomel, and then through Bryansk to Minsk. At Orel, a Russian woman took him in but for most of the time, Brandhuber slept in station waiting rooms, stealing bread from army bakeries.

The German military police regularly patrolled railway stations on the lookout for deserters, and travelling further west Corporal Brandhuber was picked up by German patrols twice, at Brest Litovsk and Warsaw. Each time the officers were persuaded that this campaign-hardened and dependable-looking non-commissioned officer had simply been separated from his unit, despite his conspicuous lack of equipment. Instead of arresting him, they bawled at him to proceed back to Orel and rejoin the 45th Infantry Division as quickly as possible. Once they were safely out of sight, Brandhuber continued westwards. At Brest, he paid an engine driver with two packets of tobacco to ride in his cab all the way to Warsaw. There, after narrowly avoiding arrest for the second time, he spotted in the sidings a passenger train bound for Vienna, which he took as far as Bludenz and Buchs. He crossed the Swiss border on 27 February, exactly ten days, 3,000 kilometres and 3 kilos of bread after he absconded at Aleksandrovka.

Anton Brandhuber was both an experienced soldier and the most unmilitary of men. He explained his motives to the Swiss military officers who interrogated him with a laconic brevity worthy of the good soldier Schweik: 'It just seemed too stupid to me.' He did not want to make a career in the Wehrmacht; and in early 1942 he was worried about how he would fare in the event of a German victory. He was not interested in becoming the administrator of a large collective farm in Russia, and he did not want to serve in an army of occupation. Nor had he developed any strong attachment to his comrades. He just wanted his old life back, on the family farm in Laa an der Thaya in Lower Austria, with its three horses, seven cows, a dozen pigs and 8 hectares of land. That was where he had grown up and where the 87-year-old Brandhuber was still to be found in the summer of 2001, as self-contained and unforthcoming as ever. He had nothing to add to the explanation he had given the Swiss military for his desertion fifty-nine years before, telling the young German historian who came to interview him in almost identical terms: 'I didn't fancy it any more.'[21]

Military pronouncements and Nazi propaganda emphasised again and again that deserters were traitors and cowards, men who abandoned and imperilled their comrades and who selfishly and cunningly undermined their efforts to hold the line. What was so remarkable about Anton Brandhuber was that he did not try to repudiate these accusations. On the contrary, he acknowledged that he fled precisely because he did not want to be a soldier and because he did not like what he saw on the eastern front in February 1942. Like others, he was dismayed by the brutality of this German war, by the devastation of the Belorussian and Russian towns and countryside and by the killing of Jews – which he had witnessed at close hand on his way through Orel. Other German deserters told stories to their Swiss interrogators which justified their flight as a response to earlier run-ins with military authority or to being mistakenly sent to court martial for things they had not done, and virtually all of them went to great lengths to repudiate the implication that deserters were selfish cowards by stressing their military records of heroic devotion to their comrades. Brandhuber stands out because he did none of these things, telling a tale which lacked any trace of the language of Nazism or the German military. Whereas another Catholic farmer's son like Albert Joos filled the pages of his diary with patriotic duty, comradeship and sacrifice, these powerful emotional appeals did not exercise a hold on Anton Brandhuber. Even amongst the idiosyncratic ranks of German deserters he stands out for being so unaffected by the values of his age.

It was extremely difficult for soldiers to escape from the front line. The proximity of the German and Soviet lines encouraged each side to use megaphones to encourage desertion. By everything from idealistic appeals to international working-class solidarity to promises of decent food, Germans were exhorted to cross the lines. It was dangerous, but not impossible: since small scouting parties went out on regular nightly patrols, men could slip away, hoping to be brought in by a raiding party from the other side. But eyewitness accounts of finding the mutilated corpses of German soldiers who had tried to surrender were told and retold within German units, acting as a serious deterrent and, in turn, legitimising further killings of Soviet prisoners. The only real prospect of successful flight lay in the German rear, but it was extremely difficult to travel along the roads and railway lines westwards, find shelter and food, without being detected. Perhaps because so few men attempted to do so, the military police patrols who stopped Brandhuber at Brest and Warsaw were inclined to believe that he had been accidentally separated from his unit.[22]

During the war several hundred other German deserters managed to cross the Swiss border, where, like Brandhuber, they were inter-rogated and interned by the Swiss military. Compared to the high stakes of appearing before a German military court, testifying to the Swiss gave these men the opportunity to craft just the kind of heroic account of themselves that Brandhuber eschewed. One such was Gerhard Schulz, who left his unit at Le Creusot and crossed the Swiss border on 15 March 1942 near St-Gingolph on Lake Geneva. He held the Swiss officers enthralled by a graphic tale of his flight, his military heroism on the eastern front and his disenchantment with Nazism. He described how the SS shot prisoners, and how they staged their fight against the partisans to provide material for the film crews of the propaganda companies. But his real ire was reserved for his own officers. Instead of eating the same food as their men, they 'always kept the best pieces for themselves'. As the non-commissioned officer responsible for provisioning, Schulz had done his best to bring rations up to his front-line unit. He told a good story, and his account of assaulting concrete bunkers so impressed his interrogators that they had it distributed to all Swiss military trainers.[23]

It was all a story. At 19, Schulz was neither a non-commissioned officer, nor had he been on the eastern front through the winter. In fact, he had been sent back to the west to recover from an intestinal infection at the end of August 1941, and it was the prospect of returning to the eastern front which actually prompted him to desert. Yet Gerhard Schulz impressed the Swiss officers so much that they decided to train him as an agent. Equipping him with a new German identity and Wehrmacht uniform, they sent him back into Germany in the summer of 1942, with instructions to gather intelligence on German anti-aircraft defences near the border. Schulz promptly did something even more surprising. He deserted for a second time, turning himself in to the German military.

In making their unusual choices, both Anton Brandhuber and Gerhard Schulz were swayed by their families. As soon as Schulz recrossed the border, he broke his cover by going home and visiting his parents and fiancée in Freiburg. Interviewed in 2002 at the age of

81, Schulz claimed that his reappearance even prompted his mother to convert to Catholicism. But whatever their fears for him, his mother and fiancée were united in persuading him to turn himself in.

Lack of family support for desertion goes some way towards explaining why it never became a mass phenomenon in Germany during the Second World War. Where mass desertion did occur – in Italy in 1943, for example, or amongst recruits to the Wehrmacht from annexed regions of Poland, Luxembourg and Alsace and members of the Bosnian SS Division in 1943–44 – it depended on the willingness of civilian society to absorb and hide men en masse, rendering the authorities relatively powerless. In the heartlands of Germany and Austria, there were no cases of mass desertion until the final weeks of the war. Until it became a mass phenomenon, the apparatus of terror remained effective precisely because it only had to target relatively isolated individuals. But exhortations of loyalty and patriotism were not just external demands imposed by the regime; they were maxims repeated within civilian society at all levels, ending with the most powerful and primary appeals of all – from mothers, fathers, wives and lovers.[24]

*

Army Group Centre, to which Anton Brandhuber was being sent, had lost 229,000 men in the push to Moscow, only 150,000 of whom were replaced. By the start of February 1942, it had lost a further 378,000 men and received a mere 60,000 replacements. Morale had plummeted: a doctor in the 2nd Panzer Army warned in early February 1942 that the 'hitherto unbounded trust of the troops in the leadership' had sunk rapidly, and their 'spiritual powers of resistance' were cracking. That month, the High Command commissioned a special report on morale in the 4th Army. Its conclusion made uncomfortable reading: 'The men [are] completely apathetic, incapable of carrying or servicing weapons; the remnants of companies are dispersed over kilometres; they hobble along in pairs using the rifles to prop themselves up, their feet wrapped in rags. When they were spoken to, they didn't hear or they began to weep.' By March, the Army High Command accepted that 104 of its 162 divisions on the eastern front were barely capable of defending themselves: no more than eight divisions were ready for offensive operations. Morale was disastrously low, and upbeat propaganda only made it worse. On 27 December, Fritz Farnbacher's artillery unit tuned their radio in, 'but you soon can't listen any more to it; what rubbish they talk!' As the High Command's special report on morale noted, among senior officers, from commanders of divisions upwards, the mood remained 'one of unanimous and intense bitterness', and the 'general tone of all criticism is: "The catastrophe this winter could have been avoided, if they had listened to us. Our warnings were as clear as they could have been. Nobody listens to us, either they are not reading our reports or they are not taking them seriously. Nobody wants to know the truth . . ."' In particular, these commanders wanted to regain the power to take decisions in the field, rather than having to spend weeks negotiating with the High Command:

> We know how to defend ourselves, but our hands are tied. We cannot act on our own initiative. The order to hold out at all costs, given solemnly to the troops and rescinded hours later under the force of circumstances, only means that instead of making an orderly withdrawal, we are being pushed back by the enemy. This results in heavy, irreplaceable losses of men and equipment.[25]

What is most extraordinary about the winter crisis, however, is what did *not* happen. The ill-clad, frostbitten, demoralised men held their lines. Morale might be at rock bottom, but very few men followed Anton Brandhuber's example. Instead, low morale expressed and dissipated itself in the world of bickering and petty conflicts, humour and violence. Helmut Paulus was irritated by his new officer, fresh from the regimental staff, 'where he definitely never sat in a foxhole', who made them do pointless inspections and drill when they were being rested from the lines in late October 1941. He told Helmut off for wearing a shabby uniform, while the sergeant major – another 'hero of the rear' – angered him by calling him, after four months' uninterrupted service at the front, a 'mummy's boy'. Even receiving the Iron Cross 2nd Class was marred by the fact that the Master of Arms, who 'himself never went on an attack but always stayed behind with the field kitchen', was awarded the decoration at the same time. In his artillery regiment, Fritz Farnbacher often felt he was the unwanted junior staff officer, caught like a 'maid of all work' between his men and the demands of his superiors. He fretted too that men below him in rank had already been awarded the Iron Cross 1st Class while he was still wearing the 2nd Class medal.[26]

Helmut Paulus's father, a veteran of the First World War, rushed to add Helmut's name to the list of those awarded the Iron Cross 2nd Class which was published in the local newspaper. Conscious of the social status to which his son ought to aspire, Paulus *père* kept urging Helmut to volunteer for officers' training. Even his mother joined the fray. As the father of an infantryman, Dr Paulus resented the preferential treatment given to the other service arms. His letters describe meeting other people's sons in the Luftwaffe and the artillery, showered with leave and decorations and given time to do specialist training or qualify in chemistry – Helmut's chosen area of study – while his son sweated it out with the infantry in the trenches. Eventually, Helmut felt obliged to reply to his parents' entreaties, explaining his refusal to take the route which his front-line service and high-school education opened up to him: 'Above all, I don't have any love of soldiering,' he wrote; he was certain that 'in time of peace, I would not make a good soldier at all'. Nor did he harbour any ambition to be promoted, preferring the egalitarianism of the trenches where he could appear 'unsoldierly and [display a] petty bourgeois' desire to be left in peace. But, he continued, the 'only exception I make to the standpoint is in battle, where I don't want anyone to have grounds to cast slurs on me'.[27]

The order of ranks may have been much the same as in the First World War but the populist ethos made it a different kind of army from the one Ernst Arnold Paulus had fought in. Helmut had become what soldiers affectionately called a '*Frontschwein*' (front pig), and he prided himself on being a battle-hardened *Landser*, 'squaddie'. Whatever his problems with his superiors, Corporal Paulus could still write that 'My comrades, whom I've lived through so much with, make me happy again.'[28] In March 1942 – at the absolute low point of German morale on the eastern front – he proudly sent a long poem home, which one of his comrades had written about the capture of Dnepropetrovsk:

The City on the Dniepr

There, where a few days before
the city proudly on the Dniepr stood,

lies, as if it had to fail,
everything in ashes and sand.
Only buildings burning still
And smoking ruins is all you are now.

. . .

If comrades fall,
we take their place.
The enemy host will fall,
we will be victors.[29]

German soldiers' optimism had reached a peak in October 1941, fuelled by the prospect of a rapid victory. In November, as the advance slowed, fewer letters home expressed such confidence. As the prospect of an early end to the war receded, soldiers still needed to believe in a duration they could bear – usually no more than another year. In place of the imminent capture of Moscow, the dream of leave acquired a new intensity. During November and early December, the High Command remained so confident in victory that it began pulling divisions out of the eastern front in order to 'refresh' them in the west, only to have to rush troops back to meet the Soviet counter-offensive. As a result both the armies and the home front were awash with rumours about leave and replacements. Erna Paulus became so convinced that Helmut might return unexpectedly on leave and not be able to get in at night that she left a key for him outside the toilet window on the ground floor. Helmut was more downbeat: he explained to his parents that as an unmarried man he would have to wait a long time before his number came up. He confirmed that 'conversation always revolves around food, post and leave', and, in the absence of leave, letters would have to do.[30]

The crisis of supply on the eastern front also impacted on the military post. Parcels, delivered to the front for free, were limited first to 2-kilo and later 1-kilo packets. By late October, Erna Paulus was sending her son up to three packets a day, containing a warm jumper, winter underwear and apples. As the mail became more erratic, she started listing the parcels she had sent him and begged Helmut to tell her which ones had arrived. Despite the interruptions and delays, the flow of sustenance from home continued: jars of honey and plum and strawberry jam; a pair of boots resoled by their trusted cobbler; the broken watch mended; the infantry campaign medal and the Iron Cross 2nd Class issued for him in Pforzheim, along with home-made Advent biscuits. By early November, Erna Paulus was sending woollens, long johns and mittens, as well as a scarf and chest warmer she had sewn.[31]

This stream of small parcels may have further burdened military transport, as the Wehrmacht attempted to streamline goods traffic and concentrate on getting munitions to the front, but it was absolutely critical to morale. Helmut was hugely appreciative. He loved the food, especially the plum spread. His mother's provisions interrupted the tedium of having 'mainly just lard or tinned sausage' to spread on his bread, and recreated maternal nurture. By early November, he confessed to his parents, he had 'turned into a pure materialist with no other interests than food and now and then the mail'.[32]

December 1941 found Helmut Paulus in a dugout in the front line of Army Group South, guarding the far bank of the river Mius. As darkness fell on Christmas Eve, he and his comrades lit the candles on the little tree which his aunt had sent, draping it with his mother's decorations. One of the men played carols on the mouth organ. Despite the enormous disappointment of not being relieved from the front line on 23 December, as promised, the men had cheered up on Christmas Eve. The post had arrived, bringing a deluge of letters and parcels. Helmut had received 'numerous parcels from home with biscuits, jam, brandy, lemons, [his sister] Irmgard's notebook, the new fountain pen, goose fat'. The new pen was particularly welcome, for just two days earlier the old one had burst when the ink froze. In addition, Helmut was inundated with offerings from friends, relatives and the pastor in Pforzheim, alongside special military rations – 'a mass of baked items, chocolate and spirits'. His second Christmas away at war Helmut preferred to the previous one, spent in St-Aubin in France, where the enforced leisure had made the separation from his family harder to bear. Although the soldiers had to take turns at sentry duty every three hours and expected the 'godless Bolsheviks' to disrupt the celebrations, the night passed quietly. On Boxing Day, they finally withdrew across the river Mius, as the last of the rearguard, to half-finished lines near Krasnyi Luch, where they would stay for the next few months.[33]

While Helmut guarded the retreat to the Mius Line, at home his family made their ritual Christmas visit to their friends the Prellers to play with their model railway. Throughout the autumn and winter, while Helmut was deepening trenches with hand grenades, his father had a garage built on to the side of the house in Pforzheim. By the early spring, Dr Paulus could consider buying a car and taking driving lessons, only to find that restrictions on engine size aimed at limiting petrol use forced him to purchase a small, overpriced, old Hansa. Far from resenting this apparent extravagance, Helmut urged him not to hesitate: as a GP, his father needed the car in order to visit his patients and was risking his health by riding the moped he had relied on throughout the winter.[34]

The huge differences between life at the front and at home did not undermine the emotional bonds between them. On the contrary, home, with all its privileges and seemingly trivial problems, made conditions at the front seem more bearable. Helmut's mother had to manage without a housemaid for much of that winter. When it all felt too much, she wrote to her son, 'then I think of you in Russia and how much a person can bear if he has to, and I think I am pretty privileged in my nice, warm house'. When her nephew Reinhard skated on thin ice and fell through, she thought of how often Helmut and his comrades 'are drenched and have no heating to warm your-selves on!' Writing to Helmut about the incident, or about the mess that Reinhard and her younger son Rudolf had made of the chemistry lab Helmut had set up in the upstairs kitchen, maintained the ties to hearth and home more strongly than any overt patriotic appeal. Helmut Paulus did not need to be told what he was fighting for.[35]

★

A week before the Red Army counter-attacked, on 29 November 1941, Fritz Todt went to see Hitler to tell him that 'this war can no longer be won by military means'. The advice was not offered lightly. As Minister for Armaments, Todt knew better than anyone the state of German materiel. He had done his best to inject new urgency into the armaments effort, but having looked at the balance of German resources and produc-tion, he concluded that Germany could not withstand a prolonged war of attrition against the Soviet Union. Others, like Friedrich Fromm, the head of the army's armaments section and commander of the training army, were telling Franz Halder the same thing.

Todt's advice to end the war did not entirely surprise Hitler. He had toyed with the same thought back in August, when he mused aloud to Goebbels as to whether the Soviet Union and Germany could ever defeat each other. Fritz Todt was one of Hitler's most effective old comrades: the architect of the autobahns and the west defences against France and, most critically, as the man in charge of boosting ammunition production ahead of the attack on France. He had the standing to deliver this bleakest of messages, and, uncharacteristically, Hitler calmly heard him out. At the end, he asked simply, 'How then shall I end the war?' Todt replied, 'It can only be ended politically', warning of the dire consequences should the United States move from supplying Britain and policing the Atlantic convoys to becoming a direct participant in the conflict.[36]

Far from heeding this sound advice, within the fortnight Hitler declared war on the United States. On 11 December, the Nazi leader announced his decision before a specially convened Reichstag, laying the blame on President Roosevelt and his Jewish lobby for 'this historical confrontation, a confrontation that will decisively shape not only the history of Germany but that of Europe, actually that of the entire world, for the next 500 or 1,000 years'. It was the Jews 'who, with Old Testament fanaticism, believe that the United States can be the instrument for preparing another Purim of the European nations that are becoming increasingly anti-Semitic. It was the Jew, in his full satanic vileness, who rallied around this man, and to whom this man also reached out.' The next day, Hitler spoke again, this time behind closed doors to a gathering of Nazi Gau and Reich leaders, offering them a general survey of the state of the war. According to Goebbels's summary notes of the speech, the Führer also reminded them of the 'prophecy' he had made to the Jews, in his Reichstag speech of 30 January 1939, 'that if they once more caused a world war, they would experience their extermination. This was not rhetoric. The world war is there, the extermination of the Jews must be the necessary consequence.' With his characteristic turn of phrase when referring to mass killing, Hitler added, 'This question is to be handled without any sentimentality.' After hearing his leader, Hans Frank went to consult with Heydrich's Reich Security Main Office to obtain confirmation of what was actually planned. He returned to Cracow to tell his officials in the General Government on 16 December:

One way or another – this I want to tell you quite openly – an end must be made with the Jews . . . We cannot shoot these 3.5 million

Jews, we cannot poison them, but we will find ways of somehow succeeding in destroying them in conjunction with the great measures being discussed in the Reich.[37]

As usual, what Hitler decided about the Jews also highlighted his view of the war as a whole. In 1939, when many people had expected him to sanction a new pogrom, he held back, still hoping to reach an accommodation with Britain and France. Once the Reich was at war with the United States, the die was cast and the 'final solution of the Jewish question' rapidly took on a new form. By New Year, Hitler was no longer prepared to listen to Todt or anyone else proposing peace, unequivocally rejecting Ribbentrop's suggestion that he should start negotiations with Moscow. Instead, he insisted, 'In the east . . . only a clear decision could be considered'. Fritz Todt visited Hitler's field headquarters once again on 7 February 1942, but on his return flight to Berlin the next morning, the plane crashed on take-off, killing Todt instantly. He was replaced by Hitler's architect, Albert Speer, a court favourite who would soon prove himself an effective technocrat, prepared to push up armaments production by the most ruthless means.[38]

Within Germany's ruling elites, where information travelled fastest, the mood remained bleak. The winter retreat took its toll on them, with a trail of heart attacks, strokes, suicides and sackings. Ernst Udet, head of Luftwaffe procurement, shot himself on 17 November 1941; in January, a key industrialist, Walter Borbet, followed suit. Among the top brass, Bock and Brauchitsch both had heart problems and were relieved of their commands. Rundstedt, far older than any of them, was 'retired' in November, only to be hastily recalled in January, when his successor Reichenau suffered a stroke and died on his way to hospital, in another air accident. Two of the most feted panzer commanders, Hoepner and Guderian, were peremptorily sacked for insubordination. When Goebbels and Hitler discussed the crisis on 20 January 1942, the Propaganda Minister and inveterate diarist noted, 'Defeatist mood in the OKW and OKH [Wehrmacht and Army High Commands] . . . General defeatism in Berlin government circles.'[39]

As news of the military debacle trickled back, a delayed sense of the crisis gripped the German home front. By mid-January 1942, mood reports were warning that the German media was no longer believed. By August, it had become clear to most people that Russia was an 'exceptionally tough opponent', in contrast to the propaganda images of defeatist masses forced into battle by Bolshevik commissars. But the Soviet counter-attack, coming just when the home front expected to hear a special announcement of the fall of Moscow, took everyone by surprise. It took German society some time to grasp the scale of the crisis. Only after Hitler issued his 'Halt Order' on 16 December, forbidding any further retreat, did people begin to ask what had gone wrong. By January, it was clear to many that the High Command had failed. In old heartlands of working-class anti-militarism, the retirement of Prussian generals on grounds of 'ill health' was greeted as a defeat for the forces of 'reaction' within the regime. Elsewhere, it was taken simply as a sign of military failure and incompetence. The public reappearance of the so recently disgraced Field Marshal von Rundstedt as Hitler's representative at the state funeral of Reichenau completed the sense of confusion. For the first time, the SD noted, civilians were abandoning official sources of information altogether. They were turning instead to 'rumours, stories of soldiers and people with "political connections", military post and the like, to construct "their picture", into which the most baseless rumours are often incorporated with astonishing lack of critical control.'[40]

With its antennae tuned to pick up the first signs of defeatism and revolution, the Nazi regime reacted anxiously to the flood of complaints from the front during the winter of 1941. Where military officials had once lauded soldiers' letters as a 'kind of spiritual vitamin' for the home front that strengthened its 'attitude and nerves', Goebbels now lamented that 'the impact of letters from the front, which had been regarded as extraordinarily important, has to be considered more than harmful today . . . Soldiers are pretty blunt when they describe the great problems they are fighting under, the lack of winter gear . . . insufficient food and ammunition.' Goebbels urged the military High Command to issue guidelines to the troops but accepted that in the face of such a tidal wave of complaint, the regime was 'powerless'. Events would prove him right. The official *Instructions to the Troops* issued in March 1942 urged men to act as propagandists to the home front and keep their worst experiences to themselves, warning them that 'whoever complains and makes accusations isn't a real soldier'. Selectively censoring the military mail only established that nothing would stop the men from writing home about such things.[41]

For Hitler and the Nazi leadership, these were uncharted waters and made them think about Germany's defeat in the First World War. Primarily, November 1918 was seen as a failure of morale and nerve, when Allied – especially British – propaganda proved superior to German. But as they faced their own first great crisis of the war, the Nazi regime confused distress, anger and depression with defeatism: they miscalculated how much soldiers and their families would be able and willing to endure. The Nazi regime's military censors and secret police reporters were predestined to make this mistake because they also grossly underestimated what German society had put up with in the previous war. For all the Nazi monopoly of propaganda, Hitler had admitted to a gathering of key media figures in November 1938 that he had no confidence that the 'chicken-hearted' German people would follow him through defeats. Whether or not his political authority and power really did depend on an unbroken string of successes, Hitler clearly went into the war believing this to be the case. Now, faced with an unresolved military crisis which made his own premature declaration of victory over Russia in October 1941 a serious embarrassment, he did his best to rally the nation.[42]

Between January and April 1942, Hitler addressed Germans four times over the radio, the greatest number of wartime speeches he made in so short a time. The first, on 30 January 1942, marked the 9th anniversary of his appointment as Reich Chancellor. Addressing an audience at the Berlin Sportpalast, Hitler admitted that even he did not know if the war could be won that year and simply asked his people to renew their trust in him. He repeated his by now famous 'prophecy' about the Jews; and for the first time, his language was less abstract. The Jews were threatened, no longer just with 'destruction' but with being 'exterminated'. Despite the new emphasis, this was not the passage which his German audience discussed afterwards. What resonated most was Hitler's exhortation to stay the course: 'God give us the strength to maintain freedom for ourselves, for our people, our children and our children's children, and not only for our people but also for the other peoples of Europe.'[43]

This echoed the propaganda of the previous war, when, in place of nineteenth-century romantic notions of heroic combat and knightly bravery, courage came to be seen as something more impassive, egalitarian and durable. In the First World War, the emphasis on 'strong nerves', 'unshakeable calm' and 'determination' created a new set of positive virtues, summed up by the slogan 'Holding out'. *'Durchhalten'* reflected the essentially defensive nature of much of the war, in which infantrymen held their trenches and endured artillery barrages and enemy attacks. Now, as *Blitzkrieg* failed in the winter of 1941–42 and the German Army in the East was forced into a static war of position, the dogged ethos of *Durchhalten* resurfaced. Without the self-sustaining highs produced by rapid advance, to 'hold out' would require a complete mobilisation of psychological and emotional commitment. In Pforzheim, Erna Paulus proudly pointed out to her son that the Führer had singled out the infantry for praise in his 30 January speech: 'As a result, it is now clear to the whole people that you are carrying the main burden of the war, and that's right and proper.'[44]

Helmut's mother had already shown her patriotic dedication when she began sewing and knitting for her son. On 20 December 1941, armed with a proclamation from Hitler, Goebbels went on the radio to call for a major nationwide collection of winter clothing and kit for the troops as 'a Christmas present from the German people to the eastern front'. Goebbels's Winter Relief campaign to provide for the troops proved remarkably successful, though it drew on more than the dedication of the German people. Across occupied Europe, the authorities lost no time in requisitioning. In occupied Poland Jews were immediately forbidden to own furs and ordered to hand them in: this yielded 16,654 fur coats and fur-lined coats, 18,000 fur jackets, 8,300 muffs and 74,446 fur collars in Warsaw alone. The Polish underground resistance took heart from this first sign of vulnerability, putting up posters depicting a German soldier huddled in a woman's fox-fur collar while he warmed his hands in her muff.[45]

There was a huge response on the German home front. By the middle of January 1942, 2 million volunteers had collected 67 million items across the Reich. Helmut Paulus's family gave generously and his mother started sewing old furs into mittens for the troops, and silk dresses into chest warmers, just as she had previously done for her son. All the women she knew were sewing and knitting too. In Berlin, the young photographer Liselotte Purper waxed lyrical: 'If only you could see the sewing rooms. From morning till late into the night, the women sit there . . . sewing camouflage jackets, caps, finger protectors, gloves, etc.' The number of volunteers was so great that 'they scarcely have elbow room'. When she wrote to her fiancé Kurt Orgel, stationed with the artillery laying siege to Leningrad, she assured him that her love for him was part of a much greater collective act:

> The German women have stood up to be counted and sent such a hot wave of love and gentleness to their soldiers in the east that it must be easy for you to fight for such women and mothers. If victory can be wrung through love and sacrifice, then ours is certain. It is a holy, yes, the holiest love which has been sent to you by all of Germany's women.[46]

Gushing with romantic idealism for such 'love donations', Liselotte also got a sense of what it must be like at the front during the cold snap in the second half of January in Berlin. As domestic coal supplies were curtailed and the thermometer plunged to −22 °C, she pulled on all her jumpers and worked on in her studio with freezing face and hands: 'For sure, no comparison to your chill, but it's enough.'[47]

The men at the front were astonished by the home front's generosity. Wilhelm Moldenhauer travelled 20 kilometres with three sledges to collect his unit's share of the fur collection and immediately replaced his worn-out mittens with an excellent pair of fur-lined leather gloves. The men marvelled at the range of items, including a 'black overcoat with velvet collar, a bright blue jacket with gold buttons and gold fastenings'. If German troops had begun to look like the Russian peasants and prisoners whose clothes they had taken, now 'the *Landser* can put on the finest masquerade'. Helmut Paulus was similarly astonished by the bales of knitwear that arrived in early February, 'a mass of knitted vests, socks and gloves', and was grateful to replace his socks with a good pair which had only been darned once. He was even happier to be given 'a pair of brand-new, hand-knitted woollen gloves, worked like mittens but with the index finger free to shoot and work the machine gun. That's really practical because I haven't had any finger gloves till now and always got cold hands when shooting.'[48]

★

The Red Army's counter-offensive finally petered out in March 1942. It had failed to exploit its stunning breakthroughs and encircle the different elements of Army Group Centre, mainly because of Stalin's insistence that it attack along the entire line of the front. With the dissipation of the Red Army's forces, the Germans were able to cling on to what for over two months had looked like hopeless positions. But every German commander knew just how very near they had come to sharing the fate of Napoleon's Grande Armée of 1812, a parallel Hitler himself drew a number of times.[49]

True to his own Social Darwinist views of war, Hitler told the Danish Foreign Minister on 27 November that 'If the German people are no longer strong enough and ready to sacrifice their own blood for their existence, then they should perish and be wiped out by another, stronger power. They are no longer worthy of the place they have won for themselves.' On 27 January 1942, over lunch with Heinrich Himmler, Hitler settled into a lengthy monologue about German national character, at the end of which he repeated this assessment: 'Faith moves mountains. In that respect I see things with the coldest objectivity. If the German people has lost its faith, if the German people were no longer inclined to give itself body and soul in order to survive – then the German people would have nothing to do but disappear!' First articulated in response to the great crisis of 1941, it would become one of Hitler's idées fixes and it would appear again in his gloomiest reactions to the final phase of the war in 1945. Hitler was careful never to voice this view in public.[50]

As Heroes Memorial Day on 15 March approached, the Catholic Church threw itself into affirming the meaning of patriotic sacrifice. Conrad Gröber, the Nazi Archbishop of Freiburg, penned a sermon explaining how Germans should acknowledge that their war dead

were heroes who believed that they were risking their lives and dying for a better German future, for a new and more just order of nations and for a potentially lasting peace on earth . . . They brought a true sacrifice, a sacrifice for all others . . . They were prepared to shed their blood so that the nation weakened with age and other ills would be rejuvenated, healthy and flourishing. They wanted to conquer Bolshevism with the battle-cry, 'God wills it', just as the liberator of

Spain Franco declared . . . They died for Europe, in order to stem the red tide and to build a protective wall for the entire Western world.

Bishop Galen of Münster took over the sermon word for word. [51]

Heroes Memorial Day itself was commemorated in the Courtyard of Honour in the Berlin Arsenal. Paying tribute to the German war dead, Hitler spoke of 'the hardest winter for 140 years' which 'was also the sole hope of the power-holders in the Kremlin, to visit on the German Wehrmacht the fate suffered by Napoleon in 1812'. For those who felt that these references to the 'fallen' were too fleeting – and the SD picked up many such complaints from bereaved relatives – there was an important coda. After the speech, the radio broadcast the Führer in conversation with wounded veterans. People were impressed by his 'warm conversational tone', his knowledge of every place and battle on the eastern front and his 'inner connection with each and every soldier'. It was indeed a surprising gesture from a dictator who generally avoided direct contact with the soldiers and later on the civilians who bore the scars of his war. Hitler had immured himself all winter far from both the front and Berlin, in the windowless room of his field headquarters in the woodland outside Rastenburg in East Prussia, drinking herbal tea to relieve his stress and insomnia. Now, on the radio, in his conversations with the wounded, Hitler came across as a 'man and a comrade'.[52]

In his speech, he remained a 'statesman and soldier' and the sentence that triggered the most enthusiastic response was the one which rallied German hopes in coming victory: 'But one thing we know today: the Bolshevik hordes, which were unable to defeat the German soldiers and their allies this winter, will be beaten by us into annihilation this coming summer!' Across Germany the mood of crisis, impending defeat and distrust of the media which had been so strong in January was receding, but there were still some who remembered the unfulfilled promises of victory of the previous autumn, or wondered aloud about the 'incalculable scale of Soviet strength'. Listeners picked over another pregnant phrase in the speech where Hitler declared 'that the Bolshevik colossus will find its final borders far away from Europe's pleasant pastures'. Did he mean that the Soviets could not be completely defeated, only pushed back and penned in behind some kind of 'East Wall'? people asked each other.

Hitler's closing declamation was simultaneously disturbing and reassuring: 'that, despite everything, the years of battle will be shorter than the time of that long and blessed peace which will be the result of the present struggle'. The admission, as the SD registered, that 'even the Führer cannot predict the end of the war and that it lies in the incalculable distance' made an enormous impression, because it buried all hope for a swift end to the war. At the same time, millions of German soldiers and civilians were already recalibrating their expectations to this, more difficult prospect. They promised themselves and their wives and fiancées that they would be compensate for all the time they had lost: 'We'll make up for it all next year, won't we?' one soldier put it. Erna Paulus reminded her son of his worry of 1940, as he had watched the triumphant campaign unfold in France, that he would miss out on the war: 'You have certainly not been "born too late"; you came at the right time and stand where it is hardest. With loving greetings and wishing you all the best, your mother.'[53]

PART FOUR

STALEMATE

8

The Shared Secret

If the German armies had disintegrated like Napoleon's Grande Armée in the winter of 1941, and the Third Reich had sued for peace, most of the soldiers and civilians who were to die in the Second World War would have lived. Germany's cities and the country's infrastructure might have emerged virtually unscathed from the bombing; as in 1918, the battles had been fought beyond its own borders. There would have been tales of Nazi atrocities: of the gassing of German and Polish psychiatric patients, mass shootings of Poles and Jews, the burning of Russian and Ukrainian villages and towns and the starving to death of 2.5 million Red Army prisoners. This would already have taken Hitler's war beyond any precedent, but far greater destruction was to come. At the beginning of 1942, most of Europe's Jews were still alive; by the end of the year, the majority were not.[1]

The killing of Jews began in the east and there, principally, it stayed – a fact which fundamentally shaped both the events of the 'final solution' and the ways in which it was perceived by contemporaries. Throughout the summer and autumn of 1941 there were many German eyewitnesses, and photographic evidence flooded back to Germany. Despite a formal directive not to take photos, spectators at mass executions routinely snapped pictures, including images of each other photographing the scene. They generally had to send the 35mm camera film home in small canisters to have it developed and printed, so that they would have been seen first in the photographic laboratories, then by family or friends who collected them, before being sent back to the eastern front. The Red Army found thousands of images of killing sites in the uniform pockets of German prisoners and dead, kept next to pictures of their fiancées, wives and children.[2]

How did people on the home front make sense of this upsurge of mass killing? When Charlotte Jarausch received letters from her husband Konrad, she would have gradually built up a picture of the murderous conditions in his transit camp for Soviet prisoners that November. He mentioned in passing the mass execution of civilians, 'above all the Jews', in the nearby forest, as 'really the most merciful thing' compared to letting them starve to death with 'nothing but their shirts to wear in the frost'. What was happening to the Jews stood out even in the generally fatal conditions of her husband's prisoner-of-war camp. It was not until the following spring that Hans Albring wrote to his friend Eugen Altrogge about the neatly stacked bodies of 'the half a thousand Jews who were shot' at one killing site. Such news had a paradoxical character. The closer these witnesses were to the events, the more fragmentary their perspective remained. Graphic and shocking as they were, the killings they witnessed might appear to be discrete or episodic, not part of an organised programme. There were many others, however, who did sense that their details were part of something more global from the outset. Already in August 1941, the reserve policeman Hermann Gieschen had placed his unit's actions in a wider context for his wife back in Bremen, telling her that '150 Jews from this place were shot, men, women and children, all bumped off. The Jews are being completely exterminated. Dear H., please don't think about it, that's how it has to be.' By the following February, Ernst Guicking had been transferred from France to the eastern front too, and wrote home to tell Irene that 'the Jews are experiencing a fiasco, as we hear. They are all being rounded up and resettled.'[3]

In the autumn of 1941, knowledge grew rapidly under the twin impact of events and public rhetoric. In October, the killing squads moved westwards, back from Soviet territory and the Baltic states to the villages and towns of Galicia in the Polish–Ukrainian border-lands: they were now operating in territory which was incorporated into the rump Polish General Government ruled from Cracow by Hans Frank. On 12 October 1941, the 133rd Police Battalion executed 10,000–12,000 Jews in Stanislau, leading them in groups of five to the ditches dug across the Jewish cemetery where the killings were watched and photographed by railway workers, soldiers and other policemen. At the same time, the deportation of Jews from the Reich itself began. From 15 October to 9 November, the first twenty-five special trains transported Jews to the Łódź ghetto, each train carrying a thousand deportees: 5,000 came from Vienna, 5,000 from the Protectorate of Bohemia and Moravia, 10,000 from the 'old' Reich; there were also 5,000 Roma from the Burgenland. Although the crisis of transport on the eastern front that winter severely curtailed the scale of deportation, a second wave of thirty-four transport trains ran from 8 November to 6 February destined for Riga in Latvia, Kaunas in Lithuania and, briefly, Minsk in Belorussia. By late November, remarkably precise information was circulating as far afield as Minden in the Ruhr in western Germany, where, it was said, the local SD office reported

> that all the Jews have been shipped to Russia, that their transport took place in passenger trains as far as Warsaw and from there in cattle trucks belonging to the German railways. The Führer is said to want to be informed by 15.1.1942 that not a single Jew remains within the borders of the German Reich. In Russia the Jews are said to have been put to work in former Soviet factories, while the elderly and sick Jews are to be shot.[4]

The details were precise – though not strictly accurate – and they were publicly discussed. As people wondered aloud what happened to their Jewish neighbours after the trains left, they made use of what they knew or surmised, recycling what they had already learned about the massacres being conducted in the 'east'. They were also quick to give the action a central logic and direction. People spoke, as if it were a fact, about the Führer wanting to see Germany cleared of Jews by 1 April 1942. These imagined dates were not so far off the mark: in discussion with his officials in Prague in early October, Reinhard Heydrich, the man detailed as head of the Reich Security Main Office with organising the deportations, told them that the Führer wanted 'the Jews to be removed from German space if possible by the end of the year'. More important than such accurate second-guessing is the fact that people immediately grasped that a central decision had been made to deport the Jews: this was not a local initiative, like so many bans on using swimming pools or park benches.[5]

The first and most dramatic of these central measures was the decree of 1 September 1941, which ordained that all Jews over the age of 5 had to wear a yellow star on the left breast of all outer garments. Even though the outbreak of the war had produced a fresh deluge of anti-Jewish ordinances, from highly restricted shopping hours to the ban on possessing radios, the yellow star was the most visible nation-wide measure taken since the November 1938 pogrom and it came into effect across the whole Reich on the same day, 19 September 1941. Its mandatory character could not be in doubt and it was immediately recognised as an important escalation, conditioning how the burghers of Minden digested the news a few weeks later of the deportation and first mass shootings of Jews from their town:

> There is much talk in the population about all Germans in America having to wear a swastika on their left breast in order to make them recognisable, along the lines of the way the Jews have been identified here in Germany. Germans in America are said to be having to pay a heavy price because the Jews have been treated so badly in Germany.[6]

This rumour that Germans were being made to wear swastika badges in the United States in retaliation for the Jewish Star arose even before the two countries were at war, and it continued to surface sporadically afterwards. One American who was still in Frankfurt that autumn found that whenever he expressed his repugnance that Jews had to wear a yellow star, his German acquaintances 'invariably replied in self-justification that the measure was not at all unusual. It was merely in keeping with the way the American authorities treated German nationals in the United States, compelling them to wear a large swastika sewn on to their coats'. Here, as Germans spoke about a world beyond their own experience, it was much easier for Nazi propaganda to shape their image of the 'Jewish' character of American politics and, with it, the notion of a 'world Jewish conspiracy'.[7]

The tenor of German anti-Americanism had become ever shriller during the summer of 1941, as the Nazi leadership watched the United States and Britain draw closer. After Congress had passed the Lend-Lease Act to supply Britain with war materiel on 11 March and American troops had occupied Iceland on 7 July, Roosevelt and Churchill met at Placentia Bay, Newfoundland on board the USS *Augusta* and HMS *Prince of Wales* between 9 and 12 August. At the end of the meeting they announced the Atlantic Charter, which affirmed that peace would be made on liberal principles of national self-determination and equal access to international trade. Without addressing the war directly, the Charter's very existence confirmed that the USA had publicly allied itself with Britain against the Axis powers, and so it was not surprising that Berlin and Tokyo interpreted it as such, especially when Roosevelt followed it up on 11 September with orders to the US Navy to attack any German submarines sighted in the Western Atlantic. With its explicit repudiation of the harsh economic terms imposed on Germany in 1919, the language of the Atlantic Charter was not in itself threatening – indeed, the RAF dropped thousands of leaflets over Germany confirming that Great Britain and the United States would 'not admit any economical discrimination against the defeated' and promised that 'Germany and the other states can again achieve enduring peace and prosperity'.[8]

Goebbels turned to his deputy in charge of radio, Wolfgang Diewerge, in order to unmask the real plan behind these anodyne assurances. Diewerge got hold of a little-known, self-published American tract, *Germany Must Perish!*, and translated key passages such as its inflammatory call for 20,000 doctors to carry out mass sterilisation of the German population, leading to 'the elimination of Germanism and its carriers' within two generations. Its author was renamed from Theodore Newman Kaufman to the unmistakably Jewish-sounding Theodore Nathan Kaufman. With a frontispiece of Churchill and Roosevelt photographed at Newfoundland, Kaufman was turned from a seller of theatre tickets who had declared himself President of the American Federation of Peace, an organisation he had also founded, into one of the American President's key advisors and Diewerge also dated the tract to August 1941 so that it appeared to be part of the Atlantic Charter.[9]

On 7 September, the Nazi Party issued as its 'weekly slogan' Hitler's prophecy of 30 January 1939: 'Should the international Jewish financiers succeed once again in plunging the nations into a world war, the result will not be the victory of Jewry but the destruction of the Jewish race in Europe.'[10] Printed up in poster format, the Führer's 'prophecy' hung in the glass display cabinets outside Party offices throughout the Reich.

As in 1939, so now it seemed to warn the Americans that Germany would hold Europe's Jews hostage. Almost certainly this escalating conflict played a part both in Hitler's decision at the end of August to authorise marking Germany's Jews and in his subsequent decision in mid-September to have them deported before the Soviet war was finished.[11]

Picturing Germans wearing swastika badges on their clothes in the USA helped to make what was being done to Jews in Germany seem less singular as people drew on their past experience of tit-for-tat retaliation. There had been a boycott campaign against German exports in the USA after the Nazis boycotted Jewish shops on 1 April 1933 and the November 1938 pogrom had led to hostile coverage in the international media. As the people of Minden considered the latest escalation, they worried that its effects would be just as they had been in 1938, 'which did us far more harm abroad than it benefited us at home'.[12]

Already during this first phase, when most of the mass shooting of Jews was still confined to the eastern front, the fate of the Jews had acquired a global significance in German discussions which was not accorded to the mass execution of other Soviet civilians. As important power-holders in Washington and London, helping to orchestrate the Allied coalition, the Jews were seen as a unified, international enemy, a way of thinking encapsulated by the use of the collective singular, 'Jewry', or, more simply, 'the Jew'. By autumn 1941, people were imagining how the Jews would orchestrate retaliation against Germany – despite the fact that it had not happened. Within three months of introducing the yellow star, Germany was at war with America.

*

The deportation of tens of thousands of Jews from the Reich involved many different administrative officials. From the outset, the Gestapo involved the local Jewish community organisations in drawing up lists of those to be deported, giving them the power to decide whom to exclude from transports as well as the responsibility for informing those whom they had included. Once they had received their summons, people selected for 'resettlement' were placed under curfew restrictions and could leave their homes only with police permission. They were kept busy settling bills, preparing food for a journey of three to five days and packing their 50 kilos of luggage. They also had to make a full list of their assets, which was cross-checked by the financial authorities. They were instructed to leave all furniture and household goods behind, and to turn their keys over to the caretaker of their block of flats before leaving. They then faced two departure dates. On the first, deportees reported to their local collection point, where they were held for days and where their luggage – and often their persons – were searched for disallowed items. Even permitted goods were frequently confiscated. Jews were charged a fee for their deportation and an additional 'donation' set at 25 per cent of the value of property being left behind was also levied by the Reich Security Main Office on the pretext of covering the transport costs of those too poor to pay; it was really just a way for the SS to claim a share before the assets were taken over by the Ministry of Finance.[13]

On the day of deportation, the Jews were driven or marched in a column to be loaded on to goods wagons. On 27 November 1941, the twelve Jews of Forchheim in Upper Franconia were marched to the local railway station, 'followed by a great number of inhabitants' who expressed their 'interest and great satisfaction', according to the contemporary police report. In many towns, the deportations were the first collective spectacle of local Jew-baiting since the pogrom of November 1938. In places where the 1938 pogrom had turned into a popular festival with Hitler Youths and BDM girls joining the throngs of ill-wishers, the deportation of the remaining Jews was now accompanied by curses and chants, mixing insults old and new – 'Just look at those cheeky Jews!' 'Now they're marching into the ghetto!' 'Just a bunch of useless eaters!' In Bad Neustadt, local activists took photographs of the elderly, undernourished Jews as they assembled on the market square. Enlarged to poster size, the photos were later displayed in the centre of town to document the action. When the column of Jews formed up, they were accompanied all the way to the station by a 'large, hooting throng of schoolchildren, who continued shouting till the train left'.[14]

The first deportations also pitted Jews against Jews. In November 1941, Marianne Strauss and her parents were waiting to board the tram in Essen taking the Jews from the collection point to the railway station when two Gestapo officials released them, to the surprise of their fellow deportees. As they left, 18-year-old Marianne could not forget 'this animal howl' that went up from the other Jews. The Strauss family was 'privileged', wealthy enough to have bought protection from a local banker and from military counter-intelligence. Others held back from these first waves of deportation included Jews working in the armaments sector, Jews with foreign, usually Western, passports, those living in 'mixed' marriages, those with outstanding records of service in the First World War and – in an attempt to preserve the fiction that the deportees were being 'resettled' in labour camps – the old and frail.[15]

The rhythm of deportation was set by the overriding priorities of military transports and the annual shortages of coal in winter. They restarted in March 1942, when another 45,000–60,000 Jews were deported from Prague, Vienna and areas of the 'old Reich' considered at risk of air raids. Many elderly Jews and war veterans were sent to Theresienstadt, a small eighteenth-century garrison town north of Prague, whose location within the Reich and away from the 'east' was deliberately used to calm German anxieties and to vitiate the numerous interventions by Nazi officials, pleading on behalf of their own favoured Jews. Far from being an 'old age ghetto', let alone the 'end station' it was claimed to be, Theresienstadt in fact served principally as a transit camp, with almost as many trains leaving as arrived. At this time, many were sent to ghettos in the Lublin district of Poland.[16]

On 21 April 1942, another transport left Essen. Among those on it was Marianne Strauss's fiancé, Ernst Krombach. Marianne tried to wave goodbye to him from the station platform and Ernst managed to post a card to her from their first stop at Duisburg to tell her that he had seen her. The next stop came at Düsseldorf-Derendorf: here the deportees were shepherded by the police into an abattoir, where their luggage was whittled down to one suitcase or rucksack with essential items. The Gestapo gave all the toiletries, medicines and surplus food to the German Red Cross; the bed linen, clothing – including 345 dresses and 192 overcoats – and umbrellas went to the National Socialist People's Welfare. Ernst managed to protect most of his family's bundles during this confiscation, at the end of which the deportees were issued with an official notification of the 11th ordinance to the Reich Citizenship Law, which informed them that once they crossed the German border, all their property would automatically be assigned to the Reich. On 23 April, the train crossed the border and the next day they arrived at Izbica, one of the ghettos in the Lublin district, from where Ernst managed to go on writing to Marianne, assuring her of his continuing love and warning her that 'the conditions here are more extreme than anything we imagined; it's simply impossible to put them into words . . . The Wild West is nothing to this.'

At the end of August, Marianne received a long and detailed account of conditions in Izbica, smuggled back to Essen by an 'Aryan' friend who drove a truck under contract for the SS. Ernst detailed how the village had been cleared of the 3,000 Polish Jews who had originally lived there in order to accommodate the transports from Poland and Slovakia, from Aachen, Nuremberg, Breslau, Stuttgart, Frankfurt and Theresienstadt. He described the ethno-national divides between Polish, Czech and German Jews, and wrote of public hangings in punishment for transgressions. At first Ernst turned down offers of a job in the Jewish police 'mainly because of the unpleasant work: Jews against Jews', but then he agreed, probably from a desire to protect his family from deportation. 'But', he told his fiancée in Essen,

> I was unable to avoid getting involved in the evacuation of Polish Jews. You have to suppress every human feeling and, under supervision of the SS, drive the people out with a whip, just as they are – barefoot, with infants in their arms. There are scenes which I cannot and will not describe but which will take me long to forget . . . I only think of these inhuman experiences in my dreams.

Meanwhile, the three German Jewish families living in their tiny wooden and clay hut on the edge of the village began to eat better and to take care of some of the other families from Essen.[17]

The households which the deported Jews left behind in Germany became sought-after spoils. From Swabian villages to the once radical city of Hamburg, locals actively lobbied to take over their property and turned up to bid at the public auctions. At least 30,000 Jewish households went under the auctioneer's hammer in Hamburg between 1941 and 1945, the lots finding approximately ten buyers for each household. Working-class housewives in the Veddel district took up trading in coffee and jewellery, and bought old furniture and carpets from the auctions. By the start of 1943, the takings in the Gestapo account at the Deutsche Bank from this trade had risen to 7.2 million Reichsmarks. As women acquired fur coats which still carried labels with the names of their original owners, they would have had to try hard not to guess what kind of people these owners had been. The press publicity advertising the auctions made no secret of the Jewish origins of the goods on sale. Meanwhile, the sealed flats became a reward to be allocated to local Nazi functionaries or the still small numbers of bombed-out families.[18]

★

Goebbels had persuaded Hitler to introduce the yellow star in the hope that it would brand the Jews in public and fan the flames of popular anti-Semitism in the same way that such measures had in Poland. It was an expectation shared by many Jews. In September 1941, Victor Klemperer could not bear to venture on to the streets of Dresden, and handed over the shopping entirely to his 'Aryan' wife, Eva. Others were so afraid that they killed themselves. There were 87 suicides in three weeks in Vienna and 243 in Berlin during the last quarter of 1941. In fact, in the first weeks Goebbels was seriously disappointed with the impact, especially in his own Gau of Berlin, which had not quite lost its secular, left-wing pre-1933 traditions and where 70,000 of Germany's population of 150,000 Jews now lived. The yellow star, the Propaganda Minister complained to Albert Speer, 'had the opposite effect from what we intended . . . People everywhere are showing sympathy for them [the Jews]. This nation is simply not yet mature; it is full of all kinds of idiotic sentimentality.' The problem, Goebbels was beginning to realise, was that society was simply not sufficiently National Socialist in outlook.[19]

To remedy this deficit, the regime's first resort was to educate by intimidation: on 24 October 1941, a decree was published banning public displays of sympathy towards the Jews, threatening Germans who did so with three months in a concentration camp. 'Anyone who continues to uphold personal contacts with him [the Jew]', Goebbels warned in his article in *Das Reich* on 16 November, 'is taking his side and must be regarded and treated as a Jew.' Having drawn a hard line, he chided his readership to grow out of any 'false sentimentalism': 'If Herr Bramsig and Frau Knöterich feel a stir of pity at the sight of an old woman wearing the yellow star, please do not let them forget that the Jews planned the war and started it.' And so Goebbels's celebrated article 'The Jews are guilty' went on, up to its matter-of-fact confirmation that Hitler's 'prophecy' about the extermination of the Jews was now being fulfilled.[20]

Goebbels was not the only Nazi leader who came close to stating bluntly that the regime's policy was to kill the Jews. Two days later, Alfred Rosenberg blurted out at a briefing of officials of his new 'Eastern Ministry' that the Jewish 'question can only be solved by a biological eradication of entire Jewry in Europe . . . That is the task which Fate has set us.' Hitler himself repeated his 'prophecy' in his public speeches no less than four times in 1942, now using the unmistakable '*Ausrottung*' – 'extermination'. The *Völkische Beobachter* followed its master's voice on 27 February 1942, screaming, 'The Jew will be exterminated!' Other Nazi leaders, like the Gauleiter of Munich, Adolf Wagner, and the head of the Labour Front, Robert Ley, followed suit. As Germans weathered the existential crisis of the eastern front in early 1942, these threats reverberated across the rhetorical landscape.[21]

To hard-line ideologues like the head of the Party apparatus, Martin Bormann, it was clear that the German people should be made to realise that they were now locked in a genocidal global conflict, which could end only with their victory or destruction. Despite the torrent of anti-Semitic arguments, the deportation of the Jews had not made the news, with no details being published in the German media about the deportees' destination, fate or the purpose of the measure. As a result, local and regional Party officials asked for guidance on how to field questions about the 'extremely harsh measures' taken against the Jews. Bormann's response was to issue them with a directive telling them that he was quite happy for them to go on the offensive and justify these actions. It is, he explained, the 'nature of the issue that these partly very difficult problems can only be solved in the interest of the final security of our people with ruthless hardness'. Instead of denying the rumours, Party officials were told to embrace 'the present opportunity for cleansing . . . the entire problem has to be solved by today's generation'.[22]

There was much to comment on, for it was during this period that the deportations reached a pan-European scale and all pretence that the

Jews were being 'resettled' was dropped. Starting on 11 May 1942, seventeen transports to Minsk no longer went to the ghetto. Instead, they stopped near the estate of Maly Trostinets, where the deportees were shot or killed in mobile gas vans. From June, transports from Theresienstadt, Berlin and Vienna were sent straight to an extermination camp at Sobibor. At the same time, the scope of deportation broadened: in March the first deportation trains left Slovakia, with selections for forced labour. In June, trains with Slovakian Jews were running directly to the Sobibor killing facility and, a month later, to Auschwitz. Six transports of Jews from France had already arrived in Auschwitz between March and July; between 19 July and 7 August, a further 125,000 people were sent there from Belgium, the Netherlands and France. Meanwhile, by far the biggest operations were more local: from 22 July, during a two-month 'action', 300,000 Jews were sent from Warsaw to Treblinka, destroying Europe's largest Jewish community. In parts of Ukraine, the 'sweeps' by the mobile squads, the *Einsatzgruppen*, went on without interruption until all the Jewish villages and towns had been wiped out. In the summer of 1942, the remaining Jewish ghettos in the Soviet territories were eliminated.[23]

The 1.9 million Jewish victims from the Soviet Union, let alone the 2.7 million from Poland, far outnumbered the Jews deported from Greater Germany – with 78,000 from the Protectorate of Bohemia and Moravia, 65,000 from Austria and 165,000 from the 'old' Reich. They also dwarfed the numbers of Jews who were transported from occupied western Europe: 76,000 from France, 102,000 from the Netherlands, 28,000 from Belgium, 1,200 from Luxembourg, 758 from Norway and 116 from Denmark. But it was the mass deportations from western Europe which spelled out that this was a centrally directed and pan-European programme, not just an extreme form of anti-partisan warfare on the eastern front. The deportations to the death camps also involved too many different authorities for them ever to have been kept secret. Whether they were soldiers observing the shootings, railwaymen running the deportation trains, or local government officials making sure that keys to apartments were handed over before their occupants left, all these people may have simultaneously hidden behind their functionally circumscribed roles yet passed their little nuggets of knowledge into the general circulation of information.[24]

In the course of 1942, Goebbels adopted a new and much more subtle approach to managing public opinion. Instead of cranking up the anti-Semitic campaign he had unleashed in the autumn of 1941, the Propaganda Minister de-escalated it. He worked hard to black out reports on specific measures from within the Reich, warning off the Gauleiter of Vienna, Baldur von Schirach, from celebrating the deportation of the Viennese Jews in a public speech to a European youth congress, lest it offer ammunition for the international press 'to jump down our throats'. Through these months when the deportation and murder of the Jews reached its height, central Nazi papers, such as the *Völkische Beobachter* and *Der Angriff*, carried no more than one or two anti-Semitic pieces a week. There was little on the Jews in the newsreels and nothing at all in the short documentaries screened before the main feature films. Why were the Nazis so concerned to conceal details, when the headlines of the main Party daily had not so long ago proclaimed that 'The Jew will be exterminated'?[25]

The most obvious motive, which Goebbels freely admitted to Schirach, was that all specific facts would be seized on by Allied propaganda and turned against Germany, as indeed they were. But there was another reason, too. In the course of 1942, two different ways of influencing the German public were tried out. There was the direct, pedagogic method of exhortation and argument, intended to bring the German people as a whole into the National Socialist fold. This was the method which Goebbels had himself tried in his November 1941 article 'The Jews are guilty' and it continued to be pursued throughout 1942 in Hitler's and Göring's speeches, Martin Bormann's instructions to the Party functionaries and, outside the Reich, in Hans Frank's official newspaper for the General Government, which did publish detailed accounts of the implementation of the deportations across German-occupied Europe.

Alongside such direct exhortation, Goebbels developed a second, more discreet and subtle form of news management. Instead of persuading their readers to endorse 'extermination' as a political and racial necessity, the German press hinted at what people already knew, fostering a sense of collusive semi-secrecy. During 1942, the press charted the 'solution of the Jewish question' by Germany's Romanian, Bulgarian, Croatian and Slovakian allies, reporting on the registration of Jews for forced labour, the ghettos and, in the case of Slovakia, even their deportation. Journalists discussed whether the 'Jewish question' had been 'completely solved' in Slovakia, or commented on the demand to deal with the 'gypsy question' in south-eastern Europe along the same lines. The incomplete and often vague reference points connected with what people already knew through rumour and hearsay. But the press avoided explicit statements. Goebbels's new tactic experimented with a tacit and collusive way of managing – and partially silencing – moral disquiet. Instead of waging an explicit propaganda campaign to win public support for the regime's action, as he had originally hoped to do, he would let awareness of the actions seep in and foster a sense of complicity.[26]

The result is perhaps best described as a 'spiral of silence'. The term was coined much later, in 1974, by post-war West Germany's most famous public opinion researcher, Elisabeth Noelle-Neumann. Although she was, of course, writing about post-war democracy, she remained deeply influenced by her own formation in 1941 and 1942, when as a young journalist she contributed articles to Goebbels's *Das Reich* on the power of the Jewish press in the USA. The element of her thinking which can be transferred back to the Nazi dictatorship is her emphasis on how public opinion is subject to private, pre-political pressures. According to Noelle-Neumann, fear of isolation and social sanctions tends to silence individuals who feel that they are in the minority, reducing their potential number; meanwhile, press reporting of the 'majority' viewpoint augments and stabilises its moral position. Her argument also highlights an important intersection between the public and private spheres of society, with much of the pressure towards conformity exercised privately, within like-minded peer groups. Through embarrassment, even humiliation, the opinion-forming relationships of family and workplace effect silent shifts in moral positions. Contrasting it with the 'bandwagon' concept which focuses on public conformism, Noelle-Neumann drew attention to the psychological importance of private pressures in fomenting an individual's fear of isolation.[27]

Karl Dürkefälden exemplifies how a general moral problem was turned into a private family affair and then buried in silence. A 40-year-old engineer with a machine-building firm in Celle, Dürkefälden was classified as 'indispensable' and spared military call-up. Coming from a working-class family with traditional Social Democratic affiliations, he had put himself through night school in the 1920s and then experienced long periods of unemployment during the Great Depression, finally achieving a family and stable working life with rearmament in the 1930s. By the summer of 1942, his firm was making oil-drilling equipment in anticipation of the conquest of the Soviet oilfields. Dürkefälden tuned in regularly to the BBC, and when he picked up a broadcast of a talk Thomas Mann had given on Voice of America about the gassing of 400 young Dutch Jews, he concluded that Hitler's public threats were not idle talk. His brother-in-law, Walter Kassler, served on the eastern front and had written saying that there were no Jews left in Kiev. When he came home on leave in June 1942, Walter talked to Karl about the mass executions he had seen and about the gassing of French Jews he had heard about from another soldier. 'Walter emphasised repeatedly,' Dürkefälden confided in his diary, '"We can be happy that we are not Jews."' Realising that Karl was shocked, Walter tried to explain to him: 'At first I didn't understand, but now I know: it's a matter of existence or non-existence.' Kassler had taken over Hitler's endlessly repeated mantra that the nation faced an apocalyptic choice: 'To be or not to be'. When Karl insisted, 'But that's murder', Walter's reply again came straight from the media: 'Certainly it has gone so far that they will do to us as we have done to them, if we should lose the war.' Karl Dürkefälden knew that he had to let it rest. To contradict his brother-in-law would have meant risking an open breach within the family. It could, in the worst case, have ended in denunciation to the Gestapo; more likely, it would have led to strained relations and ostracism.

The staple media message prevailed, not because Karl believed it, but because he had to let Walter have the last word. The many steps by which the Nazis had first destroyed the old labour movement through terror and then tried to reshape working-class identities around promises of consumer affluence, stable employment, national pride and ethnic difference had all left their mark, before the war itself had changed the perception of 'us' and 'them' being argued out across the kitchen table. Karl Dürkefälden's Social Democratic values had become old-fashioned, his humanitarian outlook embarrassing: he had become part of a beleaguered minority, silenced not by the Gestapo or by Party hacks but by the pressure to conform exerted within his own family.[28]

This version of a 'spiral of silence' worked in private because the media avoided inviting wide-ranging or open discussion of what was going on; yet at the same time, it provided a series of rhetorical justifications for extermination, and drip-fed innuendos which allowed people to connect the abstract threats of Goebbels and Hitler with the specific details of mass executions that circulated privately. What was being created was a sense of 'knowing without knowing', which did not invite any kind of public commitment, affirmation or feeling of moral responsibility; and it could work as long as no one broke the artificial limit on what could be said. The institution in the strongest position to do this was the Catholic Church. In September 1941, a month after Bishop Galen had thunderously denounced the killing of psychiatric patients from the pulpit of the Lamberti Church in Münster, he received an anonymous letter of praise for this courageous stand. The letter-writer reminded Galen of what was happening to German Jews, now that even highly patriotic ones like himself had to wear the yellow star, concluding: 'Only the senseless wish, the mad hope, that somewhere a helper will stand up for us incited me to address this letter to you. May God bless you!' There is no record of any reply. Nor did Galen utter a word in public or in private about the persecution of the Jews. Instead, he went on preaching sermons in which he depicted German Catholics as true patriots defending the Fatherland against the Bolshevik threat.[29]

It was not that Galen and the other bishops lacked knowledge. In Berlin, Margarete Sommer ran an office for relief work under the auspices of Bishop Preysing, where she compiled and passed on information on what had happened to the Catholics of Jewish descent after they were deported to the Baltic territories. She also received confidential information from Hans Globke, a high official within the Interior Ministry. Briefed by Sommer, Bishop Berning of Osnabrück concluded, on 5 February 1942, that 'There is clearly a plan to exterminate the Jews completely.' This was a mere two weeks after Heydrich had held the top-secret Wannsee Conference in order to inform high-ranking administrators about the impending murder of 11 million European Jews. But it took Bishops Berning and Preysing another eighteen months before they pushed for a petition against the 'deportation of non-Aryans in a manner that is scornful of all human rights'. In August 1943, the Fulda Bishops' Conference rejected the proposal. In any case, it was too late: by this time, most of the Jews were dead. The most influential figure in German Catholicism, Cardinal Bertram, refused to be briefed any further by Margarete Sommer, insisting that he was only willing to receive written reports from her if they were countersigned by Preysing to guarantee their authenticity. Such a procedure, as the cardinal was well aware, would also have exposed both signatories to the Gestapo. If Bertram did not know what had happened to the Jews, it was because he made every effort not to know.[30]

One of the great 'what ifs' that historians continue to debate is whether concerted action by the churches could have stopped the murder of the Jews, in the way the public protests by Catholic bishops halted the killing of psychiatric patients in August 1941. Why they chose not to act in the case of the Jews has been the subject of considerable historical speculation and moral condemnation. But the comparison is flawed. The bishops did not protest against the murder of adult psychiatric patients when it was resumed in August 1942, even though they were well aware of it. This time, the Catholic bishops avoided making the information public. What mattered most to the bishops during the confrontation of 1941 was the Nazi attack on their institutions and, by the autumn, both sides had backed away from this contest. By the time of the Fulda Bishops' Conference of August 1942, a clerical informer told the Gestapo that 'there is general contentment with the Church's successes in the year that has passed', in particular with regard to the reduced tensions with the state and the end to seizure of Church property. Nor was it was only the Jews about whose fate the German Catholic bishops remained silent. They had set an ominous precedent for themselves when they chose not to speak up about the mass shootings in Poland in 1939. Those victims had included not only teachers, officers, Girl Guides and Jews, but Polish Catholic priests. Nazi ideologues may have regarded the Church as an international conspiracy, but the German clergy knew its national identity. After the Wehrmacht's retreat from Moscow, the German Catholic Church was in no doubt about the seriousness of the war. In place of its contest with the Nazis for the spiritual leadership of the nation, it now found itself forging an uneasy, fractious alliance with the Party to rally all Germans to the urgent task of national defence.[31]

Left to their own devices, Catholics pulled in different directions. When the last, elderly Jews reported to the market square at Lemgo in the Lippe district of North Rhine–Westphalia in July 1942, their 'Aryan' neighbours looked on with disquiet. According to the local

SD, a debate erupted over whether it was really necessary to deport old people to a camp, when they were already destined to 'die out'. Spectators were split between churchgoers – some of whom even warned that the German people were inviting 'divine punishment' – and right-thinking National Socialists, who seem to have been in the minority in this case. Certainly, the SD conceded that even many 'national comrades who have previously taken every appropriate and inappropriate opportunity to express their National Socialist convictions' were advancing the humanitarian viewpoint now – perhaps because this last deportation affected objects of pity rather than fear. But Lemgo was an unusual case. In nearby Münster, where Bishop Galen had his seat, the final deportation went off without a hitch, with elderly Jews agreeing to pay the members of the SD to help carry their luggage. In Cologne, there was pressure from both laity and clerics to update the liturgy of the Catholic marriage service: they found the imprecation that the bride 'be as long-lived and faithful as Sara' to be 'absurd'.[32]

As long as no institution in occupied Europe publicly condemned the deportation and murder of the Jews, discussion in Germany could largely be contained within limits set by the media. For a time – and in Germany during the Second World War, it only ever was temporary – the 'spiral of silence' worked. This was all the more remarkable because it is not clear that the same result could have been achieved if Goebbels had gone on preaching. Merely hinting at what most newspaper readers knew, the regime's media managers found they had a better chance at shaping public opinion than through unrelenting propaganda. Moreover, Goebbels's new approach avoided the risk of exposing the moral gulf between the murderous racial utilitarianism of National Socialism and a more pervasive Christian ethic in German society that shied away from outright murder. Achieving this balance depended in great measure on the silence of the churches, the institutions which, after the Nazi regime itself, had the greatest influence across Germany and occupied Europe.

Yet there was a steady stream of information which the Nazi regime was powerless to suppress. From June to December 1942, during the very months in which the genocide was at its height, the BBC reported on the deportation and murder of the Jews. On 17 December 1942, Anthony Eden, the British Foreign Secretary, addressed the House of

Commons, describing the clearances of the Polish ghettos and the deportation of Jews from across the Continent 'in conditions of appalling horror and brutality'. No philo-Semite, Eden chose his words carefully, stating that the German government was now 'carrying out Hitler's oft repeated intention to exterminate the Jewish people in Europe'. He read out the condemnation of 'this bestial policy of cold-blooded extermination' by the twelve Allied governments – Belgium, Czechoslovakia, Greece, Luxembourg, the Netherlands, Norway, Poland, the United States, the UK, the USSR, Yugoslavia and the French National Committee – and their 'solemn resolution to ensure that those responsible for these crimes shall not escape retribution'. At his close, the House stood in a minute's silence. That week, the BBC German service broadcast several reports a day about the murder of the Jews.[33]

Three days before Eden's statement, Goebbels had anticipated the Allied response with a degree of nonchalance, telling his ministerial conference: 'We cannot reply to these matters . . . We are not in a position to get into a controversy over this, at least not in the world's media.' With an eye on media reporting in the neutral countries as well as on the home front, Goebbels called for a diversion, a German press campaign stressing Allied atrocities in India, Iran and other parts of the world. He met with a relatively weak response. The media lacked new material and German audiences were not sufficiently gripped by tales from the non-European and colonial world. German propaganda was not a complete failure, however. Its claim that the Allies were only fighting the war on behalf of the Jews hit a sensitive nerve in Britain. When Dr Cyril Garbett, the Archbishop of York, went so far as to issue a New Year's Day message calling for a 'crusade' to save the Jews, it served to underline the claim. Even in Britain, the government wanted to avoid the charge of being in hock to the Jews, and reporting on the murder of the Jews was scaled down. From now on, Allied reporting about the genocide would be carefully embedded in reports of German atrocities against other groups, so that the Allied cause remained unmistakably that of humanity as a whole. Karl Dürkefälden was not unusual in listening to the BBC for news, but not many of his fellow countrymen were prepared to take their moral bearings from enemy radio. [34]

★

By late 1942, there were many sources to corroborate the Europe-wide murder of the Jews. There had been hundreds of thousands, possibly millions of witnesses to the shooting of Jews in the occupied Soviet territories, Baltic states and eastern Poland. Even the names of the death camps in occupied Poland – Chełmno, Bełżec, Sobibor and Treblinka – as well as the new camp at Auschwitz in Upper Silesia began to be known. But information about what exactly happened in these places remained sketchy.

In Pomerania and in parts of occupied Poland and the Soviet Union, mobile gas vans were a common sight as they drove along country roads, pumping carbon-monoxide-laden exhaust fumes into their rear compartment. In Pomerania, they had been used in 1939–40 to kill psychiatric patients. From January 1942, they were used at Chełmno to murder the Jews from Łódź. In this case, considerable effort went into preserving secrecy. The old castle building which served as the camp was surrounded by a high wooden fence guarded by sentries, and military police cordoned off the roads into the area of forest where the bodies of those killed in the gassing vans were buried. The squads of Jews tasked with this work were routinely executed in their turn. Few visitors gained entry to the static gassing facilities installed at Bełżec, Sobibor and Treblinka. One of those who did leave a record was an SS officer and disinfection expert, Kurt Gerstein, who visited Bełżec on 20 August 1942. There he witnessed the arrival and gassing of a transport of Jews from Lwów. The diesel engine would not start and the Jews were kept locked in the gas chambers for two and a half hours while it was repaired. The gassing itself took a further thirty-two minutes. Gerstein's task was to advise on how to disinfect the clothing and he was accompanied to Bełżec by a part-time SS consultant, the Professor of Hygiene at the University of Marburg, Dr Wilhelm Pfannenstiel. The professor was fascinated by what was taking place and stood by the door with his eye glued to the glass peephole until it misted over. He commented that the wailing of the naked Jews crammed inside sounded 'like in a synagogue'. The two men went to view the much bigger facility at Treblinka the next day, where Pfannenstiel complimented their hosts in an after-dinner speech on 'the greatness of the work' they were doing.[35]

Gerstein returned to Berlin by night train, where he found himself sharing a compartment with the Swedish attaché at the embassy in

Berlin, Göran von Otter. Profoundly disturbed by his experience, Gerstein took the risk of disclosing what he knew to Otter, and urged him to tell the outside world. He even revealed his own identity and, as a devout Protestant, named the liberal Protestant Bishop of Berlin, Otto Dibelius, as a character reference. Back in the Reich capital, Gerstein immediately informed both Dibelius and his Catholic counterpart, Bishop Konrad Count von Preysing. He also tried to brief the Papal Nuncio and the Swiss legation; all in vain. The Swedish attaché's report to his government was promptly buried, and the bishops failed to act on the information.[36]

Gerstein's father, a retired judge, also did not want to know. Their conversation was not a success and Gerstein tried to resume it by letter. On 5 March 1944, the son wrote to his father,

> I do not know what goes on inside you, and would not presume to claim the smallest right to know. But when a man has spent his professional life in the service of the law something must have happened inside him during these last few years. I was deeply perturbed by one thing you said to me, or rather wrote to me . . . You said: Hard times demand tough methods! – No! No maxim of that kind is adequate to justify what has happened.

In a generational role reversal, the son pleaded with the father to take a moral stance, warning him that he too

> will have to stand up and be called to account for the age in which you live and what is happening in it. There would be no understanding left between us . . . if it were not possible or permissible for me to ask you not to underestimate this responsibility, this obligation on your part to answer for yourself.

The father remained unmoved, and, in a desperate attempt to reach him, the son wrote again, 'If you look around you, you will find that this is a rift that is cutting through many families and friendships that were once close.' Like Karl Dürkefälden, Kurt Gerstein's attempt to articulate a moral position was blocked by his own family: no doubt there were others like him.[37]

Only a privileged few actually witnessed how the killing was done. As news spread rapidly in the vicinity of the death camps and beyond, errors crept in about crucial details of the operations. Ten days after Pfannenstiel and Gerstein visited Bełżec, a non-commissioned officer, Wilhelm Cornides, was waiting on the platform at the nearby station of Rawa Ruska in Galicia when a train of some thirty-five cattle trucks, packed with Jews, arrived. A policeman explained to him that they were probably the last Jews from Lwów: 'That has been going on for five weeks uninterruptedly.' When he got on his own train, Cornides found himself sharing a compartment with a railway policeman and his wife, who promised to point out the camp where the Jews were being killed. After travelling for some time through a tall pine forest, he noticed a sweetish smell. 'Here it comes!' the policeman's wife called out. 'They are stinking already.' Her husband laughingly corrected her that it was 'only the gas'. 'We had gone on about 200 yards,' Cornides noted in his diary, and 'the sweetish odour was transformed into a strong smell of something burning. "That is from the crematory," says the policeman.'[38]

Rawa Ruska was only 18 kilometres from Bełżec and most trains crossing Poland had to stop at the station. When some French and Belgian prisoners of war were sent to work there that summer, they asked the middle-aged German reservists guarding them where the trains packed with Jews were going. The blunt reply was simply, 'To heaven'. Two of the Belgian prisoners managed to escape to Sweden in the spring of 1943, where they also spoke to a British agent, who filed the following report:

> What made the most impression on them was the extermination of the Jews. They had both witnessed atrocities. One of the Belgians saw truck loads of Jews carried off into a wood and the trucks returning a few hours later – empty. Bodies of Jewish children and women were left lying in ditches and along the railways. The Germans themselves, they added, boasted that they had constructed gas chambers where Jews were systematically killed and buried.[39]

French prisoners dismantling Jewish graves in eastern Galicia near Tarnopol, so as to use the stones in road-building, returned to Germany bringing their stories with them. One told a German trade unionist he trusted about the packed trains which returned empty; two others, who escaped to Sweden, informed a British agent. They did not know the details of how the killing occurred and reported that 'some said they [the Jews] had been electrocuted *en masse*'. This was not unusual. Whilst the arrival, undressing and burial or burning of corpses occurred in the open and were observed by witnesses from outside the camp, the killing itself was not. Zygmunt Klukowski, a well-informed hospital director in the nearby town of Szczebrzeszyn, heard that 'electricity' as well as 'poison gases' was being used at Bełżec as early as 8 April 1942.[40]

Tales of mass electrocution scattered far and wide, reaching the Warsaw ghetto. On the 'Aryan' side of the city, the German captain in the garrison, Wilm Hosenfeld, wrote home on 23 July, the second day of the deportations from Warsaw, telling his wife that the 'ghetto with its half-million Jews is to be emptied' on Himmler's orders: 'History has no real parallel. Perhaps, cavemen ate each other, but to simply butcher a nation, men, women, children, in the twentieth century, and that it should be us, who are waging a crusade against Bolshevism, that is such a dreadful blood-guilt to make you want to sink into the ground with shame.' Each detail he learned only made him feel worse. On 25 July, he heard that the Jews were being sent to a camp near Lublin where the victims were burned alive in electrically heated chambers, saving the work of mass shootings and burials.[41]

Such knowledge did not mean that everyone knew, but it was spreading from the vicinity of the camps, reaching far beyond the local German telephonists and railwaymen, the drinkers at taverns who fell into conversation with sozzled SS men wanting to let off steam or the German engineers working in the IG Farben plant alongside Jewish prisoners from Auschwitz. There were other rumours too – of gassing tunnels and deportation trains in which the Jews were gassed through the heating system. They cropped up in a diary from Hesse as early as November 1941, in Frankfurt in June 1942, and in the notebooks of a Viennese diarist in late 1942. In Berlin, Ruth Andreas-Friedrich noted it three times in her diary.[42]

Just as with the news of the murder of psychiatric patients in 1940 and 1941, so the information passed most rapidly amongst those with privileged bureaucratic access. The ex-ambassador to Rome and anti-Nazi conservative Ulrich von Hassell heard first of the *Einsatzgruppen* in the Soviet Union and then about the gas chambers from his high-level contacts in the military and in military counter-intelligence – Hans von Dohnanyi, Georg Thomas and Johannes Popitz. Even the head of the SD in occupied France, Werner Best, had learned of the *Einsatzgruppen* 'sweeps' informally from colleagues posted back from the east. Among less influential Germans information circulated more quickly among those who still maintained anti-Nazi networks of friends and acquaintances. On 31 August 1943, the 15-year-old daughter of Berlin Social Democrats confided to the pages of her diary, 'Mummy told me recently most of the Jews have been killed in camps, but I can't believe it.'[43]

In January 1942, one of the gravediggers at Chełmno, Yakov Grojanowski, escaped and managed to make his way to the Warsaw ghetto, where his tale reached Emanuel Ringelblum, head of the secret Jewish archives, and Yitzhak Zuckerman, a Zionist youth leader. At least two letters with similar information reached Łódź. But the warnings did not pass into mass circulation. Amongst inhabitants of the Łódź ghetto, hunger was the most important issue in early 1942, masking the true nature of the deportation of 55,000 people from the ghetto.[44]

It was not necessary for Germans to hear about death camps in order to know about the murder of the Jews. By the time the Viennese lawyer Ludwig Haydn was told, on 19 December 1942, that gas was being pumped through the heating vents of the trains in which Jews were being deported, he had already heard first- and second-hand accounts of mass shootings. At the end of June, he had tuned in to the BBC to hear one of its first reports on the extermination of the Jews. But already Haydn knew that 'With regard to the mass murder of the Jews, the broadcast merely confirms what we know here anyhow.'[45]

At the same time, even those in charge did not know for certain how much progress they had made. Dissatisfied with the internal counts compiled within the Reich Security Main Office, SS leader Heinrich Himmler commissioned his chief statistician, Richard Korherr, to provide reliable figures; an abridged – and slightly more euphemistically phrased – version of his report was sent to Hitler in early April 1943. Korherr estimated that by the end of 1942, 1.2 million Jews had been killed in the death camps and a further 633,300 Jews in the occupied Soviet Union – in the light of other evidence a considerable underestimate even at this juncture. This was a secret report for the eyes of the highest Nazi leaders, yet its estimates were broadly in line with what the Allies were saying. 'If the Jews say we have shot 2.5 million Jews in Poland or pushed them off to the east, then we obviously cannot reply that it was only 2.3 million,' Goebbels had said in his confidential press briefing on 14 December 1942. Others could only guess at the scale: Ulrich von Hassell thought that 100,000 Jews had been gassed in May 1943. Hearing an SS man boast that 2,000 were being killed every week in Auschwitz, Ruth Andreas-Friedrich estimated that 100,000 Jews were being killed in just this one camp each year. By the time the ninety-six Jews who lived on the tiny Greek island of Kos were ferried to the mainland and shipped off to Auschwitz in July 1944, it had long been clear that this was an operation to winkle out and destroy all the Jews in Europe.[46]

★

As knowledge spread, it did not automatically raise the question of moral responsibility. For that it would have needed the oxygen of public discussion. Having started in the autumn of 1941 by demanding that 'national comrades' actively support the branding and deportation of the Jews, Goebbels had realised that by turning the topic into a public issue the media was creating a space for discussion and dissent. His response had been to tone the entire anti-Semitic campaign down. In a similar fashion, he had backed away from confronting Germans directly with the 'euthanasia action' and shelved all hard-hitting attempts to do so, opting instead for a 'soft sell' approach based on the issue of voluntary assisted suicide for a terminally ill patient in the film *I Accuse*. The principal difference was that Liebeneiner's film was designed to steer a national discussion, acclimatising public opinion to the clearing of Germany's psychiatric wards. The new propaganda approach to the 'Jewish question' was more low key, leaving it to hints and rumour to work on the popular mind, promoting quiescence rather than debate. There, thanks to the silence of the churches, things remained, stalling any explicit and public moral reckoning either for or against the 'final solution'.

In some respects, Goebbels's approach seems to have worked. Both the public branding and the deportations of the Jews were irreversible, symbolic acts and they changed public attitudes slowly but fundamentally. In the autumn of 1941 there had been numerous cases of Germans getting up to give elderly Jews their seats in crowded trams and trains. A year later, such acts had become both rare and scandalous. When in October 1942 a young German woman stood up on a tram in Stuttgart for an old Jewish lady whose feet were visibly swollen, she found herself the object of a public outcry. 'Out!' shouted an angry choir of passengers. 'Servant of the Jews!' 'Have you no dignity!' The driver stopped the tram and ordered both women to get out. In Münster, the journalist Paulheinz Wantzen dated the hardening of attitudes towards the Jews to the crisis which engulfed the eastern front in the winter of 1941–42.[47]

There is another aspect to public silence: it made it harder for people to voice their moral disquiet even to themselves. The Solingen teacher August Töpperwien first heard reports about the mass shooting of Jews in Poland in December 1939, noting them again in May 1940. In May 1942, he was sent to help run a camp for prisoners of war in Belorussia and within six weeks he was reporting on the mass shooting of Jews: 'In our village 300 Jews were shot. Both sexes, every age group. The people had to take off their outer clothing (clearly so that they could be distributed amongst the remaining inhabitants of the village) and they were being killed with pistol shots. Mass graves at the local Jewish cemetery.' Later, Töpperwien was sent to Ukraine where again his way was marked by killing sites, and yet it took this reflective high-school teacher a further seventeen months before he admitted to himself what all this information meant. Only in November 1943 did he write in his diary, 'We are not just destroying the Jews fighting against us, we literally want to exterminate this people as such!' The trigger for this reflection was a conversation with a soldier from whom Töpperwien 'heard *dreadful*, apparently accurate details about how we have exterminated the Jews (from infants to the aged) in Lithuania!' August Töpperwien seems to have needed the stimulus of discussion – albeit a private conversation – to put what he had already witnessed into a general context. It was a train of thought he failed to pursue further at this point; it seems that this Protestant diarist, many of whose entries reflect extensively on the metaphysical meaning of the war, could not bear to consider what this admission meant.[48]

For non-Jewish Germans and most Europeans living under German occupation, the deportation and murder of the Jews was neither very secret nor very significant. To Jews trapped within occupied Europe – registered and labelled in the west, ghettoised in the east – their own victimisation became the central focus. On Yom Kippur 1942, as Victor Klemperer and his wife said their farewells to the last twenty-six 'old people' sitting in the Jewish community house in Dresden on the eve of their deportation, he was in no doubt about the prevailing sense common to them all: 'The mood of all Jewry here is without exception the same: The terrible end is imminent. *They* [the Nazis] will perish, but perhaps, probably, they will have time to annihilate us first.' This sense of impending doom, both collective and personal, remained fundamental to Klemperer's response to all news until the end of the war.[49]

The key asymmetry between Jewish and German responses is to be found here: for the Jews, their impending destruction shaped their understanding of all other aspects of the war; for Germans, the war framed their understanding and response to the murder of the Jews. It was not knowledge of the events which separated them, but their viewpoints, which were marked by huge asymmetries of power – and also of empathy.[50]

With the German media hinting at what people already knew, the rumours became more bizarre. In November 1942, Himmler was appalled to read a serious claim advanced by Rabbi Stephen Wise in America that the corpses of the Jews were being turned into fertiliser and soap. The SS leader immediately instructed the head of the Gestapo to investigate, asking him to guarantee that no further use was being made of corpses, beyond burning or burial. By that time, the rumour, which had reached Wise via his Swiss rabbinical informants, was already well established. In Berlin it circulated as a joke: 'Who are the three greatest chemists of world history? Answer: Jesus, because he turned water into wine; Göring because he turned butter into cannons; and Himmler because he turned Jews into soap.' Fifteen-year-olds laughed at each other under the shower after their football games, joking about how many Jews they had scrubbed in the suds of green soap. Others deciphered the initials RIF embossed in wartime bars of soap as RJF, transforming the innocuous-sounding Reichsstelle für industrielle Fette (Reich Office for Industrial Fats) into 'Rein jüdisches Fett' (Pure Jewish Fat).[51]

The soap rumour may have harked back to the First World War, when British propaganda had claimed that in German 'corpse factories' the military dead were processed into glycerine and other products. Like the rumours of mass electrocution in the special camps from which the trains returned empty, false and real details combined to convey a widespread sense that an unparalleled, industrial-scale operation was taking place. Ghoulish humour in particular provided ways of starting to assimilate the enormity of what was happening without fully accepting it as fact. With flippant remarks, people could try to displace fact into the realm of the absurd, without quite dispelling their own profound unease.

★

During 1942 and 1943, the few Jews left in the Reich were more isolated than ever. Segregated at work from their 'Aryan' colleagues, confined to unsocial hours of shopping and forced to move into 'Jewish' houses, there were few spaces left where Jews and non-Jews could meet. The Catholic convert Erna Becker Kohen found she had to quit the church choir because other members did not want to sing with her. Even communion became difficult because fellow parishioners refused to kneel beside a Jew, and some of the priests also avoided contact. After the introduction of the yellow star, Cardinal Bertram had written to Cardinal Faulhaber to say that the Church had more urgent issues to deal with than the Jewish converts; it was left to individual dioceses to work out how to handle the problem.[52]

Among the Protestant churches, only small sections of the Confessing Church affirmed the right of its Jewish converts to worship with other Christians, and Theophil Wurm, the Bishop of Württemberg, addressed several private letters to the Nazi leadership in defence of the 1,100 Jewish Christians in his see. In November 1941, Goebbels read a letter from him complaining that the measures against 'non-Aryans' played into the hands of 'Roosevelt and his accomplices': perhaps recalling Wurm's faint-hearted protest against medical killing, Goebbels saw him as a Protestant Galen: 'His letter goes into the wastepaper bin.' Further private letters by Wurm fared no better. Eventually Lammers, the head of the Reich Chancellery, sent a handwritten note warning the bishop to 'stay within the boundaries established by your profession and abstain from statements on general political matters'. Wurm fell back into line. There were two other Protestant bishops, Meiser of Bavaria and Marahrens of Hanover, who maintained their independence from the avowedly Nazi and reforming German Christians. But neither man followed Wurm's example. Even if they eschewed the racial anti-Semitism of the Nazis, all three bishops remained, like most Protestant pastors, deeply conservative and nationalist, sharing in an anti-Semitism which still identified Jews with the 'godless' Weimar Republic and saw Nazi measures to curtail their influence and 'Aryanise' their property as legitimate: there was no opposition to the deportations themselves from the Confessing Church.[53]

At the other end of the Protestant spectrum, the German Christians rushed to avow that they had 'discontinued every kind of communion with Jewish Christians', and strongly supported the persecution of the Jews. On 17 December 1941 the German Christian Church leaders of Mecklenburg, Schleswig-Holstein, Lübeck, Saxony, Hesse-Nassau and Thuringia demanded that the Jews 'be expelled from German territories' and affirmed again that 'racially Jewish Christians have no place and no right to be in the Church'. Franz Tügel, the Bishop of Hamburg, had joined the Party in 1931 and become a leading speaker at provincial rallies. Although he started to distance himself from the German Christians by 1935, he responded to the deportation of the Jews in November by reminding his readers that

> I preached once before during the time of the inflation that, in order to bring the brutal exploitation of millions of thrifty and hard-working Germans to a swift end, the banks should be shut and the Jewish stock-exchange speculators hanged . . . I have no responsibility for the Protestant members of the Jewish race, for the baptised are only in quite rare cases really members of our communion. If they have to leave for the ghettos today, then they should become missionaries there.

Two days before Christmas 1941, the Protestant Church Chancellery issued an open letter to all provincial churches calling on the 'highest authorities to take suitable measures so that baptised non-Aryans remain separate from the ecclesiastical life of the German congregations'.[54]

In his own Berlin parish church at Nikolassee on Christmas Day 1941, Jochen Klepper found 'no Jew with the star present at the service'. Thanks to her 'Aryan' marriage, his wife Johanna did not have to wear the star, but her daughter Renate enjoyed no such exemption and she did not dare accompany them. During the service, Jochen and Johanna were consumed by 'anxiety that we would not be allowed to take communion'. Klepper had returned home to Berlin two months earlier, his service in the Wehrmacht abruptly terminated because he had not broken with his Jewish wife. In September 1939 he had felt certain that Germany was fighting a justified war of national self-defence but had feared for Johanna and Renate. Certain that war would only intensify the persecution of the Jews, he was racked with guilt for having talked them out of emigrating to England while there was still time. Now, as the deportations began, his worst premonitions were being fulfilled.[55]

Desperate to use his remaining ties to the political elite, Klepper sent the last copy of his edited collection of the letters of the Prussian 'Soldier King' Frederick William to the Interior Minister, Wilhelm Frick, in March 1942: it was a fitting birthday present and served as a reminder of the promise Frick had given to help Renate to circumvent the general ban on Jewish emigration which had been introduced in October 1941. It took several months for Klepper to secure an entry visa for Renate to neutral Sweden. Eventually, on 5 December 1942, it came through and Klepper immediately contacted the British mission in Stockholm to find out if the Quakers could sponsor Renate to join her sister, Brigitte, in England. He also approached Frick about the all-important exit visa. The Interior Minister agreed to see him, acknowledged his promise and signalled his readiness to help. In Klepper's presence, he set the wheels in motion to obtain the permissions from the Reich Security Main Office. Elated and anxious in equal measure, Klepper asked him whether he would also help his wife to emigrate. Visibly agitated, Frick began to pace up and down, explaining to the writer that he no longer had the power to protect a single Jew. 'Such things by their very nature cannot remain secret. They reach the ears of the Führer and then there's a furore.' He told Klepper that, for now, his wife was protected by her marriage to an Aryan, but confided that 'there are efforts under way to push through forced divorces. And that means after the divorce the immediate deportation of the Jewish partner.'[56]

All Frick could promise was to bring his own influence to bear on the SD. This bought Klepper an audience with the head of the Jewish section, Adolf Eichmann, the following day. Warning him to speak of it to no one, Eichmann told him, 'I have not finally said yes. But I think the thing will work out.' When Klepper asked again about his wife, Eichmann told him categorically that 'A joint emigration would not be approved.' He was invited to return the next afternoon to learn the outcome of Renate's case. At his second meeting with Eichmann on 10 December, he was told that Renate's visa had been turned down. Jochen, Johanna and Renate now decided to leave on their own terms: 'Tonight we go together into death.' They placed their picture of Christ raising his hand in blessing in the kitchen, closed the door, opened the oven, and lay on the floor looking at the picture and one another, as the sleeping pills and gas took effect.[57]

The regime drew back from compulsorily dissolving Jewish–Christian marriages, an omission that was key to Victor Klemperer's survival. But signs of impending measures continued. In March 1943, 1,800 Jewish men married to 'Aryans' were rounded up in Berlin. For the next week, the women congregated in the street outside the building in the Rosenstrasse where they were held, chanting 'Give us our husbands back!' – until the Gestapo decided to release them.[58]

In Berlin, less than 10 per cent of the 70,000 Jews who were in the capital at the start of the deportations went into hiding. Those who had been spared during the great wave of deportations clung to the hope that privilege and exemption certificates could protect them. That hope was destroyed on 27 February 1943, when the 8,000 Jews still working in the city's armaments industries were rounded up. The only chance of survival now lay in going underground. Irma Simon was tipped off the day before the 'Factory Action' began and stayed home with her husband and 19-year-old son Fritz instead of reporting to Siemens. Her husband, a vet, had obtained phials of prussic acid to commit suicide. She set off down the Lehrter Strasse with a suitcase in search of rescue. Improbably, she found it, thanks to a shoemaker and his blacksmith brother, the Kossmanns, two middle-aged, working-class men with communist sympathies. They took in the three Jews and hid them. At first the couple split up, the husband staying with the shoemaker and Irma and Fritz with the smith. As Fritz was of military age, they pretended he was unfit for service. When this facade became difficult to maintain, he had to 'return' to his unit, which meant in practice hiding him in Kossmann's dark and freezing allotment shed, where his protector had to bring him food and dispose of his faeces and urine, all without attracting attention. He stayed there for two years. Irma donned the black veil of a widow and adopted the cover story that she was romantically attached to August Kossmann – a tale which in the course of 1943 became real. Against the odds, the Kossmann brothers managed to hide the three Simons until the end of the war, eking out their scanty rations, with August putting in extra hours for local farmers so as to pay off the suspicious block warden with gifts of food.[59]

The 1,400 Berlin Jews who survived in hiding had to be saved not once but many times. Often, they were supported by those who already possessed clandestine networks and were used to evading Gestapo surveillance. Growing up in Berlin as the son of an Austrian Jewish father and a mother who had converted to Judaism, Gerhard Beck was initially saved from deportation by the Rosenstrasse protests. Once released, Gerhard helped other Jews go into hiding, making use both of an underground Zionist network and one created by his 'Aryan' gay friends. Banned under paragraph 175 of the Criminal Code, male homosexuals had long become adept at keeping their social circles and sexual lives hidden to escape social discrimination, homophobia and police persecution. It was Gerhard's Jewish network which cracked first, in early 1945, when a Jewish informant betrayed them to the Gestapo.[60]

In Essen, Marianne Strauss went into hiding when the rest of her family was deported in October 1943. Rescued by a small circle of ethical socialists which called itself the Bund, she had to keep moving from flat to flat, criss-crossing Germany by train and tram, shuttling first between Braunschweig and Göttingen, and then between Wuppertal, Mülheim, Essen, Burscheid and Remscheid. During the next two years she made between thirty and fifty journeys, each one a test of her survival skills. With no form of ID apart from a post office pass, she had to continuously watch for controls. When police were checking identity cards, she learned the art of moving slowly down the carriage ahead of them in the hope that she could get off at the next station before they reached her. Each of her hosts had to invent a cover story for the out-of-town relative, or explain away the fact that she was not working by turning her into a young mother on a visit – this involved borrowing a child from another Bund member.

With so many links, even a chain constructed by dedicated activists could snap at any point, and the odds were stacked against them. What protected them from discovery by the Gestapo, however, were those aspects of their socialist utopianism which did not look overtly political. The Bund members had bought several houses in order to encourage experiments in communal living and many of them were involved in modern dance. Both of these endeavours stemmed from the movement for 'life reform' in the 1920s and convinced the secret police that they were not dealing with a political grouping. As dedicated socialists and anti-Nazis, the members of the Bund treated Marianne as a fellow German, rather than as a Jew. As socialist revolutionaries they were also waiting for Germany's defeat, a political stance which set them apart from others who chose to help Jews.[61]

The many different individuals who helped hide Jews eventually included Wilm Hosenfeld. On his arrival in Poland in September 1939 he had been shocked by the harsh treatment meted out by the new German masters, and had decided to follow his conscience. First he had helped Polish Catholics. At the start of the liquidation of the Warsaw ghetto in the summer of 1942, Hosenfeld heard that the Jews were being killed by mass electrocution. By early September, he had more accurate information: he knew that the camp was called 'Triplinka' and that the Jews were being gassed and then buried in mass graves. At first he found it hard to believe that Germans could be capable of such things, but, as the information became ever more definite, he felt deeply ashamed. He started rereading the fifteenth-century mystic Thomas à Kempis, asking himself whether God allowed mankind to go astray in order to bring it back to his teaching of 'Love One Another'.[62]

On 25 September 1942, four days after the last transport had left the ghetto for Treblinka, Hosenfeld attended a dinner party which included an SS major, Dr Gerhard Strabenow, and his lover, dressed to the nines, and wearing an outfit Hosenfeld thought was probably looted from the ghetto. As he relaxed over the meal, Strabenow portrayed himself as 'the lord of the ghetto'. 'He talks of the Jews,' Hosenfeld noted in his diary, 'as if they were ants or other pests. Of the "resettlement", that is of the mass murder, as of the eradication of bedbugs when disinfecting a house.' Hosenfeld wondered what he was doing eating at the 'richly laden table of the rich, while all around it the greatest poverty and the soldiers go hungry. Why does one remain silent and not protest?' Hosenfeld's own activities during the great deportation from Warsaw focused on the sports school he ran for the Wehrmacht. He organised a week-long sports competition, which attracted 1,200 athletes and an audience of thousands – a resounding success for military morale, after which he and his wife took a well-earned week of leave in Berlin.[63]

Unlike the small numbers of clandestine socialists, Hosenfeld took no precautions to hide his opinions from fellow officers. Despite his opposition to mass murder and his increasing readiness to equate the National Socialists, whom he had joined in 1935, with their Bolshevik enemies, he clearly thought of himself neither as a conspirator pitted against a dictatorial regime, nor as a traitor to the German cause. Rather, he told himself, the 'National Socialist idea . . . is only tolerated, because it is currently the lesser of two evils. The greater is to lose the war.' Having unburdened himself in several letters to his son Helmut, now serving on the eastern front, Hosenfeld told him how the resilience of German troops from North Africa to the Arctic 'makes one proud to belong to this nation. One may disagree,' he added, doubtless referring to the anti-Jewish action, 'with this or that, but the inner bond to the essence of one's own people lets one overlook the flaws.'[64]

It took Wilm Hosenfeld eight months before he went further and gave sanctuary to two Jews in the Wehrmacht sports school he ran. In the meantime, the ghetto uprising had been crushed and the only Jews left in the city were in hiding. One of them, Leon Warm-Warczyński, had broken out of the cattle truck of a train bound for Treblinka, and Hosenfeld readily took him in under the assumed identity of a Polish worker. For Wilm Hosenfeld – First World War veteran, Catholic schoolteacher, sometime storm trooper and member of the Nazi Party – helping to hide two Jews in Warsaw was a natural response, the kind of action his conscience finally demanded. But it did not compete with his patriotism, let alone make Hosenfeld wish for Germany's defeat, the only outcome that might secure Warm-Warczyński's survival.[65]

Few were prepared to go this far. For Ursula von Kardorff, a young journalist on the *Deutsche Allgemeine Zeitung*, helping Jews began with a personal encounter. In the dusk of a November evening in 1942, the doorbell rang and in the dim light of the hall she could see that both visitors were wearing the yellow star. They had come from

Breslau, they said, with a painting by her father, a well-known academic artist, which they now needed to sell back. 'We give them some food and slowly they thaw out,' Kardorff recounted in her diary. 'It is indescribable what these people are going through. They want to go underground, before they get picked up, live as bombed-out refugees from the Rhineland.' Her father bought the picture from them, but, as the young journalist reflected, their visitors needed not just 'material aid but also pepping up'. Occasional assistance was one thing, but the Kardorffs were not prepared to do more.[66]

Ursula had her own journalistic work for the cultural review section of the paper. Making up Christmas parcels for her brother and fiancé, both serving in the Caucasus, she decided to surprise them by popping photos of herself next to the illustrated cards in their cartons of cigarettes. However much she might want to help Jews survive, she did not want Germany to lose the war. For the New Year's cultural supplement of the newspaper she designed a page with photos ranging from the Russian snow to the North African sun to illustrate 'The German soldier on watch', and reflecting on the old year, she noted in her diary that, compared to the bombing and rationing, when it comes to the 'eradication of the Jews, the great mass [of the population] is indifferent or even approves'.[67]

Gradually, the deportation and mass murder became an event of the past. By the summer of 1943, special teams had disinterred and burned the corpses of those gassed at Treblinka, Sobibor and Bełżec and the three camps were dismantled during the following months. Even the exhuming and burning of the corpses of those shot in Galicia and Ukraine did not remain a secret from the home front. In the Reich, municipalities started to take down the quaint, out-of-date signs forbidding Jews entry to public libraries, swimming pools and parks.[68]

9

Scouring Europe

The Axis alliance emerged from the winter crisis of 1941–42 having added Japan to its allies and the United States to its enemies. The disproportion of economic resources stood at a ratio of 4:1 against Hitler's Reich. Germany could not hope to wage a successful war of attrition: that was the unalterable lesson of the First World War. As the three army groups on the eastern front struggled to withstand the Red Army's general offensive, the political leadership of the Third Reich knew that its current defensive efforts did not provide a solution to its strategic impasse: at best, they would lock the eastern front into precisely the kind of war of attrition which, over time, would tell against them.[1]

The sole grounds for strategic optimism in Germany in early 1942 lay with their Japanese ally. The day after bombing the US Pacific Fleet at Pearl Harbor, the Japanese launched an attack on Hong Kong. The island colony surrendered on Christmas Day 1941, by which time Japanese armies were sweeping through South East Asia, their string of successes culminating in the fall of Singapore on 14 February 1942. As the German leadership learned of these victories, it realised that the United States and Britain would be in no position to launch an invasion of western Europe until the autumn at the earliest, and probably not until 1943. Whatever the long-term risks of widening the war to include Japan and the United States, in the short term it bought Germany vital time in a moment of crisis. From Hitler's perspective, the United States had already covertly entered the war in September when Roosevelt committed the US Navy to securing the convoys carrying Lend-Lease military aid to Britain against German U-boats in the Atlantic. In November, the American President extended Lend-Lease to the Soviet Union. The Japanese attack on Pearl Harbor brought enormous benefit to Germany by ensuring that American resources would be sucked into the Pacific theatre before they could be deployed in Europe.[2]

Why Hitler felt it was necessary for Germany to declare war on the United States on 11 December is less clear. Given that 75 per cent of Americans were still opposed to entering the European war, Hitler certainly made Roosevelt's domestic political task easier. Japan made no matching declaration of hostilities against the Soviet Union, and, had it done so in December 1941, Stalin might have hesitated to move the Siberian divisions westwards to defend Moscow. Hitler admitted to Goebbels that he derived huge satisfaction from this act of sovereign decision-making, taking the initiative which had been denied him on 3 September 1939, when it had been the British and French leaders who had declared war on Germany. It was a strangely emotional admission, given how well the French and British declaration of war had accorded with the Nazi leadership's claims to be acting purely defensively. Declaring war on America was an unnecessary act – a provocation which threw all prior caution to the winds: it was no accident that, instead of threatening to take action against the Jews in Europe in order to curb their warmongering in America, Hitler authorised the first deportations of German Jews at this time. There would be no de-escalation, no negotiated settlement. Once again the United States, Britain and Russia were ranged against Germany, just as in 1917. If Hitler's political career had been dedicated to re-fighting and this time winning the First World War, now he had his 'world war'.

The German leadership desperately needed to rethink its military strategy. The seeming invincibility enjoyed by its often qualitatively and quantitatively inferior forces in the summer campaigns of 1940 and 1941 had derived from strategic surprise. That would be virtually impossible to recreate. By early 1942, German military intelligence and the Army General Staff knew that they had grossly underestimated Soviet military-industrial capacity, and that they could only wage a second campaign in the east if they were able to mobilise their own economic and military resources fully, on a scale usually associated with a war of attrition. In this pause for strategic stocktaking, the navy also pushed for a different strategy, one which would turn the war on the eastern front into a holding operation and devote the lion's share of resources to a new global air and sea campaign to link up with Japan in challenging British and American control of the Mediterranean, Red Sea, Indian Ocean and Atlantic Ocean. While Hitler concentrated on making his strategic choices, others in the German leadership were trying to find the labour, food, coal and steel to make any new offensive possible.[3]

By conquering the highly industrialised lands of western Europe, Germany had the real prospect of escaping from its inferior pre-war position and becoming a military-industrial superpower. Apart from the United States, all the belligerent powers were constrained by limited resources. In the German case, stocks had been run down and resources were shuffled back and forth because of short-term bottle-necks. Skilled workers moved between the army and the factory: most of the weapons deployed in the Barbarossa campaign had been produced by men released from the Wehrmacht after the 1940 victory and then called back to the colours a year later. By the end of 1941, they were meant to have returned to their factories to produce weapons for the campaign against Britain in 1942. Instead, they were combating frostbite on the eastern front. War production could be increased dramatically at home only with a massive influx of labour.[4]

It was a similar tale with material resources. In the summer campaigns of 1940 and 1941, virtually all the petrol supplies had been consumed to fuel the advancing tank columns, as reserves were staked against the chance of a decisive victory. The Royal Naval blockade continued to ensure that Europe remained chronically short of vital military supplies, like oil and rubber, as well as critically short of food. The Germans could produce synthetic rubber and biofuel, but these were costly substitutes and, heavily dependent on its limited Romanian supplies, the Wehrmacht's tanks, personnel carriers, trucks and planes all remained desperately short of petrol. Only the conquest of the Caucasian oilfields could alter this situation – and in 1942 that again became a key military goal.[5]

Coal remained the prime source of energy in wartime Europe. Nominally self-sufficient, from the outset Germany's shortage of railway rolling stock had created distribution problems. Just as in the first winter of war, there was not enough rolling stock to move military supplies in the winter and spring of 1942; even the deportation of the Jews had to wait. The general shortage of coal and steel – the basis of industrial, including weapons, production – was aggravated by the fact that firms engaged in hoarding and stockpiling in order to minimise disruption to their own production. This rational local response only exacerbated the general problem. At the same time productivity in the French and Belgian pits kept falling, limiting how much coal could be extracted and so throttling the pace of industrial expansion. The main reason was hunger. On 9–10 May 1941, there were strikes in the Belgian coal mines and steel mills, symbolically commemorating the first anniversary of the occupation. Keen to ward off any increase in communist influence, Belgian employers preferred to negotiate with the trade unions, agreeing to an 8 per cent wage rise; they also refused to hand over the lists of militants to the German military authorities.[6] But in the French and Belgian coalfields, hunger remained the dominant fear, to the point where the French factory social committees and the Belgian factory councils spent so much of their efforts setting up works canteens and allocating allotments that they were dubbed 'potato committees'.[7]

In each occupied West European country, the local German military and civil administrations jostled with each other and competed with the demands of the local Gestapo and SD, not to mention with the overarching jurisdictions of central Reich agencies, such as Göring's Four Year Planning Office, Albert Speer's Armaments Ministry, Fritz Sauckel's recruitment of foreign labour, and the Ministry of Agriculture, nominally headed by the old Nazi ideologue Walter Darré but increasingly run by his State Secretary, Herbert Backe. Moreover, the attempt to create a pan-European economy in 1942 was marked by conflict over whether to suck labour and capital into Germany or build new plants in occupied Europe, for example in the French Atlantic ports, or in the formerly Polish parts of Upper Silesia. Overshadowing all decisions loomed the issue of food.[8]

The politics of food distribution was never rationally subordinated to economic or military aims. If it had been, then French and Belgian coal miners might have been fed enough to increase their output. Instead, Germans automatically came first, their rations creating the most fundamental and enduring of their racial rights in the war. Food remained the prerogative of the Ministry of Agriculture and Herbert Backe made his career by insisting on a tough interpretation of the regime's racial-nationalist priorities. During the planning for Barbarossa, he had estimated that 20–30 million 'Slavs' would have to be starved to death in order to feed the German armies. In early 1942, German administrators were surprised that the number of deaths of Soviet civilians had not been even higher in the previous autumn and winter. The other shock was that food stocks on the home front had run dangerously low, due to the confident expectation of a short war. Backe immediately set about preparing a second 'hunger plan' for the east and imposed food delivery quotas across occupied Europe, levying them on the west as well as the east.[9]

On 6 August 1942, Hermann Göring chaired a meeting of officials from the occupied territories charged with putting Backe's food requisitioning plan into effect. Taking personal responsibility, Göring laid out the argument with brutal clarity:

> I have here before me reports on what you are expected to deliver . . . it makes no difference to me in this connection if you say that your people will starve. Let them do so, as long as no German collapses from hunger. If you had been present when the Gauleiter spoke here [yesterday], you would understand my boundless anger over the fact that we conquered such enormous territories through the valour of our troops, and yet our people have almost been forced down to the miserable rations of the First World War . . . I am interested only in those people in the occupied regions who work in armaments and food production. They must receive just enough to enable them to continue working.[10]

For added rhetorical effect, he also reminded officials, worried about the social consequences of imposing famine on a majority of the population under their control, that the extermination of the Jews would free up some food supplies in their territories. By 1942–43, Germany was drawing more than 20 per cent of its grain, 25 per cent of its fats and nearly 30 per cent of its meat from occupied Europe. The total deliveries of grain, meat and fats from France and the occupied Soviet territories more than doubled, from 3.5 million tonnes to 8.78 million tonnes over the same period. In the Kiev district of Ukraine, the greatest round of requisitioning during the whole occupation occurred ahead of the 1942 harvest itself: 38,470 tonnes of grain were collected in June, 26,570 tonnes the following month, tailing off finally to a mere 7,960 tonnes in early August. The representative for Food and Agriculture in the Reichskommissariat Ukraine returned from a tour of inspection content that the peasants of the district had no more grain, not even for seed. This had been a military-style requisitioning operation, with detachments of the mainly Ukrainian Order Police descending on houses, mills, markets, gardens and barns to search for hidden stockpiles. Much of the French and Ukrainian supplies went directly to the Wehrmacht on the spot; the General Government, whose rule had been extended from central into eastern Poland and western Ukraine, supplied more than half of the rye and potatoes and two-thirds of the oats imported into the Reich.[11]

At exactly the same time, labour recruitment increased dramatically. On 21 March 1942, Hitler appointed his old comrade Fritz Sauckel, the Gauleiter of Thuringia, to be plenipotentiary for labour mobilisation. In the eighteen months from the start of 1942 to June 1943, Sauckel's agents brought 34,000 foreign workers to the Reich every week, adding 2.8 million to the 3.5 million that were already in Germany. The number would continue to rise until there were just under 8 million foreign workers in the summer of 1944. The forced recruitment from occupied western Europe prompted raucous scenes and wildcat strikes. As the trains pulled out to take the forced drafts of French workers to Germany, crowds broke the wartime ban on national symbols and sang the 'Marseillaise'. In Belgium, the trade unions and the Catholic workers' youth movement helped hide the *réfractaires* who refused to return to Germany when they came home on leave. The numbers of those in France, Belgium and the Netherlands who did not go back rose to nearly a third. Most of them were forced to find illegal work and lodgings, often on outlying farms where their dependence made them ideal, docile labourers. With German power at its height, relatively few chose to go further and join the small resistance groups.[12]

The great majority of forced workers came from eastern Europe, however. The Polish General Government and Ukraine were particularly heavily trawled. According to Sauckel's figures, between April and November 1942, 1,375,567 civilian workers were sent to the Reich from the occupied Soviet territories, a further 291,756 from the Polish General Government and 38,369 from the Wartheland, compared to 357,940 from the Netherlands, Belgium and all but northern France. Threatened with execution if they failed to fulfil the German quotas,

in the east village leaders preferred to choose outsiders. In the predominantly Ukrainian villages of western Volhynia, as the major surviving
ethnic minority it was Poles who were often targeted. Elders faced
simultaneous pressures to deliver grain and labour to the Germans,
and therefore opted to send those who did not work in agriculture,
drafting disproportionate numbers of teenagers who were not yet in
registered employment. Over half the 1942 draft to Germany were
girls and young women aged 12–22.[13]

For the German colonial masters this was an unsustainable
strategy. Over any longer period of time, the Reich could not have
sucked both food and labour from its eastern colonies, which were
rapidly pushed into starvation and increasing mortality. There were
parallels here with Stalin's forced collectivisation and first Five Year
Plan, which had caused a huge famine in Ukraine in the early 1930s:
to Soviet planners, it had not mattered if Ukrainian peasants starved
or if agricultural output nosedived, just as long as they delivered
their quotas. But even Stalin had discovered that such a policy was
unworkable and had to reinvest and start mechanising agriculture,
to mitigate some of the losses. Despite considerable internal discussion between the different agencies involved, the Germans made no
such adjustments.[14]

The German 'east' was condemned to a spiral of economic decline,
whose pace was quickened by the unregulated brutality of colonial
rule. By the autumn of 1942, German demands on the new harvest
were becoming impossible to meet. Postal censors and the SD picked
up the impact on the countryside. 'It's harvest time, and yet we have
no bread,' a Ukrainian woman wrote to relatives working in Germany.
'The guys gather stalks, and we mill this on the hand mill, to make
some bread. This is how we've been living up to now, and we don't
know what will be next.' In almost every household private stills were
set up, and alcohol consumption soared. At least the grain they turned
into alcohol could not be seized. 'They drink "for an occasion",'
reported a Volhynian newspaper, 'and "without any reason". There
used to be one inn for the entire village; now there is an inn in every
third hut.'[15]

As villages in poorer agricultural areas, like Polissia, failed to meet
their quotas, a new and terrible war against the civilian population
began. On 2 September 1942 German and Ukrainian police entered

the village of Kaminka east of Brest Litovsk, massacred the entire population and burned all the houses as a warning to the surrounding district of the fate that awaited those who did not meet their delivery quotas or were suspected of supporting the partisans. Exactly three weeks later, it was the turn of the village of Kortelisy, near Ratne. The District Commissioner of Kovel told the peasants that as they were known to harbour partisans he had orders to burn them alive in their homes; however, he was commuting their sentence to shooting. None of the 2,900 people executed was suspected of actually being a partisan: their deaths served as a deterrent. As this strategy of pacification through terror spread across eastern and southern Europe, the number of villages burned would grow exponentially over the next two years. With different local starting points, parts of Belorussia, Greece, eastern Poland, Serbia and, later, Italy were all engulfed by German 'anti-partisan' actions, with their massive collective reprisals. In western Europe, such actions remained the exception, and the destroyed villages of Oradour-sur-Glane in France and Lidice in Bohemia and Moravia became memorials because they remained unique examples of German brutality. When it was liberated, Belorussia could count over 600 villages destroyed and their populations massacred: 2.2 million of its total population of 10.6 million died under occupation.[16]

It would take time before peasants would see the partisans as liberators, rather than as just another threat to their precarious lives. In 1942, partisan groups were still too weak and scattered to pose a serious threat to the Germans. Rather, the rival Polish, Jewish, Ukrainian and Soviet partisan groups in the forests were battling each other for control of their base areas and the food supplies of the surrounding villages. The economic, political and social collapse of Ukraine into a vortex of inter-ethnic violence followed from the untrammelled German demands. In other parts of eastern and southern Europe, the balance of causes – military, political and economic – varied, but these regions all shared a common feature: the collapse of state authority. In Belorussia, Poland, Serbia and Ukraine, no autonomous national or local government was tolerated and, reduced to mere auxiliaries, the local Order Police would eventually fracture, with many members deserting to join partisan units in the final months of German rule.[17]

In contrast to the direct colonial rule in the east, in France the state survived. Here the whole process of extracting food from farmers was carried out by French intermediaries, even in regions like Brittany and the Loire which came under direct German military administration from the start of the occupation. It involved constant negotiation between German and French officials at each level of the hierarchy, from the centralised Vichy structures manned by the director-generals of the provisioning administration all the way down to the mayors of individual rural communes. One of the great problems for the supply system was the illegal slaughter of livestock. From early on in the German occupation, new regulations were issued banning both butter-making and slaughter on French farms, in order to promote large abattoirs and dairies as instruments of control. Farmers did everything they could to avoid conforming to these rules, and in the autumn of 1941 promptly elected an ordinary farmer rather than a Vichy official to lead the new Peasant Corporation of Maine-et-Loire, which the Vichy government had instituted in order to increase its control over the countryside. Self-confident conservative Catholic aristocrats like Comte Henri de Champagny, well entrenched in the Vichy elite, had no compunction in unilaterally slashing the butter quota for his commune of Somloire in Anjou from 375 to 50 kilos. Less well connected mayors retreated to the age-old defence of the countryside – stubborn silence. Even the collective fines levied by the Germans for non-fulfilment of quotas often went unpaid for years – with relative impunity. Even though the French head of state, Marshal Pétain, remained personally very popular, his vision of conservative 'solidarity and mutual aid on a national scale' was challenged by the countryside's refusal to co-operate.[18]

In Ukraine, German demands on the countryside gradually destroyed local government, leading to an anarchic civil war; in France, power drained away from the central state in a less dramatic but still highly significant fashion. It was the local landlords and clerics who had met the invaders in 1940 and guaranteed the safety of citizens by offering themselves as hostages; now they tried to protect them from extreme economic demands. As a similar process of official exhortation and communal recalcitrance was played out across occupied western Europe, local notables re-emerged as key actors, a victory of *pays* over *patrie*.[19]

Across Europe, the countryside prospered at the expense of the cities. Urban workers in the Loire benefited from the German demand for armaments, producing ships' radios, tents, blackout material and camouflage netting, torpedo boats and destroyers, railway trucks and Heinkel III bombers, not to mention the huge projects constructing U-boat pens and Atlantic coastal fortification. But high employment, good wages and nominally better rations did not protect them from chronic food shortages and hunger. Worst off were the great cities. In Paris, a food riot broke out at the market at the rue de Buci on 31 May 1942, leaving two policemen dead. In the clampdown that followed, male communists who had helped to co-ordinate the protest were executed and female suspects were sent to Ravensbrück concentration camp. Such protests were isolated incidents, however. The numbing reality remained the queue for official allocations which increasingly ran short as supplies were diverted to the black market.[20]

Middle-class Parisians returned to areas, like Chinon, where they had been evacuated in 1940, while the bourgeois cycle-tourist with double panniers became a familiar sight in the countryside. In the absence of motorised transport, the bicycle entered a golden age. Almost every town had at least one cycling club. Most cyclists were increasingly concerned with mundane problems like how to replace worn-out tyres now the British naval blockade had closed off imports of rubber. A common, though slow and extremely bumpy, solution was to wire together lengths of garden hose.[21]

The process of economic fragmentation and regionalisation overlaid a deeper and more basic divide: that between areas of food surplus and areas of food deficit, sometimes in the same geographical region. On the European level, the Netherlands and Denmark enjoyed a surplus, whilst Belgium, Norway and Greece all suffered from deficits. Left in charge of their own affairs, Danish government administrators had adopted a pricing and rationing policy which encouraged farmers to increase the supply of pork, beef and milk and raise exports to Germany, without imposing harsh restrictions on domestic consumption or stimulating a black market. The outcome of this system of direct economic incentives was spectacular: with a population of 4 million, Denmark became an ever more important exporter to the German Reich, contributing some 10–12 per cent of its beef, pork and butter. By 1944, German cities may have drawn as much as a fifth of their meat supplies from Denmark, as other sources went into steep decline. The Netherlands, with its technologically modern agricultural sector, remained important too, though having to adapt to the constraints of the British blockade left it short of animal feed. Dutch farmers were forced to switch increasingly to arable and greenhouse crops. By 1941, they had culled their herds to the point where farmers were able to export fodder themselves, as well as large quantities of fruit, vegetables, sugar and potatoes to Germany.[22]

Norway, Belgium and Greece, on the other hand, depended on large food imports. Nazi policy-makers, their reasoning based on a mix of racial policy and economic utility, regarded Norway as more 'Aryan' than the Reich and – by German standards – the country underwent a 'model' occupation. Yet even here child mortality rates began to rise, and by the summer of 1942 German reports were noting that Norwegians were 'to a considerable extent undernourished'. In Belgium, imports from Germany were never sufficient and only reached 17 per cent of the pre-war level. As black-market prices for food soared and wage rates remained fixed, there was a wave of labour unrest.[23]

Before the war Greece had imported a third of its grain from Canada, the USA and Australia. In 1940–41, grain supplies plummeted to 40 per cent of their pre-war level, and within five months of the German occupation the first famine broke out in occupied Europe. In Athens the daily calorie intake dropped to 930, and over the next year 40,000 died in the Athens-Piraeus area. Unlike Backe's successive 'Hunger Plans' for the Soviet Union, the Greek famine was unintended, triggered by a fatal combination of military purchasing and requisitioning, alongside food hoarding by wholesale distributors. The famine was greatly exacerbated by the division of the country into three separate occupation zones – Italian, German and Bulgarian – which inhibited internal trade, in particular from the grain-rich regions of Thrace and eastern Macedonia. There was one train a day from Athens to the north, and foraging city-dwellers could bring back no more than 300–350 tonnes of food per day by rail. As post and telecommunications broke down too, the integration of the national economy went into rapid reversal. None of the three military administrations was moved to provide much assistance; nor were Backe's officials in the Reich Food Ministry in Berlin. The famine was finally relieved only when Britain agreed to lift its blockade and permit Swedish vessels to bring Canadian grain to Greece under the supervision of the International Red Cross. Whereas Belgium and Norway were of real economic and strategic importance and counted as 'Germanic' and 'Aryan' nations, the philo-Hellenism of the German officers who established their headquarters in Athens in the spring of 1941 did not extend beyond the classical period. By the spring of 1942, German-language newspapers in Greece began to speak of 'urban parasites' and 'useless eaters' – language which had so far been reserved in German parlance for the Jews.[24]

★

On 16 and 17 July 1942, French police conducted their first great round-up of Jews, arresting 13,152 foreign nationals in Paris and its suburbs. Families with children were taken to the Vélodrome d'Hiver, the famous cycling track. There, without adequate sanitation, water or food, 8,160 were held for up to six days in the sweltering heat of mid-summer, before being deported.[25]

While the Jews were still being held in the Vél d'Hiv, much of the French public was gripped by the spectacle of professional cycling. Ten days earlier, on the weekend of 5 and 6 July 1942, Parisian crowds had flocked out to the municipal stadium at Vincennes, where, overlooked by a giant portrait of Pétain urging them to 'Remain disciplined. The Marshal asks you', they watched the Dutch champion van Vliet triumph in the final. On 16 July, the first day of the round-up, a Frenchman was winning the fourteenth stage of the Tour of Spain. In the autumn of 1942, in place of the Tour de France, a smaller, six-stage version was held, billed as the Circuit de France, involving sixty-nine riders and covering 1,650 kilometres. Emile Idée and Marcel Kint slogged it out in the Paris–Roubais and Paris–Tours classics, and French riders continued to ride in the tours of Italy, Switzerland and Spain. In September, the vast Vél d'Hiv reopened to the public, for a boxing match, as if nothing had happened there.[26]

The round-ups of Jews continued until March 1943 in France: trains took Jews to transit camps at Drancy, Compiègne and Pithiviers and from there to the death camps in Poland. They departed amidst an eerie silence, quite different from the spontaneous demonstrations that had accompanied the forced drafts of French workers to Germany. Only in the Netherlands and Denmark were there public and courageous acts of support. In February 1941, hundreds of Jewish men were arrested in Amsterdam's streets in reprisal for a minor attack on a German police unit in a Jewish-owned ice-cream parlour. The Dutch Communists had called a general strike on 25 February 1941, which the Germans crushed with live ammunition and hand grenades. There was no repetition, but when the deportation of Jews began in the Netherlands, the Catholic Church protested publicly: on 26 July 1942, a letter from Archbishop de Jong of Utrecht to the Reich Commissioner Arthur Seyss-Inquart about the deportation of Jewish converts was read out in all Catholic churches. The swift German response was to arrest most of the Catholic converts: there was no recurrence, and the deportation of the Jews ran smoothly, with boisterous protest songs and shouts of 'Oranje boven!' reserved for the trains taking Dutch workers to Germany. In Denmark, anti-Semitism was so unpopular that the Germans did not attempt to deport the Jews until the summer of 1943, because they knew that it would spell the end of collaboration with the Danish constitutional monarchy. When the Reich Plenipotentiary finally took this step in September 1943, the date of the planned action was leaked and all but 485 of the country's 7,000 Jews were smuggled across the Baltic narrows to the safety of neutral Sweden.[27]

But these were exceptions to the silence and passivity which generally blanketed the Continent. Everywhere apart from Denmark the occupation tended to exacerbate pre-existing anti-Semitism. Attempting to ward off German demands for labour and food, let alone hostage-taking and reprisals for 'terrorist' acts, Europeans generally put solidarity with the Jews at the end of their list of priorities. For each institution involved there were red lines, things it would not accept. For the Catholic Church in France – whose College of cardinals had proposed taking rights away from Jews before the Vichy government took the initiative – the line was crossed on 1 February 1944 with the conscription of unmarried women for labour in Germany. The Gallican Church's assembly of cardinals and archbishops publicly condemned this 'serious attack on family life and the future of our country, on the dignity and moral susceptibility of women and their providential vocation' – motherhood. The contrast with the Church's inaction over the deportation of the Jews could not have been more marked. Under German occupation silence was as significant as protest: it signalled concessions that could be made in order to defend what really mattered.[28]

After the Jews were gone, their fate was not, however, forgotten. In parts of Poland and Ukraine, where crowds had gathered in 1941 and 1942 to watch the round-ups of Jews and acquire the property they left behind, the murder of the Jews soon became a yardstick for measuring their own possible fate. In autumn 1942, SS units returned to the Zamość district to drive Poles off the land and 'Germanise' villages, and the rumour rapidly spread that the Poles would be sent to the gas chambers at Bełżec or Treblinka, where the district's Jews had perished months earlier. In the cities of Ukraine, there were similar fears. When Kiev was occupied in September 1941, little sympathy or help had been extended when the Jews were massacred in the ravine of Babi Yar. By April 1942, with no escape from the German blockade of food to the city, a local teacher asked her diary, 'What can one do, how to live? They probably want to give us a slow death. Obviously it is inconvenient to shoot everybody.' By early autumn, after a year of German rule, Nartova chronicled what her fellow Kievans were saying: 'First they finished off the Yids, but they scoff at us for a whole year, they exterminate us every day by the dozens, they're destroying us in a slow death.'[29]

★

While maps of Europe in German classrooms were being covered with little swastikas from the Atlantic to the Caspian Sea, chronic food shortages in the Reich curbed the expression of triumph. By the end of the winter of 1941–42, none of the food requisitioning that Backe was planning for occupied Europe could save German civilians from privation. Rations were cut on 6 April 1942, sharply and across all categories. For the Nazi leadership, which drew a straight line between the 'turnip winter' of 1916–17 and the 'stab in the back' of November 1918, these were the measures it had most wanted to avoid. Within a week, the SD confirmed that it was indeed the worst single blow to civilian morale in the Reich during the war so far.

In the major cities the SD warned that the 'provisioning situation' gave rise to 'highly critical and sceptical views for the future'. Without doubt, even after weeks of preparatory leaks and rumours, the psychological shock was unprecedented. By the winter of 1941–42, fuel shortages, school closures and wearing layers of clothes to stay warm indoors – all of which had so alarmed people in the first winter of the war – had become commonplace even for a doctor's family like the Pauluses in Pforzheim. The ration cut was a shock of a different order altogether.[30]

At a single stroke, 250 grams was lopped off the weekly bread ration. Potatoes and other carbohydrates were meant to offset this, but the cut to proteins and fats was still more drastic. The weekly meat ration fell by 25 per cent for all but those who were doing 'very heavy labour'. For the category of 'normal consumers', which included housewives, the retired and white-collar workers, the meat ration fell from 400 to 300 grams a week. Despite great efforts in the media to point out the positive contrasts to the First World War, playing up the fact that rations allocated to pregnant women, nursing mothers and children had not been reduced, housewives across Germany were complaining loudly that they did not know how to feed their children.[31]

Although rationing never sank to the catastrophic levels of the First World War and although the system continued to function in most areas until the very end, this did not stop Germans from making the comparison. It was not long before an SD office in the Ruhr warned that 'in the firms a mood is growing ever stronger which is reminiscent of that in 1918'. Elsewhere, workers were heard talking loudly about how ration cuts would affect their productivity, a clear threat to go slow. Prosecutions for absenteeism and other infractions of labour discipline rose dramatically in the second half of 1942. Shortages also forced women to waste ever more time in shop queues, and employers complained bitterly about the unreliability of their German female workers. Some well-intentioned publicity drives, like the one launched in Württemberg by the Milk and Fat Trades Association urging people to collect beechnuts and extract plant oil, also reminded people of the previous war.[32]

Since consumers were registered to receive rations at particular grocery and butchers' stores, they could not shop around freely. Especially in the cities of the Rhineland and Ruhr, queues formed very early in the morning, with reports of 6 a.m., 5 a.m. and even 2 a.m. starts. Occasionally, policemen joined the queues they were meant to be controlling, so that they could obtain goods in short supply, such as fish. In August 1942 the local Nazi Party leader from Castrop-Rauxel warned that 'if the sale of vegetables etc. continues like it has so far there is a danger that women will one day succumb to rashness which could have ugly consequences'. Rather than emulating the food riots in Paris, Germans dissipated their discontent in a culture of local envy and complaint, as disgruntled shoppers checked that their neighbours were not evading the regulations.[33]

Long before the ration cuts came into force, war had lost its savour. In Germany, as in Britain, the gradual disappearance of meat, milk, eggs, fresh fruit and vegetables from the diet could be made up in calorific terms by bread and potatoes, until they accounted for over 90 per cent of the daily intake. The quality of the bread deteriorated too. In Britain, the move away from white bread to wholegrain and wheatgerm led to a considerable improvement in nutrition. In Germany, where the bread was traditionally much better, quality declined. By April 1942, virtually none of the bran was being removed from the milling process and the proportions of barley, rye and potato flour being added to the mix had increased. The coarse dough also absorbed far more water, so permitting further economies without reducing the weight of the loaf. People soon began to complain of digestive problems, especially in the south where traditionally more wheaten than rye bread was consumed. Replacing fats, proteins and vitamins with starch and yet more starch had both physical and psychological effects. Health investigators calculated that the first years of war had used up the accumulated fat reserves in urban workers' bodies. Without making good the losses in fats and essential minerals, a starch-based diet made it impossible to feel full for very long. The official 'four-fruit jam' contained increasing amounts of rhubarb, pumpkin and green tomatoes to bulk out the crushed sweepings of fruit. Minimum fat contents of milk, butter and margarine were all reduced.[34]

As the most plentiful staple, stored in cellars by the hundredweight, potatoes featured in many recipes, from soups and dumplings to sauces. In many cases, potato flour was needed, which involved grating the potatoes into a large bucket by hand, pouring in fresh water and then skimming off the dirty water from the top, before finally scooping out the white potato flour which had settled on the bottom and laying it out to dry on blotting paper. It was a process which could take all day. As sugar became harder to obtain, urban women would offer to help local farmers reap their sugar beet crop in order to receive some of it themselves. The heart-leaves, one young woman recalled, were saved for 'spinach', while the straggly outer ones were thoroughly scrubbed before being chopped fine and boiled for hours in a large tub. After they had cooled, a washing press could squeeze a thin brown liquid out of the cooked beet, which then had to be heated again for hours before it finally reduced and thickened into a sweet syrup. Demand for synthetic, chemical flavourings, such as vanilla sugar or lemon and rum essence, increased, and new recipes tried to disguise the endless repetition of the same ingredients and make them go further. 'Meatballs' and 'cutlets' were fashioned out of potatoes, lentils, turnips and white cabbage. Bored by the monotony of wartime cooking, people became obsessed with recipes and fantasy meals, dining off the memory of a lost 'golden age' of plenty.[35]

From before the war, women had passed on recipes to their daughters for making sweet and savoury preserves and conserves from berries and other fruits, cabbage, carrots, mushrooms and other vegetables, often salted. Kitchen gardens became more important as soon as war broke out, and many miners' families kept goats or piglets. Although shortage of feed now reduced their number, many households in towns as well as villages went on keeping rabbits and chickens. Even a GP like Ernst Paulus now raised chickens and tended an allotment. Stinging nettles, long collected by the Hitler Youths to make natural remedies, now began to appear in Berlin markets as a vegetable. Families went out to woodlands to collect dandelions for salads, acorns for coffee and camomile, peppermint and lime leaves for tea.[36]

The black market took on new forms. Butchers and grocers offered an under-the-counter service to favoured customers. A young woman who worked in a pharmacy traded some of its stock of black tea and sweet syrups for meat. Another, employed in the ration card section of the town hall, issued many coupons to her mother and was lucky not to be caught. Working as a clerk in the Charlottenburg ration card office, Elisabeth Hanke soon noticed that in every four-week rationing period there were people who failed to collect their cards in time. Whereas she had to obtain her superior's permission for withholding ration cards, she needed none to issue them. So she issued the unclaimed ones to herself. One evening, while going for a drink with her colleagues after work, she struck up an acquaintance with an official in the Air Ministry. The two quickly formed an economic partnership: she provided ration cards and he the contraband goods. They soon became lovers too.[37]

As the criminal police turned to combating the black market, they began to map each district of Berlin, focusing on cafés, pubs, shops and restaurants that were known for trading. Each quarter served its socially distinctive clientele, the elegant bourgeois frequenting the 'better West End', while the working-class pubs of Wedding, Neukölln and Spandau catered for their own. Whereas many traders carried out their transactions in the secrecy of the toilets, waiters sold cigarettes openly to diners – no explanation, secrecy or negotiation needed.[38]

On 1 April 1942, Martha Rebbien had to move lodgings, after falling out with her landlady on account of her black-marketeering. When the 55-year-old waitress was finally arrested two years later, she did not hesitate to incriminate her former landlady, claiming that she had kept her supplied with food while her husband, a prison warder, had used his contacts to provide 'coffee, tinned meat and chocolate'. But witness statements and successive interrogations soon revealed a local informal network, encompassing some forty business partners and associates. Most of them were working the local pubs, all within one kilometre of Gesundbrunnen station, one of Berlin's busiest railway stations and at the heart of a working-class district. Rebbien's trades usually started with personal contact and conversation, followed by a walk to her home where goods could change hands without witnesses – hence the key role played by her landlady. Despite the breadth of the network, these were small-scale black-market operations, each person responsible for just a few of them. Only one of Rebbien's contacts, a travelling salesman, turned out to be a serious trader: operating out of a café on the Danziger Strasse, he added a further fourteen contacts to her original cluster of tried and trusted clients.[39]

This still rather small black market drew on the traditional semi-open, semi-clandestine practices of prostitutes, who made their initial contacts in the same places and relied on familiar neighbourhood networks to glean information and screen outsiders, before taking their clients back to their apartments. The two networks overlapped, thanks to the sex trade's need to tap into the black market for cosmetics, dresses, hairdressing and medical care (especially in abortions).[40]

Just as in occupied Europe, those who could went to buy food in the countryside. On Sundays, the suburban railway network was crowded with people willing to trade children's toys, kitchen utensils, coats, shoes and men's civilian suits for the eggs, milk, cheese and, above all, meat which were missing from their urban diets. In cities like Ulm and Stuttgart, housewives laid in stocks of useful and unrationed goods such as detergent and glass jars for storing preserves, which they could barter at the farm gate. Already in the summer of 1941, townsfolk in Swabia were preparing for Christmas, paying the farmers in the district of Saulgau up to 20 marks per gosling and a further 40 marks once the goose had grown into a fully fattened bird. The SD monitored some of the barter, noting that in the town of Biberach 10 pounds of strawberries were swapped for a quarter-kilo of coffee beans; French shoes and fabric for fruit and vegetables; and salad oil for cherries. With so many townsfolk coming to them, farmers outside Stuttgart felt less need to sell their produce in the city's markets.[41]

In the countryside the patchy surveillance that the police maintained over German towns, cities and railways all but dried up. The authorities remained largely blind to rural trade and were correspondingly cautious about how they enforced the maze of economic regulations in the countryside. One factor which constrained their incursions into closed rural communities was shortage of manpower. For the whole of Württemberg, there were only fifteen gendarmes available at the start of the war to enforce price controls and their number continued to fall, especially after 1941, when replacements for the eastern front were desperately needed. The auxiliary policemen who replaced men sent to the front were unable to investigate cases in detail and so passed their growing caseload on to the prosecutors' offices, whose staff were facing the same attrition. By mid-1942, violations of the War Economy Decree had become the principal offences brought before the Special Courts, with illegal slaughtering chief amongst them. Yet the police and public prosecutors frequently shrank back from investigations or entered mitigating pleas for lighter sentences, preferring to pursue a softer approach of warnings and exhortations.[42]

In November 1942, the Stuttgart Special Court travelled out to Rottweil to sit in judgment on a case of illegal slaughter. It involved the mayor of the commune, his 17-year-old son, a police clerk and the local farmers' leader who, conveniently, doubled up as the local meat inspector. The four defendants were accused of having connived in systematically under-reporting the weight of slaughtered animals, mainly pigs. The meat inspector had used a common trick of recording the weights of the animals without the heads, so that when the heads were added back the equivalent weight of prime meat could be removed. It was virtually impossible to conceal the slaughter of a pig or calf on a farm: it took a butcher and the farmer a whole day to render the carcass, which was usually hung up in the open air of the courtyard. It was therefore much easier to register short-weight than not to register the slaughter at all. The Stuttgart Special Court was given evidence documenting 227 cases for the period of November 1939 to October 1941, during which almost 3,000 kilos of pork had been spirited away. At that point, the police clerk had taken over the weighing operation, allegedly defrauding the depot of 1,170 kilos of pork in just six months until his arrest in March 1942. As the official responsible for logging all cases of slaughter, the mayor had knowingly connived in the practice, employing his teenage son to do the clerical work. The boy was acquitted, on the grounds that he had simply followed his father's instructions. All three adult defendants were found guilty.

Hermann Cuhorst, the President of the Stuttgart Special Court, was a man with a fearsome reputation. A few days before this case, several people had been beheaded in Stuttgart for violating the War Economy Decree, and a month later a 60-year-old man would be executed for illegal slaughtering and 'other kinds of trickery'. In the Rottweil case, however, Cuhorst handed down relatively mild prison terms: the police clerk received a ten-month sentence, the farmers' leader eighteen and the mayor himself, as the senior official, twenty-four months. In April 1942, Hitler had publicly berated the judiciary in a speech to the Reichstag for being too lenient, which may in part explain the ruthless application of the death penalty in a regional capital such as Stuttgart. In a backwater like Rottweil, however, leniency would attract less publicity. The court also had strong motives for not antagonising an entire rural community by executing its leaders. As the judges put it, 'none of them [the defendants] wanted to break with ingrained, erroneous practice, in order to avoid conflict and strife with the farmers in their commune'. These men 'were – in a small community in which everyone knows everything [that happens], and where they are mostly related to each other by ties of blood or marriage – obviously in a difficult position in trying to fulfil their official duties when there was a conflict of interests'.[43]

Such delicacy in enforcing the regulations and softening their draconian terms was by no means unusual in the Württemberg countryside. With its intricate patterns of intermarriage across generations, the village communities in south-western Germany were particularly hard to penetrate. By conceding that local representatives of the Party and state were members of their communities first and foremost, the judges acknowledged that, unless they found mitigating circumstances to justify leniency, the regime risked losing all influence in the countryside. It was easier to reach an accommodation with these communities, long lauded as the true foundation of National Socialism's policy of 'blood and soil', than to combat them.[44]

The fact that farmers could still meet their delivery quotas and have enough surplus to trade on the black – or grey – market suggests that the SD was right to argue for increasing farmers' incentives in order to stimulate production. This, after all, was the model that proved so successful in Denmark. The Food Ministry rejected this strategy, however, seeing a system of fixed prices and delivery quotas as the guarantee that the exorbitant inflation and urban famine of the First World War would be avoided. Yet, by tolerating a widespread, if relatively modest, black market in the countryside, the police and courts were tacitly accepting the emergence of a small, illegal economy that did offer price incentives for increasing production once official quotas had been met. In practice, the regime could benefit from this development, without having to acknowledge the widening disjuncture between rhetoric and reality.[45]

Those who ran the system of food deliveries and rationing were also best placed to subvert it, not just in a Swabian village but across occupied Europe. It is much harder to map the larger-scale operations of the black market than neighbourhood trading, but their outlines are sometimes discernible. In Warsaw, a German edict banned the baking and sale of white bread from as early as 23 January 1940, yet it continued to be openly displayed in the shops and market stalls where Germans also went to buy it for themselves too. The fleet of trucks bringing in white flour each day ran on petrol issued from German-controlled stocks with permits purchased from corrupt officials in the military and civilian administrations. As a major railway junction, Warsaw also served as a fleshpot for German troops on furlough from the eastern front and had a flourishing black market. Not infrequently, the products available revealed the pan-European extent of the deals being brokered with German officials. Just before Christmas 1942, a large amount of poultry suddenly appeared on the city's markets, no doubt diverted from shipments to Germany. In 1943, news leaked out that herrings, presumably shipped by the Wehrmacht from Norway, were being sold in bulk. Occasionally, it was the goods themselves that revealed something of the scale of the enterprise. In May that year a whole consignment of tortoises sent from Greece or Bulgaria to Germany was offloaded at Warsaw. Though not part of traditional Polish cuisine, they too were sold in street and market stalls throughout the city. For weeks tortoises that had got away were spotted crawling out from behind pillars and edging their way laboriously up steps.[46]

German civilian administrators, SS officers and ordinary soldiers had celebrated their conquests of 1940 and 1941 by buying up stocks of goods that were hard to come by in the Reich; and so it continued. What impressed one teenage girl was how their table groaned under the weight of luxuries – from almonds and pears to cinnamon, pâté and carrots wrapped in ham – when her father returned from Paris; and then there was the notepaper, sewing materials, stockings, gloves, belts, detergent, shoes, soap and bed-linen that he had also brought home. Marvelling at it all, the teenager reflected that 'this has become the norm in Germany now. Wherever the men are, there they buy. Whether in Holland, Belgium, France, Greece, the Balkans, Norway, etc.' As the famished Parisians watched the hordes of German troops staggering under the weight of their luggage at the Gare de l'Est, they nicknamed them 'potato beetles'.[47]

In Ukraine, they earned the name 'hyenas'. Here the plunder began with distributing Jewish property. While tools and simple furnishings were often given to the local populace, anything of greater value was seized. The Higher SS and Police Leader for Central Russia, Erich von dem Bach-Zelewski, sent 10,000 pairs of children's socks and 2,000 pairs of children's gloves via the Reichsführer SS's personal staff to

SS men's families as Christmas presents. A delegation of Italian Fascists was awed and appalled by their tour of the Minsk opera house, where piles of looted clothes and possessions towered over them. By 1943, German postal censors were noting the way that families were taking advantage of the resources available in the east: a grandfather was urged to send his new boots to Ukraine in exchange for 8 litres of oil, which he could use to barter for a new coat for himself back in the Reich. Ukrainians sold eggs, oil, lard, ham, chickens, peas, butter, sugar, flour, noodles, biscuits, sausage, pearl barley and Persian lambs' fleeces in return for salt, matches, flints, yeast, old clothes, household utensils, women's underwear, handbags, graters, cucumber slicers, suspender belts, saccharin, skin cream, nail polish, baking powder, lipstick, toothbrushes and baking soda. Matches were being sold at 6 marks, old suits for 600 marks. A pound of salt would buy a chicken, 10 pounds a sheep, whilst it was apparently not rare for a family in the Reich to acknowledge receipt of shipments of 2,000–3,000 eggs. Germans were sending to Ukraine all their cheap jewellery, tinsel and redundant household items, with men urging their 'relatives and acquaintances to band together' to collect these things for barter.[48]

In a parody of the Nazi language of heroism, one letter-writer remarked how at least 'in this area extraordinary things have been achieved', pausing to note how the vacuum left by mass murder was being filled: 'what the Jews did previously is being pursued in a much more complete form today by the Aryans.' This was a rare insight and moral condemnation. On the whole, words like 'racketeer' and 'black-marketeer' were reserved for the black market in Germany; there was no word, pejorative or otherwise, for such activities in occupied Europe. In the west, at least in the first years of occupation, there was a degree of embarrassed self-awareness. The Münster journalist Paulheinz Wantzen noted it in a new joke in 1941: 'Two Englishmen dressed as German officers were arrested in Belgium as spies. The Germans didn't pick them out but the Belgians did because they were not carrying suitcases.' By contrast, the east was there for the taking; and it was only after the goods began to circulate within the German homeland that Germans watched and morally policed one another's activities.[49]

★

Increasingly aware of their dependence on the conquered territories, Germans embraced their new imperial mission with far less eagerness than the material advantages it brought them. By 1942, the media was trying to popularise the idea of a 'Greater Area'. In May, Hitler addressed the Reichsleiters and Gauleiters again behind closed doors, telling them that 'our colonial territory is in the east' and that it would provide coal, grain and oil. The Reich would build a massive new fortified border within which the German population could expand over the next two or three generations to reach 250 million. In public Hitler generally placed the emphasis more firmly on Germany's war of self-defence, but that same month he also told an audience of 10,000 young officers in the Berlin Sportpalast of the conquest of 'living space' in the east and the primary goods it would provide.[50]

Along with deporting the Jews, Heinrich Himmler was busy elaborating his ideas for creating agricultural colonies settled by farmer-soldiers in successive drafts of his 'General Plan for the East', providing an intellectual focus for an ambitious and talented generation of demographers, economists and historians. Germans' manifest destiny to rule over the east had been readily embraced at home when it came to Poland. Many young women, from kindergarten teachers to students, volunteered to go out and do their bit to help re-Germanise the Wartheland or, in 1942–44, the Zamość region. They had to make do with what they could find. One BDM activist in the Lublin district looking for a suitable site for a kindergarten for the children of German settlers had a Jewess ejected from her house. It was too small and so she arranged for a Jewish house in Plaszow to be dismantled and re-erected in the village.[51]

In June 1942, Erna Petri arrived with her 3-year-old son in Lwów. They had left their farm in order to join her SS husband, and they took over the former manor house of a Polish noble outside the city. With its white-pillared portico and wide meadows, it looked more like the dwelling of a plantation owner than the modest family farm she had left in Thuringia. True to the precept that the Germans should assert themselves physically over the natives, within two days of her arrival she witnessed her husband flogging his farm labourers. Soon, Erna too was beating the workers. As she served coffee and cake to her husband's SS and police colleagues on the villa's balcony overlooking the gardens, talk inevitably turned to the mass shootings of

Jews. In the summer of 1943, she was returning from shopping in Lwów when she saw a group of nearly naked children crouching by the side of the road. She stopped the carriage, calmed the six frightened children and took them home, where she gave them some food and waited for her husband to return. When he did not turn up, she took matters into her own hands. Pocketing an old service revolver which her father had given her as a parting gift, Erna Petri led the children through the woods to a pit where she knew other Jews had been shot and buried. There she lined them up in front of the ditch and went along the line firing into the back of each child's neck. She remembered that after the first two, the others 'began to cry', but 'not loudly, they whimpered'.[52]

In the Soviet territories, enthusiastic colonists like the Petris were a minority: Germans did not flock to the Crimea and Ukraine, despite the rich agriculture. If deep-seated cultural fear had served as the strongest justification for waging 'preventive' war against the Soviet Union, it also made it hard to convince Germans to go and settle there. In the first two years of war, the Nazis had successfully propagated the idea that German society needed to become a *Volksgemeinschaft*, a national community. This concept meant different things to different people, but it now clashed with talk of a wider destiny to rule a non-German 'Greater Area'. This new mission was routinely dismissed as 'imperialism', a term whose pejorative associations summoned up images of Boer women and children in British concentration camps in the 1941 film *Ohm Krüger*, and the mass starvation enforced by the Royal Navy on German children which extended after the armistice into 1919. True, there was nostalgia for Germany's former African colonies, but the tough world to be conquered and colonised in the east was another matter. Soon Himmler's SS resettlement commissions were scouring the orphanages of Poland, Ukraine and Belorussia to pick out suitably 'Aryan'-looking children they could 'Germanise' themselves. With too much 'living space' now available to Germans, Himmler told the guardians of racial purity to dilute their criteria and to 'distil' every 'drop of good blood' out of the racial 'mish-mash' of the eastern nations.[53]

There were other reasons why the Nazi empire was not a popular idea. Germany was now awash with foreigners. With much of the Nazi propaganda on racial 'purity' pandering to a narrow sense of national, or even local, identity, the influx of foreign workers could at best be tolerated as a wartime expedient, a rational but unpleasant necessity. At the same time, many domestic ills were blamed on the disruption caused by foreigners, who, it was conveniently forgotten, had been press-ganged. In a special report surveying their black-marketeering activities, the SD claimed that the French and Italians brought watches and jewellery, not to mention food and wine, into the country, or sold on the macaroni and Mediterranean fruits they received in parcels from home. As a result some of the Italian civilian workers were said to have built up large balances in their Deutsche Bank accounts. Their principal crime, in other words, had been to behave like Germans. Reversing the real bargaining power of Germans and foreign workers, the French and Italians were turned into the seducers, drawing innocent 'national comrades' into the web of their nefarious trades. This inversion of reality also accorded with the more widely shared 'doublethink' in which foreigners were blamed for sexual contacts often initiated by Germans.[54]

Many French prisoners of war had obtained German civilian suits or work clothes, and were flooding into cafés, cinemas and pubs. Outside Innsbruck, they were seen sunning themselves in the deck-chairs on the terrace of the Berg Hotel. Propagandists might exhort their national comrades to keep their distance from the foreigners in their midst but they were soon developing ever more complex ties to them, by turns opportunistic, exploitative and intimate.[55]

In late 1944, the Gestapo arrested a French worker named André after intercepting a letter he had written to his German lover. He was full of eager plans for their reunion at Christmas and promised her, 'I kiss your breasts a thousand times, we will do 69.' André was in Germany as a civilian worker and there was no actual ban on such relationships, although the fact that his lover was a married woman gave the police an excuse to intervene. The investigation revealed a clandestine love story which had begun nearly two years earlier, at the beginning of 1943, with Sunday trysts. André, it transpired, had in fact been a French prisoner of war, one of the million sent to work in Germany after the armistice of 1940. Under lax guard, it had not been difficult for him to escape, especially since his lover gave him civilian clothes. This was not so very unusual in itself – perhaps as many as 200,000 other French prisoners did the same. But André was so smitten that no sooner had he arrived in France than he decided to return to Germany. André belonged to the relatively small minority who genuinely volunteered to work in the Reich – and he must have been one of the very few to do so not from economic motives but out of love.[56]

Although relationships between Germans and French civilian workers were permitted by the complex web of police and military regulations, those between German women and French prisoners of war were prohibited. Soon after the capitulation of France, the Reich Security Main Office under Heydrich had ordered 'that in accordance with the Führer's order, French, English and Belgian prisoners should, like the Polish prisoners of war, receive the death sentence, in cases of sexual intercourse with German women and girls'. The Wehrmacht ignored Heydrich and, instead, followed the Geneva Convention, according to which representatives of the French military were entitled to take part in the proceedings of the German military courts and, more importantly, had to be informed of the verdict. Applying Article 92 of the military penal code, which covered cases of insubordination, the judges generally handed down prison terms of three years. Punishment might be lighter if it was believed that the woman had 'seduced' the man; conversely, if the woman was married to a soldier, as in this case, then the sentence imposed by the military courts was usually heavier and involved sending the prisoner to the harsh Stalag at Graudenz. An estimated 7,000–9,000 internees were sent to this fortress, where heavy labour, poor diet, exposure to the cold of winter and deficient hygiene took their toll. Despite the incriminating love letter, André tried to deny that he had had a sexual relationship: he was sentenced to three years in a fortress. We do not know how the German police treated his lover; as in other cases of this kind, much would have depended on the view of her husband.[57]

Intent on chasing down and punishing sexual misconduct, Gestapo officials launched detailed investigations, interviewing local residents in time-consuming cases which often began and sometimes ended in malicious neighbourhood gossip. In one such inquiry, a French team of glaziers had been repairing the flats in a building in Essen one after another, and, as the Gestapo officer wearily concluded after a lengthy investigation, 'It would appear that the present case is an instance of neighbours gossiping because all the apartments were not repaired simultaneously.' As RAF bombing became more frequent in 1942, such teams of glaziers were sent from town to town to replace windows and mend roofs. Many of the neighbourhood denunciations reaching the Gestapo involved minor gifts, buns, tea and sauerkraut, sometimes articles of clothing, occasionally no more than hot water to make coffee. In cases like this, the French glaziers were simply cashing in on a German wartime convention whereby handymen preferred to be paid partly in kind.[58]

In towns and cities, female French and Belgian civilian workers also began to attract the attention of the authorities. In Stuttgart the state prosecutor complained that they were rude and insulting to members of the League of German Girls, and spent a lot of time in cafés, bars and cinemas. In Ulm, there was 'lively traffic', and in Renttingen a local official was appalled by the way that German soldiers from the local barracks 'smooch and kiss French women in broad daylight'. The local Party leader appealed openly to German men to uphold their 'racial consciousness' and honour. Police who discovered that four teenage boys had been regularly dating several French women at a ski hut outside Stuttgart could only charge the three who were under 18 with breaking the curfew regulations for juveniles. The oldest could not be charged with anything, because he was over 18 and because, as the state prosecutor complained bitterly, 'sexual intercourse with female foreign workers, even when they are citizens of an enemy state and a significant affront to the public is apparent, cannot be prosecuted'.[59]

★

It was different for women from the east. Soon after the Germans took over Novocherkassk in June 1942, a local official visited Antonina Mikhailovna's home to register her family. He soon returned, collected the 17-year-old – she had only minutes to pack a few things and say goodbye to her parents – and added her to the column of those walking to Rostov-on-Don in the heat of high summer, accompanied by the local elders, Germans with rifles and guard dogs. In Rostov they were loaded into a filthy goods wagon, used for transporting pigs, which took them as far as Poland. During the 'disinfection' halt there, Antonina and the other girls were made to strip and shower, 'while men went to and fro and laughed'. Another girl, Maria Kuznetsova, told a similar story about the arrival of her transport in Munich. After being forced to shower, they were sat on a table and shaved. 'We were young and, you know, innocent and everywhere the men walked around us, though we cried and wailed. But it didn't help.'[60]

Both girls were sent to work for one of the metalworking firms supplying the armaments industry, in the Styrian town of Kalsdorf. Lapp-Finze AG was a medium-sized firm, employing a workforce of 820, including 89 'Eastern workers' and British prisoners of war, 80 Croats, and 15 French civilians. Each national group was housed separately, some in town, others in barracks on the industrial estate. There, only the three barracks for the Eastern workers were fenced off with the barbed wire which the firm produced. In summer, when they arrived, the blocks appeared spartan but clean, the wooden bunk beds covered with mattresses and pillows filled with straw. But the onset of winter was altogether different. The small wood-burning stove in each block gave off far too little heat, especially at night when they lay down to sleep. Their enclosure was right in front of the house of the camp commandant, making it easy for him to check their comings and goings.

During the working day, it was the foremen and master craftsmen who exercised arbitrary control over them, forcing the pace of work in the foundry, even though the young women were not strong enough and had not been issued with safety goggles or the right protective clothing. Some were decent sorts, like Ekaterina Berezhnova's master craftsman who had learned enough Russian as a prisoner in the First World War to talk to them. He also gave them bread. The firm followed the normal practice of monitoring the productivity of the foreign workers, rewarding the more productive ones by allowing them to wear the 'Ost' badge on the upper arm instead of the chest, but this subtle difference was lost on most of the women. In any case, the badge barred them from most of the small town and its chief recreational facility, the cinema. It was informal relationships which mattered more. Many of the forced labourers received food and clothing in return for helping out on the farms which surrounded the small town. Some of the girls made bathing costumes and swam in the canal in summer and even took photographs of their moments of recreation in the fields around the factory. They fashioned 'folk' costumes for their dances and sang Russian songs, accompanied by one of the Croatian men on a mandolin. At least eight weddings took place in the camp, benevolently presided over by the commandant.[61]

Employed often to perform semi-skilled tasks in the armaments industry, young women workers seemed unthreatening to the older, skilled German craftsmen charged with supervising and training them. One retired Krupp worker in Essen described the kind of collusive mutual aid that arose:

So there's this guy at his milling machine and they give him a woman to train. OK, she's supposed to be his replacement when he becomes a soldier. Well, you think he'll be so quick to do that? Like he says, 'Look, don't go digging my grave,' and the women had no interest in doing that either.

The SD also reported instances of 'German employees asking Russian workers to hold back on their output'.[62]

In the neighbouring coal mines of the Ruhr, much of the work was performed by Soviet prisoners of war – exhausted, emaciated men plucked from the huge, typhus-ridden Stalag holding pens. Whereas the Ukrainian miners brought in from the Krivoy Rog were hard-working, disciplined and strong, the Red Army prisoners were in no condition to withstand the task of digging coal out with pikes and picks. Mines were famous for their unrestricted brutality, and by March 1942 two-thirds of the workers sent to the Ruhr pits from Belgium and northern France had left. The German miner who controlled the bread ration and logged the output of the four or five Soviets under him enjoyed absolute power. Here, the status of Germany's coal miners, already the profession most protected from military conscription, dovetailed with interests of pit managers and the Nazi hierarchy. As the boss of the German Labour Front, Robert Ley, put it at a meeting of mine managers in October 1942, it was up to the German worker 'when a Russian pig has to be beaten'. Paul Pleiger, the head of the Reich coal organisation, remarked more smoothly, 'Below ground it is dark and Berlin is a long way away.'[63]

The German home front too became a site of mass death. At least 170,000 Soviet and 130,000 Polish civilian workers died while deployed in Germany, and the authorities did not even count those who perished on their way to and from the Reich, or were sent back home to die there; hundreds of thousands remained unaccounted for. By June 1942, typhus was spreading amongst the Soviet civilian workers. The following month, the AEG cable plant in Berlin reported that the 'Russian women employed are sometimes so weak that they collapse from hunger'. That summer, factories in Frankfurt sent back up to half the workers assigned to them 'due to illness and physical exhaustion'. By September, another official report detailed how a train bringing Eastern workers into Berlin met one taking the 'unfit' back home. This 'could have had catastrophic consequences', the report continued,

> because there were dead passengers on the returning train. Women on the train gave birth to children who were tossed from the open window during the journey, while people sick with tuberculosis and venereal disease rode in the same coach. The dying lay in freight cars without straw, and one of the dead was ultimately thrown on to the embankment. Other return transports were probably in a similar sorry state.[64]

Further down the hierarchy, the statistics were still more terrible. Almost two million Red Army prisoners were put to work in Germany. A million of them died there.

With the mass deployment of foreign labour came an exponential rise in the numbers sent to concentration camps, which became a principal means of disciplining foreign workers. The original core of German political prisoners – usually old-time Communist functionaries – alongside, and in fierce competition with, German criminals now rose above this sea of non-German inmates and vied with each other to provide the elite of prisoner functionaries, the *Kapos* and '*Prominenten*'. They wielded authority over 'eastern' and Polish workers who had tried to escape or been reported to the Gestapo for offences such as insolence or insubordination. There were two groups of Germans whose life expectancy in the camps was particularly poor – male homosexuals and petty criminals. From 1942 onwards, this greatly expanded workforce was drafted into war production as well. The Auschwitz and Monowitz camps supplied labour throughout Upper Silesia as well as to the huge IG Farben chemical works, while the Oranienburg camp in Berlin's northern suburbs serviced the Heinkel aircraft factory, Dachau BMW, Ravensbrück Siemens, Mauthausen Steyr-Daimler-Puch, and Sachsenhausen Daimler-Benz. In 1942 and 1943, the Luftwaffe industries led the way in employing camp labour, with BMW, Heinkel and Messerschmitt setting the pace.

Of the 1.65 million concentration camp prisoners deployed in Germany, at least 800,000 died; a further 300,000 prisoners were worked to death deliberately because they were Jews slated for 'destruction through labour'. Including Soviet prisoners of war and Soviet and Polish civilian workers, even the official – and therefore also inherently conservative – figures show that at least 2.4 million people were worked to death in Germany itself following the military crisis of 1941–42.[65]

One economic historian has described German use of concentration camp labour, subjected to continuous 'selections' and physical effort while provided with starvation rations, as 'not a stock but a flow'. During the rationing crisis which unfolded through most of 1942, this applied to all categories of forced labour from the east, whether military captives or civilian 'volunteers'. In an attempt to rationalise the attrition rates and select which workers would survive in a more economical fashion, the chairman of the coal organisation of Upper Silesia, Günther Falkenhahn, pioneered a system of 'performance feeding' for the 'easterners' working in his Plesschen Werke pit, taking away food from those who underperformed and redistributing it to those who exceeded their norms. He did not reduce the demand for new transports to replace the workers who died. As this cannibalistic version of Social Darwinism spread within the Silesian coal industry, it attracted Albert Speer's enthusiastic endorsement and gradually became standard practice in the German armaments industry.[66]

With starvation rations taking their toll, even managers with well-established Nazi credentials demanded better food for 'unsentimental' reasons such as labour productivity. In February 1942, Heydrich's Reich Security Main Office, which generally stood for the harshest and most ideological enforcement of racial principles, conceded that 'All German offices share the view that, given the current food rations, even those Russian workers who arrived in good condition will soon be exhausted, and no longer fully deployable.' There were early warnings throughout March, endorsed by other agencies, up to and including Hitler himself, that the 'Russians' needed to be fed enough to be able to work. But when German rations were cut on 6 April, envious gossip immediately circulated amongst 'national comrades' about the 'exceptionally good' food being allotted to the foreign workers – even after their rations had been reduced too: nothing could be allowed to erode the racial differential. Whatever economic efficiency demanded, the ethos of the 'national community' dictated that there would be no substantive rise for foreign workers until the cuts to German rations were reversed.[67]

★

The other precept for national solidarity in war was harder to enforce – equal burdens amongst Germans. On the eve of the April ration cut, Goebbels had proclaimed in *Das Reich* that the sacrifices the war imposed had to be equally shared. Otherwise, he continued, not just would 'our provisioning' be endangered but decent national comrades' 'sense of justice and their belief in the integrity and purity of public life' would be shattered. Vowing that a regime which did not proceed ruthlessly against anyone who infringed these principles 'would not deserve to be called a Government of the People any more', he proffered a yardstick by which the government could be measured. Hitler and Goebbels might remain above suspicion, with their modest meals – Goebbels's butler collected guests' ration stamps on a silver platter before dinner – but popular humour had an answer in one of the better-known replies to the famous question, 'When will the war end?' 'When Göring fits into Goebbels's trousers.' Tales of the special privileges enjoyed by the Nazi elite were also spread by British radio propaganda and its fake German station *Gustav Siegfried Eins*. Faced by a rash of rumours, Bormann reminded the Gauleiter to set a personal example of modest living within the norms of the 'people's community', especially when it came to 'food rationing'.[68]

The spectre of a major scandal began to stalk the elite. It began with August Nöthling, a grocer in the comfortable Berlin suburb of Steglitz, who was unable to provide ration coupons from his customers to cover a considerable amount of his foodstuffs. On 23 July 1942 he was fined 5,000 marks, the maximum that the Main Provisioning Office in the city could impose. Nöthling petitioned to have the administrative ruling tested in court, on the grounds that publicising the verdict would harm not only him but also his clientele, which included 'important men from the Party, state, Wehrmacht and Diplomatic Corps'. In fact, Nöthling's clients included virtually the entire political and military elite, whom he provided with venison, hams, sausages, fine wines, sweets, honey, cognac and sugar without demanding coupons. The list included the Interior Minister, Wilhelm Frick; the Foreign Minister, Joachim von Ribbentrop; the Minister for Education, Bernhard Rust; the Minister of Agriculture, Walther Darré; the Reich Labour Leader, Konstantin Hierl; Hans Lammers, Hitler's chief of staff at the Reich Chancellery; the Economics Minister, Walther Funk; the director of German radio, Eugen Hadamovsky; as well as the police chiefs of Leipzig and Berlin, and a number of state secretaries and ministerial directors. Another customer, the President of the Berlin administrative court, Gardiewski, helpfully drafted Nöthling's original petition to his own court. The Wehrmacht was well represented in the persons of Field Marshals Brauchitsch and Keitel for the army, High Admiral Raeder and Admiral Kurt Fricke for the navy, and for the Luftwaffe there were Hans Jeschonnek and Wilhelm Haehnelt.[69]

Goebbels, whose sexual adventures were a long-standing source of popular amusement, was genuinely shocked at this kind of venality and brought the matter directly to Hitler, who was sufficiently appalled to demand that those involved should be forced to explain themselves and promise to change their ways. He nominated the rather lowly figure of Otto Thierack, the Minister of Justice, to conduct an investigation. As so often, the excuses revealed more about the regime's moral compass than the scandal itself, as the Nazi elite squirmed under its betrayal of the ideal of the 'national community'. The Minister for Agriculture, Walther Darré, who had once personally intervened to make sure that his wife received her 'normal' level of service from Nöthling, denied everything, claiming to have followed the regulations – which his own ministry officials had drafted – to the letter. Others, like Ribbentrop, blustered and protested their innocence. Hans Lammers hid behind his wife's ignorance: she had not realised that the wildfowl she had accepted from the grocer was rationed. Most were forced to admit the facts but strove to minimise their responsibility. They had not known what the regulations were, or, if they had, then their wives or housekeepers had not. Viktor Lutze, head of the SA, claimed that the food had been used to make up parcels for SA men recuperating from their wounds in military hospitals. Only High Admiral Raeder accepted 'complete responsibility', but then immediately denied any direct knowledge of what his wife had purchased: nor was she responsible either, because she too had distributed the food to the wounded on her visits to naval hospitals and in parcels to men at the front. Goebbels was struck by the way they had 'mainly given only flimsy excuses', as they tried to shed responsibility for breaking the regime's own moral code. To prevent a scandal, Hitler ruled that no further action should be taken. Abandoned by his protectors, Nöthling committed suicide in prison.[70]

Meanwhile, in autumn 1942, the forced deliveries of grain from the European harvest plugged the gaping hole in German food stocks. On Sunday, 4 October 1942, Hermann Göring announced the full restoration of German rations, reversing the April cuts. The scale of rations for the lengthy hierarchy of foreign labourers below the 'national comrades' was duly increased too, securing a more viable workforce. Only the rations for the few remaining Jews in Germany were – largely symbolically – cut once more. In a major speech appropriately billed to celebrate 'Harvest Thanksgiving' and broadcast live, Göring assured the German people that 'we are feeding all of our troops from the occupied territories' – a 'small faux pas' which Goebbels instructed the media not to mention in their foreign coverage. No doubt German audiences knew what Göring meant. He then dwelt, at length, on the fact that this was above all a war against the Jews. Hammering home what would happen in the event of defeat, Göring spoke like a concerned father:

German people, you must know: if the war is lost, then you are annihilated . . . This war is not the Second World War, this war is the Great Race War. Whether the German and Aryan stands here or whether the Jew rules the world, that is what is at stake and that is what we are fighting for out there.[71]

The response to Göring's harvest festival speech within Germany was immediate and overwhelming, summed up for the SD in the comment that he 'spoke to the heart and the stomach'. His speech reconnected the population with the leadership, at a time when propaganda drives exhorting German workers to increase their productivity and 'performance' or to volunteer for sporting activities after work had been failing. Whereas civilian morale had remained depressed throughout the summer, at the start of autumn 1942 it rebounded and would continue to be upbeat and optimistic for the next few months. To most Germans, the war still remained one of national defence, but during 1942 they had adapted to its changing character, learning to scour occupied Europe for the resources to fight a much longer and deeper kind of struggle. That brought with it a half-articulated, often discomforting awareness of how imperial and genocidal their war had become.[72]

Writing to the Dead

At the beginning of April 1942, Halder put the finishing touches to a new plan of campaign in the Soviet Union. The arguments of the navy, with its proposals to join the Japanese in a 'war of continents' against the British and Americans, had been rejected in favour of the army and the land war against the Soviets. As Hitler explained to Nazi leaders a few weeks later, once the 'business in the east' was settled, 'then the war is practically won for us. Then we will be in the position of conducting a large-scale pirate war against the Anglo-Saxon powers, which in the long run they will not be able to withstand.' Hitler continued to believe that Britain would be forced to negotiate peace once the Soviet Union was defeated; and without its British ally, America would be unable to reach Continental Europe. The German leadership had gambled too far to stop gambling now.[1]

After its recent catastrophic failure to gauge Soviet strength, German Army intelligence had carried out a new assessment; but, again, the Germans severely underestimated Soviet armament, troop numbers and reserves, assuming that their principal adversary could not recover from the winter losses. Luckily for them, Soviet intelligence was equally poor and the Red Army was preparing for Army Group Centre to resume its attack on Moscow. Instead, the entire German effort was concentrated on Army Group South and the conquest of the Caucasian oilfields. 'If I don't get the oil of Maikop and Grozny,' Hitler declared to General Paulus, commander of the 6th Army, 'then I must wind up this war.' Whereas in 1941 tradition-conscious Prussian generals had wanted to focus on defeating the Red Army in a decisive battle of annihilation for Moscow, Hitler had been more interested in seizing the breadbasket of Ukraine and the oil wells. Now the two views were merged, as it was accepted that cutting the Soviet economy off from its energy lifeline would force the Red Army to stand and fight: the Wehrmacht could conquer the resources the Reich needed and it could win the war in the east.[2]

Halder's 'Operation Blue' aimed at advancing towards the Caucasus along the Black Sea coast. Its first objectives were to take Sebastopol and the Kerch peninsula so as to eliminate any attack on the German lines from the south. The focus on Army Group South was as much a matter of necessity as of design. At the end of March, 95 per cent of German divisions were still not regarded as capable of offensive action. By the start of May, the eastern front was still short of 625,000 men and 90 per cent of the vehicles which had been lost in the previous nine months had not been replaced. Army Group South garnered the bulk of the resources: of its sixty-eight divisions, seventeen had been partly rebuilt, while the great majority – forty-eight divisions in all – had been completely reconstituted. Whereas in June 1941 the invasion had taken place across a broad front, involving all three army groups, in this campaign the task of Army Groups North and Centre would be to absorb losses of materiel and hold their lines.[3]

On the northern front, the young infantryman Wilhelm Abel knew that when their precious tanks were sent south, this ruled out a ground assault on Leningrad. But he was able to tell his sister back in Westphalia that they still had enough artillery and air power to bombard the city relentlessly. He speculated whether the Russian campaign would conclude in time for them to invade England that year and wreak vengeance for all the air raids. Meanwhile, in the early May sunshine, he and his comrades went fishing in Lake Ladoga with hand grenades.[4]

Thousands of kilometres to the south, Helmut Paulus was stationed by the river Mius, on one of the most south-easterly points of the eastern front. He was one of the last to hear of the German offensive. On 1 July 1942, his sister and mother heard the special reports on the radio that Sebastopol had fallen and the long-awaited summer campaign had begun. Helmut, meanwhile, was worrying about life back in Pforzheim: he had read that potatoes were being rationed for the first time, had heard disturbing comments from a returning comrade about 'the mood and life at home' and wondered if his mother was right to give up her chocolate ration for him. Like all the other veterans in his unit, he was furious that they had just been put through another training exercise. He could hardly believe the amounts of precious artillery shells wasted in it, to say nothing of accidental casualties. One of theirs was caused by a fresh recruit throwing his hand grenade too short. A comrade had come up with an appropriate 'philosophy': 'If you don't get hit at the front, then they fire one up your arse from behind, but, in any case, you've got to go.'[5]

As the first week of July ticked by and the radio at home carried news of the huge offensive to the north-east of his lines, things continued as before in the Mius sector. Training was stepped up, with long forced marches and the occasional strafing by a Soviet biplane. When the men watched a comedy, *The Merry Vagabonds*, Helmut was struck by the change it revealed: 'Laughter has become rare amongst us . . . If you think that pretty much every one of them has at least ten Russians on his conscience, you do have to wonder a bit at this boisterousness.'[6]

Finally, on 11 July, came the order to move. In baking heat, the men waded across the Mius, the water lapping above their boots, heading for a village the Soviets had already evacuated. Soviet deserters told the German engineers where the minefields lay. A few hundred metres beyond the village, Helmut's company suddenly ran into rifle and machine-gun fire and had to dig in, spending the night shivering in their wet clothes, their shirts bathed in sweat and their trousers soaked from the river crossing, while artillery and mortars joined in the Soviet fire. They had been heading in the wrong direction, and during the night most of the company was pulled back. Helmut was one of the twenty-four men left to hold the position, cowering the next day in their foxholes with no communication to their rear and surrounded on three sides. By the end of the second day of the offensive, they had not eaten for forty-eight hours and had to keep sending men out with cooking pots on a half-hour trek to bring back brackish water.

Just as their unit was being relieved, Helmut heard an incoming mortar shell. Instinctively he leaped out of his trench. It landed 10 metres behind them and 'ripped both legs off a comrade who jumped out behind me', he wrote home, 'while nothing happened to me'. After a night spent hunting for food in the abandoned Soviet bunkers, on the next day's march they were able to beg some bread and dried biscuit from mountain troops and collect water from the streams they passed. That night they finally caught up with their baggage train and field kitchen. There was no hot food, but there was at least bread, butter, coffee and a slab of chocolate for each of them. As Helmut lay down in the shade of a wood writing his latest letter home, for the first time he heard the sounds of the major German bombardment. While the artillery barrage thundered, wave after wave of Stukas, hundreds of them, screeched down on to the line of concrete bunkers which the Soviets had built in the winter. 'Till now the enemy air force and artillery were always overwhelmingly superior wherever we were. What an indescribable feeling this barrage is for each one of us,' he wrote on the eve of their own attack.[7]

Instead of being sent in, Helmut's company was suddenly withdrawn from their trenches, squeezed into trucks and taken back all the way across the Mius again. Marching mostly at night to avoid the heat of the July sun, Helmut Paulus was being sent further south towards Rostov. He lost his metal spoon and had to ask his family for a replacement, unwilling to make do with a wooden one like the locals – 'designed for the mouth of a crocodile and with which no educated central European can eat'. The news that Krasnyi Luch – the city they had faced all winter and spring – had fallen confirmed that the 'Russians have given up their entire fortified line'. His impression, from the settlements they passed through, was that they were about a day behind the retreating Red Army, and closing. Led by a platoon of engineers checking for minefields, they had to march at the ready. They kept their machine gun assembled, however awkward and heavy it became by the end of a 40-kilometre march. When they came to a damaged bridge, they repaired it with wooden door and window frames they ripped out of the village houses nearby, and kept going.[8]

The summer heat, low casualties and rapid advance across the steppe ensured that morale remained high. On 26 July, the company reached Rostov-on-Don. Driving through the city at first light, Helmut was amazed to see the station full of abandoned locomotives and rolling stock. They crossed the Don on a large ferry and spent the rest of that night marching, often wading through the marshland on the eastern side of the great river. When they finally reached a small settlement and encountered resistance, the Stukas did most of the work, sparing them close combat.[9]

Having slept in the Soviet trenches, they moved out again the next morning at 7.30 a.m., crossing the steppe for 20 kilometres, battle-ready. The rearguard Red Army troops they met simply raised their hands in surrender. Once the Germans had left the Don marshes, things kept speeding up. Helmut watched with delight as their own tanks now came past and took over the advance across the firm terrain. Finally released from the 'Halt orders' which had hamstrung its ability to manoeuvre in 1941, the Red Army did not wait to be encircled and was in headlong retreat, making use of the supply of trucks being delivered by its new US ally. In pursuit of their motorised enemy, the German infantrymen had to make ever longer forced marches, mostly on foot. The few German trucks were used sparingly. 'Completely exhausted and over-strained, eyes burning for sleep, nerves totally overstrung,' Helmut wrote after marching well into the night. Their own artillery had not kept up and, 'as so often, we infantrymen were left to our own devices', facing the enemy on their own. Together with a neighbouring company they slowly worked their way forward towards a village, losing some wounded but taking many prisoners. They found 'eggs, milk, butter and first-rate white bread, which tasted wonderful after the strains of the last two days'. The prisoners came as a great relief: some of them were immediately set to carrying the heavy ammunition boxes across the endless grasslands.[10]

*

Such front-line deployment of Red Army prisoners was becoming increasingly common, and marked a huge shift during the first six months of 1942. The German rear was no longer swamped by huge numbers of prisoners as in 1941, because the Red Army evaded encirclement battles by continuing to retreat eastwards. The transit camps for prisoners of war, or *Dulags*, changed character. From being the sites of mass starvation, such as the one Konrad Jarausch had overseen until he was carried off by the typhus epidemic, the camps took on a new role of screening prisoners and manufacturing 'auxiliary volunteers', as they were called. Arriving in Belorussia in May 1942, the Solingen high-school teacher August Töpperwien was soon fully immersed in this work. Already in December 1941, the Germans had begun deploying prisoners in support roles and even in some combat units. Despite an explicit order from Hitler forbidding such measures, the number of 'Russians' in Wehrmacht uniform kept climbing in the spring and summer of 1942. Most 'volunteers' simply wanted to escape the festering and famine-ridden camps and were allotted menial, non-combat roles, as servants to officers, medics, cooks, translators and drivers of trucks or horse-drawn carts. It was the simplest and most practicable way of making up the chronic under-strength of German units. As the 134th Infantry Division tried to rebuild itself after its disastrous retreat to the German lines in the December blizzards, it even placed former Red Army men in combat roles. Hitler repeated his ban on further recruitment of 'Eastern troops' in February and June 1942, to no avail. Starved of German replacements to make good their losses, the Army High Command itself issued guidelines to circumvent its Supreme Commander's orders and suggested that every division in the east could take on 10–15 per cent of its strength from Red Army 'volunteers'. Once the Soviet 'volunteers' proved their value in fighting their former Red Army comrades in anti-partisan action in the rear, Army Group Centre began to create full combat units under German officers. By 18 August, Hitler relented, signing off on a directive which formally acknowledged the existence of the 'Eastern troops' and established regulations for their pay, ranks, uniforms and relations with German personnel. By the end of the year, nearly half of the men in the 134th Infantry Division were 'Russian volunteers'. In order to avoid associating the new units with Russian nationalist traditions, they were given geographical rather than historical names – 'Dniepr', 'Pripet' or 'Berezina'.[11]

Especially in the Baltic states and western Ukraine, there were many who had welcomed the Germans as liberators and were willing to fight against Bolshevism. But the problem of what they were fighting for remained. The Germans had encouraged the Organisation of Ukrainian Nationalists and both leaders of its rival factions, Andriy Melnyk and Stepan Bandera, maintained close ties to their German patrons in Military Intelligence and the Gestapo. Each man made a competitive bid for national independence after the occupation of Ukraine, and the Germans continued to support and encourage each faction's activities, as well as refusing to endorse their calls for national independence and, at times, imprisoning their leaders. In practice, Ukraine continued to be divided along similar political lines to those which had held before 1939. In the former Soviet Republic, now the Reich Commissariat of the Ukraine, the Gauleiter of East Prussia, Erich Koch, imposed his own brutally supremacist regime, taking every opportunity to enforce public floggings and executions of his 'natives'. By contrast, in the former western Ukrainian region of Galicia, which saw the German occupation as an opportunity to break away from Polish as well as Soviet rule, a more liberal cultural and political policy prevailed. With Lwów as its capital, Galicia was given its own status as a district within Hans Frank's General Government; Ukrainian nationalist publications and cultural life were encouraged. In July 1941 the SS had immediately set about raising Ukrainian Auxiliary Police battalions which played key roles in the murder of the Jews, in anti-partisan actions and in blockading the major cities in order to enforce Backe's 'Hunger Plan'. The number of these Galician police battalions grew markedly in the summer of 1942.

This was as far as any potential vehicle for Slavic nationalism was permitted to progress under German tutelage at this stage of the war. Despite pressure for a more liberal occupation regime from both Wehrmacht commanders and Rosenberg's Ministry for the Eastern Territories, Erich Koch was able to hold on to a direct and brutal policy of forced labour, food requisitioning, degrading public punishments and arbitrary terror. He knew he could count on the firm support of Göring, Bormann and Hitler. In the neighbouring fiefdom of Belorussia, Wilhelm Kube steered a middle course. In July 1942, he rejected proposals to shoot most of those aged 17–21 as '100 per cent infected with communism', opting instead to start recruiting them as industrial apprentices or to serve as auxiliary 'volunteers' for the SS and the anti-aircraft defences. But these pockets of positive engagement were tiny compared to the scale of German reprisals against the civilian population. They also kept running up against entrenched German fears that any resurgence of Slavic or Russian nationalism would automatically undermine their own plans to create areas of lasting German colonial settlement after Germany's victory over Bolshevism.[12]

Raising 'Eastern legions', as they came to be known, progressed far more rapidly and smoothly in the non-Slavic territories, especially in Muslim areas. In November 1941, Hitler authorised the raising of a 'Turkic Legion', and by the end of February 1942 the High Command was collaborating with Rosenberg's Ministry for the Eastern Territories to raise four separate legions for Turkistanis, Muslims from the Caucasus, Georgians and Armenians. Two more, the North Caucasian and the Volga Tatar Legions, followed that summer. Here the desire to rally all the non-Slav ethnic groups from the occupied Soviet territories and, later, the Balkans intersected happily with the pan-Islamic enthusiasms of the SS and the German Foreign Office, whose expertise dated back to stirring up the Middle East during the First World War. Over 500,000 men were raised in this way.[13]

When Army Group South entered the Crimea in autumn 1941, the Germans found themselves warmly welcomed by the population of 225,000 Tatars. As Sunni Muslims they had seen their mosques and madrasas desecrated, decommissioned and destroyed by the Soviets. Under German occupation, 150 mosques and a further 100 provisional prayer houses were renovated and opened in 1943 alone. The Germans drew the line at re-establishing a Muftiat in the Crimea, lest it provided a focus for political demands, but the local *ulema* helped to raise recruits for the militias attached to Manstein's 11th Army. At a conference of the Tatar Committee in Simferopol in early 1942 one of the mullahs confirmed that 'their religion and their faith commands them to take part in this holy battle alongside the Germans' against Bolshevism. The whole Tatar gathering rose to their feet and prayed for 'the achievement of a speedy victory . . . as well as for the long life of the Führer, Adolf Hitler'. By March, 20,000 Muslims had joined the militias.[14]

The Germans were impressed by the Tatar and Turkic Legions' discipline and fighting power, and they soon established a name for themselves in anti-partisan warfare. A survey of military censorship from that spring revealed men who were guided by faith in 'Allah and Adolf Effendi'. 'I fight for the liberation of the Tatars and the religion of Islam from the Bolshevist yoke,' wrote one recruit. Enthused by the capture of the Soviet naval base of Kerch in spring 1942, another man wrote, 'We have . . . shattered the Red Russian Army so that it can never recover. The word of the victor is with us. Allah has also given Adolf Effendi to us, therefore we will always remain winners.'[15]

The Wehrmacht was quick to guarantee the right of religious observance within their Muslim units, enjoining German soldiers not to stare in curiosity and, above all, not to photograph acts of daily prayer. High holidays of Ramadan and Id ul-Adha were respected and serving pork was forbidden. It was more difficult to introduce ritual slaughter of livestock, because 'animal protection' legislation had been rushed through in April 1933 by the Nazis in order to close down kosher butchers in Germany, but the Wehrmacht issued the necessary guidelines for its Muslim units. The SS, which had raised a Bosnian Muslim division of its own, followed suit. The findings of a question-naire distributed to recruits in October 1942 told a prosaic tale of motives for volunteering, such as escaping German prisoner-of-war camps and labour conscription. Among soldiers' positive reasons for fighting, especially in the Balkans, protecting their families from partisan attack predominated. At the same time, the Wehrmacht and SS set great store by the key values which they believed Nazism and Islam held in common: obedience to the leader, belief in the family and commitment to a holy war against the 'Jewish-English-Bolshevik enemy'. Heinrich Himmler even commissioned an academic study to discover whether Hitler could be set on par with the Prophet; he had to settle, for being depicted as 'the returned Isa [Jesus] who is forecast in the Qu'ran and who, similar to the type of the Knight George, defeats the giant and Jew-King Dajjal at the end of the world'.[16]

The greatest transformation occurred in the relatively small military wing of the SS, which had not played a front-line role in 1941. With a mere 170,000 members at the start of 1942, the Waffen SS began to look beyond the Reich's borders and recruit from a pool not covered by conscription to the Wehrmacht. It was helped in its efforts by a very successful illustrated magazine, Signal, published by the Wehrmacht but aimed at a western European readership numbering 2.5 million. In Paris, under Otto Abetz's expert guidance, Jean Cocteau, Henri Matisse, Pablo Picasso, Simone de Beauvoir and Jean-Paul Sartre were able to go on working, with German officers attending the opening nights of Sartre's plays. By allowing a limited cultural pluralism to flourish, ranging from such non-collaborationist radicals to out-and-out fascists and radical anti-Semites like Drieu la Rochelle and Céline, German cultural propaganda did its best to showcase their defence of West European culture against the barbarism of the East. In particular, they tried to enrol other nations' heroes, stressing the Anglophobic legacy of Joan of Arc in France, while issuing stamps with Rembrandt's head in place of the exiled monarch in the Netherlands and making a beautifully shot period film about the artist in 1942. Such cultural propaganda, with its limited scope for pluralism, may have served to dampen down support for the underground resistance movements, which remained very small at this stage. But it also proved difficult to persuade the Dutch, Belgians, French and Norwegians to volunteer for the Waffen SS divisions. It was far easier to recruit from ethnic Germans in Romania and Hungary or from Ukrainians in Galicia and Muslims in Bosnia.[17]

As the SS jettisoned its claims to 'racial' exclusivity, it had to re-educate its own members. It was a steep learning curve. In September 1941, after hundreds of Muslim prisoners of war had been executed, Reinhard Heydrich sent out a directive to all the SS *Einsatzgruppen*, warning them that 'the circumcision' and 'Jewish appearance' of the Turkic Muslims did not amount to 'proof of Jewish descent'. As Otto Ohlendorf's *Einsatzgruppe* D extended its slaughter to the Crimea, it wiped out the Ashkenazis and Turkic-speaking Krymchaks, but, on special instructions from Berlin, spared the Turkic Karaites who had converted to Judaism centuries earlier; a few hundred were even recruited into the Crimean Tatar volunteer units.[18]

Confused by the ethnically and religiously mixed, multilingual force to which they now belonged, German soldiers were often not so discriminating when it came to their own 'Asiatics'. A German train was sighted in Warsaw on which the last carriage had been daubed with the instruction, 'For Poles, Jews and Legionnaires'. Despite all the propagandists' efforts to forge a more inclusive and tolerant attitude to their new allies, German soldiers remained, for the most part, wedded to their ethno-racist preconceptions. In June 1942, Fritz Probst was in high spirits as he listened to the wail of the German Stukas striking Red Army targets when the summer offensive got under way. The Thuringian family man still found time to shudder at the sight of the Soviet prisoners as they passed the German column. 'You really have to see the Asiatic prisoners and the like, if they had come to our Fatherland, there'd have been such an enormous killing, because they aren't human and also not harmless animals; they are wild beasts.' As Fritz Probst repeated the idioms and metaphors he had imbibed since the start of the war, he could not get used to a different set of prescriptions. If anything, surviving the crisis of 1941–42 had schooled German troops in a common mindset which regarded hanging civilians, burning down villages, driving the inhabitants into the steppes or requisitioning the last of their provisions and winter clothing as natural responses to an overwhelming threat. This psychological transformation of the German soldiers on the eastern front proved irreversible: at key moments core elements of their collective outlook could be called on again, overriding all the complex, individual relations which grew up between occupiers and occupied.[19]

After six months on the eastern front, Eugen Altrogge set himself the challenge of capturing 'the essence of the Russian people' in his drawings. 'However great the store we set by curtains and culture, wooden floorboards and culture, clean fingernails and culture,' he wrote to his friend Hans Albring, 'we mostly understand nothing of the powerful primitivism, simplicity of the soul, naïve strength and terrible violence of this people.' In order to capture this exotic simplicity in art, Altrogge tried to find a new, 'less abstract, simpler' technique of drawing. The two young Catholics were searching for a kind of deep, religious purity, which they believed modern commercial civilisation had destroyed in the West. As his unit approached Stalingrad, Hans Albring went on admiring – and began to collect – icons. Both men were attracted by the physical beauty of Russian women and tried to capture its spiritual dimensions in their drawings. Yet, for all his religious and artistic sensibilities, Hans Albring was no different to Fritz Probst when he wrote about 'the dehumanised hordes [who] later perpetrated a frightful crime and murdered the helpless wounded who could not be rescued before the dark hours of this deed . . . The devil's leer is unbearable across this land.'[20]

Even such self-conscious letter-writers as Albring and Altrogge had stopped reflecting on how 'hard' they had become on the eastern front. There was no point reliving their own transformation. Instead, they looked to the emotional constants of home, family and the German culture they had been raised in. As they advanced across the steppe, Altrogge, Albring and Helmut Paulus all referred in their letters to reading Goethe and Hölderlin as well as Ernst Jünger's recently published diary of the first year of the war, *Gardens and Streets*. These young men came from different parts of Germany, different Christian confessions and held different ranks in the army but they shared a deep attachment to the literary culture they had accumulated through their families and education. Lost in the vast, alien 'deserts' of the steppes, they found refuge in the classics.[21]

To many men, the eastern front appeared a necessary trial, a ghastly ordeal, where hope rested solely on calculating when it would end. A bluff Party member and rather strict father, Fritz Probst was not much given to introspection. But he was desperately conscious of what he was losing. By 1942, his youngest child, Manfred, who had still snuggled up in his mother's bed at night in the first year of the war, was already starting school. Each new year of his service brought with it a calendar full of missed birthdays. On 6 January, it was their middle child Gundula's and Probst confessed that 'I always think of such days with horror, because the children make you realise that you are getting older and, what's more, they are getting bigger and I can't share the short time of their childhood.' It was a year since his last home leave.[22]

His absence from home seemed to affect the oldest, Karl-Heinz, most. Probst warned his wife Hildegard that she should have reined him in earlier and periodically wrote letters admonishing his son. In 1940 he had appealed in a rather schoolmasterly way to the 12-year-old's 'word of honour', promising him that 'Mummy will never refuse a request' if he would only be 'obedient'. Two years later, Probst sent off a tirade telling the 14-year-old he 'should be ashamed' for behaving 'loutishly' in his grandmother's presence. As Karl-Heinz entered the Hitler Youth, his father reminded him of the financial sacrifice they were making by letting him stay on at school beyond the normal *Volksschule* leaving age. And then there was the moral debt he owed: 'Shame on you. Your father is far away and is helping to prepare a better future for you, so that you don't have to do it later yourselves and can dedicate yourselves to other tasks, and you just don't see it. I can only say once more: shame on you.'[23]

Probst's desperation at the growing rift and his own dwindling paternal authority was palpable. A week later he was regretting that he would miss Karl-Heinz's confirmation, consoling himself with the photo Hildegard had sent him of the three children. He closed with a reminder to his wife 'not to allow yourself to be weak'. It was possible to meet the challenges of life 'only if you are hard, also against yourself . . . And that we want to be, hard and determined and to keep on hoping that we will see each other soon.' Here the 'hardness' of character embraced the dangers of the front and the domestic burdens at home in a common sense of shared familial endeavour. Three months later, Probst was encouraging Hildegard and also himself: 'We must be still harder, must not lose courage, can only keep on hoping for the day when our longing is fulfilled.' As he tried to resolve the private conflicts of family life, Fritz Probst turned again and again to the public virtues, to 'commitment', 'hardness', 'determination' and 'sacrifice'. Unable to tell his wife much about the campaign, his letters lent these common phrases his authority, and the authenticity of the front.[24]

The 20-year-old Helmut Paulus had no such cares. Miraculously, the letters and parcels from home caught up with their advance and, thanks to his father's efforts, Helmut Paulus was able to replace the campaign medal his sergeant had lost. The man was delighted. As the company neared the Caucasus, enough notepaper arrived for several months. He used the sugar his mother sent to sweeten the cherries and mulberries he and his comrades gathered in the villages. The lemon extract helped allay his thirst during the marches. He hid the volume of selections from Nietzsche in an ammunition box, and he devoured the review in *Das Reich* of Gustaf Gründgens's performance in Goethe's *Faust*. When he started to ask about the rumours that the home front was awash with complaints, his mother defended its honour, telling him that people were getting by and putting up with the shortages and long queues, with housewives often standing in line in utter silence.[25]

Compared to 1941, his parents were now much better informed and able to follow some of Helmut's campaign almost in real time, his mother predicting practically to the day when he would reach the Don marshes. His father still urged him to volunteer for officer training, but unlike a year ago, he had learned to accept no for an answer. Helmut saw himself in more populist mode as a brave 'grunt' and not a 'peacetime', parade-ground soldier. But he gradually came round to the idea of the family profession, medicine, even though it meant giving up his own desire to study chemistry. The wasted time spent at war had made him increasingly impatient to start his own career and family: 'Perhaps the war with its hardness and unfairness has made me long for quiet and settled life. Chemistry can offer that to me only after long years.' His sister Elfriede had decided to study medicine too. His mother wrote that many young men were suddenly opting for university to get out of military service. The problem was, Helmut realised, that as an infantryman he had little prospect of receiving permission: there were still too few replacements. The only option would be to request a transfer to a medical unit and then apply through their chain of command; but, he reckoned, that would take at least a further two years and he could not see the war lasting so long.[26]

Hans Albring was making plans to apply for leave to go to university. He wanted to study history, philosophy and German literature. Rather than just treat his military service as so much 'lost time', in the quiet hours of the night, when the radio in the signals van was switched off, he embarked on a fresh translation of St John's Gospel. He also reworked his sketches into illustrations for what he hoped might be a published work. He began drawing his comrades' faces and, above all, their hands. Not to be outdone, his friend Eugen Altrogge began work on the text and illustrations for a 'Book of Hours' as soon as he recovered from a bullet wound in his thigh and returned to the front. By then, however, Eugen had heard too that all study leave for soldiers on the eastern front had been stopped and he worried about Hans's state of mind, now that the 'castles of his hopes and dreams' had suddenly collapsed.[27]

*

In the Caucasus, Field Marshal Wilhelm List's Army Group A had captured the first of the oilfields at Maikop on 9 August 1942, though not before its oil installations had been destroyed. Having advanced 480 kilometres in two weeks, the German supply lines were so extended that petrol had to be brought up by camel train. Helmut Paulus's unit helped capture Krasnodar on 12 August, opening up the eastern Black Sea ports along the Taman peninsula and with them the possibility of provisioning the German and Romanian forces in the Caucasus by naval transports from the Romanian ports.[28]

By the second half of August, Helmut Paulus's infantry unit had left the seemingly endless monotony of the steppes far behind them. As they climbed the foothills of the Caucasus, he began to feel more at home. On 20 August, an artillery duel gave Helmut time to stop and take in the beauty of his surroundings, the oak forests and mountains rising behind them. He felt he 'could almost imagine being back at home. The place resembles the edge of the Black Forest so much.' That afternoon a Cherkassian forester offered to guide them along forest tracks deep into the Soviet rear. That night, while the company halted on its third peak, Helmut's platoon was sent down into the valley to spy out the military road which would lead them up to the high mountain passes. They lay the entire night in the bushes beside the road, watching Red Army trucks, artillery, marching columns and baggage trains pass by along this one major route through the mountains to the oil-rich territory to the south. At daybreak, instead of returning to the rest of their unit, they opened fire. The Soviets quickly recovered from their surprise at being attacked so far to their rear and used the woods to outflank the small group of German scouts, pinning them down in the bed of a little stream in the valley. Helmut was hit by one of the first shots.[29]

'At first,' he wrote home, 'I didn't realise that I was wounded at all. I saw the hole in the trousers. But there was no blood. Then I soon saw the underwear turn red, and so knew what was up.' A medical orderly reached him quickly, cutting away his trouser leg and bandaging the wound so that Helmut could hobble back to the gully where the doctor had set up his first aid station. The bullet had passed clean through his left thigh, missing the main artery and the bone and leaving a 5-centimetre-long flesh wound. The battalion was running out of ammunition and was gradually pushed back, hemmed in on three sides with their backs to a mountain. It was the mountain that saved them. The next morning, a column of German drivers and clerks, who had toiled all night over the hills to bring up munitions and food, reached the beleaguered skirmishers. They helped bring the wounded back. As Helmut limped along on his own, the bandage loosened and the wound rubbed against his underwear, which was drenched in sweat, caked with dried blood and unwashed in weeks. After a couple of kilometres they finally reached the carts and, with enormous relief, Helmut clambered up.[30]

The journey back, as the cart kept sliding towards the edge of the mountain road, reminded Helmut, as he lay there helplessly, of a track in the forest just to the south of Pforzheim where his sister Irmgard had nearly gone plunging over the precipice in her pram as a child. The only brake was a chain locking the cart's rear wheel. At last they reached the valley floor where they could be loaded on to German ambulances, though not before the 'Stalin organs', with their thirty-six-rocket salvos, sent them a final farewell. An hour later, Helmut was at the main dressing station, where he was given a massive tetanus injection before being taken to a military hospital in the Caucasian city of Krasnodar.

Hospital conditions in this former Red Army training barracks were spartan but comfortable, the food simple but plentiful and almost all the wounded were fellow infantrymen, many from his own company. Someone had set up a radio in the canteen and there to the sound of the light-music station, Helmut and his fellow wounded sat talking, eating apples and writing their letters home. The news took a fortnight to reach his family – still half the time letters had taken in 1941, thanks to the introduction of a special airmail service for the eastern front – and Dr Paulus immediately asked for the names and ranks of all the doctors, in the hope that he might know one of them. He also hoped that the rather friendly chief doctor might smooth Helmut's transition from the infantry into the medical corps and so back home to study. As soon as he received the certificate for Helmut's badge for having been wounded, he had the medal issued in Pforzheim and sent it to his son.[31]

Helmut was proud to have been part of the infantry assault which had taken Krasnodar, but he hated the way the rear echelon condescended to shabby *Landsers* like himself. He recalled visiting a town behind their line the previous winter and seeing 'how officers and soldiers went walking arm in arm with Russian girls. Here in Krasnodar there is even supposed to be a dance tavern. It is to be hoped this tavern will be closed soon.' Eventually boredom got the better of him and he ventured out, with one or two comrades and no crutches, to visit the market, where they gorged themselves on apples and grapes and loitered, fascinated by the 'colourful and semi-oriental' atmosphere of the streets. He found some Russian leaflets in the hospital to send back to his sister Irmgard to stick in her war album and scoured the market for an embroidered skullcap for her birthday, so that she could impress the girls of Pforzheim. At the theatre, the poor lighting hid the tatty costumes in a 'mystical half-darkness' and the largely Russian audience, as 'true proletarians had no idea how to behave in a theatre and went on talking loudly, eating snacks and smoking'. The cinema offered a pleasant diversion and, although the images of actual fighting on the *Wochenschau* suffered from the 'impossibility of taking accurate pictures' of such events, Helmut was impressed by the portrayal of advancing infantrymen. These shots, he wrote home, 'were pretty accurate . . . no dressed ranks. Everyone just walked the way they would . . . no singing of jolly soldiers' songs (which we have not ever done in the whole war so far). They were just the right shots of an infantry company which has already marched 40 or 50 kilometres.'[32]

By that time Eugen Altrogge had also just recovered from a flesh wound to his left thigh. Relieved to have taken only a minor wound, he had been excited by the flight back over the Sea of Azov in a medical transport plane, the 'Auntie Ju', as German soldiers affection- ately called the Junker 52s. Eugen was more critical of the cinenews coverage, declaring that the

> serious war artist is today replaced by the reporter, the photojour- nalist, the PK [embedded cameraman of the Propaganda Company] – the sketcher for the press. My God – how all these gentlemen lie! Yes, even the *Wochenschau* is untrue, which I saw again after a long gap. What's the cause of this untruth – doesn't one see the objective photo?

Eugen felt that the images just could not capture the emotional and physical exhaustion of war or the tension of battle. Although he admitted that 'I don't feel called upon to be a war artist', he had done one drawing which he felt was 'right'. It showed an NCO, sitting in a dugout after coming back from patrol, shirtless, his finger bandaged, his mouth open, his gaze vacant. There were other images he had not sketched but which stuck in his mind:

> Two soldiers asleep next to each other, lying on their stomachs, like the dead or like men taking cover . . . or the 'river landscape' of the Don near Rostov: the scattered remnants and ghastly remains of an army which had fled, countless bloated horses, with their outstretched hooves crying out to heaven . . . the bloated, dismembered corpses of the Russians. Every image has its laws!

he concluded, before adding falteringly, 'You can't say what they are – but they are there.'[33]

Helmut Paulus's comrades had called him 'bulletproof' for

making it all the way from Romania to the Caucasus without a scratch, and they were astonished when his luck ran out and he limped into the dressing station. Hans Albring still remained unscathed. 'I don't call that "luck" any more', he wrote to Eugen, 'but I know that Providence is at work, which has so far watched over me.' The day before a lieutenant he had liked was killed. 'Did he believe in Providence?' Albring asked himself, promising to pray for the man's soul.[34]

At the very start of the campaign in the previous summer, Albring had found it difficult to find words as he tried to reflect on the meaning of death after he he had witnessed the execution of Jews and prisoners of war. Now, as he contemplated the death of comrades, he was forced also to think about the risk to himself. Many soldiers had developed psychological defences robust enough to cope with the shock of near misses such as Helmut Paulus had experienced when a shell tore the legs off a comrade next to him in July. The egalitarianism of the trenches and the bonds of brotherly reciprocity demanded that dead comrades were treated with the highest respect: even in the worst moment of their winter retreat from Moscow, Robert R.'s comrades had carried him as long as they could, bottling up their desire to flee westwards in order to give him a decent burial and adding his note-books to their own burdens. And many would have agreed with Wilhelm Abel's sentiments, when he dedicated his role in a raid, in which they had flung hand grenades into eighteen Soviet bunkers, burning and blowing up the occupants, to 'avenging our own dead a bit'. The bond with the dead comrades became another reason to go on fighting. When Fritz Farnbacher's friend Peter Siegert was hit on 20 November 1941, Farnbacher thought about their two mothers as he enacted the final gestures of maternal care and cradled his dying friend.'[35]

However strong its mythology of honour and comradeship, like all mass armies the Wehrmacht was an assemblage of civilians in uniform: even those like Helmut Paulus, Eugen Altrogge and Hans Albring who had joined up straight after finishing high school were beginning to make choices about their futures. Above all, it was their myriad ties to home which gave a purpose and meaning to a war everyone longed to end. When Albring and Altrogge imagined meeting up again after two years of war, they pictured themselves walking through the streets of the small town in the Münsterland where they had grown up and going to a concert to hear Mozart and Haydn.[36]

★

It was not until 10 September that the Germans took the Soviet naval base of Novorossiysk on the eastern coast of the Black Sea. It was an incomplete victory: the Soviet 47th Army still held the heights south of the port as well as important coastal roads, and supply from Romania by sea continued to be hazardous. The capital of Azerbaijan, Baku, remained the real prize. It lay beyond the Transcaucasian mountains, far to the south-east on the shore of the Caspian Sea. To have any prospect of reaching it, or even the oil wells of Grozny, List's armies would need a massive influx of supplies and reinforcements. Instead, Army Group A had to send much of its armour and its entire anti-aircraft defences to assist the German 6th Army, and by late September was having to accept that its own advance had stalled. If it could not take the oil for itself, it could try to deny it to the other side. On 10 and 12 October, the 4th Air Corps set the refineries at Grozny ablaze, causing huge destruction. While Maikop and Grozny accounted for 10 per cent of Soviet supplies, Baku provided 80 per cent of Soviet supplies. Yet Baku lay at the limit of the German bombers' range and well beyond that of their fighters. To attack it, the 4th Air Corps, reduced to fewer than 200 operational bombers, would have had to fly a direct route without protection at a time when the Red Air Force had significantly increased its own presence. After the extraordinarily rapid advance from Rostov to Krasnodar, the Caucasian campaign was stalling. When Bavarian mountain troops planted their battle flag on the west peak of Mount Elbrus on 23 August, their Führer was furious at the waste of effort.[37]

With the failure of the key objective of the campaign, Franz Halder chose this as his moment to stand down as Chief of the General Staff. For Hitler, however, the real and symbolic battle was being fought far to the north of the oil wells. The German 6th Army had been tasked with shielding the advance into the Caucasus by pushing towards Stalingrad. This industrial city, which had played an important role in the Russian civil war, controlled the last great western bend of the river Volga before it flowed into the Caspian Sea. Only after a month of fighting did the 6th Army succeed, on 23 August, in crossing the river Don. With no other natural obstacles, German tanks covered the distance from the great eastern bend of the Don to the western one of the Volga the same day, reaching the northern suburbs of Stalingrad. For the next three days, Richthofen's 4th Air Fleet bombed the city, killing numerous Soviet civilians.[38]

On 30 August, Fritz Probst was approaching Stalingrad from the north-west. He wrote excitedly to Hildegard: 'I believe I'm not betraying a secret' – he was – 'if I write to you that this city will be fiercely fought over. They are on the edge of the city in the north and south but still far from it in the west. It will then become another small pocket, and when it's been gutted, then there'll be peace here.' He could not wait for it all to end, consumed by the thought that he and Hildegard were 'becoming old and the best years are passing us by, untapped'. On 12 September, the Germans entered the city and began fighting for control of it, building by building.[39]

For Probst, these weeks brought a revelation of a different kind. This gruff man with his stilted, uncomfortable style of writing had discovered a new intimacy on paper. 'If I had you here, I'd not stop kissing you,' he wrote to Hildegard. The rose she had sent him 'tells me absolutely everything, everything which is between us. Sadly, I can't express my love to you through red roses, because there are none here, but I can in these lines.' When the war was finally over, 'then, when I once more hold you in my arms and find your mouth to kiss, everything will be forgotten and I know for sure we'll then be the happiest of beings'. For now, all he could do was to wish that Hildegard would dream of him, 'for dreams are the only things that unite us'. He too had had 'some sweet dreams' but, he confessed, 'on waking the disappointment is too great.'[40]

As the couple at last found words to bridge the ever-growing distance which the German advance had placed between them, Fritz Probst felt his feelings were best expressed by Lale Andersen's new musical hit, 'Es geht alles vorüber' – 'Everything Passes':[41]

> Everything passes, it will all be over,
> After every December comes another May.
> Everything passes, it will all be over,
> But for two who love, then faithful they'll stay.[42]

Sung in her lilting, gently caressing voice, the promise of Andersen's refrain would be echoed by many other letter-writers that autumn and winter on the Stalingrad front. As he commiserated with Hildegard over their twenty months' separation, Fritz Probst told her to 'hold your head high, small, brave soldier's wife: after this autumn a new spring must come'. Fritz Probst had no idea that a few weeks later he would suddenly be granted home leave.[43]

As the Red Army ferried more and more reinforcements across from the eastern bank of the Volga at night, it began to look if the Bolshevik regime had chosen – fittingly, it seemed to the Germans – to make its final stand at the city named after their leader. Opening the Winter Relief charity drive with a speech in the Berlin Sportpalast on 30 September, Hitler promised that 'The occupation of Stalingrad, which will also be carried through, will deepen this gigantic victory [on the Volga] and strengthen it, and you can be sure that no human being will drive us out of this place later on.' He declared that

> In my eyes, in 1942 the most fateful trial of our people has already passed. That was the winter of '41 to '42. I may be permitted to say that in that winter the German people, and in particular its Wehrmacht, were weighed in the balance by Providence. Nothing worse can or will happen.[44]

For the time being the Germans looked insuperable, with the nightly barges ferrying Red Army troops across the Volga merely slowing down the inevitable loss of the city. His leave over, Fritz Probst returned to his building battalion in early November. Coming back from Görmar in Thuringia, he promptly fell ill and had to be nursed back to health in an army field hospital. With nothing to look forward to on the Stalingrad front other than the 'long and boring winter evenings in which I will think back on the beautiful hours, you know which ones I mean in particular . . .', he hesitated to say more, in case his mother happened to open the letter before Hildegard did. Instead, he encouraged her to tell him herself about these things: 'You can write as much [as you want] because I am the only one to read your letters and it'd be wonderful if you would write to me about it.'[45]

Only the huge distance they had covered and their over-extended supply lines pointed towards German vulnerability, and these formed the basis of the Soviet counter-offensive. On 19 November the Red Army launched an assault on the northern flank of the Stalingrad front; the next day, it attacked from the south too. The aim was to cut through the lines held by Romanian and Italian troops to the west at the Don, and so isolate the bulk of the 6th Army. As a radio operator, Wilhelm Moldenhauer was one of the first to hear the news, but he was also careful not to break regulations and, on 20 November, restricted himself to commenting cryptically to his wife, 'Now it's turned out differently from the way we'd figured it out.' By 22 November the million-strong Soviet offensive had cut through the enormously overstretched Axis lines. To the east, the Romanian 4th Army and the German 6th Army were now isolated in a vast no-man's-land in the Volga bend in and around Stalingrad, cut off from the rest of Army Group B to the west. At the same time, a second Red Army offensive was launched to capture the land bridge to List's Army Group A in the Caucasus: this the Germans succeeded in fighting off.[46]

The Wehrmacht thought it had been through this before. At Demyansk, an army corps of some 100,000 troops had been trapped by the Red Army's Rzhev-Vyaz'ma counter-offensive in January 1942. For four months, the German divisions there had been supplied by air, tying down five Soviet armies, until the German relief effort broke through the encirclement. Against the advice of his staff, Göring now rushed to pledge that the Luftwaffe would provide an air bridge. Reassured that the gamble might pay off, Hitler gave the order to turn the Stalingrad pocket into a 'fortress'. Just as in the previous winter, he rejected all demands to retreat.[47]

The promise of an air bridge was a powerful one and reassured soldiers' families, who had already been impressed by the special airmail service run by the military post throughout the summer's advance. The air bridge would not only bring supplies in, but also guarantee that the wounded were brought out. In early January, Liselotte Purper arrived at the airbase in Lwów to take propaganda photos of a wounded soldier being unloaded from a Ju 52 transport. It was so cold that she had trouble seeing the viewfinder. To spare the wounded man the ordeal of being repeatedly shunted in and out of the plane, Liselotte had a medical orderly bandaged up to take his place on the stretcher. After a dozen men had pushed the plane around to face the other way, she had the right light and the pictures came out well.[48]

It had taken the whole of the 1st Air Fleet to supply the Demyansk pocket. Eight months later, supplying the 290,000 troops trapped in the Stalingrad 'cauldron' was beyond the capacity of the Luftwaffe. While Demyansk had needed some 265 tonnes of supplies per day, the 6th Army required an estimated daily minimum of 680 tonnes. Operating over a much longer distance and facing a much better organised Red Air Force, the Luftwaffe had already suffered heavy losses and the relief effort would only accelerate the rate of attrition. Erhard Milch, the dynamic head of Luftwaffe procurement, took direct command, but even he could find no way of delivering more than 100 tonnes a day.

As the failure of the Luftwaffe became evident, the need to restore the land-link became still more urgent. If the 6th Army remained cut off, then it could not prevent Soviet forces from filling the gap between the two German army groups and isolating Army Group A in the Caucasus as well. On 12 December Manstein launched a counter-attack which took the Soviet forces by surprise, and made rapid progress in the first two days, coming within 50 kilometres of the encircled 6th Army. Manstein's attempt also made the Soviets break off their effort to cut off Army Group A in the Caucasus. But, despite all Manstein's urging, the commander of the 6th Army, General Friedrich von Paulus, refused to order his troops to break out of its encirclement by attacking simultaneously from the east. Faced with a lack of fuel, shells and serviceable vehicles and the onset of fierce winter blizzards, as well as a direct order from Hitler not to retreat, Paulus ignored all contrary advice and decided to wait.

Different sections of the 6th Army experienced the attrition at varying rates. Wilhelm Moldenhauer's radio truck was unheated, to conserve petrol, but he still retreated to it to hear the news and escape the confines of their dugout. At 4 by 2.5 metres, it was a tight squeeze for seven men, who took turns sleeping. The only advantage was that no one had to stand watch for more than an hour during the night; but getting your boots on and off in the dark bunker was, Moldenhauer wrote cheerfully, a real art. The tone of his letters home remained remarkably level through the weeks of December. Lack of leave and lack of post were the main concerns. Only his description of cooking would have alerted his family to his plight: they traded tobacco for horse bones to cook soups and chopped up dried white cabbage and a horse's heart or lungs for a real delicacy.[49]

By 17 December, after being cut off for four weeks in this 'muck', Fritz Probst and his comrades in the construction battalion were, he wrote home, cold, hungry but healthy. Rations were down to 200 grams of bread a day, with soup at midday. No letters were getting through to them any more, but they had heard that a relief force had broken through the encirclement. Five days later things were much the same. One of his comrades had been mortally wounded by a bomb fragment. With no laundry in five weeks, the men had not shaved or washed for four: their beards were, he wrote to his wife, 'all centimetres long, but we are keeping our hope and courage up, we know that victory is ours'.[50]

By the time that Fritz Probst had heard that relief was on its way, the chance had been lost. Its advance blocked by the 2nd Guards Army, Manstein's force itself was now threatened with encirclement. A second Soviet pincer attack, launched on 16 December, sliced through the 130,000-strong Italian 8th Army and threatened to encircle Manstein's own force. He had no choice but to send the 6th Panzer Division to save the battered remnants of the Italian army, and, on Christmas Eve, to order his own force to retreat. From now on the only link to the 6th Army was by air, but that same day a Soviet armoured raid managed to penetrate to the Luftwaffe's forward airbase at Tatsinskaya. It destroyed fifty-six transport planes and the airfield itself.[51]

That evening, the German home front tuned in to a special radio link-up, connecting thirty transmitters, among them a plane and a U-boat. From North Africa to the Arctic Sea, the front stations came in formally: 'Calling Stalingrad again!' – 'Here is Stalingrad! Here is the front on the Volga!' came the reply. Private greetings were exchanged as in the *Request Concert* broadcasts of old and at the end of the programme the different stations joined in singing 'Silent Night' and the third verse of Luther's great hymn 'A mighty fortress is our God'. Meanwhile, the word 'cauldron' was not used to describe the bitter fighting in the 'Volga–Don region'.[52]

On Christmas Day, Fritz Probst wrote to his wife again, reminding her that, in spite of the privations at home, at least they could enjoy 'a warm living room, a Christmas tree too and one is with the family'.

For all of that, he continued, 'you can only thank our dear Führer. That it remains so, that's why we are standing here.' For Wilhelm Moldenhauer, Christmas Eve brought an extraordinary surprise: two sacks of post, including five of his wife's letters and a small parcel with liver sausage, preserved cherries and a torch battery. The dugout now had to accommodate nine men, but they had excavated it a bit more and brought in car seats to sit on. They had hung a rug and newspaper photos of pretty women on the wall, and turned a bottle with silver paper and old camouflage material into their 'tree'. Cigarette papers made the decorations. A special bread ration and real coffee had put the lice-ridden men in the mood to sing carols. On 30 December, Moldenhauer also quoted Lale Andersen's hit song: 'After every December comes another May. With humour and good spirits we will also put this time behind us,' he wrote. Five days later, on 4 January 1943, under heavy air and artillery bombardment from the west, Moldenhauer could still strike an optimistic note: 'Thanks to our good leadership, we can be confident. We want to hope that the Russians' great offensive turns into a great success for us. I don't just hope that, but I am firmly convinced that's how it will turn out.' It was his last letter.[53]

Ursula von Kardorff's brother wrote to her on 23 January, reminding her of the passage in Heinrich von Kleist 'where the Prussian hussar of 1806 is depicted as representative of a soldiery which retains its splendour, independent of the failure of the whole enterprise'. 'I want', the 23-year-old went on, 'to devote my own strength to the best of my ability like that, without asking about the possible outcome.' By the time the letter reached Ursula in Berlin, his unit was being praised in the military bulletin, and 'we know what that means', Kardorff noted. The young woman asked herself where she should take spiritual refuge – 'in Bach? Hölderlin? Kleist?' – before concluding that she had to make his stance her own, 'without illusions and [yet] loyal to one's duty. Very hard.'[54]

As the Red Army pressed its advantage, it pushed the Germans and Hungarians back to the river Don. By 25 January, the city of Voronezh – captured by the Germans in early July at the start of 'Operation Blue' – was back in Soviet hands. Retreating westwards from the city, Lieutenant Eugen Altrogge was wounded in his right arm. A month earlier, he had written to Hans Albring about his latest drawings: in one, death clung to the shoulders of a sick soldier. A non-commissioned officer wrote to Altrogge's family later to tell them that Eugen had been evacuated to the main dressing station and then westwards by plane after being wounded, but this may not have been the case. In the chaos of the winter retreat, his whereabouts unknown, Eugen Altrogge joined the growing number of men who were reported as missing in action.[55]

Information reaching the home front about Stalingrad slowed to a trickle, as the Soviet encirclement tightened. On 10 January 1943, the Wehrmacht report noted merely 'local raiding parties'. Four days later the sparse military bulletins gave way to new and alarming reports of 'heroic, severe battles in the area of Stalingrad'. The SD quickly picked up a new level of public anxiety and Goebbels himself wrote an article entitled 'Total War' in *Das Reich*, praising the heroism and sacrifice of the 6th Army as it tied down Soviet forces and protected the German armies in the Caucasus. The change of tone was no accident. Having accepted that defeat was now inevitable, the Propaganda Minister persuaded Hitler to let him prepare the ground for what he called a 'heroic epic'.[56]

Saturday, 30 January 1943 marked the regime's 10th anniversary. The main event was an address by Hermann Göring, whose Harvest Festival speech the previous October had made such a strong impression. Transmitted live on all domestic and armed forces' radio stations, it was scheduled for 11 a.m. before a military audience, only to be delayed because six RAF Mosquito bombers appeared on their first daylight raid over Berlin. When Göring at last spoke, he pronouced a funeral oration over the 6th Army at Stalingrad. They would not only join the heroes of Germany's past, from the Nibelungen and Ostrogoths of legend to the student volunteers who fought at Langemarck in 1914, but also Leonidas and his 300 Spartans who held 'the narrow pass' at Thermopylae against the Persian hordes: 'even in a thousand years every German will still speak of this battle with religious awe and reverence and know that, despite everything, Germany's victory was decided there,' Göring declared. The scale of the 6th Army's heroism was the same as that of the Spartans 'two and a half thousand years ago': 'Then too it was an onslaught of hordes which broke against the nordic men.'[57]

Göring's speech marked the climax of the nationalist cult of heroic death, a tradition which the Nazis inherited but certainly did not invent. Thermopylae resonated deeply with educated Germans, brought up on the poetry of Friedrich Schiller and that of the soldier-poet of the 'liberation wars' against Napoleon, Theodor Körner. The Reich Marshal's pledge that 'In days to come it will be said thus: when you come home to Germany, tell them that you have seen us lying at Stalingrad, as the law of the security of our people ordained' deliberately echoed Schiller's rendition of the classical epitaph of Simonides, the literary heart of the Thermopylae myth: 'Wanderer, if you come to Sparta, tell them there, you saw us lying here, as the law ordained.' Hölderlin and Nietzsche had believed that the Germans were descended from the Greeks. Now Göring pronounced the Spartans to be northmen.[58]

Brought up to venerate the dead of the First World War, young recruits knew what was expected of them. As one corporal stationed with Army Group Centre wrote home on 24 January 1943:

> Here it is a matter of life and death. Russia is our fate – this or that outcome! The struggle has reached a harshness and implacability that beggars all description. 'Not one of you has the right to return home alive!' This motto has been repeated to us soldiers often enough and we know that it is meant seriously. We are completely prepared.[59]

In Croatia, a lieutenant on the regimental staff of the 721st Grenadier Regiment applauded Göring's words. 'Never before in this war has such a heroic battle been fought. From this raging cauldron no one will ever see his homeland now!! It is very true that we really do not match these immortal Stalingrad fighters.' At this time, his infantry division was embroiled in the largest dragnet operation of the war so far, 'Operation White', involving some 90,000 German, Croatian and Italian troops, who torched the villages of the Bihać region. It was a matter, he reflected, 'not of the individual but of the whole', and in that consciousness 'we can attain victory!' To young Heinrich Böll, the supreme sacrifice of the Stalingrad fighters left him uncomfortably conscious of his own physical frailties, prompting him to write, 'I feel ashamed that I'm going in for several days' medical treatment for headaches and sore eyes tomorrow.'[60]

For Peter Stölten, attending a specialised tank-training course in

Eisenach, only Attila's defeat on the Catalaunian Plains seemed to compare with the heroic event, a battle in which 'Germanic' tribes had fought alongside Roman legions to stem the 'Asiatic' Huns. But he feared that the meaning of Stalingrad was in danger of 'sinking into a bloody darkness', its spiritual expression lost. 'I believe that in a quiet, ordered time we will feel it as an enormous loss,' Stölten wrote to his parents, 'that out of these last days not a single letter reached a family. Here in the continuous face of death a true response to our time must have been found, offering an ideal standard.' While the battle was still raging Goebbels entrusted the chief reporter with the 6th Army, Heinz Schröter, with collecting and editing excerpts of soldiers' letters to satisfy exactly this kind of spiritual demand.[61]

At the time when Göring gave his address, it looked to the Nazi leadership as if events at the front might accord with the choreography they had chosen. On 29 January, General Paulus had telegraphed Hitler to offer the 6th Army's congratulations on the anniversary and to assure him that the flag was still flying over the city: 'May our battle be an example for the current and future generations never to capitulate, even in their hopes: then Germany will be victorious.' According to Nazi beliefs, a responsible commander would have to commit suicide if defeat was inevitable, and, to make quite sure Hitler promoted Paulus to the rank of field marshal, well aware that no German field marshal had ever surrendered. Paulus would earn Hitler's lasting contempt for being the first to do so. German radio did its best to give the end a different gloss, announcing merely that his southern group 'has been over-whelmed in battle by the superiority of the enemy, after more than two months of heroic defence'. On 30 January, news that the last German position had fallen at the tractor works was bathed in instransigent imagery: 'During the heroic fighting every man, up to the General, fought in the most advanced line with fixed bayonets.'[62]

Then, on 3 February, preceded by slow marches, German radio announced that the battle was finally over:

> The sacrifice of the 6th Army was not in vain. As the bulwark of the historic European mission it has broken the assault of six Soviet armies for several weeks . . . Generals, officers, non-commissioned officers and men fought shoulder to shoulder to

the last bullet. They died so that Germany may live.

These words were followed by muffled drum rolls and three stanzas of the soldiers' song 'Ich hatt' einen Kameraden' – 'The Good Comrade' – then the national anthems of Germany, Romania and Croatia, and, following the format of great victories, a three-minute silence. Three days of national mourning were declared, during which all theatres, cinemas and variety halls in the Reich would remain closed. More sombre marches and a broadcast of Beethoven's Fifth Symphony followed. Goebbels had requested a military bulletin which would stand comparison with the proclamations of Caesar, Frederick the Great and Napoleon and stir Germans' heart for centuries to come.[63]

During the three days of official mourning, the Catholic bishops responded to Stalingrad by ordering masses for the dead in all diocesan churches. Archbishop Frings of Cologne intensified his appeal to the Virgin Mary. Galen of Münster, so recently the thorn in the regime's side, penned a pastoral letter: 'Full of inner love we remember our distant soldiers, who block the onslaught of the enemy from the homeland, the violent penetration of Bolshevism.' Turning for inspiration to Thomas Aquinas, he blessed those who died 'the soldier's death in loyal fulfilment of duty' as 'near in value and worth to the martyrdom of the faithful'.[64]

The 'heroic epic' Goebbels and Göring had carefully crafted unleashed a public relations disaster of unparalleled proportions. There had been no emotional preparation for the extent of the defeat. With many of its sons serving in the 6th Army, the city of Nuremberg was seized by a paroxysm of grief. Grabbing papers from the news vendors, weeping and angry crowds turned on their leader for the first time: 'Hitler has lied to us for three months,' people railed, remembering his proud boast of 8 November that Stalingrad was virtually conquered. Across Germany, the population reacted with utter shock, dismay and an anger made all the greater by the optimistic reports which had circulated so recently. The notion that Stalingrad had been a mere battle for prestige may have concealed the full scale of the strategic defeat from many, but in the short term it also made the death of a whole army appear frivolous. To others, just as in the previous January, it now seemed as if the war had turned decisively against Germany. Goebbels realised that what might appeal to idealistic, Gymnasium-educated young men did not provide a viable myth for the whole nation: it was 'unbearable for the German people', he admitted to his diary, and he put the whole project of publishing a heroic epic of highly selected 'last letters' on ice. Stalingrad was the first and last defeat which the Nazi regime mythologised in this manner. When a quarter of a million German soldiers surrendered at Tunis a few months later the reporting was low-key and matter-of-fact; the same would hold true of the far greater defeats still to come. When Hitler finally addressed the German people for Heroes Memorial Day on 21 March, he would not mention Stalingrad at all.[65]

Goebbels realised that he needed to rally the living. At the start of the new year he had begun to rethink his own propaganda effort, telling the key media managers gathered at his ministerial conference in early January that

> Since the beginning of the war our propaganda has followed the following erroneous path:

> First year of the war: we have won.
> Second year of the war: we shall win.
> Third year of the war: we must win.
> Fourth year of the war: we cannot be defeated.[66]

The principal target of this critique could only be Goebbels himself. As he considered what might most motivate the German people, he turned for the first time to holding up the spectre of defeat, what a British observer aptly dubbed 'Strength through fear' – instead of 'Strength through joy', the pre-war slogan of the Nazi leisure organisation. But Goebbels knew that fear alone could not galvanise the nation.

On 18 February, he addressed a hand-picked crowd of Party members at the Berlin Sportpalast. Once more, the speech was amplified through the national megaphone of all radio stations. This time references to ancient Greece had nothing to do with Thermopylae. 'We now know what we have to do,' Goebbels assured his audience. 'The German people wants a Spartan way of life for everybody. For high and low, for poor and rich.' Goebbels himself had great hopes for his speech, considering it one of his best rhetorical efforts. It culminated in ten questions which turned the audience of loyal Nazis into a classical chorus, roaring their approval and standing in for the German nation as a whole. By the time he reached his tenth and final question, they were in a frenzy:

> Is it your wish that even in wartime, as the Party programme requires, equal rights and equal duties shall prevail [cries of 'Yes!'], that the home front shall give evidence of its solidarity and take the same heavy burdens of war upon its shoulders, and that the burdens be distributed equitably, whether a person be great or small, poor or rich?

It was a declaration of 'total war'. At the end, Goebbels turned to the words of the soldier-poet Theodor Körner: 'Now let the nation arise, let the storm break.' Amid wild cheers, the audience began singing the German national anthem and the Party's 'Horst Wessel Song'.[67]

Goebbels was delighted with the immediate reaction and felt it was a speech like no other he had given. The responses gathered by the SD's monitoring service, however, were less encouraging. Many felt that the wild enthusiasm of the audience looked too stage-managed to be genuine; some wondered why the regime had not taken such measures long ago; others questioned whether the speech had altered anything. During the coming weeks, Goebbels had to accept that little had changed. He had hoped to use the opportunity to persuade Hitler to vest new powers in him to override other agencies and mobilise the home front, but the management of the German war effort was not radically restructured. Hitler was not prepared to encroach on family life. The evacuation of children from bombed areas remained voluntary, to the growing frustration of officials attempting to co-ordinate civil defence. At the top of the regime, however, quiet shifts in power continued. Enraged by the Luftwaffe's failure in both east and west, Hitler did not want to hear Göring's name mentioned in his presence for days on end. But ever sensitive to the outward appearance of unity, he insisted that Göring remained 'indispensable to the supreme leadership of the Reich'. Instead of a major shake-up of the regime, the influence of some key figures grew sporadically and far beyond their functional spheres: that of Albert Speer over the war economy, Heinrich Himmler's over the agencies of coercion, and Martin Bormann's over the Party. Their competitors – Hans Lammers,

Fritz Sauckel, Robert Ley, Joachim von Ribbentrop and Alfred Rosenberg – would all gradually lose ground in this war of attrition for control of key committees, bureaucracies and access to Hitler.[68]

Goebbels failed to have himself appointed 'Plenipotentiary for Total War', but in January Hitler had appointed him to the chairmanship of the Interministerial Committee for Air Raid Damage, which allowed him to intervene and instruct other Gauleiters in civil defence matters. With this new, practical focus to the war effort, Goebbels abandoned his 'politeness campaign' to encourage model behaviour on the home front, declaring on 9 April 1943 that

> it is not important that the population should be in a good mood, but that it should preserve its bearing . . . After the fourth year of war, all men think differently of war than they did at the beginning . . . Expressions such as patriotism and enthusiasm are quite out of place. The German people simply does its duty – that is all.[69]

Increasingly, political propaganda and popular entertainment moved in opposite directions, the one becoming harder and bleaker as Goebbels emphasised the danger of defeat, while the other became lighter and fluffier. At the time of Goebbels's 'total war' speech, the three main films showing in Berlin were two romantic comedies, *Two Happy People* and *Love Me*, and a circus revue on ice, *The Big Hit*. The best hope of the Nazi leadership was that ordinary people would continue to defer their domestic utopias until after a German victory, just as the *Request Concert* had encouraged them to do in the first years of the war. The 1942 film *The Great Love* updated the story of romantic but deferred love to the eastern front and became the greatest block-buster of Nazi cinema, mainly because of the songs of Zarah Leander, the Swedish actress who took on the role of the femme fatale with her near-baritonal voice and androgynous sexuality. After Stalingrad, one of its great hits, in which Leander brings the audience in to accompany her singing 'The world is not going to end because of that', remained enduringly popular. Its carefree and raunchy, cabaret-style sense of being in it together continued to appeal. The SD noted at this time that women in Berlin had started wearing trousers as a provocative fashion statement.[70]

Stalingrad was a major defeat. For a second time, Hitler had been tempted into declaring that a crucial battle was as good as won. In military terms, Moscow in 1941 was the more critical turning point: if the Wehrmacht had conquered Moscow, it would have been very difficult for the Red Army to fight on; whereas it could have surrendered Stalingrad and continued the war. In symbolic terms, Stalingrad was worse for Hitler's reputation: in December 1941, he had taken personal command of the German armies from Brauchitsch and reaped the credit for stemming the panic through his 'halt order'; a year later, his very role as Commander-in-Chief led many Germans to question their Führer's military genius for the first time. To make matters worse, Hitler had refused to follow Goebbels's advice and allow the media to give a bleaker and more downbeat gloss to the battle in the critical months from October to December 1942. Nor had the grandiose attempt to portray the 'sacrifice' of the 6th Army as an 'epic struggle' worked either, and in February Hitler ordered that all military lectures and commentaries on the battle should cease until he had approved an official version. When the Afrika Korps surrendered at Tunis in May 1943, a press directive ordained that 'in no circumstances are references to Stalingrad to be made in the commentaries'. By June 1943, Goebbels felt confident enough to declare insouciantly, in one of his lead articles in *Das Reich* which was also read over the radio, that it was unreasonable to expect the government 'to predict the future accurately and correctly'. As he pointed out, no one had imagined in 1939 either that the war would last so long or that German troops would have fought their way to such distant fronts. Arguing that 'intentional as well as unintentional and involuntary errors are justified by victory alone', he asserted 'the leadership's sovereign right to make occasional mistakes'. A dictatorship led by a self-styled 'prophet' could not resort to this argument often. On 3 February 1944, the first anniversary of the epic battle which Göring had predicted would still be spoken of 'in a thousand years in religious awe' was passed over in silence.[71]

It was no longer clear when or how the German conquest of the Soviet Union could be achieved. Instead, people began to countenance an endless war of attrition. Goebbels's call to wage 'total war' might fall flat, but that was because in 1943, just as in 1942, Germans already had a tried and tested language for 'holding out' which had seen them through the horrors and rigours of the previous war. Popular humour was not slow to catch up, and the Münster journalist Paulheinz

Wantzen picked up the latest jokes:

> In 1999, two panzer grenadiers on the Kuban bridgehead are chatting. One of them has read the word 'Peace' in a book and would like to know what that means. No one in the bunker knows and so they ask the Sarge. He doesn't know either and so they ask the Lieutenant and company commander. 'Peace?' he asks shaking his head. 'Peace? I even attended a Gymnasium, but I don't know that word.' Next day, he is at battalion HQ and asks the commander. He doesn't know but has a recently published dictionary and there they finally discover: 'Peace, way of life unfit for human beings, abolished in 1939'.[72]

In one crucial respect, the botched attempt to create an instant myth around Stalingrad left an enduring and painful legacy. The Wehrmacht bulletin on 3 February had contained a crucial lie: that 'Generals, officers, NCOs and ordinary soldiers fought shoulder to shoulder to the last bullet.' Within a week, rumours were circulating that in fact German commanders, including Field Marshal Paulus, and many of their men had surrendered and entered Soviet captivity. Exploiting the fact that before the outbreak of hostilities the Soviet Union had not signed up to the Geneva Convention on the treatment of prisoners, the Wehrmacht insisted that it had no information that could be verified by neutral third parties and stipulated that all soldiers lost at Stalingrad should simply be classified as 'missing in action'.[73]

★

It was not the dead of Stalingrad who 'lived on', but the missing. Hildegard Probst was without news of her husband. Fritz had written to her on Christmas Day and again on New Year's Day, assuring her that although there was no wood to warm the shelter, they were still managing: 'The day must come when we are free and things get better again.' Her own letters and parcels were returned to her, undelivered. By 1 April, she had received four letters and six small, 100-gram air-freight packets back. It was the same for all the other families of men serving in his company: the last letters had been written in early January. Hoping that relatives of Fritz's comrades would come forward with news, Hildegard wrote to German radio's Comrades service and a month later heard her husband's name read aloud on the airwaves. On 29 May, she registered him with the local Red Cross office, only to receive the news that he must be regarded as 'missing'.[74]

News spread that the German embassy in Ankara, headed by the former Chancellor Franz von Papen, had successfully located a junior officer for his well-connected mother, and people turned also to the Turkish Red Crescent for help in locating their relatives. The Wehrmacht Information Office, on the other hand, did its best to block communication and suppress the fact that 113,000 German and Romanian soldiers had been taken prisoner. The Wehrmacht High Command even ordered that the few sacks of letters it had should not be delivered, so as not to spoil the choreography of the heroic last stand.[75]

But the information vacuum could not be sustained. Radio Moscow was already broadcasting 'the figure of ninety-one thousand prisoners', an official in the Press and Information Office of the Foreign Ministry noted on 2 February 1943, predicting that 'Not everyone will be able to resist the temptation to try and get news by listening to enemy broadcasts . . . In the eyes of the simple masses, "taken prisoner" is very different from "killed", no matter how many times they are told that the Russians murder all prisoners taken.' The SD agreed, charting the take-up of Soviet propaganda leaflets dropped over Germany and the pick-up of information which could only have been gleaned by listening to Radio Moscow. Both local and national reports confirmed that 'black listening' increased at this time, with both Radio Moscow and the BBC reading out the names of German prisoners. In Stuttgart, Gauleiter Murr threatened that those who 'listen to the voice of the enemy [and thus] weaken the defensive and resistance capability of our people' would be 'prosecuted and mercilessly punished'. But the local SD did not see things in such stark terms, regarding the practice as a natural response to the lack of information.[76]

As usual the Gestapo tried to discriminate in dealing with such cases, forming a view of the offender as well as the offence. In March 1943, a woman started writing to the families of German soldiers whose names and addresses were listed on a Soviet leaflet that her son had brought home on leave. She simply wanted to pass on the news that they were alive and 'doing well'. Eventually, she came to the notice of the Gestapo, which established that she was motivated

Female Red Army
prisoners, August 1941:
many were executed.

Red Army prisoners
at Mauthausen in 1941 ...

... and in 1944.

Top: Fritz Probst, engineer:
destroyed bridge over the
Dniepr at Kiev, 1941.

Left: Fritz Probst:
rebuilt Dniepr bridge, 1941.

Liselotte Purper, photo-journalist: Germans promenade through the ruins of Kiev, 1942.

Execution tourists: soldiers at Orel, winter of 1941–2.

Top: Ernst Guicking: winter retreat, 1941–2: dead Soviet soldiers and horse.

Below: Wilhelm Moldenhauer: summer advance, 1942.

Top: Deportation of Jews from Kitzingen, 24 March 1942.

Below left: Going underground: Marianne Strauss' wartime postal pass.

Below right: Germans bid for Jewish property at auction in Hanau.

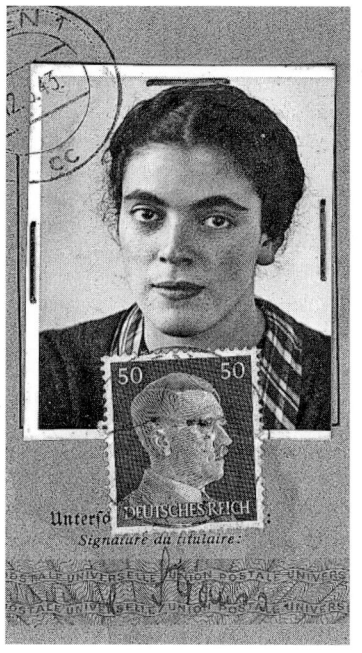

Top: Liselotte Purper: setting up her photo shoot at Lwów airbase.

Left: Liselotte Purper: a medical orderly made up as a wounded soldier being unloaded from a Ju-52.

Top: Liselotte Purper:
off-duty anti-aircraft personnel
playing duets in the bunker of
the Anhalter Bahnhof, Berlin.

Right: Queuing for
cinema tickets, Berlin.

Zarah Leander singing 'The world isn't going to end because of this' in *The Great Love* (1942).

War wedding: Liselotte Purper and Kurt Orgel, September 1943.

by the fact that she had lost two brothers in the First World War, and her youngest son the previous year. 'I wanted to help the affected persons, and I felt sorry for them that they did not have any news of their relatives,' she explained. Instead of punishing her for 'defeatism' or 'spreading enemy propaganda', the Gestapo let her go with a warning, impressed by her unblemished record of service in Nazi mass organisations.

Fritz M., by contrast, fared less well. In May 1943, the Gestapo arrested him for sending out forty-six letters to families of men listed on Radio Moscow to tell them that 'the allegedly missing German soldiers are in captivity and doing well'. This counted as 'Communist propaganda' because it challenged the 'common assumption . . . that German soldiers in Russian captivity were treated badly'. Fritz M. was also a former member of the Social Democratic Party. Given that these were potential capital offences, he was relatively lucky to be sentenced to two years in prison, a sure sign that the police did not yet want to push such cases to the extreme. He obviously did not consider his own actions to be a form of clandestine resistance: whereas some letter-writers signed themselves off as '+++', 'a national comrade' or '+++ (unfortunately I can't do otherwise)', he had provided his name and address. It was also revealing that not a single one of the recipients had denounced him, a fact that they also had to explain to the Gestapo.[77]

Despite all efforts to intercept letters and postcards from German prisoners of war in Soviet captivity, a few of them got through, some via addresses in neutral countries, some through administrative incompetence. In April 1943, the censorship office in Vienna let a letter slip through to Gisela Heitz, the wife of a senior officer in the 6th Army, General Walter Heitz. The contents of the letter were soon doing the rounds of other senior officers' families, some of whom, like Gisela Heitz herself, included the Wehrmacht High Command in their correspondence as they tried to discover how they could establish contact with their loved ones. The Wehrmacht Information Office did its best to dampen down expectations, explaining that 'due to the completely negative attitude of the Soviet Union, there have been no agreements whatsoever regarding contact with German prisoners of war in the Soviet Union'. The Heitz story soon grew into the myth that this tough-minded general served as a liaison person for the missing and prisoners in the east. The rumours persisted into the summer of 1944, revived rather than buried under the impact of new battles and defeats on the eastern front. The Army High Command finally took the highly unusual step of officially denying them.[78]

After months of waiting for news, Luise Stieber's only comfort was her diary conversations with her missing husband, and the poems she wrote to him at night:

> I sit in the room so alone
> In the night by the lamp's light
> Nearby in the bed our child
> Calls your name in his sleep.
>
>   . . .
>
> When I feel about to give up,
> Then I take down your picture,
> Call both children to me
> And see them weep for you.
> Then I know in all sorrow
> They are a comfort to me.
> So, I want to stand by my post,
> Brave and not giving up,
> For I know for sure
> The day is coming
> When we will meet again.[79]

Some historians have suggested that such irretrievable loss was the overriding collective experience of the Second World War in Germany, and that it alienated many from the regime. Yet it is hard to read either defeatism or political resistance into such reactions. It was a private grief, and in early February 1944 Luise Stieber still insisted, 'So, I want to stand by my post, / Brave and not giving up'. She consoled herself also with words Zarah Leander had sung in *The Great Love*: 'I know there'll be a miracle one day'. Twelve days later she confessed to her husband in her diary, 'Without a greeting, without a word from you, everything is unspeakably hard. I feel like an orphan.' Momentarily forgetting her two children, she added, 'Now I have no one any more who belongs to me.'[80]

Searching for an outlet after three months of fruitless, nervous waiting, at the start of April 1943 Hildegard Probst picked up the present her children had given her for Christmas, a bound notebook, and began to write to her husband. 'I want to turn it into a kind of diary,' she explained, 'to replace the letters which I can no longer write to you. I want to tell you in it what I would have otherwise written in my letters and so it ought to be a kind of bridge to the time when you are with us again. Because I still firmly believe that you will return one day.' She tried to relay the most important news items from the medieval town of Mühlhausen in Thuringia. Shops and businesses were closed as part of Goebbels's 'total war' drive, and she reported on the war deaths, some marked merely by newspaper notices, others by a 'very moving' funeral which brought the community together, complete with a detachment of soldiers who fired a volley over the empty coffin. For the families of the missing, there could be no such closure.[81]

But time did not stop. Their three children, Hildegard wrote at Whitsun, 'are able to live out the day unburdened and know nothing of my grief. And if they do occasionally see my tears, then they want to comfort me, that Daddy is going to come back again.' Their eldest son, Karl-Heinz, was taking on the kind of responsibility his father had always feared he would shirk, and applied for an apprenticeship at the Junker works in Dessau. A month later, in mid-July, Hildegard was amazed still to be receiving letters back which she had written to her husband before Christmas 1942. On Fritz's birthday, 17 August, she decorated his photo with roses as usual and thought enviously of the families of the men from the Afrika Korps: they had all received mail from the 250,000 men who had surrendered to the Americans in Tunisia back in May.[82]

Many other wives and mothers carried on with their lives like Hildegard, sending their children to school, writing to the families of other men listed as missing, sometimes passing on chain letters themselves. The birthdays and anniversaries of weddings, call-up and last leave rolled by; the small gifts and photos sent home from the front remained in prominent view. While his cabinetmaker's tools gathered dust in the workshop, Hildegard Probst was not alone in feeling she could only reach her missing husband by keeping a diary for him. Theirs was grief without mourning. Without public recognition, communal consolation and widows' pensions, they remained in limbo.

PART FIVE

THE WAR COMES HOME

II

Bombing and Retaliation

On 15 February 1943, a ceremony took place for the first time which gave a new dimension to Germany's mobilisation for war. The 15- and 16-year-old boys enrolled in classes 6 and 7 in the higher schools were sworn in as air force and naval auxiliaries. As they shed their Hitler Youth uniforms for the real thing and swore their military oaths of allegiance to the Führer, many were ecstatic. It was, one Cologne schoolboy wrote, 'a momentous day', which filled him 'with a feeling of pride, for I know that I too can take part in the defence of the homeland'. Among these first two cohorts were Hans-Dietrich Genscher from Reideburg in Saxony, who would later become German Foreign Minister, the future novelist Günter Grass from Danzig and the seminarian Joseph Ratzinger from Traunstein in Bavaria, the future Pope Benedict XVI. So many boys served with the anti-aircraft batteries, or the flak as it was universally called, that the whole levy is often refered to as the *Flakhelfer* generation, although in fact it chiefly involved the Gymnasium-educated middle classes. By the end of the war, the 1929 and 1930 cohorts had also served, including the future social theorist Jürgen Habermas and future Chancellor Helmut Kohl. The enrolment was the first of a series of adjustments to civil defence, which would indeed make Germans' experience of war 'total'.[1]

In Hamburg, 16-year-old Klaus Seidel, the son of a schoolteacher, joined the anti-aircraft battery in the middle of the city park. In Berlin Hans Joachim M. and the rest of his class were sent to man positions on an airfield. While the boys rejoiced in their new-found freedom and responsibility, their parents complained about lack of access and home visits. The press reassured them that they need not worry that their sons would be forced to take on tasks beyond their strength, while also reminding the boys that they were relatively privileged compared to those doing industrial apprenticeships. Alongside military training under Luftwaffe and naval personnel and ideological instruction by the Hitler Youth, the teenagers were supposed to continue their schooling, with a streamlined timetable. After attending a parents' evening at the Gymnasium in Cologne-Mülheim, one father was furious: 'Personally I find the whole thing outrageous,' he wrote to his elder son serving at the front. 'Hundreds and thousands of strong young men like my colleague P. are running around and avoiding service. And instead, they're taking children just out of their nappies.' The older son disagreed: even if you avoid 'all emotionalism', he admonished his father, it remained the case that 'not only the sons nowadays have to do their duty by becoming soldiers, but so do the parents too, namely by letting them go where they are needed, with their unconditional support and in the spirit of unconditional fulfilment of their duty'.[2]

Hans Joachim M. and his Berlin classmates went to assist the elderly reservists and Russian auxiliaries in servicing the huge searchlights and radar controls which supported the flak artillery. On the Führer's birthday, 20 April, Hans Joachim's battery was hit: a soldier was killed but none of his group. In the next battery the boys were not so lucky: seven of them were killed that day. In Essen, Rolf Dieter Koch saw action even sooner. At 8.45 p.m. on 5 March, the air raid sirens began to wail. At precisely 9 p.m. the first Mosquito fighter bomber dropped its red markers over the Krupp works on the southern side of the city. At short intervals until 9.36 p.m., 7 Mosquitoes, 17 Lancasters and 5 Halifax heavy bombers went on marking the site, adding an inner ring of green flares to the red outer ring. Flying in close formation, 89 Halifax bombers, 52 Stirlings, 131 Wellingtons and, last of all, 140 Lancasters arrived in three waves over the city. By 9.40 p.m., they had dropped 524.4 tonnes of incendiaries and 490.4 tonnes of high explosive and were heading home. By the end of that night, Rolf Dieter Koch was too exhausted to do more than jot down his experiences in telegraphic style: 'Strong force of oncoming planes. First deployment at the map table. High explosive and fire bombs in the position. Re-evaluation destroyed. Our barracks burned down. Putting out fires. Sleep.' The bombs killed 457 people and wounded a further 1,400; 50,000 people lost their homes that night, with 3,016 houses totally destroyed and 2,050 severely damaged. A week later the bombers returned, killing another 648 people and making a further 40,000 homeless. For days afterwards, Carola Reissner, who had mocked the RAF's efforts in 1940, was still hearing the detonation of bombs from the raid.[3]

For the RAF's Bomber Command, the Essen raids marked the beginning of an entirely new phase in the air war, the battle of the Ruhr. As the headquarters of the Krupp armament empire, Essen had been given pride of place in the string of major offensives against industrial targets. Throughout 1942, navigation equipment had proved too inaccurate to find the targets and even when pilots could see through the clouds, the enormous conurbation of the Ruhr made identification difficult. British losses to the strong anti-aircraft batteries had also been heavy. The March 1943 raids changed the balance back in the attackers' favour, the culmination of technical breakthroughs which made navigation and targeting far more accurate. The bombers plotted their route to Essen with the help of 'Oboe', a new radio guidance system. Bomber Command avoided following a straight beam towards a target. Because of the large number of potential targets within range of the North Sea coast and western Germany, plausible feints could be deployed to direct the Luftwaffe night fighters to decoy targets. By February 1943, the Pathfinders were also starting to carry 'H$_2$S', an on-board radar-imaging system which revealed whether the ground below was a built-up area or not. It was still trouble-prone, leading the Pathfinders to mistake the radar image of mudbanks in the Elbe at low tide for sections of the Hamburg docks: the bombers dropped their loads 21 kilometres downstream of the city centre. What made the raid on Essen on the night of 5–6 March more destructive than usual was that the high-speed Mosquitoes and the Pathfinders managed to mark the city accurately. For the first time in the RAF's entire bombing campaign, 153 planes, nearly half the attacking force, succeeded in dropping their bombs within 5 kilo- metres of the target zone. Over the next four months, most of the cities of the Rhineland and Ruhr would be repeatedly bombed with similar levels of accuracy. The Krupp workshops in Essen would be picked out again a week later, setting a pattern for the months to come.[4]

Even in cities like Essen, where huge ferro-concrete bunkers had been built from 1940 onwards in expectation of air attack, the great majority of the civilian population had to take refuge in the cellars

beneath their apartment blocks. That first night of 5 March, a doctor
and his wife were sharing a deckchair in their cellar in Essen-West
when a bomb blast blew the doors and windows in. The wife stopped
reacting to her husband's words of comfort and simply stared straight
ahead of her, uttering a short prayer as each new bomb whistled
through the air nearby. Holding her tightly, the doctor felt her whole
body shake and before long it transmitted itself to him and his legs
began to twitch uncontrollably too. He became one of the neuralgic
cases referred to Dr Friedrich Panse, an expert in war neuroses at
Bonn. Small children in particular felt the tremors of each explosion
and blast as they took shelter in the cellars. Here they learned to listen
for the different sounds, recognising the high explosive bombs from
their 'Crash bang!!!' and the 'muffled crack' of the incendiaries, whose
'Clack, clack clack' reminded one child of 'when someone got a juicy
slap'. They also learned fear from the adults around them. As one
boy described it, 'Then it started in the bunker where people were
crammed into every corner and crevice. With every bomb that fell
the "Our fathers" sounded louder.'[5]

The raid of 5 March knocked out all eight of Essen's emergency
soup kitchens. With only three small ones left functioning, the People's
Welfare rushed in large canteens from neighbouring cities, providing
an average of 73,000 meals per day. Local military units provided sixty
field kitchens of their own, adding a further 25,000 litres to the daily
capacity. To Carola Reissner, it was also 'really amazing with what
heroic resilience and lack of complaint everything is endured here'.[6]

The build-up to the attacks on Essen had begun the previous year
when the RAF conducted the first 'thousand bomber' raid on Cologne
on 30–31 May 1942, a demonstrative action in which even training
planes had been pressed into service in order to show the British Air
Ministry what Bomber Command could achieve if only it was given
the resources. Afterwards the editor of the local paper wrote that
everyone who walked through those streets realised 'that they had
taken their leave of their Cologne the day before'. Unlike Essen,
indistinguishable from the built-up conurbation of the Ruhr, Cologne
was easy to find. With the soaring twin spires of its Gothic cathedral
rising beside the train station on the left bank of the wide, silver strip
of the river Rhine, the city served as a convenient landmark on the
flight path of the bomber stream. Even when it was not their target,

the planes turned east over the city to bomb the industrial centres of the Ruhr, or south towards more distant targets like Nuremberg. At the end of February 1943 one young woman complained, 'the English are driving us crazy!' Every day and every evening 'alarms three, four, five and more times'. On 28 February, Heinz Pettenberg counted the 500th alarm since the start of the war and confessed, 'we are dead tired'. Many people simply fell asleep as soon as they sat down, whether it was on the tram, in the doctor's waiting room, or at a government office. There were dreadful-looking barracks on the squares to give emergency shelter to the bombed-out. Rosalie Schüttler noted the many boarded-up shops, women driving trucks and trams and the endless piles of rubble on the Neumarkt where two mechanical diggers loaded up trucks running on the tram lines. The city was emptying, its population down from 770,000 to 520,000, as people sought safety and undamaged housing in the surrounding towns and villages. The commuter trains could scarcely cope with a further quarter of a million people trying to come into work and school each day. Even before the RAF's 'battle of the Ruhr' began, the Swiss consul in Cologne, Franz-Rudolf von Weiss, described civilian morale as 'well below zero'.[7]

As the RAF bombing grew in scale during spring 1943, Rosalie Schüttler was able to 'watch the cruel game over the Ruhr' each night from her home in the south-eastern suburb of Rath-Heumar. She heard too that the raids on the Möhne and Eder reservoirs on 16–17 May had released an 'incredible deluge' and 'destroyed whole villages and caused great loss of life'. She could only guess at the death toll: while the papers printed a figure of 370–400, there were rumours of 12,000. When Dortmund was attacked on the night of 24 May, the noise of the bombing and flak was audible in Cologne, as the horizon was lit up first with the tracers and flares and then the deeper glow of the fires burning out of control 80 kilometres away. The raid made a 'profound impression' on the population, the Swiss consul concluded, not least because they felt the British had broken another rule of 'fair play': breaching the Möhne dam had flooded air raid shelters in Dortmund.[8]

As the first anniversary of the thousand-bomber raid approached, the terrified inhabitants of Cologne lay awake, waiting for the 'big one'. In the event, it was Wuppertal that was hit. In the early hours of Sunday 30 May, 13-year-old Lothar Carsten jotted down in his diary: 'In the middle of the night, at twelve o'clock, the sirens sound. This is nothing new, you turn over and go on sleeping.' He repeated what everyone said: 'The Tommies won't find Wuppertal. We lie in the valley and at night there thick fog lies over the city.' Luckily, his father did get up and rouse the family. They ran into the cellar as the first bombs fell. His mother brought their tracksuits but, in the rush, forgot the suitcase with all their important papers. As soon as it was safe to go out, Lothar immediately joined his neighbours, who formed a human chain and passed buckets from hand to hand to extinguish the fires; the water mains had been hit and the hydrants would not work. 'The whole horizon is blood red,' Lothar wrote later that morning. A total of 719 planes, most of them four-engined bombers, had succeeded in concentrating their loads on the eastern end of the long, narrow city of Wuppertal, setting the old town centre of Barmen ablaze and destroying as much as 80 per cent of its buildings. For the next few days, Lothar Carsten had no time to write up his diary. Together with the other boys in his Hitler Youth branch, he helped the bombed-out rescue their belongings and ran messages.[9]

When two SA men in Barmen went to comfort a woman who stood weeping in front of the ruins of her house where her son, daughter-in-law and 2-year-old grandson lay buried, she turned on them, shouting: 'The Brownshirts are to blame for this war. They should have gone to the front and made sure that the English could not come here.' Barmen had been totally unprepared. Within a day, news reached Rosalie Schüttler that people who had caught fire had 'jumped into the Wupper to escape the heat'. In that one night 3,400 people had been killed, by far the greatest number of casualties in a single raid until now. For Bomber Command, Wuppertal was a minor target. Its main point was to force the Germans to disperse anti-aircraft batteries from the well-defended industrial centres of the Ruhr.[10]

Listening to the constant appeal by the authorities for everyone to leave Cologne who was not employed there, Rosalie concluded that the government had decided 'to sacrifice the Rhineland'. In the city, a strange calm set in. For the next twelve days, the alarms did not sound and strange rumours flew about. There was talk of a 'secret accord' between the governments, and an Allied leaflet was said to be circulating promising to spare Cologne, because the Jews who had emigrated 'want to live there once more'. Such shared fantasies helped to create a powerful set of reference points between the persecution of the Jews and Allied bombing. Then, on the night of 11–12 June, the alarms went off again, but this time the bombers passed overhead and soon the sky to the north over Düsseldorf was 'bright with the conflagration'. On 15 June, the Swiss consul reported to his superiors, 'we are all living here on a powder keg and in Cologne everyone believes that the next major attack will be directed at us'. People were desperate to be admitted to the ferro-concrete bunkers. Meanwhile, rumours about bombing with poison gas were multiplying once again, a key indicator of plummeting morale.[11]

As news of the bombing of western Germany spread, the SD reports on the national mood became so gloomy that Goebbels took the matter up with Himmler. He tried – and failed – to persuade him to have the reports jointly vetted by the Propaganda Ministry before circulating them within the top echelon of the Nazi leadership. Goebbels did at least succeed in drastically reducing the number of government officials who were entitled to read this most prized source of news. In the Ruhr, a ditty made the rounds which pilloried the audience of Goebbels's 'total war' speech in February:

> Dear Tommy, fly further
> we are all mine workers.
> Fly further to Berlin,
> all of them cried 'Yes'.[12]

This was not a mood of entrenched hostility, however. When Goebbels toured Dortmund and Essen that spring and promised 'retaliation' for the air raids to packed halls of armaments workers, he was cheered to the rafters. Rather, it was a demand for release from the torment of air attack: in optimistic moments, many people imagined repaying the British with interest; at more pessimistic ones, they simply wished the deadly payloads would fall somewhere else. At the beginning of March, the news that Berlin had endured its heaviest raid of the war had been greeted in Cologne 'with relief and even joy', according to the Swiss consul.[13]

As chairman of the Interministerial Committee for Air Raid Damage, Goebbels was now playing a key role in organising civil defence, even though Hitler had refused to make him 'Plenipotentiary for Total War'. Responsible for bringing mobile workshops and kitchens, household goods and furniture, clothing and food supplies to the bombed cities, the committee cut red tape and requisitioned supplies from Wehrmacht stores for the 'emergency relief'. On 5 June 1943, at the height of this new campaign, Goebbels made another Sportpalast speech, promising massive retaliation against the British people. It was they who 'would have to pay for the bill marked up by [Britain's] leaders who have betrayed their own blood at the behest of those Jewish rabble-rousers and agitators'. The press began to talk about extraordinarily powerful new weapons and Goebbels's promise would remain central to orchestrating German hopes for the rest of the war: 'the hour of retaliation will come!'[14]

Four weeks after the devastating raid on Barmen, the Elberfeld end of Wuppertal was hit too. Armament workers in Zella-Mehlis near Weimar began to sing a new song, adding their own voices to the clamour for revenge:

Retaliation:
The day is coming, when the crime of Wuppertal will be avenged
And it will break over your land in a hail of iron.
Your murderers bore no sorrow in this town and its burning
Killing the child on the mother's breast
That goads us on now with wildest fervour, to hate
For you bear with all Jewish races the Wupper's mark of shame.
The dead call out for vengeance! And we stand firm by our word
And build weapons that will finally answer for this murder.[15]

In vain, Catholic bishops urged restraint. On 10 June, Archbishop Frings of Cologne issued a pastoral letter, stressing 'that the extraordinary hardships of war are a consequence of human sins, a punishment for their far-reaching falling away from God and His commandments'. As usual, Bishop Galen was more explicit, preaching a sermon at the pilgrimage site at Telgte on 4 July in which he directly challenged the ethics of 'retaliation': 'For once I must speak out in public: I can and will not make my own the calls for hatred and retaliation which have appeared repeatedly in the German press, nor may you make them your own!' Calls for revenge were 'un-Christian

and, above all, un-German, because they are unworthy, ignoble, unchiv-
alrous!' Revenge was a Jewish principle, 'the old Jewish law of "An
eye for an eye, a tooth for a tooth", expressly rejected by Christ'.
Despite tarring Nazi 'Vergeltung' – retaliation – as a 'Jewish' response,
Galen struggled as much as the other bishops to get this old-fashioned
and 'chivalrous' version of the Christian message across to his flock.
He blamed the bombing and the war on the arrogance of a secular
modernity which had turned its back on divine truths. His answer to
the question 'How can God permit this?' was to pose another question: 'In which country is God's supremacy still publicly recognised
and is He still accorded the honour He deserves?' Nationalists to a
man, the Catholic bishops had used the same kinds of arguments in
the previous war to urge contrition and repentance, hoping that the
death of so many young men on the battlefield would lead to the
resurrection of Christian society in Germany.[16]

The bishops were a generation older than the political elite of Nazi
Germany. They were men in late middle age who had been scarred
by the struggle against liberal secularisation, and their version of
ultra-conservative Catholic nationalism was out of step with the
current generation and, increasingly, with the present war. The cracks
that had begun to appear in the ranks of the lower clergy in 1942 now
widened, threatening to split the younger, more activist wing of the
Church from the ageing prelates set above them. The parish of
Fronleichnam in Aachen was ministered to by two chaplains at logger-
heads with each other. Chaplain Sparbrodt toed the episcopal line,
asking his confirmation classes, 'And what is the use of sermons of
hate?' after the thousand-bomber raid on Cologne. Gestapo informers
reported that Sparbrodt was abusing the confessional to sow doubt
in soldiers' minds by asking them testing questions such as 'Is it
permitted to perform military service for a Godless state?' By contrast,
Chaplain Hilmer preached revenge on the 'criminals from across the
Channel' for the raid on Cologne. Greeting his parishioners in the
same church with the Hitler salute, Hilmer told them that 'the psalms
calling down curses need to be brought out again and fire has to
be called down from the heavens on the island whose inhabitants are
capable of such cruelties'. Hilmer admonished his flock to be 'hard
as a diamond, faithful as a mother, not to believe foreign rumours, to
be silent in the shops, not to spread unrest and to believe in the day

when all would be avenged'. By June 1943, the chaplain was openly criticising 'the silence in Catholic circles about the destruction of the churches', going so far as to insist that the 'impression had to be avoided that this barbarism [the bombing] did not matter to German Catholics, especially to leading clergy'. For once, the Gestapo watchers could only applaud, as they reported on the 'extraordinary response' of Hilmer's congregation to his preaching.[17]

In other parishes, divisions were less overt than in Fronleichnam, but the Gestapo picked them up all the same. Some clergy wanted to see the Church's rights defended more robustly and others demanded stronger endorsements of the German war effort. In some churches, the parish priests did not even read out their bishops' pastoral letters at all. In an effort to avoid internal splits, in April 1943 Archbishop Frings encouraged Catholics to remain active members of the Nazi Party and its organisations as a way of securing the Church's place in society. After the confrontations between Party and Church in mid-1941, this move to embrace compromise was widely welcomed by both laity and clergy.[18]

There were clergymen like Dr Nattermann, the influential General Secretary of the International Kolping Society, who represented a proud nineteenth-century tradition of social action and charitable work and who now pushed for a more positive commitment to the 'national community' as part of a kind of 'reform' Catholicism. These clerics stood for a *völkisch* rejuvenation of the Church and their proposals were endorsed by a conference of lower clergy in Berensberg in June 1942. But while Protestant identities were often established at the parish level, with congregations following the lead of their pastors, over whom bishops exercised relatively weak control, it was fairly easy for the Catholic hierarchy to prevent the younger generation pushing their reform agenda any further.[19]

The price of maintaining episcopal control was a gradual erosion of influence, as the once formidably cohesive Catholic milieu fractured under the pressure of war. There was dissent from both younger clergy and laity, who could not understand why the Cologne and Paderborn archbishoprics were sending out pastoral letters in February 1943 about the immorality of extramarital sex, topics that now seemed trivial compared to the bombing. The ageing prelates, schooled in Aristotelian semantics, seemed to be speaking a language which was too abstract, whose message of forbearance was too passive and was underpinned by a vision of Christian Germany which was too aristocratic and conservative. In Aachen, Catholics complained about the clergy's comfortable accommodation, income and exemption from war work. The following month's pastoral letter fared no better: 'If they were as tired as we are, then they'd have no time to preach about morality' was one response, and, 'So you see how out of touch the bishops are that they still have time for such rubbish'. The bishops' rejection of retaliation against Britain eroded their influence further. Local Gestapo agents reported that 'the people hate the enemy and his terror methods, while the clergy defend him'. Those who had been bombed out in Essen were particularly bitter. The repudiation of the Church's position only deepened over the coming months, growing into a national phenomenon.[20]

No one knew how or when retaliation would come. The absence of real information about the secret weapon was quickly made good by rumour and speculation, with talk of massive rockets and a great gun with a 16-metre barrel being set up on the Channel coast which would half destroy London. Even after the anniversary of the thousand-bomber raid had passed, the level of tension in Cologne kept rising. On 22 June, the Swiss consul reported that the promise of 'the top-secret weapon' was played like a 'trump card' there, as the hope placed in 'retaliation' helped to subdue the terror of sitting on a 'powder keg'. The following night, Mülheim was so severely hit that even cyclists could not get in or out of the town. And then on the night of 28–29 June, a month after it had been expected, the raid on Cologne came.[21]

Thousands staggered to the first aid stations located in the city's schools, escaping from collapsing buildings and wandering through billowing smoke, falling sparks and cinders as fires burned out of control. In Immendorf, the school's chronicler was lost for words: you would need to have seen 'the refugees, their eyes soaked, even blinded by the clouds of phosphorus to have any sense of the horrors of the night'. Unlike the thousand-bomber raid the previous year, this attack was followed by two more. Over the three nights of 28–29 June and 3–4 and 8–9 July, a greater tonnage of bombs fell on Cologne than in the whole of the war till then. The first raid hit the city centre, the second the eastern bank of the Rhine and the third the north-western and south-western suburbs. In 1942, it had been the unbelievable number of planes which had overawed the people of Cologne. Now it was the number of dead.[22]

The day after the first raid, the well-connected Swiss consul guessed that at least 25,000 had been killed. A few days later, thanks to a 'highly official' source, he corrected it to 28,000. Eventually the official count would be revised down to 4,500 killed and 10,000 wounded in the first raid, with a further 1,100 killed in the two that followed. It was not surprising that even well-briefed estimates set the losses at five times this level: they accorded with the scale of physical destruction. Nearly two-thirds of the population of the city, between 350,000 and 400,000 people, lost their homes. Anneliese Hastenplug, who had just cele- brated her twentieth birthday before the first raid, wrote to her fiancé Adi in France, 'How does it look here? I can only say, 31 May last year was child's play compared to this.' There was not a single house left intact in the inner city. The theatres and cinemas were gone. Her sister Adele returned home 'completely done in' after seeing so many dead bodies in the streets: 'Now fear prevents her from taking a single step in the evening on her own,' Anneliese wrote.[23]

As refugees streamed out of the city, they took what they could on carts, bicycles and handcarts, loading themselves down with furniture, suitcases, bedding and cooking pots. To Anna Schmitz, who lived in Dünnwald between Cologne and Leverkusen, it looked like 'a mass migration'. The floodgates had opened after the second raid, with refugees camping in the woodland. As Anneliese Hastenplug discov- ered, the authorities had veered between encouraging all efforts at evacuation and ordering the police to stop those working in Cologne from leaving the city.[24]

Local Party leaders were authorised to take all measures they deemed necessary and the Hitler Youth, the League of German Girls and the People's Welfare set up food kitchens and provided temporary shelter. They tried to manage the chaos, helping the bombed-out rescue their belongings and assisting the emergency services. Prisoners from the concentration camp which the SS had established in 1942 next to the grounds of the trade fair were sent in to clear the most dangerous sites, salvage food supplies from bombed warehouses and excavate unexploded bombs. Pulling down unstable buildings without safety equipment, they salvaged tiles, metal fittings and timbers to be reused. Four days after the third raid nearly a thousand camp inmates were at work, with more prisoners arriving from Buchenwald. Dressed in their striped clothes and working under armed police and SS supervision, for the next three months they became a familiar sight in the ruins, digging out the corpses of the 4,500 dead from the rubble and laying them out in coffins knocked together in the concentration camp joinery workshop.[25]

On 8 July, ceremonies to lay the dead to rest were held simultaneously across six cemeteries, with representatives of the civic authorities, emergency services, the Wehrmacht and the Party in attendance beside the mass graves that concentration camp prisoners had dug. The *Westdeutscher Beobachter* set the tone: 'Strong hearts! The struggle demands of us' and 'From their sacrifice the bright future will come'. Such use of the language of military sacrifice for civilians broke a taboo. As recently as 1942, Bormann's office had reminded Party branches not to 'misapply the term "*Opfer*"! It is undesirable that the recognition as *Opfer* should be accorded for the efforts required by the war of the homeland . . . Only the front-line soldier bears the sacrifice in the true sense of the word.' With its double meaning of involuntary victim and active (self-)sacrifice, *Opfer* lay at the centre of the nationalist, as well as National Socialist, cult of Germany's military dead. By spring 1943 it was no longer possible to restrict the cult of 'the fallen' to them. Now military medals were awarded to civilians for their efforts in air raids and armaments production, and their dead were buried with quasi-military honours.[26]

Whatever temporary impression the mass committal of the dead made was wiped out the following night. The third raid, though by far the smallest, was also the most demoralising. As the SD discovered, the population was just beginning to put the 'horrors of the first two raids behind them, to complete the initial clearance work and get supplies moving again' when this raid 'completely disrupted the normalisation of life'. Alfons Schaller, one of the city's district Party leaders, called for his fellow citizens to join him on the Heumarkt on 10 July to demonstrate 'in the midst of the ruins of our violated city the bond between the living and the dead'. The tolling of the remaining church bells and salvoes fired by the flak guns announced the start of a minute's silence, observed across the whole city. Those who gathered on the Heumarkt found themselves listening to a speech by Gauleiter

Grohé. 'Power of resistance', 'fanatical will to fight', 'out of the brains of the most worthless of all creatures . . . the Jews', 'the end of Jewry' – the tried and tired phrases floated across the square, their staccato bravura losing itself in the mountains of rubble.[27]

Inevitably, Nazi leaders were criticised for all the failures of civil defence and propagandists for not telling the rest of Germany about the plight of the local population. Given his well-known anti-clericalism, Goebbels in particular was accused of hypocrisy for focusing so much on the damage to Cologne's cathedral. But the message of defiance itself was not altogether unpopular and was occasionally echoed in private letters and diaries. Bernd Dünnwald wrote to the front to try to describe the destruction to his son Günter. From their home he could look across the burnt-out ruins as far as the town hall. He was struck by the sculpture of the sturdy medieval peasant-burgher, armed with sword, shield, keys to the city and threshing flail, still intact and clearly visible through the ruined walls of the town hall. The potent symbolism of this 'Kölsche Boor' moved him deeply and two weeks later he wrote to his son again, quoting the words of the nationalist song: 'We are keeping watch on the Rhine'. No Nazi, but a Catholic conservative and First World War veteran, Dünnwald was moved by civic patriotism, writing of the 'artworks and countless treasures' which the 'filthy Tommy' had 'violated and destroyed' in his 'cowardly madness of destruction'. Despite much damage, the twin towers of the cathedral still stood, drawing the refugees back to their 'shadow through homesickness', whilst 'pointing in warning for all eternity' at the crime that had been perpetrated. Shaken by the detonations rocking the city as unstable buildings were brought down by the clean-up squads, Dünnwald refused to be downhearted, vowing to stand and fight: 'The day is coming!'[28]

As psychological shock waves followed the physical ones, few people were ready for such intransigent rhetoric. The Swiss consul, Franz-Rudolf von Weiss, observed the homeless sitting listlessly on their suitcases near the soup kitchens. He described the general mood as one of 'deep apathy, general indifference and the wish for peace'. He had been bombed out too and moved to the small town of Bad Godesberg. The young and newly divorced Christa Lehmacher described to her brother at the front how she and their mother had lost everything and how she had obtained a dress from the War

Reparations Office, which also paid the bills for her emergency accommodation in the Hotel Excelsior next to the cathedral. She could not help jumping at the slightest noise or when minor debris fell on her head. After the first raid, she had put all her energy into repairing the flat. Now she just wanted to look for the few belongings she had left in the cellar but was frightened that the remaining walls would collapse. Instead, she focused on getting her mother and 3-year-old daughter evacuated to the safety of Füssen in Bavaria.[29]

Christa herself stayed on, telling her brother, unperturbed at what the postal censor might read, 'It's best not to say "Heil Hitler!" here any more, or else you can expect in some situations to get a clip around the ear.' Christa's prosaic but tenacious 'holding out' bore little resemblance to the patriotic transfiguration Goebbels still hoped to inspire. She kept on updating her will and sent copies to her family, worried whether her daughter would be provided for if she died, and she went on working, rising to become business manager of her firm. In Christa Lehmacher's war, optimism would be confined to the occasional luxury of relaxing in a long, hot bath with her sister, their books, coffee cups and liqueur glasses precariously balanced on a plank across the tub.[30]

In the cities of the Rhine and Ruhr, people still talked about Goebbels's promise of massive retaliation, but without the same hope and expectation as in May and June. In Cologne at least, they no longer believed it would save them. The Gauleiter of North Westphalia, Alfred Meyer, might continue to invoke retaliation at public funeral services at the side of the mass graves, but in late June and early July, in towns like Dortmund, Bochum and Hagen, the level of anxiety about whether the promise of retaliation would be fulfilled in time reached such a pitch that the SD referred to it ominously 'as a war of nerves of German propaganda against its own population'. The ever-sensitive Goebbels called on propagandists to exercise greater rhetorical restraint.[31]

As the Nazi authorities and the churches struggled to give the bombing meaning, some terms became axiomatic and others contested. Everyone could identify with Goebbels's description of the RAF's campaign as 'terror bombing': it both reflected the Allies' declared objectives – to break the Germans' will to resist – and fitted the sense of extreme helplessness experienced by so many people, praying and trembling in the dank cellars while their blocks of flats swayed, crumbled or burned above them. But just as the Catholic bishops found it difficult to discourage an obsession with revenge, so the Party struggled in vain to transform fear and helplessness into collective defiance. Funerary rites and military medals were not enough. At the same time Nazis could not – nor did they want to – turn civilians into combatants or shake the profound conviction that waging war on civilians in this way ruptured a fundamental moral boundary. All the discussions of 1940 about who had bombed civilians first now lay in the past. What mattered urgently was whether or not Germany had the power to respond. By early July, humorists were quipping that Zarah Leander had been requested to Hitler's writing headquarters in order to sing her film hit 'I Know There'll Be a Miracle One Day'.[32]

For a regime that worshipped the right of might, 'terror bombing' raised the spectre of German weakness and demoralisation. Goebbels was anxious not to broadcast anything like the real toll on civilian life, and so the media stuck to reporting on the destruction of cultural monuments, painstakingly listing the number of churches desecrated and destroyed, and, in the case of Cologne, describing in detail the damage sustained by the cathedral. It fitted well with the Nazi message that Germany was defending European culture and heritage against Allied barbarism. In the bombed cities, some regarded such attention to cultural monuments as 'trivialising the severe damage to housing and above all the human cost'. Instead of telling them about the cathedral, the SD noted, people wanted the rest of the country to know about day-to-day conditions, 'about the necessity of walking to work over piles of debris and through clouds of dust, with no public transport running; about the impossibility of washing or cooking, because water, gas and electricity had failed, of the value that a single salvaged spoon or plate represented.' As people fled the devastation, they frequently directed their fear and rage against the Nazis. Squashed into an overcrowded train which took nearly two days to travel from Cologne to Frankfurt, an observant master craftsman from Hamm noticed a crude drawing in chalk inside the compartment: 'A gallows, on which a swastika hangs. Everyone sees it, but no one rubs it out.'[33]

Outside the bombed regions, the fundamental leap in scale of the Allied bombing was not obvious from the reports in the media: having grossly exaggerated the pinprick raids of 1940 and 1941 in order to bolster the moral case for bombing Britain, now the media was minimising their scale. Evacuees from the Rhineland and Ruhr were met with a mixture of sympathy and incredulity as they tried to tell other Germans about their ordeal. Some began to ask themselves whether the bombing had revealed a flaw in regional character. As one non-commissioned officer wrote home to Bremen, 'I was in the Rhine-Westphalian industrial area, and there the mood of the population has sunk very low and is very anxious. In North Germany, in Bremen, I could not observe anything like that. I believe the North Germans can also put up with more than any other Germans.' The flip side of appeals to 'strong hearts' and 'nerves' was to foment doubt and the divide between Germans who could and those who could not 'take it'.[34]

People who had experienced the unprecedented scale of the aerial onslaught developed a kind of pride in what they had endured and objected to the dilution of the term 'terror bombing' by applying it to anything more minor. In May 1943, when the media automatically dubbed the breach of the Eder and Möhne dams 'terror attacks', Goebbels was surprised by the storm of criticism and incomprehension which greeted this coverage. 'The population is of the opinion', the Gauleiters reported back to Berlin in late May, 'that of course dams, locks and installations count as important military targets.' Despite the rumours that as many as 30,000 people were killed by the floodwaters, even in the Ruhr region people roundly rejected the term 'Jewish terror' for the 'dambuster' raid. To quell the rumours, a 'final count' of 1,579 dead was published, 1,026 of whom were foreign workers. But, as the Gauleiters noted, the point was that people saw that 'the destruction of the dams is an extraordinary success of the English and the falsification of a legitimate attack on an important military target into a pure terror attack is not understood.'[35]

In their criticism of the media coverage, people were also showing that Goebbels's propaganda meant something real to them. To most people, it was reportedly 'incomprehensible to single out the role of a Jew' in the attack on the dams, as the German media had done. 'Jewish terror' meant nothing less than mass attacks on cities – the burning, gassing and dismembering of German women and children. 'Jewish terror' conjured up violence without moral limit. It could be

associated with Wuppertal, Dortmund and Cologne, not with a spectacular precision raid on the dams: however destructive, that had a
clear and limited military-strategic purpose, which simply did not fit
popular connotations of 'Jewish terror'.[36]

Talk of the 'Jewish' character of the 'terror attacks' broke the tacit
spiral of silence which had shrouded the Europe-wide deportation
and murder of the Jews throughout 1942. In the middle of his 'total
war' speech in February 1943, Goebbels made a verbal slip, telling his
audience that 'The aim of Bolshevism is the world revolution of the
Jews . . . Germany in any case has no intention of bowing to this
threat, but means to counter it in time and if necessary with the most
complete and radical extermi-[correcting himself] – elimination of
Jewry.' The slip was swiftly smoothed out in the printed versions of
the speech, but millions of Germans listening to it on the live radio
relay had heard the half-admission of the murder of the Jews. They
heard too how the audience in the Sportpalast applauded, shouted,
'Out with Jews,' and laughed as Goebbels corrected himself. The slip
was, perhaps, only half unintentional. It marked the beginning of a
new emphasis on the centrality of the anti-Bolshevik and anti-Jewish
nature of the war which made it a life-and-death struggle for Germany
– and for European culture.[37]

*

At the end of February 1943, a unit of the Secret Military Police came
across a mass grave in the woods of Katyn, a small town to the west
of Smolensk. The ground was frozen solid and no further investigation could be done till it thawed. Army Group Centre immediately
turned to its principal expert in forensic medicine, Professor Gerhard
Buhtz of Breslau University. Buhtz, who had further developed his
expertise by carrying out autopsies on concentration camp prisoners
at Buchenwald, began to examine the exhumed remains on 29 March.
The corpses were those of Polish officers, who had been deported
and shot by the Soviets after their invasion of eastern Poland in 1939.

A few days later Goebbels learned of the find from a visiting propagandist from Army Group Centre and immediately phoned Hitler to
obtain permission to exploit the news story to the maximum. Aiming
to split the Allies, Goebbels immediately authorised a delegation of

foreign correspondents from Berlin and a Polish delegation from Warsaw and Cracow to visit Katyn, so that they could see for themselves that this was not a German fabrication. Then, on 13 April, German radio made its announcement: the corpses of 10,000 Polish officers had been found in a mass grave measuring 28 metres by 16 metres. Still in their uniforms, they had been 'murdered' by the Soviet secret police, all of them 'with wounds to the back of the head resulting from pistol shots. The identification of the corpses poses no difficulties because the soil conditions have mummified them and the Russians left their identification documents on them.' Other Polish and international delegations would follow, most importantly an international medical commission which, under Buhtz's guidance, produced a credible forensic report.[38]

Goebbels predicted that the material was sensational enough that 'We shall be able to live on it for a couple of weeks'. There had been reports of this kind in 1941, such as those of the NVKD massacres in the three prisons in Lwów, which caught the imagination of Germans for a time. But they had been rapidly superseded by the news of the Wehrmacht's victorious advance. In the spring of 1943 there was no such distraction, but there were other considerations. At first, Goebbels planned to downplay the story at home, lest it heighten anxiety amongst the families of German prisoners of war in the Soviet Union. He changed his mind when he saw the photographs of the exhumed corpses, deciding that the German public had to be told – and shown the pictures. The story ran for seven weeks, into early June, culminating with an eight-minute film, *The Katyn Forest*. To a moving, funereal soundtrack, it showed the excavation of the trenches and the identification of the corpses. Forensic experts demonstrated the entry and exit holes of the NKVD's trademark 'shot in the back of the neck'. Most importantly, the human dignity of the victims was asserted. Photos were dug out of uniform pockets and held up to the camera to reveal the officers' waving wives and smiling children. Not only the foreign press but also former Polish soldiers, in uniform and, incongruously, wearing their steel helmets, were shown visiting the site where their comrades had been 'liquidated by Stalin's hangmen'. As the cellos playing the funeral elegy swelled, the film ended with a Polish Catholic bishop pronouncing a blessing over the open trenches.[39]

For Germans, the central message was simple and stark from the outset. 'Mass Murder of Katyn: Work of Jewish Butchers', read the *Völkischer Beobachter*'s headline. The fact that 700–900 of the Polish officers were Jews was of course suppressed. As the campaign continued, the formula of Germans' 'defence' against Jewish plans to destroy them became ever more explicit. At the end of a long article for *Das Reich* on 'The War and the Jews' in early May, Goebbels reminded his readers of the Führer's 'prophetic word' that

> if World Jewry succeeded in provoking a Second World War, it would lead not to the destruction of Aryan humanity but to the extinction of the Jewish race. This process is of a world-historic significance and, given that it will probably entail unavoidable consequences, it also takes time. But it can no longer be halted.

This was, Goebbels told his readers, not a matter of '*Ressentiment*' or 'naïve plans of revenge', but of a 'world problem of the first rank' in which 'sentimental considerations are irrelevant'. When the Jews, Goebbels concluded, 'laid their plan against the German people for their complete destruction, they signed their own death warrant. And here too world history will be a world court.'[40]

Katyn provided the centrepiece to a fresh anti-Semitic propaganda campaign which harnessed older themes, such as the Jews' guilt for instigating the war, and newer ones, such as the fate awaiting Germany should the Jews ever take revenge. Increasingly, journalists assumed a more explicit knowledge amongst their readership about what had happened to the Jews than in 1942. The Badenese Gau paper, *Der Führer*, carried a commentary by the well-known journalist and sometime academic Johann von Leers in which he broached a point of popular criticism: 'Yes, but the methods? Anyone talking about methods is always wrong. What matters is the result. For a doctor the result has to be the complete elimination of cholera, the result for our people the complete elimination of the Jews . . . Between us and the Jews the issue is who will survive whom.' Victor Klemperer was so struck by Leers's insistence that 'If the Jews are victorious, our whole nation will be slaughtered like the Polish officers in the forest of Katyn' that he excerpted a whole chunk of his rhetoric, making a note for his intended study of the 'Language of the Third Reich': 'Every sentence, every expression of this lecture is important. The feigned objectivity, the obsessiveness, the populism, the reduction of everything to one denominator'. Leers was no exception. The respectable Berlin daily the *Deutsche Allgemeine Zeitung* carried an editorial on 29 May reminding its readers that 'we have carried out our anti-Semitic campaign systematically'. Four days later, it printed an article by a reporter serving with an SS unit in the east, who explained that now was 'not yet the time to open the reports which cover the operations of the Security Police and the SD. Much will certainly remain unsaid, since it is not always advisable to reveal one's strategy.' In May and June 1943, whether discussing the need to tackle the 'gypsy question' in south-eastern Europe in the same way as the 'Jewish problem had been solved' or commenting on the incompleteness of the Slovaks' measures against their Jewish population, the German media was awash with allusions to the 'final solution'. The uncomfortable silences of 1942 had been replaced with a semi-open affirmation of collective complicity.[41]

Hitler's enthusiasm for this campaign was enormous. Treating his Propaganda Minister to a long disquisition on *The Protocols of the Elders of Zion* – about whose authenticity Goebbels had previously harboured some reservations – the Führer ventured on to an extended analogy between Jews and potato beetles. This latest in a long line of parasitical metaphors soon travelled from the privacy of the Führer's luncheon table across the European airwaves when Goebbels spoke in the Sportpalast on 5 June promising retaliation against Britain for the bombing: 'Just as the potato beetle destroys potato fields, indeed has to destroy them, so the Jew destroys states and nations. Against this there is only one remedy: radical removal of the threat.' Again, he left no doubt about what this meant: 'The complete elimination of Jewry from Europe is not a moral question but one of the security of states.'[42]

To the delight of the Nazi leaders, Katyn created strains in the Allied coalition, with General Sikorski's Polish government-in-exile in London endorsing German calls for the International Red Cross to investigate the massacre and challenging the denial which the Soviet Information Bureau had issued. Stalin responded by breaking off diplomatic relations with the London Poles. But it did not break up the Allied coalition. Whatever their private misgivings, Churchill and Roosevelt blocked the involvement of the International Red Cross in the investigation of the massacre, at the same time as they resisted Soviet pressure to withdraw recognition from the Polish government-in-exile. But for the Western Allies, Katyn remained an enduring embarrassment, because it challenged their own claim to be fighting for all mankind. By mounting a case for the human rights of the Poles, Goebbels scored a propaganda coup on the international stage.[43]

German audiences found it all rather confusing. Suddenly the 'Polish trash' who had massacred ethnic Germans at the outbreak of the war deserved their sympathy. This new-found solidarity only made sense, according to the SD, to those 'in intellectual and religious circles' who felt guilty on account of the 'far greater numbers of Poles and Jews eliminated by the German side'. It was easier to hold to the view formed in the autumn of 1939 that the Poles deserved what they got because they had 'murdered 60,000 national comrades'. As the SD also noted:

> A large section of the population sees in the [Soviets'] elimination of the Polish officers . . . the radical extinction of a dangerous opponent, unavoidable in war. One could set it on the same plane as the bombing attacks of the English and Americans on the German cities and, finally, also our own battle of annihilation against the Jews.[44]

★

Just before 1 a.m. on 25 July, Klaus Seidel's flak battery in the Hamburg city park went into action. Flying from north to south over the city, 740 RAF bombers dropped 1,346 tonnes of high explosive and 938 tonnes of incendiaries, while the 54 heavy and 26 light flak batteries – supported by 24 searchlight batteries – shot over 50,000 rounds into the night sky. During the 58-minute raid, they brought down only two planes. That night the RAF had used 'Window' for the first time, dropping a cascade of short aluminium strips cut to a length which jammed the radar guidance for the searchlights and guns. At 3 a.m., 16-year-old Klaus Seidel was called to fight the fires at the Stadthalle. Dressed hastily in his 'pyjamas, tracksuit, steel helmet and boots', the young air force auxiliaries attempted to salvage goods and fight the fire with hoses. Luckily another boy had sprayed Klaus for a lark and this protected him from the sparks from falling timbers. After an hour and a half, they returned to the battery, where Klaus ran messages until 6 a.m. He snatched three hours' sleep and returned to duty, preparing the guns in the Stadtpark again.[45]

The next attack came much earlier, at 4.30 p.m., when ninety American 'flying fortresses' appeared over Hamburg. Another fifty-four followed at midday on 26 July. That day Ingeborg Hey's parents wrote to Wehlen on the Elbe, where the young teacher had been evacuated with her pupils, telling her that they were safe and sound. They wrote again the next day describing how the sirens kept sounding in a confused succession of signals – pre-warning, alarm over, alarm, alarm over. Despite the stream of people leaving the city, they decided to follow the authorities' advice and stay. Exhausted by the last three days and nights, they asked Inge and her friends to keep their fingers crossed for them. After two nights in which the RAF had only sent out six fast-flying Mosquitoes, just after midnight on 27–28 July, 722 bombers came. Flying from east to west, they targeted neighbourhoods which had gone virtually unscathed till now. In Rothenburgsort, Hammerbrook, Borgfelde, Hohenfelde and Hamm, freak weather conditions and the intense heat of the fires transformed the conflagration into a firestorm of unprecedented proportions. Objects and people simply vanished. Trees up to a metre thick were flattened. Those who stayed in their cellars and air raid shelters risked being asphyxiated by carbon monoxide gases or baked inside them. Those fleeing often did so below ground, breaking through walls and doors into other cellars as the buildings above them caught fire. Those who fled on to the streets risked being hit by debris from collapsing house fronts or trapped in the melting road surface. Many jumped into the canals to extinguish falling sparks which caught in their hair and clothes. Among the 18,474 people killed that night were Ingeborg Hey's parents.[46]

The next day, Klaus Seidel wrote to his mother advising her against returning from her summer holidays in Darmstadt. Although he could report that the flak had proved to be more effective this time, he had to tell her that Hamburg had suffered large-scale destruction. That day the Gauleiter of Hamburg, Karl Kaufmann, reversed his earlier orders to remain and issued instructions to enlist every available means to evacuate the city. As the Stadtpark filled up with those who had been bombed out and were waiting to be evacuated, Klaus Seidel watched as lorries simply dumped large heaps of bread on the ground for them. It had become policy to issue extra food and materials in areas affected by air raids – without counting them against ration entitlements – in order to shore up morale. Yet Seidel was shocked by the way the refugees, so accustomed to wartime shortages, wasted the extra food: he found tins of half-eaten meat slung into the bushes and heaps of plums left to rot on the ground.[47]

On the night of 29–30 July, the RAF returned in force again. That night Klaus wrote to his mother without candlelight, by the glow of the 'fire-cloud'. On 31 July he finally had enough time off duty to check that his mother's flat was intact and carry their valuables down to the cellar. Klaus professed not to understand why their neighbours still wanted to leave, arguing with cool logic that they were protected by a firebreak now that the surrounding buildings had been destroyed.[48]

By the time the final wave of British bombers dropped their payloads at 2.55 a.m. on 3 August 1943, the Reich's second-largest city lay in ruins. Half of its buildings had been destroyed during the previous week and 900,000 people had fled. On 1 August, Gauleiter Kaufmann had spoken of 'people in their panic running in a kind of psychosis like animals into the flames'. He struck Goebbels as 'a broken figure'. As the authorities panicked, the Chief Prosecutor even released 2,000 convicts and remand prisoners, including fifty members of an underground Communist group. Stories abounded of Party 'big shots' misusing the refugee transports to ship out their furniture and belongings. When enraged civilians harangued Party officials, even ripping off their insignia, the police did nothing, preferring, as Hamburg's chief of police and SS told Himmler, to take a 'deliberately cautious' approach.[49]

A trio of Gauleiter Kaufmann, his deputy, State Secretary Georg Ahrens, and Mayor Krogmann quickly recovered their nerve and improvised the evacuation and clean-up operation with their own style of pragmatism. Using whatever personnel they could find, including soldiers, forced labourers and concentration camp inmates, the Hamburg authorities moved to extinguish the fires, clear the rubble from the streets and reconnect the main utilities. Fire brigades were sent from Kiel, Lübeck and Bremen, with volunteer firefighters arriving from the rural hinterland. It had been clear for over six months that the 'self-protection' system developed by the Reich Air Defence Association, with buckets of sand on every landing and human chains for passing buckets of water from street pumps, could not cope with severe air raids. But its mass organisation, counting 22 million volunteers nationwide, offered a crucial reservoir of labour, alongside the Hitler Youth, the SA, the National Socialist People's Welfare, and the Party's women's organisations. They set up first aid points, found shelter for the bombed-out, fed orphaned children and evacuated refugees. On 10 August, sections of Hamburg's tram line began running again. On 15 August, the water mains were back; by the beginning of September, gas was being delivered to industry and most sections of the city; and by mid-September all habitable houses were receiving electricity.[50]

Special brigades of concentration camp prisoners, for the most part forced foreign workers who had fallen foul of their German employers, did the dirtiest jobs. Seventeen-year-old Pavel Vasilievich Pavlenko was sent from the nearby camp at Neuengamme to defuse bombs in Wilhelmshafen. His squad would dig a circle around the unexploded device before one of them was chosen by lot to unscrew the detonating fuse. Pavlenko was also one of the prisoners sent into the firestorm area, a 4-kilometre-square 'dead zone' comprising Rothenburgsort, Hammerbrook and Hamm-Süd. Here the streets were littered with dead bodies, often clustered in groups of twenty-five to thirty where a fireball had caught them. Some, overwhelmed by heat, were hardly scarred; others were charred beyond recognition. By 10 September, 26,409 corpses had been recovered, mainly from the streets and squares. But the most difficult and dangerous work was opening up the cellars in which people had sought refuge, and where most had died of carbon-monoxide asphyxiation as the oxygen was consumed in the fires. Pavlenko recalled how 'we collected the bones in a bucket and carried them outside'. Elsewhere, workers found 'doll-like' corpses, reduced to less than half their normal size and yet still quite recognisable, a phenomenon attributed to the proportionate dehydration of all the internal organs as the cellars turned into ovens.[51]

To Georg Henning Graf von Bassewitz-Behr, the city's police president, it was like a modern-day Pompeii and Herculaneum. The Protestant Bishop of Hamburg, Franz Tügel, turned to biblical imagery, writing in his pastoral letter that 'Some have been reminded of images from the Old Testament when the summer sun is literally darkened by the clouds of fire and brimstone.' Addressing his shattered parish of Hamm, Pastor Paul Kreye considered the story of Sodom and Gomorrah:

'I am reminded of the story of Lot's wife,' one of you wrote to me. 'The Lord let fire and brimstone rain down from the heavens and covered the cities. And he spoke to Lot: Save your soul and do not look back, so that you perish not.' And his wife did look back and became a pillar of salt. – No glancing backwards, only forwards.

Kreye and Tügel could not know that Arthur Harris, with his penchant for biblical code names, had called Bomber Command's raids on Hamburg 'Operation Gomorrah'.[52]

The authorities erected a wall around the 'dead zone' and barred all unauthorised personnel from entering it, but parts of the devastated area were visible from the single-track railway line which began running again on 15 August through the ruins of Hammerbrook and Rothenburgsort to the Hauptbahnhof. Rumours abounded of 100,000 to 350,000 dead. The real number, 34,000–38,000 people, still dwarfed the destruction caused by any air raids in the war so far. Many soldiers who returned on compassionate leave to search for family members, the Hamburg police president reported, 'found only a few bones'. As survivors searched provisional morgues full of dismembered bodies for relatives, often only the chance recognition of a wedding ring or a fob watch made it possible to identify a severed arm or torso. It took Klaus Seidel a fortnight to discover that his grandparents had survived.[53]

Evacuation was still under way when the population began to return. In mid-August, numbers climbed from 600,000 to 800,000. By the end of November, over a million residents were back in the city, creating an acute housing crisis. The densely packed working-class neighbourhoods which had burned down could not be rebuilt, and even the rushed production of prefabricated, two-room wooden cabins fell pitifully short of the one million new homes per annum promised for the whole of Germany in September; by June 1944 only 35,000 homes had been completed, with a further 23,000 under construction. Forced to rig up makeshift accommodation in half-destroyed buildings, people dubbed them 'cellar quarters'. Others took up permanent residence in Hamburg's concrete bunkers or their workplaces. More than half the city was still standing, including much of the belt of middle-class villas beyond the city centre, prompting much bitterness amongst workers at the reluctance of the better-off to give up their privileges. Wehrmacht and SS officers had to be exhorted to get their families to take in the bombed-out wives of their own comrades.[54]

With the emphasis firmly on restarting production, the Hamburg docks were able to boast their highest output figures for U-boats that year. It scarcely seemed to matter that the battle for the Atlantic was over and the submarines had been called back to their bases. Gauleiter Kaufmann handed over the reconstruction of industry to leading members of the Hamburg economic elite such as Rudolf Blohm, whose famous naval shipyard employed thousands of concentration camp prisoners from Neuengamme. Blohm requisitioned school buildings for housing, turned the Museum for Hamburg's History into a department store, and set up a community hall where dances and concerts were held and films screened. Crucially, the employers now became responsible for allocating housing and food as well as emergency clothing, household goods and furniture for their workforce. But labour discipline remained poor, with even the new economic managers appreciating that 'People don't have any possessions any more and want to buy something first.'[55]

Recycling Jewish goods played a role in the relief operation too. When the Jews were deported from France, Belgium, the Netherlands and Luxembourg in 1942–43, their furniture was seized and redistributed under 'Aktion-M' (for *Möbel*), under the auspices of the 'Western Office' of the Eastern Ministry and the SS. From Bamberg to Frankfurt am Main, the authorities reported that people were calling for the warehouses holding Jewish goods to be opened up to help the bombed-out. The fabled prosperity of the Jews convinced many that 'this furniture is sufficient to re-equip all those who have suffered loss through bombing', and they argued that leaving them in storage ran the risk that the whole lot would be bombed. By 1944, 18,665 wagons of Jewish goods had been shipped to cities particularly affected by the bombing, 2,699 of them to Hamburg. Instead of being grateful, the beneficiaries were often aggrieved at what they received. In late September 1943, reports were reaching Berlin from Münster and Frankfurt on the Oder, about how 'disappointed the population was with the used furniture reaching them from the occupied territories, especially the Jewish furniture'. Either the pieces came from large villas and would not fit into small flats, or they were infested with vermin, smashed in transit, or simply too old and shabby to be suitable for Germans: it seemed that the Jews had either been too rich or too poor.[56]

Across the Reich, disappointed covetousness turned quickly to envy and anger. From an iron foundry in Kitzingen, the SD reported that Nazi officials were accused of 'laying their arses in the Jewish beds after they have exterminated the Jews'; there were rumours that 'they carried off the valuable carpets, furniture and silver from the Jewish flats by night and fog', redeploying an older idiom which the Nazis had borrowed. In Hitler's adopted home town of Linz the local Party leader was forced to beat a hasty retreat from a condolence visit in the face of a torrent of abuse: the cause of his outrage, the bereaved father claimed, was not his son's death, but the fact that the Nazi Party had recently prevented his sister from buying 'a Jew's house'. If thwarted greed provoked rage, guilt crept up on those who had got what they craved. People frequently told themselves that if the Jews won the war, then they would want their homes back.[57]

*

On 6 August 1943, Goebbels caused panic in Berlin by ordering an immediate, partial evacuation of the capital. Instead of preaching the usual sangfroid of heroic defiance and 'strong hearts', the newspapers astonished their readers by warning that Berlin was about to suffer the same fate as Hamburg. 'Acts of hysteria, flight, panic. Concrete terms: complete hospitals and private clinics have been evacuated from Berlin along with the most ill patients, staff and doctors,' noted the publisher Hermann Kasack. All the schools were declared closed. Branches of firms and ministerial departments were relocated. As train after special train pulled out of Berlin, those, like Kasack, who chose to stay distributed furniture, wardrobes, cooking pots and bedding around their friends and relatives to spread the risk. They arranged to spend the nights in the suburbs, even if it meant sleeping in the stations at the ends of the underground lines. Striking a balance, it was, Kasack thought, a 'still organised panic'. Those areas which had already been inundated with refugees from the Ruhr, Rhineland and Hamburg now had to take in yet more evacuees arriving from cities like Berlin and Munich which had so far been spared heavy raids.

Berlin women brought the news to Frankfurt am Main that lime pits had been dug in advance to serve as mass graves. Soon there were rumours that soldiers were being sent from Frankfurt in order to deal with the expected unrest in the capital. It was what many people across the Reich thought had already happened in Hamburg. From as far afield as Innsbruck, Königsberg, Weimar and Würzburg, as well as Braunschweig and Berlin, it was reported that the Allies had issued an ultimatum that unless the government resigned by 15 August, Berlin, Leipzig, Munich and other major cities would be 'erased' just like Hamburg. The threat Hitler had made against Britain in September 1940 was well remembered by Germans now. There was some truth to these tales: by the end of the month, the Allies were dropping leaflets threatening other cities with the fate of Hamburg, mocking the regime's own heroic slogans: 'The choice is: capitulation or destruction. Tunis – or Stalingrad. Palermo – or Hamburg. Life or death.'[58]

On 22 July, Palermo had fallen to Allied troops without resistance and three days later, at the same time as the first raid on Hamburg, Mussolini had been voted out of power by the Fascist Grand Council and arrested. Predictably enough, Italian civilian workers in German cities broke into 'tears of joy' and held all-night celebrations. According to the secret police, 'even Fascists declared that, for all his political achievements, the Duce had failed militarily'. In Breslau and other cities, French prisoners of war drank and sang late into the night and refused to turn up for work the next day. In Warsaw, the Polish Resistance began chalking up the slogan 'October' to warn that the November 1918 revolution would come a month earlier to Germany this time. Germans too were caught up by the events in Italy, scanning the news for information on the momentous regime change engulfing their closest ally. Many noted a minor item reporting the banning of the Fascist Party. If this could occur overnight after twenty years of Fascist rule, then, people were speculating quite openly, 'National Socialism could be got rid of even more quickly after a ten-year rule'.[59]

Most ominously for a Security Service primed to prevent a repeat of the 1918 revolution, during the course of August 1943 it reported growing public dissent. When the Lord Mayor of Göttingen boarded a train from Hamburg, refugees spotted his golden Party badge and told him quietly that there would be a reckoning. A woman even held her sleeve up to his nose so that he could smell the stench of the smoke on her clothes. Party officials were so often abused and threatened in public, especially in cities which had recently been bombed, that in the late summer of 1943 many stopped wearing their uniforms and Party badges in public. A rash of new jokes ridiculed their fright, such as the mock classified ad: 'Swap Golden Party badge for seven-league boots'. In Marburg, Lisa de Boor was thrilled: 'Everywhere in the streets, in the shops, at the station, people are talking to one another saying that it can't go on like this.' Even among Germans in Warsaw, Wilm Hosenfeld picked up the undercurrent of hope in an Italian-style change of regime: a post-Nazi military dictatorship, like that taking shape under Marshal Badoglio in Italy, could then negotiate a separate peace with the British and Americans. According to the weekly confidential reports on 'popular sentiment' compiled by the SD, hope that a military dictatorship offered Germany 'the best', or possibly even 'the last', way of reaching a 'separate peace' with the Western Allies was gaining traction. The fact that Badoglio had already announced that the war would continue and confirmed the alliance with Germany also calmed popular anxieties about the danger of an Italian 'betrayal'. In Braunschweig, two women at the weekly vegetable market were heard complaining noisily about the complete failure of German promises to retaliate against Britain for the bombing of German cities, when a group of railway workers standing nearby joined in, calling out loudly, 'Of course there's a way, our regime has got to go. We have to have a new government.'[60]

As Germans shrugged off the lessons of ten years of Gestapo repression and began to say such unheard-of things in public, its political leaders began to waver. Albert Speer, who had taken over armaments in the shadow of the crisis before Moscow and who had remained unshaken by the defeat at Stalingrad, warned Hitler now that armament production would come to 'a total halt' if six more cities were attacked on this scale. Hans Jeschonnek, the Luftwaffe Chief of Staff, considered that 'Stalingrad was trifling' by comparison to Hamburg. In mid-August, following the RAF's precision strike against the centre for German rocket development at Peenemünde, he committed suicide. On 6 August Goebbels confessed that 'the air war is a sword of Damocles hanging over our heads' and that since the raids on Hamburg, 'a large part of the Continent is gripped by a panic-struck terror of the English air force'. For once the Nazi leadership held back: despite all the rumours of counter-insurgency measures Himmler waited apprehensively on events.[61]

But Germany was not Italy. For all their war-weariness and hopes for a compromise peace in the west, Germans did not talk about ending the war in the east. Instead, the crisis impelled them to bring their most powerful fears out into the open. The equation of Allied bombing with the murder of the Jews, which had first emerged in the spring, attained key importance now. On 15 August 1943, after returning from Hamburg to his translation work for the naval command in Berlin, the Far Eastern merchant Lothar de la Camp wrote a circular letter to his siblings, friends and acquaintances. He described what he knew of the fire-bombing of Hamburg, including an estimate of 200,000–240,000 dead, before turning to what people were saying about the raids:

> Whatever the rage against the English and Americans for their inhuman way of waging war, one has to say quite objectively that the common people, the middle classes, and the rest of the population make repeated remarks in intimate circles and also in larger gatherings that the attacks count as retaliation for our treatment of the Jews.[62]

As evacuees from northern and western Germany brought tales of horror they had endured to the unscathed south and east of the country, everywhere 'terror bombing' was ascribed to 'the Jewish retaliation'. Nazi propaganda had played its part in preparing this response by insisting that the Jewish lobby in London and Washington was behind the bombing in an attempt to exterminate the German nation. But the tenor of popular reasoning was now different: it was what the Germans had done to the Jews that had provoked them to use their power to bomb German cities. Often this sense of acute vulnerability was given a local twist. People in the small Bavarian town of Bad Brückenau, for instance, were deeply affected by the tales told by the evacuees from Frankfurt (to their west) and in 'their mood of deep pessimism and growing fatalistic apathy' they saw the bombing of Frankfurt as 'retaliation to the nth degree for the Jewish action of 1938'. Under the immediate impact of the Hamburg raids, the inhabitants of Ochsenfurt wondered whether neighbouring Würzburg would be next. While some claimed it was being spared

because 'in Würzburg no synagogues were burned', others warned
'that now the airmen would come to Würzburg too, given that the
last Jew recently left Würzburg'. For good measure, he was even
reported to have 'declared before his deportation that now Würzburg
would also receive air raids'.[63]

Such rumours reflected a particular sense of helplessness, a far
cry from the kind of hatred and resistance Goebbels had hoped his
anti-Semitic campaign would instil. In the cities this popular state
of mind manifested itself in urban myths that greatly exaggerated
the accuracy of Allied targeting. At a time when British bomber
crews were having great difficulties delivering their payloads within
the prescribed 5-kilometre radius of their targets, Berliners imagined
that they were deliberately targeting particular streets and neighbourhoods which they wished to punish. The same sense of naked vulnerability animated the rumours about what specific Jews had said
before their deportation or whether particular cities had burned or
spared their synagogues.

Time and again, people linked the bombing to the pogrom of
November 1938, a connection which might seem strange in a society
awash with rumours about the mass killing of Jews in the east. But
1938 had been the last anti-Semitic action which many people had
witnessed and actively participated in throughout Germany: in its
aftermath, most of the Jews who remained in the Reich had moved
to larger cities. In some places there was also a direct connection to
the bombing war: in Wetzlar, Braunschweig, Solingen, Frankfurt am
Main, Berlin, Siegen, Cologne, Emden and Hamburg, massive
concrete bunker towers had been erected on vacant sites where
synagogues had stood until November 1938. In Cologne and Aachen,
people connected the burnt synagogues with the churches destroyed
in the air raids, evoking a sense of divine retribution. As a clerical
informer summarised such views for the local Gestapo: 'Yes, it's
deserved . . . everything avenges itself on earth.' Thus, many people
saw 1938 as the *start* of the German war against the Jews, which set
in motion the chain of escalating mutual retaliation. By the late
summer and autumn such hitherto rare admissions of German
responsibility and guilt had spread to parts of Germany which had
not been bombed at all.[64]

In early June, Goebbels had rallied the beleaguered cities with promises of 'retaliation' against Britain. The burning of Hamburg turned those hopes upside down: it was clear that the power to 'retaliate' was in the hands of the Jews and the Allies. This catastrophic military failure inverted the popular hope placed in German retaliation a month earlier, transforming it into the fear of 'Jewish retaliation'. As they spoke about this throughout the Reich, people inadvertently disclosed something which had previously been half concealed – their own knowledge that all the abstract Nazi rhetoric about exterminating the Jews had been literally accomplished. In 1941 and 1942, when the deportations were at their height; when many people had bid at auctions in Hamburg and other cities for Jewish furniture and fittings; when many witnesses had returned with details of the mass graves and mass shootings in the east; and when, above all, any widespread German opposition to the killing might have saved Jewish lives, people had spoken about the unfolding genocide differently: piecemeal, behind closed doors, through rumours and in relation to specific killings. Now in the third quarter of 1943, all this lay in the past: 'what we did to the Jews' provided the public acknowledgement that had been withheld at the time.

The public conversations reported to the Nazi leadership in the summer of 1943 were not a direct commentary on the 'final solution'. It was no longer a contemporary event; the 'measures carried out against the Jews', as the report writers euphemistically called them, already lay in the past and could not be reversed. The real point of such talk was to express the fear that Allied bombing was both vengeful and possibly even exterminatory in intent. It was their own predicament, not that of the Jews, which remained of primary concern. As people felt impelled to express a sense of culpability and regret, their admissions of guilt were also irretrievably entwined with an overwhelming sense of their own vulnerability and victimhood.

The popular search for literal and moral equivalence was helped by the absence of hard facts about the numbers of dead either from bombing or the murder of the Jews. The SS's own statistical count of April 1943 was top secret; yet people were aware that only a tiny number of Jews still remained in Germany. The authorities, on the other hand, did not divulge the police count of the numbers killed in air raids or publish photographs of the dead for fear of destroying civilian morale. Rumour filled the vacuum, inevitably exaggerating the numbers. Informal estimates by well-connected and well-informed witnesses set the number of dead from the raids on Dortmund at 15,000; on Düsseldorf at 17,000; on the dams between 12,000 and 30,000; on Wuppertal at 27,000; on Cologne at 28,000; and on Hamburg at between 100,000 and 350,000. In each case the police's official counts were much lower, but were not released. In the information vacuum these inflated figures acquired wide currency, adding to the conviction that all prior moral boundaries had been crossed.[65]

Goebbels did not have an answer to the raft of public criticism. Depicting the bombing with various shadings as Jewish terror, revenge or retaliation was not the difficulty. That was axiomatic to all his media messages. Rather, it was the gloss put on it. The sentiment – 'if only we had not treated the Jews so badly' – expressed an impossible wish. By searching for a way back through a cycle of escalation which could not be reversed, Germans were acknowledging precisely the bind that Goebbels had wanted to place them in. 'Above all in the Jewish question, we have gone so far that for us there's no escape. And that is just as well,' Goebbels had consoled himself back in March. 'Experience tells that a movement and a people, which has broken the bridges behind itself, fights much more unreservedly than those which still possess the possibility of retreating.' But it did not seem to be working out like this. The SD reports on the public desire for a separate peace, change of regime and regret about the murder of the Jews all spoke of retreat.[66]

Since the spring, Goebbels and Hitler had been making propaganda with what they most fervently believed, allowing the media to speak ever more openly about the war against the Jews, even if Goebbels still took care to prevent specific details from being mentioned. For German society at large, the murder of the Jews did not fulfil the role Goebbels imagined when he spoke of breaking the bridges. It did not herald a new sense of purpose, galvanising Germans to wage 'total war': rather these conversations on market squares conveyed a sense of doom, a sense of impending defeat and crisis. Even loyal supporters who sent in their own suggestions to Goebbels on how propaganda could be improved started criticising the anti-Semitic campaign. Some of them also pointed out that the Germans were now being punished for what they had done to the Jews.[67]

From the Nazi point of view, talk about 'Jewish retaliation' during the crisis after Hamburg marked German failure. It was both a military failure and denoted a crisis of legitimacy, as the regime was found wanting according to its own core values. Goebbels had deliberately played with popular knowledge of the genocide, encouraging a 'knowing but not knowing' kind of collusion. Yet, the price of success-fully embedding the 'Jewish enemy' within the common sense of everyday life was to lose control over how people made use of the notion. Goebbels could neither confirm nor deny what had happened to the Jews, any more than he could answer the wish to undo their murder. All he could do was hope that this tide of depressing comment would cease.[68]

.Throughout August, the Nazi regime stepped back. The Gestapo did not swoop in to arrest people for saying the things the SD was reporting, even when they called for regime change. Then, in early September, the propaganda machine began to answer back. On 3 September 1943, the Gau paper in Baden, *Der Führer*, chided its readers: 'It is said, if National Socialist Germany had not solved the Jewish Question so radically, international World Jewry would not be fighting us today.' Only a 'senile fool' could believe such stuff, the paper jeered, pointing out that the Jews had caused both world wars, with the present one 'no more than a continuation of the first'. This was a risky tactic, which could have sanctioned a semi-open debate about the 'final solution'. Instead, Goebbels stepped in with an article in *Das Reich* on 26 September, in which he explained the virtues of 'silence' on certain key questions. 'Only a few people know the secrets of the war,' he told his million-odd readers:

> It is therefore extremely unfair and damaging to the general good to try, by spreading rumours, to force the government to make public statements about a question of importance, or indeed of decisive significance, for the outcome of the war. They would be useful to the enemy and cause the gravest harm to our own people.[69]

The new Minister of the Interior, Heinrich Himmler, went on the radio in early October, threatening that 'Defeatists must die in expiation of their actions' and 'as a warning to others'. A flurry of exemplary sentences soon followed to underline exactly what he meant. A middle-aged Munich woman was sentenced to three years in prison for derogatory remarks about Hitler and for having said: 'Do you think then that nobody listens to the foreign broadcasts? They have loaded Jewish women and children into a wagon, driven out of town, and annihilated them with gas.' An accountant from Brackwede was convicted by the Special Court in Bielefeld for alleg- edly saying that 'What happened with the Jews is being avenged now.' He had heard from soldiers at the front 'that the Jews were murdered in their thousands'. On 6 October 1943, Himmler took the unprece- dented step of addressing the wider Nazi leadership gathered in Posen, telling them how he had dealt with 'the problem of defeatism' through a small number of exemplary executions of those talking out of turn:

> We will never catch every winger and neither do we want to do so
> . . . Those who are caught have to pay the price – that is after all the
> point of any law – and by their death serve as a lesson and a warning
> to thousands of others, so that they don't unwisely do the same.

The small, selective wave of terror against individuals accused of spreading the same 'defeatist rumours' which the SD continued to report from all across Germany was meant to demonstrate where the limits of public speech lay. In the same address at Posen, Himmler made the first explicit announcement about the extermination of the Jews. This was hardly news to his audience, but it was different for the Reich leaders and Gauleiters to be told officially and bound to secrecy. Himmler told them, 'I believe it is better, we – we collectively – have done this for our people, have taken the responsibility on ourselves – the responsibility for a deed not just for an idea – and we then carry the secret with us to our graves.'[70]

The regime could demand silence from the German people, but it could not alter the fact that the shared secret of the murder of the Jews had been broached openly across Germany and that such talk did not strengthen support for the regime. But it did not provoke real action either: dissent never progressed beyond idle talk of regime change and a separate peace. Meanwhile, that autumn the Swiss consul in Cologne observed that the knowledge 'that the evacuated Jews had been murdered in their totality' was 'seeping through ever more'. The more it informed the common stock of knowledge, the more it fed the bleakest of expectations about how genocidal the war would become.

What Germans wanted above all was a solution to the war in the west, which would strengthen their position to fight the war in the east through to a conclusion. The crisis of August 1943 was unprecedented. And yet it proved to be a brief interlude. Events in Italy brought the German crisis to a close. Marshal Badoglio's moment of popularity in August 1943 grew from rekindled hope in peace. On 8 September 1943, the associations with his name changed unalterably, when news came through that he had signed an armistice with the Allies. Many Germans would have liked to do so too, but for their closest Axis ally to do so was pure 'treachery'. The Wehrmacht's response was swift, decisive and a real boost to morale at home, as twenty divisions completed the German occupation of the Italian peninsula, engaging the Allies at Salerno.[71]

The lightning military response did not resolve the moral quandary about the meaning of 'Jewish retaliation' but it did end the domestic crisis by showing that Germany was not as helpless as it had appeared a month earlier. A million Italian soldiers were equally swiftly 'interned' by their former German allies, and 710,000 of them sent to the Reich. There they found themselves at the bottom of the hierarchy of foreign workers: like Red Army prisoners, they were denied Prisoner of War status under the Geneva Conventions. Their appalling treatment was accompanied by a new German nickname for traitors: 'Badoglios'. Universally reviled as old prejudices were let loose on former allies, the Italians were punished, above all, for the failure of German hopes.[72]

12

'Holding Out'

Remembrance Sunday fell on 21 November 1943, a Lutheran memorial introduced to Prussia at the end of the Napoleonic wars. For Hamburg, nearly four months after the raids, it served as the first collective act of commemoration and the pastor of St Peter's invited all the city's churches to join him in a communion service to unite the scarred parishes with those that had been spared. Exceptionally, given its central location between the Alster and the Zollkanal, St Peter's, with its iconic fourteenth-century bronze lionhead door handles, had survived relatively intact. The service attracted just ninety-one people.[1]

Despite the religious significance of the day, the churches could not compete with the Party-led ritual which unfolded at the same time in front of the burnt-out shell of the town hall on Adolf Hitler Square. Gauleiter Karl Kaufmann led the mourning and remembrance in a choreography which fused the secular and sacred, the Party and the city. In front of a huge crowd, state and city officials, the Party and its organisations and all three branches of the military were marshalled in serried ranks, their flagpoles pointing at the ground, while across the city flags flew at half mast. A bass-voiced actor intoned the words of the Nazi poet Gerhard Schumann's 'Immortality':

> Birth wants death, to die is to give birth.
> You may mourn now, but do not despair.

When Kaufmann took the podium, the standard-bearers on the square swung their banners aloft, the flags on the buildings were hoisted to full mast, and the tone shifted from remembrance to resilience. The Gauleiter promised that Hamburg's citizens would remain worthy through all the demands of the war. Echoing the religious liturgy, he claimed that they had withstood 'the great hour of trial' during the nights of July. He pledged that Hamburg would be rebuilt, reminding his audience that much of the city – including both the town hall and St Peter's – had been destroyed in the great fire of 1842:

The city has a difficult history behind it, but also one that binds us. It has borne many sacrifices in war, destruction, struggle and hardship, and it has always arisen again in more radiant beauty and increased greatness. These ruins around us and the dead are an everlasting covenant for our mission.

Afterwards, people gathered in their thousands at the Ohlsdorf cemetery for the official wreath-laying. Here the city architect Konstanty Gutschow had created an enormous cruciform grave – measuring 280 metres from north to south and 240 metres east to west – to hold the 34,000 victims. It had been dug at great speed to avert the risk of epidemics in the summer heat, with the dead delivered by the truckload. The workforce was kept supplied with cigarettes and alcohol to offset the 'very bad taste in your mouth' produced by decomposing corpses. 'We have had the best luck with rum,' a local administrator reported. In Hamburg, as in other cities, most of the burial squads were made up of prisoners of war and concentration camp inmates. When their work was complete, along its length wide oak boards were positioned at intervals across the grave, carved with the names of the destroyed quarters of the city: HAMMERBROOK, ROTHENBURGSORT, HAMM, BARMBECK. Creating this aesthetic had meant clearing away the many private memorials relatives had erected in the meantime, decorated with the names and photographs of the deceased.

In this collective act of commemoration, perhaps the most important element was time. Göring had held his 'Thermopylae' speech while remnants of the 6th Army were still surrendering at Stalingrad, profoundly shocking a public emotionally unprepared for the military disaster and the loss of a whole army. Whereas Göring and Goebbels had wanted to enact the rites over Stalingrad immediately, in order to use the shared moment to create a collective experience of heroism, the scale of the crisis after the Hamburg bombing enforced a delay of months and gave time for the initial shock to pass. It allowed the bereaved to embrace the joint mourning which local Nazi leaders in Hamburg now offered the whole community: by promising reconstruction, resilience and rebirth, they also steered away from the overblown martyrology expended on Stalingrad. The mass pilgrimage to the Ohlsdorf cemetery was repeated on 25 July 1944, the first anniversary of the attack, and has been every year since, the ritual's success evident in the fact that its Nazi origins would be gradually forgotten.[2]

In other respects, the Hamburg memorial was unusual. Mass graves were deeply unpopular: like paupers' graves, they seemed shameful and their anonymity left no individual headstone for relatives to visit and mourn. In Berlin and other cities, the bombing dead continued to be buried individually – thanks to a combination of family pressure and official sensibilities. The bodies were laid out in a 'respectful' way in the huge halls for identification and families were then permitted to have their relatives buried by private undertakers: the right to provide a private coffin had been upheld in an emergency decree of July 1943. Only those at the bottom of the race hierarchy were shovelled into anonymous collective graves: 122 'Eastern workers' were interred at one such site at the Wilmersdorf cemetery in Berlin. Avoiding such ignominy had been one of the aesthetic challenges in designing the Ohlsdorf memorial in Hamburg.[3]

In Hamburg on Remembrance Sunday 1943, the Party was able to marginalise the Church, something it set great store by. But while Party leaders insisted on their prerogative to deliver the news of military deaths to families in person, the bereaved continued to turn to their local churches. A month after Gertrud L. received the news of her husband's death, his memorial service was held in the church where the couple had married eight years earlier, presided over by the same pastor. He posed the question of faith directly: 'You have to ask yourself is there a Lord God, who permits the loving husband of such a young woman to be taken and four children to lose their father?' Where another widow might have doubted, Gertrud felt 'comforted' by his answer. 'God', he assured them all, 'does not place greater burdens on us than we can carry.' It was May and the church had been decorated with branches of laurel. As the congregation filed out, they passed a single steel helmet and a pyramid of rifles, representing the fallen soldier and his absent comrades.[4]

Pastors and priests drew upon a repertoire of texts and prayers which had stood the test of the wars of national unification and the

First World War, often taking their theme from Matthew 5:4: 'Blessed are they that mourn: for they shall be comforted'. One sermon closed with a contemporary soldier's prayer:

> All who have fallen on sea and on land
> Have fallen into your hand.
> All who fight in a far-off place
> Your mercy face.
> All who in the dark night weep
> Are by your mercy shielded.
> Amen.[5]

In their competition to serve grieving communities, the Party and the churches borrowed from each other, with the SD noting that church memorials generally used a swastika flag draped over the empty coffin in front of the altar, topped by a steel helmet and 'two crossed sidearms, or, for officers, swords'. And the churches preached patriotic defiance too: there could be no escape from death and mourning, for 'Our nation is engaged in a war of life and death'. In the Rhineland, Catholic priests gradually realised that the turnout for funerals and services of remembrance was greater than it was even on high holidays, including Good Friday services. Bishops started to worry that such large congregations said more about Catholics' need for collective acts of remembrance than it did about their religiosity.[6]

The first weeks after the Hamburg air raids saw an upsurge in Protestant church attendance. Members of the civil and military elite came, wearing uniform for the first time in ages, and workers, 'long closed to religion', felt a need to talk and engage with pastors. The churches explained the bombing as a trial sent by God. As Pastor Heinrich Zacharias-Langhans told his congregation in Fuhlsbüttel:

Our home town is dying. Should we accuse the Royal Air Force? . . . But where is the sense in that? Here it is more than the English . . . The hand!! The Hand, not of the enemy. No, His hand! And all complaining is out of place now. For here . . . at the end, in darkness about His mysterious guidance, we are called by God to end our Godlessness. To return to Him with our innermost convictions.

The Lutheran demand for repentance differed little from the pastoral letters issued by the Catholic bishops to their flock in the Rhineland. Both Catholics and Lutherans laid the blame for the sufferings of the air war not on the enemy so much as on godless materialism and hubristic secularism. Both denominations called on the German people to return to God.[7] It was a message which was ill equipped to deal with communities of the bombed. Whereas battlefield deaths were remote and letters readily sanitised – soldiers' final moments becoming pietà-like accounts of men cradling their dying comrades in their laps – the reality of the bombing dead was not so easily cleansed or sacralised. Too many people had seen scattered limbs on the street or gone to identify charred, semi-naked corpses in the morgues. No familiar language or set of rituals was adequate to express what the population of Germany's north-western cities had experienced. To many, the bleak message of religious repentance did not offer comfort. It did not channel their outrage. And it did not promise protection. Protestant attendance in Hamburg rapidly fell again. After the three massive raids on Cologne in late June and early July 1943, Archbishop Frings convened a special meeting of Catholic clergy. In the words of one Gestapo informant, 'The outlook is general within the clergy that the bombing is not accompanied by a renewal of religious thought. Threatened to the core of their being, people are becoming like animals, turning back to their primal instincts.' Theologians and religious leaders of all Christian denominations had hoped for the 'spiritual rebirth' of the nation, just as they had in the First World War, but they feared they were witnessing the triumph of 'materialism'.[8]

While both the Party and the churches continued to provide the public rituals of commemoration, neither found that they enhanced their own moral authority. By the autumn of 1943, Catholic parishioners regularly walked out of church in the middle of the sermon, and citizens turned angrily against uniformed Party officials in the street. While there was no questioning the basic legitimacy of Germany's war, a change was taking place as momentous as any of the waves of political hope and fear sweeping the country. Neither the churches nor the Nazi Party could provide a meaningful interpretation of mass death. The crises of 1943 precipitated a search for personal meaning.[9]

★

On the night of 22–23 November 1943, the government district of the German capital burned. Unlike previous heavy raids in late August and early September, this one was concentrated and most of the payload of 1,132 tonnes of high explosive and 1,331 tonnes of incendiary bombs fell on Berlin's central districts. A sharp, frosty wind threatened to turn the fires into an inferno. When the all-clear sounded, a young woman living just south of the Tiergarten near the epicentre of the raid noticed that 'the sky on three sides was blood-red'. Forewarned that the danger of a firestorm would become greatest in a few hours' time, she and her father went back inside and filled every available container in their apartment with water. As the smoke grew thicker and the air hotter in the streets outside, the father, an imperturbable, ageing Russian émigré, climbed out on to the roof to watch for fire. His daughter finally lay down to sleep in the early hours, assailed by wind whose 'roar outside was like a train going through a tunnel'. Shortly afterwards, RAF planes returned to drop leaflets, repeating the threat that they would 'Hamburgise' Berlin.[10]

To the north of Berlin's central park, the working-class district of Wedding was badly hit. The school for apprentices offered shelter and food to the silent, almost apathetic victims – a 'flood of misery', as the teachers described them. A Red Cross nurse brought in a young woman hugging a small child, her face an expressionless, staring mask. 'My sister, where is my sister?' she kept on asking. Terrified horses from a carter's yard were brought into the school compound and calmed down by girls on air raid duty. Four cows stood quietly to one side chewing the cud. As the flood of homeless people continued, the school building filled from the cellar to the third floor. A woman who had been brought in unconscious came round and could not find her child. A clean-up squad arrived, deathly pale and utterly exhausted. Trucks delivered bread, butter and sausages to the school hall where women volunteers prepared them for general distribution. Men stowed people's possessions in the gym.[11]

The photojournalist Liselotte Purper was one of those bombed out: 'The most terrible night! We have lost everything save our lives,' she wrote to her husband on the Leningrad front the next day, pleading with him, 'If you can come – I need you utterly'. Liselotte had been lucky to be caught by the raid at Anhalter station, trying to collect her suitcase of valuables from the left luggage. Once again, their

guiding star had protected her, she wrote. She had been quickly shepherded down to the station's four-storey concrete bunker, where she
had sat the raid out. Afterwards, with surrounding buildings ablaze
and railway lines blocked, all she could do was to check her suitcase
back into left luggage and make her way along partially blocked streets
to Schöneberg. Their faces covered in handkerchiefs, she and her
companion picked their way through the broken glass in the dark
streets, sheltering behind stationary trams, ambulances and advertising
pillars from the smoke, sand, cement and plaster dust blown by the
rising wind. Near the Nollendorfplatz the storm became too much
for the two women and they ducked into the entrance of a house,
where they rested on upturned buckets in the foyer, unexpectedly
plied with cups of tea by acquaintances who lived there. At dawn, the
wind fell and they continued towards the flat belonging to Liselotte's
parents in Martin Luther Strasse.[12]

As they approached the corner, her heart dropped: 'My God! Now
I see it! Burnt out, totally burnt out!' Other houses were still on fire.
There were beams strewn over the street, empty windows gaping out
of the brick facades which were threatening to topple over. The school
opposite had been hit by a high explosive bomb. In the middle of the
street Liselotte met her parents' caretaker and was relieved to learn
that they had escaped the building alive. Later that day she found
them staring at the ruins of their home, starting to count their losses.
All of Kurt's letters and war diaries were gone. Her professional archive
of 6,000 photos, the negatives from their wedding, a mere two months
earlier, had all been destroyed – as had her books and pictures, the
mementoes from her travels, her collector's edition of *Faust*, her record
collection, 'the beautiful lamp, oh everything, everything which I
loved'. Worst of all was the loss of her violin, her 'dear friend'. For
months afterwards, in between her recurring nightmare of being
caught in the open during air raids and watching buildings go up in
flames, Liselotte dreamed of her violin.[13]

Kurt Orgel, an adjutant with an artillery regiment besieging
Leningrad, had followed the bombing of Berlin with growing alarm.
Liselotte's two letters about the raid arrived at the end of three weeks
of anxious waiting. He was elated at her good fortune. Everything
she had lost could be replaced, even his letters: 'I will write you new
ones, as many as you like' – 'Our wedding photos – we have enough

prints! Pictures of our honeymoon – we'll have a new, still more beautiful one . . . Books, pictures, radio, lamp – everything can be and will be replaced – by us two. We are just beginning! And no one can take our memories from us.' It was different for her parents who had lost so much more, he added dutifully.[14]

Army units and the fire brigades arrived in Berlin from as far off as Stettin, Magdeburg and Leipzig, but the destruction in the city centre was so great that they could hardly get through. The fires were only extinguished shortly before the bombers returned the next night. Between 22 and 26 November, 3,758 people were killed in the capital; a further 574 were listed as missing and nearly half a million were made homeless. To cope with the enormous numbers bombed out and with nowhere to go, the municipal authorities erected temporary shelters in the city's outer suburbs and its green belt.[15]

When Ursula von Kardorff reported for work at the *Deutsche Allgemeine Zeitung* on 23 November, she realised that 'Berlin is so big that many colleagues have seen nothing of the attacks'. Her house had survived, although she had no gas, electricity, running water or any way of silencing the banging of the empty window frames. Nightfall felt like 'the witching hour', and she fled to the security of white sheets and a clean bed with friends in Potsdam. On 29 January, her father's flat was hit. Just as the bookcases in their living room caught fire, friends arrived in time to throw beds, books and pillows down from the windows. Then they carried what they could down the staircase, over the charred beams which had fallen from the roof. They slung silverware, cutlery and porcelain into laundry baskets, as the blue-green phosphorus-tinged flames began to lick the window frames. Unable to return to their floor, they helped salvage their neighbours' heavy furniture, passing around the remaining bottles of schnapps. With fire hoses trained on the upper storeys, an impromptu party unfolded under the protection of umbrellas on the first floor. Washing at a street pump afterwards, as the smoke and mist mingled in a dawn drizzle, a gaunt woman asked Kardorff and her friends: 'When will the retaliation come? When we're all dead?'[16]

After four days of rest in the country, Ursula von Kardorff rebounded: 'I feel a wild vitality welling up within me, mixed with defiance – the opposite of resignation.' She felt the indiscriminate attacks, 'which fall on Nazis and anti-Nazis alike', were welding the population together, and the special distributions of cigarettes, real coffee and meat after each attack helped people bear it all too; the young woman concluded: 'if the English believe they can undermine morale, then that's a miscalculation.' Within a week she was back in Berlin in a tiny but beautiful ground-floor flat next to the Foreign Ministry, thanks to her patrician connections. Her newspaper, whose offices had been destroyed in the same raid, had also relocated and continued to appear daily.[17]

Liselotte Purper was able to call in favours, securing two bright rooms in a quiet eighteenth-century country house in the Altmark. It belonged to a relative and it was where Liselotte and Kurt had held their wedding back in September. With its elegant facade and its half-mile of wooded parkland with winding walks around the fishing lake, it was the right place to recuperate. As she settled in, she prayed that she would become 'hard' and that the 'new weapons' would come soon. As a bombed-out husband, Kurt was granted compassionate leave, and the couple were able to spend Christmas and New Year together.[18]

Three weeks after Kurt had returned to Army Group North, Liselotte began to hope for a baby and started thinking of children's names. She was unpleasantly struck, on a shopping expedition with her friend Hada in Prague, by 'the extraordinary fertility of the Czech women': even the 19- and 20-year-olds all seemed to be pregnant – just 'like rabbits'. It was a eugenics propagandist's bad dream and Liselotte duly fell back on well-worn nationalist expressions, writing to her husband that 'the best of our nation are being lost without producing any progeny or only one while in the East the inferior are propagating themselves by the dozen'. She confessed to Kurt that she did not know whether she really wanted children for herself, or whether they would only distract from their perfect relationship. An attractive young woman of 30, with a successful career as a photojournalist and well-connected, amusing friends, Liselotte was also profoundly lonely.[19]

She made up for it by taking the night-sleeper to Vienna with Hada, where, enchanted to be in a city 'without rubble, without ruins and without permanent threat of air raids', they put up at the smartest hotel they could find. By late February 1944, she was busy at a photo shoot of soldiers convalescing in the Austrian Tyrol. Her hair bleached by the sun off the snow, her face tanned and her blue eyes once more clear and relaxed, Liselotte's only worry was how people might react to her appearance when she returned to Berlin. In her search for new home furnishings to replace the ones she had lost, she braved an air raid warning to make a special trip to Braunschweig to buy a table lamp from the same craft workshop which supplied Göring and Hitler. Liselotte was delighted by her coup.[20]

★

RAF's Bomber Command continued its 'battle for Berlin' until 24 March 1944, launching a total of sixteen major attacks on the city, interspersed by seventeen smaller ones. These were the heaviest, most prolonged bombing missions on a single target in the European theatre. But Berlin survived. Despite the massive fires that engulfed parts of the city in late November, Berlin was not Hamburg or Kassel, which had been destroyed in a firestorm on 22 October. Much of the city had been built with steel and brick, rather than half-timbered medieval houses, and its wide avenues served as firebreaks. Berlin was also beyond the range of 'Oboe', the land-based guidance system on which Bomber Command relied. The Pathfinders' on-board radar sets were often not accurate enough to find the city, and unanticipated strong winds also blew the bombers off course. Although the same central and south-western districts of Charlottenburg, Kreuzberg and Wilmersdorf were hit again on the night of 16 December, on 2–3 and 23–24 December many of the planes missed the city altogether or bombed the southern suburbs. Raids on the first two nights of January resulted in major losses for the RAF, as the German fighters followed the bomber stream all the way to Berlin. On 20–21 January, the RAF did not find the city at all. So heavy was the winter cloud cover that, during the whole five months of the 'battle for Berlin', only two reconnaissance flights yielded aerial photographs of the bomb damage. Instead of creating a single great catastrophe, the bombing of Berlin turned into a war of attrition, in which both sides tried to calculate their respective rates of loss of aircraft – and both speculated how long civilian morale would hold.[21]

Paradoxically, as the raids continued and the tonnage of bombs and the material damage mounted, casualties began to fall. On the night of 15 February 1944, over 800 bombers reached Berlin, pounding a wide swathe from the working-class districts of Wedding and Pankow in the north to leafy Zehlendorf in the south-west. This time, 169 people were killed – a far cry from the 1,500 killed in the much smaller raids of August and September 1943. Berliners had become adept at navigating the city with an eye for where and when to take shelter. Visitors were struck by the new atmosphere of humour, vitality and resistance. In February, Liselotte Purper returned to the capital for the first time since being bombed out in November. The building she had occupied in Schöneberg was so badly damaged that she barely recognised it: the whole of the front facade and entrance were gone. Climbing across piles of stones and planks, she found a middle-aged neighbour in the cellar, wearing a black cap and boiler suit as he tried to rescue the family's belongings. 'Covered in dust and run-down but with a bearing like a soldier at the front,' she wrote to Kurt. 'And that is just how it is in Berlin too. It is a life at the front, if one can still speak of life.'[22]

As the battle for control of German airspace continued, Milch and Speer disregarded Hitler's injunctions to concentrate on producing bombers, and quietly shifted resources towards ground defence and the Luftwaffe's fighter squadrons. Production of single-engined fighters peaked at 851 planes per month in the second half of 1943. Up to a third of Germany's optical industry and half of its electronics industry were diverted to home-front defence, as each side kept leap-frogging the other's innovations in the radar war. By the end of 1943 the flak artillery had built up 7,000 searchlights and 55,000 guns, receiving three-quarters of the 88 mm guns which had earned a fear-some reputation as tank-busters on the eastern front. Manning the guns occupied the majority of the 1.8 million air force personnel as well as 400,000 auxiliaries, including 80,000 schoolboys and 60,000 prisoners of war. Mixed crews served each of the large cannon, with Soviet prisoners of war fetching the shells, boys acting as gun-layers and soldiers acting as master gunners. The flak was consuming 12 per cent of total German ammunition production, twice as much as the army's field guns, even though the success rates were relatively low, with 16,000 artillery rounds needed on average to shoot down a single plane. But they gave civilians a greater sense of security.[23]

By late March 1944, RAF Bomber Command was forced to call off the 'battle for Berlin', because of mounting losses to German defences.

Harris had estimated what he would need for the operation relatively correctly. The RAF flew 14,562 sorties where Harris had called for 15,000. He had predicted that the battle would cost 400–500 aircraft; in fact, 496 bombers were shot down, with a further 95 crashing on their return to England. By February and March 1944, Bomber Command's losses from individual raids on Leipzig and Berlin were over 9 per cent; a few days after the 24 March raid on Berlin, they climbed to 11.8 per cent during a raid on Nuremberg. For the crews themselves, these statistics meant that they had a low chance of surviving a tour of operations. Berlin was a defeat for the concept that strategic bombing alone could defeat Germany.[24]

To the Germans this turning point was not immediately evident, because it coincided with the USAAF's resumption of the bombing campaign it had halted in the autumn. The Liberators and Flying Fortresses were now accompanied by new long-range Mustang fighters, which could take on German fighter squadrons over German airspace. Although the Americans bombed Berlin in March, their principal objective remained defeating the Luftwaffe, targeting aircraft factories, airfields and, with great effect, synthetic oil installations. As the character of the air war changed in the spring of 1944, many Germans drew comfort from the end to the nightly onslaught on the cities.[25]

The writer and journalist Margret Boveri chose that moment to return to the capital from Madrid, where she gave up a plum job at the German embassy. Against the advice of friends and family, including her American mother, Boveri committed herself 'to stay in Berlin and really get to know German life under the bombs' and started writing for *Das Reich*. In April, Goebbels devoted one of his own articles in the weekly to the 'indestructible rhythm of life' and 'unbreakable will to life of our metropolitan population', setting a theme which the paper's editor, Boveri and others expanded upon as they celebrated the capital's ability to hold out.[26]

★

The great prize of strategic bombing was always psychological and political: to spread defeatism and engineer the collapse of regimes. In retrospect, Harris's over-confident claims that Germany would capitulate by 1 April 1944 appear hubristic. But he did have a precedent. Bomber Command had started attacking the northern Italian industrial cities of Genoa, Turin and Milan in the autumn of 1942 and, by the following spring, the campaign had provoked mass flight, violent riots and spontaneous demonstrations against the Prefects and the Fascist Party, with demands for political rights. During August 1943 it looked as if the bombing of Hamburg might have a similar effect in Germany, as people openly discussed copying the Italians and installing a military regime. But that was as far as the parallel went: talk and a few symbolic assaults on Party officials did not turn into collective action.

What made Germany different from Italy? An estimated 50,000–60,000 people died as a result of the air raids in Italy throughout the war; this was comparable to the losses sustained in Britain and France. By September 1944, the civilian death toll from bombing in Germany was closer to 200,000. What made Germany so different from Italy was not the absolute number killed, but the social impact of bombing. Italian cities lacked civil defences: there were few shelters, little anti-aircraft artillery and almost no fighter squadrons. Their absence made people feel utterly undefended. As the Fascist state failed to organise adequate defensive and evacuation measures, the population turned to the extended family, the black market and the Church for shelter, food and security.[27]

Nazi Germany did not implode in this way in 1943–44. Not only were German cities better defended and supplied, but – despite all the inefficiencies and rivalries engendered by their overlapping jurisdictions – the institutions of the state, Party, local government and the military co-operated effectively to mobilise millions of Germans to participate in civil defence and mass evacuation. This was a triumph of organisation and mass mobilisation. Young German women were mobilised in ever greater numbers. Alongside the 400,000 female Red Cross auxiliaries, by 1944 there were 500,000 women serving with the Wehrmacht. Most of them – 300,000 – became air force auxiliaries, mainly on the home front. A slightly older cohort served with the Reich Air Defence Association, the Reichsluftschutzbund. In the town of Aschaffenburg, these were mostly married women, aged between 25 and 30, who did not work. Despite the patriarchal values of Nazism, there were too few men to fill all the higher positions in air defence and more and more active duties fell to the young women. In the town of Trier, all the full-time personnel were women; in Füssen, two-thirds were. Some women continued to avoid service, pleading age, poor health or having to care for young children or elderly relatives. Others enjoyed their new responsibilities. One young Red Cross nurse who had rescued twenty-one people from a collapsed cellar recalled how proud her whole unit was when she was awarded the War Merit Cross in the summer of 1942: it was the first time a woman was decorated with this medal. With their military-style jumpsuits, steel helmets, belt buckles and norms of duty, obedience and sacrifice, these women had literally joined the nation under arms. By 1944 there were 620,000 of them, almost all unpaid volunteers.[28]

Since 1942, soldiers at the front had to get used to female radio announcers addressing them as 'comrades'. 'We're happy to be spoken to by girls with delicate, whispery soprano voices or other young ladies,' one soldier complained, 'but don't you think it's a bit ridiculous when a (hopefully!) well-brought-up, dainty little thing like that speaks to us rowdies as "comrades"?' By late 1943, the neat demarcation of men 'out there' and women and children 'back home' had broken down in much of urban Germany. 'Home' had ceased to be a place of automatic safety. Women and teenagers had become 'heroic defenders' to be mobilised and militarised.[29]

During 1944, a young psychiatrist in Leipzig studied his patients to determine whether or not bombing had led to a rise in 'psychological and nervous reactions' among German civilians. A 50-year-old businessman described how he had started having speech problems a week after rescuing his mother from the flames and being knocked unconscious by the blast of a bomb. 'I find it particularly difficult to get out words that begin with a vowel and I have to force them out or else I would be completely unable to speak,' he explained to Dr Feudell. Since then, air raid sirens produced an immediate reaction, with 'blood rushing to the head, heart pains and trembling'. Feudell was sympathetic to his patients but he concluded that they tended to be people who had been nervy and fragile before the war. He was also mindful that 'the demands of the community must take precedence over subjective suffering', postulating that the 'impetus given by a völkisch attitude' had helped to mobilise the nation's psychological resources and that there were in fact fewer 'hysterical' people than during the First World War – the common reference point for measuring when 'hysteria' had triggered defeatism and revolution. Feudell also concluded that rumours, especially the 'irresponsible passing on of horror stories and exaggerated statistics', were more dangerous than the actual experiences people had undergone. So he recommended that patients should repress their experiences and deal with them in silence rather than talk about them and stir up anxiety in others. A parallel study conducted in Erlangen was even more upbeat, marvelling at Germans' powers of psychological resistance and discounting the notion that the bombing had given rise to any new or specific kind of illness: rather, the terrifying experiences which healthy people had gone through would soon fade.[30]

By September 1943, 800,000 people had left Berlin. Over the coming months, until March 1944, a further 400,000 people were evacuated, as the population of the capital dropped from 4 to 2.8 million. By the end of the year, there were over six million German evacuees from the bombing nationwide. Many decided to leave in the immediate aftermath of air raids, even if their houses had not been hit. Whilst men were expected to assist in firefighting, rescue and salvage operations after the all-clear sounded, many women headed straight for their local reception centre. Staffed by municipal social workers and volunteers from the National Socialist People's Welfare (the NSV), these centres provided first aid, hot drinks, sandwiches, emergency camp beds and an opportunity to immediately log losses and claim compensation from the municipal officials stationed there. They also registered those who wanted to leave. Given the acute housing pressure on the cities, the local Nazi Party and air defence associations encouraged the exodus. Would-be evacuees had to have the requisite departure permit, which would be issued only if they were not bound by a contract of employment. Without this permit, they would not be registered or issued with ration cards in their new abode. The requirement was only waived on the few occasions when the system collapsed entirely: the rarity of such cases – after the Hamburg raids of July 1943 and the raid on Nuremberg in August – itself offers striking commentary on the effectiveness of this decentralised way of organising civil defence and evacuation. Not surprisingly, men counted for a small percentage of evacuees: 10 per cent of 200,000 people who left from Munich, and just 5 per cent of those from Schweinfurt. Almost certainly the men who were evacuated had either passed retirement age or were disabled. If evacuation was aimed principally at children and women, it also divided women into two classes: those in work and those who were not, or, exceptionally, who were able to persuade their employers to let them go.[31]

The great majority – as many as 78 per cent – of evacuees were brought to safety by the mass organisations of the Nazi Party. This was true even of those who were able to rely on family networks and find their own accommodation. Women's experience of the assistance provided by the NSV was often positive. As one woman from Karlsruhe recounted just after the war: 'Everything was arranged and paid for. We got a slip of paper and were told where to go and when to leave. We were put up in the house of a woman who had a big farm.' The stepdaughter of a seamstress in Münster had similarly positive memories of her evacuation – 'and all was done by the NSV', she recalled in 1945. Since the first wartime evacuations from the Saarland in the autumn of 1939, the People's Welfare had prided itself on maintaining posts at railway stations, staffed by women volunteers who would dispense hot drinks and sandwiches. As the trains of evacuees came through, these volunteers were reinforced by members of the Nazi Women's Organisation and the League of German Girls, who helped carry luggage, watch over children and find overnight accommodation.[32]

At times of acute overload, such as the summer of 1943, both the railway network and the volunteers were overwhelmed. The SD highlighted the story of one Hamburg mother fleeing with her three children. Arriving in the south, she was unable to obtain clean nappies for her 1-year-old baby. By the time she reached Linz in Austria, she and the children had nowhere to sleep but the floor of the railway station. Predictably, the children began to fall ill. The woman begged her husband to send her the money for her fare home, assuring him that the basement of their ruined house in Hamburg would be a 'thousand times better than here'. Above all, she asked him to 'Stop, wherever you can, the poor people from travelling to regions which lie in deepest peace . . . No one here in the Ostmark understands. I wish that they would get bombed here too.' This was not how things were meant to be. Indeed, the fact that the story was relayed by the SD to the highest level of government indicates the regime's resolve that such cases should remain the exception.[33]

By the summer of 1943, the Nazi evacuation effort was receiving support from one of the least likely sources – the Catholic Church. The Church had initially put up fierce resistance to the KLV programme to evacuate children, seeing the homes run under the auspices of the Hitler Youth as a gigantic exercise in anti-religious indoctrination. The suspicions of the clergy did not lessen but, faced with mass bombing, they dropped their opposition. In late July 1943, the chairman of the Diocesan Caritas Association for Cologne and Aachen praised the work of the National Socialist People's Welfare and this new-won clerical support helped to turn this new phase of evacuation into a mass migration. Unlike the earlier KLV evacuations, stints were no longer limited to six months: they became open-ended. Without surrendering the voluntary principle or challenging the prerogative of parental consent, local Party and Education Ministry officials now embarked on the wholesale closure and evacuation of entire schools, with their teachers, from the end of the summer holidays.[34]

In September 1943, the Pestalozzi Gymnasium for Girls in Berlin-Rummelsburg was relocated to the Wartheland, where they took over the residence of a Polish count at Schloss Streben. Everything was improvised, and the girls were bitten by fleas from the straw mattresses they had to sleep on at first, before wooden bunk beds were built for them. They soon settled in to the structure of their 'camp', jointly run by the head teacher and the youth leader, who read them ghost stories at bedtime by the flickering light of kerosene lamps. The headmaster, now always dressed in his SS uniform, was relaxed, never bothering to censor the girls' letters home or stop them from sliding down the bannisters of the grand staircase.[35]

With their boarding-school atmosphere and absorbing single-sex group dynamics, the KLV camps offered young teenagers an all-encompassing atmosphere which protected them from much of the social reality of the home front. They were out of the cities, often out of the 'old' Reich itself, and as an age cohort of 10- to 14-year-olds they developed an outlook steeped – just as the Church had feared – in the slogans and propaganda of the Hitler Youth. Keeping a diary in his KLV camp in the Bistritz area of the Hungarian–Romanian Danube, Friedrich Heiden was fascinated by the ethnography of the village: with its Hungarian shop; the small, round and squalid mud-brick huts of the Romanians and Roma on the edge; and, at the centre of the village, the spacious, stone-built farmsteads of the Germans grouped around the Lutheran pastor's house and Protestant church. Much of the boys' time was spent in organised activities, especially sport, war games and hiking. Designed to cultivate 'comradeship', the long days in the foothills of the eastern Carpathians seemed like an extension of the summer camps which the Hitler Youth had organised in the pre-war years. With its system of drill and ranks, marked out by the different colours of braid worn on the shoulder of the uniform, it was all meant to prepare the boys and girls for labour service or the flak. At Werner Kroll's camp at Dürrbach/Dispe in Hungary, the boys were encouraged to duel with willow wands in the headmaster's temporary absence: the Hitler Youth leader said it was 'character-building'. A few days later, the boy Werner had beaten in his duel smashed the window of a Jew's house. That night the whole group of thirty boys returned, throwing – Werner guessed – eighty to ninety stones at the house. They were not punished.[36]

*

In acknowledgement of the huge reversal of population movements, the formerly unpopular rural provinces of eastern and southern Germany were affectionately named 'Reich air raid shelters'. Mass evacuation helped to alleviate the acute crisis of accommodation in the bombed cities, only to create a new one in small-town and rural Germany. A survey carried out in early 1943 by the People's Welfare had revealed that most of the guest houses, hotels and monastic buildings in safe areas of the Reich were already full. In September 1943, for example, 1,241 evacuees from Bochum, Hagen, Berlin, Stettin and other cities arrived in Rügenwalde on the East Prussian coast, a town with 8,000 residents. As numbers of evacuees grew, locals became ever more reluctant to take them in, and the village mayor and local Party leader – often in fact the same person – had to exert ever greater pressure to find them lodgings.[37]

When 12-year-old Erwin Ebeling arrived in Lübow near Stargard in Pomerania, his group of women, children and teenagers was taken to an inn, where they were 'auctioned off' to the local farmers. Most wanted to have a woman with only one child, in order to derive most benefit on their farms. Erwin and ten other boys failed to find takers and had to sleep on bundles of straw in the swineherd's house until families could be found for them. In Naugard in August 1943, no one wanted to take in 13-year-old Gisela Vedder and her sister. Finally, the mayor gave them a bed in his kitchen, where he also conducted his business. While he sat drinking with his visitors in the evening, the two girls hid under the covers. Unable to find anyone willing to intervene on their behalf, they decided to return home, setting off on a hot and dusty walk to the station, dragging their wooden trunk along behind them. In the Bayreuth district, two women and a child were outraged at having to share a tiny room while no one was prepared to offer them a warm meal. They returned to Hamburg in disgust.[38]

Mass evacuation may have been an organisational triumph. It was not, however, a victory of the 'national community'. On the contrary, the experience of evacuation in particular would engender whole new areas of conflict within German society. Time and again, the refusal to share kitchens and laundries with evacuees became flashpoints of conflict, and local Party officials had to mediate. The Nazi Women's Organisation and the People's Welfare set about establishing sewing centres, communal kitchens and laundries to defuse these conflicts.[39]

It would take much more to engender any sense of affinity between evacuees and their hosts. Locals in Pomerania referred to mothers as 'bombing women' and called the girls and boys 'shrapnel kids', routinely blaming them for all acts of vandalism. In Bavaria, they shouted other, traditional insults like 'Prussian sows' at the girls as they marched in their junior youth league uniforms through the countryside. Evacuee women were accused of neglecting their children and carrying on with local men, a theme which soon found its way into the reports filed by the SD and the Catholic Church, two organisations united in mutual loathing and in their shared conviction that 'loose women' undermined social order and national morale. It was an accusation that had already been well rehearsed in relation to another group of single women – soldiers' wives – and so it was a handy stone to cast at unwelcome intruders. In Swabia, farmers' wives complained that the evacuee women would not even help with domestic chores like washing and mending, let alone with the field-work, even when all hands were needed to bring in the harvest. To them, the idle city women 'seem to think that they should be waited on hand and foot, as in a hotel'. By contrast, to working-class women from Essen, Düsseldorf and Hamburg, the peasant women seemed 'simple and stupid because they work so hard', and they complained that there were no cafés, hairdressers or cinemas. In the Rhineland Palatinate, a young woman evacuated from Bremen with her young daughter found the unfriendliness of the farmers' families in the village as difficult to bear as their cold and damp lodgings. Homesick and isolated, she wrote to her mother-in-law of how 'the farmers don't want to be visited. On some farmsteads, they simply slam the door in your face.'[40]

Representatives of Church and Party were soon overstretched trying to dissolve the social tensions engendered by mass evacuation. Catholic priests visiting women and children from the Rhineland in Upper Swabia in the autumn of 1943 reported that they spent most of their time 'clear[ing] up difficulties, resentments, hostilities and incomprehension on both sides'. Most of the Catholic priests from the Rhineland were elderly men, who found the rigours of cycling around the villages to minister to their scattered flock physically exhausting. The priests were troubled that women in Saxony preferred to take the train to Dresden and Pirna to go the cinema and hairdresser.[41]

In the German Christian stronghold of Thuringia, evacuees from Barmen welcomed the arrival of their pastor, Johannes Mehrhoff, who visited 400 of his parishioners in seventeen different places. Serving as an information point, he passed on news and addresses of other evacuees, occasioning contact between people evacuated to different regions. Many women wrote back to express their thanks. For some, steeped in the pietist traditions of the Wuppertal, it was an opportunity to voice their own search for a religious meaning in an alien Protestant region. Others thanked him for the pleasure they felt 'each time that a greeting from you and our dear ones in the parish at home reaches us'. One young mother who had been evacuated with her two small children wrote that 'Then our hearts feel differently again, knowing that we are being thought of back home. Otherwise, it would be easy to give up, but this certainty always gives us fresh courage again.' Thuringia proved much harder for the Catholic priests trying to minister to their Rhineland flock. Sometimes, they were picked up and warned off by police and local Party officials who shared local animosities towards the 'Papists'.[42]

Beyond the clashes of city and countryside, and of north and south

– with all their attendant cultural divisions evinced by different dialects, cuisine, religiosity and dress sense – the conflicts between the evacuees and their hosts also quickly developed a socio-economic dimension. Evacuees complained that local shopkeepers often refused to sell them goods, failing to grasp that they were also disturbing the balance within a food-rich but cash-poor countryside. Whereas a farmer's wife with five children had to make do with between 45 and 60 marks a month, the childless wife of a white-collar worker had about 150 to 180 marks to spend.[43]

Much of this imbalance in purchasing power stemmed from the elaborate system of subsidies and payments devised by central government and first applied to the Saar evacuees in 1939. The Nazi regime created payments under the heading of 'evacuee family support' in order to ease the additional costs incurred by families: for travel and transport, replacing furniture and other household items, the loss of income from evacuation, or the extra cost of running a second home in cases where the husband was still living in the city. All these costs could be factored into calculations of financial entitlement. As the state strove to make evacuation work, having to eat out or buy meals in became defrayable expenses alongside journeys home to place belongings in safe storage. As many people availed themselves of the opportunity – a chance also to see friends and relatives and take stock of conditions in their home towns – the railway network buckled under the additional load.[44]

The scale of resources being paid out by the state reflated – perhaps even inflated – local, rural economies, with regional price control commissions setting rates for rent, cooking facilities, heating and bedding in order to provide incentives for locals to take in evacuees. Intent on equipping the 'national community' with the means to face the test of the bombing war, the regime issued no fewer than thirty-nine directives and amendments to regulate the 'evacuee family support'. Calculations became so complex that municipal authorities issued multiple model examples for a mother with four children to show how the payments varied depending on whether the father was in the military, worked in a reserved occupation or was deceased. Minor discrepancies between the levels of entitlement fuelled envy and jibes, while in fact the sums being paid out were almost as great as, and in some cases greater than, the breadwinner's peacetime earnings.[45]

Using the male breadwinner's wages as a yardstick was designed to preserve the pre-war social order. As with the payment of 'family supplements' to the wives of soldiers, such massive spending by the state was designed not to dislodge existing distinctions of pay, class and rank, but to leave them intact without causing hardship. This was not egalitarian social welfare; nor was it targeted at either individuals or communities. Rather, as Nazi policy quietly replaced its expectations of spontaneous communal solidarity with state provision, it put the family at the centre of welfare.[46]

In other respects, the family remained an obstacle to those like Goebbels, Albert Speer and the SD who would have liked to institute a simple, compulsory system of evacuation. As it was a power Hitler never granted them, local authorities were forced to persuade parents to sanction the evacuation of their children. Party officials soon found that meetings with parents were most successful when they were conducted by an experienced teacher or head teacher who already commanded local respect. Despite a great deal of effort, however, parents did not always give their consent and local Party and Education Ministry officials often had to put pressure on them to comply. When the schools were closed and evacuated wholesale to the countryside in the early autumn of 1943, recalcitrant parents were warned that they remained legally liable for sending their children to school. Many families complied, but others sent their children to out-of-town schools. In Goebbels's own Gau of Berlin, some children travelled as far as Oranienburg to attend the schools there or boarded with foster families in nearby towns like Nauen.[47]

Parents were not slow to enforce their rights. On 11 October 1943, 300 women protested vehemently at the municipal offices in Witten, demanding that ration cards be issued to their children and themselves. In an effort to stem the return of children, the Gauleiter and Reich Defence Commissioner for South Westphalia, Albert Hoffmann, had ordered that ration cards should be withheld from those who lacked serious reasons for coming home. When the police arrived on the scene, they refused to intervene, pointing out that the mothers were 'in the right' and that there 'was no legal basis' for withholding their ration cards. Similar scenes unfolded at the municipal provisioning offices in Hamm, Bochum and Lünen. Mothers brought their toddlers and babies with them. Some of their coal-miner husbands also came, and threatened to stage a sit-in until the ration cards were issued. Since evacuation remained voluntary, the authorities had to give way.[48]

The presence or absence of their husbands made a big difference to women's choices at this time. After the firestorm, men from Hamburg serving in the Wehrmacht were anxious for their wives and children to leave the city, while most of those who came back had husbands working there who wanted their wives to return. Then there were the women who were prevented by their reserved occupations from leaving at all. In Munich, working mothers petitioned, demanding the same liberty to go as women who were not working. Others simply upped and left, exacerbating the chronic shortage of labour in the war industries. In August 1944, the Plenipotentiary for Labour, Fritz Sauckel, stipulated that children and infants should be allowed to go in order to safeguard these 'bearers of the German future', but that mothers of children of over 1 year old would have to stay, unless the employer gave them permission to leave. While Goebbels officially upheld the letter of the regulations which entitled the authorities to refuse to register women for rations and accommodation who did not have a valid departure permit, he clearly lacked the appetite for a battle with mothers who had accompanied their small children. Instead, he proposed a face-saving gesture, making them liable for labour service in their new place of evacuation.[49]

To compensate for absent housewives in the increasingly empty cities, the Nazi Women's Organisation ordered its local sections to provide meals and home help for grass widowers, while the press carried simple recipes for men as well as practical tips on how to sew and mend. Across the denuded cities of the Reich, works canteens, which had proved so unpopular to the family-minded industrial workers in the early years of the war, gained ground rapidly. By providing hot meals and shelter, workplaces were becoming a kind of substitute home.[50]

By early 1944, the whole model of evacuation underwent a fundamental rethink. The grand scheme that Goebbels's Interministerial Committee for Air War Damages had devised a year earlier had divided the Reich into 'sending' and 'receiving' regions. This had proved unworkable, as 'receiving' areas were swamped by successive waves of evacuees. Goebbels now began trying to limit evacuation itself, by restricting it to large cities which appeared particularly at risk. In fact, the evidence showed that many people would do everything they could to remain in or near their home town. In Ludwigshafen, the special trains and chartered buses had stood empty for days after heavy bombing while people tried to rescue property and find alternative housing within the city – in school halls, cellars, the basements of offices, or in the bunkers themselves. After the June and July 1943 raids on Cologne, Gauleiter Josef Grohé reported that most of the 300,000 people who had left the city were staying in the nearby countryside, with many still clinging to the idea of setting up some kind of abode in Cologne – 'be it a cellar room or an allotment garden shed'. In the same spirit, Grohé permitted evacuees from the neighbouring Gau of Düsseldorf to stay in his region rather than moving them on, as planned, to Thuringia, Kärnten and Württemberg.[51]

By the winter of 1943–44, such ad hoc local measures were becoming the basis of a different model of evacuation, and the *Reichsbahn* was encouraged to ferry commuters travelling short distances and link up with local bus and tram networks. The railways – already buckling under the trans-European demands of conveying military transports, war materiel, evacuees, forced labour convoys, food shipments and Jews – engaged in another round of planning and improvisation. Cattle trucks were refitted as commuter carriages: with their wooden benches, light bulbs and pot-bellied stoves, they became carriage model MCi 43. Commuting soon provided a new source of envy and dispute: were evacuees who continued to come to work in the city from the surrounding countryside entitled to the special ration supplements issued to pep up those who were living in the bombed cities? In Mannheim, these special allowances included a bottle of wine, 50 grams of real coffee beans, cigarettes, as well as half a pound of veal or a pound of apple purée. The issue was referred all the way to the Reich Chancellery before a negative decision was reached. Naturally, some zealous citizens took it on themselves to inform on neighbours they thought were cheating.[52]

Such lack of 'organic solidarity' not only challenged the Nazi ideal of the 'national community'. It also challenges the schemas of historians who divide between those who see the regime as a 'consensual dictatorship' and those who depict a regime pitted against growing defeatism and social opposition. For all their differences, both of these concepts suffer from the same flaw: they imagine that German society as a whole either supported or opposed the regime. The collective protest of the coal miners' wives in Witten – to demand their children's ration cards – was highly unusual. And even in this case, they expected the state to abide by the law and recognise the justice of their claims, as it indeed did. Most kinds of wartime social conflict were not directed against the authorities at all. Instead, people generally wanted the authorities to step in and put other categories of 'national comrades', whom they accused of behaving unfairly, firmly in their place. As the demand for places in Germany's bunkers grew, people in war work began to challenge the principle that mothers with children had first claim on access: petitioners pointed out that, whereas they had no choice themselves, women with children ought already to have left for the safety of evacuation. Göring's 'chivalrous' ruling in favour of women and children remained in force, however. The pattern was similar elsewhere. Rising demand for cinema tickets generated complaints about ticket-touting, advance queuing and whether enough seats had been reserved for soldiers on leave. As each constituency petitioned the authorities about the unfairness to which it felt exposed, the professional magazine the *Film-Kurier* commented that 'There is no shortage of attempts to help every national comrade get his rights.'[53]

With their petitions, complaints and occasional denunciations, Germans drew the authorities into their conflicts with one another, expecting them to impose a 'fair' solution. This pattern of behaviour gave the notion of a 'national community' a certain legitimacy, because it provided the framework for staking a claim – just as it automatically excluded Jews, Poles and other foreigners. At the same time, the increasing bitterness of complaints and apparent pettiness of conflicts amongst Germans tells of a beleaguered nation which rarely felt like a 'national people's community' and made the more grandiose claims of propagandists ring hollow. But this did not mean that society had become 'atomised': family ties, religious congregations, professional networks and circles of friendship continued to function, as did communities based on apartment block, urban neighbourhood or village. As expectations of spontaneous 'national solidarity' were progressively disappointed, people became more conscious of the immediate, everyday communities on which they could draw.

German society was still held together on the national level by the voluntary mass organisations like the Air Raid Defence League and the People's Welfare, by the churches and the Party, all of whom had to work at bridging the new social conflicts caused by bombing, homelessness and evacuation. All this produced ambivalent responses to Nazism. Hitler had stopped speaking often in public and seemed too distant to impinge on daily life. Goebbels, whose sexual adventures and mendacious propaganda furnished material for many jokes, was widely admired for visiting bombed neighbourhoods of Berlin each night and for rallying the population. Local leaders were judged on their appearance – with tales of corruption, crass luxury or crude behaviour colouring jokes about the 'Bonzen' – the 'big shots' – while most Germans imagined themselves, by contrast, as 'little' people. But most of the structures of the Nazi regime simply seemed normal – down to the urban sub-camps for concentration camp prisoners who worked to clear bomb sites. The Party-state, in all its local manifestations, remained a primary source of rights, entitlements and racial privileges, whether dispensed by the volunteers of the NSV or the municipal ration card offices. Efforts at change focused on improving one's lot within the scale of ration supplements or simply finding the woman in the department store who had control over the scarce supply of winter coats.

*

The thirst for private, non-political entertainment was irrepressible. People might turn to the Party, the Führer or the churches on key ritual occasions such as memorial services for the victims of bombing or annual events like Heroes' Memorial Day or Hitler's New Year's Day addresses. But for years people had tried to cope with the burdens of war through private, non-political means. The first radio programme with a mass following of this kind had been the *Request Concert for the Wehrmacht*. On 31 December 1939, the Vienna Philharmonic gave their first New Year's Eve concert of Strauss waltzes to raise money for the Party's Winter Relief charity. Performed under the baton of their long-standing conductor, Clemens Krauss, the concert proved such success that, a year later, it was moved to New Year's Day and broadcast live across the Reich.[54]

As the battle for German morale entered this key phase, the search for personal, private fulfilment became more intense. When the

Marburg writer Lisa de Boor visited the capital in April 1944, she was amazed to find the undamaged cinemas in the Kurfürstendamm opening at 11.30 in the morning to full houses. The film to see in the winter of 1943–44, *The White Dream*, was an escapist musical on the ice rink, its hit song 'Go buy a coloured balloon / and hold it in your hand / imagine it carries you off / into a strange fairytale land'. By the autumn of 1943, even the newsreels shied away from coverage of the front, prefering to dwell on what the SD called 'peacetime matters' such as sports, trivia and current events.[55]

Goebbels had always been prepared to spend huge sums on live performance in order to keep the theatres going. By 1942–43, he was allocating 45 million marks to the theatres – up nearly a hundredfold from a decade earlier. This sum, which the Gaus and the municipalities were meant to top up, amounted to a full quarter of Goebbels's entire budget. It was more than he spent on propaganda itself, and more than twice the amount spent on film – for where the film industry was profitable, theatre would have folded without subsidies. And while the regime called for theatre to be opened up to the masses, it tolerated the enduring cultural grip of the middle classes, which they exercised through the tradition of renewable annual subscriptions for seats. The scale of resources allocated to theatre shows just how seriously the Nazi regime took the notion of 'German culture' and satisfying the educated classes who embodied it. Most of the Reich's 300 theatre companies operated all year round, performing two or three times every day. To keep the show on the road, on average one new production was needed every fortnight: with over 13,000 new productions during the war years, this average was sustained across the Reich. A flagship house such as the Vienna Burgtheater inaugurated a dozen new productions during the 1943–44 season. In February 1944, the latest of the Third Reich's new theatres opened its doors in the industrial town of Gleiwitz in Upper Silesia.[56]

Two-thirds of the Berlin theatres had been seriously damaged by the end of 1943, but restoration work began immediately. By mid-1944 seventeen theatres were operating normally again, with a further five still being rebuilt. The repair of the Comedy House was only abandoned after it was hit for the fourth time in January. Improvisation was the order of the day. When the Schiller Theatre was beyond repair, performances were held in its vast canteen where a stellar cast was assembled for Goethe's *Faust*. By the summer, Goebbels, who demanded detailed monthly reports on the state of the theatres in his Gau, suggested additional night-time performances around the full moon, when it would be easier for audiences to pick their way home through the rubble-strewn streets in the blackout. Meanwhile, several actors from the German Theatre were sleeping at the Friedrichstrasse station – happy to be in a heated dormitory close at hand.

Live performance had never been more memorable. In the depths of winter 1943, Berliners started queuing on Saturday afternoon in front of the box office of Gustaf Gründgens's Prussian State Theatre, relieving each other periodically through the night, in order to be there at 10 a.m. on Sunday when tickets went on sale. In April 1944, Goebbels persuaded star actors to come to Berlin from Vienna and perform Shakespeare's *The Winter's Tale*. Ursula von Kardorff managed to attend, only hours after enduring a heavy American air raid. To reach the theatre she had to clamber over rubble, 'past blood-spattered people with green-tinged faces', as she noted in her diary that night. But it was worth it: 'I felt almost physically lifted out of my present existence and transported into a dream world'. This elation united actors and audiences, inadvertently providing a sense of emotional intensity which theatre directors, critics and Nazi propagandists had long craved. Shakespeare was as eagerly consumed in Berlin as in London, the search for spiritual meaning and for moments of inner reprieve just as crucial in the intervals between air raids.[57]

Live performance also provided a means of expressing nonconformity. During performances of Goethe's *Faust* at the Berlin State Theatre, audiences stood up and applauded ostentatiously when Mephistopheles, played by Gustaf Gründgens, declared, 'Of the rights with which we are born / sadly of them it is never a question.' In *Don Carlos* Schiller had the Marquis of Posa confront Philip II of Spain with the tyranny of the Inquisition, scripting a demand for political and religious freedom which so often brought audiences to their feet that theatre directors began to shy away from putting on the play. In Vienna's Burgtheater, which – despite all of Goebbels's efforts in Berlin – still remained the premier stage in the Reich, dissent took a more separatist turn. Franz Grillparzer's *King Ottokar*, a play about the tragic fall of the last King of Bohemia, gave conservative Viennese the opportunity to stand and applaud von Hornek's patriotic soliloquy in praise of Austria. They cheered still more loudly when the first Austrian emperor, Rudolf von Habsburg, came on to plead that 'justice and the rule of law prevail in German lands'. The SD took note of this 'demonstration by various reactionary elements'.[58]

The regime took it all in its stride. When an enraged Hitler Youth leader in Bremen wrote to Rainer Schlösser, Goebbels's head of theatres, denouncing the city's Schauspielhaus as a 'hotbed of reactionary sentiment', it was Schlösser himself who explained that 'Theatres with a pronounced liberal atmosphere are essential because they cater for a certain section of the audience and ensure that [these people] ultimately remain under our control.' Goebbels and Schlösser might criticise the choices of repertoire made by their favoured theatre directors, especially the galaxy of actor-managers in Berlin, but on the whole they let them run their own houses as they saw fit.[59]

Wanting an uncensored theatre, even standing up for a traditional version of Schiller, was not necessarily a political protest so much as a rediscovery of a kind of national identity: the 'apolitical German', profoundly nationalist but in an axiomatic rather party-political sense. It was a self-identity which had served the educated classes well during the previous war. Two writers who were widely read both at home and at the front and to whom educated Germans returned to again and again for inspiration were the contemporary Ernst Jünger, who continued to publish during the war, and the Romantic poet Friedrich Hölderlin, who had studied with Hegel and Schelling in the 1780s and been influenced by Goethe and Schiller in the early 1790s.[60]

During the nineteenth century much of Hölderlin's oeuvre remained unpublished and he had been less well known than his early-nineteenth-century contemporaries such as Joseph von Eichendorff or Theodor Körner. They were also more strident, celebrating the military heroism of the war of 'national liberation' against Napoleon, where Hölderlin was more elegiac and lyrical. But it was precisely the mystical and elusive qualities of his writing that appealed to the poet Stefan George, who started the Hölderlin cult as a patriotic, mysterious and exclusive endeavour before the First World War. One of George's disciples, Norbert von Hellingrath, helped to edit and publish Hölderlin's unpublished work during the war. When he showed it to Rainer Maria Rilke, the poet was so moved by the hymns and elegies that he composed

his first two 'Duino Elegies' as a kind of late-Romantic tribute.
Hellingrath asserted that many of Hölderlin's works 'only share their
secret with a very small number, indeed remain completely silent for
the majority. And are utterly inaccessible for non-Germans.' Hellingrath
was killed at Verdun, but his version of Hölderlin entered public
consciousness in Germany via the elitist 'George circle', which vener-
ated a Hellenistic, aristocratic 'secret Germany'. When the three hand-
some Stauffenberg brothers – Berthold, Alexander and Claus – joined
the circle in the 1920s, they were immediately welcomed as the descend-
ants of the Stauffen Emperor Frederick II – whose biography another
member of the circle, the historian Ernst Kantorowicz, was writing.
The cult of a 'secret', 'other Germany' entered public circulation.
Associated with another young officer who had served in the First
World War and the *Freikorps*, Ernst Jünger, it became the literary
touchstone of the anti-Weimar nationalist Right, creating an inherit-
ance with an enduring – and deeply personal – appeal.[61]

The centenary of Hölderlin's death in June 1843 was marked by
celebrations of his work across Germany, with Tübingen, where
Hölderlin had lived for the last thirty-six years of his life, at their centre.
One sharp-tongued graduate student, Hellmuth Günther Dahms, wrote
to a friend disparaging the Nazi epigones' efforts to kidnap the poet
and 'declare Hölderlin the first SS man' during the crass official lectures
which accompanied the Tübingen Hölderlin festival. But Dahms found
the festival's final concert 'deeply moving', especially its culmination
– Brahms's setting of the 'Song of Fate' from *Hyperion*. The first stanza
established the harmony of the divine world, where 'Fateless, like
sleeping / infants, the divine beings breathe', sealing it off from the
mortals down below. Their fate is described in the second stanza:

> Yet there is granted us
> no place to rest;
> we vanish, we fall –
> the suffering humans –
> blind from one
> hour to another,
> like water thrown from cliff
> to cliff,
> for years into the unknown abyss.

Brahms repeated the final words four times, that plunge 'into the unknown abyss' – 'ins Ungewisse hinab'. The performance left Dahms 'quietly convinced that the effect of this hour was so powerful that nothing contemporary can compare with it, that this one true figure can say more than all the stupid clap-trap of our days, that morally speaking Hölderlin's centenary is on the same level as Katyn'. This was a strange, jarring comparison – placing the lyric poet next to the mass grave of Polish officers shot by the NKVD. Presumably, the brief reference to Katyn – which had been in the news for the previous seven weeks – made perfect sense to his friend, however odd it sounds in retrospect. If Hölderlin was the culture they were fighting for, then Katyn represented the overwhelming threat facing Germany of 'Jewish-Bolshevik annihilation'. Dahms did not have to be a Nazi to believe this: indeed, what he resented was not the mobilisation of his cultural values but the crude attempt to Nazify Hölderlin.[62]

In Marburg, the writer Lisa de Boor turned to Hölderlin's 'Song of Fate' to chronicle her own reaction to the news of the fire-bombing of Wuppertal: 'Yet, how horrific is the path for us in Germany into the abyss. "Into the unknown depths."' Wishing for the defeat of the Nazi regime she detested and dreading what that would mean for Germany, Lisa de Boor turned to Hölderlin because he expressed the fundamental dilemma of living on the edge of the abyss, drawn down into it yet morally resisting the pull of fate. When Ursula von Kardorff heard that a close friend – and a private critic of the regime – had been killed in action, she remembered the volume of Hölderlin's poetry she had given him, and her dedication: 'You all know the wild grief that besets us when we remember times of happiness. How far beyond recall they are, and we are severed from them by something more pitiless than leagues and miles.' The words were not hers. They came from Ernst Jünger's *On the Marble Cliffs*, a work that Lisa de Boor was also reading with a mixture of repulsion and admiration.[63]

In December 1943, Lisa de Boor's daughter, Monika, was arrested along with other doctors in Hamburg belonging to a group called 'Candidates of Humanity'. Wolf and Lisa de Boor drew on all their connections to gain access to Monika, to write to her and to find a good Nazi lawyer to defend her when her case came to trial.

Meanwhile, Lisa sat for a portrait and went to concerts of Schubert, Beethoven and Chopin in Marburg. She was delighted when a young officer wrote to tell her that her playful articles in the *Neue Schau* had meant more to him on the eastern front than all the propaganda slogans dinned into their ears. For her own part, 'moved by the millions of German dead with whose bodies Russian soil is now being nurtured', she felt drawn to her 'old idea of composing ballads'. She felt too that the ruins of Kassel and other German cities were heralding 'a new birth of Christ', and that 'the trials must be undergone'. In January 1944, it was Ernst Jünger's novel *The Worker* which told her of 'the demonic, transcendental entities that overpower mankind'.

By 1942, the young General Staff officer Claus von Stauffenberg was turning against the Führer he had formerly revered, drawing spiritual strength to resist Hitler from the poetic sources which had nurtured his opposition to Weimar democracy: Pindar, Dante, Hölderlin and Stefan George. Meanwhile, in Munich the student Sophie Scholl turned to Hölderlin for inspiration when she wrote a long letter to her boyfriend Fritz Hartnagel to explain why she had to oppose the Nazis. Comparing the poet to the boxer Max Schmeling, she pointed out that Schmeling may have been physically stronger but insisted that Hölderlin remained superior: 'We do not believe in the victory of the stronger, but the stronger in spirit. And the fact that this victory may perhaps come to pass in a world other than our own limited one (beautiful though it is, it is nonetheless small) makes it no less worthy of attainment.' She continued to distribute the leaflets of the White Rose urging Germans to engage in peaceful resistance to Nazi rule until she and other members of the group were arrested on 18 February 1943. They were executed four days later.[64]

But neither Hölderlin nor Jünger inspired everyone on the path towards anti-Nazi resistance. Helmut Paulus had taken the poet's works with him as he marched across Ukraine. In the winter of 1943–44, another young infantryman found himself in dialogue with the same writers when he sat down to turn his war diary into a memoir. Willy Reese was a 23-year-old trainee bank clerk from Duisburg, who had four tours of duty on the eastern front behind him and would return for a fifth. A lapsed Catholic who had abhorred Nazi parades and avoided drilling with the Hitler Youth, Reese had gone to war in 1941 expecting to measure his own 'baptism of fire' by the yardstick set by Jünger in his best-selling accounts of the First World War. In 1922, in *The Struggle as Inner Experience*, Jünger had scripted a paean to the erotic charge of pulsing blood and 'a frenzied orgy' of killing, describing how 'The sight of the opponent brings not only ultimate horror but also release from a heavy and unbearable pressure. This is the voluptuousness of blood that hangs over war like a red storm-sail over black galleys, in its boundless verve akin only to love.' For Reese, keyed up to expect their first, frenzied infantry charge at Soviet lines to be like this, the reality 'was not harrowing and stirring enough, and yet everywhere horror leered at us'.[65]

As each tour of duty was ended by illness and wounds and periods of rehabilitation in Germany, Reese's view of the war changed. After surviving his 'Russian Passion' during the winter of 1941, Reese chose to model himself on a harder, more cynical version of Jünger when he returned to the front in the summer of 1942. As the troop train brought them eastwards he took in the huge stockpiles of weaponry and munitions being shipped forward and grasped the gigantic scale of the war for the first time. This realisation brought him back to Jünger's stark 1932 novel, *The Worker*. Challenging the Weimar vogue for seeing industrial society in terms of the Marxist notion of alien-ation, Jünger had celebrated the willing subjugation of worker-warriors to a totally mobilised machine age. Reese had no trouble transposing that description to the military build-up he now observed in the east. Reese and his comrades consciously play-acted Jünger. They called themselves 'heroic nihilists', made speeches about crusades and wore red roses in their buttonholes.[66]

By the next winter, none of that bravado was left. 'Unshaven, lice-ridden, sick, spiritually destitute, no more than a sum of blood, guts and bones', they were bound together by 'forced dependence on one another . . . our humour . . . born of black humour, gallows humour, satire, obscenities, mordancy . . . a play with the dead, spattered brains, lice, pus and excrement, born of spiritual void . . . Our ideals were me, tobacco, food, sleep and France's whores.' As 'dehumanised cari-catures', Reese and his comrades had 'stupefied existences'. He had finally reached the state so many soldiers on the eastern front had described as 'rough' and 'hard'. But even in this piercing self-description there was a strain of lyricism, mixed with self-pity.[67]

Reese also felt transfigured, more alive and at home than he had ever imagined in the world Jünger had depicted: 'In the battle of materiel life proved stronger in a wild lust for being. War led us into a dream-like realm and some who were peaceable at heart' – he was referring, presumably, to himself – 'experienced a secret longing to suffer and do terrrible things. The primitive awoke in us. Instinct replaced mind and feeling and we were borne up by a transcendental vitality.'[68]

Saved from the front by a sniper's bullet, Reese returned to Germany a second time. Despite being plagued by nightmares in which, he wrote, 'again and again I relived the horrors of the winter war, heard the shells' howl, the cries of the wounded, saw soldiers advancing and dying, and saw myself like a stranger in my fate on the edge of no-man's-land', Reese volunteered to return to the eastern front for a third time in the summer of 1943. He now believed only in the spiritual journey which the war afforded him: 'I wanted to conquer fire with fire, the war with the war,' he wrote. Returning to the front became 'a crazy means to an inner homecoming'.[69]

By this point Reese had long outgrown Jünger's illiberal values and narrow range of empathy. He was horrified and guilt-ridden by the war they were fighting. In 1942, he tossed off 'Carneval', one of the most extraordinary German poems written during the war. Reese chose a light, lilting rhythm to jar with the brutal directness of the words:

> Murdered the Jews
> Marched into Russia
> As a roaring horde
> Muzzled the people
> Sabred in blood
> Led by a clown
> We are his envoys
> Of the one everyone knows
> And are wading in blood.[70]

After surviving for so long, Reese had finally, hesitantly, found the cause he was fighting for. Writing home in a complete, uncensored confession of faith, he set out an anti-Nazi patriotism:

For that I want to live and fight for Germany, for the spiritual, secret Germany, which only after defeat, after the end of the Hitler-period, can exist again and will regain the place in the world which belongs to Germany. If I fight, then for my life; if I should fall, then because it was my destiny. And I want to sacrifice myself too for the future, free, spiritual Germany – but never for the Third Reich.

But he did not know how to square his war for a 'free, spiritual Germany' with the 'mask of the laughing soldier' in Wehrmacht uniform who joined his comrades in burning villages and assaulting Russian women. By the time Reese ended his manuscript in Duisburg in February 1944 to return for a fifth tour of duty, he closed his memoir with another affirmation of his vitality: 'The war continued. Out once more I wandered. I loved life.'[71]

Part of the appeal of Ernst Jünger's existentialist epic and Hölderlin's classical 'fate' for literary-minded Germans was that they avoided questions of responsibility and causation: they turned war into an elemental force, a natural disaster, beyond human morality or power. Lisa de Boor, Ursula von Kardorff and Willy Reese each regarded themselves as anti-Nazi. But, unlike the Scholls or Stauffenbergs, they had not come to regard the war as a 'Nazi war' or feel that they had to make a political choice. They could not wish for Germany's defeat, even as their sense of profound vulnerability grew.

*

The sense of crisis after the Hamburg firestorm forced many Germans to talk about their own guilt for the murder of the Jews. But this was a political assessment, dependent on an external shock and sense of doom. What educated Germans were looking for in their literary and musical canon were answers unfettered by time and connected to their 'inner' moral certainties. German awareness of the external, 'Jewish war' did not abate, but it changed character. The murder of the Jews had become established, irreversible fact to be assimilated and understood, or, if that was impossible, to be put to one side.

Sent to work on the production line of a cardboard-box-making factory in Dresden, Victor Klemperer learned to overcome his conservative fears and middle-class disdain for the working class, finding many of his new 'Aryan' co-workers more critical, less Nazi and more generous towards him than his former academic colleagues. The foreman, an old-time trade union type, expressed his sympathies with Klemperer in March 1944 for having lost his academic job just because he was Jewish. A week later, this same man would turn to the idea of Jewish 'billionaires' as he cast about helplessly for a reason for the latest, senseless American bombing of Hamburg. For people like him, the abstract idea of a foreign 'Jewish plutocracy' offered an explanation which cut across their personal liking for individual German Jews. To make sense of the ferocity of the aerial onslaught on the civilian population, the 'terror bombing' required a conspiracy by an enemy who was filled with an implacable hatred of Germans and Germany.[72]

By spring 1944, comparisons of the bombing with the murder of the Jews had a different ring from the previous autumn. Gone was shock and panic after Hamburg, and those wishes to reverse the mutual escalation – as if the murder of the Jews could somehow be undone in order to stop the bombing. After twelve months of sustained mass raids on German cities, they had become a fact of life and the 'Jewish' character of the bombing had become axiomatic. Instead of blaming themselves, some people offered advice on how to turn the screw further. In May 1944, when the Wehrmacht occupied the Hungarian capital Budapest, the ghettoisation of the Jews sparked much comment, not for what it meant for the Jews, but solely for what it might mean for Germans. Workers in Würzburg greeted the news that Jews were being held very close to factory sites in Budapest with comments like 'the Hungarians are ahead of us; they're handling the issue the right way'. There were calls to hold Jews as human shields in German cities too. A string of letters to Goebbels survives from May and June 1944, advising the regime to inform 'the British and American government [sic] after every terror attack in which civilians are killed that ten times as many Jews and Jewesses and their children have been shot'. And a number of letter-writers explicitly argued that such measures should have the effect on the British and Americans which the 'new weapons' and 'retaliation' had so far failed to deliver. Irma J., who called on Goebbels 'on behalf of all German women and mothers and the families of those living here in the Reich' to 'have twenty Jews hanged for every German killed in the place where our defenceless and priceless German people have been cowardly and bestially murdered by the terror-flyers', also confessed to her own feelings of helplessness: 'because we have no other weapon available'. The underlying pessimism about German air defences was palpable, but so too was a strengthening commitment to resist.[73]

Listening to Hyperion's 'Song of Fate' or reading Jünger provided a glimpse into the abyss and a retreat into reverie, a safe haven in which readers could surrender – momentarily – and marshal their own inner, moral reserves. Hiding the war behind a veil of lyrical abstractions, this literary canon helped 'apolitical Germans' to reinvent themselves, unwilling to be preached to by the Nazi hacks, but at the same time blocking out the possibility that the war might confront them with immediate moral and political choices. Instead, they ransacked their cultural heritage to help bear its burdens.

13

Borrowed Time

At the end of May 1944, the Third Reich still controlled Europe from the Arctic north of Norway to south of Rome, from the Black Sea to the Channel ports. On 3 November 1943, Hitler had issued General Directive Number 51, requiring that the eastern front take care of itself while fresh troops and new supplies of weaponry were sent west. The Red Army had held the initiative since counter-attacking from the Kursk salient the previous summer, but this time all the German forces in the east pulled back much faster than they were being pushed, giving up huge areas of Ukraine in order to retreat behind the natural barrier of the river Dniepr. Hitler and his generals hoped that this new, fortified 'Panther Line' would hold the Red Army, while precious armoured and combat divisions were sent west to repel the Allied landing in Italy and to defend the coastlines of Greece and France. The Dniepr defensive line, Hitler told his generals in September 1943, was to be the last barrier against Bolshevism. The withdrawal began on 15 September.

Along the entire line of their retreat, the Germans set everything alight, using precious time and munitions to destroy as much as possible. Guarding the German retreat, Willy Reese felt 'torn apart by guilt', appalled by a 'scorched earth' policy far worse than the Germans' first efforts of 1941–42. He drank as he watched the villages and towns turned into a 'depopulated, smoking, burning desert covered in ruins'. At the same time, he wrote, the line of burning villages at night 'created magical images and so, with my old delight in paradoxes, I called the war an aesthetic problem'. Looting the villages for food and the German warehouses for alcohol, tobacco and new uniforms, the men turned the great retreat into an orgy of feasting, making 'grotesque speeches about war and peace', becoming melancholy and confiding their home-sickness and love worries. As they drank and danced in the cattle trucks carrying them westwards towards Gomel, they found a woman prisoner and stripped her naked to dance for them, smearing her breasts with boot fat and making her 'as drunk', Reese wrote, 'as we were'.[1]

Through that autumn and winter, the new Dniepr defensive position held, as Gotthard Heinrici deployed his scant forces with remarkable skill in the face of massive frontal assaults on the centre of the German line. The experience encouraged Wehrmacht commanders to believe that the seemingly inexhaustible reserves of the Soviets were finally running out and that their generals had learned little. Entrenched beyond Vitebsk, Mogilev and Pinsk, the Wehrmacht still occupied much of Belorussia and Ukraine, preparing for the inevitable attack once the summer had dried out the boggy ground. In the east, Hitler's directive acknowledged, the Germans could afford to sacrifice, 'if worst came to worst, even large losses of space without deadly danger to German survival'. In the west, they could not.[2]

Some of Germany's crack armoured units were kept in readiness in France. Huge quantities of steel, concrete and labour were devoted to fortifying the French and Belgian coast, which the German commanders in the west, Rommel and Rundstedt, toured to the cameras of the *Wochenschau*. Newsreels, radio and press repeated the mantra that the Atlantic Wall was 'untakeable' – some witty Viennese began to quip that so was their synthetic coffee – and the image of 'Fortress Europe' sheltering behind the sea bastions from the British and American air and sea 'pirates' convinced even sceptical German observers. The extraordinary reputations of Rommel and Rundstedt – neither a Nazi – in themselves inspired trust.[3]

In the relative quiet of spring 1944, for the first time in over a year, bombing gradually ceased to be the centre of conversations about the war; instead, complaints dwelled on the seasonal shortage of potatoes and fresh vegetables. The expected invasion in the west supplanted it. The Allies would choose the time and place, but hopes ran high that if they could be driven back into the sea, then it was unlikely that they would be able to launch another invasion in 1944, if at all. An Allied invasion appeared to offer Germans the most tangible prospect of regaining the initiative and turning the tables on their adversaries: if only they could be 'lured' on to the European continent, the British and Americans would be decisively defeated on the same ground as the French and British in 1940. It would be a fitting response to the destruction of German cities.

The overriding anxiety in the spring of 1944 was that the Allies would not take the bait, preferring the greater safety of continuing their long war of attrition. Behind the expectant optimism about the coming confrontation on the Channel coast lay an uneasy pessimism about the Reich's ability to withstand an air war of unlimited duration.[4]

★

On the home front, the SD's anxieties about social revolution had been superseded by new worries about sexual unrest; so much so that in April 1944 it filed a special report on the 'Immoral behaviour of German women'. The problem stemmed, its authors in the Reich Security Main Office opined, 'from the length of the war' and the fact 'that a large number of women and girls are ever more inclined to live it up sexually'. The wives of serving soldiers apparently led the way, with every town boasting well-known pubs where they went to meet men. Unmarried young women and teenagers were following their example: the SD pointed to rising rates of teenage pregnancy and sexual disease amongst 14- to 18-year-olds. These were classic grounds for sending girls to reformatories, and the SD confirmed that this was just what the Youth Welfare Boards in some cities were doing. The SD continued to worry too that German women were engaging in sex with foreign men, a slur on national honour even in those cases when it did not enfringe race laws. And they also worried about how children, neglected and left to 'run wild' themselves, were affected by their mothers making love to passing Germans in cramped cellar quarters with only the flimsiest of screens, sometimes no more than an umbrella. The SD was concerned about how news of their wives' infidelities would impact on the morale of husbands serving in the armed forces.[5]

Other impressions confirmed this picture. One of the men in Kurt Orgel's artillery unit came to seek his advice after receiving a devastating letter from his wife: 'Leave is blocked,' she had written:

Who knows when you can come? Perhaps not till after the war. I don't need to wait for you. I could have four men, if I wanted, at any time. I've had enough, I want it now too! Finally, I want to have a couple of strapping boys now too. At this moment I don't know what else to write!

Kurt told the soldier to let his wife go, pointing out to Liselotte Purper that 'What we demand of him, he can expect from his wife' – loyalty and steadfastness. But, as Kurt admitted, so many 'war marriages' had failed that the very term was used with cynical smiles and allusions. What, Kurt asked Liselotte, made theirs so different? Was it that others mistook sexual attraction for 'true, deep love'? Were other couples too young, or had they simply had too little time to get to know each other? But he did not dare ask how the war had altered things between Liselotte and himself. Liselotte had recently complained that she had been living 'like a nun' for the last six years. She had noticed that hardly anybody asked her about her husband. By 1944, even wearing a wedding ring in Germany was not a clear marker. 'Perhaps', she reflected, 'most people have bad experiences and prefer "not to ask".' Death and infidelity had made everything more complicated.[6]

Germany's moral guardians in the SD and the Catholic Church could broadly agree in their misogynistic diagnosis of sexual disorder. The SD urged withholding 'family support payments' from soldiers' wives who misbehaved and appealed to the military honour of soldiers not to sleep with the wives of comrades. They also demanded that the Propaganda Ministry 'de-eroticise' press, radio and film by getting rid of songs with 'erotic' couplets. But both the Nazi and Catholic guardians were floundering and did not know how to restore self-restraint. Their frustrations apart, in the context of early 1944 they were actually describing a society which was still managing to absorb the strains and tensions of total war. Its structures were largely intact, and expectations and aspirations for the post-war future remained modest, focused on finding homes, families and careers within local worlds to which the men at the front would one day return.[7]

The SD was also describing a problem which had grown partly through the German cult of 'love tokens', the official encouragement given to teenage girls to write and send parcels to unknown and unmarried young soldiers. 'Dear, unknown Miss Gisela! You will be quite astonished to receive mail from an unknown soldier and will rack your brains over how I came by your address,' began one letter in October 1943. Heinz was a young submariner stationed in Arctic Norway; Gisela a young woman in Berlin, still living with her parents. During the entirety of their four-year correspondence, they seem to have met only once, when Heinz finally got leave in June 1944. But the rest of the time they waited impatiently for each other, trying to work out when they could meet again, sending and receiving photos. He fixed hers to his bunk, his one bit of private space, 'so that I can always see you, when I get up and in the evening when I go to sleep, I have to see you. And then I can think, "Gisel is now thinking of me too".'[8]

Kurt Orgel and Liselotte Purper continued to write to each other love letters whose erotic content markedly increased as the frustrations of separation grew. They affirmed their commitment to each other and they promised to wait, continuing to put their 'real' life on hold. Dreams and fantasy came to their rescue. Kurt dreamed that he was walking along Liselotte's street in Krumke at night, when she and Hada appeared in the sidecar of a motorbike. He hugged them intensely before they could even get out – 'you can see how great my need for love is!' he commented. Kurt assured Liselotte that he found her far more attractive than Hada, whom he had still not met. When his letter arrived, Liselotte told him, she was sitting on the balcony of the country house – sunbathing and 'half naked'. Laughing at him and telling him that 'you don't have to be called Siegmund [sic] Freud' to read lots of meanings into the dream, she described one of her own:

> I dreamed last night about more super things than just sitting in a sidecar and waving . . . I beg for forgiveness, but last night another man took me in his arms and smothered me with kisses, though I did manage to protect myself gently all the same by telling him that I am married! (I didn't forget!)

Later that year, after a night working on a photo-story together, Hada and Liselotte each wrote to Kurt, pretending that he could see them through the eyes of his photo on the wall: Liselotte was warming her long bare legs against the tiled stove; Hada undressing for the night – 'and you didn't look at her the way a husband should', Liselotte wrote. 'Next time, you'll have to turn around or cover your prying eyes with a cloth.'[9]

Others were experimenting with different ways of expressing them-selves. Born in Bremen in 1926, Reinhard had spent his teens without his father, who was killed in 1941. He trained as a radio operator two years later and was then posted to the relative quiet of Hungary. From there he kept up a regular correspondence with six young women, who

all knew of each other and yet all wrote love letters to him. They wrote
of their 'many admirers', their disappointments and their flirtations
with others and imagined how 'dashing' he looked: 'I would so like to
see you in your uniform,' Eva flattered him. Ina pictured Reinhard in
his steel helmet as 'cute'. They quoted snatches of romantic film songs:
for Hannelore, training to be a nurse in Königsberg, it was hearing 'Girl,
I'm coming straight back / when the enemy is beaten I'll always stay
with you' on the radio that made her think of him. To them, the war
appeared even in 1944 more an adventure than a threat – having brought
them all greater freedom of a personal kind. Even the youngest of the
six, 16-year-old Ina who still lived at home, was in work, training to be
a secretary. They all smoked – though they meekly accepted his rebuke
– and made their own choices. Hannelore instinctively rejected the
advances of a French prisoner of war: although he was an officer, she
seemed alive to the injunctions to defend the honour of German women
without needing to say so explicitly.

Reinhard and his admirers did not quote political slogans or tell
each other to 'hold out', as older couples like the Guickings or Kurt
Orgel and Liselotte Purper did. And they spoke less of their longing
for peace. The search for privacy may have been 'apolitical' in its
indifference to official messages, but it was certainly not anti-war. The
correspondents accepted their obligations and moral duties, moulding
their self-images around the appealing 'soft' propaganda of popular
film and music with its combination of eroticism and gratification
deferred until the war's end. They had grown up during the war and
they treated it as a normal, almost natural, state of affairs: in the
spring of 1944, it afforded them the freedom to be young. Their play
at promiscuity would have shocked their parents – but it hardly resembled the spectre of moral dissolution painted by the SD.[10]

On Saturday, 5 February 1944, the post arrived at the little airbase
at Aschersleben, a town below the north-eastern escarpment of the
Harz, and, in the eyes of Hans H., deadly dull. The 23-year-old climbed
up on to his bunk to read the letters in privacy. When he had finished,
he began them all over again. Then he threw on his greatcoat and
walked in the woodland under the pale winter sun for an hour till he
reached a village station where he caught a train to another town.
Carefully avoiding all chance conversations, Hans managed to stay in
his unbroken reverie, finding a quiet café where he could dwell on his

girlfriend's letters. As he described it to Maria the next day, he could see with his 'inner eye' how she got up before dawn and travelled to the village station at Michelbeuern, where she worked in the ticket office and where she had to hide her own letters from Hans's father, the stationmaster. 'If I had only the inner eye to transmit impressions, then I'd only see beauty all day,' he promised. The railwayman's son from a village to the north of Vienna had a knack of drawing Maria close with the vividness of his imagination, putting himself in the scene near her, helping her to issue the tickets.[11]

Hans needed all his ability to woo her. Neither was certain of the other. Like most new couples, they began to cement their courtship by creating an instant store of memories: on 16 January, it was two weeks since their first kiss; by 23 July, it was already twenty-nine weeks. In January, Hans was seriously worried that it might not mean as much to Maria as it did to him: though her later kisses were freely given, that first time he had simply grabbed her and refused to let her go. She had not pushed him away but it was clear from his half-apologies that she had not responded either. And there was another problem: keeping the relationship a secret from his father, her boss. It could not be kept from his mother and sister, however, and by July, Maria felt that both his parents were giving her 'funny looks' and making 'loaded remarks'.[12]

With so few days together, snatched at the station in Michelbeuern on whose upper floors Hans's family lived, it was the thousands of kisses sent by mail which made their relationship real. Hans was cheered by songs broadcast on Sunday afternoons and hoped Maria might have heard Zarah Leander singing 'I Know There'll Be a Miracle One Day'. He was worried about his reputation as the village lover-boy, and assured Maria that military service had changed him for the better. Maria, who was two years younger, had had her share of local admirers too. Hans confessed that the very idea that he might lose her to someone who managed to avoid the army and stay at home was like 'theft during the blackout', and he vowed to Maria that if anyone 'goes and takes my girl from me, I'll kill him. I'll do him in like a Russian.' Although she suspected the village postmistress of steaming open and holding back Hans's letters to her out of spite, somehow Maria succeeded in evading the prying eyes of a small Austrian village. In old age, Maria confessed that she had also corresponded with nine other young men at the time. As with Reinhard's six female admirers, this was not so unusual when none of their futures was secure.[13]

After serving in Russia and then Italy, where his 2nd Paratrooper Division had seized control of Rome in September 1943, life on the airfield at Aschersleben was boring and Hans detested his comrades' taste in music. The young veterans were not keen to exert themselves in the menial clear-up work, where they answered to civilian engineers. At the end of May 1944 they were moved west to another airbase near Cologne, where Hans sunned himself and was deeply impressed by the stoicism of the population. He told Maria that the air raids on Vienna which she had seen from a distance were no worse than what the Rhinelanders had been enduring day and night for the last three years. Then, scarcely a week after he and his comrades had arrived at the Rhine, their division was sent to France.[14]

*

In May 1944, Lieutenant Peter Stölten stopped off in Paris, tramping from the Champs-Elysées to Montmartre, taking in Notre Dame and the Moulin de la Galette and washing down lobster with burgundy, followed by real coffee. He was part of the Panzer-Lehr Division which had just returned to the west after participating in the occupation of Hungary. It had taken seventy trains to carry the men and their equipment. The young, aspiring painter from Berlin was thrilled by the Parisians' sense of style and by the 'elegant world' which had long since vanished from German cities. Scarcely bothered by the string of air raid alarms, Stölten and his friend Hermann had explored the capital for fifteen hours before crashing into their beds; as they fell asleep, they kept repeating the enchanted city's name aloud, 'just like soldiers in a patriotic film murmuring the name of their loved ones on the battlefield'.[15]

Peter Stölten was almost two years younger than Willy Reese, who at this moment was being moved up to the front too. His unit quit the village of Jurkovasteno where he had spent several quiet months, sharing the bed of a Russian girl. 'It was hard,' he wrote in a letter to his uncle the next day,

> for all involved. The evening before, I lay with Klara in bed and comforted her till she fell into a troubled sleep, but when I kissed her goodbye yesterday morning, she cried all the same . . . the father

wished me luck and the mother blessed me – such people, and they are meant to be enemies? Never.

Willy Reese was headed for Vitebsk, the sector of the front he most wanted to avoid.[16]

Stölten and Reese had both started their military service at the same time, on the eastern front in 1941. A motorbike despatch rider with a tank division, Stölten was twice invalided out with suppurating boils, after which he succeeded in being admitted to officers' training, doing well enough to jump up the rungs from non-commissioned officer to lieutenant in short order. The year 1943 had seen him mastering Goliaths, which, belying their nickname, were in fact minature, remote-controlled vehicles loaded with high explosive which were used for attacking fortified structures. Having gone on to train with the most valued heavy tank, the Tiger, Peter Stölten gained entry into one of the most elite armoured divisions of the Wehrmacht, despite his lack of battlefield experience. Its 316th Company, which Stölten joined, specialised in using both Goliaths and Tiger tanks. From Paris, Stölten and his comrades were sent to the Département d'Eure-et-Loir in Normandy, where the division formed part of the armoured reserve of Rommel's Army Group B. Against a backdrop of old mills, chateaux and trees in full blossom, Stölten felt a pang of nostalgia and the old tug to get out his sketchbooks and settle into the landscape.[17]

On 5 June, the weather was so appalling in the English Channel that the Germans called off their air and sea reconnaissance. Having lost their long-range ability to monitor the weather out in the Atlantic, they did not know that a brief window was about to open into the storm. Into this the huge Allied convoys with their six battleships, twenty-three cruisers and eighty destroyers in attendance embarked that night. The landings depended on surprise, speed and concentration of force if the Normandy beaches were to be won from the superior numbers and firepower of the fifty-eight divisions of the Wehrmacht.[18]

Two days after the invasion began, Peter Stölten was in the thick of the battle with the British 2nd Army for control of Caen. Facing units of the British 7th Armoured Division in front of Bayeux, the Panzer-Lehr Division was exposed to bombardment from the ships at sea, field artillery and the massive bomber fleets which gave cover to the British and American landings. On 10 June Stölten wrote home to tell his parents that his few belongings had been shredded by aerial machine-gunners and that, with his stubble, he resembled the leader of a robber band. 'The responsibility is enormous. But everywhere, iron calm,' he wrote. Despite his three years of military service, it was Stölten's first full-scale battle, and calm nerves under fire became the guarantee that the line would be held. To their west, the 352nd Infantry Division had crumbled under the onslaught, opening a gap in the German line, which the British exploited, launching a flanking incursion into the rear and briefly occupying the village of Villers-Bocage before being driven back by a company of SS heavy tanks. The German line held, just.[19]

On 20 June, Stölten wrote home that 'We are still all very grave, but we are calm in a way that exists only on the western front. I don't have any cases with [bad] nerves.' In the same letter he reported that the day before he had participated in a failed counter-attack during which his own vehicle had fallen into a ditch, its gun pointing downwards, while he had watched helplessly as two of his closest friends were burned in their tank. He told his parents how another close friend had been 'shot up next to me' in his machine five days earlier.[20]

On 26 June, the American 7th Corps captured the heavily destroyed and, for now, unusable port of Cherbourg. Even so, Caen, one of the first objectives of the landing force, continued to block the Allied breakout from the Normandy peninsula. Controlling the Caen Canal and the river Orne as well as a road hub, it gave the Germans a defensive position while denying the Allies the flatter, less wooded land where they would be able to establish airfields. On 2 July, Peter Stölten learned that his division was being pulled out of the line and sent westwards to shore up the defence of Saint-Lô against the Americans. Complaining about the break in the fighting and relishing his buccaneering role, he treated his family to a cheerful turn of phrase worthy of Ernst Jünger, declaring that 'a life without exciting impressions has become unbearable for un-bourgeois like us'.[21]

It would take the British until 18 July to drive the Germans out of Caen, and the Americans would not capture Saint-Lô from the Panzer-Lehr Division until the day after that. Hemmed in by the high hedges and copses of this bocage country, both sides were constrained by poor manoeuvrability and visibility. By now, Peter Stölten was no longer in the front line: in early July, his company was withdrawn in order to rebuild another unit, the 302nd Panzer Abteilung. Set on staying with his comrades and defending heroically to the very end, Stölten objected strenuously and jumped on a motorbike to persuade his regimental commander to rescind this 'most senseless, stupid and upsetting order of my life'. He failed. On his furious ride back, Stölten crashed. '[Your] Son in field hospital, unfortunately not wounded … but result of accident', he wrote sadly and laconically home from the military hospital at Le Mans on 8 July.[22]

Shocked by the accident and afraid that he might lose his left eye, Stölten also feared that he would be court-martialled for his reckless-ness in riding a motorbike alone. He spent the first week in Le Mans lying in bed and imagining 'all eventualities from a penal battalion to prison to reduction to the ranks'. He also knew that the accident had let him escape almost certain death. When the colonel consigned the charges against him to the waste paperbasket, he could not rejoice. Instead, he told Dorothee how he and the group of young officers who had gone through training together had appraised their military situation at the beginning of the invasion and

> came to the sober and simple conclusion that none of us would draw his head out of the noose and that our lives were now over … And now that not one of these lieutenants is still alive and all the Tigers are missing, I know that only my accident … saved me from what we expected.

He also found the enforced break from the fighting difficult to bear, confiding to Dorothee that he needed the comradeship, the tension and the oblivion of the front-line.[23]

While Stölten was recuperating, the remnants of his proud division were slowly ground down by the overwhelming superiority of the 140,000 Allied troops attacking them. On 25 July, 2,000 Allied bombers flew in to pound the German positions in the most devastating demon-stration of airpower on the battlefield so far. The Panzer-Lehr Division lay directly in their path. By the time its shattered remnants were finally ordered back to Alençon for rest and refitting on 5 August, the division had virtually ceased to exist: it emerged from Normandy with twenty functioning tanks. After penning the American and British forces onto the Cotentin peninsula for six weeks, the rest of the German 7th Army now found itself virtually encircled in the Falaise pocket.

Peter Stölten's eyesight was saved and he was released from the field hospital in Le Mans. Convalescing in a hotel at Verdun, he was plunged into depression, plagued by a sense of guilt for his friends and no longer sure what he was fighting for. On 24 July, he wrote to Dorothee that the 'world' seemed 'hardly interesting any more, just monotonously sad and composed of an indescribable mixture of apathy and tension'. Two days later he told her that he hoped she would forget him, because 'I am ashamed that for a whole week I am just nothing, anything but a strength inside . . . It is so paltry what I can give you.'[24]

He found his release, not in his chosen métier of drawing or painting, but by writing feverishly into the night. He was composing not a diary or a memoir but a dramatic dialogue between three young men, all soldiers, and two young women. Giving two of the men the names of his dead friends, Theo and Karl, and one of the women the captivating vitality of his fiancée Dorothee, he let his characters argue out his own dilemmas amongst themselves. Karl got the best lines, claiming that there was neither God nor purpose in war, in men crawling towards their own death like flies towards a gigantic swatter. Theo took the opposite, religious stance, insisting that men fall back in awe of the mystery of the divine:

'My ways are not your ways, for as high as the heavens are above the earth, so are my thoughts above your thoughts.' All that we find and say bears the imprint of the limitations of man. But religious awe is the first step beyond the painful experience of man's boundaries: to want to know the infinite – but only to be able to know the finite.

In the character of Angelika, Stölten dwelt on Dorothee: 'Imagine yourself as a flower, which flowers, ripens, spreads its seed, withers and falls back to the earth.' Not surprisingly, it was Angelika's love of life which brought the three young men back on track, and led the quietest of the three, Michael, to make his impassioned plea for the transfiguring quality of human love. Only love could escape the physical and mortal confines of the human body: 'Love! It is the longing for a union with the better and the will to melt into the beautiful. In this feeling and will we want to learn to overcome the world like Empedocles.'[25]

Stölten admitted to Dorothee that he had made his literary challenge of giving meaning to war 'easy by giving the last, most important word to Hölderlin (not the Bible), and insuring myself with good odds'. If Stölten turned to the lyric poet's drama *Empedokles* for inspiration, it was Hölderlin's *Hyperion* which provided the measure by which Stölten had tried to live in Normandy: 'You are now put to the test, and must show who you are.' By the time his division had been destroyed and his closest friends killed, Stölten knew that the Allies enjoyed a technological superiority which the Germans could not expect to defeat: 'over time it is the material [advantage] that wins', he had written to Dorothee. He saw how profoundly the war had changed from the adventure which he – and his whole cohort of boys out of high school – had feared that they would miss out on in 1939–40. But in one key respect, he remained unchanged. He had been educated in the patriotic virtues of 'devotion', 'courage', 'readiness for action', 'self-sacrifice' and 'loyalty' – and these still held good.[26]

Raised in German pietism and educated in theology in Tübingen in the the late 1780s and early 1790s, Hölderlin had lost his faith. So too had Willy Reese and Peter Stölten, who turned away from the Catholic and Protestant churches of childhood. This had not turned them into materialists or nihilists, despite Reese's flirtations with Jünger. 'For it is certain', Stölten wrote in his dramatic dialogue, 'that one thing does not exist: nothingness.' These late-Romantic 'wanderers' remained fixated on their own spiritual journeys.[27]

★

On 19 June, while Stölten followed the Normandy battles from his field hospital, in Belorussia Soviet partisans went into action, laying more than 10,000 charges under the railway tracks west of Minsk. For the next four nights they returned, inflicting heavy damage on the tracks supplying the German front, between Vitebsk and Orsha, Polotsk and Molodechno, as well as those back towards Minsk, Brest and Pinsk. Although German rear units fought off many of the attacks, over a thousand transport points were severed, preventing the Germans from moving reinforcements and supplies up the line. They hampered the lateral movement of troops across the front as well as the retreat.

Mustering over 140,000 men, the 150 Soviet partisan brigades in Belorussia were amongst the most powerful resistance forces in German-occupied Europe and had survived large-scale efforts to clear them out of the forests. In the brutal struggle to control the rear, the German 9th Army had cleared entire regions, designating them 'dead zones' and forcing the adult population into mobile 'work camps'. By rounding up the children and holding them hostage in separate 'villages', the Wehrmacht prevented their parents from running away or joining the partisans. As the German occupation became ever more murderous – culminating in forcibly transfusing blood for the wounded from children – even local Belorussian collaborators and police units began to join the partisans. The German methods also had a military price: by committing significant forces to 'pacification' in the rear, the overstretched German armies no longer possessed reserves which could be rushed in to resist a Soviet attack.

During the night of 21–22 June the Red Air Force began bombing the German rear with relative impunity. As day dawned on the third anniversary of the 1941 invasion, Soviet reconnaissance battalions began to penetrate the German lines. Wehrmacht commanders were expecting the Red Army to renew their attack where it had proved most successful in the winter and early spring of 1944: either in the north, where the siege of Leningrad had been lifted and where the Red Army had begun an offensive against the Finns on 10 June; or in the south, where the German armies had been pushed out of the Crimea and far back across the Dniepr, so that they now lacked any natural defensive barrier to protect them. In confirmation of German expectations, the heaviest concentrations of Soviet armour remained in the south. But the main attack fell where the Germans least expected it: against Army Group Centre, which had defended itself so effectively during the autumn of 1943.

This time, Soviet commanders did not launch mass human-wave attacks on the German guns as they had done previously. They had lost too many men and Soviet generals had finally learned some key tactical lessons from the Germans. The way through the German minefields was opened by specially adapted tanks with ploughs attached to detonate the mines in their path. The infantry was protected and supported by tanks, self-propelled guns, artillery and bombers acting as an integrated unit. These were the tactics which the Wehrmacht had deployed so successfully in 1941, but now the Soviets enjoyed huge superiority in armour and firepower. The assault continued at night, lit by searchlights and flares.[28]

At a strategic level too, fundamental lessons had been learned. The main points of attack were carefully chosen and took the German High Command completely by surprise. At Bobruisk, Rokossovsky's 1st Belorussian Front used wooden bridges and causeways to attack through the seemingly impenetrable Pripet marshes, a flanking movement which brought them into the German rear. Meanwhile the Soviet 3rd Army broke through the German lines further north. It was the first time the Red Army had launched a classic German 'pincer' attack and the result was the destruction of the German 9th Army. Trapped in a pocket around Bobruisk, it was rapidly pushed into fighting for the ruins of the town itself. When the town fell on 29 June, the journalist and writer Vasily Grossman witnessed the results:

> Men are walking over German corpses. Corpses, hundreds and thousands of them, pave the road, lie in ditches, under the pines, in the green barley. In some places, vehicles have to drive over the corpses, so densely they lie upon the ground . . . A cauldron of death was boiling here, where the revenge was carried out.

Shelled and bombed in a confined area, some 50,000 Germans died. Another 20,000 were captured; only 12,000 men were able to escape westwards, abandoning almost all the weaponry.[29]

To the north, the breakthrough at Vitebsk and Orsha was no less successful, with Soviet forces crossing the Dvina river late on 24 June. By the 27th, both towns had fallen and Soviet commanders were in a position to pour fresh mechanised armies through the enormous gaps ripped in the German front line. As they rushed westwards to Minsk and secured the river crossings over the Svisloch, they bypassed the bulk of the German 4th Army, the pride of Army Group Centre, which was pinned down in a series of battles to the east of the city. By 4 July, it was trapped in just the kind of massive envelopment which it had meted out to Soviet armies in Belorussia three years earlier. And just as the Red Army's plight had been made worse by Stalin's repeated 'halt' orders in 1941, so on 27 June 1944 Hitler issued yet another stand-fast directive, refusing to let Bobruisk, Vitebsk, Orsha, Mogilev or Minsk be surrendered until it was too late to save most of the troops. Even if Hitler had been more flexible – and not mistaken the situation for the one his armies had faced in the retreat from Moscow in December 1941 – it is doubtful whether this could have saved Army Group Centre. Between 22 June and 4 July, it lost twenty-five divisions, more than 300,000 men. It would lose at least another 100,000 soldiers in the following weeks, dwarfing the defeat of Stalingrad by comparison, as the German death toll for the first time topped 5,000 for every day of fighting. Willy Reese met the onslaught on the Vitebsk sector and belonged to the large number of those officially listed as 'missing in action'; in the end, they would be counted amongst the 740,821 German soldiers who died on the eastern front in the second half of 1944.[30]

Lack of reserves meant that the Germans were unable to prevent the Soviets from exploiting their breakthrough. Rokossovsky's forces drove on from Minsk south-westwards along the few key roads across Belorussia to Baranovichi as well as north-westwards into the Baltic states. The Red Army liberated Vilnius on 13 July, threatening to isolate Army Group North on the Baltic coast. On that day, Konev launched his long-awaited attack on the two German army groups in the south, pushing them back into Hungary and Romania and deploying the full weight of his tank armies to drive towards Lwów, Lublin and the river Vistula in the west.

On 17 July, 57,000 German prisoners were paraded through the streets of Moscow in an unprecedented demonstration of the Soviet victories and mockery of the racist hubris of their enemies. But that summer, many Red Army units simply slaughtered their German captives before they could be registered as prisoners. A young Red Army woman recalled years later how she had watched the men of her unit hack their German prisoners to pieces with bayonets. 'I waited,' she remembered, 'waited long for the moment when their eyes would burst with pain. The pupils. You are appalled to hear that? Is it cruel? If a great fire had been lit in the middle of the village before your eyes and your mother thrown into it? Your sister? Your beloved teacher?'[31]

On 27 July, Lwów was finally liberated. Over the next three days, the 47th Army under Radzievsky raced on towards Warsaw from the south-east. In a final, exhausted flanking effort, the general sent his 8th Guards Tank Corps and 3rd Tank Corps to spring the city from the north-east. But when the two corps reached Wołomin on 30 July, they were pinned down by German counter-attacks. Warsaw was still 15 kilometres away, but the Soviet troops who had advanced 300 kilometres in five weeks – from the banks of the Dniepr and Dvina to the Vistula – were exhausted and outrunning their own supply lines.

On 1 August, the Polish underground armies launched an insurrection in Warsaw, catching the German garrison off guard. Attacking in full daylight at 4 p.m., the lightly armed insurgents failed, however, to capture key positions. To make matters worse, the rising quickly turned out to have been militarily mistimed. Within an hour of sending out the order for the uprising, General Bór-Komorowski, the commander of the Home Army, learned that the Soviet tanks that had been sighted at Wołomin were not about to liberate the Praga district on the eastern bank of the Vistula. It would take the Red Army until 13–14 September to take the Praga district. With bridgeheads over the Vistula at Sandomierz and Magnuszew, the Red Army could bypass Warsaw, rather than fight a costly battle to dislodge the Germans from the city. It was not obvious what the Soviets had to gain here.[32]

Bór-Komorowski, acting without the endorsement of the exiled Polish Government in London, had also miscalculated politically. The uprising was intended to present the Polish Home Army as armed liberators rather than passive spectators to a Soviet conquest. But the Soviets had already shown that they would not tolerate any independent, non-Communist forces when they had promptly arrested the Home Army units they found patrolling Lublin on 22 July. Having broken all relations with the Polish Government in London in the aftermath of the Katyn revelations, they were not predisposed to acknowledge their legitimacy now, and had installed their own puppet government, the 'Polish Committee of National Liberation'. There was no prospect that they would tolerate representatives of the London-based exiled government in Warsaw itself. Whether the Red Army was militarily ready to intervene more vigorously in the first weeks of the uprising is a moot question. As the uprising dragged on into September, it certainly could have done so. Instead, Soviet forces took the Praga district, occupying positions along the eastern bank of the Vistula; there they waited, while Stalin did his best to block British and American attempts to drop aid for the Poles from the air.

Having spent most of the war in the Polish capital, Captain Wilm Hosenfeld suddenly found himself on the commander's staff, experiencing active service for the first time since September 1939. On 4 August 1944, he wrote home, 'Till now I have not witnessed the horrors of the war. And that's why the experiences of these days have shaken me.' Two days later, he told his family that he expected the Poles to fight stubbornly, noting that 'even the deployment of tanks and heavy bombardment seems to have made no real impression on the rebels. When streets of houses are deliberately burned down and the civilian population flees somewhere, rebels occupy the rubble and go on firing. Anyone sighted on the streets is shot.'[33]

As an Army Intelligence officer, it was one of Hosenfeld's duties to interrogate Polish prisoners. During the first week the Germans did not take any. On 8 August, Hosenfeld noted in his diary that the Germans were clearing the civilians from the cellars as they retook parts of the city: 'yesterday only the men, in the days before also the women and children were killed'. In the Wola district of Warsaw, the Dirlewanger Brigade – a special unit composed of German professional criminals, poachers and SS men on probation – executed all the civilians it could find, from patients in hospitals to young children, accounting for 30,000–40,000 deaths. As Hosenfeld looked out from the headquarters at the 'long columns of civilians' being taken towards the western outskirts of the city, he recorded what a German police officer had told him: 'the civilians are to be sorted out. There is said to be an order from Himmler to kill all the men.' The commander of the SS units telephoned the commander of the 9th Army, asking, 'What should I do with the civilians? I have less ammunition than prisoners.'[34]

For the first time, Hosenfeld began to censor what he wrote to his wife and daughters, sparing them this particular detail, while trying to give them an accurate overall picture: 'From hour to hour the city is sinking through conflagrations and bombing into rubble. Streets of houses have to be systematically burned down. You have to close your eyes and your heart. The population is being destroyed pitilessly.' Struggling to establish a moral scale of comparison, Hosenfeld pointed out that 'countless German cities also lie in rubble!' In fact, it all reminded him of the biblical Flood, brought on by 'human sinfulness and pride'. Duty and red wine with each meal – the alcohol a new addition to his diet – were proving sufficient to relieve the stress for the time being: 'Come what may, I am in good cheer.' Meanwhile, the fighting itself had reached an impasse, neither side strong enough to dislodge the other. While most of the officers around him predicted that they would quash the uprising and then hold the Red Army on the Vistula, Hosenfeld remained convinced that the Soviets would soon sweep through the weakened German lines. He entrusted his valuable watch to a fellow officer on his way home to send on to his wife.[35]

On 21 August, Peter Stölten's 302nd Panzer Abteilung reached the outskirts of Warsaw, having been pulled out of Normandy and sent east. This was not a good posting for a young man who had just declared his 'will to merge with beauty'. As soon as he arrived, he wrote to tell Dorothee that 'the fighting is meant to be particularly hard – scarcely imaginable. Tomorrow', he added philosophically, 'we'll see.'[42] Within days of his arrival, Stölten was wounded again and six of his men were killed. One of their miniature Goliaths had detonated its cargo of high explosives near to his own command vehicle. A few days later, the same thing happened again and two more men were killed. 'The enemy fired at us, detonating a thousand kilos of explosives just three metres from my vehicle,' Stölten wrote home:

> I don't consider myself at fault. But it makes no difference. If you bring bad luck you'll be stigmatised, as if you really were guilty. It's a curse. You can see it in everyone's faces. After the explosion, I was lying for hours, blinded, among the groaning wounded. Now I'm safe and calm. I believe that ill fortune and responsibility educate a man.

Stölten felt this sudden loss of confidence even more keenly as he busily wrote letters of condolence to the families of his dead men.[36]

The cruelty and violence of the house-to-house fighting outdid anything Peter had seen before, he told Dorothee on 26 August, even the bombing of the German cities. But he felt able to write about 'the war in Warsaw, a heroic struggle of the Poles, only satirically and to a woman not at all'. He was not joking. Once again, he turned to writing to dramatise his moral crisis. Amid the battles, losses and anxiety of these first days in Warsaw, he somehow found the time to write a sixteen-page work which he called 'Satire – Jungle fighting'. Stölten sent it to his father, asking him not to show his writing to his mother, sticking to the code of sparing women details he found truly disturbing.[37]

Stölten's 'Satire' could not have been less like the elegiac dialogue he had written a mere five weeks earlier. The protagonists were a motley bunch, ranging from old German infantrymen, few with all their limbs intact, and German police units, occupied with 'setting alight the not

completely burnt-out house frontages again', to 'cossacks and auxiliaries
. . . their arms covered with bracelets and watches like the neck of a
female giraffe'. Looting was the order of the day, with 'soldiers of all
nationalities lugging every conceivable object around in bed sheets'. He
learned not to interfere with the Kaminski Brigade, who 'rape women,
cut off their breasts or throw them bodily out of the window!'

In the wake of Stalingrad, Bronislav Kaminski's unit of police
auxiliaries had been expanded into a 'brigade' of some 10,000–12,000
'volunteers', drawn mainly from camps for Soviet prisoners of war
and equipped with captured Soviet tanks and artillery; in June 1944,
the unit had been absorbed into the Waffen SS. The 'Eastern legions'
had grown in a similar way as the Germans relied increasingly on
foreign fighters to take over the bitter and brutal struggle against the
partisans. The 1st Cossack Division was formed in April 1943, the
Estonian SS Division in May 1944: by the end of the war, half of all
Waffen SS troops, some 500,000 men, did not come from the Reich.
Many – but by no means all – of the atrocities committed in Warsaw
were ascribed to such ill-disciplined units.[38]

As Stölten realised, the Germans were reconquering Warsaw thanks
entirely to their 'tanks, dive-bombers, anti-tank and anti-aircraft guns firing
horizontally, artillery, rocket-launchers' and 'above all, deserters who reveal
the entrances to the underground passages. Then a water main is ruptured
and all are drowned.' Or the Germans threw in Molotov cocktails 'and
let the bodies blow apart in the explosions'. Stölten modelled his prose
on the macabre, expressionist poetry of Gottfried Benn, but his 'Satire'
collapsed under the weight of his own shock. Horror-struck and
profoundly ashamed, Stölten was unable to maintain the lightness of tone
and ironic distance with which he began and dropped all self-censorship
about Warsaw, writing home about what the fighting was really like for
the first time. 'Those [Polish fighters] who surrender are shot – Bandits!
Shot in the back of the neck – the next ones lying down – shot in the
back of the neck!' Like Hosenfeld, Stölten witnessed the separation of
the captured civilians by sex before they were marched off, and he hinted
at yet further atrocities perpetrated on them: 'Some have also seen other
things – but that is no concern of ours – THANK GOD!!!'[39]

He did not want Dorothee, his mother or sister to see his satire,
but on 28 September, after five weeks of fighting in the ruins of the
city, he confessed to his fiancée:

One is accustomed to male corpses, they have long belonged to the natural order. But when you still recognise the once radiant beauty among the mangled remains of women, a completely different, loving, harmless life; still more, when you find children, whose innocence draws my most intense love even in the darkest hours irrespective of their appearance or language, . . . You will already see – and say I shouldn't and oughtn't to write about it.

Stumbling over his utter breach of self-imposed norms, he argued against those 'men who forbid their own and women in general from reading books about war' on the grounds 'that you also need to have your eyes opened and need to know the danger', implying already that what the Germans were doing in Warsaw others could perpetrate in Berlin. As he challenged his received notions of male and female roles in this war, Stölten noticed for the first time that such prescribed norms drew their validation from the 'aura of male heroism' in which he had grown up – and continued, in many ways, to believe.[40]

Wilm Hosenfeld also subscribed to the official description of the Polish insurgents as 'bandits' who forced the civilian population to shield them. More than Stölten, he claimed that the Wehrmacht had retained its honour in Warsaw and that all the worst deeds were committed by the Russian 'volunteers' in the Kaminski Brigade, or by the SS and police units. But, after watching German artillery set the cupola of a large church aflame, Hosenfeld relayed the shocking news that 1,500 people had been sheltering inside. He was also disturbed by the brutal treatment of female prisoners. On 27 August, three girls, mere high-school pupils, were brought in for interrogation for distribu-ting leaflets and maps. He hoped, Hosenfeld wrote home to his wife and daughters, that he could prevent them from being shot. He could get nothing out of the prisoners, and concluded that he lacked the 'mercilessness which is fitting here and is usually deployed'. All, he noted, had a religious medallion or a picture of the Virgin.[41]

Stölten enjoyed a brief respite when his commanding officer, an interior designer in civilian life, sent him off to find quarters in the finest apartments of central Warsaw, which he furnished with 'statues, sofas, Gobelin tapestries, etc.' 'Soon,' Stölten told Dorothee, 'every-thing will be burned.' In his temporary abode, he tried to replicate his parents' flat in Berlin's leafy neighbourhood of Zehlendorf and soon 'furnished a living room in the style of our dining room'. Ransacking the record collection, he danced through foxtrots, tangos, waltzes and polkas in the room on his own, accompanied only by the deep shadows cast by the light of a 1.5-metre beeswax candle. Beethoven also came to the rescue: Stölten was so moved by listening to the *Egmont* overture that he wrote to Dorothee suggesting that it should be broadcast 'instead of all the National Socialist speeches' – 'it is the source of strength'. In between the fighting he and his superior wandered through the half-wrecked apartments, their boots crunching on the glass, the air filled with acrid plaster dust, looking at the extraordinary artworks that had remained oddly intact. More than once, the two men picked up photos of a fair-haired child and found themselves saying in unison, 'Let's hope he is all right.' As Stölten began distractedly ripping the plates out of volumes of art history, hoping to preserve some small part of the cultural heritage of Warsaw from the flames, he became convinced that this was an urban culture which 'Germany really does not match'. It was an inversion of every-thing that Germans had been led to believe about Poles.[42]

After taking the eastern, Praga side of the Vistula, General Rokossovsky sent Polish volunteer units across on the night of 14–15 September, where they were mown down by the Germans, an action in which Peter Stölten took part. With no further assistance from the Soviets, no heavy weapons, far too few rifles, scant ammunition and food, the remaining insurgents stood no chance. The district of Mokotów fell on 27 September, Żoliborz three days later. On 2 October, after frantic negotiations to secure German concessions regarding the treatment of their fighters and civilians, the Polish forces in the city centre finally agreed to capitulate. All fighting ceased that evening.[43]

Both Wilm Hosenfeld and Peter Stölten witnessed the Polish surrender. As Hosenfeld stood and watched the 'endless columns of the insurgents', he was astonished by their

> proud bearing . . . Young people, only officers around my age, and not many of them . . . 10-year-old boys wearing their military caps with pride: they had done their duty as messengers and for them it was an honour to march into captivity alongside the men. Behind each squad of sixty men came the young girls and women . . . They sang patriotic songs and not one showed the terrible things they had gone through.

Throughout the sixty-three days of the rising, Hosenfeld had stuck to the official terminology, calling the insurgents 'bandits', describing the young female prisoners he wanted to save as misguided, and explaining all civilian support as coerced. Now that the German command had finally recognised them as a legitimate force to be accorded prisoner-of-war status, Hosenfeld felt free to express his full admiration: 'What national spirit is and in what true spontaneous form it can express itself, when a people has endured five years of undeserved suffering, that one could experience here.'[44]

Stölten was no less moved by the Poles' demonstration of 'unbowed national pride' as they marched into captivity, feeling that they had fully earned their military honour – 'for, God is my witness, they fought better than we'. After fighting in Warsaw for forty-two days himself, Stölten felt he was watching an event which 'put all the theatrical effects of a great tragedy in the shade'. Like Hosenfeld, what drew him to identify with the Poles was the fact that they manifested the values he believed in, in a purer, still more self-sacrificing form: 'We', he concluded, turning to the Germans, 'are still not the people that incorporates bearing and nationalism, sacrificial courage and strength.' The realisation that a defeated nation was still capable of heroic resistance also prompted him for the first time to see German occupation from the other side: 'I too would not want to live under German administration,' he wrote. Whereas on the battlefields of Normandy he had seen German 'spirit' vanquished by Allied 'matériel', here, he confirmed, it was German 'matériel' which had crushed Polish 'spirit'. Having lived in the conviction that national will and unshakeable faith would triumph over matériel adversity, he could not accept this obvious lesson. 'Is there any justice in history?' he asked Dorothee, falling back temporarily on a mystery which he had rejected out of hand a few months earlier in Le Mans: 'The thoughts of God are not our thoughts.'[45]

While Stölten's unit was sent off to defend the hamlets of East Prussia, Wilm Hosenfeld returned to the centre of Warsaw, where his old garrison regiment was ordered to turn the front-line city into a 'fortress'. The army and SS simultaneously busied themselves with fulfilling the Führer's order to erase Warsaw from the face of the earth. The entire civilian population was forcibly evacuated. Hosenfeld's first job was to take the German and neutral press on a tour of the ruins. It was the little things which brought the destruction home to him, like stumbling upon the piles of ruined costumes and musical scores in the rubble of the theatre. As he brooded on the destruction in his letters to Annemie, he asked, 'Is it any different at home? What might Aachen look like now?'[46]

Hosenfeld had trouble finding houses to serve as billets and offices for the regiment's new headquarters. While he was looking over a house in the Niepodległości Avenue on 17 November, Hosenfeld came upon the skeletal figure of a Jew searching for food in the kitchen – and, after hearing him play Chopin, helped him to hide in the attic. That night, as Hosenfeld lay awake in the dark, he imagined conversations with his dead comrades. 'It is incredibly comforting to speak with them,' he told his wife. 'I feel fully alive and held in this closed company . . . And then I see my loved ones at home, you and the children. I see the little ones asleep, the tired boys, the big girl and you with large, wakeful eyes looking into the night and coming to me.' He was careful not to mention that he was hiding a Jew in case his letters were opened by the censor. Hosenfeld had previously hidden Jews in the sports stadium he had run before the uprising; this one turned out to be a well-known pianist, Władysław Szpilman, and for the next few weeks Hosenfeld regularly brought food to him, while the garrison used the lower floors of the house as offices. Meanwhile, Wilm Hosenfeld's confidence returned and for the first time since the uprising had begun he felt that the Germans could hold the Soviets on the Vistula.[47]

*

The carpet-bombing of Peter Stölten's Panzer-Lehr Division near Saint-Lô on 25 July marked the beginning of the American breakout of the Normandy peninsula. After three days of battle, the over-stretched German divisions were unable to plug the gaps in their lines. As with the Soviet breakthrough in Belorussia, in Normandy too the Wehrmacht lacked sufficient mobile reserves to stop the Americans from developing enormous momentum. Avranches fell on 30 July and the next day the armoured divisions of Patton's US 3rd Army captured the bridge at Pontaubault and poured into Brittany.[48]

On 7 August, the US 8th Corps laid siege to the port city of Brest. With its harbour and U-boat pens, it was a major German asset and

Hans H. belonged to the 40,000 German troops defending it. The young Austrian paratrooper's morale remained high, as he wrote to Maria back in her ticket office in Michelbeuern: 'Now the Tommy is trying to kill us with bombs and artillery. But that doesn't bother us much cos we're sitting deep underground.' They had enough to eat and drink – although the forced march across Brittany had cost Hans his rucksack; he had lost all of Maria's letters, as well as his shaving gear and half a dozen socks. He was delighted to receive another eight letters from her in Brest. Writing back, Hans promised Maria that their love and luck would see them through: 'I won't let my courage sink. I have had luck, you are my luck-bringer. And I know you will continue to bring me luck.' Hans's letter left Brest by U-boat. It was to be his last. Brest held out for six weeks, and when it fell on 19 September, almost nothing in the city was left standing.[49]

On 15 August, the US 7th Army landed on the Mediterranean coast between Marseilles and Toulon under Major-General Alexander Patch. Whereas the best German forces had been concentrated in the north, in Army Group B, south-western France was occupied by the ill-equipped divisions of Johannes Blaskowitz's Army Group G. Hitler immediately accepted that Blaskowitz would have to retreat, if he still could, eastwards towards Alsace-Lorraine, or risk being caught in a pincer between the armies of Patton and Patch.

After a day of alarms and inexplicable delays, Ernst Guicking set off on 17 August, driving one of the last trucks transporting the 19th Army's field hospital no. 1089. At Avignon, the bridge was so badly damaged that, in order to reduce the weight, he had to leave half his load behind and then repeat the journey to Orange. Rumours of landings by paratroopers were rife, and the menacing air presence was constant. On 18 August he was stuck in the middle of another long bridge when it was bombed, and sat in his cab as he watched the bombs falling into the water. Along the road to Valence the column of vehicles carrying German wounded had to stop and fight off attacks by 'terrorists', as Ernst generally called the Maquis in his diary. Even now, in headlong flight from an overwhelming American force through hostile countryside held by the French Resistance, Guicking's charac-teristic confidence did not desert him. Having seen his first American prisoners and learned that they had come from Grenoble to try and cut off the German retreat at the Rhône, Guicking remained optimistic: they 'can only fire into the valley with artillery', he wrote. 'The infantry is too cowardly for open battle.'[50]

In the north, the German 7th Army was now caught in a pocket around Falaise. Surrounded on three sides, with only a narrow corridor to escape eastwards between Falaise and Argentan, the best German forces in the west were in danger of being completely encircled. Replacing Kluge with Walter Model – the 'fireman' who had just shored up the new defensive lines along the Vistula in the east – Hitler finally authorised a withdrawal. As many as half the remaining German forces, some 40,000–50,000 men, got through the gap before the British and Canadians were able to seal the pocket. They had to abandon almost all their armoured vehicles and heavy equipment. Between 10,000 and 15,000 German soldiers were killed. It was the first battle of encirclement that the Western Allies had fought since returning to the European continent and they were appalled by the carnage. When the Supreme Commander of the Allied Expeditionary Force, General Dwight D. Eisenhower, visited the battlefield on foot, he experienced a similar sensation to Vasily Grossman at Bobruisk, recording that it 'was literally possible to walk for hundreds of yards at a time, stepping on nothing but dead and decaying flesh'. Four days later, on 25 August, Paris was liberated.[51]

In the south, the Americans tried to cut off the German retreat eastwards and Blaskowitz's army group had to rely on just one armoured division, the 11th Panzer, to cover the entire retreat of the 1st and 19th Armies from Montélimar. The tanks kept the road open long enough for most of the German troops to get through. The 27th of August found Ernst Guicking in Lyons, delivering wounded to the field hospitals, avoiding shoot-outs in the streets with 'terrorists' and rescuing engine parts from the strafed wreck of a hospital bus. 'These swine take no notice of the Red Cross,' he noted, though in fact his diary entries showed that such attacks were still rare. Every day of his retreat was accompanied by visits from 'Jabos', fighter-bombers, but most of the time they merely buzzed overhead. Guicking somehow found time to send a parcel of tobacco and two letters home, the parcel via the trusted route of a soldier going home on leave, the letters through the normal field post, which still functioned at least in the major towns along the line of retreat.[52]

On 3 September, Ernst Guicking crossed the Rhône, driving through the town of Dôle – 'infested with terrorists' – in moonlight. Besançon, Vesoul, Champagne and Épinal followed. By Remiremont, the bearings on the front wheel of Guicking's vehicle were gone and had to be rebuilt out of scavenged parts. On 10 September Patch's and Patton's armies linked up, but the 11th Panzer Division continued to defend the German retreat. On 13 September, Guicking's little convoy reached the pass in the western Vosges which marked the Franco-German border, where they were greeted by waving Hitler Youths. Guicking and his comrades waved back. 'Now we stand on German soil,' he jotted down that day. 'A dreadful feeling.' Exhausted and depressed by their retreat, relieved to have escaped, the men fell asleep in their vehicles. In spite of all Allied attempts to outflank it, the last-minute retreat of Blaskowitz's army group had succeeded.[53]

In the north, Army Group B was also able to pull back, the last of its units crossing the Seine at the end of August. But it was no more able to defend the river barrier than the French and British had been when they had tried to regroup on the other bank of the river in June 1940. Brussels was abandoned by the Germans on 3 September and the key port city of Antwerp the following day. Now, as the Wehrmacht began falling back towards the German border, the German High Command ordered the hasty reactivation of the Belgian fortifications along the Albert Canal between Antwerp and Aachen and of the German West Wall from Aachen down to Trier and Saarbrücken. Instead of defending 'Fortress Europe' from the Channel to the Black Sea, the German armies had retreated beyond the former armistice line of Ghent–Mons–Sedan, which they had still held on 11 November 1918.[54]

Panic gripped Germany's western borderlands as the Allied armies swept onwards from Antwerp. Suddenly, the whole of the border from Aachen to Trier was becoming a front line. In early September, the weekly opinion reports to the Propaganda Ministry indicated that the mood of the German population had reached its lowest recorded point. Negative attitudes, 'concealed criticism' of the leadership and defeatist comments were on the rise. Indeed, morale was so low that Goebbels blacked the news of the first V-2 rocket attack on London, rather than risk frittering away its propaganda value. At the same time, the reporters to the Propaganda Ministry continued to claim that the population was not ready to 'throw in the towel' and risk enslavement; they wanted to know whether they could be defended. Given that the far stronger Atlantic Wall had not stopped the Allied invasion in June, what purpose, they asked, would the West Wall serve now? For many, it was merely a matter of whether the British and Americans or the Soviets would invade the Reich first.[55]

On 11 September, the first US troops crossed the German border, just south of Aachen. Tens of thousands of Germans had already fled eastwards, away from the approaching front. That day, Hitler gave permission for Aachen to be evacuated, and a further 25,000 people left the city over the next two days. Any semblance of an orderly evacuation soon broke down, and by late evening, local Party functionaries, policemen, fire brigades and even Gestapo officers were joining the exodus, instead of directing it. Similar scenes unfolded in Luxembourg and Trier. On a lightning tour of the area, Albert Speer found that Nazi officials pointed the finger at the army for the calamitous loss of France, accusing all officers of treachery. But, as he reported to Hitler, he was also struck by the contrast between the weary soldiers in the worn-out field grey and the strutting Party functionaries in their immaculate gold-braided uniforms.[56]

In Aachen, it was the Wehrmacht which restored order. On 12 September, the 116th Panzer Division – a once proud force reduced to a mere 600 men, 12 functioning tanks and no artillery – arrived just in time to halt the 'wild evacuation'. They directed tens of thousands of civilians still in the city to bunkers until they could be evacuated properly, cleared the streets and prepared to face the 3rd US Armored Division. By 13 September, when both Trier and Aachen were under artillery fire, ditches were still being hastily dug. The next day, Rundstedt, reinstated as Commander-in-Chief of the Western Front, proclaimed that the West Wall had to be held 'down to the last bullet and complete destruction'. On 16 September, Hitler turned the order into a general directive to all the armies in the west: 'Every bunker, every block of houses in a German town, every German village, must become a fortification in which the enemy bleeds to death or the occupiers are entombed in man-to-man fighting.'[57]

PART SIX

TOTAL DEFEAT

14

Digging In

In late August and September 1944, the Germans dug in, literally. Hundreds of thousands of civilians were sent out to dig trenches and build fortifications, a massive effort directed by the Gauleiters in their role as regional Reich Defence Commissioners. By 10 September, there were 211,000 civilians at work on the West Wall alone, mainly women, teenagers and men too old for military service. A further 137 units of the Hitler Youth and the Reich Labour Service, for which both young men and women were liable, were also sent to work. In the east, another half-million Germans and foreign workers were conscripted to dig. In September the theatres were closed across the Reich so that actors, musicians and stagehands could be drafted. While Goebbels tried to protect part of the film industry and Hitler constructed his own list of exceptional artists to exempt, in the Führer's adopted city of Linz actors and singers were enlisted in the SS and sent off to do guard duty at the nearby concentration camp of Mauthausen.[1]

Applying the lesson of the Soviets' bitter defence of Stalingrad, in March 1944 Hitler had designated Mogilev, Bobruisk and Vitebsk as 'fortresses', which 'will allow themselves to be surrounded, thereby holding down the largest possible number of enemy forces and establishing conditions for successful counter-attacks'. All three had been lost in the devastating defeats of the summer, but the model had worked better on the western front. Capturing Brest had cost so many American lives – and the port had been so badly destroyed – that the German garrisons were left in control of their other Atlantic ports at Royan, La Rochelle, St-Nazaire and Lorient. As the Wehrmacht fell back to the Vistula in the east, a further twenty towns were now designated as 'fortresses' in the eastern German provinces and in Poland. In Silesia, Danzig-West Prussia and the Wartheland, much of the work was done by forced Polish labour. In East Prussia, extensive fortifications dated back to before the First World War but had to be renovated and, where possible, re-equipped. Here the 200,000 Germans racing to finish that task before the autumn rains came complained about the coercive quality of the works. Criticism was mainly aimed at local Party officials who drove out to the sites in their immaculate uniforms and bawled out commands without venturing to pick up a spade and join in. Poor food, accommodation in barns on straw mattresses and excessive hours all took their toll, as German civilians got a mild taste of what they had inflicted on others. But the corvées of labour also renewed a sense of common endeavour, as restaurant waiters and students, printers and university professors trooped out of cities like Königsberg to pick up shovels. By the end of the year, their number had risen to 1.5 million.[2]

The collecting drives for Winter Relief, summer camps and communal stews had long prepared Germans for such an effort. Years of war had completed the training in shared sacrifice. In Lauterbach, Irene Guicking wrote to her husband Ernst, 'I would so like to set a good example going forwards. I am convinced I would shame the others.' But looking after two small children left her wondering 'what I should do so as not to be left on the margins in the total war drive'. At least the German retreat from France meant that her husband could no longer be tempted by the elegant French women. The hills of the Vosges looked so close on the map in her atlas and, gazing at it several times a day, she mused, 'Just a bit further east and you will be behind the protective border. You know, it must be a funny feeling to know that the border of the Reich is near.'[3]

It was a time of exceptional measures. In mid-July, Goebbels still felt thwarted by Hitler's reluctance to impose 'total war' measures on the home front. But on 20 July 1944 Hitler's attitude changed, after he narrowly survived an assassination attempt. A bomb planted by Colonel Claus Schenk von Stauffenberg went off in the conference room at his field headquarters in East Prussia, fatally wounding three officers and the stenographer. Like most of the twenty-four people in the room, Hitler suffered a burst eardrum and blast injuries; otherwise, he escaped unscathed. A profound weakness in the conspiracy lay in its lack of high-level support. Whereas in Italy in July 1943 there had been clear consensus within the military that they had to oust

Mussolini, no such view had crystallised in the Wehrmacht. Indeed, although they tested out many senior officers, most of the conspirators were officers of mid-rank.

Its organising brain was Henning von Tresckow, who used his role as chief of operations on the Staff of Army Group Centre in 1942–43 to have men like Rudolf Christoph von Gersdorff, Carl-Hans von Hardenberg, Heinrich von Lehndorff-Steinort, Fabian von Schlabrendorff, Philipp and Georg von Boeselager and Berndt von Kleist placed in key positions there. Linked by a web of aristocratic family connections, these younger officers were both held back and tolerated by senior commanders such as Bock, the uncle of Tresckow's wife, and by Bock's successor as commander of Army Group Centre, Field Marshal Günther von Kluge, who vetoed their plan to assassinate Hitler when he visited the Smolensk headquarters in March 1943. The plotters failed to win over any high-level military commanders, with the exception of Erwin Rommel and the military commander in France, Carl-Heinrich von Stülpnagel. This lack of support and comprehension was still more evident lower down the chain of command: the conspirators might have been well connected but they were always an isolated minority.[4]

The plotters attempted to circumvent their weakness by misappropriating an operational plan, code-named 'Valkyrie', which had been designed to suppress internal disorder, such as a coup attempt or an uprising by foreign workers, by automatically ordering military units under the command of the Reserve Army to surround government buildings in the capital. It was a fairly flimsy plan. It only took one loyal major, Otto-Ernst Remer, to question the *raison d'être* of his deployment for the plot to collapse. When Remer went up to arrest Goebbels, he was put through on the telephone to Hitler, whose voice he recognised, and the major immediately accepted responsibility for crushing the plot whose unwitting instrument he had been made. By the early evening of 20 July the rest of the coup attempt had unravelled: the key conspirators were either dead, under arrest or frantically trying to destroy evidence that might implicate them. Remer and his men reached army headquarters in the Bendlerstrasse in time to provide the firing squad. Stauffenberg was in no doubt that his contemporaries would not understand their actions, explaining that he was acting 'in the knowledge that he will go down in German history as a traitor'. Among his contemporaries, he was not wrong.[5]

News of the attempted coup broke at 6.30 p.m. with a short radio announcement. Then, just after midnight, Hitler's baritone voice – measured, if slightly breathless – could be heard. 'German national comrades, I do not know how many times now an attempt on my life has been planned and carried out,' the Führer began. 'If I speak to you today it is, first, in order that you should hear my voice and that you should know that I myself am unhurt and well; second, in order that you should know about a crime unparalleled in German history.' He went on to tell how 'a very small clique of ambitious, irresponsible, and at the same time senseless and criminally stupid officers have formed a plot to eliminate me and, with me, the German Wehrmacht command' and to reassure the nation that 'I myself am completely unhurt. I regard this as a confirmation of the task imposed on me by Providence to continue on the road of my life as I have done hitherto.' Hitler promised to 'exterminate' the perpetrators. The six-minute-long speech and those by Hermann Göring and the Commander-in-Chief of the navy, Karl Dönitz, which followed straight afterwards, were re-broadcast throughout the following day. They came as an earthquake.[6]

In Berlin-Zehlendorf, Peter Stölten's father expressed his shock tersely, writing to his son, 'How can they endanger the front so?' In his diary, he expressed his thoughts more fully: 'It looks as if they regard the war as lost and want to save what can be saved or what appears salvageable to them. But the whole thing . . . can only lead at this moment to civil war and inner division and create a new stab-in-the-back myth.' It was a measured response, and he was not alone in fearing defeat or even civil war. According to the SD report from Nuremberg, even those who were critical of the Nazis were convinced that 'only the Führer can master the situation and that his death would have led to chaos and civil war'. This local report added an interesting note of candour: 'Even the circles which have looked favourably on a military dictatorship are convinced by the more than dilettantish preparation and execution of the coup that generals are not equipped to take over the helm of state in the most serious of times.' Clearly, the loose talk about regime change from the summer of 1943 was over. In the streets and shops of Königsberg and Berlin, women were said to have burst into tears of joy at news of Hitler's survival: 'Thank God, the Führer is alive' was the typical expression of relief.[7]

The Propaganda Ministry and the Party rushed to organise 'spontaneous' rallies and thanksgivings for Hitler's 'providential salvation'. But the huge turnouts and effusive expressions of gratitude seem to have been genuine enough. Even Catholic bastions such as Paderborn and Freiburg, where the Party had previously struggled to hold public rallies at all, recorded unprecedented numbers. Families wrote to each other en masse expressing their relief and joy at Hitler's miraculous escape: no military censor or propagandist could force them to do so. The Allies, applying 'scientific' techniques to measure the success of their own propaganda amongst German prisoners of war, found – to their dismay – that trust in Hitler's leadership rose from 57 per cent in mid-July to 68 per cent in early August. By this stage, the regime did not make the mistake of confusing such trust and relief with confidence in Germany's military position. As the President of the Nuremberg provincial court reported, 'that the *mood* of the people is very gloomy is no surprise given the position on the eastern front'. But the crisis had a galvanising effect. All the reports confirmed that people expected that 'now finally' all obstacles to full mobilisation for total war would be swept aside.[8]

Army Group Centre, from which many of the plotters came, had just lost half its divisions in the huge encirclement battles in Belorussia. The regime was not slow to attribute the defeats to the treachery of these officers. According to the SD reports, 'national comrades' now looked admiringly at Stalin's 1937–38 purge of the officer corps of the Red Army, passing comments such as 'Stalin is the only clear-sighted one among all the leaders, the one who made betrayal impossible in advance by exterminating the predominant but unreliable elements'. The resolutely plebeian Robert Ley promptly amplified such sentiments in an article in the house paper of the German Labour Front, in which he ranted in terms he had previously reserved for the Jews:

Degenerate to their very bones, blue-blooded to idiocy, repulsively corrupt and as cowardly as all base creatures, this is the clique of nobles which the Jew sends forth against National Socialism, arms with bombs and turns into murderers and criminals . . . This vermin must be exterminated, destroyed root and branch.

Ley's tirade remained the exception, and Goebbels instructed the press to be careful not to attack the officer corps as a whole. Hitler had called the conspirators 'a very small clique' – and so they were. They had lacked the support of any major part of the German state: although many of the plotters came from the army and the Foreign Office, the senior ranks of both institutions remained firmly loyal through the crisis.[9]

In its aftermath, Hitler relied not just on out-and-out Nazi generals, like General Ferdinand Schörner, the new commander of Army Group North, but more 'apolitical' figures such as the veteran tank commander Heinz Guderian, whom he had immediately appointed as his new Chief of General Staff on 21 July. The ageing conservative nationalist Gerd von Rundstedt was recalled too, first to chair the officer corps's purge of its own ranks, and, in September, to take command of the western front once more – this, despite having been dismissed at the beginning of July for telling the High Command that the Allied invasion could not be halted. Despite his deep distrust of the military caste in general and the General Staff in particular, Hitler still knew how to use the loyalty and skills of these men. There was even room for General Johannes Blaskowitz, who had been sacked from his Polish command in 1940 for repeatedly challenging the atrocities carried out by the SS. In the aftermath of the July assassination attempt Blaskowitz had pledged 'after this dastardly crime to rally to him [the Führer] yet more closely'. Having proved himself during the retreat from southern France, Blaskowitz was entrusted with commanding Army Group H in the Netherlands: with the British in Belgium, it was vital to prevent them from bypassing the Rhineland defences by swinging through the southern Netherlands and into northern Germany. Blaskowitz would repay Hitler's confidence in full.[10]

When Schörner took command of the 500,000-strong Army Group North in Estonia and Latvia, he issued orders which reflected Hitler's own apocalyptic views, insisting on the absolute necessity of stopping the 'Asiatic flood-wave' of Bolshevism. To halt the German retreat and the desertion of Latvian auxiliaries and to instil obedience through fear, Schörner meted out unprecedented numbers of death sentences for cowardice, defeatism and desertion. For the first time German soldiers did not just face the firing squad. Increasingly Schörner's command ordered that the condemned should be hanged, with

demeaning placards attesting to their crime for all to see: a 'dishon-
ourable' death which had so far been reserved for Jews and Slavs. But
Schörner was merely an extreme exponent of a growing trend, as
Wehrmacht commanders fought to stop their armies from breaking.
Even the pious Protestant Blaskowitz turned to draconian methods
to halt mass flight. He too would have increasing numbers of his own
soldiers shot during the coming months for desertion. On 31 October,
Rundstedt proposed placing the relatives of deserters in concentration
camps and confiscating their property – so far a measure which had
only been used against a handful of families of the July plotters, with
most of their wives and children being released within a few weeks.[11]

Although this principle of family liability was also canvassed by
other senior generals, the widespread introduction of the policy was
ultimately thwarted, and from an unlikely quarter. The SD, the institution empowered to take family members into custody, refused to
operate a system of collective reprisals against Germans. Instead of
immediately resorting to such measures on the German home front,
the Gestapo and SD continued to weigh its decisions on the basis of
individual assessments of 'character'. In Würzburg, for example, the
Gestapo refused to act against the parents of a soldier who had deserted
on the Italian front because it found no evidence that they were 'anti-
National Socialist'; after dragging out the investigation for nine
months, the Gestapo closed the case. Despite new levels of coercion,
the Nazi regime was still not ready to deploy at home the techniques
of indiscriminate mass terror it had pioneered in occupied Europe.[12]

In other respects, the Nazi leadership emerged from the bomb
plot imbued with a more radical sense of purpose, as the most
ruthless and efficient group of leaders now formed a virtual
'quadrumvirate'. With more and more responsibility for the defence
of the German regions given to the Gauleiters, Martin Bormann's
control over the Party machine made him a key player. Now adding
the command of the Reserve Army to his control over the Interior
Ministry, police and SS, Himmler had a near-complete monopoly
over the means of coercion within the Reich. Goebbels finally became
Plenipotentiary for Total War, a role he had coveted since early 1942.
He was now able – at least in principle – to give a new impetus to
setting the needs of the civilian economy and cultural consumption
aside in favour of unchecked mobilisation for the defence of the

Reich. The fourth member of this inner group was Albert Speer, the Minister for Armaments, whose abilities in getting the most out of inadequate resources would be tested as never before. With Hitler focused ever more on micromanaging his military commanders, these four key leaders – all inclined to expand into the others' spheres of control – would be forced to run the home front in competitive collaboration.[13]

In August, the Hitler Youth leader, Artur Axmann, issued a call for boys born in 1928 to volunteer for the Wehrmacht. Whole cohorts of Hitler Youths answered the summons and within six weeks 70 per cent of the age group had signed up. Parents may have viewed the call-up with horror, but few tried to stop the teenagers from going. In the earlier years of the war, especially after the victories in the west, military recruitment offices had been besieged by teenagers desperate to sign up and do their bit for the Fatherland; for many this sense of patriotic adventure continued into 1945. Then on 25 September a new people's militia was announced, the Volkssturm, its name a populist merging of the romantic tradition of the 1813 'War of Liberation' against Napoleon and the traditional Prussian militia, the Landsturm. As military strategists in the 1920s had examined Germany's failure to make a 'last stand' in 1918, there had been calls for just such a 'total mobilisation' of the civilian population. Unlike Axmann's earlier appeal for volunteers, however, recruitment for the Volkssturm was not voluntary, and by the end of 1944 parents were being threatened with legal sanctions if their sons did not enlist. But these threats affected a small minority: by that time most Hitler Youths had already volunteered. As call-up was extended to boys and men between the ages of 16 and 60, the Gauleiters were entrusted with raising this final levy to form a militia numbering up to six million. Its potential reservoir was even larger: if every able-bodied German man had been called up, the Volkssturm would have grown to 13.5 million – greater in size than the Wehrmacht with its 11.2 million officers and men.[14]

The Volkssturm levy, intended to help make good the losses the army had sustained that summer, was simply too large to be equipped. Indeed, the Wehrmacht itself was short of 714,000 rifles in October 1944. At a monthly output of 186,000 standard infantry carbines, German production could no longer keep pace with the ambitions of this 'rising of the people'. By the end of January 1945, the Volkssturm had managed to accumulate a mere 40,500 rifles and 2,900 machine guns: a heterogeneous array of mainly foreign and out-of-date weapons, often with little, if any, compatible ammunition, giving recruits little chance to practise with live rounds. While more effort was lavished on inducting the teenagers as future soldiers, who were sent to separate training camps, far less went on the middle-aged men, who were treated as cannon fodder; few of them received more than ten to fourteen days' training. Improvisation was the order of the day: the quadruple batteries of 20mm anti-aircraft guns were frequently converted to infantry use, machine guns from planes remounted on tripods and even flare pistols used for firing grenades.[15]

The flak auxiliaries already included 10,000 women volunteers from the Nazi Women's Organisation, who ran messages and worked the searchlights and radar guidance systems of the heavy batteries. As boys headed off to train for the Volkssturm, their anti-aircraft positions were often taken over by girls from the BDM and Reich Labour Service. Unlike the smart attire worn by the women already posted to the military telephone exhanges and typing pools, this new levy of female recruits simply inherited the oversized uniforms left by their male forerunners. Now, as German women put on pistols to defend their gun emplacements, the myth that German men 'out there' were protecting women and children 'at home' completely crumbled. In 1941, audiences at home had unhesitatingly seen the 'Bolshevik gun-woman' as a freak against nature and a perversion of women's vocation to nurture. As German women broke this final cultural barrier, it hardly seemed remarkable any more.[16]

The establishment of the Volkssturm also sat uncomfortably with Nazi measures to protect Germany's children: what was the point in evacuating them from the cities, only to send them out against tanks on bicycles with a brace of anti-tank grenades strapped to the handlebars? With the nation's future at stake, service and sacrifice became the overriding virtues. The new Commander-in-Chief of the Reserve Army and of the Volkssturm, Heinrich Himmler, told military recruiters why they should share his determination 'to send 15-year-olds to the front': 'It is better that a young cohort dies and the nation is saved than that I spare a young cohort and a whole nation of 80–90 million people dies out.' Hitler had warned in his decree establishing the Volkssturm that the enemy's 'final goal is to exterminate the German people' and now his political *idée fixe* that 'there must never be another November 1918' had been put to the test.[17]

As girls as well as boys took their military oaths, after the parade-ground ceremonies the immediate problem was to find uniforms and equipment. In the Rhineland, 15-year-old Hugo Stehkämper and his comrades were given pre-war black SS uniforms, brown Organisation Todt coats, blue Air Force Auxiliary caps and French steel helmets. Across the country, the stores of the Wehrmacht, police, railways, border guards, postal service, storm troopers, National Socialist truck drivers, the Reich Labour Service, the SS, the Hitler Youth and the German Labour Front were all turned over to provide uniforms for the Volkssturm. What made this quest all the more important was the fear that members of the Volkssturm would otherwise be shot as 'irregulars', in the way Germans had executed Polish volunteers in 1939.[18]

The regime also realised that the Wehrmacht could learn about ideological control from the Red Army, and in the autumn of 1944 rapidly expanded its own – rather weak – version of political commissars, the National Socialist Leadership Officers. These were volunteers who took on the role of part-time morale-raiser and educator alongside their normal military duties, but they lacked the authority to countermand superior orders. One of the new volunteers was August Töpperwien. Although the high-school teacher from Solingen detested the anti-Christian thrust of Nazism and was appalled by the murder of the Jews, like many other Protestant conservatives Töpperwien still counted 'world Jewry' amongst Germany's enemies. As early as October 1939, he had divided Europe into three blocks, 'the Western democracies, the National Socialist centre and the Bolshevik east', and concluded that only Germany would have the determination to defend European culture from 'Asiatic barbarism' – this at a time when Germany was allied to the Soviet Union. Believing that 'World Jewry' had corrupted the Western democracies, his analysis foreshadowed Goebbels's later propaganda, but Töpperwien was no Nazi. His views stemmed from conservative nationalism, with its own anti-liberal, anti-Semitic and anti-socialist precepts. Moreover, Töpperwien shared one other fundamental tenet with many of the senior Wehrmacht commanders, like him all veterans of the First World War: he remained committed to preventing any repetition of the revolutionary disintegration of 1918. In October 1944, as the German front lines stabilised again, he noted proudly in his diary, 'But thank God, the spirit of revolt is still far off!' Töpperwien had periodically expressed doubts in Hitler's leadership throughout the war, but by early November he admitted to himself that 'The clearer it becomes that Hitler is not the God to whom people prayed the more I feel bound to him.' As Töpperwien worried about people's loyalty to the German cause, he realised that there was no room for any other leader than Hitler: he might not be a messianic saviour, but no one else could now save Germany.[19]

Another unusual volunteer for the new propaganda role within the Wehrmacht was Peter Stölten. He had, he quipped to his mother, become 'one of the Doctor's [Goebbels's] boys'. By the end of 1944, their number had swelled to 47,000 officers. The prime task of these part-time 'political commissars' was to educate their men in an 'unconstrained will to destroy and to hate' the enemy. Stölten was certain that the Soviets had to be stopped at all costs. Despite his growing conviction that the war was lost, he forbade himself from doing anything to hasten that result. On the contrary, he admired the Polish fighters in Warsaw for the lesson they had provided in heroic self-sacrifice. He assured his fiancée Dorothee that he had not lost his 'inborn aversion to NS-sloganeering' and left 'all the information sheets' unread and 'just improvised', but his talks may have been all the more credible for not sounding hackneyed; after all, they came from a tank commander with an impressive record of front-line service.[20]

Stölten was not alone in looking to the Poles for an example. Even Heinrich Himmler, entrusted by Hitler with wiping Warsaw from the map, now turned to the Polish 'Untermenschen' for inspiration, telling an audience of Party, military and business leaders that

> Nothing can be defended so outstandingly as a major city or a field of rubble . . . Here we must defend . . . the country . . . The saying 'till the last cartridge and bullet!' must be no idle phrase, but a fact. It must be our sacred duty to ensure that the sorrowful and costly exemplar which Warsaw gave us is enacted by the Wehrmacht and Volkssturm for every German city which has the misfortune to be encircled and besieged.

The comparison was not a hyperbolic one. That autumn, under Guderian's guidance, German military strategy on the eastern front shifted away from digging continuous entrenched lines, like the positions so recently abandoned along the river Dniepr. Instead, military engineers were using their corvées of civilian workers to turn key cities such as Warsaw, Königsberg, Breslau, Küstrin and Budapest into strongpoints. They were to become the 'fortresses' that would hold back the Soviets the way that Moscow and Stalingrad had stopped the Wehrmacht.[21]

★

Into October 1944, the new defensive lines held and, against all expectations, blocked the advance of both the Soviets and the Western Allies into the Reich. Partly because of the Wehrmacht's strong position in the southern Vosges, it was not easy for Patton's force advancing on the Saar to link up with Patch's troops in Alsace. The British and American armies also struggled with their own logistical bottleneck: all supplies were still being shipped by road from Normandy and Marseilles. Although the port of Antwerp had been captured on 4 September, before the Germans could blow it up, the Wehrmacht controlled its harbour mouth until November. While the Allies concentrated on reopening Antwerp and shortening their supply lines, the Germans re-equipped the West Wall and began to mass their divisions on the western front.[22]

On the eastern front, in early October the Red Army suddenly turned its northern assault across the marshlands, rivers and tough defences protecting Army Group North in the Baltic states around to the west. As Soviet troops crossed the pre-war German frontier for the first time, penetrating the East Prussian district of Gumbinnen and taking the town of Gołdap and the village of Nemmersdorf, they also cut off thirty German divisions on the Memel peninsula. Scratch units of the new, East Prussian Volkssturm managed to hold the Russian advance around Treuburg, Gumbinnen and along the Angerapp river until mobile reserves could move up to give them support. Then, in mid-October, the Wehrmacht counter-attacked in East Prussia, threatening to encircle the Soviets and forcing them to retreat to the border. With Berlin still over 600 kilometres away the

Red Army's summer offensive had come to a halt along the Vistula and the line of the Carpathians.[23]

Compared to the mass panic which had gripped many of its units on the western front in September, a month later the Wehrmacht presented a very different opponent. Allied commanders were shocked by the stiffening resistance of an enemy that they had assumed was on the point of collapse. At Supreme Headquarters of the Allied Expeditionary Force, Eisenhower called a crisis summit in November to ask why nothing had destroyed the 'will of the Wehrmacht to resist'. The psychological war experts, responsible for debriefing German prisoners of war and profiling their beliefs, were at a loss to explain it. Earlier in the year they had been similarly baffled as the Allies slowly fought their way up the Italian peninsula: there too the morale of their German prisoners had kept rising, the complete oppos-ite of what they had predicted and hoped. Asked if they believed in the existence of 'new weapons', in October 1943, only 43 per cent of prisoners had answered in the affirmative, but by February 1944 that proportion had risen to 58 per cent. After the initial shock of the Allied landings in southern Italy, German morale had stabilised. Now, Eisenhower was told, at least half of the captives on the western front still displayed 'loyalty to the Führer' and spoke confidently of the Red Army as a spent and defeated force.[24]

It seemed clear that the findings in Italy were now being replicated on the western front. In late August and early September, while ordinary German infantrymen were downcast, morale remained high amongst the core cadre of junior officers, not to mention elite formations such as paratroopers and Waffen SS divisions. But even before German resistance at the front stiffened, most of the prisoners being questioned affirmed the absolute necessity of national defence and the righteousness of their cause. Allied insistence on Germany's 'unconditional surrender' and the leaking of the Morgenthau Plan to strip Germany of all industrial capacity played a part; but the most important factor, now as ever, remained the fear of conquest by the Russians. The exiled novelist Klaus Mann was one of those German-speakers in the US Army tasked with debriefing prisoners of war on the Italian front. In late 1944, he asked his New York publisher: 'Why don't they finally stop? What are they waiting for, the unfortunates?

This is the question which I don't just ask you and me, but always pose to them too.' Other Western experts were equally baffled. Henry Dicks, a veteran of the Tavistock Clinic and the leading British Army psychiatrist, who had interviewed hundreds of German prisoners and written the standard analysis of their outlook, now took refuge in the rather vague concept of the 'German capacity for repressing reality'. What neither Klaus Mann nor Henry Dicks considered was that, in the absence of a separate peace in the west, German troops considered blocking the British and Americans as essential to holding the Soviets in the east.[25]

In mid-October 1944, the Western Allies could not be sure whether the stiffening German resistance amounted to a temporary pause or a real change in the balance of forces. Military historians now know that the defeats of the summer had ripped the Wehrmacht apart, its fighting power sapped beyond recovery. In the three months from July until the end of September, German military deaths reached a new peak of 5,750 per day. The Army High Command knew in part how disastrous the summer had been – and it was Guderian who first suggested raising an East Prussian Landsturm. Even with bitter fighting in the west, it was on the eastern front that the real haemorrhaging had occurred: 1,233,000 German troops died there in 1944, accounting for nearly half the German fatalities in the east since June 1941.[26]

At home, Goebbels's highest priority as Plenipotentiary for Total War was to 'comb' men out of the civilian economy for military service. By the end of September, 500,000 extra men had been called up; by the end of December, the number had doubled. Exercising his new powers as commander of the Reserve Army, Himmler ordered that all men who had become detached from their units – irrespective of whether they belonged to the Wehrmacht, the police, Waffen SS, the Organisation Todt or the Reich Labour Service – were to be turned over to the Replacement Army. Meanwhile, Party leaders at local, district and Gau level were busy rounding up 'stragglers' and sending them back to their units: by mid-September there were 160,000 of them. While none of these measures could compensate for the losses of the previous summer, the reinforcements did help. The Wehrmacht remained a powerful fighting force, bound together by increasingly draconian discipline and hardened *esprit de corps*.[27]

The new 'quadrumvirate' of Goebbels, Himmler, Speer and

Bormann drew their authority from Hitler, who remained largely remote, intervening, if at all, to soften the impact of their final mobilisation on society: the Führer queried whether Bavarians' 'nerves' could cope with a cut in their beer ration; and he added names to Goebbels's 'Noah's Ark' of German musicians and actors who were to be spared conscription. But even now, implementing such 'total war' measures depended on mass participation and a degree of popular belief in their legitimacy.

Although the regime had set out from the beginning to reshape the values and loyalties of its citizens, it was neither propaganda nor Hitler's popularity that played the decisive part in this process. Belief in Hitler in the 1930s or even in 1940 did not depend on sharing his radical anti-Semitism or his view of war as a spiritual necessity for a great nation. On the contrary, Nazism was most successful and popular when it promised peace, prosperity and easy victories. It took the mass bombing of 1943 and the military defeats of 1944 to make large numbers of Germans share in their Führer's apocalyptic vision of 'victory or annihilation'. In the autumn of 1944, as Germans realised that they had to secure their own national defence, there was a spike in denunciations of colleagues and a small flurry of new entrants joining the Party. Even though many Nazi functionaries remained deeply unpopular and the leaders were being criticised more frequently too, their failures to defend the home front seemed to galvanise people into taking more initiative themselves. It was the regime's failures rather than its successes which imprinted the moral brutality of its core values on so many who did not see themselves as Nazis.

As the ruthless logic of defending Germany at its borders took hold, there was a new murderousness in the air. On 14 October 1944, the Duisburg Volkssturm seized a 'suspicious-looking' Russian working in a clean-up squad after an air raid on the city. They stood him against a wall in the street and shot him, merely because they had been told that some Russian prisoners of war had been eating stolen jam in the basement of a demolished house nearby. The upsurge in violence went hand in hand with a new sense of vulnerability and fear. On a walk through the long underground passages of Berlin's Friedrichstrasse station, Ursula von Kardorff was fascinated and scared by the polyglot world of foreign workers she saw in this 'Berlin Shanghai'. As young men with bright scarves and long hair laughed and sang, bartered and traded with one another in the large beer halls, she remembered the rumours she had heard about their secret weapons caches. 'Twelve million foreign workers in Germany,' she mused, inflating the real figure by 50 per cent. 'An army in itself. Some call them the Trojan Horse of this war.' Indeed, rumours circulated that the foreign workers were about to be sent to concentration camps to prevent an uprising.[28]

On one of her trips into the capital from Krumke, Liselotte Purper was exhilarated by the carefree atmosphere in the city: 'Berlin remains Berlin,' she announced to Kurt. As loyal supporters of the regime, the couple also felt entitled to voice their opinions. Liselotte admitted to Kurt that she found the logic of Goebbels's view that 'We will win because we have to win' unconvincing, proposing instead a more positive message of her own: 'We can take our fate into our own hands.' Kurt too had not been impressed by a Goebbels speech that November; to him weapons mattered more than words.[29]

But words still mattered, binding Germans into patterns of rationalisation which they seemed unable to escape. Goebbels's new slogan was 'Time against space': the promise that the soaring military casualty rate and bitter defensive battles of 1943 and 1944 had bought time for 'new weapons' to come on stream. On 30 August, the *Völkischer Beobachter* published a piece on 'The secret of the last phase of the war' by the veteran war correspondent Joachim Fernau. Fernau fed the hunger for uplifting news with promises of weapons of unequalled power. He quoted Winston Churchill as saying that 'We have to end the war by the autumn, or else.' Germany only had to hold out till then. 'Victory', Fernau confided as if letting his readers in on a secret, 'is really quite close.' In some schools, his piece was read aloud in class; in Berlin, Ursula von Kardorff was astonished by the extraordinary excitement which greeted his revelation that Germany was readying itself to use the 'secret weapon'. When he read the article in Dresden, Victor Klemperer responded with his typical mixture of sceptical disbelief about the 'fact' and curiosity about its propaganda value, noting in his secret diary, 'That's the richest yet. Popular secrecy . . . All the same: with the slogan "time against space" and with the secret weapons one can make the people keep at it.' But even Klemperer was not sure what was real and what was propaganda: 'Germany is playing poker. Is it bluffing or does it really have trumps?'

Throughout the late summer and autumn, other Germans asked the same question.[30]

Meanwhile, the home front demanded that its borders be vigorously defended. As Kurt Orgel's unit retreated along the Baltic coast, his men could not bring themselves to shoot the cattle in front of the Latvian farmers, although they knew that the Red Army would gain from their compassion. Liselotte's reply was prompt and forthright:

> Rage fills me! I have to tell you: close your soft German heart with hardness to the outside. No one in the whole world values or cares for soft fine feelings more than the Germans. But think of the cruelties to which your homeland is delivered, if . . . Think of the brutality with which we will be raped and murdered, think of the terrible misery, which the air terror alone is already bringing upon our country. No, let the farmer wail, if you have to kill their animals. Who cares about our suffering which you are adding to? – yes, you with your genuine German fine feelings. No, do the enemy harm where you can, that's what you are there for, not to make it easier for him in his struggle against you.

By 24 October, Kurt and the rest of the 18th Army had retreated into the Memel peninsula and he was aware that it was not only Latvian farmers who were suffering: every shell they fired now hit a German village or farm. It felt, he wrote to Liselotte, like the worst burden the war had laid on them. Despite his experience over the previous three years in which his battery had helped shell Leningrad, this was the first time that Kurt mentioned the human cost of the war.[31]

Peter Stölten was now fighting on German soil too. To reach the East Prussian farm where he was quartered, he had had to pass the 'treks' of German evacuees. He had driven over squashed geese, past a nervous girl in a fur hat looking around all the time for ground-attack aircraft, past children driving carts and kilometre-long herds of lowing cattle. Stölten also knew that the farms burning in the distance were German ones. After the Normandy battles and in the midst of the Warsaw Uprising, Stölten had tried to express and resolve his own moral crises in literary form. Now, he picked up books left behind by fleeing civilians and leafed through his favourite authors – Lichtenberg, Oscar Wilde, Dostoevsky, Hoffmannsthal, Binding, Edgar Allan Poe and Hesse – but he felt that they did not 'speak' to him. Instead, he was left with a depressing sense of 'how much poorer I am'. Even Rilke and Hölderlin no longer moved him. In the relative quiet of the East Prussian farmstead, he gave in to his exhaustion. 'If you knew how tired everyone is,' he told Dorothee. But as soon as the next attack came, Stölten's tiredness gave way to a renewed intensity, his senses heightened to 'see more beauty of a morning' in the moments between action; yet another part of him was now looking on with Olympian detachment: 'I see death and destruction, the mass murder of Europe.' Increasingly, Stölten tried to school himself in a kind of faith he had lacked after Normandy and to learn 'that all fate comes from God and to be content with not being able to escape it – and *yet* to love, to plan and to build'. He accepted his role, but his own sense of a future was invested in Dorothee. In one of his dreams, he had seen her waiting to meet him off the S-Bahn in Berlin, her straight-cut, white woollen coat standing out against the tunnel entrance and accentuating the contrast between her dark hair, eyes and lips and her fair skin – 'a pretty picture', he told her.[32]

In December, Stölten found himself suddenly reunited with Dorothee, thanks to an unexpected spell of leave. It was strange to be back in his beloved atelier in the Zehlendorf attic, which his parents had kept just as he had left it. He still wanted to paint, even though 'the paintbrush has become as foreign to me as a fish-fork to an Eskimo'. And he was painfully conscious too of how little his artistic knowledge and skills had developed in the previous year. It felt to him that 'my goal does not lie on the path which I have been forced to follow for years'. Seeing Dorothee reaffirmed that life was worth living, but it also threw him into a new crisis, as he contemplated – for the first time – his return to civilian life after the war. How could he ask Dorothee to share the life of a penniless artist in a future that would be 'dark and poor in hope and full of unheard-of poverty'? For the first time, Stölten seems to have been contemplating Germany's defeat. 'After this war will soon come, perhaps in twenty years, another, which is already faintly discernible today,' he warned Dorothee after his return to the front in his first post-leave letter. 'In any case, the life of this generation seems to me to be measured by catastrophes.' Yet imagining the catastrophe to come did not mean that he was ready to capitulate yet.[33]

Rescuing possessions
from a destroyed house
in Cologne, 1943.

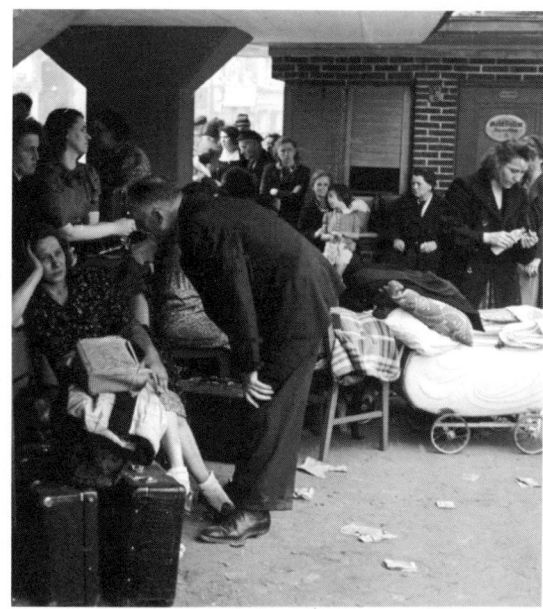

Hamburg firestorm – the living:
in the Reeperbahn bunker, July 1943.

Hamburg firestorm – the dead:
concentration camp prisoner
gathering up remains, August 1943.

Top: Evacuation: bidding farewell at Hagen railway station, July 1943.

Left: Girls from Hagen on the Baltic coast.

Top: Commemorating the dead of the
Hamburg firestorm, 21 November 1943.

Right: Female anti-aircraft personnel
repairing a search light.

Flight from East Prussia across the Frische Nehrung, January/February 1945.

Death march to Dachau: dead concentration camp prisoners on a train, April 1945.

Top: Teenage soldiers surrender at Veckerhagen.

Right: Eva and Victor Klemperer outside their home in Dölzschen in Saxony, *c*.1940.

Left: Red Army Lieutenant
Vladimir Gelfand and Berlin girlfriend.

Below: Berliners swimming near
the remains of the Zoo bunker, 1945.

Black market in Berlin.

Missing children poster.

Cellar dwelling in Hamburg for two families, July 1947.

Liselotte Purper: rehabilitation of a war amputee.

As the bombing of the cities began again in the autumn of 1944, Lisa de Boor found strength in German culture. When she learned that the house in which Goethe was born had been destroyed, she told herself that the writer 'can only be sought and found through what he gave to the world, through *Faust*, *Wilhelm Meister*, in *Poetry and Truth* and in the *West-East Divan*. All that cannot be destroyed by terror-flyers when one has already imbibed its substance, treasured it and brought it to life.' Hoping for a quick defeat and the end of Nazism, as she had since 1939, she turned to her spiritual guide, Rudolf Steiner, who had founded his Anthroposophical Society on an esoteric reading of Goethe. For all her humanitarian internationalism, the Steiner quotes which she found apposite now had a strong ring of German nationalism: 'It belongs to the most miraculous stroke of fate that the German always brings his inner strength, the power of his spirit, to fruition when the trends of the outward world are most unfavourable. As with her admiration for Hölderlin and Ernst Jünger, so here too de Boor found a sense of national identity in the words of a writer with no connection to National Socialism. On 25 November, she commemorated Remembrance Sunday by finally writing the poem she had long planned in memory of the German war dead:

> Now gathering on the other side
> The young, the beloved dead,
> They went silently in black boats
> And looked gravely back to this side,
> At the fiery glow on our shores.
>
> With no word of complaint, silently they went.
> But their bright footprints remain
> And words – their legacy – flutter,
> Inwardly directing those who love them
> To do their duty to the dead.[34]

Although Marburg itself had not yet been bombed, Lisa de Boor knew that it was now only a matter of time before the war caught up with her too. She reread Thomas à Kempis and the last letter from a painter who had gone missing in action in Russia. Ever practical, she busied herself with drying fruit, and making up beds for the steady stream of friends fleeing from the west. As she waited for news of her daughter in Gestapo custody and met a mother whose own daughter had been killed while serving in a flak battery, Lisa asked herself, 'What plans does the divine world have for the German people that it lays such heavy trials upon it?'[35]

When Irene Guicking wrote to Ernst, her language was more home-spun: 'This war puts us through such a hard test.' Frustrated by their separation, she found solace in the verse: 'Let him be tested, who binds himself for ever.' During the day, she had her hands full with their two small children but when she went to bed alone she had time to dwell on how much she missed him. She comforted herself with memories of their courtship but she could not conceal her fear: 'I love you so. But then these painful thoughts fill me. You are a man. You love me above all. But all the same, how can you manage the desires which swirl in your head? I dare not think further. You are a man, after all.' By contrast, her tone when she told Ernst that their flat in Giessen had been bombed was quite light: she and the children had long since moved to the relative safety of her parental home in Lauterbach.[36]

On 4 and 5 November 1944, August Töpperwien's home town of Solingen was bombed, the second raid destroying the town centre. Margarete wrote to her husband that she believed that 6,000 people had died; their house and furniture had survived largely intact. She and their 16-year-old son Karl Christoph had managed to reach the safety of the Lower Saxon countryside, humping their eiderdowns, rucksacks, suitcases and bags on overcrowded night trains and through waiting rooms full of exhausted soldiers and civilians. She was grateful simply to have 'the hell of the west' behind them, and found it incompre-hensible 'how people here cope with their overstrung nerves in the long run . . . Before each lunch we had to go to the cellar. And yet life goes on.'[37]

As Liselotte Purper counted the 'jewels' of German cities destroyed by Allied air attacks – Strasbourg, Freiburg, Vienna, Munich, Nuremberg, Braunschweig, Stuttgart, 'not to mention our Hamburg' – she was filled with impotent rage at 'the global criminal conspiracy' which revealed 'such a bottomless hatred, such a fanatical will to destroy as there never has been in the world. They know not what they do! . . . One day perhaps – if the veil of their senseless rage falls from their eyes – they may look with distress on what they have done.' It was a different tone from her defiant letter of September, proclaiming that 'Berlin remains Berlin'. 'And us?' she asked. 'We are proud but powerless. If we had wings again . . .'[38]

On the night of 12 September, the RAF returned to Stuttgart. In 31 minutes, they released 75 heavy mines, 4,300 high explosive bombs and 180,000 incendiaries over the old town centre, utterly destroying a 5-kilometre-square area. It was a repeat of the raids of 29 July, which had taken off many roofs and caused widespread fires in the city. This time, the heavy, late-summer air helped to ignite a firestorm in the steep-sided valley. As in Rostock, Hamburg and Kassel, many of those trying to flee were immolated by the flames. Many of the city's air raid shelters rapidly overheated too. An estimated 1,000 people were killed, many of them from carbon monoxide gases seeping into the cellars of their blocks of flats where they had taken refuge.[39]

The loss of France and Belgium meant that German forward fighter bases had become Allied airfields. With the loss of flak batteries and warning systems along the Channel coast, the British and American bomber fleets were now free to pick out targets that had never been hit before, and with little warning. From a strategic point of view, the bombing of the Ruhr, Hamburg and Berlin from March 1943 to March 1944 had marked the most important single phase of the bombing war. But the continued expansion of the British and American bomber fleets allowed them to carry fourteen times the payload of bombs and target them with six times the accuracy of 1941–42. Over half the total tonnage of bombs dropped on Germany rained down during the last eight months of the war.[40]

The result was a death toll that stood no comparison with the previous phase of the air war. In Darmstadt, a firestorm was unleashed on the night of 11 September 1944, killing 8,494 people: their dead on this single night outstripped all the bombing casualties in Essen of the entire war. In Heilbronn, 5,092 were killed on the night of 5 December; on 16 December, some 4,000 lost their lives in Magdeburg. Over half the German civilians killed in the air war died after August 1944: 223,406 of an estimated 420,000 for the duration of the war.[41]

Alongside the scale of the firestorms, the element of surprise accounted for a disproportionate number of the civilians killed in these raids. The populations of the cities which had been most frequently bombed, like Essen, Düsseldorf, Cologne, Kassel, Hamburg and Berlin, had had years to learn when it was dangerous to be out on the streets and where they could take shelter on their way to work. In Munich, Augsburg, Stuttgart, Vienna and Salzburg, people now had to adjust much faster, under far worse conditions. There was neither time nor materials to build new bunkers in cities that were being attacked for the first time. As the Allies targeted areas of the Reich which until now had served as centres of evacuation, Germans found that nowhere was truly safe.

As the air war worsened, rumours about Germany's 'new weapons' centred on what was most obviously lacking – fighter planes. 'The view is widespread and general that unless the enemy control of the air can be broken, no change in the fortunes of war can be brought about,' ran a national report to the Propaganda Ministry in November. The rumours were not baseless: a squadron equipped with the Me 262 jet fighter was training at this time and even fought on a few occasions between August and November but, beset with chronic engine failures, it would not enter active service till the New Year. Engineers used all their skills in designing new models of jet aircraft, including Alexander Lippisch's ramjet, the first model with a revolutionary delta wing. But Germany was now cut off from its Turkish and Portuguese supplies of chrome, wolfram and bauxite, so that production of high-grade steel alloys and aluminium could only continue from existing stocks. In early September, the USAAF carried out three devastating raids on synthetic oil plants, the Luftwaffe's lifeline, setting the scene for a final shift in the strategic control of German airspace. Lack of aero fuel curtailed available flying time, which meant that new, under-trained pilots were sent into combat against overwhelming odds. In the second half of 1944, the Luftwaffe was effectively destroyed, losing 20,200 planes.[42]

In this febrile atmosphere that veered precipitously between hope and helplessness, Goebbels launched a new propaganda offensive about 'Bolshevik terror'. It had the same ingredients as the Katyn publicity of April and May 1943; except this time the victims were not Polish officers but German civilians. During the Soviet incursion into East Prussia in October 1944, two tank battalions had taken the small village of Nemmersdorf. They held it and its bridge for two days, 21–23 October, before retreating in the face of Wehrmacht counter-attacks. Most of the village's 637 inhabitants got away, some of them waved through by Soviet troops after they had occupied the village. Some of the occupiers and occupied established normal relations – food was accepted with thanks and broken conversations were held – but elsewhere Germans were beaten, robbed, raped or killed. When German troops retook the village, Volkssturm men gathered the corpses of 26 civilians and laid them in an open grave in the village cemetery. The news spread like wildfire and, the next day, Heinrich Himmler's personal physician, Professor Dr Karl Gebhardt, arrived along with several commissions from the Party, SS and police. On 25 October, a unit of military police arrived and conducted its own search, finding no further bodies. The 13 women, 5 children and 8 men were raised from the open grave and laid out on the ground so that they could be photographed, identified and examined by medical personnel. They found that, apart from the mayor, most of the men and women killed were elderly and had been executed by shots to the head. Although they suspected rape only in the case of one of the younger women, the photographers suggested otherwise, taking pictures of the female victims – who had already been moved at least twice – with their skirts raised and their stockings down. It was the kind of thing that Gebhardt, who combined serving as President of the German Red Cross with conducting experiments on female concentration camp prisoners, may well have ordered before the photographers arrived.[43]

This was a massacre similar to those which many of the German investigators had themselves carried out in Soviet territory. One of the many high-ranking German visitors claimed in his diary to have seen women and children nailed to barn doors. Though the military police did not record any such evidence, stories of crucified women and children furnished the material for the blanket coverage in the German media. The journalists covering the story were so short on detail that Goebbels urged them to make it up in order to convey 'poetic truth'. For the first but not the last time East Prussia furnished evidence which made the ceaseless invocation of the Soviet threat ring true to German ears. And, as with Katyn, the normal embargo on showing footage of atrocities was lifted and both the papers and newsreels carried photographs of the twenty-six bodies. The *Völkische Beobachter* put the murdered children on its front page, as Nemmersdorf became synonymous with the deeds of 'Asiatic hordes' whipped into a frenzy by 'Jewish commissars'.[44]

In East Prussia itself, both the reality of the Soviet incursion in October and the successful German counter-attack left a profound mark. The commander of the reconstituted Army Group Centre, Colonel-General Reinhardt, wrote to his wife of the 'rage, the hatred which fills us since we have seen how the Bolsheviks have wrought havoc in the area that we have retaken, south of Gumbinnen'. Elsewhere in the Reich, the impact of the Nemmersdorf story was more varied. So many people doubted whether the news was real that Goebbels admitted in his diary that 'the reports from Nemmersdorf have only convinced a part of the population'. People also blamed the Nazi Party for not evacuating civilians from the area in time. Then there were those in other, more distant regions of the Reich who asked why they should worry about the Russians just 'because they killed a couple of people in East Prussia'.[45]

To the population of Stuttgart, on Germany's western border, the Gumbinnen district was as remote as it had been possible to travel within the pre-war Reich, and here traditional Swabian hostility to everything Prussian had become stronger as the war dragged on. Above all, Stuttgarters were still reeling from the fire-bombing of 12 September, and were profoundly sceptical of all propaganda messages. According to the vox populi relayed by Stuttgart's particularly downbeat SD office, the leadership

> should realise that the sight of these victims will remind every thinking person of the atrocities we have committed in enemy territory, even in Germany itself. Have we not murdered thousands of Jews? Don't soldiers again and again report that Jews in Poland have had to dig their own graves? And how did we treat the Jews in the [Natzweiler] concentration camp in Alsace? Jews are human beings too. By doing all this we have shown the enemy what they can do to us if they win.[46]

This sounded like the talk of the summer and autumn of 1943, which Goebbels and Himmler had silenced through a mixture of admonition and exemplary punishment. Now that the next crisis had hit, it emerged again. As the regime tried again to combat defeatism by using Nemmersdorf to stoke up fears of annihilatory 'Jewish terror', once more it encountered a wave of criticism of its own role in escalating the cycle of murder. In this febrile atmosphere, an argument over seats on a Berlin tram was enough to prompt some passengers to point out that 'One has to remain humane, because we have already weighed ourselves down with enough guilt for our treatment of the Jews and Poles, which will yet be paid back to us.' Moments such as this, where strangers argued in public over who was to blame for the 'Jewish war', marked the periodic lows of German morale. Unlike Katyn, the twenty-six corpses at Nemmersdorf were not a significant enough atrocity to garner international attention.[47]

On 24 July 1944, the Soviet 2nd Tank Army had liberated a camp on the outskirts of Lublin, where they found 1,500 Soviet prisoners of war whom the fleeing SS guards had left behind. They showed their liberators the commandant's house and building materials depot; the barracks for SS guards and for prisoners; the three gas chambers, the crematorium and behind it the trenches for mass shootings; the piles of clothes, the heaps of shoes and the mounds of human hair. Majdanek had served mainly as a concentration camp for Poles and Soviet prisoners of war employed in Lublin's factories, but it was also a death camp in which some 200,000 Poles, Slovaks, Jews, Roma and Red Army prisoners had been killed. The Soviet advance had been so rapid that the SS had had no time to destroy the camp. Majdanek was the first and – as events would show – the most intact of the death camps to be liberated. The Soviets immediately realised the significance of what they had found. Foreign journalists were invited in, and photographs and film footage of the site were transmitted around the world. Allied leaflet drops made sure that, from late August, the details of the gas chambers and crematoria at Majdanek reached Germany.[48]

For the soldiers of the Red Army, Majdanek became an emblem of how the Germans had treated their comrades, confirming that they had murdered people of many nationalities, but had singled out Soviet citizens. Alongside the exhortations penned by Ilya Ehrenburg and other writers, to revenge themselves on the Germans for the crimes of occupation, the images of Majdanek became seared into many an imagination. Yuri Uspensky, a young officer with the Soviet 5th Artillery Corps, added Majdanek to the horrors he had seen in the villages he had liberated in the Smolensk region; as his unit fought its way towards the borders of East Prussia he would not forget 'the German cold-bloodedness in Majdanek', which he found 'a hundred times worse' than the worst actions committed by his own side – which indeed appalled him too.[49]

That December, Ursula von Kardorff locked herself in the toilet of a friend's flat and read her copy of the *Journal de Genève*, which detailed the gassing of thousands of women and children at Auschwitz-Birkenau. It was based on a detailed report by two Slovak prisoners who had escaped from the camp in April. Even though Kardorff already knew that the mass murder of the Jews was a fact – and was herself helping Jews to hide in Berlin – the stark details were too much for her. 'Is one to believe such a ghastly story?' she asked herself in her diary. 'It simply cannot be true. Surely even the most brutal fanatics could not be so absolutely bestial.'[50]

For many, disbelief was often the first step to acknowledging what had been done. Instead of fading away, news of death camps in which the victims were killed by mass electrocution or gassing grew during 1944, spreading throughout the Reich; it was even picked up by Allied observers of German prisoners of war in Italy. Curiosity drove people to broach the taboo subject of what actually happened in these secret locations. They spoke of pillars of corpses, probably without realising that they were formed by victims struggling in the darkness to reach the remaining oxygen near the ceiling of the gas chamber. As even correct details were misunderstood, the conversations disclosed how hard – and imaginatively – people were trying to join up the fragments into a coherent account. Like marked banknotes, tales of mass electrocution give a sense of how widely, yet partially, news of the death camps circulated.[51]

As Germans continued to equate Allied bombing with the murder of the Jews, they cast themselves as victims, seeing both as the cause of their own woes. In the harsh climate of police measures after the failed July bomb plot, Germans might have been expected to censor themselves. Ursula von Kardorff, who sympathised with the plotters, certainly feared arrest, and was careful what she said in public. But, as glimpses from Stuttgart and Berlin reveal, it did not take much prompting for people without conspiratorial connections to talk openly about the murder of the Jews. Whether they were impelled to do so by existential fear, or simply caught up in a public debate triggered by stories in the media which juxtaposed 'Jewish terror' and mass execution sites, this social response reveals one thing very clearly: this was not, or at least not yet, an 'atomised' society forced by dictatorial terror alone to continue the war. Many Germans felt entitled to air their views and, whatever their criticisms of the regime, they assumed that their own loyalty had not become suspect.

Then there were those who felt that the regime could benefit from their advice. By November and December 1944, well-intentioned citizens were writing in to the Propaganda Ministry tendering suggestions, even enclosing drafts for leaflets to be dropped over the Allied armies. 'Englishmen, Americans, Russians, listen to our voice,' ran the text proposed by the director of the engineering institute in Kaiserslautern:

> Don't sacrifice your lives any longer for the Jewish bloodsuckers who are only driving you to the butcher's block so that they can enjoy ruling the whole world . . . *Christians, you should never fight for Jews!* . . . help us found the *United States of Europe in which there are no more Jews.*

It was eye-catching enough for someone in the Propaganda Ministry to underline key turns of phrase. The text ended with an adaptation of Marx's famous slogan: 'Europeans of all countries unite!' In place of the collective reprisals proposed back in May and early June 1944, Goebbels's correspondents now believed in persuading British and American 'workers and soldiers' that they were being duped into fighting against their natural ally, Germany. But as an old doctor from Hamburg sadly lamented, there was always the danger that the English would not get the message: so, any leaflet would have to address them 'in the style of someone who is slow on the uptake' and even then it might all fail, because 'We Germans are used to talking to educated nations . . . The English-speaking peoples do not come up to this level.'[52]

Across the Reich, those monitoring the public mood for the SD, the Propaganda Ministry, the Party Chancellery and the presidents of the higher provincial courts busied themselves with mapping the shifting balance of opinions of their increasingly distraught 'national comrades'. Some, like the SD in Stuttgart, were distinctly and consistently pessimistic, cataloguing much criticism of the regime; some others, like their colleagues in Freiburg, wrote in Panglossian terms. In September, the Wehrmacht persuaded Goebbels to let it expand its own propaganda operation to monitor and to try also to steer public opinion. Goebbels's willingness to tolerate this incursion into his domain was an acknowledgement that, despite the July plot, the Wehrmacht still enjoyed higher public standing than the Party. Military events continued to determine civilian morale. In the west, it recovered from the retreat from France slowly and hesitantly. In places where, in early September, people had openly declared that all was lost, they were still not listening to the news three weeks later; instead, they buckled down and 'obediently did their duty'.

On 15 December, Irene Guicking wrote to Ernst with more news of the bombing of Giessen. Everyone who had sheltered in the cellar of the town hall had been killed. Irene had heard that 2,500 people had died and 30,000 had been made homeless by the raid. Their own home was not so badly hit as she had first thought. A bomb had landed in the courtyard just in front of the building and, although the house was uninhabitable, the contents were virtually unscathed. Only Ernst's straw hat, a pre-war souvenir, had been sucked out by the blast. It had landed, fittingly, in the crater out in the street. Meanwhile, all their furniture had been safely stowed in her aunt's home. Only the kitchen fittings, sofa and sideboard proved too heavy for them and remained in the bombed flat. In this reckoning of good and ill luck, the worst immediate inconvenience was having Irene's aunt Johanna to stay: three days with her seemed far too long. By the time she left, on 17 December, Irene was cheered by other news. The papers were reprinting an article which had appeared in the Swiss press about 500 enemy planes downed by the new German fighters. Her spirits rose at the very thought that now – finally – they could be defended against attack from the air.[53]

The number of air raids on Germany had indeed fallen dramatically on 17 December, because the previous day the Wehrmacht launched a major counter-offensive in the west. In his proclamation on the eve of battle, Rundstedt exhorted: 'Soldiers of the western front! Your great hour has struck. Strong attacking armies are marching today against the British and Americans. I don't need to say any more. You all feel it: it's all or nothing!' Careful not to stoke public expectations prematurely, Goebbels held the press back. The first public announcement of the offensive was a short mention in the Wehrmacht radio bulletin on 18 December. Newspaper headlines did not follow until the next day. Even the *Völkischer Beobachter* dispensed with its usual bombast by simply announcing an 'Offensive in the west'. People were delighted and amazed that the Wehrmacht was still capable of launching a major attack; many felt 'released from an oppressive weight'. As Sepp Dietrich's 6th SS Panzer Army struck northwards and Manteuffel's 5th Panzer Army broke the American lines and advanced on the town of Bastogne in the south, the reports to the Reich Propaganda Ministry described the public response as like news of 'rainfall after a long drought'. In Berlin, almost the whole of the schnapps ration for the Christmas period was consumed in toasts to what many happily dubbed the 'Führer's Christmas present'.[54]

Cooped up with the remains of Army Group North in the Courland peninsula, Kurt Orgel reported that even the hardened old veterans were excitedly clamouring, 'Man, I want to be there too!' As they looked at the map to follow the progress of the offensive, Kurt realised that his battery had advanced along the same road through Luxembourg during the 1940 campaign. By 21 December he had heard that 20,000 Americans had been captured in the west. Ernst Guicking reported that the number of prisoners was 60,000. What was immediately evident to him was that the offensive had ended the harrying attacks on the Alsatian bridgehead he and his comrades were holding at Issenheim. As the joyful reports poured in, the Propaganda Ministry realised that the analogies being drawn with the rapid conquest of France in 1940 were highly dangerous. Goebbels immediately set about dampening expectations, using plain-clothes agents on the streets to prepare people for a more limited success. Yet, with their hopes suddenly rekindled, in Reichenberg, Brandenburg, Dessau, even in pessimistic Hamburg and Stuttgart, people wanted to imagine a swift strategic victory which could end the war in the west. It was the same hope that had been invested in the Atlantic Wall in May, or, with less confidence, in miracle weapons in the autumn. As it resurfaced again in mid-December, the strategic calculation remained much the same: if only the British and Americans could be forced to sue for peace, then the full resources of the Wehrmacht could be thrown on to the eastern front.[55]

In fact, Hitler's own thinking in launching the offensive was not far removed from these popular hopes. To suggestions by Goebbels and the Japanese ambassador that it was time to sue for peace with the

Soviets he had responded by insisting that the war in the east had to be fought to the finish and that a peace in the west could only be made from a position of strength. The aim of the Ardennes offensive was to drive northwards to Antwerp. If the port could be regained, then the British and Americans would again become bogged down by the trials of slow overland transport. In this optimistic scheme, German strength in the west might force the Western Allies to negotiate a separate peace.[56]

By 23 December, German troops reached Buissonville and Celle, with the Meuse less than 8 kilometres away. But they never crossed the great river. As the fog which had protected the German armoured divisions from bombing cleared on Christmas Eve, Antwerp remained a distant goal. Even the loyal Walter Model admitted that the offensive had failed. With 5,000 British and American planes pounding the German tanks, airfields, artillery positions and supply lines, Rundstedt conceded on 27 December that no reinforcements could be moved up the line. The offensive was effectively over. The fact that the Allied losses of 76,890 were slightly higher than the 67,461 men captured, wounded and killed on the German side testified to the remaining effectiveness of the German Army as a fighting force. But it could not replace its losses from the operation.[57]

Hitler had told Albert Speer that everything depended on the Ardennes offensive, admitting that 'If it doesn't succeed, I see no other possibility of bringing the war to a favourable conclusion.' Speer knew that coal was no longer reaching the power stations and that the loss of iron and steel from France, Belgium and Luxembourg could not be offset: German arms production was now in irreversible decline. Increasingly, the Armaments Minister devoted his efforts to keeping the rail network from collapsing completely. By halting the construction of the new generation of U-boats, he tried to boost the production of ammunition and tanks. This was far worse than the crisis management of the first winter of the war, when coal and steel had also been in short supply. Alfred Jodl, acting characteristically as Hitler's voice, had admitted to the commanders in the west in early November that the Wehrmacht lacked the 'available forces' for the counter-attack, simply pointing out that 'in our current situation we can't shrink from staking everything on one card'.[58]

Now it had been played, Hitler and the High Command returned to their prior strategy of holding the line. Halt orders, which declared towns to be 'fortresses' to be held to the last bullet, followed one after another as the British and American advance restarted in the west. German soldiers, returning on leave from the west, still talked excitedly about reaching Paris before the New Year; 'absolute rubbish' was Goebbels's estimate, as he ordered the media to lower expectations. On 29 December, the press acknowledged that the offensive had, in fact, stalled.[59]

★

On New Year's Eve, the great actor Heinrich George read over the radio the words which the founder of modern military theory, Carl von Clausewitz, had written in February 1812:

I believe and confess that a people can value nothing more highly than the dignity and liberty of its existence; that it must defend these to the last drop of its blood; that there is no higher duty to fulfil, no higher law to obey; that the shameful blot of cowardly submission can never be erased; that this drop of poison in the blood of a nation is passed on to posterity, crippling and eroding the strength of future generations.

Clausewitz had written these lines to his patron and mentor, Scharnhorst, to explain why he was resigning from the Prussian service in order to take up arms against Napoleon in Russia. He had also penned them in the expectation of defeat. What was left to him was a romantic belief in the greater moral victory and faith in the future of the nation. As the letter, which became known as Clausewitz's *Confession*, went on: 'Even the destruction of liberty after a bloody and honourable struggle assures the people's rebirth. It is the seed of life, which one day will bring forth a new, securely rooted tree.'[60]

As Heinrich George reached the final sentence, violins began to play the national anthem, quietly at first, the sound then swelling before the twelve strokes that saw out the Old Year. The last stroke was sounded by the unmistakable bronze Rhine bell. The nineteenth-century Prussian soldiers' song 'Oh Germany High in Honour' followed, its choral injunction, 'Hold out! Hold out!', more fitting than ever. Then, prefaced by a brief rendition of the Badenweiler

March, at five past midnight Hitler spoke. His message for the New Year was brief. The Führer dwelt on the threat of the 'Jewish international world conspiracy', repeating his prophecy that its attempt to 'destroy Europe and eradicate its peoples' would fail and lead only to 'its own destruction'. This was neither news nor particularly comforting; it merely underlined the fear many felt that there would indeed be no negotiated end to the war, or, as Hitler once more affirmed, 'a 9 November in the German Reich will never be repeated'. He promised a change of fortune, but offered no details, made no promises about the deployment of new weapons and none about how or when the Allies' air attacks would be halted. And he did not mention the offensive in the west. The war was described in the bleak and apocalyptic terms he had employed so often: 'A matter of death and life, to be or not to be, and victory will be ours, because ours it must be.' The Propaganda Ministry swiftly issued instructions that the obvious lack of concrete detail which might have comforted German listeners should be explained away as a security precaution.[61]

While he heard the broadcast on the Courland front, Kurt Orgel was filled with thoughts of Liselotte, rather like couples during the *Request Concert* broadcasts of the first years of the war. 'I imagined', he wrote to her on 1 January 1945, 'how lovely it is that we both can simultaneously hear the same man! Were you delighted as well to hear the voice of the Führer again?' During the whole of 1944, Hitler had spoken publicly only once, briefly and immediately after the assassination attempt of 20 July. That he now stepped before the microphone brought a kind of reassurance to many; it felt like a sign that a battle had been won. Otherwise, people assumed on the basis of their experience of 1943–44, he would have remained silent. Across the country, report-writers for the Propaganda and Justice Ministries, as well as for the Wehrmacht, concurred. Many people entered 1945 buoyed up and hoping, once more, that the war might yet end well for Germany.[62]

In Marburg, Lisa and Wolf de Boor disagreed. To Lisa, Hitler's voice sounded as 'hollow as the grave'. They had sat by their Christmas tree, while they watched the candles slowly burn down in their holders and drank a glass of vermouth, a special allocation for the over-sixties. Their three children, all medics, were scattered. Hans, the youngest, was on the Baltic coast, qualifying in medicine with the Wehrmacht at Greifswald. The older son, Anton, a staff doctor, had been posted to a tank division and was cut off in Courland. But the parents remained most anxious about their daughter Monika, who had spent the last twelve months on remand in a Gestapo prison. To her mother's delight, Monika had turned to religion during her imprisonment, using the time in solitary confinement to read and pray. As her parents reread her Christmas letter together, it allayed their fears for a while, Lisa jotting down how 'profoundly impressed' they were 'by the way she used the opportunities offered by contemplation not just to withstand this time but to elevate it'.[63]

In Lauterbach, Irene Guicking was roused from her bed at 5.30 on New Year's morning: Ernst had come home. She had taken his advice and sent a telegram to say that they had been 'totally bombed out' and it had done the trick. Ernst was granted ten days' compassionate leave, and it had taken him just an afternoon and a night to reach her from Alsace. The front was moving closer.[64]

15

Collapse

Weakened by its own tremendous efforts during the Ardennes offensive, the Wehrmacht returned immediately afterwards to strategic defence. Simply absorbing the Allied onslaughts was once again the primary aim, just as in January 1944, but with a key difference. After twelve months of trading 'space against time', the lines had shifted from the Dniepr and the Atlantic to the German borderlands. The Germans still held Warsaw and the Vistula in the east and on the Italian front could defend a line along the river Po. In the west, the Allied advance was blocked by the German defensive lines of the West Wall, especially the powerful triangle formed around Trier by the confluence of the Saar and Moselle rivers. In the panic of September 1944, Trier had looked as vulnerable as Aachen. Through the autumn and winter, however, it weathered numerous attacks, anchoring the northern apex of the fortified triangle. Behind these defences lay the Rhine, the final natural obstacle facing the British and Americans. Crossing the great rivers – the Po, Vistula and Rhine – became the key to defeating and occupying the Reich. For the Allies, these were still formidable barriers. For the Germans, they provided the last lines in a defensive strategy.

Even though German tank production had reached a new peak in late 1944, the Allies' massive superiority in weaponry was increasingly obvious to everyone, as the American and British bomber fleets quite eclipsed their massed air attacks of a year earlier, targeting the railway network, synthetic oil plants and Germany's cities. It was devastatingly clear that the prospect of defending Germany until their own side could wrest a military or technological advantage was now minimal. Instead, German hopes dwelt on purchasing time during which the Allied coalition might – just – disintegrate under its own inner tensions. This optimistic scenario depended on history repeating itself. Frederick II of Prussia had been saved from certain defeat in the Seven Years War when Tsarina Elizabeth of Russia suddenly died in 1762 and the overwhelming Franco-Austro-Russian coalition had miraculously disintegrated. Through films like the 1942 biopic *The Great King*, Germans had been encouraged to see their Führer as the successor of Frederick the Great. It was also a parallel which inspired Hitler, and he sent a print of the film to Mussolini. When he returned to Berlin on 15 January from his western headquarters, he took the Prussian King's portrait into his study in the bunker deep below the Reich Chancellery. Anticipating the clash of the capitalist West with the communist East was not entirely baseless, as decades of Cold War would later demonstrate. But in their desperation to find an exit strategy from the cul-de-sac of their own making, the Nazi leaders forgot that they themselves were the threat which had forged this 'unholy alliance' in the first place. When Roosevelt died on 12 April, Hitler, who had come to see the American President as his Jewish-aided nemesis, celebrated briefly, anticipating the moment when the events of 1762 would begin to replay.[1]

Hoping that America would join Germany in saving Europe from Bolshevism offered a final reason to play for time and spend lives. Though the Wehrmacht High Command no longer knew the scale of its own losses, in 1945 each day of fighting would cost the lives of 10,000 German soldiers. As long as the Rhine held, the Wehrmacht was defending a coherent, if greatly shrunken, territory, in which every week kept the prospect alive that the Grand Alliance against the Reich might still fall apart. And it was the most formidable of the remaining German armies, Walter Model's Army Group B, that was entrusted with defending the western front.[2]

From December to March, the British and Americans fought their way from the river Saar to the Rhine. The great river barriers of the Vistula and Rhine fell in near-simultaneous offensives which unfolded from January to the end of March 1945. The greatest breakthrough came in the east, as the Soviets bridged the Vistula and swept through Poland, conquering the eastern German provinces and seizing bridgeheads over the Oder by late January. It would take until late March for the rest of the Soviet front to anchor itself along this new front line, a mere 80 kilometres from Berlin. It was conceivable that the

German armies in the east could still fall back to the Elbe from the Oder, but the armies in the west had no such option. Beyond the Rhine lay nothing but the North German Plain all the way to the Elbe. Along the Rhine lay the heartland of German industry, with the great river itself serving as a major shipping route for coal and other goods. The Rhine remained the key barrier without which no German defensive position could be mapped out, let alone sustained.

After going through a final flowering during the autumn of 1944, national solidarity disintegrated under the force of the Allied invasion. The collapse of the Reich, region by region, naturally exacerbated local loyalties and robbed people of any sense of belonging to a larger 'community of fate', to use one of Goebbels's favoured terms. Even before the final assault on the Reich began, regional differences were growing: the shake-up of government after the July bomb plot strengthened the powers of the Gauleiters at the expense of central government, a trend which was greatly magnified once the battle for Germany began. Of far greater impact was the increasingly divergent experience of the fighting itself. With Soviet, American, British and French armies invading different parts of the Reich, Germans did not face the same enemies everywhere or run the same risks. Moreover, the conquest of Germany, region by region, completed the elevation of family and *Heimat* above *Reich* and *Volk*. Throughout the war, men had justified their military service above all in terms of a patriotism grounded in the family and where they came from. Mass evacuation from the cities – with all its attendant conflicts between town and village, Catholics and Protestants, north and south and east and west – had only underlined the extent to which Germany remained a nation of provincials. By 8 May 1945, Germany had become a nation of migrants and refugees, as millions of displaced soldiers and civilians tried to survive far from home, and calls to self-sacrifice and national solidarity were finally exhausted. The German nation state was destroyed not only by the four-power occupation which was to come, but by its own disintegration in the final months of the war. Defeat did not destroy German nationalism; many of its exclusive hatreds could not be so easily excised. But its positive meanings, its ability to harness social effort and motivate self-sacrifice for a national cause, promptly collapsed. Just as workers in the Ruhr had wished for someone else to be bombed in 1943, so, as the fighting crossed into the Reich in January 1945, everyone wanted to escape the war zone themselves.

★

Since taking command of his own company, Wilm Hosenfeld felt rejuvenated. Scattered across Warsaw in small groups, guarding seven depots and two radio stations, the company was hard to weld together. Even though it was full of 'all sorts of good-for-nothings', Hosenfeld had started licking the middle-aged men into shape with early-morning gymnastics and sport. He was in his element, doing what he had longed for during the years of rear service. He even rescued the harmonium from the ruined sports school, to accompany their Christmas carols, and he encouraged both the Catholic and the Protestant chaplains to speak to the men. Before taking over the company, he had made sure that the Jewish pianist he was hiding in the freezing attic above the Warsaw staff HQ was provided with food, a German greatcoat and blankets. Now, in the quiet of early January, as a thick shroud of snow covered the destroyed city, Hosenfeld wrote to Annemie about his fears for her and the children back in Thalau. The Wehrmacht bulletin had reported a further air raid on nearby Fulda. 'What's still left of the city?' he asked on 7 January, worrying that the bombing would strike Thalau too.[3]

The Soviet High Command had mustered nearly 6.5 million troops for its winter offensive on Germany, double the number fielded by the Wehrmacht for its invasion of the Soviet Union in June 1941. Along the Vistula front, 2,250,000 Red Army soldiers faced 400,000 German troops. Cramming 250 artillery guns to every kilometre around their bridgeheads over the Vistula at Magnuszew and Puławy, Zhukov's divisions used their huge superiority in firepower to deliver a shattering twenty-five-minute barrage early on 14 January, before sending infantry and armour to shatter the thin defensive lines of the German 9th Army along the river and bypass the 'fortress' of Warsaw altogether. On 16 January General Smilo von Lüttwitz ordered the 9th Army to abandon the city. Leading his company westwards, Hosenfeld covered the 30 kilometres to Błonie by the following day, only to find that the Red Army was already there. After a brief skirmish most of the German troops surrendered, and Wilm

Hosenfeld was taken prisoner. He would spend the next seven years in Soviet captivity. The same day the 1st Polish Army ended the German occupation of Warsaw. During those five years and three and a half months, 350,000 Jews had been killed, most of the city destroyed and its overall population had fallen from 1.3 million to 153,000. One of the emaciated survivors to emerge from the ruins was the pianist Hosenfeld had helped, Władysław Szpilman.[4]

Further south, Konev's 1st Ukrainian Front had launched its assault across the Vistula two days earlier, exploiting his bridgehead at Sandomierz and attacking through dense forest, which the German General Staff had assumed would protect their elevated positions in Małopolska. Advancing on the German lines in gaps between their own artillery fire, Soviet infantrymen lured the Germans out of their bunkers in order to defend their trenches, where they were then completely exposed to a further Soviet artillery barrage. By the end of the first day, Konev's forces had advanced to a depth of 20 kilometres along a 35-kilometre-wide front. By the end of 13 January, the Soviet breakthrough was 60 kilometres wide and 40 kilometres deep. Their prime goal was the 'black gold', as Stalin called it, of Upper Silesia – its coal and steel industry. In order to capture it intact, Konev's forces embarked on a huge encirclement of mines and factory towns from the east, north and south, leaving the Wehrmacht with a narrow escape route westwards. Cracow fell on 19 January, the Germans for once simply pulling out, surrendering their defensive positions and the capital of Hans Frank's General Government without destroying it.

The previous night, as snow fell, the SS guards had marched their prisoners out of the main gate of the concentration camp at Auschwitz: 14,000 were sent to Gleiwitz and 25,000 prisoners were marched the 63 kilometres to Loslau. The SS were so afraid of being caught by the Red Army that they did not stop for the first two nights, clubbing the exhausted stragglers and shooting those who fell down in the snow. At least 450 prisoners died on the road to the railheads. They had quickly learned to expect nothing from the German villages they passed, where people stayed off the streets and closed their doors. By contrast, Polish villagers often offered the prisoners bread and milk; some even managed to escape from the column, slipping into the knots of Poles lining the streets.[5]

At the railway yard in Loslau, the prisoners were packed a hundred to each open goods wagon, and, as soon as the train began to move, they huddled still closer to keep out the sharp wind. On the night of 22–23 January, the first of Konev's armies reached the river Oder and established a bridgehead at Brieg, cutting the main train line to the west and breaching the last natural barrier en route to Berlin; German trains now had to take the minor, southern line out of Silesia. Each night the Auschwitz prisoners began to freeze and each morning brought a new count of the dead. Fifteen-year-old Thomas Gève had survived the selection for the gas chambers thanks to the protection of German Communist prisoners in the camp, who assigned the tall German Jewish boy to work alongside them on their building brigade. As their open goods wagons pulled through the crowded Silesian stations, Gève was struck by something unprecedented. German civilians were looking at the freezing prisoners in their striped concentration camp clothing with envy and resentment: for they had places on a train.[6]

With over 200,000 Germans walking along the ice-bound roads in the hope of boarding trains at the small stations from Ratibor through Schweidnitz to Liegnitz, many had to wait days before they could clamber aboard. Their sheer numbers overwhelmed the volunteers from the National Socialist People's Welfare who had come to offer food, hot drinks and blankets. On 20 January, the Gauleiter of Lower Silesia, Karl Hanke, finally gave the order to evacuate his capital, Breslau, completing its transformation into a 'fortress'. Ten-year-old Jürgen Illmer and his mother were lucky enough to find places on a train out of Breslau and reach the relative safety of Saxony. At Leipzig, they were helped through the chaotic crush on the platforms by groups of Hitler Youths and Red Cross nurses. Glancing across the tracks as he got off his train to take shelter from an air raid, Jürgen saw an open goods train filled with motionless, snow-covered figures in striped clothing. He wondered if they had frozen to death. As the air raid siren sounded and the Germans went down to the shelter under the great station hall, the conversation turned to the prisoners they had all seen. When someone suggested that they might be Jews, a woman replied coldly, 'They weren't Jews. They have all been shot in Poland already.' She was wrong. One of the prisoners on the train may have been Thomas

Gève. He too was left with memories of Leipzig; how the prisoners called out, begging for water from the German Red Cross nurses whose hospital train stood at the next platform. The nurses ignored them.[7]

On 21 January Breslau's aged prelate, Cardinal Bertram, departed for Jauernig in Moravian Silesia, while the most valuable items in the city's churches were shipped out to Kamenz in Saxony. The wounded recovering in the city's military hospitals were moved too, alongside the tax office, municipal administration, the radio station and the post, telegraph and rail authorities. Over 150,000 civilians remained. The next day Gauleiter Hanke called 'on the men of Breslau to join the defence front of our Fortress Breslau', vowing that 'the Fortress will be defended to the end'. Its defenders consisted of 45,000 troops, ranging from raw recruits to battle-hardened paratroopers and Waffen SS veterans. To the west of the city, the Wehrmacht fought bitterly to drive the Soviets back across the Oder at Steinau for another two weeks. On 9–11 February, Kanth, Liegnitz and Haynau fell and on 15 February the Red Army captured the Sudeten mountain passes, cutting Breslau off from the west. The next day, the city came under siege, with the attacking Soviets swiftly occupying the outer suburbs before grinding to a halt as the defenders made them fight for every building and street crossing. From 15 February, the Luftwaffe began an airlift which lasted 76 days and some 2,000 flights, bringing in 1,670 tonnes of supplies – mainly ammunition – and evacuating 6,600 wounded.[8]

Alfred Bauditz was one of the civilians who stayed in Breslau, equipped with a horse and cart and tasked with clearing buildings that interfered with the line of fire. In late January he used the cart to bring his wife, 14-year-old daughter Leonie and 9-year-old son Winfried out of the city to Malkwitz, where two of his brothers owned farms. On 9 February, Malkwitz was occupied and all the inhabitants were questioned one by one by a Soviet officer who spoke fluent German and took down their personal details. Despite the Germans' fears of rape and murder, the Red Army men behaved correctly. Leonie's ordeal began when the next armoured unit arrived. Most of the thirty Soviet soldiers were friendly, but two terrorised the women. Despite hiding in a barn at night and having her hair cut short and going about dressed as a boy by day, Leonie was discovered and raped multiple times. For a while a well-spoken Soviet lieutenant protected her and her mother, but when his unit left, the women and girls were drafted into a work brigade and sent out to thresh grain and shell peas on different farms – a seemingly inescapable routine of fieldwork, laundry, cooking duties and forced sex.[9]

★

The start of the Soviet winter offensive found Peter Stölten at the southern end of the East Prussian front near Praschnitz, 100 kilometres north of Warsaw. On 14 January, while things were still quiet on their sector, Stölten snatched time to write to his family:

> Daily the Russians begin an attack at a new point . . . Now it's gradually becoming clear and we're awaiting the main build-up at one of the bridgeheads. We're sitting on our warm vehicles and packed clothes and spinning our theories and whiling away the hours that remain to us and we are waiting – for, yes, he is coming to *us* . . . And now there's a pretty big noise coming from over there, which we're waiting for, smiling and completely calm.[10]

East Prussia would see the most bitter fighting of the winter offensive, and in preparation for what the Soviet High Command knew would be a gruelling frontal assault on multiple lines of German fortifications, it allocated its greatest strength to this front. The Red Army's 1,670,000 men, 28,360 guns and heavy mortars, 3,000 tanks and self-propelled guns and 3,000 aircraft outnumbered the much-depleted forty-one divisions of Army Group Centre, which could only muster 580,000 men, 700 tanks and self-propelled guns and a mere 515 aircraft. During the first week of the attack, the Red Army ground its way westwards from one fortified position to another. Its progress was slow and costly.[11]

The Soviet offensive in the north was transformed by Zhukov's and Konev's breakthroughs in central Poland. The rapid push westwards towards Cracow and Silesia opened up the German southern flank in East Prussia, allowing Rokossowsky's armies to bypass the strong lines of east-facing fortifications. On 20 January, the 5th Guards Tank Army drove directly northwards through the centre of East

Prussia, heading through the fortified German line around Allenstein the next day, taking Prussian Holland on 23 January and reaching Tolkemit on the shore of the lagoon at the mouth of the Vistula, the Frisches Haff.

Having cut East Prussia in two, the Red Army immediately widened its corridor in order to encircle the eastern half of the province and take its besieged capital, Königsberg. The commander of the reconstituted German 4th Army, Friedrich Hossbach, responded by abandoning the heavily fortified eastern defences around Lötzen – disobeying his direct orders – and pulling back to the west in a series of forced marches through deep winter snow. Peter Stölten and his tank unit were sent to shore up a German infantry position east of Osterode, as Hossbach tried to break through the thin Soviet line to the east of Elbing and stop the port from being completely surrounded. The critical battle for East Prussia was fought through innumerable skirmishes.

The morning of 24 January found Stölten's men cooking potatoes, having been driven out of the little village of Jadden. Ordered to mount a counter-attack, they left the potatoes for their return. Their four tanks led the German infantry assault across the snow-covered fields and up a small hill into the village. A drift had filled a ditch, into which three of the tanks fell. Only Stölten's made it across, helping to retake Jadden. In a lull after the battle, when they were still in the centre of the tiny village, an artillery shell hit his tank. Stölten and the rest of his crew did not make it out of the burning vehicle.[12]

The next day, the Red Army retook Jadden and by 30 January the survivors of Stölten's unit, together with the rest of the 4th Army and some units of the 2nd Army, were penned into a pocket formed around the coastal towns of Heiligenbeil and Braunsberg on the Frisches Haff. It measured no more than 20 kilometres across at its greatest extent. There they dug in. Harried by ground attack aircraft and hurried onwards by news of the Soviet advance, hundreds of thousands of refugees headed for this enclave, which the remnants of twenty-three German divisions defended stubbornly for the next two months.[13]

Erich Koch, the Gauleiter of East Prussia, had prohibited civilian evacuation until 20 January, by which point it was too late to put most of the plans into operation. By then, the Soviet breakthrough to Elbing had ruptured the overland routes for the majority of the province's 2.5 million inhabitants. There were now only two ways out of East Prussia. Refugees from the northern districts headed towards Königsberg and, to its north, the Samland peninsula, hoping to leave by sea from the Baltic port of Pillau. Those from the south-east and central districts made for the Frisches Haff, attempting to cross the ice to the long, thin sandspit, or Nehrung, which separated the Vistula lagoon from the Baltic Sea.

Lore Ehrich set out for the Haff from Braunsberg on 12 February with her two small children, grateful to the SA men who forced German farmers at gunpoint to take refugees on to their carts. The Haff lay within range of Soviet artillery and the Red Air Force, and so their group, like most others, aimed to cross during the long winter night. The engineers of the 4th Army had reinforced a road over the ice, but within the first half-hour on the ice the colt ambling along beside their cart broke both legs and had to be left behind. Later on one of the two carthorses fell through a hole in the ice in the dark. Trembling with fear at losing his horse – and with it the ability to pull his remaining possessions – the farmer carefully cut the horse free with an axe. By now the ice had begun to thaw and the freezing surface water was gradually rising. In the light of widely spaced torches, the slow-moving column looked like a long funeral procession. As the cold enveloped them, creeping into their limbs, Lore Ehrich kept her thoughts focused on the farmer's broad back in front of her. The morning light revealed the wreckage of trucks and cars that had broken down, their former passengers trudging across the ice on foot. Wounded soldiers lay on top of hay wagons, exposed to the wind and snow.

After a second night out on the frozen lagoon, Lore Ehrich's two children fell quiet, exhausted by the cold. By the time they reached the small summer resort of Kahlberg, which lay on the sandspit of the Nehrung, they were suffering from the 'highway illness', chronic diarrhoea. Lore Ehrich went on a hopeless tour of the port and the District Party Leader's office, which was besieged by frustrated and frightened refugees. Tormented by thirst even more than by hunger, they did not dare drink the water for fear of typhoid. The refugees inched further along the narrow, boggy road down the sandspit, with more carts falling into holes or overturning ahead of them. The whole column had to stop continually and wait for damaged wheels to be repaired and loads to be repacked. The soldiers they passed had no bread to give them. That first day they managed no more than 4 or 5 kilometres. Their cart, with its rubber wheels, two horses and solid roof, was one of the strongest, but the farmer's fear for his horses was palpable. As they passed more wreckage they saw old people and mothers huddled with their young children, lying beside dead horses.[14]

On their right lay the military road and the tree break of evergreens that protected them from the vicious wind off the Baltic. To their left lay the glittering ice of the Haff, over which occasional artillery shells flew. At one of the many long halts on the road, they were passed by a column of thousands of Red Army prisoners. Lore Ehrich saw many of them go up to the dead horses to cut off and eat strips of raw flesh. She was terrified that they might overpower their guards and fall on the trek. The Nehrung road eventually brought her to a huge assembly camp at Stutthof, where she left the farmer. Lore realised that no one was willing to queue on her behalf for the soup and bread that was distributed and she could not leave her sick children alone. Then her luggage and her handbag, containing all her jewellery, savings books and money, were stolen. Against the odds, thanks to the successive assistance of an SS officer, a policeman and a railway official, Lore Ehrich made it to Danzig. Here, too, connections helped. Acquaintances saw their names on the arrivals list, plucked Lore and her boys from the refugee camp and looked after them until they were well enough to board a ship for Denmark three weeks later.

Until the ice began to melt at the end of February, over 600,000 refugees ventured out from Heiligenbeil and Braunsberg towards Danzig. Some 10,000–12,000 fled along the Nehrung in the other direction, heading eastwards to Neutief, where the lagoon opened on to the sea. There they had to abandon their horses, carts and most of their belongings and make the short crossing to the Samland peninsula and the port of Pillau, where the German Navy continued to rescue civilians long after Gauleiter Koch had fled by ship from there.[15]

On 1 February, Liselotte Purper received a telegram to say that her husband had been wounded and was waiting for transport from Pillau. Kurt Orgel had greeted the start of the Soviet offensive with equanimity, mistaking it at first for a small, local counter-attack. Standing outside his dugout smoking his pipe as he watched the Red Air Force bomb their regimental headquarters, he exuded confidence that they could hold the Memel bridgehead. The sight of female Red Army prisoners had once again rekindled the old hope that the Soviets were finally running out of reserves. Only after the Soviet break-through to the coast near Elbing did Kurt Orgel admit that he had underrated the scale of the offensive and ask whether the leadership had been taken by surprise too. Even now, he found words to re-assure Liselotte. The failed Ardennes offensive had at least protected Germany from simultaneous attacks from east and west, he told her – 'I believe that could have been the end'. Now, they just had to hold on till 'new weapons' came, 'and I can tell you I am delighted at the confident trust which governs the front! Despite everything!' On 24 January, as his unit was retreating towards the East Prussian coast with the temperature falling to −13°C, Kurt was wounded in both buttocks and the right thigh.[16]

On 12 February, Kurt managed to scrawl a brief note to Liselotte, telling her that, for the last week, he had been on a hospital ship off the Pomeranian coastline near the island of Rügen. The next day he was able to tell her more. Despite the dreadful transport across the Baltic, he was confident that his flesh wounds would heal in two to three months and was looking forward to spending that time with her. 'Let's hope all goes well. Our star has looked after us once more,' he assured her. On 14 February, the hospital ship reached Copenhagen. Kurt admitted that during the journey his wounds had become infected and he had arrived at the naval hospital reduced to 'skin and bones'. In Copenhagen the food 'is quite excellent, only it's of no use to me because I have no appetite. Instead, mostly a high fever.' His restless mind worried that Liselotte could not visit him in Denmark when he needed her most; their reunion would have to wait until he was well enough to return to Germany.

Liselotte's letters to him described the trouble brewing with her neighbours over who should give up a room to accommodate some of the refugees pouring in from the west; she refused to vacate Kurt's room. On 22 February, Liselotte received his letter from Rügen and could see in the awkward scrawl how much effort it had cost him to write the few lines to her – 'My one, my love!' She began writing a reply. In Copenhagen, she promised, he would have the 'calm and order' he needed to recover. Reaching across the distance from the quiet country estate at Osterburg, she told him to concentrate on eating enough, 'so that I don't have to bruise myself against your hard bones in our future love-making'. Then she paused to answer the door, leaving her unfinished letter on the table. A telegram had arrived: 'Captain Orgel died on 19.2.45 in Copenhagen.'[17]

Even before she knew Kurt was dead, Liselotte had lost her customary self-confidence. She dated it back to a delayed reaction to raids on Berlin in November 1943. 'Since then,' she had explained to Kurt, 'I know that everything can be shaken . . . Does harm only come to others? Why should I not be hit by bombs? Only because I do not wish it, because I am full of the greatest vitality? Did the thousands of people who were hit not have "self-confidence" too?' Quoting Goethe 'as saying something like, "Only he who conquers the fear of death has completely won life"', she tried to buoy herself up; yet the fear remained. 'Against the devilish thunder from the air,' she confessed, 'I feel unarmed. My self-confidence deserts me and I often stand there ashamed in front of all my friends and acquaintances, who get through terror attack on terror attack without being seriously disturbed, or hurrying to escape it. They are firmly convinced that they will emerge unscathed.' Both the solitary, gnawing fear which Liselotte observed in herself and the matter-of-fact coping she saw in others were increasingly evident among other Berliners, both the result of their long schooling in air raids.[18]

On 3 February, the capital endured its heaviest raid of the war, leaving 3,000 dead. As Ursula von Kardorff went to check on her editorial colleagues afterwards, she watched the bombed-out emerge from clouds of swirling dust. She glimpsed their grey, drawn faces and bodies bowed under the weight of their possessions in the light of the fires on Potsdamer Platz, before they disappeared again into the dust clouds. Yet, even now, there were those who repeated the old slogan: '"Holding out", the most senseless of all words,' Kardorff fumed at the end of that long day. 'Well, they will hold out until they are all dead, there is no other salvation.' Her fellow journalist

Margret Boveri would not have agreed. With her angular features and small stature, Boveri stood out in the editorial offices for her direct gaze, sensible shoes and lack of make-up. She never went anywhere without her canvas bread bag, in which she carried her most important documents and possessions – which included that rarity, an intact light bulb. Like Kardorff, she too went to the editorial offices at Tempelhof, which *Das Reich* shared with the *Deutsche Allgemeine Zeitung*, determined to make sure that the next issue of the paper appeared without errors and on time. Having chosen to return to Berlin ten months before, Boveri was determined to hold out and positively relished the heightened feeling of being alive, watching the air raids at night from her balcony.

According to military reports on civilian morale in the capital, Berliners were similarly divided. Two well-dressed ladies were observed on a street in Zehlendorf arguing about whether or not they had voted for the Nazis in 1933, as if this should decide their lot in the event of defeat. Some Berliners were prepared to fight to the 'last drop of blood to stop the Russians', while others spread pessimistic rumours that the government had failed to take up a British and American offer to sign a separate peace and join the battle against the Soviets. Still, everyone was ready to point the finger at groups of foreign workers and, even worse, foreign soldiers lounging around in public and talking loudly in foreign languages.[19]

On 13, 14 and 15 February 1945, Dresden was attacked. Twenty-five thousand people died in the inferno. Victor Klemperer had spent the earlier part of 13 February delivering deportation notices to the handful of Jews in privileged mixed marriages who were still living in the city. As the full-scale alarm sounded, one of the condemned women in their cramped 'Jews' house' in the city centre exclaimed bitterly, 'If only they would smash everything up!' Then, as the humming of the planes grew louder and the lights went out, they knelt on the cellar floor with their heads underneath the chairs. A window was blasted open, exposing the burning city and the gusts of a strong wind. Victor and Eva Klemperer were separated during the second raid, which set their house ablaze. He followed the trail of refugees clambering up through the public gardens – forbidden to Jews – towards the cooler air on the Brühl terrace. Wearing a woollen blanket over his rucksack and clutching a grey bag with his

precious manuscripts and Eva's jewellery, Klemperer spent the rest
of the night watching the city centre burn. Some buildings glowed
red, others silvery white. From 40 kilometres away, a small German
girl was quite bewitched by 'that theatre', riveted by the 'blood red'
of the sky, while 'the city itself looked like a drop of white-hot iron.
And into this light fell "Christmas trees" of all colours.'[20]

Victor Klemperer watched, too dazed to take it in. He accepted
the gift of a napkin for his wounded face from another Dresden Jew
and listened as a young Dutchman, clutching the waistband of his
trousers, told his tale of escape from police custody. Further along
the terrace, in the first grey light of winter dawn Victor and Eva
found each other. She cut his Jewish star off with her pocket knife.
Reassured that the Police Headquarters and all the Gestapo files
inside it had burned and knowing what Jews with a star risked in the
wake of such a raid, the couple became bombed-out Germans like
everyone else. Slowly they joined the throngs of people heading for
the banks of the Elbe. Chronicling his own state of shock, the inveterate diarist noted how a corpse looked just like a bundle of clothes,
a severed hand like 'a model made of wax such as one sees in barbers'
shop windows'. Later an ambulance man dispensed eye-drops, wiping
the dirt out of Klemperer's eye. The couple weathered the succeeding
raids in the catacomb-like cellars of the Albertinum, where doctors
operated on the wounded while soldiers and ambulance men came
and went, bringing in more and more people on stretchers. Packets
of sandwiches finally arrived from the National Socialist People's
Welfare. Then the lights gave out and in the candlelight the men
cranked the generator, which powered the lighting and the fans,
casting huge shadows on the walls. The next day, 15 February, the
Klemperers joined the evacuees who were taken by truck to
the Luftwaffe base at Klotzsche.

A week later, on 22 February, Lisa de Boor and her husband sat
out a raid in the cellar of their house in Marburg, while she fretted
about the fate of their daughter Monika. They had just heard that
Monika had been moved from the prison in Cottbus to Leipzig in
preparation for her trial before the People's Court. But Monika's case
was delayed again after the presiding judge, Roland Freisler, was killed
by a falling beam in his own courtroom during the 3 February raid
on Berlin. Meanwhile on the Baltic front the de Boors' son Anton

had been wounded in the pelvis, stomach and thighs. After enduring two operations, he was suffering from pus and fever, exacerbated no doubt by poor sanitation and lack of antibiotics. Unlike Kurt Orgel, he would survive. The air raid on Marburg hit the station and a military hospital nearby. Many of the patients, Lisa de Boor heard, were killed as they sheltered in slit trenches. They took in an architect friend whose house had burned down in an earlier raid in Cologne and whose eldest son had been killed aged 18; the second son was reported missing in Italy and the third was now listed as missing on the western front. Meanwhile, the thunder of the guns in the west was becoming more audible.[21]

On 23 February, Ernst Arnold Paulus returned home earlier than usual from his GP practice in Pforzheim, hoping to be in time to see his two daughters off at the station. Both Elfriede and Irmgard had started studying medicine, following in his footsteps, just as he had once hoped their brother Helmut would. There had been no news of Helmut since he had been reported missing in November 1943 soon after returning to the eastern front from a spell of home leave. In the mobilisation drive of autumn 1944, Elfriede and Irmgard had both been called away from university to serve as Red Cross nurses, and were now working together in the same military hospital in Heilbronn. Their train left before their father could get to the station. It was just before the air raid began at 7.50 p.m. That coincidence saved their lives – and his. Instead of being in the centre of Pforzheim when the raid started, Dr Paulus had just driven back to their home on the outskirts of town. The attack, which came unexpectedly early, only lasted twenty-two minutes and involved 368 aircraft. As soon as the drone of the planes grew fainter, Ernst Paulus went out to man his emergency medical post in Pforzheim's high school. As he approached the town centre, he was driven back by billowing smoke and had to change direction. When he finally reached the high school, its upper floors were on fire. Undeterred, Paulus set his first aid centre up in the basement, working through the night and the next day treating the walking wounded as they streamed in, until finally a second doctor came to relieve him.[22]

Ernst Paulus's surgery had been hit, along with everyone in it, and his wife counted fourteen other doctors they knew among the dead. The fire hydrants had not functioned, leaving the fire brigade watching helplessly as the old town, with its narrow streets, family workshops and half-timbered houses, was engulfed in flames. An area measuring 3 by 1.5 square kilometres was completely destroyed. It would take many months, until beyond midsummer, to clear the rubble and remove the dead. The initial police estimates set the death toll at between 7,000 and 8,000 but the count gradually rose, reaching 17,600, about 20 per cent of the total population: it was one of the deadliest tolls inflicted on any German city.[23]

While Erna Paulus and the maid set about patching their torn blackout blinds and nailing up cardboard over their gaping windows, her husband held his morning open surgery at home with equipment donated by the emergency post in the high school. With no tradesmen and no shops, Pforzheim felt like a dead city. The Pauluses relied on food donated by family, friends and patients from the surrounding villages and local farms who saw to it that they received precious eggs and meat. Despite the devastating demonstration of Allied air supremacy, despite the ongoing uncertainty about Helmut's fate, despite their worries for their second son Rudolf, who was also now serving at the front, Erna and Ernst Paulus showed no signs of defeatism. Erna busied herself mending clothes for her daughters in Heilbronn, darning the family's stockings and socks and ironing while the electricity was on. At the end of March, they still listened to the German military bulletins keenly: when the electricity failed, they could now hear them only on their nephew's crystal set.[24]

Erna Paulus's sister, Käthe Wurster, was appalled by the news from Pforzheim, even though, as she put it, 'Punctually every evening for weeks now we have our attack on Berlin. In between, from time to time, a major day attack. But Berlin is large,' she explained from her leafy, south-western suburb: 'there have been many, many raids without hitting Zehlendorf.' That month, in the local cinema, safely located in the underground station at Onkel Toms Hütte, the audience refused to watch the newsreel before the main feature. According to an officer reporting for the Wehrmacht, 'A number of visitors forced a change of programme through thoroughly vulgar behaviour such as stamping, whistling, bellowing etc. People wanted to see the main film . . . first. Who is still interested in the newsreel, it is all fraud, propaganda, etc.' Their protest was not an expression of political opposition: the audience did not want the regular evening air raid to interrupt the feature film, the premiere of *The Soloist Anna Alt*, a classical music romance loosely based around the fraught relationship of Robert and Clara Schumann. When the sirens duly sounded, it was the newsreel which had to be stopped. Other cinemas found that trying to abandon their programme after long air raid interruptions precipitated 'tumultuous scenes, in the course of which there was no shortage of blunt remarks'.[25]

Demand for cinema tickets remained as high as ever, despite the air raids. If anything, the bombing only made filmgoers more vociferous in asserting their sense of entitlement, especially now that the theatres had been closed since the autumn. But there were few new films to watch. One anti-British offering, *Titanic*, fell victim to the air raids. Lovingly shot on a cruise liner in the Baltic, it had been released in 1943 but was only screened in occupied France, where the depiction of the rigid class divisions, with the third-class passengers being left to drown, was intended to stiffen Anglophobia. But before it was released in Germany, Goebbels decided that the scenes of mass panic amongst the passengers trapped in the third-class decks of the sinking ship might trigger all the wrong associations in the bombed cities. The film was pulled from the schedules.[26]

In a more positive vein, Goebbels had commissioned by far the largest and most lavish colour film to date in response to defeats of the summer. Set during the Napoleonic conquest of Prussia, it centred on the siege of Kolberg in 1807, which was eventually taken by the French. The film celebrated the new spirit of resistance that had been born there and which led to the German 'war of liberation' of 1812–13. In the film, the mayor of Kolberg tells the Prussian commander, General von Gneisenau, that he 'would rather be buried in the ruins than surrender', and only rises from his knees once the legendary Prussian general has replied: 'That's what I wanted to hear from you, Nettelbeck. Now we can die together.' The premiere was symbolically held in another German coastal 'fortress', the French port of La Rochelle, on 30 January 1945. Few Germans saw the film, though its central motifs of romantic patriotism had become ubiquitous, with the same lines of Theodor Körner's Romantic poetry appearing in the film as Goebbels had quoted at the end of his 'total war' speech two years earlier: 'Now let the nation arise, let the storm break!' While the brave Pomeranian farmer in the film torched his own farmstead in order to inflict 'scorched earth' on the French, the German farmers now fleeing from Silesia, East Prussia and Pomerania in their hundreds of thousands had other concerns.[27]

The arrival of their treks in the diminished Reich led to the demise of another anti-British film. In January 1945 the Propaganda Ministry decided that 'scenes of [Boer] refugees', depicted in the 1941 blockbuster *Ohm Krüger*, 'for the time being fitted "into the landscape" very badly'. Yet as the Propaganda Ministry tried to keep imaginary scenes of civilian panic and mass death off the cinema screens, it busily inflated the death toll in Dresden, letting the German Foreign Office feed photographs of the destruction, including close-ups of badly burnt children, to the press in neutral Sweden. For the first time, the Germans also decided to exaggerate, rather than to minimise, the loss of life. By 17 February, the *Svenska Morgonbladet* was telling the world that 'currently 100,000 dead are talked of'; on 25 February, the *Svenska Dagbladet* reported that, 'according to information compiled a few days after the destruction, the figure is closer to 200,000 than 100,000'. On 4 March, *Das Reich* carried a story written by its editor-in-chief entitled 'The death of Dresden: A beacon of resistance'. The Allied raids, the article declared, represented 'four acts of a coolly calculated plan of murder and destruction', with the second wave of British planes deliberately targeting the refugees sheltering on the banks of the Elbe and causing 'a bloodbath'. The high casualty figure rapidly entered German public consciousness; it was registered by both the Paulus and de Boor families.[28]

Goebbels had plucked his statistics from the air. In February the military and police in Dresden had only just begun to build up an accurate picture by counting the dead, street by street, block by block. As they did so, they came under pressure from the local military commander, General Karl Mehnert, to find more bodies. The destruction and the concentration of bodies within the narrow inner city was so great that it would have seemed to him – and many others – that the scale of destruction was even worse than it was. A special SS unit was brought in to oversee the cremation of the remains of 6,865 people by concentration camp prisoners in the Altmarkt square. As the *Sonderkommando* brought back to one of the Reich's finest baroque cities the methods pioneered for disposing of the Jews gassed in Treblinka, it added another involuntary image to the store of German parallels between their own victimhood and what they had done to the Jews.[29]

But the actual death toll did not match Mehnert's and Goebbels's guesses. By 10 March, the police had discovered 18,375 bodies; five days later, their 'final report' confirmed this number, predicting that the total would probably rise to 25,000. A further report on 22 March brought the actual number of the dead to 20,204 and repeated the estimate of a maximum total of 25,000. This was to be the final wartime report. To substantiate the exaggerated claims it had already made, the Propaganda Ministry simply added a zero to these numbers, setting before the world an utterly unprecedented death toll of 202,000, rising to a probable 250,000; it explained the large numbers by claiming that the population of the city had been tripled by a huge influx of refugees from the east. Yet in the twenty years after the war only a further 1,858 bodies were recovered, confirming the accuracy of the local police's original estimate. Both in Germany and outside it, however, Goebbels's mythical claims would enjoy a long run.[30]

This quest to influence international opinion, especially the public in Britain and the United States, was remarkably successful. Support came from an unexpected direction, when journalists were told at a press briefing at Eisenhower's headquarters that Dresden amounted to 'terror bombing', a term the British and Americans had always rejected in public – even though Churchill did use it privately. The British media responded to pressure not to report the slip, yet it got out in the United States via Associated Press, triggering a major debate on the ethics of 'area bombing'. Articles in the *Manchester Guardian* followed and on 6 March the Labour MP Richard Stokes used a question in the House of Commons to place all the information he had obtained about Dresden on the official record. On 28 March, Churchill bowed to public pressure and ordered a halt to the bombing of German cities. The heroism of Bomber Command had been lauded when Britain had possessed no other effective weapon against Germany, but now there was a queasy sense that an ethical line had been crossed.[31]

★

After three months of fighting in the Vosges hills, the Americans were forcing the Germans back to the Rhine at Colmar. Ernst Guicking was still defending the western, Alsatian bank of the Upper Rhine and, for the next few weeks, his wife Irene was torn between her fears for him and her anxiety that the Allies might manage to cross the great river. She confessed that her dearest wish was that he could turn into a mole and dig an underground tunnel to her in Lauterbach: 'I would bathe you in the laundry, rid you of all the bits of soil and then, yes then, I would dig you into the soil again, or hide you somewhere else, till no danger threatened you any more.' On 4 February, Ernst was at last able to write to tell her that his unit had crossed the Rhine to the Badenese side at Neuenburg and that they were now stationed in the relative safety of the Black Forest. They were still involved in fighting, but, as Ernst's private account veered into the language of the military bulletins with their calming talk of 'planned withdrawals', he assured Irene: 'Yes, the bridgehead has been cleared in the best order and with intelligent foresight. Over there they may shout about another victory, but on our side everything was already planned long in advance.'[32]

Irene was not perhaps a natural reader of *Das Reich*, but the young florist found herself forced to think about politics by the approaching front. She pored over an article Goebbels had written:

> We do not doubt for an instant that we will succeed in smashing the global threat from the east. When and how is a matter of the means which have been set in motion. The [hordes from the] steppes will be brought to a halt, and at the very moment when the danger has reached a peak and so is clear to everyone. Till then, keep a cool head.

The piece only half reassured Irene. She could not help asking Ernst if he thought that there were still 'elements in the Wehrmacht' who wanted to 'plot another 20 July'. 'Will Himmler pay enough attention?' she asked too, wondering why there were still 'so many healthy, young chaps running around here' when they could be at the front. Lauterbach remained relatively quiet, with occasional bombs dropped near the station, but Irene's main concern was getting in enough wood from the forest to see her through to the end of winter.[33]

While Guicking's Upper Rhine sector remained relatively quiet,

much heavier fighting was under way to the north. Along the wide
Lower Rhine, Canadian and British forces pushed from Nijmegen on
8 February. The American advance across the river Roer towards the
Cologne plain was delayed for a further twelve days when German
engineers opened the dams, flooding the valley. The German armies
under Rundstedt fought bitterly to hold on to their positions west
of the Rhine, continuing to inflict heavier casualties on the Allies
than they were suffering themselves. Such continued 'fighting power'
was all the more striking given the huge imbalance of forces: by
February, 462,000 German troops were facing 3.5 million Allied
soldiers. To make matters worse, many of the German divisions had
a high proportion of raw recruits, who had not been hardened in the
difficult rearguard battles for which their commanders, Model,
Blaskowitz and Hausser, were famous. Nor could they rely on the
same level of artillery or armour as their opponents. Indeed, having
starved the eastern front of tanks and artillery in December and
January in order to mount the Ardennes offensive, Hitler and Keitel
were now sending heavy weapons eastwards again, in a desperate
attempt to block the Red Army in Silesia and Hungary. On 2 March,
the Americans reached the western bank of the Rhine south and
north of Düsseldorf, and occupied Krefeld. Three days later, they
broke through the weak defences around Cologne and took the city
in a day, the Wehrmacht hurriedly detonating the main Hohenzollern
bridge as soon as they had crossed to the eastern bank.[34]

The Saar–Moselle defensive triangle had held all winter, its southern
side sealed by the Orscholz line. After months of fighting in snow-
drifts, the Americans finally breached this sector of the West Wall
on 22 February, when assault battalions of the 302nd US Infantry
crossed the Saar at Taben in the dense fog before dawn. As German
troops were rushed to counter different American attacks, Trier was
left undefended and, after a five-month siege, the city fell with virtually no fighting on 2 March. Having finally broken through, the US
3rd Army exploited its success, advancing rapidly along the Moselle
valley to where the river joined the Rhine at Koblenz.

In late February and March, as the Wehrmacht pulled back in the
west, there was no repeat of the mass civilian panic of early September
1944. This time, the local population refused to flee. White flags
were hung out from houses to prevent the destruction of villages.

In some places, people stopped German troops from shooting; in one village, local farmers with pitchforks set on the soldiers trying to detonate charges. A group of soldiers who reached the German lines after escaping from encirclement was greeted with shouts of 'You're prolonging the war!' In late February, when the Wehrmacht retook Geislautern near Völklingen, the local SS commander learned that, after the brief enemy occupation, the Americans were popular for treating the houses where they were quartered with more respect than the German troops had done and for sharing their rations, their chocolate, jam and cigarettes, with the famished population. He reported that the US forces' good repute was preceding them throughout the territory. A tank commander reported from near Mayen that civilians had tried to sabotage the defensive measures of the local command and offered civilian clothes to soldiers so that they could abscond.[35]

It quickly became clear that this was a very different situation from the previous autumn. As reported to the Commander-in-Chief in the West, 'then the soldiers flooding back from France influenced the civilian population negatively with their pessimistic judgement of the situation', whereas now 'the civilian population is having a depressing effect on the fighting morale and attitude of the German soldiers'. On 15 February, the Minister for Justice issued a decree establishing summary court martials for civilians, placing them under the same penalties as soldiers who deserted or undermined military morale. By 11 March, Goebbels realised that propaganda could no longer prevent morale from collapsing, noting in his diary that 'something can now only be achieved in the west through brutal measures'. Defeatism was spreading further along the Rhine as soldiers withdrawing from its western bank told of the flight of Nazi Party functionaries and the sea of white flags that had greeted the Americans in Neuss and Krefeld. They described their own powerlessness in the face of their enemies' incredible fire-power and control of the air. In Bochum, the local Party propaganda department conceded the hopelessness of dragooning workers to listen to set-piece speeches by uniformed Party officials. Instead, in mid-March it sent out thirty trained public speakers wearing plain clothes, to spread 'word-of-mouth propaganda' at railway stations, on trains, in air raid shelters – wherever people gathered and opinions were noisily exchanged. By 21 March, the weekly report to the Propaganda Ministry from the right bank of the Rhine accepted that even this kind of subtle approach 'would not help much any more'.[36]

Koblenz fell on 17 March. Within a week the economically vital Saar industrial area was encircled. As German forces fell back, Goebbels noted that 'tens of thousands of soldiers, allegedly stragglers but in reality wanting to avoid front-line service, are said to be in the big cities of the Reich'. Army commanders redoubled threats of summary justice. Nazis like Ferdinand Schörner led the way in hanging soldiers from lamp posts with demeaning placards such as 'I didn't believe in the Führer' or 'I am a coward'. But he had no monopoly on this. On 5 March, even the pious Protestant Johannes Blaskowitz warned the men of Army Group H that anyone who deserted his post would be 'summarily condemned and shot'. Shortly before Hitler retired him for the third – and final – time, Rundstedt issued another last-ditch order: 'The enemy must have to fight for every step in German land through the highest possible bloody losses.' On 10 March, Albert Kesselring replaced Rundstedt as Commander-in-Chief in the West and immediately established a special motorised unit of the military police to round up 'stragglers'. A few days earlier a new 'flying court martial' executed four officers for failing to detonate the bridge across the Rhine at Remagen before the Americans could cross it. A fifth officer was already an American prisoner of war and, on 25 March, Kesselring personally ordered that his family should be imprisoned. The local Gestapo and Reich Security Main Office in Berlin continued to oppose such measures and, as the Waffen SS General Paul Hausser pointed out, holding relatives liable did little when 'the family of the soldier was already within enemy-occupied territory'.[37]

Immediately after the Dresden raids, Hitler and Goebbels wanted to abrogate the Geneva Convention in the west and execute British and American prisoners of war in retaliation for German civilian dead. By inciting the Allies to execute German prisoners in turn, Hitler hoped to replicate in the west the mix of terror and dogged self-sacrifice which imbued German soldiers on the eastern front. The draft order ran into the united opposition of Jodl, Dönitz and Keitel, however, who succeeded in talking their Führer out of it:

they might countenance the lynching of Allied pilots – by now commonplace even in areas which had hardly been bombed before 1944, such as Austria – or push for reprisals against the families of German deserters but they baulked at endangering German prisoners of war. This crossed some invisible line in their sense of a professional ethical code.[38]

As Goebbels and the Propaganda Ministry tried to keep pace with military events, they recalibrated the message: reports of the good behaviour of American front-line troops in the Moselle–Saar borderland were countered with the warning that they would be followed by rear services ready to commit atrocities when 'the Jews' took control – as if the US armies would deploy their own Jewish *Einsatzgruppen*. Increasingly, German hopes centred on the prospect that the enemy alliance might break up. German officers in British captivity told each other that 'the British and Americans will one day . . . awaken to the real situation and will join the Germans in holding off Russia'. The Chief of Staff of Wehrmacht Armament, Colonel Kurt Pollex, knew how depleted his arsenals were and harboured no illusions about 'miracle weapons'; but he too hoped that conflict between the Americans and Russians could still give Germany a chance. As he put it, it was like a car race decided 100 metres from the finishing line by a puncture. The flimsy simile echoed something Goebbels himself had said in a national broadcast on 28 February, in which he compared the nation to a marathon runner, with 35 kilometres behind him and only 8 kilometres to go.[39]

After cutting off his Jewish star, Victor Klemperer was terrified that he would be killed if he was picked up by the Gestapo. To avoid contact with the mass organisations of the Party, he and his wife turned to their former domestic servant, Agnes, who lived in the Wendish-speaking village of Piskowitz in Saxony. There Klemperer listened to the clear cadences of the Propaganda Minister on the radio: 'Only the greatest willpower keeps him going, drives him on, perhaps he will collapse unconscious at the finishing post, but he must reach it! . . . We are strained to the utmost, the terror attacks have become almost unbearable – but we must stay the course.' With its combination of metaphysical metaphors about the meaning of History, practical consolation that 'Our enemies were "just as tired as we were"', hints at a massive German counter-offensive and threats to '"coldly and calmly put a rope round the neck" of anyone who tries to sabotage us', Goebbels had ceased to claim that the war could last much longer. Indeed, the ever-alert Klemperer was struck by his message of 'utter despair'. His own hopes that he and Eva would live to see their liberation revived once more.[40]

In 1943 and 1944, Goebbels had repeatedly proposed that Hitler open negotiations with either the Soviets or the British and Americans in order to secure a separate peace. He was perhaps the only Nazi leader who could risk making such a suggestion so frequently in their private meetings: although Hitler had never accepted that the time was right, he had not banned the topic. But Goebbels now realised that time to negotiate was running out: the Rhine had to be held if there was to be any prospect of persuading the Western Allies that it was better to negotiate than to go on losing men. Defending Germany west of the Rhine had cost the Wehrmacht half its forces on the western front: 60,000 soldiers were wounded or dead, and 293,000 had been taken prisoner, including 53,000 in a single encirclement near Wesel.[41]

What remained of Hitler's 'Great German Reich' was bounded by two major rivers, the Oder and the Rhine, both of which had already been breached by enemy bridgeheads. In between lay 540 kilometres of the North German Plain, punctuated by only one natural obstacle: the river Elbe. A German General Staff officer told his Allied captors in mid-March that the German High Command

> believed that the line of the Elbe at the east and of the Rhine in the west could be held for as long as proved necessary. It was envisaged that sooner or later a split would occur between the US and UK on the one hand and the USSR on the other, which would enable Germany to restore her position.

In order to safeguard the re-emergence of the Luftwaffe and its jet fighters in this next phase of fighting, oil refineries and other key installations had been equipped with heavy anti-aircraft defences. On 20 March, Hitler appointed General Gotthard Heinrici to command the Oder front, replacing Himmler, on whose 'defeatism' and military incompetence he blamed the loss of Pomerania. Heinrici, who had proved his skill in tactical defence time and again, also believed that as long as German forces held the Rhine, his defence of the Oder made strategic sense.[42]

Albert Speer was steeling himself to warn Hitler that the German economy would unwind in just four weeks; but he too joined in the optimistic talk and suggested rushing back the divisions in Italy and Norway to defend the Rhine and Oder fronts. As the Armaments Minister put it in a memo for Hitler on 18 March, 'Holding out tenaciously on the current front for a few weeks can gain respect from the enemy and perhaps thus favourably determine the end of the war.' The two men met the same day, with Hitler asserting that the war would continue and the army would wage a 'scorched earth' policy without regard to Germany's future needs: 'If the war is lost, then the people too is lost.' If the German people proved too weak, he declared, then the 'future belongs exclusively to the stronger people of the east'. This sentiment, first expressed in a moment of despair during the retreat from Moscow in the winter of 1941–42, had become one of Hitler's *idées fixes*. He had expressed it in a private address to the Gauleiters on 24 February, and would repeat it verbatim when drafting his political testament a few weeks later. But it remained an idea which Hitler and Goebbels expounded only to that inner circle of leaders whom they considered responsible enough to think of their final hour in terms of heroic suicide.

After speaking to the Gauleiters, Hitler was too exhausted to broadcast his customary speech to the German people on 24 February, a date which commemorated the promulgation of the Party programme. Instead his proclamation had to be read over the radio by his old Party comrade, Hermann Esser. It was redolent with the Führer's recognisable phrases: 'this Jewish-Bolshevik anni-hilation of peoples and its West European and American pimps'; 'freedom of the German nation'; fighting till 'the historical turning point'. 'The life left to us can serve only one command,' the Führer demanded at the close: 'that is to make good what the international Jewish criminals and their henchmen have done to our people.' Even the local Party boss in Lüneburg was driven to quip bitterly, 'The Führer is prophesying again.'[43]

Goebbels's most loyal correspondents continued to pin their hopes on leaflet drops to persuade British and American troops not to allow themselves to serve as the pawns of 'world Jewry'. Suggesting ways of getting the message across to enemy soldiers that they were being made to pay the 'blood sacrifice' of 'Jewish Bolshevism' and 'Jewish plutocracy', they all emphasised that the only hope for Western civilisation lay in Britain and the United States forging an alliance with Germany against Stalin. One letter to the Propaganda Ministry closed with the pseudo-Marxist slogan: 'Goy awake! Non-Jews of the world unite!'[44]

Ernst Guicking wrote to Irene about the coming spring counter-offensive, advising her just to bunker down, make sure that their furniture was safe and lay in enough provisions. He was confident that they would be able to withstand the coming Allied assault. 'If we can survive the summer,' Ernst wrote to Irene on 9 March, 'then we have also won.' Promising her that Germany still possessed a 'miracle weapon' which would turn the tables on the Allies even if Berlin fell, Ernst affirmed that those who doubted the German cause did not 'belong among us any more'. Without ceasing to talk up their hopes, for the first time Ernst and Irene began to consider their post-war future. On his last leave, the ever-practical Ernst had noticed that many young men would never return to his father's village of Altenburschla. With the prospect of farms lying vacant, he suggested to Irene that they sink their savings into a plot of land. 'If we win the war,' he explained, 'then we have what we most need, namely land. If we go to the dogs, then everything goes to the dogs.'[45]

On 22 and 23 March, the US 5th Infantry Division under Patton crossed the Rhine at Nierstein and Oppenheim. The troops met with little resistance but found it hard to exploit their success, because there were few roads in this rural area to the south of the river Main. In addition to the bridgehead established at Remagen on 7 March, a further crossing was forced along the middle Rhine where it ran through a gorge at St Goar. The main assault in the north came as expected on the Lower Rhine, where the British crossed the river at Wesel and Rees late on 23 March. The following day, engineers bridged the wide river and marshy terrain. Without reserves or air support and with few tanks or artillery, the German 1st Parachute Army was ill equipped to oppose the 1,250,000 men under Montgomery. The German commander, General Günther Blumentritt, agreed with

Blaskowitz, his superior, that they could neither counter-attack nor continue to hold a broken line: by 1 April he had disengaged and pulled back to the far side of the Dortmund–Ems Canal, leaving the way into the Ruhr open from the north.

American progress in the south was even swifter. The bridges over the Main at Aschaffenburg and Frankfurt were taken on 25 and 26 March, allowing the forces that had just crossed the Upper and Middle Rhine to link up. During the previous two weeks, Model had used up precious artillery and armour trying to regain control of the Remagen bridgehead. Here Hodges' US 1st Army began its breakout on 25 March. But, instead of attacking northwards into the powerful Ruhr defences established by Model, the Americans went for a wide encirclement, driving eastwards. By the end of the second day, they had broken through the German lines and were racing towards the river Lahn and the cities of Giessen and Marburg.

As the news of the first crossings over the Rhine came through on 25 March, Joseph Goebbels could only note that 'The situation in the West has entered an extraordinarily critical, ostensibly almost deadly, phase.' In Münster the newspaperman Paulheinz Wantzen had been driven to despair when he had heard that the Americans had taken the bridge at Remagen: 'Everyone hoped that they would halt the Americans and English; if not totally, then at least for a long time and somehow support the front. These hopes are over now.' As he filled pages of his diary with accounts of the air raids on Münster and the surrounding towns, he felt 'pretty shaken' by the news of the Allied crossings. Yet, somehow, Wantzen still had the energy to record a political joke: 'The Führer is pregnant. He is carrying Little Germany.' It was as if the calamity of the military collapse was too great to express in any other way. In Lauterbach, Irene Guicking told Ernst that she could no longer believe in the war, even though she knew he still did and feared his reaction: 'The British and Americans have forced their way too deep into Germany. Do you know that we all hope that there isn't a successful counter-offensive from our side? Then we'd have total war. Not just from the air: the battle waged on German land would be much worse.' Lauterbach lay between Giessen and Fulda: Irene could not yet know it, but the American tanks would arrive soon.[46]

In the small university town of Marburg, the warm weather encouraged Lisa and Wolf de Boor to dig their vegetable garden and start their spring planting. Whatever happened, they would need food, particularly as Lisa had taken in refugees and friends. When the water and electricity were knocked out in the town's barracks, she had brewed coffee for the soldiers. A friend in the local administration reassured her that the men had neither the ammunition nor artillery to make a stand. But the couple worried most about their daughter Monika. There was no current news: the last card they received from Cottbus prison had been sent weeks earlier, on 6 February, and it was not reassuring. Reduced to skin and bones, Monika had joked that she made 'an object for an osteological study'.

On 26 March, the Marburg garrison was sent out to meet the Americans advancing along the Lahn valley from Limburg. Lisa had already heard on the BBC that Churchill had crossed the Rhine with the British forces and that Scots pipers had given a concert on the east bank. The following day, she noticed that there were more classified adverts in the local newspaper offering English lessons. As she sat in the sunshine enjoying the first buds of spring, Lisa watched a 'flood of vehicles, cars, bicycles, soldiers and civilians' pour along the road from Giessen. Marburg itself felt like 'a swarm of bees that have been roused'. That night the de Boors heard on the BBC that the Americans were beyond Giessen. In bed, they listened to the ceaseless drone of the German retreat, confident that the next day the Americans would reach them.[47]

On the morning of 28 March, Lisa was in the garden picking lamb's lettuce when she heard the thudding of shells. She was so excited that, instead of taking shelter, she ran upstairs into the house to watch for the American tanks. About noon, she finally spotted them entering the town. Clutching the Stars and Stripes flag which her sister had brought her years before from America, Lisa ran down the empty streets to the Barfüssertor, joined by a Polish worker from a nearby coal merchant's. They were the first to greet a long column of Red Cross vehicles. Calling out their few words of English as they ran across, they were joined by French prisoners of war, Italian military internees and more Poles. The Americans distributed piles of German coats, blankets and clothing to the forced labourers. Returning home, Lisa found that a column of American infantrymen and German prisoners had halted in front of her house, where she was able to provide them with food and drink. At 5 p.m., the de Boors walked through the city reading the new orders pasted to the walls, announcing the banning of all Nazi organisations, the closure of schools and the university, and, to their delight, permission to hold religious services. They could immediately start setting up a meeting room for the small Steinerian 'Christian Community' to which they belonged. As Lisa de Boor stepped out on to the balcony at dusk, the clouds dispersed. The moon appeared large and reddish as it rose over the dark woods to the east of Marburg. 'This', she wrote at the end of that momentous day, 'is the spring full moon which is followed by Easter Sunday and the Resurrection. We know that the coming period will be hard, very hard. Yet, on this evening my heart rejoices.'[48]

Irene Guicking's home town of Lauterbach was occupied by the leading tanks of the US 3rd Army on the same day, leaving Ernst, a mere 90 kilometres to the south near Bad Kissingen, on the other side of the lines. On 3 April, he took the precaution of sending Irene an early birthday letter, which he hoped would make it across to 'the area of the other world view'. He also hoped 'that you and the little ones are OK and you are well and in good spirits'. And he promised her, 'I know one thing, Irene: we will both come through everything.' The next day, certain that he was about to be either captured or killed, he managed to send one more note: 'This will be the last letter. Please, please, stay brave. You will hear from me. It will be through the International Red Cross.'[49]

The sheer speed of the American breakthrough was astonishing. On 29 March, the US 1st and 3rd Armies met between Giessen and Marburg. Patton's tanks continued their push eastwards into Thuringia, while those of Hodges turned north-east towards Paderborn to link up with Simpson's 9th Army, which was encircling the Ruhr from the north. Despite bitter resistance from a Waffen SS unit with sixty tanks near Paderborn, the junction was rapidly made. At 3.30 p.m. on 1 April, the American tanks met at Lippstadt, closing the ring. It was Easter Sunday.[50]

In Braunschweig, Bochum and Hanover, people were burying their valuables in preparation for occupation even before the British and Americans crossed the Rhine. The Propaganda Ministry knew that no one believed the war could continue once the Ruhr was in Allied hands. It did not matter that much manufacture had been dispersed to other regions: it was on the coal mines and steel mills of Upper

Silesia, the Saar and the Ruhr that the German war economy depended. As the American encirclement of the Ruhr tightened from the east, 400,000 German troops were pinned against the Rhine barrier they had tried to defend. They lacked the artillery and armour to break out, and conditions in the cities became increasingly violent and desperate.[51]

The last days of Nazi rule in this strategically vital region resembled the collapsing beehive Lisa de Boor had witnessed in Marburg. Hamm and Dortmund held out against occupation, with units of Hitler Youths fighting on till they were overwhelmed and the cities had been virtually destroyed by artillery and bombing. Bochum, Mülheim and Duisburg all surrendered, as leading industrialists joined forces with old-time trade unionists and labour activists to pressure Nazi mayors and military commanders to safeguard what was left. In Oberhausen, retreating German troops began to plunder, drinking any alcohol they could find and destroying equipment in a haphazard application of Hitler's 'scorched earth' orders. Elsewhere in the Ruhr, German miners, engineers and managers quietly co-operated, often staying underground and manning pumps to prevent their pits from being flooded by the retreating Wehrmacht. At the Frederick the Great mine, eighty men turned out with hunting guns and old Belgian rifles to prevent the District Leader's order to destroy the mine from being carried out. These men were instinctively doing the same thing as the metalworkers in Kiev in 1941, when they had hidden machinery to foil Stalin's 'scorched earth' orders. In January 1945, the coal miners and steelworkers of Upper Silesia were some of the few who did not flee from the Red Army: having seen their Polish colleagues 'Germanised' in 1939–40, they assumed that their vital role in production would prove more important to the occupiers than their national identity. In each of these different conditions of occupation, workers and managers regarded their expertise as their most valuable asset, seeing it as a rational guarantee in the face of overwhelming military force. Only the Kievans, facing ruthless application of racist ideology, calculated wrongly.[52]

In 1945 there were still 7.7 million forced workers in the Reich. On 7 and 10 February, the Gestapo shot twenty-four 'Eastern workers' in Duisburg whom they suspected of being members of gangs, some of which had been waging running battles with the police in the semi-uninhabited shells of cities like Cologne, Essen, Düsseldorf and Duisburg. The gangs arose out of the conditions created by the renewed bomber offensive of September 1944. When barracks and workplaces were destroyed, German and also West European workers were generally given assistance and rehoused. Many of the 'Eastern workers' simply became vagrants or, in a minority of cases, took to petty crime or worked in the black market. As the gangs grew, they hid in abandoned scrapyards, obtained money and military weapons, sometimes co-operating with German gangs. The better-organised ones included former Red Army soldiers and inflicted heavy casualties on the Gestapo squads sent to arrest them.

From the autumn of 1944, the Reich Security Main Office in Berlin delegated decisions about executions to individual Gestapo offices, further increasing local autonomy. Even before the Allies reached the west bank of the Rhine, the Gestapo began shooting the Soviet workers it held in remand. As the Allies occupied the western bank, the executions increased. In Essen, the head of the local Gestapo chose a firing squad from officers who had never participated in executions before to shoot 35 prisoners, thereby ensuring that responsibility was equally shared. On 20 March, 30 prisoners were executed near Wuppertal; 11 in Gelsenkirchen on 28 March; and the following day, 29 prisoners were shot in the bomb crater in Duisburg's Waldfriedhof cemetery: none was accused of having done more than give shelter to gang members. Officers at the Gestapo's head office for the eastern Ruhr at Dortmund were even more active, executing an estimated 230–240 prisoners between February and April, including members of a French theatre troupe. But the great majority of their victims were civilian workers or prisoners of war from the Soviet Union. In Dortmund, Bochum and elsewhere, as the Allied encirclement of the Ruhr tightened, the Gestapo carried out a last frantic round of executions on 7 and 8 April, hours before the secret policemen were all pulled out of their towns to gather at a high school at Hemer. Here they executed a further nine prisoners, again allotting the task of shooting them to several detectives who had only recently been transferred to the Gestapo and had yet to carry out an execution. Then they stayed at the school, watching each other lest anyone abscond, as they awaited the arrival of the Americans.[53]

Düsseldorf straddles the Rhine and, on 3 March, the Americans had captured the neighbourhoods on the left bank of the river, but the Wehrmacht destroyed the bridges and dug into its positions on the eastern bank. As luck would have it, Marianne Strauss, the young Jewish woman who had gone into hiding in October 1943 when her family was deported from Essen, had arrived in the city in February. The small socialist resistance group, the Bund, had decided to send her to Düsseldorf as the Allies approached the Rhine, in the hope that she would be liberated soon. Marianne had landed on the doorstep of a teacher whom she had never met before, clutching a letter of introduction. She was lucky. Hanni Ganzer unhesitatingly offered her sanctuary. After taking the western bank, US forces shelled and bombed Düsseldorf every day for the next six weeks. One by one, all the utility mains – gas, electricity and water – were cut. Having perfected her skills at 'passing' on the street, despite her lack of corroborating identity documents, Marianne went with Hanni to the bunker. In the overcrowded, claustrophobic concrete rooms they slept on chairs, sometimes only coming out into the acrid air, full of the dust from destroyed buildings, for an hour each day. Although most of the authorities' coercive surveillance was targeted at deserters and gangs of foreign workers, they had not forgotten that there might be hidden Jews too. On 15 April, an army unit found a 72-year-old Jewish man: he was promptly hanged on the Oberbilker market square.[54]

Essen alone had over 300 camps for foreign workers, who constituted up to 70 per cent of the workforce in heavy industry. Here, ten days before the Allies crossed the Rhine, six young women escaped from the Krupp works during an air raid. They were Hungarian Jews who had been deported in the summer of 1944 to Auschwitz-Birkenau but, along with tens of thousands of other camp prisoners, were then selected for labour and sent back to the 'old' Reich and put to work at the Krupp steelworks. They were the first Jews to come to parts of Germany which had been triumphantly declared 'free of Jews' in 1942 and 1943. Then, on 15 March 1945, those who had survived the winter learned that they were about to be deported again, this time to the parent camp at Buchenwald. Threatened by the SS guards that they would not survive the war, the six young women fled while the streets were deserted during an air raid. They hid in the wrecked mortuary of the Jewish cemetery – and endured days without water or food. Finally, one of them found her way to the flat of Erna and Gerhard Marquardt, who had given them food at the Krupp works. Marquardt turned to an acquaintance in the SS, who lent him a spare uniform. Thus attired, the two men went unchallenged as they lugged two sacks of bread across to the six Jews hiding in the cemetery. The Marquardts found an odd assortment of people to take the women in: a work colleague, a grocer, even an SA man. Each of these helpers would have had different – and probably confused – motives, ranging from anti-Nazi sympathies and humanitarian compassion to the search for a useful excuse to cover membership of the SS and SA when the Allies arrived.[55]

In early April, thousands of concentration camp prisoners were sent out on forced marches across the Reich. There was virtually no chance of further exploiting their labour: most prisoners were no longer capable of work and, in any case, factories were being abandoned. Himmler's own agenda veered between fulfilling Hitler's demands that no prisoners should fall into enemy hands alive and using them as hostages to trade in secret peace talks with the Americans, which he hoped to start through Scandinavian intermediaries. Increasingly, such decisions fell to the local SS guards, as all semblance of central control disintegrated in areas already encircled by the Americans. On 4–5 April all the prisoners working at the underground factories at Mittelbau-Dora producing the V-2 rockets were evacuated from the western Harz. When the Americans arrived on 11 April they found 700 prisoners, too ill and emaciated to be moved, and discovered the tunnels into the Harz rock which had been dug by the prisoners in order to secure rocket production from air raids. Two days later, some 40 kilometres north of Magdeburg, a motley collection of guards, drawn from military personnel, the Hitler Youth and the Volkssturm as well as the local fire brigade, locked a thousand prisoners from Mittelbau-Dora into a barn in the village of Mieste and burned them alive. The local Nazi Party District Leader had decided that it was easier to be rid of them than to wait for the railway line to be repaired and transport them further to the camps at Bergen-Belsen, Sachsenhausen and Neuengamme.[56]

As the remaining territory of the Third Reich dwindled, the forced marches of prisoners became more pointless and murderous. Many of the guards now included older SA men, grounded air force personnel, members of the Volkssturm and the Hitler Youth. They were both inexperienced and determined to follow their instructions not to let their prisoners escape. For years, labour details of concentration camp prisoners had been an increasingly common sight in German town and cities; now the evacuation marches tore the last veil of secrecy away from their treatment. Many onlookers were shocked by the emaciated, shambling figures and the brutality of their guards, and recoiled behind closed doors in quiet horror. But feelings of compassion and guilt were less prevalent than fear. Even the prisoners' suffering damned them. Germans told themselves, 'What crimes they must have committed to be treated so cruelly!' When the prisoners from Auschwitz were marched through Polish towns in Silesia in January, they were sometimes hidden and often given food and drink by sympathetic locals; but as the exhausted columns wound their way through German towns and villages in the spring of 1945, the general reaction was revulsion and fear. More people jeered, spat and threw stones at them than offered assistance. On the night of 8–9 April, local civilians helped the SS, Volkssturm, SA, local police, soldiers and Hitler Youths to hunt down and shoot over 200 prisoners who had fled into the woodland near Celle after their train was bombed.[57]

As the Nazi order in the Ruhr collapsed, the victims of German violence continued to fit the Nazi profile of its enemies: German deserters and communists, French prisoners of war, and, overwhelmingly, 'Eastern' workers. Sometimes the vague sense of threat was enough, as crowds of famished and ragged forced labourers tramped eastwards to escape the bombing. SS General Kammler, commander of the V-2 rocket site near Suttrop, decided that 'this riffraff ought to be eliminated' before it could commit acts of terror in Germany, after his car was held up by crowds on the road in the Sauerland. In late March, more than 200 men, women and children were killed by his ZV2 Division in three mass executions: far from posing a terrorist threat, the victims were those who had stepped forward in response to a request for labour volunteers.[58]

Such violence extended beyond the ranks of the army, SS, police and Gestapo. So many German men and women played active roles in the mass organisations of the Party that no sharp line can be drawn between regime and society. Even after the Gestapo withdrew from the Ruhr to the schoolrooms at Hemer, their murderous role was filled by others. In early April 1945, four 'Eastern' workers were seen leaving a house in Oberhausen during a bombing raid. A group of German men, on air raid watch, set off in pursuit, seizing one of the men and beating him till he confessed to having stolen some potatoes. He was then beaten again by a group of German youths, before a telephone operator took the man first to the police and then on to a Wehrmacht office where he was loaned a pistol. Harried and beaten once more by a crowd with clubs and wooden fence slats, the 'Eastern' worker was led out to a sports field. There, in a bomb crater, the telephone operator shot him in the stomach and the crowd continued to beat him until he died.[59]

★

On 18 April, August Töpperwien's son, Karl Christoph, turned 17. By coincidence, that day a letter from him reached his father in the quiet Czech backwater of Petersdorf. Karl Christoph described how he and his comrades had been inducted into the Volkssturm and taken their military oaths, having undergone fourteen days' training in a former Reich Labour Service camp. He tried to show that he was true to his father's religious and moral standards, even if they made him feel isolated from his comrades. 'It is not made easier for one to obtain inner peace, but that is only to the good,' he wrote. 'Success does not lie in our hand. But Goethe was surely right: "He who truly strives, him we can save".' Karl Christoph bemoaned his comrades' irreligiosity and love of 'Jazz – or hot nigger music', as he called it, but felt compelled to defend their patriotism:

> On the matter of the Fatherland, I believe the fact that many want to get out to the front stems from insolence and utter ignorance of what the front means. Nonetheless, a certain patriotism is present. How else to explain the exemplary deeds of the 1927 and 1928 cohorts and older.

He admitted that 'There are some who aren't happy to do it', before hurriedly assuring his father: 'I don't have this misgiving. But all the same, it did cost me a real effort . . . Commanded by God! What more could we wish for ourselves. And our Fatherland commanded by God. Yours, Karl Christoph.'[60]

By now, August Töpperwien had finally ceased to trust in the

Führer and his prophecies. On 15 April, as the Americans approached Solingen, he had admitted to himself that 'The battle of arms can now only be about defeat with honour!' For Karl Christoph's birthday, he had sent Joseph von Eichendorff's poem 'The Soldier', whose final lines promised:

> And when it is darkest
> [and] I am tired of the earth . . .
> We will storm heaven's gate.

Somehow the words shielded August Töpperwien from the fact that his son was about to face the danger and terror of an overwhelming and unwinnable battle.[61]

As the Americans approached Pforzheim in late March, Ernst Arnold and Erna Paulus continued to mourn their son Helmut, missing in action since November 1943. Erna confessed that 'thinking of Helmut is frightful': his sacrifice no longer made sense to her, as she and her husband finally realised that the war was irretrievably lost. 'We want to wait here quietly and see what fate has in store for us, and not give up hope that we all meet again one day and that our beautiful house remains intact,' she wrote to her two daughters in Heilbronn, where they continued to work in the main dressing station. She had no news from them, but the radio reported again and again that the city was being bombed.[62]

When Jürgen Heitmann's Volkssturm unit was out training north of Fulda, they saw American tanks firing into their camp. The seventy boys simply ran away with the weapons they were carrying, reaching a Reich Labour Service camp at mid-afternoon on the next day. There they were plied with food and sweets, but the locals were keen for them to move on, telling them that US tanks had already reached their village. Jürgen's company split into small units to make their way through the Thuringian forest undetected, where they passed a forced march of concentration camp prisoners. From the bodies in the ditches, he could see that the SS had been shooting stragglers and, as they passed, Jürgen witnessed another killing. Taking their food from passing Wehrmacht units and sleeping in farms, on the floors of school buildings and in the forest, Jürgen's small unit pressed on into Thuringia for another ten days. Finally, they realised from the noise of American lorries roaring along the nearby autobahn that they had been overrun. While a major wearing a Knight's Cross organised other groups to make a last stand, on the morning of 16 April their own leader ordered them to bury their weapons and uniforms in the woodland. Releasing the boys from their service oath, he left them to get home as best they could.[63]

By mid-April, two-thirds of Army Group B lacked weapons and ammunition, and troops were simply melting away into the woods and cities of the Ruhr. On 15 April, in August Töpperwien's home town of Solingen local citizens began tearing down the tank barriers; by the following day almost all the soldiers there had obtained civilian clothes. Even the senior commander discarded his major's uniform for an ill-fitting suit and sports cap as he abandoned his command. Walter Model avoided actually surrendering to the Americans by ordering his army to 'dissolve' itself on 17 April, the day Solingen fell: 317,000 men were taken prisoner, including thirty generals. Torn between common sense and proud loyalty, Model followed the course of action Hitler had wished Paulus to take at Stalingrad: he went into the woodland and shot himself. That day, the US 97th Infantry Division entered Düsseldorf. Marianne Strauss had become so used to the constant threat of being caught that it took her ten days to realise she was finally safe.[64]

16

Finale

On 9 April 1945 Goebbels described the Reich as a narrow band running from Norway to the Adriatic coast of northern Italy. Along the Oder front, Heinrici's armies waited for the Soviets to renew their offensive. Entrenched in three deep defensive lines, the Germans deployed a million men, with 1,500 tanks and armoured vehicles, 10,400 artillery guns and 3,300 fighter planes. It was a formidable force, but they faced armies three times their size with over 6,000 tanks, 41,000 artillery pieces and 7,500 planes. When news came that the British and Americans had crossed the Rhine and trapped the strongest German armies in the Ruhr, the strategic value of defending the Reich at the Oder also evaporated: with no clear front line in the west, holding the Red Army at the Oder could no longer protect what was left of the Third Reich. The British pushed across the North German Plain to Hamburg and the river Elbe; the Americans and French into the Ruhr, Hesse and the south. These stark military facts greatly exacerbated the distinct local and regional character of the German defeat, as it unfolded during the final three weeks of the war in Europe.[1]

In the west, battles became delaying tactics, attempts to hold particular places for as long as possible or, conversely, to disengage and fight through to safety somewhere else. Army Group G under its new commander, Friedrich Schulz, tried to hold the river Main south of Aschaffenburg but, despite dogged resistance, it was soon outflanked to its east by the US 3rd Army and began a headlong retreat southwards. Heilbronn was defended for a week by Wehrmacht and Volkssturm units, whilst Karlsruhe fell without a shot. By mid-April, the American armies were already pressing eastwards into Thuringia, taking Erfurt, Weimar and Jena, and southwards into Saxony and Bavaria: Halle, Chemnitz, Leipzig, Coburg and Bayreuth all fell in quick succession. On 11 April, American troops reached the Elbe. By 16 April, Nuremberg was a battleground, with the former editor of *Der Stürmer* and Gauleiter of Franconia, Karl Holz, organising the resistance. For five days, a mixed group of German and Russian 'volunteer' troops held on against the American artillery barrage, even after the old city was surrounded and bombed.[2]

In this febrile atmosphere, in which SS troops were often the last to surrender and committed a growing number of atrocities against prisoners and German civilians, Himmler quietly tried to kick-start secret peace talks with the Americans. In February and March he met the Vice-President of the Swedish Red Cross and member of the royal family, Count Folke Bernadotte, and agreed to the release of Scandinavian prisoners in the concentration camps, including a small number of Jews. On 20 April, Himmler was so desperate to find a way of approaching Eisenhower and brokering an armistice that he left Hitler's birthday celebrations in Berlin for a meeting with Norbert Masur, the Swedish representative on the World Jewish Congress, a body whose influence and power in America the Reichsführer SS doubtless hugely overrated. Ribbentrop too became increasingly active, first proposing an anti-Bolshevik alliance to the Western powers through the German embassy in Stockholm and, when that got nowhere, telling the deputy ambassador to approach the Soviets instead. Unlike Himmler, who continued his machinations in secret, Ribbentrop sought Hitler's sanction – and was forced to desist. Goebbels too had hoped that Hitler might make a separate peace with one side or the other and had raised this option with his Führer at regular intervals since August 1941. He was also realistic enough to shelve the idea after the fall of the Rhine. In public, he continued to encourage German hopes that Allied infighting might yet save the Reich, but he clearly no longer believed that the Nazi leadership had the power to engineer this result. Following Hitler's lead, he refocused his own efforts on imbuing the imminent defeat with a tragic heroism which could inspire future generations. Above all, it was clear that the temptation to repeat the cowardly capitulation of November 1918 had to be resisted at all costs. While senior Nazi leaders like Göring, Speer and Himmler wanted to save what they could from total destruction, Hitler and Goebbels were not alone: there were many officers in the Wehrmacht who, though not Nazis themselves, were prepared to act out the 'final battle' now which they believed should have been fought in 1918.[3]

While the fighting in the west was turning into a series of gigantic mopping-up operations for the Western Allies, as long as the Oder front held, Germans still wanted Heinrici's armies to halt the 'Asiatic hordes' from the 'steppes'. This imperative continued even after the military map of a defensible 'Reich' had been erased in the west: in the final weeks of the war, German soldiers fought on for a variety of motives – out of automatism, because this was what they had been instructed to do, because they were still trying to hold back the 'red tide', or because they wanted to be conquered and taken prisoner by the Western Allies. To the east of the Oder front, the besieged fortress cities fell one by one. In Upper Silesia, Oppeln fell on 24 January while Ratibor held out for another two months. In West Prussia, Graudenz and Posen were captured in the first week of March. Danzig, where the war had begun on 1 September 1939, was taken in the Soviet offensive on eastern Pomerania in March, while the East Prussian capital of Königsberg finally surrendered after an intensive three-day assault on 9 April. On 5 March General Hermann Niehoff was sent to the capital of Lower Silesia, Breslau, to renew the fighting spirit of the defenders. Niehoff deployed thousands of forced workers to turn the principal Kaiserstrasse into an alternative airstrip so that the Luftwaffe could continue to supply the inner city once the suburbs fell. They razed the churches and grand university buildings under continual strafing attacks by the Red Air Force, and the Luftwaffe continued its perilous daily flights into Breslau. The German armoured divisions in the city used Goliaths, the miniature remote-controlled tanks they had deployed to reconquer Warsaw, but this time to destroy buildings occupied by the advancing Soviets. While the less reliable and experienced German troops were held in reserve to plug gaps in the line, the elite units of paratroopers and Waffen SS continued to mount counter-attacks, halting the Red Army's advance in the southern suburbs: a single apartment block on the corner of the Höfchenplatz and Opitzstrasse was fought over for eight days.[4]

Holding the line was not just an imperative for fanatical Nazis and military commanders hardened on the eastern front. Workers in Berlin could be overheard talking approvingly on the S-Bahn about the three soldiers and the local Party leader who had been hanged from telephone poles in Fürstenwalde on the Oder, bearing placards proclaiming their desertion from the front. Others called for the press to publish the numbers of deserters executed. The months of fighting on German soil had already created divisions between those civilians engulfed by combat in the borderlands and those sheltering behind them in the hinterland. As the conquest of the Reich entered its final, critical phase, these divisions became still more acute and violent.[5]

In the quiet flatlands of the Lüneburg Heath, where the teacher Agnes Seidel had been evacuated with her Hamburg schoolchildren since March 1944, a strange calm reigned. Seidel saw no tangible signs of the approaching front, even though she knew from the Wehrmacht report that the British and Canadians had crossed the Lower Rhine and that Blumentritt's 1st Paratroop Army was fighting a slow, tenacious retreat eastwards. Her son Klaus, who had manned a flak gun in the middle of Hamburg throughout the firestorm, had last written from Pomerania, a short postcard sent on 1 March on his way to the front. On Sunday 1 April, the day the Ruhr was encircled, the children had their Easter egg hunt as usual in the garden and farmyard but a few days later, on the 5th, parents began to fetch their children home after the Hamburg educational authority gave in to their lobbying. Within two days, only five remained in the village. If it had not been for the sixteen boys and girls who had arrived with the refugees from East Prussia and Pomerania, Agnes Seidel would have had no one to teach. On 11 April, 1,500 British prisoners of war arrived at the farm where Agnes lodged. Like the German refugees before them, they were fed – potatoes and broth with milk in it – before continuing on their way. That night Agnes joined the farmer's family, celebrating the birthday of one of the other teachers by drinking more heavily than usual. As the SD noted in their last attempt at a nationwide report at the end of March, across the Reich any occasion now seemed a good opportunity to uncork bottles which had been carefully put by for so long to celebrate 'final victory'.[6]

Agnes had ordered packing crates for her own possessions but she did not begin to grasp the gravity of the situation until 12 April, when the soldiers at the nearby Wehrmacht base blew up their ammunition dump and left. People started arriving at the farm laden with cloth, cooking pots, pails, buckets and bundles of clothing. She realised that they were looting the shops and the army warehouse at Melzingen.

That night she could hardly sleep. The next day the police accepted her gift of cigarettes to transport 2 hundredweight of potatoes on their truck to Hamburg – her post-war provisions. On 16 April, a local foster mother came to complain that she had no butter or meat and hardly any bread to feed the boy she had taken in from Hamburg. Trust in the system of payments which had worked for the last two years was clearly evaporating. Exhausted and no longer bothered by the frequent noise of low-flying aircraft overhead, Agnes took an afternoon nap. At 4 p.m., she woke to a different sound – the roar of British trucks and tanks pouring through the village in an endless stream. She was outraged when the polite English officers and an aggressive American 'half-nigger' came to the farm later that afternoon to arrest the German officers, including two 17-year-old SS men. She ran after the car to pass some food to them both and to shake their hands one more time. As the new occupiers claimed the best rooms in the farmstead, she had to move upstairs. Over the next two weeks, as one set of occupiers followed another, the reserved English were replaced by unfriendly Americans, most of them, Agnes thought, of Polish origin. In the stillness of the night in the house, she found the noise of singing and dance music coming from the barn where the Polish farm workers still slept unnerving.[7]

Margarete Töpperwien was not in Solingen when the town fell. She and her daughter Bärbel had let out the house and repaired to the quiet of her mother-in-law's in the Harz town of Osterode the previous autumn. In early March she could still write that 'we are living incredibly peacefully here, in spite of all the overflights, in spite of all the refugees'. But, like Agnes Seidel, she too felt that 'the flood is rising'. Placing her trust in God that all would be well, she reassured her husband August that 'inner integrity is more important than external preservation'. Now in the quiet Czech backwater of Petersdorf, August was reduced to watching with mounting anxiety from afar the Americans' conquest of western Germany: 'All of mine in the field of fire and I – as a soldier – in what looks like deepest peace!'[8]

After being evacuated from Dresden, the Klemperers had spent late February and March in the tiny, one-up, one-down house of their former domestic servant Agnes in the Wendish-speaking village of Piskowitz. They gradually put on weight and rebuilt their strength on a diet of the excellent rye bread, unlimited amounts of butter, curd cheese and honey, even enjoying meat every day. When the village was cleared of refugees to accommodate troops, they journeyed on to Pirna, where old friends took them in for the night and gave Victor shoes and new trousers. Next they stayed with their old pharmacist friend Hans Scherner at Falkenstein in the Vogtland until 1 April, when once again their room was requisitioned.[9]

Until now, the Klemperers had been using their real names. Eva, with her 'Aryan' passport and identity card, had acted as their 'tour guide', dealing with the local authorities and buying train tickets, while Victor hid his 'Jewish passport' and proffered only the 'Aryan' ration card he had been issued with after the Dresden raid. They were aware that their name sounded suspiciously Jewish. Before leaving Falkenstein, they decided to falsify their documents. Ironically, the idea came from a dispensing chemist, who had made a slip a year before, spelling their name as 'Kleinpeter'. Eva realised that she only had to dot the 'm' and lengthen the 'r' to achieve the transformation. Having doctored their police registration of departure and their ration cards, on 2 April they embarked once more, to all the world just another weary couple in their sixties who had been caught in Dresden during the raids, Victor a secondary-school teacher from his real birthplace of Landsberg an der Warthe. With Landsberg already in Soviet hands, their cover story was safely uncheckable. Still, they decided to keep their real passports and one of Victor's Jewish stars at the bottom of a bag. It was a huge risk, but they wanted to hang on to them for when the Allies arrived, 'because we shall need this evidence to save ourselves, just as much as we need the Aryan identity'.[10]

Travelling on to Munich, the 'Kleinpeters' found themselves unwittingly journeying ever deeper into what remained of the Third Reich. A night in a waiting room at Marktredwitz 'made a great impression on me', Victor noted, 'because of the crowding together and the different groups mixed up on the floor: soldiers, civilians, men, women, children, blankets, suitcases, kitbags, rucksacks, legs, heads jumbled together, the picturesque centrepiece a girl and a young soldier sleeping gently shoulder to shoulder'. As they stood or sat on slow-moving trains, sometimes forced to get off and walk along sections where the line had been bombed, it was the same picture, just on a progressively larger scale, in Eger, Regensburg and Munich. After years of being marked out, Klemperer could finally blend in as a 'national comrade', a participant-observer of how 'ordinary Germans' talked amongst themselves. On the night of 4–5 April, he recorded the conversation that unfolded in the dark of a second-class compartment of the train:

> A young man beside me: My father still believed in victory, never listened to me. But now even he doesn't believe any more . . . Bolshevism and international Jewry are the victors . . . A young woman sitting some distance away: She still believed in victory, she trusted in the Führer, her husband was fighting in Breslau, and she believed.

Klemperer's interest in how people talked was fuelled by an enduring need to know how much they believed Goebbels's propaganda, how far it chimed with or shaped their common sense of the war. As he jotted down these increasingly unstable oscillations between hope and despair he became ever more attentive to the odd juxtapositions and split-mind-sets they entailed, uncertain himself whether the people he was listening to were ready to abandon or continue the war.[11]

Trekking to and from the Bavarian capital over the next week, the 'Kleinpeters' found themselves increasingly dependent on precisely the kind of public assistance they had tried so hard to avoid in order to escape the notice of Nazi officialdom. In Munich they slept in the vast underground shelter of the main station run by the National Socialist People's Welfare: Eva with her thick glasses and short, grey hair, wearing a fur coat with bald patches singed by flying sparks during the Dresden raid; Victor sprouting white stubble and clad in a heavy but threadbare old overcoat. As they adjusted to Munich in early April 1945, they discovered a kind of spontaneous social order underlying the apparent chaos. They found out where the National Socialist People's Welfare dispensed soup, bread and coffee. There was the improvised tram service after the heavy bombing: 'tracks laid on the streets, little locomotives, giving off black clouds, pull trains of wagons, each truck converted into a primitive carriage by means of box boards, all the seats packed, also clusters of people hanging between and on the wagons'. In Munich, Eva and Victor managed to track down the last link in their network of pre-Nazi friends and acquaintances: Klemperer's old doctoral supervisor, Professor Karl Vossler, a Catholic keen to air his anti-Nazi views over lunch in his grand apartment but unwilling to provide any further support for his former pupil.[12]

After the Vosslers, the Klemperers' private network was exhausted and they had no choice but to turn to the People's Welfare office and hope that no one became too curious about them. What is remarkable is how effectively the system of resettlement still operated in Bavaria in early April 1945. The trains, although irregular and overcrowded, still ran and people grudgingly made space for each other and told each other their stories in the darkness. In the small villages they were sent to, local police and mayors did their best to help them, although they struggled to find a room. But each time the 'Kleinpeters' returned, defeated, to the People's Welfare in Aichach, a town not far from Augsburg, apologetic assistance was at hand; the volunteers clearly wanted to solve their problem and find them lodging, rather than just pass them on to someone else. On 12 April they arrived at the village of Unterbernbach in the evening, where the local farmers' leader, a big, gaunt, grey-haired man called Flammensbeck, and his wife 'immediately took care of us with touching kindliness (a Quaker, says Eva)'. Exhausted, Victor and Eva were deeply relieved: 'It was a matter of course for straw beds, pillows and blankets to be laid down on the living room floor for us', but soon they were billeted in an attic room at the end of the village.[13]

They continued to take their meals at the Flammensbecks' table, and the food they provided was wholesome and generous. Over the next few days, Victor learned that Flammensbeck had been one of the first and most ardent Nazis in the village; now a son was missing in Russia, one son-in-law had been killed in action, and the other wounded five times and back in the village with his wife and baby. A few days after the 'Kleinpeters' arrived in Unterbernbach, large sections of the Vogtland from which they had just come were occupied by the US 3rd Army. They had reached one of the remaining heartlands of the Third Reich.[14]

The day that Eva and Victor reached Unterbernbach brought news that President Roosevelt had died on 12 April. Goebbels rushed to cheer Hitler with the news, pointing out the miraculous parallel with the death of Tsarina Elizabeth in 1762 and the collapse of the coalition facing Frederick the Great. With his usual care to control the reporting of good news, the Propaganda Minister instructed the press not to make this overly explicit in case it prompted 'premature hopes and exaggerated expectations'. Meanwhile, in the capital, graffiti with

Soviet stars started to appear on formerly communist housing estates. More generally, most Berliners vented their bitterness at their plight on the Party and its meddling in military affairs, but there was still a clamour for Hitler, or even Goebbels, to speak 'now in the hour of greatest need'. Flight seemed pointless: 'Where should one flee to?' The only hope lay in the very speed of the Americans' advance towards the Elbe during the previous week, as people canvassed the possibility 'that the Anglo-Americans will still reach Berlin ahead of the Soviets'.[15]

★

On 16 April, at 3.30 a.m., the Soviet heavy guns began their initial bombardment of the German position along the Seelow Heights, the low but steep hills on which the German 9th Army was entrenched above the swampy ground of the Oder valley. Lacking tanks and artillery, reserves and battle-hardened troops, the Germans withstood the initial massive barrage by retreating to their rear lines and leaving the shells to fall into empty trenches. It was a technique Heinrici had used to hold the Dniepr line for seven months in 1943–44. Now it bought him three days. Further south, the Soviets broke through Ferdinand Schörner's 4th Panzer Army, threatening to encircle Heinrici's troops. As it too was forced back, giving up the Seelow Heights, the German 9th Army was broken up. Then, on 20 April – Hitler's birthday and the day so many Germans had been led to believe the Wehrmacht would launch its own counter-offensive – Zhukov's 1st Belorussian Front broke through the outer defence ring of the capital. At the same time, the 1st Ukrainian Front under Konev was approaching Berlin from the south.[16]

While some 85,000 German troops attempted to defend the capital against the 1.5 million Soviet troops converging on it from three sides, in Wilmersdorf the novelist Hertha von Gebhardt and her daughter Renate took their coffee at the bakery on the corner. The owner had donned his SA uniform and medals and was holding forth to his customers, while the 'sad herds' of the Volkssturm assembling outside caught Gebhardt's eye. In her block of flats, there was no gas and the neighbours had all erected shaky stoves on their balconies; bunk beds were being erected in the cellar for all of the twenty people living there. For the next week, Gebhardt would chronicle the transformation of her heterogeneous collection of neighbours into a 'cellar community', increasingly cut off from any wider 'national community'.[17]

On Sunday 22 April, the shops reopened so that people could stock up between air raids and attacks by dive-bombers. That day the electricity came on again too, allowing them to listen to Mozart's *Magic Flute* on the radio. The news reported that the fighting had reached the northern suburb of Berlin-Weissensee. Monday brought rumours of workers fighting the SS in the old 'red' districts of the city and the men of the neighbourhood took turns to stand watch. Other rumours doing the rounds of the queues outside the shops heralded an imminent armistice and a new German alliance with Britain and America against Russia. Hertha and Renate used the lull in the bombing to eat their noodle soup upstairs at their dining-room table, before taking their coffee again at the local bakery. Soon they had a new worry: the soldiers were moving into their neighbourhood, setting up flak guns, building street barricades and establishing a command post at the street corner. 'All this, highly unpropitious,' Gebhardt commented drily. As she calculated their chances of surviving such a defence it suddenly did not seem worth eking out the week's meat ration, and she and Renate ate half of it for dinner. The 49-year-old novelist felt confident that the older Volkssturm men would throw away their weapons in good time, but she was not so sure about the 14 to 16-year-olds, as she watched them lugging rifles almost as big as they were while their greatcoats trailed on the ground behind them. 'The Americans don't seem to be coming. Unbelievable,' she noted in her diary, seized with gloom.[18]

The less there was left to defend, the more draconian the orders. Keitel, Bormann and Himmler instructed the military, Party officials and the SS to defend every town to the last man and reject all offers to surrender. Himmler told the SS to shoot all men 'in a house where a white flag appears', dropping his earlier reluctance to impose collective reprisals on Germans. In the west, as the Wehrmacht retreated towards first the Main and then the Danube, the fate of each town and village depended on a local constellation: on the military commander, the Nazi leadership, other civic officials and, sometimes, the local population. How the war ended would be decided city by city, town by town, and village by village. In Schwäbisch Gmünd, the

Party leader and military commander had two men executed hours before the Americans arrived on 20 April. In nearby Stuttgart, local notables managed to sideline the Gauleiter of Württemberg by persuading the city's mayor to negotiate secretly with the Wehrmacht commanders and so ensure a peaceful handover. In Bad Windsheim in Lower Franconia, the population itself took the initiative. Between 200 and 300 women came out to demonstrate, some with their children, until the local commandant gave in and agreed not to defend the town – but not before a Gestapo unit from Nuremberg had executed one of the women as a ringleader.[19]

Much of the terror that engulfed Swabia, Bavaria and Baden in these final weeks came not from local Nazis, but from the sudden arrival of units like Max Simon's 13th SS Army Corps, as they pulled back to the Danube and then to Munich, and the 'flying court martials' conducted by Major Erwin Helms, who patrolled the south in a grey Mercedes looking for deserters. In the village of Zellingen, Helms had a 60-year-old farmer and Volkssturm member hanged from his own pear tree simply for making disparaging remarks about further military defence. In the village of Brettheim, Simon executed three inhabitants, including the local Nazi Party leader and mayor, and posted placards threatening retaliation against the families of anyone guilty of defeatism.[20]

In Unterbernbach, Victor Klemperer had also heard the rumour that the German counter-offensive would start on 20 April. The following day, after it had failed to materialise, an elderly Volkssturm man insisted that military strategy 'could not be grasped with a "slide rule" and with "common sense": that was no use at all – one simply had to "believe in the Führer and in victory"! I was really rather depressed by these speeches,' Klemperer added. He noted too that Germany now 'basically consists of no more than a generously defined Greater Berlin and a part of Bavaria'. By 22 April, even the old Nazi Flammensbeck lost heart as he read Goebbels's article for Hitler's birthday. Discussing the piece around the kitchen table, Klemperer was struck by the change in the farmer's outlook: 'New weapon, offensive, turning-point – he had believed it all, but "now he didn't believe in anything any more". Peace must be made, the present government must go. Did I think we would all be deported?'[21]

Meanwhile the wheels of ordinary administration continued to turn. Although the Bavarian Finance Ministry had resorted to printing banknotes itself, salaries were paid on time for all public sector employees, from army generals to the office cleaning staff in the Munich police department. On 23 April, Bayern Munich beat TSV 1860 in a football derby by three goals to two. Despite the regime of terror that gripped Bavaria in April 1945, people went on expressing opinions for and against the war. As the front approached each town and village, it became increasingly clear that the immediate threat now came from German not American soldiers. When part of a Hitler Youth division arrived in Unterbernbach, Klemperer could not decide if they looked more like marauders from the Thirty Years War or the Children's Crusade. On 23 April, Regensburg was surrendered and the Americans pushed on south of the Danube towards Augsburg. On 27 April, an old man from Tyrol asked Victor Klemperer 'whether the Americans and Russians will fight when they meet'. It was the final legacy, Klemperer thought, of Goebbels's efforts to encourage belief that Germany might be rescued by the Americans; as yet, no one in Unterbernbach knew that the Russians and Americans had met near Torgau on the Elbe two days earlier.[22]

As the sixth day of battle for Berlin broke on 25 April, Hertha von Gebhardt heard that, just to the south of Wilmersdorf, the station at Steglitz had been taken. She was gripped by fear: what would happen if someone foolishly decided to defend their block of flats? Could she trust all her 'house community' not to try? A neighbour returned having seen five women lying in the street with their shopping bags beside them, their bodies ripped open by shrapnel. The news from Steglitz was more encouraging: they heard that the Russians were being 'very friendly to the civilian population'. In an attempt to reverse the reputation they had earned in East Prussia and Silesia, the Red Army was sending civilians and even German prisoners of war back across the lines to assure Berliners that they would be treated well. In the meantime, the Wilmersdorf shops were open and selling off their remaining stock while they could: men's underwear, long scarce, was suddenly available.

That night, fifteen bombs and shells hit their block. The small 'house community' slept fitfully as they waited for the attack, and Gebhardt roused them at 6 a.m., just before the Katiusha rockets opened up.

She persuaded her neighbours to move into the adjacent cellar, where they would be safer. At midday they divided up all the schnapps and tobacco they had left and then searched the flats for weapons, uniforms, Nazi insignia and military maps, anything that might provoke the Russians. The 'house community' also suffered its first casualties. A man and a 19-year-old girl were hit by shrapnel as they tried to make it back inside from queuing for water at the street corner. Two nurses and a woman dentist came from neighbouring houses to tend them, before they took them to the nearest hospital. The girl was operated on and saved, while the man bled to death in the hospital corridor. Late in the evening as they sat in the cellar of the neighbouring house someone mentioned to Hertha that the bomb which had injured them had also destroyed their apartment building. It did not seem to matter any more – or not yet. All she could find to say was, 'So?'[23]

At 5 a.m. on Friday 27 April, Hertha von Gebhardt heard the crump of tank shells nearby. The men went upstairs to ply the Volkssturm soldiers posted in the entrance to the building with schnapps and talk them into leaving. They took the schnapps but moved on reluctantly. While many of the older men destroyed their militia armbands and paybooks, threw away their weapons and equipment and went home, those along the Teltow Canal made a stand. Further to the west, the Hitler Youth battalions continued to defend the Pichelsdorf and Charlotte bridges over the Havel. Elsewhere in Berlin, looting was under way, as soldiers, civilians and Volkssturm men elbowed each other aside to empty shops and warehouses before the Soviets arrived. In the cellars of Kleiststrasse, they stood up to their ankles in drink, pouring wine and spirits into the dirty buckets they had brought with them. By the end of that day Berlin was completely surrounded, cut off from the archipelago of territories which now constituted the 'Reich'.[24]

In Wilmersdorf the stillness that afternoon was broken by rifle shots ricocheting in the street outside the Gebhardts' building. 'The Russians are there,' the neighbours whispered to one another in the cellar. Women who had been quarrelling earlier now kissed and hugged. Even a neighbour who had not spoken to Gebhardt for weeks now came over and offered her a cigarette, as the moment they had all dreaded for so long finally arrived. Everyone rummaged in their bags to find white material – towels, napkins, handkerchiefs. Then a single Russian soldier entered their cellar. He calmly asked in German about soldiers and weapons and then left. As the fighting moved on to the Fehrberliner Platz, some of the women ventured out to fetch water from the pump outside the bakery. For Hertha von Gebhardt and the 'house community' of 8 Geroldstrasse the war ended that Friday afternoon.[25]

When Adolf Hitler committed suicide on 30 April, there was little left to defend in Berlin. While sailors, Hitler Youths and SS units fought on in the Reichstag building and held the Zoo bunker, Goebbels initiated the first negotiations with the victor of Stalingrad, Vasily Chuikov, to surrender the German capital. By a quirk of fate, that same day American troops entered Hitler's private flat on the Prinzregentenplatz in Munich; during the previous week, the headline of the *Völkischer Beobachter* had still been proclaiming 'Fortress Bavaria' and 'Germany stands firm and loyal to the Führer'.[26]

On 29 April, as the US 45th 'Thunderbird' Division had approached Munich from the north-west, it reached Dachau, the centre of a major SS training facility and stores and Himmler's first, 'model' concentration camp. Outside the camp the troops came upon an abandoned train of forty cattle trucks loaded with 2,000 prisoners evacuated from the concentration camp at Buchenwald. Those who had made it out of the doors had been shot by the SS; inside the trucks only seventeen people showed any signs of life. Dachau had become the final destination for the death marches from camp to camp. Among the dying and the dead the Americans found 32,000 survivors. Appalled and enraged by what they saw on entering the camp, some of the US soldiers simply gunned down the SS guards or shot them in the legs and let the prisoners finish them off.

On the first evening of their liberation, prisoners took Colonel Bill Walsh on a tour of the camp. He was shown the kennels of the bloodhounds, the interior of one of the dark, overcrowded and infested barracks, the corpses lying in rows outside the sick bay, and finally the thousands of corpses neatly stacked to over two metres high like firewood around the crematorium, its ovens full of ash. Nothing had prepared the American soldiers for these sights. In the next few days, as local residents pushed their bicycles down the camp road to collect loot from the SS warehouses, US soldiers were astonished to see them passing the goods train with its freight of dead with no apparent concern.[27]

Berlin capitulated on the night of 1–2 May. Here too local residents spent their first day of peace plundering the remaining shops and military depots. The SS had set fire to their central stores in the Schultheiss Brewery in the Prenzlauerberg district during the fighting, but now it was overrun with civilians eager to salvage what was left and put something by for the starvation conditions they expected defeat to bring. Children who witnessed the turmoil and sudden violence were shocked. Outside the water tower in the Prenzlauerberg district, one 12-year-old watched as the looters were robbed by other civilians who fell on them 'like hyenas'. Another boy felt ashamed when he saw Red Army soldiers taking pictures of the fighting crowds: 'Germany's conquerors did not get a good impression,' he observed.[28]

As in the other great capitals of Budapest and Vienna, which had fallen on 13 February and 13 April respectively, in Berlin conquest was accompanied by mass rape. As many as 10–20 per cent of the women fell victim. During the battle for Berlin and the first weeks of May, women were raped in cellars, in their flats and on the street, in front of neighbours, husbands, children and strangers. In Wilmersdorf too the rapes started the night Red Army soldiers arrived. As Hertha von Gebhardt tried to hide her daughter Renate behind her, she hoped each time a Russian entered their cellar that he would take another woman. In Zehlendorf, a friend of Ursula von Kardorff who had hidden behind a heap of coal was betrayed by a neighbour anxious to protect her own daughter, and then gang-raped by twenty-three soldiers. Like many of the victims, she had to be taken to the hospital to stop the haemorrhaging. She told Kardorff four months later, 'I never want to have anything to do with a man again.' The journalist Margret Boveri, who had relished watching air raids from her balcony, became so anxious that she started taking sleeping tablets to get through the night.[29]

The weeks of unbridled fear in Berlin were seared deeply into popular consciousness, leading middle-aged women of the polite and educated classes to discard their reticence and discuss how they could protect themselves and what they had had to endure. One Communist militant, Hilde Radusch, reported that some women defended themselves by inserting into their vagina a copper stopper which they had obtained from a plumber. The copper rim would then cut the penis of their assailant. 'And then the Russian came out howling,' Radusch recounted with a certain *Schadenfreude* thirty-six years later, 'with no idea what had happened to them. And from then on the house was called "the house with the crazy women".' Mothers cut short the hair of their adolescent daughters and dressed them as boys to protect them. When a woman doctor helped hide several young women by putting up signs on the door in German and Russian warning of typhoid, news of this haven spread like wildfire among the women gathered at the water pump in the street. Such survival stratagems became legendary precisely because women's powerlessness and fear of rape and assault were universal.[30]

One of the least famous but most common forms of safety was provided by Soviet officers determined to restore order. A Russian officer agreed to sleep in the cellar next to Hertha and Renate von Gebhardt for the first few nights to protect them. In Schwerin, the war reporter Vasily Grossman noted that 'A Jewish commander whose whole family was killed by the Germans, is quartered in the apartment of a Gestapo man who has fled. The wife and children are safe with him and the whole family weeps and pleads with him to stay when he wants to leave.' Such protection was partly a matter of goodwill, partly a centrally directed policy. Shortly before the attack across the Oder, Soviet propaganda had changed dramatically: in place of inciting troops to kill Germans, the message was to distinguish between Nazis and ordinary Germans. The final conquest of Germany was meant to be more orderly. By comparison with the chaos and massacres of civilians during the winter conquest of East Prussia and Silesia, it was. Nonetheless, it still took weeks to bring the troops under control in Berlin, Vienna and Budapest.[31]

Christa J. later recalled that in the Prenzlauerberg district many of her class of 14- and 15-year-olds were raped. Unable to speak about it, some teenagers constructed stories in which other girls and women were raped but not the narrator herself. 'I too was hidden, somewhere in the cellar,' Christa explained. In Vienna, 14-year-old Hermine told how she and a friend were discovered hiding behind a curtain when a Soviet soldier burst into their flat. Hermine's mother then placed her baby in her teenage daughter's arms, hoping that he would protect her. 'The soldier gestured to make clear that I should pass the infant on,' Hermine recalled over fifty years later. After some further altercation, the soldier – inexplicably – left. Whereas many adult women spoke matter-of-factly of their own rape, those who were teenagers at the time often found it far harder to do so either then or subsequently.[32]

Gabriele Köpp had fled from Schneidemühl in West Prussia in February 1945, but they had been overrun by the Red Army. The 15-year-old was raped multiple times. Even afterwards when she stayed with her cousin on a farm in Pomerania, she had to hide each time Soviet soldiers came to the farm because the farmer's wife tried to protect herself by pointing Gabriele out to them. In the following months, she consoled herself by composing a letter to her mother. 'I am not that big and old. I can't really talk properly about everything with anyone,' she wrote. 'I am so alone. I am so frightened, because I am not getting my time of feeling unwell. Soon it'll already be ten weeks [since my last period]. You could help me for sure.' She was never able to send the letter and it took another fifty-eight years before she was able to talk about what had happened to her in 1945.[33]

★

By the end of April, Unterbernbach stood in a kind of no-man's-land, skirted by the fighting and unoccupied, the village a transit point for German stragglers trying to get home. On 28 April, German troops had fled from their positions in the meadow and woodland after a brief skirmish, and, even though a few SS men were still in the village, the mayor had the swastika emblem removed from the gable of the district office. Flammensbeck was busy shedding his Nazi persona and rediscovering his Catholic heritage. As Victor Klemperer noted, the farmers' leader now accused the Nazis of having 'been "too radical", they had deviated from their programme, they had not treated religion with consideration'. To escape the hothouse atmosphere, Victor and Eva found solitude by retreating to the small wood to the north of the village, where they read aloud to each other. When three soldiers came out of the trees to ask if the Americans were already in Unterbernbach, the Klemperers advised them to get hold of civilian clothes, and which places to avoid. The couple were struck by the young soldiers' helplessness: 'all three have good faces, undoubtedly from good families, perhaps students . . . as ardently as we have longed for the loss of the war and as necessary as this loss is for Germany (and truly for mankind) – we nevertheless felt sorry for the boys.' For Victor Klemperer they were an allegory of the lost war.[34]

Cut off in Flensburg, Grand Admiral Karl Dönitz was as surprised as anyone to learn that he was Hitler's final choice as heir. Aware that one of his Führer's final acts had been to order the arrest of Göring and Himmler for trying to negotiate with the Western Allies, Dönitz circumspectly waited till Bormann confirmed by telex on the afternoon of 1 May that the 'testament was in force', before approaching the British and Americans himself. There was a prospect that the German divisions cut off in Courland could be brought back to Copenhagen, which was still under German occupation, or to the German North Sea ports. But when the British crossed the Elbe and advanced into Schleswig-Holstein, they cut the link to Denmark and the passage through the narrows of the Baltic to the North Sea. Bremen had already been comprehensively destroyed in a week of fighting, and holding the North Sea ports no longer served any purpose. Dönitz persisted in demanding that Breslau and the 40,000 civilians besieged there since January should continue to 'hold out' against the Soviets, but on 3 May he agreed to surrender Hamburg to the British.

The next day, the surrender of the Wehrmacht in northern Germany, Denmark and the Netherlands was agreed with the commander of British forces, Field Marshal Bernard Montgomery, and set to come into force on 5 May, the day that Army Group G also capitulated to the Americans in the south. Dönitz, Jodl, Keitel and Schwerin von Krosigk, the remaining military and political leadership of the Third Reich, still hoped that they were concluding a separate armistice in the west, so that they could execute a fighting withdrawal from the eastern front and save as many divisions from surrendering to the Soviets as possible. It was a complex and dangerous manoeuvre, but during the first week of May as many as 1.8 million German soldiers managed to disengage from the Red Army and surrender to the Western powers.[35]

In Breslau itself, a delegation of Protestant and Catholic clergy called on General Niehoff on 4 May, asking him: 'Is continuing the defence of Breslau something which you could justify to God?' Niehoff took heed and quietly set about negotiating a ceasefire, despite the pressure from Dönitz to hold out – transmitted by both the new Commander-in-Chief of the Wehrmacht, Field Marshal Schörner, and Gauleiter Hanke, the new head of the SS. In his proclamation to his troops on 5 May, Niehoff pointed out that 'Hitler is dead, Berlin has fallen. The Allies of East and West have shaken hands in the heart of Germany. Thus the conditions for a continuation of the struggle for Breslau no longer exist. Every further sacrifice is a crime.' With a gesture to Simonides' epitaph to the 300 Spartans at Thermopylae, he concluded, 'We have done our duty, as the law demanded.' The next day, the Germans handed over their positions.[36]

August Töpperwien had been shielded by the battle for Breslau. As he carried on running his prisoner-of-war camp at Petersdorf in Upper Silesia, on 2 May he had listened to Dönitz's appeal to the German people to go on fighting the British and Americans as long as they sided with Bolshevism. Töpperwien finally acknowledged that Hitler's 'terrible miscalculation' – underlined in red in his diary – was 'to make war against the Anglo-Americans when his real enemy is Bolshevism!?!' In his despair at Germany's impending defeat, the Gymnasium teacher returned once more to his belief that 'A mankind who wages war like this has become godless. The Russian barbarities in the German east – the terror attacks of the Anglo-Americans – our struggle against the Jews (sterilisation of healthy women, shooting everyone from infants to old women, gassing of Jewish transport trains)!'[37]

Töpperwien had acknowledged the full scale of the German extermination of the Jews once before, back in November 1943. Whatever knowledge he had accumulated about transport trains and gas chambers he had pushed aside until Germany's final defeat forced him to reflect once more on what he knew. But by equating the murder of the Jews with Allied bombing and Bolshevik terror, morally condemning these acts of extreme immorality as 'godless', his words acknowledged and simultaneously dissipated guilt by relativising and diffusing it. And his own *völkisch* belief in Germans' 'civilising mission' meant that he could never equate the nations which had committed these acts. On 3 May, he tuned in to hear the radio appeal of the new German Foreign Minister, Schwerin von Krosigk, to the Western powers to fight Bolshevism jointly and he asked himself: 'Would it have been possible to get England and America to join the anti-Bolshevik front in spite of Liberalism and World Jewry?!?!' Whatever his sense of moral horror at the murder of the Jews, August Töpperwien still counted them amongst Germany's most powerful adversaries. On 6 May, the same day that Breslau fell, Captain August Töpperwien was taken prisoner by the Soviets, abandoning his diary in the attic of a house where it was discovered by Polish schoolchildren fifty years later.[38]

While the farmers slaughtered their pigs in Unterbernbach so that the Americans would not take them, on the afternoon of 2 May Victor Klemperer walked to the next village to go shopping. In the church square he saw his first Americans, a column of repair vehicles. Most of them were black soldiers. Falling into conversation with a young German woman in a side street, he learned that apart from ransacking the shops on the first day, the troops 'had been altogether decently behaved. "The blacks too?" She almost beamed with delight. "They're even friendlier than the others, there's nothing to be afraid of."' Since the shops were likely to remain closed for a week, she showed him how to buy bread at the back door of the bakery.

On his return to Unterbernbach Klemperer found two more stragglers at Flammensbeck's table, young men in their early twenties, one of them a law student. They were trying to get home to the Sudetenland and confirmed that Hitler was dead and Berlin had capitulated. As ever, Klemperer was trying to gauge what they believed:

> The student declared: 'If anyone had told me that, even four weeks ago, I would have shot him down – but now I don't believe anything any more . . .' They had wanted too much, there had been atrocities, the way people had been treated in Poland and Russia, inhuman! 'But the Führer probably knew nothing about it' . . . Neither quite believed in the 'turning-point' and the imminent war between the USA and Russia, but they did a little bit nevertheless.

It was clear to Klemperer that these soldiers were unable to imagine life beyond the war and the impending German defeat. By now, Flammensbeck was beginning to 'talk as if Hitlerism had been essentially a Prussian, militaristic, un-Catholic, un-Bavarian cause'. Klemperer had to remind himself that the movement had originated in Munich. Still unwilling to reveal his Jewish identity in what he took to be a traditionally anti-Semitic, Catholic village, he quietly told the local teacher and Flammensbeck that 'perhaps I could be of assistance . . . At some point, my name was respected, and the Nazis had forced me out of my post.' Meanwhile, the village was 'revelling in meat and fat and every kind of food surplus'.[39]

On 6 May, the Commander-in-Chief in the West, Kesselring, surrendered the so-called 'alpine redoubt' at Berchtesgaden, where the Allies had feared that the Nazi leaders would make their last stand. That same day, Dönitz sent Jodl to Reims to negotiate a general armistice in the west with Eisenhower. Unlike Montgomery, Eisenhower refused point-blank to negotiate anything that suggested a separate peace; demanding complete capitulation, he threatened to resume the bombing of German cities. At 2.41 a.m. on 7 May, Jodl signed. Later that day the remaining German garrisons surrendered the French ports of St-Nazaire, Lorient and La Rochelle. Only in Prague did German troops continue fighting, partly in the hope of crossing the Soviet lines and into American captivity. Sixteen minutes after the complete ceasefire had come into effect at midnight on 8–9 May, the surrender ceremony itself was repeated at Zhukov's headquarters outside Berlin at Karlshorst. This time a full surrender document had been drawn up which representatives of all three arms of the Wehrmacht and, most importantly, all of the Allies signed. The following evening, at its normal slot of 8 p.m., the Wehrmacht broadcast its final bulletin of the war from Flensburg:

> Since midnight the weapons on all fronts are now silent. On the orders of the Grand Admiral, the Wehrmacht has given up the fight which has become hopeless. Thus the heroic struggle which lasted nearly six years has come to an end . . .
>
> The German soldier, true to his oath and with the greatest dedication, has performed deeds which never will be forgotten. The home front supported him to the last with all its powers and suffering the greatest sacrifices.
>
> The unique achievement of the front and home front will find its ultimate appreciation in a future just verdict of history.[40]

This time the home front had stood the test: there had been no repeat of November 1918. Out on the farm on the Lüneburg heath, Agnes Seidel had spent the day sorting out and repairing her worst clothes to donate to a compulsory collection for 'foreigners, Jews and inmates of concentration camps'. As she helped with the collection, she was surprised at the quantity and quality of what others gave. She was not ready to spare a thought in her diary about the intended recipients. Since the beginning of the British occupation, the farm had seen a kind of uneasy peace between the twenty-two Poles and the thirty Germans, twenty of whom were children. The former forced labourers were increasingly unwilling to work, and, by late April, Agnes was outraged that she was having to butter bread for them. But nothing had occurred here to compare with the reports of armed attacks and robberies coming in from neighbouring farmsteads. As elsewhere, the Germans quickly turned to their conquerors as guarantors of their safety. On 8 May, Agnes Seidel took her children on a hike for the first time since the occupation had begun and the British soldiers showered them with gifts of chocolate and sweets. On 14 May, the old Nazi schoolteacher borrowed some English textbooks to start learning the language of Germany's enemies.[41]

When 14-year-old Leonie Bauditz and her mother heard that all the women on their work brigade were about to be sent from Silesia to Russia, they managed to escape, thanks to the help of one of their Russian guards. They returned to Breslau, walking through streets, comprehensively destroyed by the twelve weeks of fighting, until they reached their old apartment block. Not only was the house still standing, but the store of textiles and wool that Leonie's father had laid by against hard times was still intact. Despite her terrible experiences the teenager soon struck up a friendship with a young Soviet officer who wanted to learn German. They sat together on a bench in the sunshine or, if it rained, on the staircase; but he was only allowed to enter the apartment itself if Leonie's mother was present.[42]

Berliners were surprised by the speed with which the Soviet military authorities restored the food supply and set about clearing the streets, repairing the tram and underground lines and restarting the gas, electricity and water supplies. On 3 May, Anneliese H. saw that the Russians had already begun distributing 'flour, potatoes, bread and goulash' to 'long queues'. The writer and war correspondent Vasily Grossman arrived to find women already sweeping the pavements of Berlin and clearing the rubble, and noticed that a girl's dismembered legs, clad in shoes and stockings, were still lying in the road. The theatre director Gustaf Gründgens and the musician Karla Höcker helped dismantle street barricades which forced labourers had erected weeks earlier. In the quiet and sunshine of early May, Höcker noted 'the crassness of the situation: we the musicians, artists, bourgeois . . . are clearing away the barricades as pointless traffic obstacles . . . And Asia triumphs!' By mid-May, Hertha von Gebhardt no longer felt afraid to go out on to the street alone during the day and the nightly break-ins by Soviet soldiers had abated. Now her block of flats would only be robbed by her own 'national comrades', as Germans faced a new wave of crime perpetrated by their fellow countrymen. Gebhardt had the impression that every Russian who wanted a girlfriend had now found one, noting that 'many are wandering along arm in arm . . . Overall, everyone is delighted. Russians are so nice,' she wrote with a trace of irony as well as surprise.[43]

Her status as a writer secured for Gebhardt privileges on the new scale of rationing instituted by the Soviet Command in Berlin, and through her network of German acquaintances she found an empty flat in a former artists' colony. Having rescued most of their possessions from the old Geroldstrasse flat and cellar – only their violin had been stolen – Hertha and Renate carried their two wicker chairs, many suitcases, a hundredweight of brickettes, firewood, manuscripts and a small library to the new flat – only to have it broken into and plundered by Germans. Mother and daughter had learned to step around the dead horse in the Heidelberger Platz and the corpses of Soviet and German soldiers still lying in the streets. They noticed the many improvised graves in the gardens. The mains were still not connected to the houses, and at the water pump a new ordinance permitted Jews and foreigners to go to the head of the queue. 'Vox pop,' Gebhardt noted on 12 May. 'That is only right! The poor Jews! All of a sudden everyone had always sympathised. All of a sudden no one was a Nazi!'[44]

On 18 May, the Klemperers finally left Unterbernbach, armed with Victor's yellow star, Jewish identity card and a paper from the local American administration attesting that he was a famous and persecuted professor. They cadged a lift to the outskirts of Munich, where they found that everything was more chaotic than six weeks earlier. Against the grey thundery sky of a Saturday afternoon, the white ruins of the city looked to Victor like a scene from the Last Judgement. The roaring of the American trucks and jeeps 'made the picture of hell complete; they are the angels of judgement,' he noted. Smothered by the dust of the rubble churned up by the motor vehicles, sweating in the summer heat and burdened by their suitcases and heavy winter clothes, the Klemperers trudged along, looking for shelter, food and permits to cross the new border into the Soviet zone of occupation. They hoped that they could reclaim their home outside Dresden, and Victor his professorial chair. Against the odds, they would succeed, but for now, dimly aware of his own residual nationalism, Victor reflected bitterly on how much liberation felt like defeat: 'Curious conflict within me: I rejoice in God's vengeance on the Henchmen of the Third Reich . . . and yet I find it dreadful now to see the victors and avengers racing through the city which they have so hellishly wrecked.'[45]

Epilogue: Crossing the Abyss

On 9 May 1945, Germans awoke to defeat. The stillness was remarkable. No shell bursts, no bombs, no blackout. It was neither the peace which had been so longed for, nor the annihilation which had been so dreaded. For 16-year-old Wilhelm Körner it was so hard to grasp that he wrote nothing in his diary for another week. When he picked it up again it was to vent his anguish:

> The 9th of May will definitely count amongst the blackest days of German history. Capitulation! We youths of today had struck the word from our vocabulary, and now we have had to experience how our German people after an almost six-year encirclement has had to lay down its arms. And how bravely has our people borne all hardships and sacrifices.

'Now it is up to us not to give up the spirit which has been planted in us and to remember that we are Germans,' he continued. 'If we forget that, then we are also betraying the dead who fell for a better Fatherland.' The son of a headmaster in Bremen who had gone through the Hitler Youth, the flak and finally the Volkssturm, Wilhelm was young enough to believe he could hold on to his wartime patriotism beyond the reality of complete defeat.[1]

In its final report on morale at the end of March 1945, the SD had broached the question of defeatism, the spreading certainty that nothing could rescue the war effort any more. Far from the revolutionary response the Nazis had always feared, they found 'deep-seated disappointment at misplaced trust, a feeling of grief, despondency, bitterness and growing rage, above all amongst those who have known nothing in this war other than sacrifice and work'. The first response was not rebellion so much as a rush of self-pity, with people quoted as saying, 'We did not deserve to be led into such a catastrophe.' Such sentiments were more self-righteous than anti-Nazi, as people of all classes 'excused themselves of any guilt for the course the war had taken', insisting 'that it was not they who had had responsibility for war leadership and politics'. For now the question of 'guilt' revolved around the agents of Germany's greatest disaster. And for those who remembered Goebbels's weekly articles in *Das Reich* in which he called on the German people to trust the Nazi leadership through all of the crises of the war, it was clear where responsibility for the nation's defeat lay.[2]

Listening to conversations on the streets of the eastern suburb of Friedrichshagen in late April, while the battle for the centre of Berlin was still raging, Liselotte Günzel was appalled by the speed with which people changed political allegiance, now 'cursing Hitler'. 'From one day to the next. First they are all Nazis and suddenly Communists. Out of the brown skin into the red one,' the 17-year-old noted in her diary, resolving that 'I will keep clear of the whole infatuation with the Party. At the most a Social Democrat like my parents.' As news of the suicide of Hitler and Goebbels spread, people's sense of rage at having been abandoned by their leaders rapidly grew; so too did the feeling that having lived under a dictatorship absolved one of personal responsibility for all that had happened.[3]

It was their first encounters with their victors which exposed Germans to a different kind of guilt. While the battle for Aachen was still raging in mid-October 1944, a US Army psychological warfare unit filed one of the first reports from German territory. It found 'a latent and possibly deep-seated sense of guilt, owing to the brutalities committed by the German armies in Europe, particularly in the east and against the Jews', adding that: 'Germans have resigned themselves to the idea of retribution and only hope that the Americans would moderate the rage of those who will punish them. But the idea of punishment they do accept.'[4]

One of the stranger elements of personal encounters between Allied victors and vanquished Germans in the early summer of 1945 were the sporadic attempts to instigate a moral reckoning. The writer and publisher Hermann Kasack described one such meeting, which took place in June 1945 at his villa in Potsdam. Here a Soviet officer began to tell of his sister:

At 17 years of age, she had . . . been tormented and abused by a German soldier; the soldier, as he put it, had 'red hair and eyes like an ox'. We sat there in anguish as the Georgian officer exclaimed in anger that just thinking of it made him want to wring people's necks. 'But', he added after a pause, 'you – good, you – good.' And he alluded to the fact that he knew how to behave, as we had to admit that he did. His rage at the suffering of his unfortunate sister kept boiling over again, and as so often in these days and weeks and in fact in all the Nazi years, we experienced again the shame of being Germans. After a time which felt unbelievably long to us but hardly lasted more than an hour and a half, he bade farewell, promising to return the next day, and departed . . . What a disgrace and what a humiliation to have to be born amongst the Germans.

What was remarkable in the summer of 1945 was the victors' frequent need to start some kind of dialogue with the conquered enemy, to force individual Germans to understand what they had done. In Hertha von Gebhardt's cellar, a Soviet soldier spent hours talking to his captive audience, frequently threatening to execute them. In another case, a 29-year-old nurse recorded how an officer, who had proved himself 'always friendly and lovable' to her children, came into her room, cradled the smallest in his arms and, gesturing at the other two, said, '"Pretty children! – I too wife and child, one year [old]! The Germans killed them both. Like so!" And he imitated slitting the stomach open!! "SS?" I asked. He nodded. (He was a Jew).'[5]

While the threat of violence forced Germans to see themselves as collectively guilty, it also created new barriers, deterring people from rethinking what their particular roles and responsibilities had been. On 12 April 1945, with the Americans and British across the Rhine and the Red Army on the Oder, Ursula von Kardorff was quite explicit about both her fear and her sense of guilt: 'And when the others [Allies] come with their boundless hatred and gruesome accusations, we will have to keep quiet because they are true.' But for many Germans it was an all-too-brief moment of openness, which did not endure beyond the immediate aftermath of defeat. By the time Hannah Arendt visited Germany in 1949, she was struck by her former fellow countrymen's lack of emotional engagement and unwillingness to discuss what had happened. And when Ursula von Kardorff prepared her diary for publication in 1962, she quietly cut her acknowledgement of German guilt.[6]

Even in 1945, there were two quite different conversations about guilt in Germany. One concerned the lost war and who bore responsibility for the German 'catastrophe': this was the self-pitying conversation within the German 'national community' that the SD had picked up in the final weeks of the war. The other concerned German war crimes and involved a sense of moral reckoning, which Germans expected to be enforced upon them by the victorious Allies. As Göring had warned in October 1943,

> Let no one be under any illusions and think he can come along later and say: I was always a good democrat under these dreadful Nazis. The Jew will give you the correct answer irrespective of whether you say you have been the greatest admirer of Jews or the greatest hater of Jews. He will treat the one like the other. For his thirst for vengeance encompasses the German nation.[7]

This dissonant dualism of German guilt – the crimes committed against the Jews and the greater crime to have lost the war – became more, not less, entrenched in the post-war years. Despite the markedly different ideological approaches to 're-education' pursued by the occupying powers, by the time the Third Reich's three successor states had been founded in 1949 in all of them a sense of German victimhood came to overshadow any sense of shared responsibility for the suffering of Germany's victims. Mass death, homelessness, expulsion and hunger rendered defeat and the first years of occupation far worse for many German civilians than their experience of the war itself. And there was now no greater national cause which could be invoked to justify or compensate for enduring such suffering.

*

As the Allies fixed new borders in post-war Europe, both Soviet Ukraine and Poland were moved westwards, with the cattle truck continuing to service the demographic reordering of eastern Europe. The Soviet Union resettled 810,415 Poles, many of them from historical centres in eastern Galicia, from Lwów and Rivne. In parallel, 482,880 Ukrainians were moved eastwards into the newly enlarged Soviet Ukraine. In the deeply 'mixed' Polish-German region of Upper Silesia, the influx of Polish settlers from the east acted as the administrative trigger to expel the ethnic Germans in fairly orderly fashion. Elsewhere, expulsion was more punitive and symbolically laden. The liberated Czech Jewish ghetto of Terezín – Theresienstadt – now interned Germans, who pleaded with the local Russian commandant not to withdraw, fearful that the Czechs would kill them all. Czechs forced German civilians to sing and dance, crawl and do gymnastics, as they awaited the cattle trains to deport them to Germany. On 30 May 1945, all 30,000 Germans living in Brno – or, as they would have called it, Brünn – were roused from their beds and driven out on foot. They were beaten as they walked to the camps on the Austrian border. Some 1,700 of them died on what Germans soon called the 'Brünn death march'. Leonie Bauditz and her family were expelled from Breslau in the snows of January 1946. It took five days for their cattle truck to reach Frankfurt on the Oder. By 1947, the rump Germany of the four Allied occupation zones had had to absorb 10,096,000 German refugees and expellees from Poland, Czechoslovakia, Hungary and Romania. In addition, as late as 1946, over three million wartime evacuees were still living in the countryside, unable or unwilling to risk returning to the ruined cities they had left two or three years earlier, especially if this meant crossing the tightly policed borders between the different occupation zones.[8]

In May 1945, 8 million foreigners had been liberated in Germany. During their first encounters with Allied troops, German farmers often asked their forced labourers to act as mediators with the invaders. Within weeks, the German population turned to their conquerors to protect them from roving gangs of foreign workers who appeared suddenly on outlying farms at night, demanding food, clothes and money, or simply wanting revenge for years of abuse. Their number continued to fall steadily, as the Allies implemented their policy of repatriating all 'Displaced Persons' (DPs). By early 1947, there were just under a million foreigners in Germany. Most of those who remained were in western Germany, with 575,000 in the US and 275,000 in the British zones. Their numbers were augmented by Jews fleeing westwards to escape the pogroms which swept post-war Poland: the worst excesses were in Cracow and Kielce, where 42 Jews out of a 200-strong community were killed in early July 1946. By October 1946, over 160,000 Jews had arrived in western Germany. Against a general policy to repatriate all East Europeans from Germany, the US Military Government permitted this one group to migrate westwards. The US Zone was also unique in establishing separate DP camps for Jews. In the French and British Zones, they were placed in camps by nationality, a toxic recipe as Jews lived alongside former German collaborators who had their own reasons to resist 'repatriation'.[9]

But even in the US Zone, Jewish DPs did not have an easy time. As Jews became a larger proportion of the remaining DPs, so the old image of the Jew as the archetypal swindler gained new currency. On 29 March 1946, 180 German police accompanied by dogs raided a Jewish camp in the Reinsburg Strasse in Stuttgart looking for black-market goods. Although they found only a few eggs, they provoked a full-scale fight with the Jewish DPs. One concentration camp survivor who had only recently been reunited with his wife and two children was killed. The American Military Government immediately responded by barring German police from entering Jewish camps.[10]

With the collapse of the Third Reich, the black market took off on a scale which eclipsed its rather modest wartime dimensions. The German economy was in chaos and heavy industry was at a standstill. In Berlin, centres of the black market sprang up on the Alexanderplatz and at the Tiergarten. Sewing needles, nails and screws ranked amongst its luxury goods. Just as in occupied Poland during the war, so now in Germany factories began to pay workers partly in kind, to allow them to enter the barter trade themselves. Children's games quickly caught up with reality, with cops and robbers giving way to 'coal thief and engine driver', as shoals of children pilfered coal from the railway sidings. The Western Allies debated whether to 'pastoralise' the country along the lines of the Morgenthau Plan in order to prevent any future German threat or whether to restart industrial production in the Ruhr. In its zone, the Soviet Union dismantled industrial plant and shipped it back as reparations. As the cash economy fell apart, firms made wholesale barter arrangements with one another, further disrupting any chance of restoring an integrated market. The food supply was also critical. Germany had lost some of its most produc-tive agricultural regions to Poland in the Allied settlement of national borders at Potsdam in 1945. During the first three post-war years, as crisis after crisis hit transport, food, heating fuel and clothing, Germans experienced levels of hunger which were far worse than anything they had endured during the war itself – mainly because the Nazi requisitioning of food had displaced shortages on to other Europeans.[11]

Cardinal Frings's sermon in Cologne on New Year's Eve 1946 authorised stealing the essentials of daily life, and he was commemorated for his gesture by a new local verb for theft: *fringsen*. No one group was responsible for the black market: its causes lay in the conditions of defeat and occupation. German police and local politicians blamed the racketeering and violent crime that engulfed Germany in 1945–48 on the DPs, as if they possessed the economic and institutional power to run the black market on their own. The rates of criminal conviction did not substantiate such assertions, even in courts run by an unreformed West German judiciary not given to thinking kindly about impoverished and downtrodden foreigners.[12]

In the semi-lawless conditions that prevailed in all four Allied occupation zones, two crimes struck the Chief State Prosecutor for Freiburg, Professor Karl Bader, as emblematic of the time: robbery and bigamy. With 8.7 million German men in prisoner-of-war camps in the summer of 1945, there were huge gender disparities. In Sachsen-Anhalt, there were three times as many women as men in the 20–30 age group and twice as many among 30 to 40-year-olds. Bigamy was most common amongst men who had been displaced by war and had been separated from their original families. Sometimes they simply wanted to legitimise children who had been born during the war. In other cases, people resorted to bigamy to hide their past identities. Equipped with false papers, the former Nazi mayor of a town in Saxony attested to his own death, after which he proceded to remarry his now 'widowed' wife, without fear of arrest for his Nazi activities. He even landed a job in the British Zone dealing with inter-zonal trade, where he went on to do well out of bribes and the black market.[13]

In a society desperate for moral anchors and respectability, the appearance of false doctors and pastors was particularly worrying. Former Wehrmacht medical orderlies masqueraded as doctors, surgeons and obstetricians, gaining access to drugs like morphine to feed their own needs or to sell on the black market. One former mechanic managed to persuade the Bishop of Mecklenburg of his clerical bona fides, serving as pastor in a parish near Schwerin until the end of 1945. Germany was awash with soothsayers. In July 1947 there were claims that

> In Berlin there is one *fortune-teller* for every 1,000 people. 99 per cent
> of their customers are women who wish to learn something of the
> uncertain fate of their relatives. One fortune-teller in Neukölln has a
> daily income of 5,000 marks and was forced to employ four assistants
> in order to deal with the queue in front of his house each day.

Besieged by people seeking guidance, one pastor with the Protestant
Inner Mission in Berlin remarked in 1946: 'Earlier such people
always had a goal or at least plans and wishes. These people do
not. They cannot find their feet; they don't want anything any
more, they don't wish for anything any more, they simply do not
know any more.'[14]

In Pforzheim there had been no news of Helmut Paulus since 1
November 1943. His commanding officer wrote twice to tell Erna and
Ernst Arnold Paulus how their eldest son had gone missing in action.
He had just returned from a spell of home leave when he ran into
an ambush; two search parties failed to find any trace of him and
there was a possibility that he had been taken prisoner. In May 1945,
Helmut's two sisters, Elfriede and Irmgard, arrived home together,
exhausted from tending the wounded in Heilbronn during the twelve-
day battle for the town. Their younger brother Rudolf had managed
to leave his army unit at Leipheim on the Danube and make his way
back thanks to civilian clothes given him by a farmer. Only Helmut
remained unaccounted for. His parents wrote to the Soviet Red Cross,
to Bishop Dibelius in Berlin and to Helmut's former comrades, all to
no avail. It was not until September 1976 that the Search Service of
the German Red Cross finally confirmed that Helmut had been killed
in November 1943.[15]

In Görmar in Thuringia, Hildegard Probst admitted on 1 July 1945
that 'I don't want to write any more because every day I ardently
await your return. For every day soldiers come home.' But she was
not yet ready to close the diary she had started when her husband
Fritz was reported missing in action after Stalingrad. Their son Karl-
Heinz was also unaccounted for: he returned; his father did not.[16]

Families pinned photos to the noticeboards of railway stations in
the hope that a returning comrade might bring them news of their
loved ones. Clergymen published prayers for the missing in their parish
newsletters and in September 1947 the Protestant Inner Mission dedi-

cated a week of prayer to them. The services were to take Jeremiah, 29:14 as their first reading. Its last verse ran:

'I will be found by you', declares the Lord, 'and I will restore your fortunes and will gather you from all the nations and from all the places where I have driven you', declares the Lord. 'And I will bring you back to the place from which I sent you into exile.'[17]

Some clergymen gave permission for headstones to be laid over empty graves for men who had not returned, including those whose status was never clarified. While she awaited the return of her son in Hildesheim, Frau R. wrote to a Catholic priest on 2 September 1947 about her conversations with men who had come home. She had become convinced that conditions of captivity in the USSR were 'much worse' than in the 'German concentration camps'. Whereas 'innocent people who had only done their duty at the front' had to suffer for a long time, 'the people in the concentration camps were immediately anaesthetised in the gas chambers', even though, she added, 'it was terrible and not nice to treat people like that'.[18]

The majority of the 17.3 million Wehrmacht soldiers had served on the eastern front, but only 3,060,000 men entered Soviet captivity. Most managed to switch across the fronts and surrender to the Western powers in the final weeks of fighting: 3.1 million prisoners were taken by the Americans, 3,640,000 by the British and 940,000 by the French. In the United States and Britain, prisoners were deployed in agricultural labour; in France and the Soviet Union they were rebuilding the shattered infrastructure. Although their labour was in breach of the Geneva Convention, the victors continued to use these men for several years after the war ended. By the end of 1948, however, most prisoners of war had returned to Germany from Western and Soviet captivity.[19]

In December 1949, Dr August Töpperwien was released from his prisoner-of-war camp in Poland and returned to Solingen. His house had been bombed, but Margarete and their two children had survived the war. Töpperwien rejoined the staff at his old grammar school in the position, as a senior high-school teacher, a *Studienrat*, which he had occupied for the fourteen years before he was called up to the Wehrmacht.[20]

Returning prisoners of war soon became a source of medical and psychiatric concern, as German psychiatrists turned to the term 'dystrophy' to describe their plight. Malnutrition and the endless space of the Russian landscape brought on apathy, depression and a loss of all moral inhibitions. Apparently, even German prisoners' 'nature and facial expressions have become Russian' and they 'had lost much of their actual humanity'. Psychologists, who had lauded the superiority of German manly virtues over Soviet barbarism such a short time before, now feared that the sex instinct might have died among the German prisoners held in the east. It was one thing to diagnose Germany's military casualties; quite another to listen to them. The medical files of former soldiers reveal the extreme anguish and guilt they continued to feel about the war, usually towards comrades who had been killed. According to his doctor, Helmut G. carried 'a strong sense of guilt around with him'. Helmut's first tour of duty had come right at the end of the war when in May 1945 he and his men were ordered to make their way back to the Elbe to surrender to the Americans rather than the Soviets. The 19-year-old felt he had failed the mix of very young and late-middle-aged men under his command by only saving those who could keep up with the forced marches. He felt he had broken the first rule of 'comradeship'.[21]

Rudolf B. sought out psychiatric help in 1949. He had signed on as a professional soldier and been wounded in the upper arm in early 1943. In his hospital bed he kept dreaming of the events which led up to his being wounded and shouted out military commands in his sleep. Some of his obsessive preoccupations surfaced in his fragmentary and rambling account to the psychiatrist who admitted him: 'Involuntarily I have to think that it's over. Am I imagining it all? Why all the sacrifices and losses? All for nothing. Betrayal, sabotage. I cannot . . .' A moment later, Rudolf raised his voice in anger: 'Is that so then. All for nothing, yes, yes. Am I mad or am I going mad? . . . (Have people changed?) People, people are worth nothing. And I tell you, Doctor, it was so, we did have the secret weapon.' In the end, he switched from Goebbels's slogans to the Ten Commandments, 'yes, yes, you shall not kill', before lapsing into silence. Everything he had believed in – the value of true sacrifice, the betrayal of the officers' plot, comradeship and Germany's possession of 'secret weapons', the guarantee of 'final victory' which justified every death and every escalation – remained vividly present four years after the end of the war. Unlike the rest of German society, Rudolf B. could not stop repeating the ideas and beliefs that had sustained him since 1939.[22]

Wilm Hosenfeld had been captured on 17 January 1945. In May he was sent to a camp for officers at Minsk, where he was questioned three times by NKVD interrogators over the next few months. His rank as an intelligence officer on the Staff Command of the Warsaw garrison suggested to them that he had been involved in running anti-Soviet intelligence operations; they did not believe that he had only organised sporting events and educational programmes. Held for six months in solitary confinement, his health deteriorated rapidly. When he rejoined the camp's other 2,000 prisoners at the end of 1945, he was able to write regularly to his family. His health improved and he was moved to a new camp at Bobruisk.

His wife Annemie turned to those her husband had aided and protected, locating a former concentration camp prisoner and a Communist, Karl Hörle, who had served under her husband from December 1943 and could vouchsafe Hosenfeld's anti-Nazi political outlook, despite his Party membership. In October 1947, Hörle drew on his position as chairman of the local 'Union of Victims of Nazi Persecution' to lobby the new rulers of East Germany to intercede with their Soviet patrons. It took longer to establish contact with those whom Hosenfeld had helped in Poland. In November 1950, Leon Warm-Warczyński, a Jew he had hidden in the Warsaw sports stadium, used a visit to the West to thank his rescuer. Astonished to find that Hosenfeld was still a prisoner, he wrote to Władysław Szpilman, who had re-established himself as a composer and pianist in post-war Warsaw. Szpilman pleaded in person with the much-feared head of the Polish secret police, Jakub Berman, only to be told that there 'was nothing to be done, because he is with the Soviet comrades'.[23]

The Soviets treated Wehrmacht intelligence officers like Hosenfeld on a par with the Gestapo and SD. On 27 May 1950, the military tribunal carried out an administrative review of Hosenfeld's case without a hearing and gave him a twenty-five-year sentence in a labour camp, mainly for his part in interrogating prisoners during the Warsaw Uprising. Hosenfeld had suffered a major stroke in July 1947 and although he received prompt medical treatment and recovered, from then on he suffered from unstable blood pressure, dizzy spells, headaches and a series of minor strokes. In August 1950, he was sent to serve his sentence in Stalingrad, where 2,000 German prisoners lived in stone huts and in bunkers dug out of the earth while they helped rebuild the city and construct the Volga–Don Canal. By June 1952, Hosenfeld's handwriting had deteriorated so much that he could only sign his name and had to dictate the rest of his card. His final message to his wife closed reassuringly: 'Don't worry about me, I am OK in the circumstances. I send you all my love, all the best! Your Wilm'. Hosenfeld died of a ruptured aorta on 13 August.[24]

On 26 October 1950, when the new West German Parliament held a day of remembrance for the German prisoners of war in the Soviet Union, Chancellor Konrad Adenauer asked in his official address whether 'ever before in history millions of people have been sentenced with such chilling heartlessness to misery and misfortune?' He was referring not to the murder of the Jews but to the fate of German prisoners in the Soviet Union, even though by this time there were only 30,000 prisoners still in Soviet captivity. Most of the 3 million taken prisoner by the Red Army during the war had already returned to Germany and Austria. Approximately 750,000 had died of illness and exhaustion: this was particularly true of the 110,000 exhausted prisoners taken at Stalingrad, of whom only 5,000 survived. When parts of the Soviet Union were gripped by famine in 1946–47, German prisoners were subjected to the same harsh conditions as the rest of the population: yet there was no retaliation for the policy of deliberate starvation which the Wehrmacht had inflicted on the 3.9 million Soviet prisoners of war it captured in 1941, and which had killed 2.8 million of them by early 1942. By the end of 1953, another 20,000 German prisoners had been released, leaving just 10,000 in the Soviet Union. But as their numbers fell, public agitation in the newly founded Federal Republic for the release of those remaining in Soviet captivity grew. Minutes of silence brought the bustle of traffic and urban life to a halt. Vigils and marches were held, while special prayers were said in churches for both the prisoners of war and the missing.[25]

Part of the problem was that during the final phase of the war the Wehrmacht had lost track of its own losses: by the summer of 1944, it had under-reported military deaths by 500,000. Losing whole army groups in the summer's retreats had meant also leaving both dead and wounded behind. By December, the Wehrmacht's internal count was a million adrift. The first four months of 1945 were even worse, with the Wehrmacht reporting that 200,000 men had died, when the reality was 1.2 million: in each of these months, on average 300,000–400,000 German soldiers had died, compared to the pre-June 1944 peak of 185,000 lost in January 1943 at Stalingrad. The result was that the Wehrmacht thought it had lost 3 million men compared to the reality of 4.8 million soldiers and 300,000 Waffen SS men. Because so many of these deaths occurred in the last phase of the war – especially in the fighting for the former eastern provinces – and because the military post had continued to function until the end of 1944, both relatives and experts thought that there were many more prisoners in Soviet custody than there were. When the Soviet Union announced at the Moscow conference of 1947 that it now only had 890,532 German prisoners of war, this came as a huge shock. It was widely assumed in Germany that there were still at least 2.5 million prisoners of war in Soviet camps. Expert opinion fuelled such sentiments: in 1947, a Hessian statistician published an estimate that an additional 700,000 prisoners of war must be in the Soviet Union, and this statistic was then taken up to confirm the lower estimate of German losses claimed by the Wehrmacht in the standard West German history.[26]

The same statistical error led to an exaggerated estimate of the numbers of civilians who had died in the flight and expulsion from the eastern provinces: based on demographic data, the Federal Office for Statistics estimated in 1958 that 2 million Germans had died, of whom 500,000 were soldiers: only in 1999 did it become clear that 1.4 million German soldiers from the eastern territories and provinces had died, thereby reducing the probable number of civilian deaths to 600,000. A similar process of revising the estimated death toll from Allied bombing downwards also had to wait until the 1990s, leading one reputable German historian to conclude then that 370,000–390,000 Germans and a further 40,000–50,000 forced foreign workers and prisoners of war were killed in the bombing. As with military deaths, most of these civilians had been killed in the final phase of the war.[27]

In the Cold War atmosphere of the 1950s the notion spread that there were secret Soviet camps where German prisoners were killed or deliberately worked to death. The emaciated faces, hollow eyes and shaven heads on the posters for films such as *Taiga* and *The Doctor of Stalingrad*, both released in 1958, or the 1961 offering *The Devil Played*

Balalaika, did not depict the victims of the Nazis but German prisoners of war. As if to displace the real concentration camps in Germany, which the Americans had made some local residents visit, special travelling exhibitions were mounted so that Germans could walk up to the barbed-wire fences and the watchtowers of models of Soviet prison camps. It was German men and women who were sent to the left and to the right, German corpses that were piled in makeshift mortuaries and their gold teeth that were pulled out before the bodies were interred in a Soviet camp's mass grave. While the tales of suffering of the prisoners of war in the 1950s or those of German expellees, carefully compiled and published in a multi-volume edition by the West German government, were widely publicised, few Germans wanted to discuss the genocide of the Jews, whose details had been silently borrowed for the tales they were now telling about their own suffering.[28]

★

On 20 November 1945, when the trial of the major war criminals opened at Nuremberg, it garnered unparalleled international publicity. That day, a mother with three small children wrote to her husband, a German officer in an American prisoner-of-war camp:

> *No* nation – however free of guilt it feels (which in any case never happens – guilt is *always* on both sides!) – is entitled to damn a *whole* nation, to take away all its freedoms, just by the right of the victor. Woe to the vanquished! Neither before nor since do *I* feel guilty for the war and all the horrors in the concentration camps as well as the shameful deeds committed in our name. – You, Mummy, my brothers and many, many among us bear just as little guilt. That's why I also categorically reject collective guilt!

Her one regret remained that she had not been able to walk the streets of her home town with her husband after he was promoted to the rank of general. Now a dependent evacuee mother, it would have gone a long way to compensating her for the status she had lost. But more fundamentally, she believed that 'A nation without a military is unarmed and that means the same as being without honour.'[29]

Public agitation against the Nuremberg trials began in the Western occupation zones with the first signs of the conflict between the British and American side and the Soviets, which Goebbels had so confidently predicted. In the West, the running was made by the German churches. With the banning of the Nazi Party and all its mass organisations by the Allies, they had come to enjoy unrivalled public influence. Within two weeks of Churchill's 'Iron Curtain' speech in March 1946, Catholic bishops in the West were using their freedom to attack the precepts underpinning Allied denazification and occupation policy. Cardinal Frings issued a pastoral letter in which he asserted, 'To ascribe collect- ive guilt to an entire people and to treat it accordingly is to usurp the powers of God.' The Münster journalist and diarist Paulheinz Wantzen noted the steady trickle of news about the deaths of Nazi functionaries in the Allied 'concentration camps' where they had been 'treated no differently from the former concentration camp inmates'. He reported that 'among the people sympathy for the "accused" at Nuremberg is growing by the hour'. In this atmosphere of vanishing terror and abiding powerlessness, the Church was seen to stand up for German rights. On 4 July 1946, Cardinal Frings wrote directly to the Nuremberg tribunal, trivialising their task and challenging the notion that 'someone should be considered worthy of punishment merely on account of his membership in the SA or other National Socialist organisations'. At the local level, prominent clerics like the General Vicar of Cologne argued that 'the SA rules of manly behaviour were quite compatible with Christian philosophy and were approved by the Bishops'.[30]

As early as June 1945, Bishop Galen of Münster had restated his respect for the patriotic example set by German soldiers. 'We want to deeply thank our Christian soldiers too,' he declared, 'those who in good conscience of doing right have risked their lives for the nation and Fatherland and who even in the hubbub of war kept their hearts and hands clean of hatred, plundering and unjust acts of violence.' The Allies set about dismantling not just the explicitly Nazi emblems of the Third Reich but also the memorial culture of sacrificial death that had sustained it. The inscription 'Germany must live, even if we must die' vanished from the military cemetery at Langemarck along- side the elaborate monuments the Nazis had erected for the dead of the First World War. But the symbolism of sacrifice could not be so easily eradicated. By October 1945, Galen was reminding Catholic congregations that 'the soldier's death stands in honour and value next to the martyr's death'. In February 1946, Pope Pius XII elevated Galen, Frings of Cologne and Konrad von Preysing of Berlin to the College of Cardinals, further enhancing their national and international standing. The following month, Galen, now seriously ill, was welcomed back to Münster with floral arches and garlands, like nothing the former journalist Paulheinz Wantzen had seen since visits by the Führer. Once again, the ailing cardinal preached a sermon on the sacrifices made by German soldiers. Germany's defeat might have been the result of the 'inner foulness' of National Socialism, he declaimed, but the honour of its soldiers remained unbesmirched: 'Nevertheless, what our soldiers did in loyal fulfilment of their duty will stand for ever and through all time as heroism, as loyalty and adhering to conscience which we honour and acknowledge.'[31]

In September 1946, Cardinal Frings became the first German to address a postwar audience in London, when he was handed the pulpit in Westminster Cathedral. Frings used the opportunity to affirm that 'We German Catholics were not National Socialists but we love our Fatherland. We love it all the more now that it is in deepest need and we fight for the inalienable rights which it has retained.' A few weeks later, an ecumenical delegation of British clergy, which included Bishop Bell of Chichester and the Roman Catholic Bishop of Nottingham, toured the Rhineland and Westphalia. They argued that the Allies had to support the churches' efforts to rebuild Germany, endorsing their claim that they had 'resisted its [the Nazi regime's] inhumanities'. Meanwhile, Catholic and Protestant leaders, especially men like Martin Niemöller who had themselves been imprisoned by the Nazis, became much-sought-after intercessors for those convicted of war crimes.[32]

As a leading Protestant theologian, Paul Althaus also felt obliged to offer intellectual leadership and published a short article addressing the issue of 'Guilt'. Like others, he had been quick to blame the Nazi 'leadership' for 'terrible mistakes' and 'serious injustice' in his early post-war sermons, but now looked for reasons why that same leadership should not be judged at Nuremberg. Althaus focused not on the war crimes and their consequences, but on the human nature of which they were a mere manifestation, claiming that 'all evil that occurs somewhere in my nation, yes, somewhere in humanity, stems from the same roots in the human soul which is the same everywhere and in all ages'. Having made specific acts disappear into an abstract, universal and timeless sense of human sinfulness, it was easy for him to conclude that only God Himself could judge the evil of these acts, for 'this community of guilt in its depth and breadth is beyond the understanding and justice of a human court. Human judges cannot and may not speak to me about it.'[33]

As a leading protagonist of nationalist Protestantism, Althaus had warned his fellow Germans after the First World War that 1918 meant more than just defeat: God had judged them and found them wanting. Whereas the God he evoked after the earlier war had been the punitive deity of the Old Testament, after 1945 Althaus came to emphasise His 'merciful will'. 'We cannot atone in any other way,' he wrote in 1946,

> than that we, Christianity in Germany, first of all step humbly under Christ's cross representing our entire people with our needs and shame over the terrible things which have happened: 'Christ, you lamb of God, who takes away the sins of the world, have mercy upon us and lift the curse, the ban from our land.'[34]

It is possible that Althaus's rediscovery of mercy was perfectly genuine: his disabled daughter had been lucky to escape the selections of psychiatric patients for medical murder. Yet during the rest of 1945 the theologian reminded his congregation about the 'blood sacrifice' of 'millions of dead German soldiers', without mentioning the millions of soldiers and civilians Germans had killed. When he preached about the '6 million from the east', he was speaking of the German refugees, although the number he chose related to the murdered Jews. When he spoke of the Polish 'hangmen' who had shot eighteen Germans in 1939 in Thorn, he made no reference to millions of Poles killed by the German occupiers. And when he referred to the 'guilt' of the American and British bombing, he did not mention how the Germans had waged war. Althaus was entrusted by the Americans with chairing the denazification tribunal at Erlangen: although they then suspended him from his professorial chair for lack of action, it was restored to him in 1948. During this tumultuous time, no colleague broke ranks and denounced Althaus as one of the principal authors of the 'Aryan paragraph' which had excluded converted Jews from the Protestant Church. Nor did anyone signal that his 'theology of order' and 'theology of creation' had provided intellectual legitimacy to Nazism and to anti-Semitism. Instead, Althaus remained a key player in German Protestantism long after his academic retirement in 1956.[35]

When Martin Niemöller asked an audience of Erlangen students in January 1946 why no clergyman in Germany had preached about 'the terrible suffering which we, we Germans caused other peoples, over what happened in Poland, over the depopulation of Russia and over the 5.6 million dead Jews', he was shouted down. Niemöller remained a radical and outspoken figure. Within the Confessing Church, he had become the sharpest critic of Nazi religious policies; for this he was arrested in July 1937 and sent to Dachau. Niemöller also remained a German nationalist, volunteering to serve again in the German Navy on the outbreak of the Second World War. On his release in 1945, Niemöller admitted at a press conference in Naples that he had 'never quarrelled with Hitler over political matters, but purely on religious grounds'. In October 1945, however, he persuaded the other ten members of the Council of the Evangelical Church in Germany to sign the Stuttgart Declaration of Guilt, which admitted:

> Through us infinite wrong was brought over many peoples and countries. That which we often testified to in our communities, we express now in the name of the whole Church: we did fight for long years in the name of Jesus Christ against the mentality that found its awful expression in the National Socialist regime of violence; but we accuse ourselves for not standing by our beliefs more courageously, for not praying more faithfully, for not believing more joyously, and for not loving more ardently.

It was a controversial document, wrung from its signatories by the insistence of representatives of Protestantism in the Netherlands, Switzerland, France, Britain and the USA, who attended the synod, that they could re-establish ties with the German Protestant Church only if their co-religionists accepted moral responsibility. Beyond the general confession, the document avoided all reference to the war, but even so, it went too far for most German Protestants, who felt it amounted to a humiliating concession to the Allies on a par with the Versailles Treaty's clause about German war guilt in 1919. Not until 1950 did the synod concede that 'through acts of omission and silence'

German Protestants 'have been guilty before the God of mercy for the iniquity which has been perpetrated against the Jews by members of our nation'. It would take decades to evoke a more candid and openly self-critical admission.[36]

Although the political Left rode a wave of popular support in both Eastern and Western occupation zones, even in its old heartlands of the Ruhr, Saxony and Berlin it was building on very different cultural foundations from those that existed before 1933. The new generation who joined the Social Democrats, the Communists and the trade unions were very different from the leaders who returned from exile or imprisonment. These were people who had gone through the Hitler Youth, BDM, the Reich Labour Service and the flak or had served in the Wehrmacht. The old associational life of the Left could not be rebuilt; nor could its old moral values.[37]

In April 1945, after the US Army occupied Düsseldorf, Marianne Strauss emerged from hiding. Immediately she threw herself into political activity, spending her evenings and weekends at meetings, eager to seize the moment and bring about the transformation of German society that she and the other members of the small socialist organisation which had hidden her since August 1943 had awaited. Marianne tried to recruit for the Bund by joining the re-founded Communist Party and becoming an activist in its Free German Youth movement. In April 1946, she started writing full-time on the arts for the Communist newspaper *Freiheit* and also worked for the German service of the BBC in the British Zone. But already she was admitting in a letter to one of her British cousins that 'one recognises how illusory were the hopes we placed in Germany's ability to develop and change. Sometimes I feel that the Germans have learned nothing.' Within a year, Marianne, who in May 1945 had automatically identified herself as a German rather than presenting herself to the Allies as a Jew, was no longer sure about counting herself amongst them and began thinking of leaving Germany.[38]

Wartime beliefs had not disappeared with Nazi rule. In June 1945, a Catholic priest in Münster told Allied investigators how widespread the view still was in his area that their wartime bombing represented 'the revenge of World Jewry'. In August, US Intelligence in Germany reported that only the Russians were hated more than the Americans. Germans were willing to accept that Britain and France had been forced into the war but could not understand US intervention. No one seemed to remember that it was Hitler who had declared war on the United States. Interviewers found that the 'Jewish war' still provided the key explanation for American actions against Germany, and German defeat seemed only to have confirmed the 'power of world Jewry'. Hardly anybody thought that the German people as a whole were responsible for the suffering of the Jews, although 64 per cent agreed that the persecution of the Jews had been decisive in making Germany lose the war. Still, there was a large minority of respondents – 37 per cent – who, even in conditions of Allied occupation, were prepared to endorse the view that 'the extermination of the Jews and the Poles and other non-Aryans' had been necessary for 'the security of the Germans'. It was clear that most Germans still believed they had fought a legitimate war of national defence.[39]

This was not what any of the victorious Allies had intended. The Americans had pursued the most ambitious re-education and denazification policy in 1945 and 1946, forcing Germans to visit the liberated concentration camps or, sometimes, to view film footage from Buchenwald and Dachau before receiving ration cards. Many turned their faces away, unwilling or unable to look. Others began to disparage the films and photographs as propaganda staged by the Allies. Even the word 're-education', with its connotations of sending juvenile delinquents to reformatories or 'asocials' to concentration camps, sounded offensive to German ears. The Americans found that their efforts were bearing little fruit. Between November 1945 and December 1946 they had conducted eleven polls, finding that on average 47 per cent endorsed the proposition that National Socialism had been 'a good idea carried out badly'; in August 1947, 55 per cent of those polled endorsed this view. The level of support amongst those under 30, those with high-school education, amongst Protestants, and those living in West Berlin and in Hesse was even higher, reaching 60–68 per cent – and this at a time when openly advocating National Socialism still potentially carried the death penalty.[40]

★

In the Soviet occupation zone, a quite different political and ideological course was pursued, as Communist leaders like Wilhelm Pieck and Walter Ulbricht returned from Soviet exile determined to transform the country and prevent the re-emergence of fascism by creating a new cult and set of norms based around the heroic example of Communist fighters against fascism. In April 1945 Pieck affirmed the German people's 'deep implication' in Nazi crimes, and the view that Germans had brought their sufferings on themselves was disseminated in *Dresden*, a short documentary film made in 1946 about the bombing of the city. Hopes that the German people would embrace the heroic example of the 'Anti-fascist Resistance Fighters' persisted and particular emphasis was placed on education and propaganda efforts amongst German prisoners of war. In his attempt, however, to establish effective rule over the Soviet occupation zone, Pieck now welcomed returning prisoners of war instead of continuing to blame them, explicitly confining German guilt to a small circle, the 'Hitler clique'. As early as 1946, he went so far as to equate the innocent suffering of 'millions of German people' who 'had been driven to death on the battlefields and in the *Heimat* by the Hitler government' with that of 'millions' – he did not say of what nation or ethnicity – who 'had been murdered and tortured to death by an inhuman terror in the concentration camps'.[41]

Here the shift from 'collective guilt' was effected far more smoothly than in the West. From 1947, East Germans were encouraged to commemorate their war dead on Remembrance Sunday as 'victims of fascism', exploited and sent to their death by the 'Hitler clique'. Out of the heroic 'Anti-fascist Resistance', socialist Germany had been born. With its overblown language of sacrifice, rebirth, optimism and collective endeavour, many of the phrases had a ring familiar from Nazi appeals to the 'national community', although the Communists' goals of peaceful reconstruction were more bathetic and achievable. By this point, actual veterans of the 'Anti-fascist Resistance' such as German-Jewish Communists who had fought in the International Brigades in Spain were met with suspicion when they opted to return to East Germany from exile in Britain.[42]

Austria followed an even shorter route to transforming its citizens from perpetrators into victims. Taking its cue from the Allies' Moscow Declaration of 1943, on 27 April 1945 Austrian independence from the Reich was declared, with the assertion that the *Anschluss* of March 1938 had made Austria the 'first victim' of National Socialist aggression. Ten years later, a State Treaty was signed, giving formal Allied recognition to the non-aligned Second Republic, and its first article enshrined this myth. When Austria opened a permanent exhibition in the Auschwitz concentration camp in 1978, it once more presented itself as a pure victim of the Nazis.[43]

The formal creation of two German states in 1949 was rapidly overshadowed by the outbreak of the Korean War in June 1950. Now both the Soviet Union and the United States urged their German clients to rearm. Official pronouncements in East Germany shifted dramatically. In February 1949, the official Socialist Unity Party paper, *Neues Deutschland,* dedicated half its Sunday supplement to commemorating the destruction of Dresden four years earlier. There were photographs, which would soon become iconic, of the dead piled up in the Altmarkt square to be burned, eyewitness reports and an article by the city's mayor. For the first time, the wanton and needless destruction was blamed on the British and Americans. It set the tone for the new Cold War confrontation and there was again talk of the 'Anglo-American terror attacks' – only the 'Jewish' epithet was omitted from Goebbels's original turn of phrase. In 1964, a new memorial was unveiled at the Heide Cemetery where the remains of those killed in the Dresden raids were interred. Its circle of fourteen stelae gave visual form to the equivalence Pieck had drawn between victims of Nazi persecution and the German war dead. Seven columns bore the names of concentration camps, the other seven the names of bombed cities from around the world. Across the open circle of stelae Dresden faced Auschwitz.[44]

In the West, Chancellor Adenauer responded to the American pressure to rearm by asserting in the Federal Parliament in 1951 that 'there has been no breach in the honour of the former German Wehrmacht'. Members of Parliament welcomed the opportunity to proclaim that 'the age of collective guilt is now at an end'. As the new democracy paid court to the corps of non-commissioned officers and senior commanders it needed to form its own armed forces, the cult of 'sacrifice', 'duty' and 'honour' re-emerged. Meanwhile the other old professional elites were also welcomed back into the West German state. In 1951–53, the West German Parliament guaranteed the employment rights and pensions of former civil servants and military personnel, including those who had been transferred to the Gestapo or Waffen SS. Ingeborg T. might never have had the pleasure of walking with her husband down the streets of Soest in the few months that he ranked as a Wehrmacht general in 1945, but he did secure a general's pension. Old networks proved strong within the professional elites. Soon 43 per cent of the West German diplomatic corps were former SS men and another 17 per cent had served in the SD or Gestapo. In Bavaria, where American efforts at denazification had gone further than in the other Western zones, 77 per cent of Finance Ministry officials and 94 per cent of judges and state prosecutors were former Nazis. The Federal Republic had taken over Allied decrees recognising the persecution of political prisoners and Jews and its courts and administration complied, reluctantly, with survivors' compensation claims: Marianne Strauss began her legal claim in September 1945 and, redefined by successive Federal laws and rulings, it continued into the 1970s. No ruling by the Allies had been made on behalf of the Roma, Jehovah's Witnesses or homosexuals, and for decades West German courts held out against recognising their claims, as many of the same civil servants and judges who had persecuted them as 'asocials' or 'pacifists' under the Third Reich continued to rule over their cases until they finally retired in the late 1950s and early 1960s. Uniquely amongst former political prisoners, communists' claims were also routinely rejected on the grounds that they supported a 'totalitarian' regime. The Cold War also altered the status of claimants in East Germany: Frieda Rimpl's husband Josef – a Jehovah's Witness – had been executed in December 1939 for refusing to serve in the Wehrmacht. She had duly been recognised as a 'victim of National Socialist perse-cution' and paid a widow's pension by the Saxon Social Security Office; in November 1950, she received a letter informing her that she had been 'de-recognised' and the payments terminated.[45]

Despite the bitterness of Cold War polemics, it was hard to persuade the young on either side to become soldiers, especially not when a future German–German war lay in prospect. In East Germany, the 950,000 members of the Communist youth movement responded to calls to join the new National People's Army by resigning en masse: they were not willing to jettison their ideals of 'democractic pacifism'. Although most West Germans still regarded military service in the Wehrmacht in positive terms, rearmament and the reintroduction of conscription in 1956 were opposed by a loose coalition of Social

Democrats, Christian pacifists and conservatives. Some, like Gustav Heinemann, who resigned from Adenauer's government in protest, and Martin Niemöller, wanted Germany to remain unarmed and neutral in the hope that this would lead to national reunification. It was a coalition which would further build over the next few years to oppose the presence of an American nuclear arsenal on German soil.[46]

Now, instead of contributing to a new militarism, the cult of the 'fallen' became steeped in a pathos which, however nationalist in its cultivation of German victimhood, was shorn of bellicosity. In February 1943, Goebbels had entrusted the propagandist for the 6th Army, Heinz Schröter, with compiling a suitable selection of letters from German soldiers fighting at Stalingrad. Anticipating the creation of a 'heroic epic of Stalingrad' to rival the Nibelungen legend, Goebbels abruptly shelved the whole project once he realised how negatively the German public was responding to this way of mythologising defeat. In 1950, Schröter published the selection himself as *Last Letters from Stalingrad*. It was brought out by a small West German publishing house, but when it was taken up by the Bertelsmann book clubs in 1954 it reached a mass audience. There were thirty-nine letters, just as Schröter had originally proposed to Goebbels. Some contained signs of fabrication: the authorial voice was too uniform, factual inaccuracies too jarring, the kitschy episodes too dominant. Nonetheless, the collection was soon accepted as *the* authentic voice of the doomed warriors, their letters prized for their elegiac, tragically heroic tone, perfectly suited to being read aloud at commemorations. But they never served the purpose Goebbels had intended.[47]

There was no 'Stalingrad syndrome', no real desire to avenge the defeat. Instead, the letters became part of a culture of reconciliation, translated into numerous languages and recrossing the Iron Curtain to appear in Russian and East German collections; they were even made obligatory reading in Japanese schools. In the same year as Schröter's volume appeared, the war veteran Heinrich Böll published a short story about a severely wounded soldier who returns to be operated on in an improvised hospital which the dying man gradually realises is his former school. Eventually he recognises his own hand in the incomplete chalked sentence on the board of the drawing class: 'Come wanderer to Spa . . .', Schiller's version of the Simonides epitaph for the 300 Spartans – the verse which Göring had invoked for the Stalingrad fighters and which had moved Böll at the time. By puncturing the myth at its source, the young writer was accusing the humanistic Gymnasium of mis-educating the young in patriotism; it was a reprise of an accusation Erich Maria Remarque or Wilfred Owen had levelled it the previous war. 'Opfer' never quite lost its double connotation of active 'sacrifice' and passive 'victim'. But even if reference to 'the fallen' still carried an echo of active, patriotic sacrifice, commemoration of the war was gravitating towards seeing soldiers as unwitting, passive and innocent victims. There was a certain inevitability here: defeat had shattered all wartime hopes, leaving only suffering, the shadow of futile heroism more potent than any general's post-war assertions that the war in the east could have been won. And so, after all the apocalyptic prophecies, Germans found themselves not in but, somehow, on the other side of Hölderlin's 'unknown abyss'.[48]

*

At the end of the war Liselotte Purper was still young, a widow at 33. After the Red Army occupied the estate of Krumke in May 1945, she kept a low profile in order to avoid being recognised as a Nazi propaganda photographer and worked on the estate and as a dental assistant. In 1946, she moved to West Berlin and began to work as a photographer again, for the first time in her professional career using her married name, Orgel. Among her early post-war subjects, she chose to photograph men in a Berlin rehabilitation centre, the Oskar Helene Home. One man she photographed had lost his right forearm and was learning to use a file to do metalwork. The horrific injuries of war had been shown before, by Ernst Friedrich in his militantly anti-war tract of 1924, War against War, where his emphasis on the terrible destruction of life made him a particular object of hatred for the Nazis. Now, Liselotte Orgel used her wartime technique of angling the shot from below to accentuate the sense of strength and purpose in the man, conjuring up an uplifting message: simple manual work could reconstruct not just Germany's shattered landscape but also Germans' shattered bodies.[49]

Ernst Guicking's luck held. After only a few weeks' incarceration as a prisoner of war, he returned, finding Irene and their two young children at her parents' home in Lauterbach. Her training as a florist and his childhood on the farm saw them through the post-war years: they began to grow flowers and vegetables on a strip of land next to the house. In 1949, Irene realised her pre-war dream and opened a modest flower shop of her own. When asked in 2003 whether she and Ernst had ever talked to their children about the war, Irene replied: 'I don't think so, I don't think so, no. I don't remember that, no. And then we were just so busy from morning to night in the market garden and the shop.' She did not call to mind the letters she and Ernst had written in early 1942 about the deportation of the Jews and what happened to them in the east, or their anxiety that Germany should hold out in early 1945. What Irene did want to talk about was love, and this was the principal reason why she wanted to see their wartime correspondence archived and published.[50]

As families like the Guickings retrieved the private lives they had put on hold during the war years, they were also redeeming one of the promises they had made to each other at the time. In their 1950s version of the patriarchal nuclear family West Germans were keen to recompense themselves for having deferred personal life for so long. It was not untypical that, having finally secured the economic foundations of their family idyll, parents did not know what to tell their children. They might continue to believe that what they had done was justified but in many families new barriers of silence were erected between generations. While the next generation began to ask why Germans had unleashed such a calamity on the world, the older one was still locked into the calamity they had themselves suffered.

Notes

Abbreviations

AEK	Historisches Archiv des Erzbistums Köln
BA	Bundesarchiv, Berlin
BA–MA	Bundesarchiv-Militärarchiv, Freiburg
DAZ	*Deutsche Allgemeine Zeitung*, Berlin, 1861–1945
DHM	Deutsches Historisches Museum, Berlin
DLA	Dokumentation lebensgeschichtliche Aufzeichungen, University of Vienna, Department of Economic and Social History
DRZW	Militärgeschichtliches Forschungsamt (ed.), *Das Deutsche Reich und der Zweite Weltkrieg*, 1–10, Stuttgart / Munich, 1979–2008
DTA	Deutsches Tagebucharchiv, Emmendingen
FZ	*Frankfurter Zeitung*, Frankfurt, 1856–1943
Goebbels, *Tgb*	*Die Tagebücher von Joseph Goebbels*, ed. Elke Fröhlich and the Institut für Zeitgeschichte, Munich, 1987–2008
IfZ–Archiv	Archiv, Institut für Zeitgeschichte, Munich
IMT	*Trial of the Major War Criminals before the International Military Tribunal, Nuremberg, 14 November 1945–1 October 1946*, 1–42, Nuremberg, 1947–9
JZD	Jehovas Zeugen in Deutschland, Schreibabteilung-Archiv, 65617 Selters-Taunus
KA	Kempowski-Archiv, formally at Nartum, now Akademie der Künste, Berlin
LNRW.ARH	Landesarchiv Nordrhein-Westfalen, Abteilung Rheinland
LNRW.AW	Landesarchiv Nordrhein-Westfalen, Abteilung Westfalen
LWV	Landeswohlfahrtsverbandarchiv-Hessen, Kassel
MadR	Heinz Boberach (ed.), *Meldungen aus dem Reich, 1938–1945: Die geheimen Lageberichte des Sicherheitsdienstes der SS*, 1–17, Herrsching, 1984

MfK–FA	Museum für Kommunikation Berlin, Feldpost-Archiv
RA	Wilhelm Roessler-Archiv, Institut für Geschichte und Biographie, Aussenstelle der Fernuniversität Hagen, Lüdenscheid
RSHA	Reichssicherheitshauptamt (Reich Security Main Office)
Sopade	Klaus Behnken (ed.), *Deutschlandberichte der Sozialdemokratischen Partei Deutschlands (Sopade) 1934–1940*, Frankfurt, 1980
UV, SF/NL	Sammlung Frauennachlässe, University of Vienna, Department of History
VB	*Völkischer Beobachter*, 1920–45
VfZ	*Vierteljahreshefte für Zeitgeschichte*, Munich, 1953–
YIVO Archives	YIVO Institute for Jewish Research, New York

Introduction

1   Rethinking the final phase of the war: Kershaw, *The End*; Geyer, 'Endkampf 1918 and 1945', in Lüdtke and Weisbrod (eds), *No Man's Land of Violence*, 35–67; Bessel, 'The shock of violence' in ibid., *No Man's Land of Violence*, 69–99, and Bessel, *Germany in 1945*.

2   On bombing, Groehler, *Bombenkrieg gegen Deutschland*; Friedrich, *Der Brand*; on rape, Sander and Johr (eds), *BeFreier und Befreite*; Beevor, *Berlin*; Jacobs, *Freiwild*; women's experience of the war, Dörr, '*Wer die Zeit nicht miterlebt hat . . .*' 1–3; flight, prompted by Grass, *Im Krebsgang*; e.g. Schön, *Pommern auf der Flucht 1945*; interviews with German children, Lorenz, *Kriegskinder*; Bode, *Die vergessene Generation*; Schulz et al., *Söhne ohne Väter*; for critical discussions, Kettenacker (ed.), *Ein Volk von Opfern?*; Wierling, '"Kriegskinder"', in Seegers and Reulecke (eds), *Die 'Generation der Kriegskinder'*, 141–55; Stargardt, *Witnesses of War*: introduction; Niven (ed.), *Germans as Victims*; Fritzsche, 'Volkstümliche Erinnerung', in Jarausch and Sabrow (eds), *Verletztes Gedächtnis*, 75–97.

3   Joel, *The Dresden Firebombing*; Niven, *Germans as Victims*, introduction; on 1950s, Moeller, *War Stories*; Schissler (ed.), *The Miracle Years*; Gassert and Steinweis (eds), *Coping with the Nazi Past*; 1995 Wehrmacht exhibition and debate, Heer and Naumann (eds), *Vernichtungskrieg*; Hartmann et al., *Verbrechen der Wehrmacht*; historical research began with Streit, *Keine Kameraden* (1978); and continued to Römer, *Der Kommissarbefehl* (2008).

4   Hauschild-Thiessen (ed.), *Die Hamburger Katastrophe vom Sommer 1943*, 230: Lothar de la Camp, circular letter, 28 July 1943; Kulka and Jäckel (eds), *Die Juden in den geheimen NS-Stimmungsberichten*, 3693, SD Außenstelle Schweinfurt, o.D. [1944] and 3661, NSDAP Kreisschulungsamt

Rothenburg/T, 22 Oct. 1943; Stargardt, 'Speaking in public about the murder of the Jews', in Wiese and Betts (eds), *Years of Persecution*, 133–55.

5   Kershaw, 'German popular opinion', in Paucker (ed.), *Die Juden im nationalsozialistischen Deutschland*, 365–86; Bankier, *The Germans and the Final Solution;* Himmler, *Die Geheimreden,* 171: speech at Posen, 6 Oct. 1943; Confino, *Foundational Pasts.*

6   Orłowski and Schneider (eds), *'Erschießen will ich nicht!'*, 247: 18 Nov. 1943.

7   Ibid., 338: 17 Mar. 1945.

8   *MadR,* 5571, 5578–9 and 5583: 5 and 9 Aug. 1943; Stargardt, 'Beyond "Consent" or "Terror"', 190–204.

9   Kershaw, *'Hitler Myth';* Kershaw, *Hitler,* I–II; Wilhelm II, 'An das deutsche Volk', 6 Aug. 1914, in *Der Krieg in amtlichen Depeschen 1914/1915,* 17–18; Verhey, *The Spirit of 1914;* Reimann, *Der grosse Krieg der Sprachen.*

10   Most important contributions to this overall interpretation: Steinert, *Hitlers Krieg und die Deutschen;* Martin Broszat, 'Einleitung', in Broszat, Henke and Woller (eds), *Von Stalingrad zur Währungsreform;* Joachim Szodrzynski, 'Die "Heimatfront"', in Forschungsstelle für Zeitgeschichte in Hamburg (ed.), *Hamburg im 'Dritten Reich',* 633–85; most recently, Schneider, *In der Kriegsgesellschaft,* 802–34. On capital punishment, Evans, *Rituals of Retribution,* 689–96.

11   Kater, *The Nazi Party;* Benz (ed.), *Wie wurde man Parteigenosse?;* Nolzen, 'Die NSDAP', 99–111.

12   Peukert, *Inside Nazi Germany;* Gellately, *Backing Hitler;* Wachsmann, *Hitler's Prisons;* Caplan and Wachsmann (eds), *Concentration Camps;* Evans, *The Third Reich in Power,* chapter 1.

13   Oswald, *Fußball-Volksgemeinschaft,* 282–5; Havemann, *Fußball unterm Hakenkreuz.*

14   *Sopade* 3, 836: 3 July 1936; Schneider, *Unterm Hakenkreuz.*

15   Sontheimer, *Antidemokratisches Denken in der Weimarer Republik;* Wildt, 'Volksgemeinschaft', in Steber and Gotto (eds), *Visions of Community in Nazi Germany,* 43–59; Schiller, *Gelehrte Gegenwelten;* Eckel, *Hans Rothfels.*

16   Ericksen, *Theologians under Hitler;* Hetzer, *'Deutsche Stunde';* Stayer, *Martin Luther;* Schüssler, *Paul Tillich.*

17   Strobl, *The Swastika and the Stage,* 58–64, 104, 134–7.

18   Ibid., 187.

19   Martina Steber and Bernhard Gotto, 'Introduction', and Lutz Raphael, 'Pluralities of National Socialist ideology', both in Steber and Gotto (eds), *Visions of Community in Nazi Germany,* 1–25 and 73–86; Noakes, *Nazism,* 4, *The German Home Front,* 355–9.

20   Bentley, *Martin Niemöller;* Gailus, 'Keine gute Performance', in Gailus and Nolzen (eds), *Zerstrittene 'Volksgemeinschaft',* 96–121.

21   Althaus, *Die deutsche Stunde der Kirche*, 3rd edn, 5; Gailus, *Protestantismus und Nationalsozialismus*, 637–66.

22   Brodie, 'For Christ and Germany', D. Phil., Oxford, 2013.

23   Conflict, see Kershaw, *Popular Opinion and Political Dissent*, 185–223; Stephenson, *Hitler's Home Front*, 229–64; antagonistic co-operation, Süß, 'Antagonistische Kooperationen', in Hummel and Kösters (eds), *Kirchen im Krieg*, 317–42; Kramer, *Volksgenossinnen an der Heimatfront*; Brodie, 'For Christ and Germany', chapter 3.

24   Stargardt, 'The Troubled Patriot', 326–42.

25   MfK–FA, 3.2002.0306, Fritz to Hildegard P., 6 Oct. 1939; see also Latzel, *Deutsche Soldaten*; Goltz, *Hindenburg*.

26   Latzel, *Deutsche Soldaten*, 323 and 331–2; Irrgang, *Leutnant der Wehrmacht*, 235–6: Peter Stölten to Dorothee Ehrensberger, 21/22 Dec. 1944.

1 *Unwelcome War*

1   Kleindienst (ed.), *Sei tausendmal gegrüßt*, Ernst to Irene, 25 Aug. 1939: all references to their letters are given by date only, because the full correspondence is held on the CD-rom which accompanies the published selection.

2   Breloer (ed.), *Mein Tagebuch*, 32: Gerhard M., 26 Aug. 1939; Hosenfeld, '*Ich versuche jeden zu retten*', ed. Vogel, 242–3: 27 and 30 Aug. 1939.

3   Breloer (ed.), *Mein Tagebuch*, 32–3: Gerhard M., 27 Aug. 1939.

4   Klepper, *Unter dem Schatten deiner Flügel*, 797 and 792–4: 1 Sept., 26 and 27 Aug. 1939; Wecht, *Jochen Klepper*, 52 and 222–5.

5   Kershaw, *Hitler*, 2, 200–3; Chu, *The German Minority in Interwar Poland*.

6   Blaazer, 'Finance and the End of Appeasement', 25–39.

7   Kershaw, *The 'Hitler Myth'*, 139–40; Kershaw, *Hitler*, 2, 173.

8   Kleindienst (ed.), *Sei tausendmal gegrüßt*: Irene to Ernst, 3 Sept. 1939.

9   *Sopade*, 6, 561, 818 and 693: May and July 1939.

10   Baumgart, 'Zur Ansprache Hitlers vor den Führern der Werhmacht am 22. August 1939'; 'Hossbach Niederschrift'; Bussmann, 'Zur Entstehung und Überlieferung der Hossbach Niederschrift', 373–84.

11   Schmidt, *Statist auf diplomatischer Bühne*, 469; Kershaw, *Hitler*, 2, 220–1 and 208.

12   Klepper, *Unter dem Schatten deiner Flügel*, 796: 1 Sept. 1939; Domarus (ed.), *Hitler*, 1307–18; Kershaw, *Hitler*, 2, 222.

13   Pospieszalski, 'Nazi attacks on German property', 98–137; Runzheimer, 'Der Überfall auf den Sender Gleiwitz', 408–26; Sywottek, *Mobilmachung für den totalen Krieg*, 219–32.

14   Hosenfeld, '*Ich versuche jeden zu retten*', 245–6: to Helmut, 1 Sept. 1939.

15   Ibid. 245–6: to Helmut, 1 Sept. 1939, 245; Verhey, *The Spirit of 1914*;

Stenographische Berichte des Reichstages, 13. Legislaturperiode, 306/ 2. Session 1914, 1–12: Wilhelm II to the Reichstag, 4 Aug. 1914.

16 Klepper, *Unter dem Schatten deiner Flügel*, 792–3 and 798: 26 and 27 Aug. and 3 Sept. 1939; Klepper, *Der Vater*; Klepper, *Kyrie*; Endlich et al. (eds), *Christenkreuz und Hakenkreuz*.

17 Klepper, *Unter dem Schatten deiner Flügel*, 794 and 797: 27 Aug. and 1 Sept. 1939; Shirer, *Berlin Diary*, 154: 31 Aug. 1939; *DAZ*, 1 Sept. 1939; Steinert, *Hitlers Krieg und die Deutschen*, 84–7.

18 MfK–FA 3.2002.0279, Liselotte Purper to Kurt Orgel, 4 Sept. 1939.

19 Klepper, *Unter dem Schatten deiner Flügel*, 797: 2 Sept. 1939; Klemperer, *I Shall Bear Witness*, 1, 374 and 377: 3, 10 and 13 Sept. 1939.

20 Breloer, *Mein Tagebuch*, 33: Gerhard M., 3 Sept. 1939.

21 Ibid., 33–5: Gerhard M., 4–5 Sept. 1939.

22 Orłowski and Schneider (eds), 'Erschießen will ich nicht!', Introduction and 37–8: 3–5 Sept. 1939; Ericksen, *Theologians under Hitler*; Forstman, *Christian Faith in Dark Times*.

23 Evangelisches Zentralarchiv Berlin, 2877, Doc. 1, *Gesetzblatt der Deutschen Evangelischen Kirche*, 6 Sept. 1939; on Meiser in 1934, Kershaw, *Popular Opinion and Political Dissent*, 156–84.

24 On 1914, see Fuchs, 'Vom Segen des Krieges'; Brodie, 'For Christ and Germany', 37–51; Löffler (ed.), *Galen: Akten, Briefe und Predigten*, 2, 747; *MadR*, 467–8 and 555–6: 17 Nov. and 11 Dec. 1939.

25 Kleindienst (ed.), *Sei tausendmal gegrüßt*: Ernst Guicking to Irene Reitz, 5 Sept. 1939; Irene to Ernst, 3 Sept. 1939.

26 Kershaw, *The 'Hitler Myth'*, 142.

27 Ibid., 123–4; Hitler, 'Rede vor der deutschen Presse', *VfZ*, 2 (1958), 181–91; Domarus (ed.), *Hitler*, 1217; Kershaw, *Hitler*, 2, 197.

28 Breloer (ed.), *Mein Tagebuch*, 35–6: Gerhard M., 7 Sept. 1939.

29 Ibid., 36–8: Gerhard M., 10 Sept. 1939.

30 Ibid., 38–40: 11 Sept. 1939; for his location: http://www.lexikon-der-wehrmacht.de/Gliederungen/Infanterieregimenter/IR26-R.htm.

31 Rohde, 'Hitlers erster "Blitzkrieg"', *DRZW*, 2, 79–126.

32 Hosenfeld, 'Ich versuche jeden zu retten', 247–8: 14 Sept. 1939.

33 Ibid., 250: 16 Sept. 1939.

34 Baumgart, 'Zur Ansprache Hitlers vor den Führern der Wehrmacht am 22. August 1939'; *Akten zur deutschen Auswärtigen Politik 1918–1945*, Serie D, 7, Baden-Baden and Göttingen, 1956, no. 193.

35 Böhler, *Auftakt zum Vernichtungskrieg*, 56–7 and 60–1; Toppe, *Militär und Kriegsvölkerrecht*, 417.

36 See Strachan, 'Clausewitz and the dialectics of war', in Strachan and Herberg-Rothe (eds), *Clausewitz in the Twenty-First Century*, 14–44; *DAZ*, 8 Sept. 1939; *FZ*, 7 Sept. 1939; Shirer, *Berlin Diary*, 166: 9 Sept. 1939; Böhler, *Auftakt zum Vernichtungskrieg*, 147–53; Datner, 'Crimes committed by the

Wehrmacht'; Umbreit, *Deutsche Militärverwaltungen*, 197–9; Rossino, *Hitler Strikes Poland*, 174–5 and 263.

37 Hosenfeld, *'Ich versuche jeden zu retten'*, 247–8 and 256: 14 and 30 Sept. 1939; Bergen, 'Instrumentalization of "Volksdeutschen"'.

38 Jarausch and Arnold (eds), *'Das stille Sterben . . .'*, 100–1: to family, 16 Sept. 1939; Krzoska, 'Der "Bromberger Blutsonntag" 1939'; Jatrzębski, *Der Bromberger Blutsonntag*.

39 Krausnick and Wilhelm, *Die Truppe des Weltanschauungskrieges*, 36; Mallmann et al., *Einsatzgruppen in Polen*; Rossino, *Hitler Strikes Poland*.

40 Smith, *The Butcher's Tale*, 214–15.

41 Jansen and Weckbecker, *Der 'Volksdeutsche Selbstschutz'*, 116–17 and 135–8; Lukas, *Did the Children Cry?*, 17.

42 Wachsmann and Caplan (eds), *Concentration Camps in Nazi Germany*; Rieß, 'Zentrale und dezentrale Radikalisierung,' in Mallmann and Musial (eds), *Genesis den Genozids*, 127–44.

43 Longerich, *Politik der Vernichtung*, 245–7; Jansen and Weckbecker, *Der 'Volksdeutsche Selbstschutz'*, 127–9 and 212ff.; Wildt, *Generation des Unbedingten*, 419–85.

44 Jansen and Weckbecker, *Der 'Volksdeutsche Selbstschutz'*, 83–93.

45 Ibid., 117–19.

46 Ibid., 83–5: Oberstabsarzt Dr Wilhelm Möller to Hitler, 9 Oct. 1939; Engel, *Heeresadjutant bei Hitler*, 68: 18 Nov. 1939, also in Broszat, *Nationalsozialistische Polenpolitik*, 41; Blaskowitz, notes for speech to Wehrmacht commanders on 15 Feb. 1940, in Jacobsen and Jochmann (eds), *Ausgewählte Dokumente zur Geschichte des Nationalsozialismus*, II; Clark, 'Johannes Blaskowitz', in Smelser and Syring (eds), *Die Militärelite des dritten Reiches*, 28–50; Giziowski, *Enigma of General Blaskowitz*; Hürter, *Hitlers Heerführer*, 184ff.; occupation forces, see Madajczyk, *Okkupationspolitik Nazideutschlands in Polen*, 239–40.

47 Hlond (ed.), *The Persecution of the Catholic Church in German-occupied Poland*; Blet, *Pius XII and the Second World War*, 89–90; Brodie, 'For Christ and Germany', 47–51; *MadR*, 555–6: 11 Dec. 1939; Körner, 'Katholische Kirche und polnische Zwangsarbeiter', 131–2.

48 Hosenfeld, *'Ich versuche jeden zu retten'*, 286: 10 Nov. 1939.

49 Ibid.

50 Böll, *Briefe aus dem Krieg*, 1, 78–9, and 62: to parents and sisters, 16 July and 2 May 1940; Defalque and Wright, 'Methamphetamine for Hitler's Germany'.

51 *VB*, 13 and 18 Aug. 1939; on the Wehrmacht Untersuchungsstelle, see forthcoming Oxford doctoral research of Jacques Schuhmacher, 'Nazi Germany and the Morality of War'; de Zayas, *Die Wehrmacht-Untersuchungsstelle*, is an entirely uncritical and tendentious selection from this source.

52   Bergen, 'Instrumentalization of "Volksdeutschen" in German propaganda in 1939'.

53   Auswärtiges Amt (ed.), *Dokumente polnischer Grausamkeit*, Berlin, 1939 and (2nd edn) 1940, 7; *VB*, 11 and 16 Feb. 1940; *MadR*, 5145: 19 April 1943; Schuhmacher, 'Nazi Germany', chapter 1.

54   *Der Feldzug in Polen*, 1940; *Feuertaufe – Der Film vom Einsatz unserer Luftwaffe in Polen*, 1940; *Feinde*, Viktor Tourjansky, 1940; *Heimkehr*, Gustav Ucicky, 1941; Kundrus, 'Totale Unterhaltung?', 125; Trimmel, *Heimkehr*; Fox, *Film Propaganda in Britain and Nazi Germany*.

55   Evangelisches Zentralarchiv Berlin, 2877, *Gesetzblatt der Deutschen Evangelischen Kirche*, Berlin, 28 Sept. and 9 Nov. 1939.

56   *Sopade* 1939, 6, 980.

57   Shirer, *Berlin Diary*, 185–6: 6 Oct. 1939; Kershaw, *Hitler*, 2, 238–9; 265–6; Domarus (ed.), *Hitler*, 1377–94.

58   Shirer, *Berlin Diary*, 185–6: 6 Oct. 1939.

59   *MadR*, 339–40 and 347–8: 11 and 13 Oct. 1939; Shirer, *Berlin Diary*, 189: 15 Oct. 1939.

60   *MadR*, 382: 23 Oct 1939.

61   Hartmann, *Halder*, 162; Martin, *Friedensinitiativen und Machtpolitik im Zweiten Weltkrieg*, 82ff.

62   Strobl, *The Swastika and the Stage*, 170–98; Goebbels, radio broadcast, 1 April 1933, in Hippel (ed.), *Freiheit, Gleichheit, Brüderlichkeit?*, 344–5. The cast included Bernhard Minetti (Robespierre), Gustav Knuth (Danton), Gründgens himself (St Just), Marianne Hoppe (Lucile Duplessis), Kitty Stengel (Julie Danton) and Maria Koppenhöfer (Marion); sets were by Traugott Müller. Reviews: Hermann Pirich, *Der Angriff*, 11 Dec. 1939; Bruno Werner, *DAZ*, 9 Dec. 1939; Franz Köppen, *Berliner Börsenzeitung*, 11 Dec. 1939; also Strobl, *The Swastika and the Stage*, 192.

63   Georg Büchner, *Dantons Tod*, Act III, sc. ix: Danton; Act IV, sc. ix: Lucile Duplessis.

64   Strobl, *The Swastika and the Stage*, 192.

2 Closing Ranks

1   Orłowski and Schneider (eds), '*Erschießen will ich nicht!*', 38–9: 5 Sept. 1939; Lange and Burkard (eds), '*Abends wenn wir essen fehlt uns immer einer*', 22–3; letters, 13 and 22 Sept. 1939.

2   Kleindienst (ed.), *Sei tausendmal gegrüßt*: Bernhard Guicking to Ernst, 12 Sept. and 18 Dec. 1939; Brodie, 'For Christ and Germany', 272: Bishop of Fulda, 12 Oct. 1939; *MadR*, 438–41: 8 Nov. 1939.

3   Wildt, 'Volksgemeinschaft', and Herbert, 'Echoes of the Volksgemeinschaft', both in Steber and Gotto (eds), *Visions of Community in Nazi Germany*, 43–69.

4   Winter and Robert (eds), *Capital Cities at War*, 487–523; Offer, *The First World War*; Cox, 'Hunger Games', *Economic History Review*, Sept. 2014: doi: 10.1111/ehr.12070; Collingham, *The Taste of War*, 18–32.

5   Kleindienst (ed.), *Sei tausendmal gegrüßt*: Irene to Ernst, 5 and 28 Sept. 1939.

5   Ibid., Irene Reitz to Ernst Guicking, 28 Sept. 1939.

6   Werner, '*Bleib übrig*', 51–4; Kleindienst (ed.), *Sei tausendmal gegrüßt*: Irene Reitz to Ernst Guicking, 24 Sept. 1939.

7   *MadR*, 377–9: 20 Oct. 1939; Berth, *Biografien und Netzwerke im Kaffeehandel*.

8   Tooze, *The Wages of Destruction*, 353–4; Corni and Gies, *Brot – Butter – Kanonen*, 556–7; Kleindienst (ed.), *Sei tausendmal gegrüßt*: Irene to Ernst Guicking, 31 Oct. 1939.

9   *MadR*, 353–4, 370, 378–9, and 436: 13, 18 and 20 Oct. 1939 and 8 Nov. 1939; Keil, *Erlebnisse eines Sozialdemokraten*, 2, 558.

10   Werner, '*Bleib übrig*', 129; *Sopade*, 1939, 6, 978; Steinert, *Hitlers Krieg und die Deutschen*, 110–21; *MadR*, 580–1: 15 Dec. 1939.

11   *Sopade*, 1939, 6, 979–80: Grohé was Gauleiter of Cologne and Aachen from 1931 to 1945. *MadR*, 421: 6 Nov. 1939.

12   Strauss, 'Jewish emigration from Germany', 317–18 and 326–7; Kaplan, *Between Dignity and Despair*, 118, 132 and 150–5; Rosenstrauch (ed.), *Aus Nachbarn wurden Juden*, 118; Klepper, *Unter dem Schatten deiner Flügel*, 794–5: 28 Aug. 1939; Herbert, *Hitler's Foreign Workers*, 88–94.

13   Corni and Gies, *Brot – Butter – Kanonen*, 555–7; Werner, '*Bleib übrig*', 134, 126–7 and 198–9; *MadR*, 2, 354 and 424: 13 Oct. and 6 Nov. 1939; Kundrus, *Kriegerfrauen*, 279–81 on *Familienunterhalt*, and the Interior Ministry's determination that state subsidies should not replace private earnings.

14   Werner, '*Bleib übrig*', 128–36.

15   Ibid., 127–8.

16   *MadR*, 363 and 384: 16 and 23 Oct. 1939; Mason, *Arbeiterklasse und Volksgemeinschaft*, 980–1234; Mason, *Social Policy in the Third Reich*, ed. Caplan, 345–6.

17   Werner, '*Bleib übrig*', 53–4; Steinert, *Hitlers Krieg und die Deutschen*, 120; Shirer, *Berlin Diary*, 219: 9 and 11 Jan. 1940; at the same time, he broadcast that the crisis was easing: Shirer, *This is Berlin*, 182–3.

18   Werner, '*Bleib übrig*', 54–5 and 129: Hess forbade this practice, 17 Feb. 1940.

19   Steinert, *Hitlers Krieg und die Deutschen*, 121; *MadR*, 357: 16 Oct. 1939; *Sopade*, 1939, 6, 983: report from south-west Germany.

20   *MadR*, 416: 3 Nov. 1939.

21   Bock, *Zwangssterilisation im Nationalsozialismus*; Weindling, *Health, Race,*

and German Politics; Usbourne, *The Politics of the Body in Weimar Germany*; Kühl, *The Nazi Connection*. For a comparative context, see Mahood, *Policing Gender, Class and Family*; Abrams, *Orphan Country*, Fishman, *The Battle for Children*; Mennel, *Thorns and Thistles*; Ceretti, *Come pensa il Tribunale per i minorenni*; Wachsmann, *Hitler's Prisons*, 364–9. On the Barnardo's homes and migration to Australia and Canada, see Coldrey, *Child Migration*; Dunae, 'Gender, generations and social class', in Lawrence and Starkey (eds), *Child Welfare and Social Action*; on racist policies in Australia and the United States, see Haskins and Jacobs, 'Stolen generations and vanishing Indians', in Marten (ed.), *Children and War*, 227–41; Haebich, 'Between knowing and not knowing', 70–90.

22   See Stargardt, *Witnesses of War*, chapter 2; Dickinson, *The Politics of German Child Welfare*, 213–14; Hansen, *Wohlfahrtspolititk im NS-Staat*, 245.

23   Ayass, *Das Arbeitshaus Breitenau*, 162–9.

24   LWV 2/8253 Ronald H., Weimar Amtsgericht, 10 Mar. 1942.

25   LWV 2/8868, Anni N., 8–9, Kriminalpolizeibericht, 31 July 1940; Jugendamt Apolda, 13 Oct. 1941.

26   LWV 2/8868, Anni N., 30: Direktor Breitenau to Jugendamt Apolda, 24 Feb. 1942; LWV 2/9565, Liselotte W., Hausstrafen, 3; LWV 2/9009, Waltraud P., d. 12 Sept. 1942: 57–8; LWV 2/8029, Ruth F., d. 23 Oct. 1942; LWV 2/9163, Maria S., d. 7 Nov. 1943: 30 and 32; Liselotte S. in LWV Bücherei 1988/323, Ulla Fricke and Petra Zimmermann, 'Weibliche Fürsorgeerziehung während des Faschismus – am Beispiel Breitenau', MS, 86–7.

27   LWV 2/9189, Lieselotte S., 16–19: letter to mother, 14 Jan. 1940.

28   Winkler, 'Frauenarbeit versus Frauenideologie', 99–126; Westenrieder, *Deutsche Frauen und Mädchen!*; Bajohr, *Die Hälfte der Fabrik*; Sachse, *Siemens, der Nationalsozialismus und die moderne Familie*; Dörr, 'Wer die Zeit nicht miterlebt hat', 9–37 and 81–99; Kershaw, *Popular Opinion and Political Dissent*, 297–302; Noakes (ed.), *Nazism*, 4, 313–25 and 335–8.

29   MfK–FA, 3.2002.0306, Fritz P. to family: 13 Sept. 1939.

30   MfK–FA, 3.2002.0306, Fritz P. to family: 30 Nov. 1939.

31   MfK–FA, 3.2002.0306, Fritz P. to family: 29 Sept. 1939.

32   Ross, *Media and the Making of Modern Germany*, 355–6; MadR, 334: 9 Oct. 1939.

33   Kris and Speier (eds), *German Radio Propaganda*, 203–4 and 328: 4 Feb. 1940.

34   Ross, *Media and the Making of Modern Germany*, 331–7; Goebbels, *Goebbels Reden*, ed. Heiber, 94–5: 25 Mar. 1933.

35   Kleindienst (ed.), *Sei tausendmal gegrüßt*: Irene to Ernst Guicking, 13 Oct. 1939.

36   Goedecke and Krug, *Wir beginnen das Wunschkonzert*, 36 and 39; Bathrick,

'Making a national family with the radio'. See also Noakes, *Nazism*, 4, 502–3, 551–2 and 558–65.

37 Kleindienst (ed.), *Sei tausendmal gegrüßt*: Irene to Ernst, 15 Oct. 1939.

38 Ibid.: Irene to Ernst, 29 Oct. 1939; Paula Reitz to Irene, 27 Nov. 1939 and to Ernst Guicking, 27 Nov. 1939; Ernst to Hermann Reitz, 29 Nov. 1939; Hermann and Paula Reitz to Ernst Guicking, 6 Dec. 1939; Ernst to Irene, 29 Nov. 1939.

39 Ibid.: Anna Guicking to Irene Reitz, 10 Dec. 1939.

40 Goedecke and Krug, *Wir beginnen das Wunschkonzert*, 43–5 and 128; Kundrus, 'Totale Unterhaltung?', 134.

41 Koch, *Das Wunschkonzert im NS-Rundfunk*, 221; Kundrus, 'Totale Unterhaltung?', 138; SD report, April 1940, cited in Diller, *Rundfunkpolitik im Dritten Reich*, 343.

42 See the excellent analysis in Bathrick, 'Making a national family with the radio'.

43 MfK–FA, 3.2002.0306, Fritz P. to family: 6 Oct. 1939.

44 MfK–FA, 3.2002.0306, Fritz P. to family: 7 Oct. 1939; in general, Latzel, *Deutsche Soldaten*.

3 *Extreme Measures*

1 JZD, Karl Kühnel to family, 23 Oct. 1939, and to Wehrmeldeamt in Freiberg, 1 Jan. 1937; also Herrberger (ed.), *Denn es steht geschrieben*, 300.

2 JZD, Josef Rimpl, Rupert Sauseng and Karl Endstrasser to families, 14 Dec. 1939; Herrberger (ed.), *Denn es steht geschrieben*, 296–302.

3 Garbe, *Between Resistance and Martyrdom*, 410–12; *VB*, 16 Sept. 1939.

4 Gerwarth, *Hitler's Hangman*; Godau-Schüttke, *Ich habe nur dem Recht gedient*, 188–9; Welch, '"Harsh but just"?', 378; for the First World War, see Ziemann, *Gewalt im Ersten Weltkrieg*.

5 Garbe, *Between Resistance and Martyrdom*, 349–61 and 379–82; Kalmbach, *Wehrmachtjustiz*; Messerschmidt, *Wehrmachtjustiz 1933–1945*; Klausch, '"Erziehungsmänner" und "Wehrunwürdige"', in Haase and Paul (eds), *Die anderen Soldaten*, 66–82; Ausländer, '"Zwölf Jahre Zuchthaus!"', in ibid., 50–65.

6 JZD, Bernhard Grimm to parents and brother, 20–21 Aug. 1942; executed 21 Aug. 1942; Herrberger (ed.), *Denn es steht geschrieben*, 265–72; Garbe, *Between Resistance and Martyrdom*, 378–9.

7 Lichti, *Houses on the Sand?*, 1–3, 46–7, 65; Röhm, *Sterben für den Frieden*; Brantzen, *Pater Franz Reinisch*; Maislinger, 'Der Fall Franz Jägerstätter', Dokumentationsarchiv des österreichischen Widerstandes, *Jahrbuch*, 1991. Stöhr was executed on 21 June 1940; Reinisch on 22 Aug. 1942;

Jägerstätter on 9 Aug. 1943; Jentsch, *Christliche Stimmen zur Wehrdienstfrage*, 17–84.

8   Garbe, *Between Resistance and Martyrdom*, 370; 229–30.

9   Ibid., 361–2: Fromm, 17 Oct. 1939; Keitel, 1 Dec. 1939; BA–MA, RH 53-6/76, Bl. 168.

10   Riedesser and Verderber, 'Maschinengewehre hinter der Front', 104–5; Kalinowsky, 'Problems of war neuroses in the light of experiences in other countries', *American Journal of Psychiatry*, 107/5 (1950), 340–6, cited in Shephard, *War of Nerves*, 303.

11   Forsbach, *Die medizinische Fakultät der Universität Bonn im 'Dritten Reich'*, 213–16; Emmerich, 'Die Wittenauer Heilstätten', in Arbeitsgruppe zur Erforschung der Geschichte der Karl-Bonhoeffer-Nervenklinik (ed.), *Totgeschwiegen 1933–1945*, 82; Richarz, *Heilen, Pflegen, Töten*, 134–5.

12   Riedesser and Verderber, 'Maschinengewehre hinter der Front', 112, 116–21 and 126–9.

13   Althaus, 'Pazifismus und Christentum', 456; Ericksen, *Theologians under Hitler*; Hetzer, 'Deutsche Stunde'; Forstman, *Christian Faith in Dark Times*.

14   Orłowski and Schneider (eds), 'Erschießen will ich nicht!', 16–26, 38 and 52: 5 Sept. and 22 Nov. 1939.

15   Sontheimer, *Antidemokratisches Denken in der Weimarer Republik*; Hetzer, 'Deutsche Stunde', 171–204; Stayer, *Martin Luther*, 86–90.

16   Fieberg et al. (eds), *Im Namen des deutschen Volkes*, 149–50; Evans, *Rituals of Retribution*, 690; Peukert, *Inside Nazi Germany*; Gellately, *Backing Hitler*; Wachsmann, *Hitler's Prisons*.

17   Gellately, *Backing Hitler*, 78–9; Evans, *Rituals of Retribution*, 696–700; Wachsmann, '"Annihilation through labor"'.

18   Johnson, *Nazi Terror*, 310; Stephenson, *Hitler's Home Front*; 206; Wöhlert, *Der politische Witz in der NS-Zeit*; Kershaw and Lewin (eds), *Stalinism and Nazism*.

19   Shirer, *Berlin Diary*, 209: 21 Dec. 1939; *MadR*, 366, 358 and 421–2: 18 and 16 Oct. and 6 Nov. 1939; Kundrus, 'Totale Unterhaltung?', 144–7; Latour, 'Goebbels' 'Außerordentliche Rundfunkmaßnahmen'; Michael Hensle, *Rundfunkverbrechen*; Mechler, *Kriegsalltag an der 'Heimatfront'*.

20   Reissner in Krüger, 'Die Bombenangriffe auf das Ruhrgebiet', in Borsdorf and Jamin (eds), *Kriegserfahrungen in einer Industrieregion*, 92; RAF in Weinberg, *A World at Arms*, 68–9; Overy, *Why the Allies Won*, 107–8; Strobl, *The Germanic Isle*; Kris and Speier (eds), *German Radio Propaganda*, 243: Ley, 24 Mar. 1940, 'der Lügen-Lord'; Löns song: *MadR*, 384: 23 Oct. 1939.

21   Johnson, *Nazi Terror*, 329–32; Maas, *Freizeitgestaltung*, 240.

22   Evans, *Rituals of Retribution*, 690; Wrobel (ed.), *Strafjustiz im totalen Krieg*, 1, 46–9; Gruchmann, *Justiz im Dritten Reich*, 910–11; Dörner, *Erziehung durch Strafe*, 199–215 and 257–64; Wagner, *Volksgemeinschaft ohne Verbrecher*, 311.

23   Wachsmann, *Hitler's Prisons*, 364–9, 204–6, 223–6 and 276–83; Orth, *Das System der nationalsozialistischen Konzentrationslager*, 97–106.

24   Faulstich, 'Die Zahl der "Euthanasie"-Opfer', in Frewer and Eickhoff (eds), *'Euthanasie' und aktuelle Sterbehilfe-Debatte*, 223–7.

25   Schmidt, 'Reassessing the beginning of the "Euthanasia" programme', 543–50; Burleigh, *Death and Deliverance*, 93–101; Sander, *Verwaltung des Krankenmordes*, 532–3; Mausbach and Bromberger, 'Kinder als Opfer der NS-Medizin', in Vanja and Vogt (eds), *Euthanasie in Hadamar*, 145–56; Richarz, *Heilen, Pflegen, Töten*, 177–89; Berger and Oelschläger, '"Ich habe eines natürlichen Todes sterben lassen"', in Schrapper and Sengling (eds), *Die Idee der Bildbarkeit*, 310–31 [269–336]; Sick, *'Euthanasie' im Nationalsozialismus*, 57–9; Roer and Henkel (eds), *Psychiatrie im Faschismus*, 216–18; Benzenhöfer, *'Kinderfachabteilungen' und 'NS-Kindereuthanasie'*.

26   Forsbach, *Die medizinische Fakultät*, 493–517.

27   Riedesser and Verderber, 'Maschinengewehre hinter der Front', 109 and 113–14; Klee (ed.), *Dokumente zur 'Euthanasie'*, 70–1; Klee, *Was sie taten – Was sie wurden*; Burleigh, *Death and Deliverance*, 130–2; on Weimar, Weindling, *Health, Race, and German Politics*, 381–3, 444 and 578; Usbourne, *The Politics of the Body in Weimar Germany*, 134–9; Harvey, *Youth and the Welfare State in Weimar Germany*, 253–4.

28   Burleigh, *Death and Deliverance*, 11–53; death in First World War: Faulstich, *Von der Irrenfürsorge zur 'Euthanasie'*, 77.

29   Sick, *'Euthanasie' im Nationalsozialismus*, 73; Schmidt, *Selektion in der Heilanstalt*, 118–19.

30   Nowak, *'Euthanasie' und Sterilisierung im 'Dritten Reich'*, 138–48.

31   Burleigh, *Death and Deliverance*, 166–71; Süß, *Der 'Volkskörper' im Krieg*; Aly, *Die Belasteten*, 78–81.

32   Hetzer, *'Deutsche Stunde'*, 189–91 and 232.

33   Nowak, *'Euthanasie' und Sterilisierung im 'Dritten Reich'*, 138–48; Scholz and Singer, 'Die Kinder in Hadamar', in Roer and Henkel (eds), *Psychiatrie im Faschismus*, 228–9; Otto, 'Die Heilerziehungs- und Pflegeanstalt Scheuern', in Böhme and Lohalm (eds), *Wege in den Tod*, 320–33; Sandner, *Verwaltung des Krankenmordes*, 458–9; Kaminski, *Zwangssterilisation und 'Euthanasie' im Rheinland*, 420–2; Winter, 'Verlegt nach Hadamar', 116; Burleigh, *Death and Deliverance*, 163–4.

34   Gruchmann (ed.), *Autobiographie eines Attentäters*; Kershaw, *Hitler*, 2, 271–3; *MadR*, 441: 10 Nov. 1939.

35 Lauber, *Judenpogrom: 'Reichskristallnacht'*, 123–4; Friedländer, *Nazi Germany and the Jews*, I, *Years of Persecution*, 275–6; Wildt, 'Gewalt gegen Juden in Deutschland'.

36 Kaplan, *Between Dignity and Despair*, 150–5; Gève, *Youth in Chains*, 21.

4 Breaking Out

1   Wantzen, *Das Leben im Krieg*, 73.

2   Ibid., 71–5: 10 May 1940.

3   Shirer, *Berlin Diary*, 263–4: 10–11 May 1940; *MadR*, 1128: 14 May 1940; Hoch, 'Der Luftangriff auf Freiburg am 10. Mai 1940'.

4   MfK–FA, 3.2002.7209, Helmut Paulus to parents, 11 May 1940; Erna to Helmut Paulus: 12 May 1940.

5   Hosenfeld, 'Ich versuche jeden zu retten', 344–5: 10 May 1940.

6   *MadR*, 1127: 14 May 1940.

7   *Die Wehrmachtberichte 1939–1945*, I, 144–5.

8   Frieser, *The Blitzkrieg Legend*, 241–3.

9   Jackson, *The Fall of France*, 25–39; Frieser, *The Blitzkrieg Legend*, 245–6.

10 Hartmann, *Halder*, 172–4 and 191–6.

11 Frieser, *The Blitzkrieg Legend*, 154–61; Jackson, *Air War over France*.

12 Frieser, *The Blitzkrieg Legend*, 258; Jackson, *Fall of France*, 42–7.

13 *MadR*, 1139, 1127 and 1151: 16, 14 and 20 May 1940.

14 Frieser, *The Blitzkrieg Legend*, 179–239.

15 Hooton, *Luftwaffe at War*, 2, 67; Frieser, *The Blitzkrieg Legend*, 252–90; Pieper (ed.), *Nazis on Speed*.

16 *MadR*, 1153–4, 1162–6: 20 and 23 May 1940.

17 Kleindienst (ed.), *Sei tausendmal gegrüßt*: Ernst to Irene Guicking, 28 May, 9, 2, 7, 15, 21, 24 and 15 June 1940.

18 MfK–FA, 3.2002.0211, Hans Albring to Eugen Altrogge, 21–22 Mar., [n.d.] May 1940; MfK–FA, 3.2002.210, Eugen Altrogge to Hans Albring, 21 April 1940; Robert Grosche, the General Vicar at Cologne, was also an admirer of Newman: Grosche, letter 10 July 1941, in AEK, Nachlaß Grosche, 285, 36.

19 MfK–FA, 3.2002.210, Eugen Altrogge to Hans Albring, 16, 23 and 1 May 1940; Kreuzer, *Verdi and the Germans*.

20 MfK–FA, 3.2002.0306, Fritz to Hildegard P., 3 June, 17 July 1940; also 15, 19, 22, 26, 28 May, 19 and 24 June 1940.

21 Hoffmann, 'Der Mythos der perfekten Propaganda', in Daniel (ed.), *Augenzeugen*, 169–92; Kundrus, 'Totale Unterhaltung?', 102–3; Kris and Speier (eds), *German Radio Propaganda*, 151–2: 19 June 1940; *MadR*, 1166–8

and 1221–3: 23 May and 6 June 1940; Ross, *Media and the Making of Modern Germany*, 343.

22   Gardner, *The Evacuation from Dunkirk*; Franks, *The Air Battle of Dunkirk*.

23   MfK–FA, 3.2002.0211, Hans Albring to Eugen Altrogge, Whitsun [12] May and 2 June 1940.

24   *MadR*, 1266–7: 17 June 1940; Kleindienst (ed.), *Sei tausendmal gegrüßt*: Irene to Ernst Guicking, 23 June 1940.

25   MfK–FA, 3.2002.0306, Fritz to Hildegard P., 3 June, 17 July 1940; also 15, 19, 22, 26, 28 May, 19 and 24 June 1940.

26   Hosenfeld, 'Ich versuche jeden zu retten', 51–4; 357–60: letters to wife and son, 11, 14 and 16 June 1940.

27   MfK–FA, 3.2002.7209, Helmut Paulus to his parents, 17 June 1940; target practice, Helmut Paulus to parents, 16 April 1940; KA, 3931/2, Dierk S., 'Auszüge', 5–6 and 12–15: 1 July, 25–26 Sept., 29 Nov. and 21 Dec. 1940; Kershaw, 'Hitler Myth', 156.

28   *MadR*, 1167 and 1283: 23 May and 20 June 1940; Kris and Speier (eds), *German Radio Propaganda*, 234; *Die Deutsche Wochenschau*, No. 511, 20 June 1940.

29   *MadR*, 1221–2: 6 June 1940; MfK–FA, 3.2002.0306, Fritz to Hildegard P., 22 May 1940; Scheck, *Hitler's African Victims*; for poster, Theweleit, *Male Fantasies*, 1, 94.

30   Shirer, *Berlin Diary*, 328–36: 21–23 June 1940; *Die Deutsche Wochenschau*, No. 512, 27 June 1940; *MadR*, 1306–7: 27 June 1940.

31   *MadR*, 1284: 20 June 1940, and also 829–30, and 4, 978–9, 1179–80 and 1221–3: 1 Mar., 10 Apr., 27 May and 6 June 1940; cinema attendance, see Welch, *Propaganda and the German Cinema*, 196; Carter, *Dietrich's Ghosts*, chapter 7; Regierungspräsident of Swabia, 9 July 1940 and reports on the *Wochenschau*, cited in Kershaw, 'Hitler Myth', 155 and 158–9.

32   Orłowski and Schneider (eds), 'Erschießen will ich nicht!', 73 and 70: 21 June and 15 May 1940; Evangelisches Zentralarchiv Berlin, 1/2877: Ansprache von Landesbischof D Meiser bei der 49 Tagung des bayerischen Pfarrervereins, 26 June 1940.

33   Gildea, *Marianne in Chains*, 72, citing *Sturmmarsch zur Loire: Ein Infanteriekorps stürmt, siegt und verfolgt. Erinnerungsbuch des XXXVIII. Armeekorps vom Feldzug über Somme, Seine und Loire*, Berlin, 1941, 142; Kleindienst (ed.), *Sei tausendmal gegrüßt*: Ernst to Irene Guicking, 30 June 1940.

34   Germany's official tally of military deaths in the First World War amounted to 1,885,245, with an additional 170,000 soldiers missing, presumed dead: *Statistisches Jahrbuch für das Deutsche Reich 1924–5*, 44, Berlin, 1925, 25. In 1944, the Wehrmacht calculated that 15,500 of its

soldiers were killed in the Polish campaign and increased its estimate of those killed in France from 26,500 to 46,000: Overmans, *Deutsche militärische Verluste im zweiten Weltkrieg*, 304.

35   Shirer, *Berlin Diary*, 354–5: 18 July 1940; Richie, *Faust's Metropolis*, 492–3.

36   Kris and Speier (eds), *German Radio Propaganda*, 388; Shirer, *Berlin Diary*, 360: 22 July 1940; Hitler, *Reden und Proklamationen*, 1540–59: 19 July 1940.

37   *MadR*, 1412 and 1402: 25 and 22 July 1940; Kershaw, *Hitler*, 2, 298; Kleindienst (ed.), *Sei tausendmal gegrüßt*: Irene to Ernst, 23 June 1940; Hosenfeld, 'Ich versuche jeden zu retten', 362 and 260: 26 and 16 June 1940.

38   Churchill, BBC, 14 July 1940: http://www.winstonchurchill.org/learn/speeches/speeches-of-winston-churchill/126-war-of-the-unknown-warriors; Thomas, 'After Mers-el-Kébir', 112/447, 643–70; Osborn, *Operation Pike*, 198–9.

39   Overy, *Bombing War*, 60–6 and 237; Shirer, *Berlin Diary*, 263–4: 10–11 May 1940; Hoch, 'Der Luftangriff auf Freiburg am 10. Mai 1940'; Hahnke, *Luftkrieg und Zivilbevölkerung*, 187–90; Werner Jochmann (ed.), *Monologe im Führer-Hauptquartier*, 394: 6 Sept. 1942; Auswärtiges Amt, *8. Weissbuch. Dokumente über die Alleinschuld Englands am Bombenkrieg gegen die Zivilbevölkerung*, Berlin, 1943.

40   *MadR*, 1309, 1424 and 1441: 27 June, 29 July and 5 Aug. 1940; Overy, *Bombing War*, 84; Shirer, *Berlin Diary*, 364: 4 Aug. 1940.

41   *MadR*, 1307, 1293, 1362–3 and 1412 and 1402: 27 and 24 June, 11, 25 and 22 July 1940; Kershaw, *Hitler*, 2, 298; Goebbels, *Tgb*, I/8, 202: 3 July 1940.

42   Hubatsch (ed.), *Hitlers Weisungen*, 46–9 and 71–6; Förster, 'Hitler turns East', in Wegner (ed.), *From Peace to War*, 117–24; Shirer, *Berlin Diary*, 366: 11 Aug. 1940.

43   Overy, *Bombing War*, 81–3; Göring, *VB*, 4 Aug. 1940; Shirer, *Berlin Diary*, 365: 5 Aug. 1940.

44   *MadR*, 1525: 2 Sept. 1940. On Göring, Fleming, *August 1939*, 171; Steinert, *Hitlers Krieg und die Deutschen*, 172 and 366–7; Klemperer, *The Language of the Third Reich*, 128 and 278.

45   Hitler, *Reden und Proklamationen*, 1574–83: 4 Sept. 1940; Shirer, *Berlin Diary*, 388–9: 5 Sept. 1940.

46   Shirer, *Berlin Diary*, 385–6: 31 Aug. 1940.

47   Kris and Speier (eds), *German Radio Propaganda*, 399; Shirer, *Berlin Diary*, 391–2: 7–8 Sept. 1940; Overy, *Bombing War*, 86–8.

48   Shirer, *Berlin Diary*, 394 and 391: 11 and 7 Sept. 1940.

49   Groehler, *Bombenkrieg gegen Deutschland*, 238–54; Blank, 'Kriegsalltag und Luftkrieg an der "Heimatfront"', 401–6; Krüger, 'Die Bombenangriffe auf das Ruhrgebiet', in Borsdorf and Jamin (eds), *Überleben im Krieg*, 93.

50   Wantzen, *Das Leben im Krieg*, 163: 10 July 1940.

51 Kock, 'Der Führer sorgt für unsere Kinder . . .', 71–81.

52 Ibid., 120–22.

53 Parental attitudes and rumours, MadR, 1648: 7 Oct. 1940; numbers of child evacuees, Kock, 'Der Führer sorgt für unsere Kinder . . .', 136–8.

54 Rüther (ed.), KLV, Cologne, 2000, electronic resource only: Anneliese Mayer, letters home, 28 and 30 Jan. 1941; Gisela Eckmann (Henn), Bericht.

55 Sollbach, Heimat Ade!, 14.

56 Ibid., 136–7: Rudolf Lenz: 19 Feb. 1997.

57 KA 2073, Ilse-W. Pfofe, KLV-Tagebuch, 27.4.–18.11.1941, MS, 7 May, 3 and 13 June, 29 July, 18 and 25 Aug., and 19 Oct. 1941.

58 KA 2073, Ilse-W. Pfofe, KLV-Tagebuch, 1, 3, 4, 5, 11, 25 and 28 May, 2, 16, 22 and 29 June, 6 and 20 July, 8 and 14 Aug. 1941.

59 Kris and Speier (eds), German Radio Propaganda, 400.

60 Ibid., 64–5, 394 and 398–401: 7–12 Sept. 1940.

61 MadR, 1526 and 1530: 2 Sept. 1940.

62 Kris and Speier (eds), German Radio Propaganda, 393: 15 Aug. 1940; MadR, 1527 and 1583: 2 and 19 Sept. 1940.

63 MadR, 1646–7: 7 Oct. 1940; also, 1608, 1619, 1633: 19 Sept.–3 Oct. 1940. 'Die lügen und wir lügen auch'.

64 Strobl, The Germanic Isle, 141–60 and 175–89; Die verlorene Insel: Das Gesicht des heutigen England, Berlin, 1941; Sopade 1939, 6, 843: 6 July 1939; MadR, 1526 and 1530: 2 Sept. 1940.

65 Wantzen, Das Leben im Krieg, 164: 10 July 1940; Strobl, The Germanic Isle, 188–93; Strobl, The Swastika and the Stage, 153 and 192; Jochmann (ed.), Monologe im Führer-Hauptquartier, 45: 22–23 July 1941.

66 Ohm Krüger, 1941, directed by Hans Steinhoff, Karl Anton and Herbert Maisch, with Emil Jannings.

67 Hitler cited in Halder, Kriegstagebuch, 98–100: 14 Sept. 1940; Maier, 'Luftschlacht um England', in Maier et al. (eds), Das deutsche Reich und der zweite Weltkrieg, 2, 390–1; Kris and Speier (eds), German Radio Propaganda, 66–7 and 401–2; Overy, The Bombing War, 98; MadR, 1595: 23 Sept. 1940.

68 Goebbels, Tgb, I/8, 410: 24 Nov. 1940; MadR, 1834 and 1916: 5 Dec. 1940 and 20 Jan. 1941.

69 Overy, Bombing War, 98, 108 and 113–15; Kris and Speier (eds), German Radio Propaganda, 398: fig. xxix 'Frequency of stereotypes during the Battle of Britain'.

70 Wantzen, Das Leben im Krieg, 256 and 164–5; Eggert, Der Krieg frißt eine Schule, 92–3; Reissner, in Krüger, 'Die Bombenangriffe auf das Ruhrgebiet', 92–3; Gève, Youth in Chains, 17; Middlebrook and Everitt, Bomber Command War Diaries, 31–8 and 56–130; statistics in Groehler, 'Bomber über Berlin', 113; Overy, Bombing War, 113.

71 DHM, D02 96/1861, 'Tagebuch von Liselotte Purper aus dem Zeitraum September 1940 bis Januar 1943': 17 Oct. 1940 and 25 July 1941; Reissner, in Krüger, 'Die Bombenangriffe auf das Ruhrgebiet', 92; Wantzen, *Das Leben im Krieg*, 321–2: 29 Dec. 1940; falling numbers, Kock, *'Der Führer sorgt für unsere Kinder . . .'*, 137.

5 *Winners and Losers*

1   Jureit, 'Zwischen Ehe und Männerbund', 61–73: Robert to Mia, 13 Aug., 5 Oct. and 7 Sept. 1940.

2   Jureit, 'Zwischen Ehe und Männerbund', 66: Robert to Mia, 12 Sept. 1940.

3   Jureit, 'Zwischen Ehe und Männerbund', 66: Mia to Robert, 1 Oct. 1940.

4   Ute Dettmar, 'Der Kampf gegen "Schmutz und Schund"', in Neuhaus (ed.), *Die Kinder- und Jugendliteratur in der Zeit der Weimarer Republik*, 565–86; Adam, *Lesen unter Hitler*; Herzog, *Sex after Fascism*.

5   See Marszolek, '"Ich möchte Dich zu gern mal in Uniform sehen"', 41–59; here 51; Latzel, *Deutsche Soldaten*, 332 and 337–8.

6   Jureit, 'Zwischen Ehe und Männerbund', 68–9.

7   Latzel found that none of his correspondents in either world war discussed this topic: Latzel, *Deutsche Soldaten*, 339; Meinen, *Wehrmacht und Prostitution im besetzten Frankreich*; Gildea, *Marianne in Chains*, 49, 77; Virgili, *Naître ennemi*, 40, 55 and 59.

8   Gildea, *Marianne in Chains*, 76, 49 and 60.

9   Ibid., 73; also Morin, *Les Allemands en Touraine*, 196; similarly in Simone de Beauvoir's account of Germans arriving in Paris: Virgili, *Naître ennemi*, 18, 60–3; de Beauvoir, *La Force de l'âge*, 457.

10 Gildea, *Marianne in Chains*, 88; Virgili, *Naître ennemi*, 57–9.

11 Lulu Anne Hansen, '"Youth off the rails"' in Herzog (ed.), *Brutality and Desire*, 158 and 145–6: Børge Hebo, report of 2 Aug. 1940; Hartmann, *The Girls They Left Behind*, 61: she found that 51 per cent said they preferred Germans over Danes, with 19.1 per cent citing the Germans' courtly manners; 5–6 per cent thought the Germans were better lovers. For a critical analysis of her results, see Warring, *Tyskerpiger*, 31ff. and 131.

12 Hansen, '"Youth off the Rails"', 150–7.

13 Maren Röger, *Kriegsbeziehungen: Intimität, Gewalt und Prostitution im besetzten Polen 1939 bis 1945*, Frankfurt am Main, 2015, especially Ch. 2.

14 Kleindienst (ed.), *Sei tausendmal gegrüßt*: Ernst to Irene Guicking, 2, 7 and 13 Aug., 3 and 7 Sept. 1940.

15 KA 3931/2, Dierk S., 'Auszüge aus dem Tagebuch', 5–6: 21 July and 28

Sept. 1940; Dennler, *Die böhmische Passion*, 31; Aly, *Hitlers Volksstaat*, 117–18.

16 Kleindienst (ed.), *Sei tausendmal gegrüßt*: Ernst to Irene Guicking, 11 and 24 Nov., 6 and 17 Dec. 1940.

17 Tooze, *Wages of Destruction*, 353–6.

18 Michel, *Paris allemand*, 298; Aly, *Hitlers Volksstaat*, 114–32.

19 Aly, *Hitlers Volksstaat*, 115, 131–2: report of Nuremberg customs post, 3 Sept. 1943.

20 Ibid., 114, 118–19 and 128; Böll, *Briefe aus dem Krieg*, 1, 90, 101, 108, 111: 5 and 21 Aug., 4 and 7 Sept. 1940.

21 MfK–FA, 3.2002.0211, Hans Albring to Eugen Altrogge, n.d. [July 1940]; Gordon, 'Ist Gott Französisch?', 287–98; Torrie, '"Our rear area probably lived too well"', 309–30.

22 MfK–FA, 3.2002.0211, Hans Albring to Eugen Altrogge, 16 Aug. 1940 and n.d. [Aug.] 1940.

23 MfK–FA, 3.2002.210, Eugen Altrogge to Hans Albring, 12 Aug. 1940; J.W. von Goethe, *Von deutscher Baukunst*, Darmstadt, 1989 [1772]; Jantzen, 'Das Straßburger Münster', in Busse, *Das Elsaß*, 271; Beutler, *Von deutscher Baukunst*; Williams, 'Remaking the Franco-German borderlands'.

24 DHM, Do2 96/1861, 'Tagebuch von Liselotte Purper', 17–19 Sept. 1940; also 8, 14 and 16 May 1940.

25 Ibid., 2 Oct. 1940; Madajczyk, *Die Okkupationspolitik Nazideutschlands*, 261–2; Aly, *'Final Solution'*, 45–7; Adelson and Lapides (eds), *Łódź Ghetto*, 30–41.

26 Harvey, 'Seeing the world', in Swett et al. (eds), *Pleasure and Power in Nazi Germany*, 177–204; Hugo Jaeger sold his collection to *Life* magazine, which has placed them online: http://life.time.com/history/world-war-ii-color-photos-from-nazi-occupied-poland-1939–1940/#1.

27 Epstein, *Model Nazi*; Madajczyk, *Die Okkupationspolitik Nazideutschlands*, 407–8 and Table 15. A further 367,592 Poles were evicted – mainly from rural areas in central Poland near the new Soviet border with the General Government, to make way for military training grounds and SS camps; and citing Tadeusz Norwid, *Kraj bez Quislinga*, Rome, 1945, 30–2. See also Oskar Rosenfeld in Adelson and Lapides (eds), *Łódź Ghetto*, 27; Hrabar et al., *Kinder im Krieg – Krieg gegen Kinder*, 82–3; Pohl, *Von der 'Judenpolitik' zum Judenmord*, 52.

28 DHM, Do2 96/1861, 'Tagebuch von Liselotte Purper', 2 Oct. 1940.

29 Ibid., 1 Nov.–6. Dec. 1940; Harvey, '"Ich war überall"', in Steinbacher (ed.), *Volksgenossinnen*, 138–53.

30 DHM, Do2 96/1861, 'Tagebuch von Liselotte Purper', 2 Oct. 1940. See Harvey, *Women and the Nazi East*, 155–6.

31 Epstein, *Model Nazi*; Wolf, *Ideologie und Herrschaftsrationalität*; Wolf, 'Exporting *Volksgemeinschaft*', in Steber and Gotto (eds), *Visions of Community in Nazi Germany*, 129–45.

32 Hohenstein, *Wartheländisches Tagebuch*, 293: 10 July 1942; Harten, *De-Kulturation und Germanisierung*, 192–6.

33 Madajczyk, *Die Okkupationspolitik Nazideutschlands*, 245–9; Herbert, *Hitler's Foreign Workers*, 61–4 and 86–96.

34 Hämmerle et al. (eds), *Gender and the First World War*, 1–15; Daniel, *The War from Within*; Nienhaus, 'Hitlers willige Komplizinnen', in Grüttner et al. (eds), *Geschichte und Emanzipation*, 517–39; Maubach, 'Expansion weiblicher Hilfe', in Steinbacher (ed.), *Volksgenossinnen*; Maubach, *Die Stellung halten*.

35 Theweleit, *Male Fantasies*, 1, 70–79; Cited in Rothmaler, 'Fall 29', in Justizbehörde Hamburg (ed.), 'Von Gewohnheitsverbrechern', 372. Przyrembel, 'Rassenschande'.

36 Cited in Hansch-Singh, *Rassismus und Fremdarbeitereinsatz*, 138; Kundrus and Szobar, 'Forbidden company'.

37 Herbert, *Hitler's Foreign Workers*, 132; Gellately, *Backing Hitler*, 172–3 and 176.

38 Lüdtke, 'Denunziation – Politik aus Liebe?', in Hohkamp and Ulbrich (eds), *Der Staatsbürger als Spitzel*, 397–407; Przyrembel, 'Rassenschande', 65–84; Gellately, *Backing Hitler*, 134–40 and 155–66; Gordon, *Hitler, Germans and the 'Jewish Question'*, 241.

39 Virgili, *Naître ennemi*, 88–9.

40 Gellately, *The Gestapo and German Society*, 243; Gellately, *Backing Hitler*, 169–70 and 179–80; Herbert, *Hitler's Foreign Workers*, 129.

41 Gellately, The *Gestapo and German Society*, 242; van Dülmen, *Theatre of Horror*; Evans, *Rituals of Retribution*, chapter 2.

42 Gellately, *Backing Hitler*, 179: SD Bayreuth, 17 Aug. 1942; Fenwick, 'Religion in the Wake of "Total War"'.

43 Kundrus and Stobar, 'Forbidden company', 210; cited also in Hochhuth, *Eine Liebe in Deutschland*, 63; Gellately, *The Gestapo and German Society*, 238–9.

44 Gellately, *Backing Hitler*, 180 and 160: Düsseldorf, Oct. 1942; Schweinfurt, Aug. 1941.

45 Nowak, '*Euthanasie' und Sterilisierung im 'Dritten Reich'*, 158–63; Löffler (ed.), *Galen: Akten, Briefe und Predigten*, 874–83; Brodie, 'For Christ and Germany', 103; citing LNRW.AW, *NSDAP Kreis- und Ortsgruppenleitungen*, 125, 11 Sept 1941; LNRW.ARH, *RW 35/08*, 17.

46 Sick, '*Euthanasie' im Nationalsozialismus*, 73; Gerhard Schmidt, *Selektion in der Heilanstalt*, 118–19; Sandner, *Verwaltung des Krankenmordes*, 457, 488–505, 595–6 and 642–3; Burleigh, *Death and Deliverance*, 163–4.

47 Noakes, *Nazism*, 3, 431; Trevor-Roper (ed.), *Hitler's Table Talk*, 555: 4 July 1942; Goebbels, *Tgb*, II/2, xxx, 27 and 29 Sept., 5 Nov. and 14 Dec. 1941.

48 Nowak, *'Euthanasie' und Sterilisierung im 'Dritten Reich'*, 168–70; Adolph, *Kardinal Preysing und zwei Diktaturen*, 168–70: Preysing, 2 Nov. 1941.

49 Burleigh, *Death and Deliverance*, 183–219; Brodie, 'For Christ and Germany', 103–8; Joachim Kuropka (ed.), *Meldungen aus Münster*, 539.

50 *MadR*, 3175–8: 15 Jan. 1942; Rost, *Sterilisation und Euthanasie*, 208–13; Nowak, 'Widerstand, Zustimmung, Hinnahme', in Frei (ed.), *Medizin und Gesundheitspolitik in der NS-Zeit*, 235–51.

51 Schmuhl, *Rassenhygiene, Nationalsozialismus, Euthanasie*, 210 and 437; Nowak, *'Euthanasie' und Sterilisierung im 'Dritten Reich'*, 138–48, 152–7, 164 and 171.

52 Mertens, *Himmlers Klostersturm*, 21 and 388; Süß, *Der Volkskörper im Krieg*, 127–51; Griech-Polelle, *Bishop von Galen*, 78–9; Stephenson, *Hitler's Home Front*, 236 and 257; Kershaw, *Popular Opinion and Political Dissent*, 332–3.

53 Zahn, *German Catholics and Hitler's Wars*, 83–7; Nowak, *'Euthanasie' und Sterilisierung im 'Dritten Reich'*, 173.

54 Kershaw, *Popular Opinion and Political Dissent*, 341–55.

55 Ibid., 349–57.

56 Brodie, 'For Christ and Germany', 108–17, citing LNRW.AW *Politische Polizei im III. Reich*, 408, SD report, 20 Aug. 1941; Hosenfeld, *'Ich versuche jeden zu retten'*, 530–1: 17–19 Sept. 1941; MfK–FA, 3.2002.0211, Hans Albring to Eugen Altrogge, 14 Sept. 1941.

57 Kuropka (ed.), *Meldungen aus Münster*, 545; Brodie, 'For Christ and Germany', 114–21, citing LNRW.AW, 'NSDAP Kreis- und Ortsgruppenleitungen, 125', 15 Aug. and 14 Nov. 1941; LNRW.AW, 'Gauleitung Westfalen-Nord, Hauptleitung', 11 Nov. 1941; Winter, *'Verlegt nach Hadamar'*, 159; Redemann (ed.), *Zwischen Front und Heimat*, 295.

58 Kershaw, *Hitler*, 2, 428; Nowak, *'Euthanasie' und Sterilisierung im 'Dritten Reich'*, 173–4; Süß, *Volkskörper im Krieg*, 311–14.

59 Faulstich, 'Die Zahl der "Euthanasie"-Opfer'; Burleigh, *Death and Deliverance*, 242; Sandner, *Verwaltung des Krankenmordes*, 607–25; Winter, *'Verlegt nach Hadamar'*, 118–54; Roer and Henkel (eds), *Psychiatrie im Faschismus*, 58–120.

60 Sick, *'Euthanasie' im Nationalsozialismus*, 73; Schmidt, *Selektion in der Heilanstalt*; 118–19; Sandner, *Verwaltung des Krankenmordes*, 457, 488–505, 595–6 and 642–3.

61 Schmidt von Blittersdorf et al., 'Die Geschichte der Anstalt Hadamar', in Roer and Henkel (eds), *Psychiatrie im Faschismus*, 58–120, here 112.

62 Lutz, 'Eine "reichlich einsichtslose Tochter"'; in George et al. (eds), *Hadamar*, 293–304; case of Maria M., LWV-Archiv, Kassel, K12/ 2581.

63 Lutz, 'Eine "reichlich einsichtslose Tochter"'; for other cases of children, see Stargardt, *Witnesses of War*, chapter 3.

6 German Crusade

1   MfK–FA, 3.2002.7209, Helmut Paulus to parents, 27 June 1942; and diary, 24 June 1941.

2   MfK–FA, 3.2002.7209, Helmut Paulus, diary, 24 June 1941; *DRZW*, 4 (1983), 470–6; Graser, *Zwischen Kattegat und Kaukasus*; on comradeship and 'primary groups', see Shils and Janowitz, 'Cohesion and disintegration', 12/2, 280–315; Kühne, *Kameradschaft*.

3   Overy, *The Bombing War*, 70, 110–11; Domarus (ed.), *Hitler*, 1726–32; Kershaw, *Hitler*, 2, 386–7; Wette, 'Die propagandistische Begleitmusik', in Ueberschär and Wette (eds), *Der deutsche Überfall auf die Sowjetunion*, 111–29.

4   Klemperer, *I Shall Bear Witness*, 1, 475–6: 22 June 1941.

5   MfK–FA, 3.2002.7209, Erna and Irmgard to Helmut Paulus, 21 and 29 June, 30 July and 9 Aug. 1941.

6   *MadR*, 2426–8: 23 June 1941; Wantzen, *Das Leben im Krieg*, 407: 22–23 June 1941.

7   Wantzen, *Das Leben im Krieg*, 400–5: 20–21 June 1941; Goebbels, *Tgb*, I/9, 336–7 and 387: 12 and 19 June 1941; Kershaw, *Hitler*, 2, 386.

8   For a survey, see Ueberschär and Bezymenskij (eds), *Der deutsche Angriff auf die Sowjetunion 1941*.

9   Wilhelm Düwell, *Vorwärts*, 28 Aug. 1914; cited in Goltz, *Hindenburg*, 16; Stargardt, *The German Idea of Militarism*.

10 Brodie, 'For Christ and Germany', 113 and 123–4; Kershaw, *Popular Opinion and Political Dissent*, 356; although the SD was deeply involved in the conflict, see also its assessments: *MadR*, 2517–19, and 2822–4: 14 July and 29 Sept. 1941; Löffler (ed.), *Galen: Akten, Briefe und Predigten*, 2, 850–1, 863, 883 and 901–2: 13 and 20 July, 3 Aug. and 14 Sept. 1941.

11 *MadR*, 2472–4, 2507 and 2704: 3, 7 and 14 July 1941. 'Wilden', 'Untermenschen', 'Zuchthäusler'.

12 Krausnick et al. (eds), *Anatomy of the SS State*, 512–13; Schuhmacher, 'Nazi Germany and the morality of war', citing BA–MA, RW 2/148, 335–81.

13 MfK–FA, 3.2008.2195, Manfred von Plotho to wife: 30 June 1941.

14 Schuhmacher, 'Nazi Germany and the morality of war'; *VB*, 5 and 8 July 1941; *DAZ*, 5 July 1941; *Westdeutscher Beobachter*, 7 and 14 July 1941.

15 Raschhofer, *Der Fall Oberländer*, 66; *Deutsche Wochenschau* no. 567 (16 July 1941); *MadR*, 7, 2564: 24 July 1941.

16 MfK–FA, 3.2002.0211, Albring to Altrogge, 8 July 1941.

17 Ibid., Albring to Altrogge, 5, 8, 12 July and 4 Aug. 1941; Bistumsarchiv Münster, Abt. 101 Sekretariat des Generalvikars, A 101–1, 92–3, diocesan pastoral letter, 15 Oct. 1941.

18 MfK–FA, 3.2002.0211, Albring to Altrogge, 30–31 Aug. 1941.

19 BA–MA, MSg 2/13904: Friedrich Farnbacher, 'Persönliches Kriegstagebuch des Hauptmanns der Reserve Friedrich Farnbacher, Panzer-Artillerie-Regiment 103 (seit 12. Jan. 1945 Kommandeur II./Pz. Art. Rgt. 103), für die Zeit vom 22. Juni 1941 bis 8. Mai 1945': 20 July 1941, 470.

20 Römer, Der Kommissarbefehl; Farnbacher, 'Persönliches Kriegstagebuch', 20 July 1941, 471–6.

21 Ibid.; BA–MA, MSg 2/13904, Farnbacher, 'Persönliches Kriegstagebuch', 20 July 1941, 471–6.

22 BA–MA, MSg 2/13904, Farnbacher, 'Persönliches Kriegstagebuch', 2 July and 13 Aug. 1941, 349–50 and 681; Hartmann, Wehrmacht im Ostkrieg, 259.

23 MfK–FA, 3.2002.0211, Albring to Altrogge, 28 Oct. 1941.

24 On shortage of military chaplains to provide spiritual guidance, Bergen (ed.), The Sword of the Lord; Böll, Brief an einen jungen Katholiken; MfK–FA, 3.2002.0211, Albring to Altrogge, 1 Jan. and 21 Mar. 1942.

25 Ebert (ed.), Im Funkwagen der Wehrmacht, 20–22, 136.

26 Eiber (ed.), '". . . Ein bisschen die Wahrheit": Briefe eines Bremer Kaufmanns': Nr 9 HG to Hannah, 7 Sept. 1941, 4–5 July and 7 Aug. 1941; Schneider, 'Auswärts eingesetzt'.

27 Eiber (ed.), '". . . Ein bisschen die Wahrheit"', 79–81: 8 Oct. 1941.

28 Ibid., 76, 7 Sept. 1941, Nr 9; Deutsche Wochenschau, No. 567 (16 July 1941); MadR, 7, 2564: 24 July 1941.

29 Eiber (ed.), '". . . Ein bisschen die Wahrheit"', 74, 81–3: 22 Aug. 1941, 25 Oct. and 18 Nov. 1941.

30 The most famous collection of letters used to show that German soldiers approved of the murder of the Jews is Manoschek (ed.), 'Es gibt nur eines für das Judentum: Vernichtung', which contains 103 anti-Semitic letters, about 20 per cent of which mention the murder of the Jews; cited widely in Friedländer, The Years of Extermination. They were taken from the Sterz Collection at the Bibliothek für Zeitgeschichte in Stuttgart, which contained 50,000 soldiers' letters at that time. One of the major problems of working on this collection, however, is that the letters are not organised by correspondent but by date, and are one-sided: hence, the development of the relationships at the centre of any correspondence cannot be evaluated: Humburg, 'Feldpostbriefe aus dem Zweiten Weltkrieg'; Latzel, Deutsche Soldaten, 201–4; also Müller, Deutsche Soldaten und ihre Feinde, 194–229; MfK–FA, 3.2002.7209, Paulus to parents, 4 Sept. 1942 and 28 June 1941.

31 Latzel, 'Tourismus und Gewalt', in Heer and Neumann (eds), Vernichtungskrieg, 447–59; Haydn, Meter, immer nur Meter!, 123–5: 19 Dec.

1942; Hilberg, *Sonderzüge nach Auschwitz*, 188; Diewerge (ed.), *Feldpostbriefe aus dem Osten*, 38, cited in Weinberg, *A World at Arms*, 473.

32 Hürter, *Ein deutscher General*, 62: letter, 21 June 1941.

33 Hartmann, *Wehrmacht im Ostkrieg*, 271–8.

34 Jefim Gechtman, 'Riga', in Grossman and Ehrenburg (eds), *Das Schwarzbuch*, 684; Mühlhäuser, *Eroberungen*, 74–86.

35 Longerich, *Holocaust*, 179–205; Wildt, *Generation des Unbedingten*, 578–91; Dieckman, 'The war and the killing of the Lithuanian Jews', in Herbert, *National Socialist Extermination Policies*, 242–6; Klee et al. (eds), *'The Good Old Days'*, 27–37 and 46–58.

36 Longerich, *Holocaust*, 206–39; Klee et al. (eds), *'The Good Old Days'*, 54–7.

37 Chiari, *Alltag hinter der Front*; Dean, *Collaboration in the Holocaust*, 2000; on the First World War precedent, see Kramer and Horne, *German Atrocities, 1914*; Hartmann, *Halder*, 160–72.

38 Klee et al. (eds), *'The Good Old Days'*, 138–54.

39 Noakes and Pridham (eds), *Nazism*, 3, 495.

40 Hürter, *Hitlers Heerführer*, 579, and Pohl, *Die Herrschaft der Wehrmacht*, 261; Ueberschär and Wette, *Unternehmen Barbarossa*, 339 ff.; Guderian issued the order to the 2nd Panzer Army on 6 Nov. 1941, and it took a further five to seven days to reach its divisions: Hartmann, *Wehrmacht im Ostkrieg*, 10 and 316.

41 Glantz, *Barbarossa Derailed*; Glantz, *When Titans Clashed*, 293.

42 Reinhardt, *Moscow*, 41–2.

43 Bock, *Zwischen Pflicht und Verweigerung*, 255: 22 Aug. 1941; Hartmann, *Halder*, 281–4; Hartmann, *Wehrmacht im Ostkrieg*, 285; Hürter, *Hitlers Heerführer*, 302–10; Wallach, *The Dogma of the Battle of Annihilation*, 1986, 265–81.

44 Hammer and Nieden (eds), *'Sehr selten habe ich geweint,'* 242–4: Robert R., diary, 21 Aug. 1941.

45 Hammer and Nieden (eds), *'Sehr selten habe ich geweint'*, 242–4: Robert R., diary, 21 Aug. 1941.

46 Ibid., 246–7: Robert R., diary, 28 Aug. 1941.

47 Ibid., 244–5: Robert R. to Maria, 23 Aug. 1941.

48 Ebert (ed.), *Im Funkwagen der Wehrmacht*, 159–60: Wilhelm to Erika Moldenhauer, 14 Sept. 1941.

49 Ibid., 161–2: Wilhelm to Erika Moldenhauer, 17 Sept. 1941.

50 Hartmann, *Wehrmacht im Ostkrieg*, 289–91.

51 Ibid., 289–91: IfZ–Archiv, MA 1589: 4. Pz. Div., Stab, Gefechtsbericht für den 22.9.1941; Kühne, *Kameradschaft*, 147; BA–MA, MSg 2/13904, Farnbacher, 'Persönliches Kriegstagebuch', 22 Sept. 1941.

52 Hartmann, *Wehrmacht im Ostkrieg*, 297–9: Reinert, diary 19 and 21 Sept.

1941; numbers in *DRZW*, 4 (1983), 751; Ebert (ed.), *Im Funkwagen der Wehrmacht*, 163–5: Wilhelm to Erika Moldenhauer, 19 and 20 Sept. 1941.

53   MfK–FA, 3.2002.0306, Fritz to Hildegard P., 25 Sept., 5 and 8 Oct. 1941, Feldpostbrief-Archiv, Museum für Komunikation, Berlin, Sig. 3.2002.0306.

54   Arnold, 'Die Eroberung und Behandlung der Stadt Kiew'; Hartmann, *Wehrmacht im Ostkrieg*, 299–301: Reinert diary, 24 and 26 Sept. 1941; Bibliothek für Zeitgeschichte, Sammlung Sterz, 04650, L.B., 29 Sept. 1941.

55   Hartmann, *Wehrmacht im Ostkrieg*, 299: Bibliothek für Zeitgeschichte, Sammlung Sterz, 04650, L.B., 28 Sept. 1941; Klee et al. (eds), 'The Good Old Days', 63–8; Hamburg Institute for Social Research, Johannes Hähle, Propagandakompanie (PK) 637, 6th Army: http://www.deathcamps.org/occupation/byalbum/list01.html.

56   Berkhoff, *Harvest of Despair*, 147, 153, 155–6.

57   Ibid., 173 and 169–72.

58   Gerlach, *Krieg, Ernährung, Völkermord*; *Trial of the Major War Criminals before the International Military Tribunal, Nuremberg, 14 November 1945–1 October 1946*, Nuremberg, 1947–9, v. 31, 84: 2718-PS, and v. 36, 135–57.

59   Hubatsch (ed.), *Hitlers Weisungen*, 148; Ueberschär and Wette, '*Unternehmen Barbarossa*', 333; Halder, *Kriegstagebuch*, 3, 53: 8 July 1941; Reinhardt, *Moscow*, 96.

60   Ziegelmayer in Aly, *Hitlers Volksstaat*, 198; Ziegelmayer, *Rohstoff-Fragen der deutschen Volksnährung*; Ganzenmüller, *Das belagerte Leningrad 1941–1944*, 42–52, citing KTB der Oberquartiermeisterabteilung der 18 Armee, 11, 14 and 18 Sept. 1941; Wagner to home: 9 Sept. 1941; Goebbels, *Tgb*, II/1, 359 and 392: 5 and 10 Sept. 1941; Ganzenmüller, *Das belagerte Leningrad*, 20–53 and 73–6.

61   Ganzenmüller, *Das belagerte Leningrad*, 53–64; Jones, *Leningrad*, 42–3 and 127; Biernacki et al., *Generalny plan wschodni*, 82–110: summary by RSHA (27 April 1942); Hans-Joachim Riecke, 'Aufgaben der Landwirtschaft im Osten', in *Probleme des Ostraumes. Sonderveröffentlichung der Bücherei des Ostraumes*, Berlin, 1942; Herbert Backe, *Um die Nahrungsfreiheit Europas: Weltwirtschaft oder Grossraum*, Leipzig, 1943.

62   Ganzenmüller, *Das belagerte Leningrad*, 69–73; Jones, *Leningrad*, 131 and 129; Kershaw, *War without Garlands*; Lubbeck, *At Leningrad's Gates*.

63   Reinhardt, *Moscow*, 182–5 and 95–6.

64   Ebert (ed.), *Im Funkwagen der Wehrmacht*, 167: Wilhelm to Erika Moldenhauer, 3 Oct. 1941; Hartmann, *Wehrmacht im Ostkrieg*, 307–8.

65   Stahel, *Operation Typhoon*, 100–2.

66   Streit, *Keine Kameraden*; Hartmann, *Wehrmacht im Ostkrieg*, 516–634.

67   Jarausch and Arnold (eds), '*Das stille Sterben . . .*', 343 and 329: 25 Nov. and 25 Oct. 1941.

68   Ibid., 336 and 325–6: 7 Nov. and 12 Oct. 1941.

69   Ibid., Arnold, introduction, 86, 335, 346 and 345: 6, 7, 28 and 25 Nov. 1941.

70 Ibid., 339: 14 Nov. 1941.

71 Guderian, *Erinnerungen eines Soldaten*, 231; Seitz, *Verlorene Jahre*, 104.

72 Grossman, *A Writer at War*; Wagner (ed.), *Soviet Air Force in World War II*, 68 ff.; Hartmann, *Wehrmacht im Ostkrieg*, 313.

73 Reinhardt, *Moscow*, 367–70; Hartmann, *Wehrmacht im Ostkrieg*, 255–6.

74 Reinhardt, *Moscow*, 148–9 and 92–4.

75 Hartmann, *Wehrmacht im Ostkrieg*, 313; Neumann, *Die 4. Panzerdivision*, 299 and 314; Schüler, *Logistik im Rußlandfeldzug*.

76 Humburg, 'Siegeshoffnungen und "Herbstkrise" im Jahre 1941', citing Bumke, 28 Sept. 1941; BA–MA, RH 20–2/1091–1095, Tätigkeitsberichte der Feldpostprüfstelle beim AOK2 1 Aug.–1 Dec. 1941; only in Nov. did morale fall: BA–MA, RH 20–2/1095, Tätigkeitsbericht der Feldpostprüfstelle beim AOK2 für den Monat November 1941.

77 MfK–FA, 3.2002.7209, Dr Ernst Arnold to Helmut Paulus, 5 Nov. 1941 and Helmut Paulus to parents, 11 Nov. 23 and 31 Oct. 1941.

78 DTA, 148, Albert Joos, 'Kriegstagebuch, 28.8.1939–1.3.1945', Vorwort and 28 Aug., 1 and 18 Sept., 24 Oct. and 26 Nov. 1939 and 15 Oct. 1941.

79 DTA, 148, Joos, 'Kriegstagebuch', 3, 4, 5, 6, 7–12, 13, 15, 16, 20, 21 and 23 Dec. 1941.

80 Hartmann, *Wehrmacht im Ostkrieg*, 312–14 and 347.

81 BA–MA, MSg 2/13904, Farnbacher, 'Persönliches Kriegstagebuch', 1, 20, 21 and 23 Nov. 1941; Kühne, *Kameradschaft*, 166–9.

82 Hartmann, *Wehrmacht im Ostkrieg*, 317 and 733: points for an address to officers, 17 Nov. 1941.

83 Hammer and Nieden (eds), *'Sehr selten habe ich geweint'*, 255–7: Robert R., diary, 27 Oct. 1941.

84 BA–MA, MSg 2/13904, Farnbacher, 'Persönliches Kriegstagebuch', 17 Nov. 1941. Hartmann; *Wehrmacht im Ostkrieg*, 10 and 2–3.

85 Hartmann, *Wehrmacht im Ostkrieg*, 733: BA–MA, MSg 2/13904, Farnbacher, 'Persönliches Kriegstagebuch', 9, 13, 24, 25 and 30 Nov. 1941; Hartmann, *Wehrmacht im Ostkrieg*, 317–19.

86 BA–MA, MSg 2/13904, Farnbacher, 'Persönliches Kriegstagebuch', 27 Oct. 1941; Kühne, *Kameradschaft*, 151–2; Hartmann, *Wehrmacht im Ostkrieg*, 351; Seitz, *Verlorene Jahre*, 105; Guderian, *Erinnerungen*, 231.

87 Hitler, *Reden und Proklamationen*, 1771–81: 8 Nov. 1941.

88 Goebbels, 'Die Juden sind schuld!', *Das Reich*, 16 Nov. 1941.

89 Hammer and Nieden (eds), *'Sehr selten habe ich geweint'*, 258–64: Robert R., diary, 28 and 9–11 Nov. 1941.

90 Ibid., 260: Robert R., letter to Maria, 18 Nov. 1941.

91 Ibid., 265, 267: Robert R., letter to Maria, 30 Nov. 1941.

92 Reinhardt, *Moscow*, 224–6; Hartmann, *Wehrmacht im Ostkrieg*, 350–2; Lüttwitz to wife, 1 Dec. 1941; Guderian, *Erinnerungen*, 233ff. and 257; also Overy, *Russia's War*, 124.

7 The First Defeat

1   Hartmann, *Wehrmacht im Ostkrieg*, 353–4.

2   Ibid., 361–3: Reinert, Tagebuch, 9 Dec. 1941.

3   Cited Reinhardt, *Moscow*, 288–9.

4   Reinhardt, *Moscow*, 293: Kriegstagebuch, Panzer-Gruppe 3, 14 Dec. 1941.

5   BA–MA, MSg 2/13904, Farnbacher, 'Persönliches Kriegstagebuch', 20 Dec. 1941; Hartmann, *Wehrmacht im Ostkrieg*, 354–7.

6   Hartmann, *Wehrmacht im Ostkrieg*, 363–6: 296th Infantry Division, Diary, 21 Dec. 1941; Reinert, 20 and 22 Dec. 1941.

7   Reinhardt, *Moscow*, 310: Heeresgruppe Mitte, Kriegstagebuch, 19 Dec. 1941.

8   Reinhardt, *Moscow*, 291–5, 320–4 and 349.

9   Ibid., 297–8; Hartmann, *Wehrmacht im Ostkrieg*, 370–1.

10 Reinhardt, *Moscow*, 298; Hartmann, *Wehrmacht im Ostkrieg*, 370–1 and 374–9.

11 Hürter (ed.), *Ein deutscher General*, 128–9: Heinrici, 16 Dec. 1941; BA–MA, MSg 2/13904, Farnbacher, 'Persönliches Kriegstagebuch', 6 Dec. 1941.

12 Jarausch and Arnold (eds), '*Das stille Sterben . . .*', 359–67: 1, 4, 5, 8, 10 and 11 Jan. 1942.

13 Ibid., 366–7: 13 Jan. 1942; death rates, see Gerlach, *Kalkulierte Morde*, 820ff.; Streit, *Keine Kameraden*.

14 Hartmann, *Wehrmacht im Ostkrieg*, 765 n.2: 17 Dec. 1941.

15 Rass, '*Menschenmaterial*', 88–134 and 378–80; BA–MA, MSg 2/13904, Farnbacher, 'Persönliches Kriegstagebuch', 7, 9 and 30 Dec. 1941 and 5 Jan. 1942; Hartmann, *Wehrmacht im Ostkrieg*, 357–8.

16 Hartmann, *Wehrmacht im Ostkrieg*, 356–7 and 382: BA–MA, MSg 2/13904, Farnbacher, 'Persönliches Kriegstagebuch', 21 Dec. 1941; Seitz, *Verlorene Jahre*, 116; Reese, *Mir selber seltsam fremd*, 57–66 and 92–3.

17 DTA, 148, Joos, 'Kriegstagebuch', 3, 4, 5, 6, 7–12, 13, 15, 16, 20, 21 and 23 Dec. 1941 and 1 Jan. 1942.

18 DTA, 148, Joos, 'Kriegstagebuch', 4, 6, 12, 20, 22, 24 and 26 Jan., 5, 10–11, 14–18 and 22 Feb., 5, 6 and 11 Mar. 1942.

19 MfK–FA, 3.2002.0211, Albring to Altrogge, 1, 21 Mar. and 13 April 1942.

20 Koch, *Fahnenfluchten*, 325–51.

21 Ibid., 325 and 351.

22 Rass, '*Menschenmaterial*', 169–204.

23 Koch, *Fahnenfluchten*, 191 n. 49.

24 Ibid., 198; and Rombach's rejection by his family, 131–4; Ziemann, 'Fluchten aus dem Konsens zum Durchhalten', in Müller and Volkmann (eds), *Hitlers Wehrmacht*, 589–613; Motadel, *Islam and Nazi Germany's War*, 310–11.

25   BA–MA, MSg 2/13904, Farnbacher, 'Persönliches Kriegstagebuch', 26 and 27 Dec. 1941; Seitz, *Verlorene Jahre*, 115; Hartmann, *Wehrmacht im Ostkrieg*, 356 and 421; Steinert, *Hitlers Krieg und die Deutschen*, 272–3, and Reinhardt, *Moscow*, 365–6, citing Oehmichen's report; BA–MA, MSg 2/13904, Farnbacher, 'Persönliches Kriegstagebuch', 27 Dec. 1941.

26   MfK–FA, 3.2002.7209, Paulus to parents, 27 Oct., 13 Dec. 1941 and 7 Mar. 1942; BA–MA, MSg 2/13904, Farnbacher, 'Persönliches Kriegstagebuch', 14 Aug, 22 Sept., 3 Oct., 10 and 21 Dec. 1941, 15 Jan. and 7 Feb. 1942; Kühne, *Kameradschaft*, 149–51.

27   MfK–FA, 3.2002.7209, Ernst to Helmut Paulus, 3 and 8 Mar. and 7 Jan. 1942; Helmut Paulus to his parents, 17 Mar. 1942.

28   MfK–FA, 3.2002.7209, Helmut Paulus to parents, 27 Oct. and 13 Dec. 1941, 7 Mar. and 15 Sept. 1942.

29   MfK–FA, 3.2002.7209, Helmut Paulus to his parents, 12 Mar. 1942.

30   MfK–FA, 3.2002.7209, parents to Helmut Paulus, 5 Nov. 1941, 17 Dec. 1941 and 6 April 1942; Erna to Helmut Paulus, 5 Jan. 1942; Helmut to parents, 11 Nov. 1941; Reinhardt, *Moscow*, 365: Oehmichen report.

31   MfK–FA, 3.2002.7209, Erna to Helmut Paulus, 23 Oct. 1941; Helmut to parents, 11 Nov. 1941.

32   MfK–FA, 3.2002.7209, Helmut to parents, 11 Nov. 1941.

33   MfK–FA, 3.2002.7209, Helmut Paulus to parents, 25 Dec. 1941; Helmut Paulus, Tagebuch, 2 Jan. 1942.

34   MfK–FA, 3.2002.7209, Elfriede and Erna to Helmut Paulus, 27–28 Dec. 1941; Helmut Paulus to parents, 1st letter of 12 Mar. 1942; Erna to Helmut Paulus, 15 Mar. 1942; Ernst to Helmut Paulus, 22 Mar. 1942.

35   MfK–FA, 3.2002.7209, Erna to Helmut Paulus, 8 and 1 Feb. 1942; Erna to Helmut Paulus, 25 Jan. 1942.

36   Rohland, *Bewegte Zeiten*, 77–8; Goebbels, *Tgb*, II/1, 260–3: 19 Aug. 1941; Kershaw, *Hitler*, 2, 440–1; Tooze, *Wages of Destruction*, 507–8.

37   Hitler, *Reden und Proklamationen*, 1793–1811: 11 Dec. 1941; Goebbels, *Tgb*, II/2, 498ff.: 13 Dec. 1941; Frank, *Das Diensttagebuch*, 457–8: 16 Dec. 1941.

38   Ribbentrop, *Zwischen Moskau und London*, ed. von Ribbentrop, 261; Tooze, *The Wages of Destruction*, 349–3; 508–9.

39   Goebbels, *Tgb*, II/3, 154–5: 20 Jan. 1942.

40   *MadR*, 3193–6: 22 Jan. 1942; 2704 and 2489: 14 July and 29 Aug. 1941; Steinert, *Hitlers Krieg und die Deutschen*, 267 and 272.

41   Fritzsche, *Life and Death in the Third Reich*, 149; Goebbels, *Tgb*, II/2, 483: 12 Dec. 1941; Steinert, *Hitlers Krieg und die Deutschen*, 273: 'Mitteilungen für die Truppe', 11 Mar. 1942.

42   Hitler, 'Rede vor der deutschen Presse', *VfZ*, 2 (1958), 181–191.

43   Domarus (ed)., *Hitler*, 1826–34.

44   Reimann, *Der große Krieg der Sprachen*, 39–44; Lipp, *Meinungslenkung im Krieg*; MfK–FA, 3.2002.7209, Erna to Helmut Paulus, 3 Feb. 1942.

45   Goebbels, *Tgb*, II/2, 554: 21 Dec. 1941; Hitler, *Reden und Proklamationen*, 1813–15; Szarota, *Warschau unter dem Hakenkreuz*, 147–8.

46   Bramsted, *Goebbels and National Socialist Propaganda*, 250; Fritzsche, *Life and Death in the Third Reich*, 276; MfK–FA, 3.2002.7209, Erna to Helmut Paulus, 24 Dec. 1941 and 9, 18 and 19 Jan. 1942; MfK–FA 3.2002.0279, Liselotte Purper to Kurt Orgel, 11 Jan. 1942.

47   MfK–FA 3.2002.0279, Liselotte Purper to Kurt Orgel, 21 Jan. 1942.

48   Ebert (ed.), *Im Funkwagen der Wehrmacht*, 197–8: Wilhelm to Erika Moldenhauer, 11 Feb. 1942; MfK–FA, 3.2002.7209, Helmut Paulus to parents, 12 Feb. 1942.

49   Reinhardt, *Moscow*, 128: Hitler to Ciano, 25 Oct. 1941; Hillgruber (ed.), *Staatsmänner und Diplomaten bei Hitler*, 47: to Antonescu, 11 Feb. 1942.

50   Hillgruber (ed.), *Staatsmänner und Diplomaten bei Hitler*, 1, 657; Jochmann (ed.), *Monologe in Führer-Hauptquartier*, 239: 27 Jan. 1942; ibid., 260: 27 Jan. 1942.

51   Hirtenwort zum Sonntag dem 15. März 1942, *Kirchliches Amtsblatt für die Diözese Münster*, 12 Mar. 1942.

52   Hitler, *Reden und Proklamationen*, 1848–51; *MadR*, 3486–8: 19 Mar. 1942; Kershaw, *Hitler*, 2, 505–6.

53   *MadR*, 3487: 19 Mar. 1942; Latzel, *Deutsche Soldaten*, 331; MfK–FA, 3.2002.7209, Erna to Helmut Paulus, 3 Feb. 1942.

8 *The Shared Secret*

1   Browning, *Origins of the Final Solution*; Roseman, *The Villa, the Lake, the Meeting*.

2   MfK–FA, 3.2002.7209, Helmut Paulus to parents, 11 July 1941, 15 April, 8 May and 4 June 1942; Erna to Helmut Paulus, 23 and 30 Oct. and 30 Nov. 1941; Irmgard to Helmut Paulus, 24 Mar. 1942, and Ernst Arnold to Helmut Paulus, 11 July 1942; Reifahrth and Schmidt-Linsenhoff, 'Die Kamera der Täter', in Heer and Naumann (eds), *Vernichtungskrieg*, 475–503; Knoch, *Die Tat as Bild*, 50–122.

3   Jarausch and Arnold (eds), '*Das stille Sterben . . .*', 339: 14 Nov. 1941; MfK–FA, 3.2002.0211, Albring to Altrogge, 21 Mar. 1942; Eiber, '". . . Ein bisschen die Wahrheit"', HG to Hannah, 7 Aug. 1941; Schneider, '*Auswärts eingesetzt*'; Kleindienst (ed.), *Sei tausendmal gegrüßt*: Ernst to Irene Guicking, 3 and 22 Feb. 1942.

4   Pohl, *Nationalsozialistische Judenverfolgung in Ostgalizien, 1941–1944*, 138–75. Sandkühler, '*Endlösung' in Galizien*, 148–65; Longerich, *Holocaust*, 286; Kulka and Jäckel (eds), *Die Juden in den geheimen NS-Stimmungsberichten*,

3388: SD Außenstelle Minden, 12 Dec. 1941. (The full set of reports is on CD-rom and so references are by document, not page, number).

5   Bankier, *The Germans and the Final Solution*, 131; Adler, *Theresienstadt*, 720–2: n. 46b: Heydrich, 10 Oct. 1941.

6   Kulka and Jäckel (eds), *Die Juden in den geheimen NS-Stimmungsberichten*, 3388: SD Außenstelle Minden, 12 Dec. 1941.

7   Bankier, *The Germans and the Final Solution*, 128.

8   Sauer, *Grundlehre des Völkerrechts*, 407.

9   Doenecke and Stoler, *Debating Franklin D. Roosevelt's Foreign Policies*, 130–6; Longerich, *'Davon haben wir nicht gewußt!'*, 167–9; Benz, 'Judenvernichtung aus Notwehr?', 618; Goebbels, *Tgb*, II/1, 116–17: 24 July 1941.

10   Wiener Library, London: Nazi Party Slogan of the Week, 7 Sept. 1941; Kershaw, *Hitler*, 2, fig. 45.

11   Longerich, *Holocaust*, 266–7.

12   Kulka and Jäckel (eds), *Die Juden in den geheimen NS-Stimmungsberichten*, 3387: SD Außenstelle Minden, 6 Dec. 1941.

13   Adler, *Verwaltete Mensch*, 354–437; Longerich, *The Holocaust*, 287; Friedländer, *The Years of Extermination*, 306–7.

14   Kulka and Jäckel (eds), *Die Juden in den geheimen NS-Stimmungsberichten*, 3475: Landrat Bad Neustadt/Saale, 23 April 1942; Schultheis, *Juden in Mainfranken*, 467; Fritzsche, *Life and Death in the Third Reich*, 253–7; Wildt, *Volksgemeinschaft*; Longerich, *'Davon haben wir nichts gewußt!'*, 219.

15   Roseman, *The Past in Hiding*, 152–5.

16   Roseman, *The Villa, the Lake, the Meeting*, 113: Heydrich at Wannsee Conference, 20 Jan. 1942; Longerich, *Holocaust*, 321.

17   Roseman, *The Past in Hiding*, 195–230.

18   Bajohr, *'Aryanisation' in Hamburg*, 277–82 and 279–80; Becker, *Gewalt und Gedächtnis*, 77–140; Seydelmann, *Gefährdete Balance*, 105–6; Sielemann (ed.), *Hamburger jüdische Opfer des Nationalsozialismus*, xviii: Karl Kaufmann to Hermann Göring, 4 Sept. 1942; National Archives Washington, Misc. German Record Collection, T84/7; Longerich, *'Davon haben wir nichts gewußt!'*, 199.

19   Klemperer, *I Shall Bear Witness*, 524–5: 15 Sept. 1941; Goeschel, *Suicide in the Third Reich*, 106–10; Kwiet, 'The ultimate refuge', 173–98; Baumann, 'Suizid im "Dritten Reich"', in Rürup (ed.), *Geschichte und Emanzipation*, 500; Speer, *Spandau*, 287; Bankier, *The Germans and the Final Solution*, 125–7; also Goebbels, *Tgb.*, II/2, 194–5: 28 Oct. 1941; Longerich, *'Davon haben wir nichts gewußt!'*, 181–5.

20   Goebbels, 'Die Juden sind schuld!', *Das Reich*, 16 Nov. 1941, in Martens, *Zum Beispiel Das Reich*, 61–4.

21   Wilhelm, *Rassenpolitik und Kriegsführung*, 131–2: Rosenberg, 18 Nov.

1941; Longerich, 'Davon haben wir nichts gewußt!', 201; Domarus (ed.), Hitler, 1821, 1828–9, 1844, 1920, 1937: 30 Jan., 24 Feb., 30 Sept. and 8 Nov. 1942; Kershaw, 'Hitler Myth', 243; Münchener Neuesten Nachrichten, 16 Mar. 1942.

22 Vertrauliche Informationen der Parteikanzlei, 9 Oct. 1942, printed in Huber and Müller (eds), Das Dritte Reich, 2, 110.

23 Longerich, Holocaust, 320–69; Friedländer, The Years of Extermination, 359–60; Paulsson, Secret City, 73–8.

24 Numbers, Noakes and Pridham (eds), Nazism, 3, 629; see Latzel, Deutsche Soldaten, 203–5; Friedrich, '"Die Wohnungsschlüssel sind beim Hausverwalter abzugeben"', in Wollenberg (ed.), 'Niemand war dabei und keiner hat's gewußt', 188–203, and Lichtenstein, 'Pünktlich an der Rampe', ibid., 204–23.

25 Longerich, 'Davon haben wir nichts gewußt!', 211–17 and 202–3: Goebbels, Tgb, II/5, 505, 15 Sept. 1942.

26 Longerich, 'Davon haben wir nichts gewußt!', 205–6.

27 Noelle-Neumann, 'The spiral of silence: A theory of public opinion'; also Becker, Elisabeth Noelle-Neumann.

28 Dürkefälden, 'Schreiben wie es wirklich war!', 107ff.: Feb. 1942; also 109, 114, 115, 117, 125, 126 and 129; Kershaw, 'German popular opinion', in Paucker (ed.), Die Juden im nationalsozialistischen Deutschland, [365–86] 379; Bankier, The Germans and the Final Solution, 108; Fritzsche, Life and Death in the Third Reich, 265.

29 Friedländer, The Years of Extermination, 303, citing Löffler (ed.), Galen: Akten, Briefe und Predigten, 2, 910–11.

30 Longerich, 'Davon haben wir nichts gewußt!', 227; also Friedländer, The Years of Extermination, 303 and 515–16; Phayer, The Catholic Church and the Holocaust, 70–1.

31 Nowak, 'Euthanasie' und Sterilisierung im 'Dritten Reich', 151; Brodie, 'For Christ and Germany', 140–4 and 162: citing LNRW.ARH, RW 58, 3741, 120.

32 Kulka and Jäckel (eds), Die Juden in den geheimen NS-Stimmungsberichten, 3508: SD-Außenstelle Detmold, 31 July 1942; Stephenson, Hitler's Home Front, 145–8; Wantzen, Das Leben im Krieg, 30 July 1942; LNRW.ARH, RW34/03, 17: SD rept, Cologne, 7 July 1943.

33 Bankier, The Germans and the Final Solution; on BBC coverage, 113.

34 Longerich, 'Davon haben wir nichts gewußt!', 256–61 and 267: Goebbels, Tgb, II/7, 651 and 675, and II/8, 42: 27 and 31 Mar. and 3 April 1943; Rubinstein, The Myth of Rescue, 131.

35 Arad, Belzec, Sobibor, Treblinka; Friedländer, Kurt Gerstein, 100–29; Pfannstiel in Klee et al. (eds), 'The Good Old Days', 238–44.

36 Friedländer, Kurt Gerstein, 100–29.

37 Friedländer, *Years of Extermination*, 539–40.

38 Wilhelm Cornides, diary, 31 Aug. 1942, in 'Observations about the "Resettlement of Jews" in the General Government', in Hilberg (ed.), *Documents of Destruction*, 208 ff.; Friedländer, *The Years of Extermination*, 399–400.

39 Bankier, *The Germans and the Final Solution*, 110.

40 Klukowski, *Diary from the Years of Occupation*, 8 April 1942; the same rumour circulated locally amongst the Jewish population: see Bankier, *The Germans and the Final Solution*, 109 and 179, n. 51, citing testimony of Wohlfuss, *Memorial Book of Rawa Ruska*, 238.

41 Hosenfeld, *'Ich versuche jeden zu retten'*, 628, 630–1, 640–1, 650, 653–5, 658: diary and letters to family, 25 and 29 July, 13 Aug., 1 and 26 Sept. 1942.

42 Wagner, 'Gerüchte, Wissen, Verdrängung', in Frei et al. (eds), *Ausbeutung, Vernichtung, Öffentlichkeit*, 231–48; Steinbacher, *'Musterstadt' Auschwitz*, 246–52 and 318–20; Bankier, *The Germans and the Final Solution*, 111–14: Ludwig Haydn, 1942; Salazar Soriano, June 1942; Fermin Lopez Robertz, Mar. 1943; Hahn, *Bis alles in Scherben fällt*, 338: 30 Nov. 1941; Andreas-Friedrich, *Der Schattenmann*, 96: 22 Dec. 1942; 111 and 125–8: 10 Aug. 1943 and 4 Feb. 1944.

43 Bankier, *The Germans and the Final Solution*, 109; Herbert, *Best*, 313; Niewyk (ed.), *Fresh Wounds*, 176; Liselotte G. in Hammer and Nieden, *'Sehr selten habe ich geweint'*, 278–9: 31 Aug. 1943.

44 Yakov Grojanowski, testimony on Chelmno camp, 6–19 Jan. 1942, in Gilbert, *The Holocaust*, 252–79; Katsh, *Diary of Chaim A. Kaplan*, 360, 369–72 and 379: 25 June, 10–12 and 22 July 1942; Hilberg et al. (eds), *Warsaw Diary of Adam Czerniakow*, 'introduction', 62; Adelson, *The Diary of Dawid Sierakowiak*, 142, 161–2 and 258: 19 Oct. 1941, 1–2 May 1942 and 15 Mar. 1943; Corni, *Hitler's Ghettos*, 179–82; on ignorance and knowledge within the ghettos during Mar.–Aug. 1942, see Arad, *Belzec, Sobibor, Treblinka*, 241–4.

45 Haydn, *Meter immer nur Meter*, 6, 9–11, 53, 123–4 and 129–31: 29 June, 31 July, 19 and 24 Dec. 1942.

46 Longerich, *'Davon haben wir nichts gewußt!'*, 259; Hassell, *The von Hassell Diaries*, 272: 15 May 1943; Andreas-Friedrich, *Der Schattenmann*, 125–6: 4 Feb. 1944; Scholl, *Die weiße Rose*, 91–3: second manifesto: 300,000 Jews murdered; Haydn, *Meter immer nur Meter*, 51: 30 July 1942; Aly, 'Die Deportation der Juden von Rhodos nach Auschwitz', 79–88.

47 *Stuttgart NS-Kurier*, 4 Oct. 1941; Bankier, *The Germans and the Final Solution*, 130; Haag, *Das Glück zu leben*, 164: 5 Oct. 1942; Wantzen, *Das Leben im Krieg*, 610: 5 Nov. 1941.

48 Orłowski and Schneider, *'Erschießen will ich nicht!'*, 247: 18 Nov. 1943.

49   Klemperer, *To the Bitter End*, 141–2: 21 Sept. 1942.

50   Stargardt, 'Speaking in public about the murder of the Jews', in Wiese and Betts (eds), *Years of Persecution, Years of Extermination*, 133–55.

51   Heiber, *Reichsführer!*, 169; on Wise's information, Feingold, *Politics of Rescue*, 170; Himmler, *Der Dienstkalender Heinrich Himmlers 1941/42*, ed. Witte, 619 n. 43; Friedländer, *The Years of Extermination*, 462–3; Hilberg, *The Destruction of the European Jews*, 623–4; Neander, 'Seife aus Judenfett', in *Fabula: Zeitschrift für Erzählforschung*, 46 (2005), 241–56; Harig, *Weh dem, der aus der Reihe tanzt*, 203.

52   Bankier, *The Germans and the Final Solution*, 122–3; for more of her story, Kaplan, *Between Dignity and Despair*, 223–8.

53   Klee, *Die SA Jesu Christi*, 148; Goebbels, *Tgb*, II/2, 362–3: 25 Nov. 1941; Wurm in Gerlach, *And the Witnesses Were Silent*, 204; Hermle, 'Die Bischöfe und die Schicksale "nichtarischer" Christen', in Gailus and Lehmann (eds), *Nationalprotestantische Mentalitäten*, 263–306; Gailus and Nolzen (eds), *Zerstrittene 'Volksgemeinschaft'*.

54   Gutteridge, *Open thy Mouth for the Dumb!*, 231–2; Gerlach, *And the Witnesses Were Silent*, 194: Church Chancellery, open letter to all provincial churches, 23 Dec. 1941; Düringer and Kaiser (eds), *Kirchliches Leben im Zweiten Weltkrieg*, 82–3; Bergen, *Twisted Cross*.

55   Klepper, *Unter dem Schatten deiner Flügel*, 1008–9: 25 Dec. 1941; also Wecht, *Jochen Klepper*, 292–320.

56   Klepper, *Unter dem Schatten deiner Flügel*, 1041, 1043, 1127–32: 10 and 15 Mar. and 5–8 Dec. 1942; Klepper (ed.), *In Tormentis Pinxit*.

57   Klepper, *Unter dem Schatten deiner Flügel*, 1132–3: 9–10 Dec. 1942.

58   Gruner, *Widerstand in der Rosenstrasse*; Stoltzfuss, *Resistance of the Heart*.

59   Kaplan, *Between Dignity and Despair*, 217–20.

60   Ibid., 203 and 228; Kwiet and Eschwege, *Selbstverwaltung und Widerstand*, 150; Beck, *An Underground Life*.

61   Roseman, *The Past in Hiding*, 306–92; Roseman, 'Gerettete Geschichte', 100–21.

62   Hosenfeld, 'Ich versuche jeden zu retten', 630–1, 640–1, 650, 653–5, 658: diary and letters to family, 25 and 29 July, 13 Aug., 1 and 26 Sept. 1942.

63   Hosenfeld, 'Ich versuche jeden zu retten', 657–8: diary, 26 Sept. 1942; Paulsson, *Secret City*, 79, and further details in his 'Hiding in Warsaw,' DPhil. Thesis, Oxford, 1998, 278; SS-Untersturmbannführer Gerhard Stabenow, born 26 Jan. 1906 in Halle, had a PhD and a doctorate in law, and was still alive to be interviewed in 1950: *Der Spiegel*, 31 Aug. 1950, 35/ 1950. He wrote two short books: *Das Ostreparationen: Ein Inaugural-Dissertation*, n.p., 1930; *Die Olympiaberichterstattung in der Deutschen Presse unter besonderer Berücksichtigung der Provinzpresse und*

die Entwicklung der Sportberichterstattung in der Provinzpresse 1936 bis 1940, Mitteldt. National-Verlag, 1941.

64   Hosenfeld, '*Ich versuche jeden zu retten*', 659, 637, 641–3 and 660: diary, 1 Oct. and 7 and 18 Aug. 1942; letter to Helmut, 5 Oct. 1942.

65   Ibid., 250: 16 Sept. 1939, and 81–3.

66   Kardorff, *Berliner Aufzeichnungen*, 44: 20 Nov. 1942: this incident may be a post-war addition; there is nothing in her original pocket diary.

67   Ibid., 52, n. 3 and 59: 31 Dec. 1942 and 12 Jan. 1943, dramatised this dilemma at length.

68   On *Sonderaktion* 1005, see Arad, *Belzec, Sobibor, Treblinka*, 170–8, 370–6; Hilberg, *Destruction of the European Jews*, 3, 976–7; Kulka and Jäckel, *Die Juden in den geheimen NS-Stimmungsberichten*, #3652, SD Außenstelle Bad Neustadt, 15 Oct. 1943.

9   Scouring Europe

1   Tooze, *Wages of Destruction*, 639–40; also Overy, *Why the Allies Won*, 1–24.

2   Kershaw, *Hitler*, 2, 442–6.

3   Wegner, 'Hitlers Strategie zwischen Pearl Harbor und Stalingrad'.

4   Tooze, *Wages of Destruction*, 513–15; Mazower, *Hitler's Empire*, 259–72.

5   Tooze, *Wages of Destruction*, 380–93, 402–15.

6   Gildea et al.(eds), *Surviving Hitler and Mussolini*, 46–7.

7   Gillingham, *Industry and Politics in the Third Reich*; Gildea et al. (eds), *Surviving Hitler and Mussolini*, 50.

8   Tooze, *Wages of Destruction*, 513–51.

9   Gerlach, *Krieg, Ernährung, Völkermord*; Kay, *Exploitation, Resettlement, Mass Murder*.

10   IMT, 39, doc. 170-USSR, 384–412; Gerlach, *Krieg, Ernährung, Völkermord*, 175; Tooze, *Wages of Destruction*, 546–7; Gerlach and Tooze have taken this intervention as an announcement of policy, and argued that German food requirements became a major driver of the Holocaust. Against this interpretation is the fact that the mass deportation of European Jews to the death camps had already started weeks before this meeting: for a critique, see Stone, *Histories of the Holocaust*, 140–2.

11   Berkhoff, *Harvest of Despair*, 122; Brandt, *Management of Agriculture*, 610 and 614.

12   Herbert, *Hitler's Foreign Workers*, 167–204; Gildea et al. (eds), *Surviving Hitler and Mussolini*, 62–70.

13   Berkhoff, *Harvest of Despair*, 259–64; Herbert, *Hitler's Foreign Workers*, 192–8; Tooze, *Wages of Destruction*, 517–18.

14 Davies and Wheatcroft, *The Years of Hunger*; Davies et al., *The Years of Progress*.

15 Berkhoff, *Harvest of Despair*, 135.

16 Ibid., 134 and 280–12; Chiari, *Alltag hinter der Front*; Gerlach, *Kalkulierte Morde*, 11; Mazower, *Hitler's Empire*, 282–4.

17 Chiari, *Alltag hinter der Front*, 36–48 and 268; Berkhoff, *Harvest of Despair*.

18 Gildea, *Marianne in Chains*, 126.

19 Ibid., 111, 126–32.

20 Ibid., 83–5; Schwartz, 'The politics of food and gender in occupied Paris', 35–45.

21 Gildea, *Marianne in Chains*, 116–18, 148–9; 27; Reg Langlois (Jersey) and Daphne Breton (Guernsey): bbc.co.uk/ww2peopleswar archive of stories, A3403946 and A4014091.

22 Nissen, 'Danish food production in the German war economy', in Trentmann and Just (eds), *Food and Conflict in Europe in the Age of the Two World Wars*; Brandt, *Management of Agriculture*, 300–11; Collingham, *The Taste of War*, 174–6.

23 Aly, *Hitlers Volksstaat*, 123, citing VR der RKK, 1 July 1942, BA R 29/3, Nl. 223f; Bohn, *Reichskommissariat Norwegen*; Voglis, 'Surviving hunger', in Gildea et al. (eds), *Surviving Hitler and Mussolini*, 21–2, and Gildea, Luyten and Fürst, 'To work or not to work?', in ibid., 50.

24 Voglis, 'Surviving hunger', in Gildea et al. (eds), *Surviving Hitler and Mussolini*, 23–4, 29–30; Mazower, *Inside Hitler's Greece*, 23–52; Hionidou, *Famine and Death in Occupied Greece*; Mazower, *Hitler's Empire*, 280.

25 Friedländer, *The Years of Extermination*, 414–16; Kaspi, *Les Juifs pendant l'occupation*, 222–7.

26 Bobet, *Le vélo à l'heure allemande*, 105–35.

27 Klarsfeld, *Vichy – Auschwitz*; Friedländer, *The Years of Extermination*, 123–4, 178–9, 410–11 and 545–7; Longerich, *The Holocaust*, 397–9; Gildea et al. (eds), *Surviving Hitler and Mussolini*, 45 and 64–9.

28 Cointet, *L'Eglise sous Vichy*, 291.

29 Madajczyk, *Die Okkupationspolitik Nazideutschlands*, 427 and annexe 29A, 317–20; Berkhoff, *Harvest of Despair*, 183, 184.

30 *MadR*, 3613 and 3639: 13 and 20 April 1942; Boelcke, *Wollt ihr den totalen Krieg?*, 295: 1 April 1942; MfK–FA, 3.2002.7209, Ernst Arnold to Helmut Paulus: 6 and 7 April 1942; Erna to Helmut Paulus: 12 April 1942.

31 Corni and Gies, *Brot – Butter – Kanonen*, 562–3, and Werner, *Bleib übrig!*, 194–6; complaints, *MadR*, 3613: 13 April 1942.

32 Werner, *Bleib übrig*, 196; Stephenson, *Hitler's Home Front*, 184.

33 Werner, *Bleib übrig*, 204: 22 Aug. 1942.

34 Ibid., 202–3 and 303–11.

35   Dörr, 'Wer die Zeit nicht miterlebt hat . . .', 2, 24–6; Franz Ruhm, *Kochen im Krieg. Eine Sammlung einfacher und dennoch schmackhafter Gerichte für den Mittags- und Abendtisch*, Vienna, 1940.

36   *MadR* 38/9–22, 3882, 3917–20, 3923–4 and 4006: 4 and 29 June, 8, 9 and 27 July 1942; Dörr, 'Wer die Zeit nicht miterlebt hat . . .', 2, 13; MfK–FA, 3.2002.7209, Ernst Arnold to Helmut Paulus: 9 June 1942; Erna to Helmut Paulus: 17 July 1942; DLA, Helga F., 'Bericht eines zehnjährigen Kindes zur Zeit des 2. Weltkrieges', 2 and 9; DLA, Friedl H., 10.

37   Dörr, 'Wer die Zeit nicht miterlebt hat . . .', 2, 18, 20; Zierenberg, *Stadt der Schieber*, 116–18.

38   Zierenberg, *Stadt der Schieber*, 135–51.

39   Ibid., 86–90.

40   Harris, *Selling Sex in the Reich*, 98–113.

41   Stephenson, *Hitler's Home Front*, 204.

42   Ibid., 206, 210–11.

43   Ibid., 213–15: 24 Nov. 1942.

44   Ibid., 211.

45   Bauer, *Nationalsozialistische Agrarpolitik und bäuerliches Verhalten im Zweiten Weltkrieg*, 93–6; Stephenson, *Hitler's Home Front*, 202.

46   Szarota, *Warschau unter dem Hakenkreuz*, 123–5; Aly, *Hitlers Volkstaat*, 123.

47   Mellin in Bauer, *Alltag im 2. Weltkrieg*, 14; Michel, *Paris allemand*, 298; Aly, *Hitlers Volksstaat*, 114–24; Drolshagen, *Der freundliche Feind*.

48   Gerlach, *Kalkulierte Morde*, 679–83; Hilberg, *Die Vernichtung der europäischen Juden*, 378, n. 324; Chiari, *Alltag hinter der Front*, 245 and 257–63; Hohenstein, *Wartheländisches Tagebuch aus den Jahren 1941/42*, 251; Gross, 'A tangled web', in Deák et al. (eds), *The Politics of Retribution in Europe*, 88–91; Aly, *Hitlers Volksstaat*, 134–8.

49   Aly, *Hitlers Volksstaat*, 138; Wantzen, *Das Leben im Krieg*, 324: 2 Jan. 1941.

50   Domarus (ed.), *Hitler*, 187–8: 23 and 30 May 1942; Goebbels, *Tgb*, II/4, 354–64: 24 May 1942.

51   Madajczyk, 'Introduction to General Plan East', 391–442; Rössler and Schleiermacher (eds), *Der Generalplan Ost*; Aly and Heim, *Architects of Annihilation*; Harvey, *Women and the Nazi East*, 241–4 and 255.

52   Lower, *Hitler's Furies*, 131–3.

53   Hans Grimm, *Volk ohne Raum*, Munich, 1926: it sold 220,000 copies by 1933 and a further 330,000 during 1933–44: Schneider, 'Bestseller im Dritten Reich', 85; Lilienthal, *Der 'Lebensborn e.V.'*, 219–21.

54   *MadR*, 5639–43: 17 Aug. 1943; Kundrus, 'Forbidden Company'.

55   *MadR*, 3323–20: 16 Feb. 1942; Spoerer, *Zwangsarbeit unter dem Hakenkreuz*; Plato et al. (eds), *Hitlers Sklaven*.

56   Virgili, *Naître ennemi*, 52–3.

57   Ibid., 84–7; Herbert, *Hitler's Foreign Workers*, 129–30; Boll, '". . . das gesunde Volksempfinden auf das Gröbste verletzt"', 661; Gellately, *Backing Hitler*, 169–70.

58   Aly, *Hitlers Volksstaat*, 120; Herbert, *Hitler's Foreign Workers*, 127.

59   Waite, 'Teenage sexuality in Nazi Germany', 456.

60   Knoll at al., 'Zwangsarbeit bei der Lapp-Finze AG', in Karner et al. (eds), *NS-Zwangsarbeit in der Rüstungsindustrie*, 111–14: citing interview conducted in 2001 and 2002.

61   Ibid., 45, 126–56.

62   Herbert, *Hitler's Foreign Workers*, 228; different analysis of same trend, *MadR*, 4305–6: 8 Oct. 1942.

63   Abelshauser, 'Rüstungsschmiede der Nation?', in Gall (ed.), *Krupp im 20. Jahrhundert*, 412.

64   Herbert, *Hitler's Foreign Workers*, 175.

65   Kaienburg, *Die Wirtschaft der SS*, 114–38 and 434–5; Schulte, *Zwangsarbeit und Vernichtung*; Wagner, *IG Auschwitz*; Tooze, *Wages of Destruction*, 519–23.

66   Tooze, *Wages of Destruction*, 530–3.

67   Herbert, *Hitler's Foreign Workers*, 172; *MadR*, 3715–17: 7 May 1942.

68   Goebbels, 'Offene Aussprache', *Das Reich*, 29 Mar. 1942; Gruchmann, 'Korruption im Dritten Reich', 578; Corni and Gies, *Brot – Butter – Kanonen*, 558–60: edicts of 21 Mar. 1942 and 10 May 1943; *MadR*, 3688: 30 Apr. 1942; Sefton Delmer, *Black Boomerang*; Steinert, *Hitlers Krieg und die Deutschen*, 281; Bormann, 5 June 1942, in Partei-Kanzlei (ed.), *Verfügungen, Anordnungen, Bekanntgaben*, 640.

69   Gruchmann, 'Korruption im Dritten Reich'.

70   Ibid.; Goebbels, *Tgb*, II/8, 326: 19 May 1943.

71   Boelcke, *Wollt Ihr den totalen Krieg*, 377: 4–5 Oct. 1942; Goebbels, *Tgb*, II/6, 72, 127: 4 and 15 Oct. 1942; Göring, 4 Oct. 1942, in Longerich, *'Davon habe wir nichts gewußt!'*, 203–4; Aly, *Hitlers Volksstaat*, 202.

72   *MadR*, 4291–2 and 4309–11: 8 and 12 Oct. 1942.

10 Writing to the Dead

1   Wegner, 'Hitlers Strategie zwischen Pearl Harbor und Stalingrad'.

2   Kershaw, *Hitler*, 2, 514–17; Domarus (ed.), *Hitler*, 1887–8: 23 May 1942; Goebbels, *Tgb*, II/4, 362–4: 24 May 1942.

3   Wegner, 'Hitlers "zweiter Feldzug"'; Pahl, *Fremde Heere Ost*.

4   MfK–FA, 3.2002.201, Wilhelm Abel, letters home: 21, 24, 28 April, 5 and 31 May 1942.

5 MfK–FA, 3.2002.7209, Helmut Paulus to parents, 1 July and 29 June 1942; Irmgard and Erna to Helmut Paulus, 1 July 1942.

6 MfK–FA, 3.2002.7209, Helmut Paulus to family, 6 July 1942; Elfriede to Helmut Paulus, 6 July 1942.

7 MfK–FA, 3.2002.7209, Helmut Paulus, 14 July 1942; Grossjohann, *Five Years, Four Fronts*, 50–4.

8 MfK–FA, 3.2002.7209, Helmut Paulus, n.d. [21–22 July 1942].

9 MfK–FA, 3.2002.7209, Helmut Paulus, 20, 26 and 27 July 1942.

10 MfK–FA, 3.2002.7209, Helmut Paulus, 27, 29 and 31 July 1942.

11 Dallin, *German Rule in Russia*, 534–8; Neulen, *An deutscher Seite*.

12 Gerlach, *Kalkulierte Morde*, 1082–5; Quinkert, *Propaganda und Terror in Weißrußland*.

13 Hoffmann, *Die Ostlegionen 1941–1943*; Müller, *An der Seite der Wehrmacht*; Lepre, *Himmler's Bosnian Divison*.

14 Motadel, *Islam and Nazi Germany's War*, 150–66 and 225–6; Kunz, *Die Krim unter deutscher Herrschaft*.

15 Motadel, *Islam and Nazi Germany's War*, 302–3.

16 Hoffmann, *Die Ostlegionen*, 111–12; Motadel, *Islam and Nazi Germany's War*, 306; 52–72 and 88–9; Ernst Kaltenbrunner to Heinrich Himmler, 6 Dec. 1943: BA, NS 19/3544.

17 Rutz, *Signal*; Boltanski and Jussen (eds), *Signal*; Riding, *And the Show Went On*; Rembrandt, 1942, Ufa/dir. Hans Steinhoff; Kedward, *Resistance in Vichy France*; Jackson, *France: The Dark Years*; Hirschfeld (ed.), *Nazi Rule and Dutch Collaboration*; Mazower, *Hitler's Empire*, 455–60.

18 Kunz, *Die Krim unter deutscher Herrschaft*, 187–94; Mühlen, *Zwischen Hakenkreuz und Sowjetstern*, 49–51; Motadel, *Islam and Nazi Germany's War*, 171–2.

19 Motadel, *Islam and Nazi Germany's War*, 308; MfK–FA, 3.2002.0306, Fritz to Hildegard P., 30 June 1942; similar, 12 April 1942.

20 MfK–FA, 3.2002.210, Altrogge to Albring, 28 Oct. 1942; MfK–FA, 3.2002.0211, Albring to Altrogge, 25 May 1942.

21 MfK–FA, 3.2002.0211, Albring to Altrogge, 15, 25 May and 17 June 1942; MfK–FA, 3.2002.210, Altrogge to Albring, 18 Sept. 1941, 29 Sept. 1942; MfK–FA, 3.2002.7209, Helmut Paulus to parents, 4 Sept. 1942; Jünger, *Gärten und Straßen*.

22 MfK–FA, 3.2002.0306, Fritz to Hildegard P., 5 Jan. 1942.

23 MfK–FA, 3.2002.0306, Fritz to Karl-Heinz P., 16 Feb. 1940; 11 Feb. 1942.

24 MfK–FA, 3.2002.0306, Fritz to Hildegard P., 18 Feb., 15 May and 15 Feb. 1942.

25 MfK–FA, 3.2002.7209, Helmut Paulus to parents, 23, 18, 20, 26 July 1942; Elfriede, 13 July 1942; Erna to Helmut Paulus, 5, 22 and 12 July 1942.

26 MfK–FA, 3.2002.7209, Helmut Paulus to his parents, 17 Mar. and 27 June 1942; Ernst Arnold Paulus, 16 June, 3 and 11 July 1942; urges Helmut to study medicine: 7 Jan., 9 June 1942; Elfriede decides to do so: 21 Jan. 1942; Erna on medicine, 15 June 1942.

27 MfK–FA, 3.2002.210, Altrogge, 4 and 31. Aug., 5 Dec. and 14 Oct. 1942.

28 Wegner, 'Hitlers "zweiter Feldzug"'.

29 MfK–FA, 3.2002.7209, Helmut Paulus to parents, 20 Aug. 1942.

30 MfK–FA, 3.2002.7209, Helmut Paulus to parents, 23 and 30 Aug. 1942; to Aunt Käthe Wurster, 28 Aug. 1942.

31 MfK–FA, 3.2002.7209, parents to Helmut Paulus, 11, 15, 16, 20 and 24 Sept. 1942.

32 MfK–FA, 3.2002.7209, Helmut Paulus to Aunt Käthe Wurster, 28 Aug. 1942; to parents, 23 Aug., 2, 11 and 23 Sept. 1942.

33 MfK–FA, 3.2002.210, Altrogge to Albring, 4 and 31 Aug. 1942.

34 MfK–FA, 3.2002.201, Abel to home, 11 Jan. and 17 June 1942; MfK–FA, 3.2002.0211, Albring to Altrogge, 29 April 1942.

35 Hammer and Nieden, 'Sehr selten habe ich geweint', 267; MfK–FA, 3.2002.201, Abel to home, 8 Jan. 1942; BA–MA, MSg 2/13904, Farnbacher, 'Persönliches Kriegstagebuch', 1, 20 and 23 Nov. 1941; Kühne, Kameradschaft, 166–9.

36 MfK–FA, 3.2002.0211, Albring to Altrogge, 1 Sept. 1942.

37 Hayward, 'Too little too late'; Wegner, 'Hitlers "zweiter Feldzug"'.

38 Beevor, Stalingrad.

39 MfK–FA, 3.2002.0306, Fritz to Hildegard P., 30 Aug. 1942.

40 MfK–FA, 3.2002.0306, Fritz to Hildegard P., 13 and 26 Aug. 1942.

41 MfK–FA, 3.2002.0306, Fritz to Hildegard P., 30 Aug. 1942.

42 'Es geht alles vorüber, es geht alles vorbei': Lale Andersen, conducted by Bruno Seidler-Winkler, Electrola 1942. Source: http://www.youtube.com/watch?v=fy6BQgERi6E.

43 MfK–FA, 3.2002.0306, Fritz to Hildegard P., 3 Sept. 1942.

44 Domarus (ed.), Hitler, 1913–24: 30 Sept. 1942; Kershaw, Hitler, 2, 536–41.

45 MfK–FA, 3.2002.0306, Fritz to Hildegard P., 15 Nov. 1942.

46 Ebert (ed.), Im Funkwagen der Wehrmacht, 269: Wilhelm to Erika Moldenhauer, 20 Nov. 1942; Beevor, Stalingrad, 239–65.

47 Wegner, 'Hitlers "zweiter Feldzug"'; Kershaw, Hitler, 2, 543–5; Overy, Goering, 218–19.

48 DHM, Do2 96/1861, 'Tagebuch von Liselotte Purper', 12–13 Jan. 1943.

49 Ebert (ed.), Im Funkwagen der Wehrmacht, Moldenhauer, 269–73: 20 Nov.–16 Dec. 1943.

50 MfK–FA, 3.2002.0306, Fritz to Hildegard P., 17 and 22 Dec. 1943.

51 Glantz, When Titans Clashed, 140; Beevor, Stalingrad, 291–310.

52   Kundrus, 'Totale Unterhaltung?', 138.

53   MfK–FA, 3.2002.0306, Fritz to Hildegard P., 25 Dec. 1943; Ebert (ed.), *Im Funkwagen der Wehrmacht*, 277 and 280; 30 Dec. 1942 and 4 Jan. 1943.

54   Kardorff, *Berliner Aufzeichnungen*, 64: 6 Feb. 1943.

55   MfK–FA, 3.2002.210, Altrogge to Albring, 29 Dec. 1942; W. Ernst to Gertrud and Hans Salmen, n.d. and 12 May 1943; M. Altrogge to Delmer, 30 Sept. 1949.

56   Ebert (ed.), *Feldpostbriefe aus Stalingrad*, 341–2; Goebbels, 'Totaler Krieg', *Das Reich*, 17 Jan. 1943; Wette, 'Massensterben als "Heldenepos"', in Wette and Ueberschär (eds), *Stalingrad*, 43–60.

57   Deutsches Rundfunkarchiv, Frankfurt a.M., Nr. 52/8920: Göring, 30 Jan. 1943, also Göring, 'Stalingrad-Thermopylä: Aus dem Appell des Reichsmarschalls an die Wehrmacht am 30. Januar 1943', in Vacano (ed.), *Sparta*, 2nd edn, 1942 (*sic*), 120; cited in Ebert (ed.), *Feldpostbriefe aus Stalingrad*, 345; Domarus (ed.), *Hitler*, 1974–6.

58   Deutsches Rundfunkarchiv, Frankfurt a.M., Nr. 52/8920: Göring, 30 Jan. 1943; Rebenich, 'From Thermopylae to Stalingrad', in Powell and Hodkinson (eds), *Sparta beyond the Mirage*, 323–49. Also, Gehrke, 'Die Thermopylenrede Hermann Görings zur Kapitulation Stalingrads', in Martin (ed.), *Der Zweite Weltkrieg*, 13–29.

Simonides' epitaph has been translated in many versions and used in many different traditions of patriotic death:

Ὦ ξεῖν', ἀγγέλλειν Λακεδαιμονίοις ὅτι τῇδε
κείμεθα, τοῖς κείνων ῥήμασι πειθόμενοι.

The standard German translation was Schiller's: Friedrich Schiller, 'Der Spaziergang', 1795:

Wanderer, kommst du nach Sparta, verkündige dorten, du habest uns hier liegen gesehn, wie das Gesetz es befahl.

59   Behrenbeck, *Der Kult um die toten Helden*; Obergefreiter F.B., 24 Jan. 1943, in Buchbender and Sterz, *Das andere Gesicht des Krieges*, Nr 304, 151.

60   Buchbender and Sterz, *Das andere Gesicht des Krieges*, 105; Brajović-Djuro, *Yugoslavia in the Second World War*, 109–14; Schubert, *Heinrich Böll: Schriftsteller*, 599: Heinrich Böll to Annemarie Böll, 29 Jan. 1943.

61   Irrgang, *Leutnant der Wehrmacht*, 153: Peter Stölten to his parents, 5 Mar. 1943.

62   Kershaw, *Hitler*, 2, 548–50; Diedrich, *Paulus*.

63   Kris and Speier (eds), *German Radio Propaganda*, 341; Ebert (ed.), *Feldpostbriefe aus Stalingrad*, 346–48; *VB*, 3 Feb. 1943.

64   Löffler (ed.), *Galen: Akten, Briefe und Predigten*, 2, 970; Brodie, 'For Christ and Germany', 157–63.

65   Nadler, *Eine Stadt im Schatten Streichers*, 73–6; *MadR*, 4720, 4750–1 and 4760–1: 28 Jan., 4 and 8 Feb. 1943; Goebbels, *Tgb*, II/7, 266: 5 Feb. 1943; Domarus (ed.), *Hitler*, 1999–2001: 21 Mar. 1943; Kershaw, *Hitler*, 2, 551–6; Ebert (ed.), *Feldpostbriefe aus Stalingrad*, 349.

66   Boelcke, *Wollt Ihr den totalen Krieg*, 417–18: 6 Jan. 1943.

67   Noakes (ed.), *Nazism*, 4, 490–4, based on original radio transcript; Bramsted, *Goebbels and National Socialist Propaganda*.

68   Goebbels, *Tgb*, II/7, 378–80, 440, 444–5, 450–9, 554–7: 20 and 28 Feb., 1, 2, 12 and 16 Mar. 1943; *MadR*, 4832–3, 4843–5, 4902–3: 22 and 25 Feb., 8 Mar. 1943; Overy, *Goering*, 216–23; Kershaw, *Hitler*, 2, 561–4.

69   Blank, 'Kriegsalltag und Luftkrieg an der "Heimatfront"', 391; Kris and Speier (eds), *German Radio Propaganda*, 208: 9 April 1943.

70   Kundrus, 'Totale Unterhaltung?'; Carter, *Dietrich's Ghosts*, 196–7; *MadR*, 4870: 1 Mar. 1943; *Zwei glückliche Menschen*, 1942, Vienna, with Magda Schneider and Wolf Albach-Retty; *Hab mich lieb!*, 1942, Ufa/Harald Braun, music Franz Grothe, with Marika Rökk and Viktor Staal; *Die grosse Nummer*, 1942, Karl Anton/Tobis, Berlin, with Rudolf Prack and Leny Marenbach; *Die große Liebe*, 1942, dir. Rolf Hansen; Leiser, *Nazi Cinema*, 61.

71   Baird, 'Myth of Stalingrad'; Goebbels, 'Vom Reden und vom Schweigen', *Das Reich*, 20 June 1943; broadcast 19 June 1943: Kris and Speier (eds), *German Radio Propaganda*, 45; reprinted in Joseph Goebbels, *Der steile Aufstieg. Reden und Aufsätze aus den Jahren 1942/43*, Munich, 1944, 331–8.

72   Wantzen, *Das Leben im Krieg*, 1176: 15 Sept. 1943.

73   *MadR*, 4751, 4760–2, 4784: 4, 8 and 11 Feb. 1943; Baird, 'The Myth of Stalingrad', 201–2: Koblenz to Propaganda Ministry, 11 Feb. 1943; Bormann to all Reichsleiter, Gau- and Kreisleiter, 28 May 1943.

74   MfK–FA, 3.2002.0306, Fritz to Hildegard P., 25 Dec. 1942; Hildegard P., diary, 1 April, 3 and 29 May 1943; Ebert, *Stalingrad*, 56 ff.

75   Biess, *Homecomings*, 19–28; BA–MA, RH 15/310 11 and BA–MA RH 15/310 114, Franz von Papen to Frau Pöpsel, 20 Aug. 1943.

76   Studnitz, *While Berlin Burns*, 7–8: 2 Feb. 1943; BA–MA, RH 15/340, 6: 'Bericht über die Stimmung bei den Angehörigen der Stalingrad-Kämpfer', 8 Dec. 1943; Serrano, *German Propaganda in Military Decline*, 29; Gellately, *Backing Hitler*, 185–6; Biess, *Homecomings*, 26; Stephenson, *Hitler's Home Front*, 187–9.

77   Both cases in Biess, *Homecomings*, 26–7; BA–MA, RH 15/340, 6: 'Bericht über die Stimmung bei den Angehörigen der Stalingrad-Kämpfer', 8 Dec. 1943.

78   Biess, *Homecomings*, 28; Haller, *Lieutenant General Karl Strecker*, 105; BA–MA, RH 15/310, 150: Oberkommando der Wehrmacht to Abwicklungsstab der 6. Armee und H.Gr.-Afrika, 8 July 1944; Boddenberg, *Die Kriegsgefangenenpost deutscher Soldaten in sowjetischem Gewahrsam*, 44.

79   DTA, Luise Stieber, diary, 10 Feb. 1944.

80   Jarausch and Geyer, *Shattered Past*, 216; Biess, *Homecomings*, 22 and 30–31 for a nuanced view; DTA, Stieber, diary, 2 and 22 Feb. 1944; see also MfK–FA, 3.2002.0369, Auguste Rath, 1 and 10 Feb. and 10 April 1943.

81   MfK–FA, 3.2002.0306, Hildegard P., diary, 1 April, 3, 14, 17 and 20 May, 8 Sept., 31 Dec. 1943.

82   MfK–FA, 3.2002.0306, Hildegard P., diary, 13 June, 17 and 19 Aug. 1943.

11 *Bombing and Retaliation*

1   See Noakes (ed.), *Nazism, 4, The German Home Front*, 409–12; Klönne, *Gegen den Strom*, 143–4; KA 1997, Werner K., '20 Monate Luftwaffenhelfer: Tagebücher 5. Januar 1944–20. August 1945', 1–20; Trapp, *Kölner Schulen in der NS-Zeit*, 138–9: based on 1985 testimony in Matzerath (ed.), '. . . *Vergessen kann man die Zeit nicht* . . .', 247 and 249: testimony by 'Z27'.

2   KA 4709/2, Klaus S., b. 1926, 'Gomorrha. Bericht über die Luftangriffe auf Hamburg Juli/August 1943', MS. Hamburg, 1993, based on diary and letters to his mother; Rüther, *Köln im Zweiten Weltkrieg*, 260–1: Hans to Rudolf Haas and Rudolf to Hans Haas, 9 and 23 Feb. 1943.

3   Hans Joachim M., born 1930, cited in Arbeitsgruppe Pädagogisches Museum (ed.), *Heil Hitler, Herr Lehrer*, 180; Koch in Krüger, 'Die Bombenangriffe auf das Ruhrgebiet', in Borsdorf and Jamin (eds), *Überleben im Krieg*, 95; Groehler, *Bombenkrieg gegen Deutschland*, 93–103; Blank, 'Kriegsalltag und Luftkrieg', 366 and 421; Reissner in Gepp (ed.), *Essen im Luftkrieg*, 36; Blank, *Ruhrschlacht*.

4   Groehler, *Bombenkrieg gegen Deutschland*, 93–103; Süß, *Death from the Skies*, 300–3.

5   Estimates at bunker capacity, Groehler, *Bombenkrieg gegen Deutschland*, 238–54; Müller, *Der Bombenkrieg 1939–1945*, 135; Friedrich Panse, *Angst und Schreck*, Stuttgart, 1952, 39, cited in Krüger, 'Die Bombenangriffe auf das Ruhrgebiet', 96; see chapter 2 above on Panse; Gröschner (ed.), *Ich schlug meiner Mutter die Brennenden Funken ab*, 35; RA, Berufschule M2/6, 1, 16 yrs, essay, 21 Jan. 1956; RA Burg-Gymnasium Essen, UII/519, 18 yrs., 24 Feb. 1956, 1.

6   Reissner in Gepp (ed.), *Essen im Luftkrieg*, 36; Blank, *Ruhrschlacht*.

7   Rüther, *Köln im Zweiten Weltkrieg*, 167–8, 256–7 and 276: Weiss, 3 Mar. 1943; Anna Schmitz, 28 Feb. 1943; Heinz Pettenberg, 28 Feb. 1943; Rosalie Schüttler, 26 May 1943.

8   Ibid., 277: Rosalie Schüttler, 26 May 1943; Weiss, 26 May 1943.

9   Institut für Geschichte und Biographie, Aussenstelle der Fernuniversität Hagen, Lüdenscheid, Lothar C., diary, 30 May and 3 June 1943; Friedrich, *Der Brand*, 13–20.

10   *MadR*, 5356: 17 June 1943; Rüther, *Köln im Zweiten Weltkrieg*, 277: Rosalie Schüttler, 31 May 1943.

11   Rüther, *Köln im Zweiten Weltkrieg*, 277–9: Weiss, 10 and 15 June 1943; Schüttler, 9 June 1943; Annemarie Hastenplug, 18 June 1943; *MadR*, 5216: 6 May 1943.

12   Goebbels, *Tgb*, II/8, 117–18, 279–80 and 379–80: 17 April, 12 and 28 May 1943; Boberach, introduction, *MadR*, 36 and 5217: 6 May 1943; Steinert, *Hitlers Krieg und die Deutschen*, 361–3.

13   Rüther, *Köln im Zweiten Weltkrieg*, 256: Weiss, 3 Mar. 1943.

14   Blank, 'Kriegsalltag und Luftkrieg', 391–4 and 434; *DAZ*, 6 June 1943; *VB*, 6 June 1943: Heiber (ed.), *Goebbels Reden 1932–1945*, 225–8.

15   *MadR*, 5426 and 5432; Kulka and Jäckel (eds), *Die Juden in den geheimen NS-Stimmungsberichten*, #3614, RHSA, Amt III (SD), Bericht Berlin, 2 July 1943.

16   Brodie, 'For Christ and Germany', 165–6 and 188–9; citing Frings: AEK, DA Lenné 164, 'Hirtenwort zum Herz-Jesu-Zeit': AEK, CR II 25.18, 1, 227; Löffler (ed.), *Galen: Akten, Briefe und Predigten*, 2, 983–5.

17   Brodie, 'For Christ and Germany', 22–5, 151–5, 168, 172 and 184: citing LNRW.ARH, RW 35/09, 49 and 44 and 184–5.

18   Ibid., 179–80 and 183–6: citing LNRW.ARH, RW 35/09, 28.

19   Ibid., 173–4; Sister M. Irmtrudis Fiederling, 'Adolf Kolping and the Kolping Society of the United States', MA Dissertation, Catholic University of America, Washington, DC, 30 July 1941; Gailus, *Protestantismus und Nationalsozialismus*; Gailus and Nolzen (eds), *Zerstrittene 'Volksgemeinschaft'*.

20   Brodie, 'For Christ and Germany', 178–85: citing LNRW.ARH, RW 35/09, 128, 147 and 182–4; *MadR*, 5886: 18 Oct. 1943.

21   Rüther, *Köln im Zweiten Weltkrieg*, 279: Weiss, 18–22 June 1943; later rumours, *MadR*, 5833: 4 Oct. 1943.

22   Rüther, *Köln im Zweiten Weltkrieg*, 282–3: Chronik der Volksschule Immendorf.

23   Ibid., 283–9: Anneliese Hastenplug, 29 and 30 June 1943, and Weiss report to Bern, 30 June and 5 July 1943.

24 Ibid., 290: Anna Schmitz, 5 July 1943; Anneliese Hastenplug, 6 July 1943.

25 Ibid., 284 and 305–8.

26 Ibid., 294; Behrenbeck, *Kult um die toten Helden*, 469.

27 Rüther, *Köln im Zweiten Weltkrieg*, 292 and 294; *MadR*, 5515–18: 22 July 1943; BA, R22/3374, 102ff., Lagebericht des Oberlandesgerichtspräsident, 30 July 1943.

28 *MadR*, 5515–18: 22 July 1943; Rüther, *Köln im Zweiten Weltkrieg*, 291–3 and 842–55: 22 and 25 July 1943; LNRW.ARH, RW35/09, 187: 10 July 1943.

29 Rüther, *Köln im Zweiten Weltkrieg*, 294: 12 July 1943.

30 Ibid., 290–1 and 697–708: letter of Christa Lehmacher to her brother: 18–19 July 1943.

31 Blank, 'Kriegsalltag und Luftkrieg', 435: 22 June 1943, Gauleiter of North Westphalia, Alfred Meyer, at the cemetery in Marl for the dead of a US raid on the Buna Works; *MadR*, 5428: 2 July 1943; Goebbels in Thiessen, *Eingebrannt ins Gedächtnis*, 45; Boog, *DRZW*, 7, 383ff.

32 On Churchill, Hastings, *Bomber Command*, 46–7; Overy, *The Bombing War*, 257–9; *MadR*, 5446: 8 July 1943.

33 *MadR*, 5515: 22 July 1943; Blank, 'Kriegsalltag und Luftkrieg', 380–1: Willi Römer, diary: 6 July 1943.

34 BA–MA, Tätigkeitsbericht der Feldpostprüfstelle beim Oberkommando der 1. Panzerarmee für Juni 1943, Uffz. FPNr. 31682. Tessin, *Verbände und Truppen*, Bd. 2: *Die Landstreitkräfte*, 1–5, 9.

35 Goebbels, *Tgb*, II/8, 337: 21 May 1943; *MadR*, 5277, 5285 and 5290: 23 and 30 May 1943; Kulka and Jäckel (eds), *Die Juden in den geheimen NS-Stimmungsberichten*, #3595, NSDAP Parteikanzlei II B 4, Bericht Munich, 23–29 May 1943; published 'final toll' in *Hagener Zeitung*, 1 June 1943, cited in Blank, 'Kriegsalltag und Luftkrieg', 367.

36 Kulka and Jäckel (eds), *Die Juden in den geheimen NS-Stimmungsberichten*, #3595, NSDAP Parteikanzlei II B 4, Bericht Munich, 23–29 May 1943.

37 Noakes (ed.), *Nazism*, 4, 491, based on the original radio transcript; Jewish listeners in Friedländer, *The Years of Extermination*, 473–4.

38 Fox, 'Der Fall Katyn und die Propaganda des NS-Regimes', 462–99.

39 Goebbels, *Tgb*, II/8, 2, 104: 14 April 1943; *Im Wald von Katyn: Dokumentarische Bildstreifen* (1943): https://archive.org/details/1943-Im–Wald–von–Katyn.

40 *VB*, 15 April 1943; Baird, *The Mythical World of Nazi War Propaganda*, 198; Longerich, *'Davon haben wir nichts gewußt!'*, 267–81; Fox, 'Jewish victims of the Katyn massacre', 49–55; Goebbels in *Das Reich*, 9 May 1943.

41 Longerich, 'Davon haben wir nichts gewußt!', 278–80; Sennholz, *Johann von Leers*; Klemperer, *To the Bitter End*, 223: 29 May 1943.

42 Goebbels, *Tgb*, II/8, 287–90: 13 May 1943, and *VB*, 6 June 1943: speech of 5 June 1943; cited in Longerich, 'Davon haben wir nichts gewußt!', 274 and 281.

43 Official statement of the Polish government, on 17 April 1943: http://web. archive.org/web/20080616072503/http://www.electronicmuseum.ca/ Poland-WW2/katyn_memorial_wall/kmw_statement.html; Carlton, *Churchill and the Soviet Union*, 105; and Benjamin B. Fischer, 'The Katyn controversy: Stalin's killing field', *Studies in Intelligence*, Winter 1999–2000: posted 14 April 2007 on CIA website: https://www.cia.gov/library/ center-for-the-study-of-intelligence/csi-publications/csi-studies/studies/ winter99-00/art6.html; Goebbels, *Tgb*, II/8, 331–2, 341, 377–8, 416 and 484–5: 20, 22, 28 May, 4 and 17 June 1943; Longerich, 'Davon haben wir nichts gewußt!', 276.

44 *MadR*, 1073–4 and 5145: 29 April 1940 and 19 April 1943; for both Catholic and Protestant objections to Nazi inhumanity, see Kulka and Jäckel (eds), *Die Juden in den geheimen NS-Stimmungsberichten*, #3604, NSDAP Parteikanzlei II B 4, Report, 6–12 June 1943, Munich; #3571, SD Außenstelle Bad Brückenau III A 4, 22 April 1943; #3567, 3568, 3570, 3574, 3589.

45 KA 4709/2, Klaus S., b. 1926, 'Gomorrha. Bericht über die Luftangriffe auf Hamburg Juli/August 1943', MS. Hamburg, 1993, based on diary and letters to his mother: 25 July 1943. For statistics and background, see Groehler, *Bombenkrieg gegen Deutschland*, 106–21; also Middlebrook, *Battle of Hamburg*; Friedrich, *Der Brand*, 192–5.

46 KA 2020, parental letters to Ingeborg Schmidt, née Hey, 26–27 July 1943; Groehler, *Bombenkrieg gegen Deutschland*, 106–21; Lowe, *Inferno*, 185–232.

47 KA 4709/2, Klaus S. to mother, 1 Aug. 1943.

48 KA 4709/2, Klaus S. to mother, 30, 28 July, 10 Aug., 31 July and 1 Aug. 1943.

49 Szodrzynski, 'Die "Heimatfront"', in Forschungsstelle für Zeitgeschichte in Hamburg (ed.), *Hamburg im 'Dritten Reich'*, 656; Thiessen, *Eingebrannt ins Gedächtnis*, 46–51 and 38–9; Johe, 'Strategisches Kalkül und Wirklichkeit', in Müller and Dilks (eds), *Großbritannien und der deutsche Widerstand 1933–1944*, 222.

50 Brunswig, *Feuersturm über Hamburg*, 286–8; Blank, 'Kriegsalltag und Luftkrieg', 383–6; Kramer, *Volksgenossinnen*; Büttner, '"Gomorrha"', in Forschungsstelle für Zeitgeschichte in Hamburg (ed.), *Hamburg im 'Dritten Reich'*, 627–8.

51   Pavel Vasilievich Pavlenko, in Diercks (ed.), *Verschleppt nach Deutschland!*, 97; Brunswig, *Feuersturm über Hamburg*, 275; Police President of Hamburg, in Noakes, *Nazism*, 4, 554–7; Schröder, *Die gestohlenen Jahre*, 756–69; Gräff, *Tod im Luftangriff*, III and 116.

52   Thiessen, *Eingebrannt ins Gedächtnis*, 36–8 and 73.

53   Brunswig, *Feuersturm über Hamburg*, 295; Dröge, *Der zerredete Widerstand*, 130; KA 4709/2, Klaus S. to mother, 10 Aug. 1943.

54   Büttner, '"Gomorrha"', 627; Szodrzynski, 'Die "Heimatfront"', 647–58; Wolff-Mönckeberg, *Briefe, die sie nicht erreichten*, 160ff.; Thiessen, *Eingebrannt ins Gedächtnis*, 46–51.

55   Bajohr, 'Hamburg – der Zerfall der "Volksgemeinschaft"', in Herbert and Schildt (eds), *Kriegsende in Europa*, 323–5; Büttner, '"Gomorrha"', 629–30.

56   Seydelmann, *Gefährdete Balance*, 105–6; Bajohr, *'Aryanisation' in Hamburg*, 277–82 and 284 n. 34: a performance report of the Western Office, 8 Aug. 1944; Kulka and Jäckel (eds), *Die Juden in den geheimen NS-Stimmungsberichten*, #3624, Oberlandesgericht Bamberg, Report 2 Aug. 1943; #3680, Stimmungs- und Gerüchteerfassung, Bericht, Frankfurt/M, 11 Dec. 1943; *MadR*, 5815, 5821: 27 Sept. 1943.

57   Kulka and Jäckel (eds), *Die Juden in den geheimen NS-Stimmungsberichten*, #3644, SD Außenstelle Kitzingen, Report, 13 Sept. 1943; #3646, SD Abschnitt Linz III A 4, 24 Sept. 1943; #3648, SD Hauptaußenstelle Würzburg III A 4, 7 Sept. 1943.

58   *MadR*, 5569–70 and 5619–21: 5 and 16 Aug. 1943: 5 Aug. 1943; Nossack, 7–8 Aug. 1943, in Szodrzynski, 'Die "Heimatfront"', 655; Thiessen, *Eingebrannt ins Gedächtnis*, 45 n. 59; Allied leaflets, Kirchner, *Flugblattpropaganda im 2. Weltkrieg: Europa*, 5, 184, 196–9, 210–17, 233–6 and 273–81: 'July 1943' or 'Hamburg' used as threat of complete destruction in others; Goebbels, *Tgb*, II/10, 360, 26 Nov. 1943.

59   Szodrzynski, 'Die "Heimatfront"', 656; Thiessen, *Eingebrannt ins Gedächtnis*, 46–51; *MadR*, 5560–9, 5573–4 and 5620–1: 2, 5 and 16 Aug. 1943.

60   *MadR*, 5560–9, 5573–4 and 5620–1: 2, 5 and 16 Aug. 1943.

61   Overy, *Bombing War*, 120; Goebbels, *Tgb*, II/9, 226: 6 Aug. 1943.

62   Lothar de la Camp, circular letter, 15 Aug. 1943, in Hauschild-Thiessen (ed.), *Die Hamburger Katastrophe*, 230.

63   See Bankier, *The Germans and the Final Solution*, 148; Kulka and Jäckel (eds), *Die Juden in den geheimen NS-Stimmungsberichten*, #3592, Regierungspräsident Schwaben, Bericht für Mai 1943 ('Monatsbericht (Lagebericht)'), Augsburg, 10 June 1943; #3571, SD Außenstelle Bad Brückenau, 22 April 1943; #3647, SD Außenstelle Schweinfurt, 6 Sep. 1943; #3661, NSDAP Kreisschulungsamt Rothenburg/T., 22 Oct. 1943;

#3693, SD Außenstelle Schweinfurt, [1944]; #3573, SD Außenstelle Schweinfurt, 16 April 1943; #3648, SD Hauptaußenstelle Würzburg, 7 Sept. 1943; #3708, SD Außenstelle Bad Brückenau, [2?] April 1944; #3628, SD Außenstelle Würzburg, 3 Aug. 1943; #3718, SD Außenstelle Lohr III, 15 May 1944. For a different interpretation, reading these sources as expressing moral indifference, see Kershaw, *Popular Opinion and Political Dissent*, 369; and Longerich, *'Davon haben wir nichts gewußt!'*, 284–7.

64   Wildt, 'Gewalt gegen Juden in Deutschland 1933 bis 1939', 59–80; Wildt, *Volksgemeinschaft als Selbstermächtigung*; Blank, 'Kriegsalltag und Luftkrieg', 404; Brodie, 'For Christ and Germany', 189; *MadR*, 5449; LNRW.ARH, RW 35/09, 191: Aachen, 26 July 1943; Kulka and Jäckel (eds), *Die Juden in den geheimen NS-Stimmungsberichten*, #3722, SD-Außenstelle [Bad Brückenau] III A 4, [?] June 1944.

65   Blank, 'Kriegsalltag und Luftkrieg', 368–9; *MadR*, 4983: 22 Mar. 1943; Beck, *Under the Bombs*, 59; Goebbels, *Tgb*, II/7, 491 and 570, II/8, 358: 7 and 18 Mar. and 25 May 1943.

66   Goebbels, *Tgb*, II/7, 454, 2 Mar. 1943; Longerich, *'Davon haben wir nichts gewußt!'*, 263–7.

67   Bankier, 'German public awareness of the final solution', in Cesarani (ed.), *The Final Solution*, 222; Steinert, *Hitlers Krieg*, 143–4; 288, 305; Kershaw, *Popular Opinion and Political Dissent*, 369; Trommler, '"Deutschlands Sieg oder Untergang"', in Koebner et al. (eds), *Deutschland nach Hitler*, 214–28.

68   *MadR*, Boberach, 'Einleitung', 36.

69   Hermann Hirsch in *Stuttgarter NS-Kurier*, 2 Sept. 1943; *Der Führer*, 3 Sept. 1943; also Klaus Schickert, 'Kriegsschauplatz Israel' in the Hitler Youth journal *Wille und Macht* for Sept./Oct. 1943. Joseph Goebbels, '30 Kriegsartikel für das deutsche Volk', *Das Reich*, 26 Sept. 1943, Art. 8; reprinted in Goebbels, *Der steile Aufstieg*, 464–73.

70   Kris and Speier (eds), *German Radio Propaganda*, 210: 6 Oct. 1943; Marxen, *Das Volk und sein Gerichtshof*, 36 and 42–3; Schlüter, *Die Urteilspraxis des Volksgerichtshofs*, 175–82; Dörner, 'Heimtücke', 33, 144–5 and 233–40; Kershaw, *Popular Opinion and Political Dissent*, 367; Himmler, *Die Geheimreden*, 170–2: speech to Reichsleiters and Gauleiters, Posen, 6 Oct. 1943.

71   Schmitz and Haunfelder (eds), *Humanität und Diplomatie*, 208.

72   Schreiber, *Die italienischen Militärinternierten im deutschen Machtbereich 1943–1945*; reactions to the Armistice in Germany amongst Germans and foreign workers, see *MadR*, 5745–6 and 5764–9: 13 Sept. 1943.

12 'Holding Out'

1   For this and the following, Thiessen, *Eingebrandt ins Gedächtnis*, 61–6.

2   Blank, 'Kriegsalltag und Luftkrieg', 383–4; Thiessen, *Eingebrandt ins Gedächtnis*, 67–9.

3   Black, *Death in Berlin*, 112–22.

4   *MadR*, 4875: 1 March 1943; Black, *Death in Berlin*, 102–3.

5   Dörr, 'Wer die Zeit nicht miterlebt hat . . .', 2, 219–21: interview with Gertrud L. (b. 1910), 'Gedächtnisgottesdienst von Karl K.' (no date).

6   *MadR*, 4875: 1 Mar. 1943; Black, *Death in Berlin*, 102–6; Brodie, 'For Christ and Germany', 196–207 and 223–41 on failure of religious revival in Catholic Rhineland.

7   Thiessen, *Eingebrandt ins Gedächtnis*, 85 and 77–8; Büttner, '"Gomorrha"', 32; Zacharias-Langhans, *Hoffen auf den kommenden Christus*, 38–40.

8   Goebbels, *Tgb*, II/11, 527, and II/12, 355: 22 Mar. and 25 May 1944; Brodie, 'For Christ and Germany', 223; citing LNRW.ARH, RW 34/03, 23.

9   Brodie, 'For Christ and Germany', 183–4 and 221.

10   Goebbels, *Tgb*, II/10, 360: 26 Nov. 1943; Groehler, *Bombenkrieg gegen Deutschland*, 183; Vassiltchikov, *Berlin Diaries, 1940–1945*, 105–9: 23 Nov. 1943; Kirchner, *Flugblattpropaganda im 2. Weltkrieg*, 196–9, 210–17, 233–6 and 273–81.

11   Handelsanstalt Berlin-Wedding, cited in Arbeitsgruppe Pädagogisches Museum (ed.), *Heil Hitler, Herr Lehrer*, 206–7.

12   MfK–FA, 3.2002.0279, Liselotte Purper to Kurt Orgel and Kurt Orgel to Liselotte Purper, 23 Nov. 1943.

13   MfK–FA, 3.2002.0279, Liselotte Purper to Kurt Orgel, 25 Nov. 1943 and 11 Mar. 1944.

14   MfK–FA, 3.2002.0279, Kurt Orgel to Liselotte Purper, 10 Dec. 1943.

15   Groehler, *Bombenkrieg gegen Deutschland*, 183; Middlebrook, *The Berlin Raids*; Moorhouse, *Berlin at War*, 321–5.

16   Kardorff, *Berliner Aufzeichnungen*, 129–34: 25–27 Nov. 1943. On her work as a journalist, editing the feuilleton of the *DAZ*, see Frei and Schmitz, *Journalismus im Dritten Reich*, 150–4. Kardorff, *Berliner Aufzeichnungen*, 155–9: 1 Feb. 1944.

17   Ibid., 160–2 and 181: 3 and 10 Feb. and 20 April 1944.

18   MfK–FA, 3.2002.0279, Liselotte Purper, 4 and 16 Dec. 1943; Kurt Orgel, 4 Dec. 1944.

19   MfK–FA, 3.2002.0279, Liselotte to Kurt Orgel, 14 and 24 Mar. 1944.

20   Ibid.

21   Groehler, *Bombenkrieg gegen Deutschland*, 190–5; Webster and Frankland, *The Strategic Air Offensive against Germany*, 2, 198–211, and 3, 9–41;

Middlebrook and Everitt (eds), *The Bomber Command War Diaries*, Dec. 1943–Jan. 1944.

22   MfK–FA, 3.2002.0279, Liselotte Purper to Kurt Orgel, 25 Feb. 1944.

23   Overy, *Why the Allies Won*, 90–7 and 129; Müller, *Der Bombenkrieg*, 140–5; Hastings, *Bomber Command*, 308 and 348.

24   Overy, *Bombing War*, 338–55; Webster and Frankland, *The Strategic Air Offensive against Germany*, 2, 190 and 196: Harris to Churchill, 3 Nov. 1943; Hastings, *Bomber Command*, 258–61; Overy, *Bombing War*, 338–41.

25   Overy, *Bombing War*, 357–77; Hastings, *Bomber Command*, 341–8 and 356; Webster and Frankland, *The Strategic Air Offensive against Germany*, 2, 193.

26   Görtemaker, *Ein deutsches Leben*, 199–203; Goebbels, 'Das Leben geht weiter', *Das Reich*, 16 April 1944; Rudolf Sparing, 'Ich lebe in Berlin. Ein Bericht', *Das Reich*, 30 July 1944; Frei and Schmitz, *Journalismus im Dritten Reich*, 110.

27   Baldoli, 'Spring 1943', *History Workshop Journal*, 72 (2011), 181–9; also Baldoli and Fincardi, 'Italian society under Anglo-American bombs', *Historical Journal* 52: 4 (2009); Baldoli et al. (eds), *Bombing, States and Peoples in Western Europe 1940–1945*; Baldoli and Knapp, *Forgotten Blitzes*; Gribaudi, *Guerra totale*.

28   Kramer, 'Mobilisierung für die "Heimatfront"', in Steinbacher (ed.), *Volksgenossinnen*, 69–92; Maubach, 'Expansion weiblicher Hilfe', in Steinbacher (ed.), *Volksgenossinnen*, 93–111; for a more downbeat view, Stephenson, *Hitler's Home Front*, 225. She was the first female auxiliary in Nuremberg to be awarded the medal.

29   Lacey, *Feminine Frequencies*, 205–6; Kramer, *Volksgenossinnen an der Heimatfront*.

30   Süß, *Death from the Skies*, 362–7.

31   Kock, 'Der Führer sorgt für unsere Kinder . . .', 213–25 and 253–5; Süß, *Der 'Völkskörper' im Krieg*, 279; Kramer, *Volksgenossinnen an der Heimatfront*, 259–80; Krause, *Flucht vor dem Bombenkrieg*, 103–4.

32   Kramer, *Volksgenossinnen an der Heimatfront*, 283–6; Krause, *Flucht vor dem Bombenkrieg*, 182; for older estimates of 5 million evacuees, Bundesministerium für Vertriebene, Flüchtlinge und Kriegsgeschädigte (ed.), *Dokumente deutscher Kriegsschäden: Evakuierte, Kriegssachgeschädigte, Währungsgeschädigte*, Bonn, 1958, 1, 103–5; *United States Strategic Bombing Survey: The Effects of Strategic Bombing on German Morale*, 1, Washington DC, 1947, 10.

33   MadR, 5643–6: 19 Aug. 1943; Kramer, *Volksgenossinnen an der Heimatfront*, 282: incident from June 1943.

34   *United States Strategic Bombing Survey*, 2, 72; Kramer, *Volksgenossinnen*

an der Heimatfront, 282–4; *MadR*, 5828: 30 Sept. 1943; Kock, '*Der Führer sorgt für unsere Kinder . . .*', 213–25 and 253–5; Brodie, 'For Christ and Germany', 244–7: Albert Lenné report, 28 July 1943; Sollbach, *Heimat Ade!*, 30.

35 KA 2808/1, Renate S., b. 1931, 'Ein Schloß voll kleiner Mädchen: Erinnerungen an die Kinderlandverschickung 1943–1945', MS, 2–16.

36 KA 1997, Werner K., 26 and 29 Nov. 1943.

37 Klee, *Im 'Luftschutzkeller des Reiches'*, 117–21; Mertens, 'NS-Kirchenpolitik im Krieg', in Hummel and Kösters (eds), *Kirchen im Krieg*, 245–6; Sollbach, *Heimat Ade!*, 52 n. 180.

38 Erwin Ebeling, Inge Reininghaus and Gisela Schwartz (née Vedder), testimony in Sollbach, *Heimat Ade!*, 13, 41, 135, 144–5 and 154–9; *MadR*, 5643–6: 19 Aug. 1943.

39 Kramer, *Volksgenossinnen an der Heimatfront*, 290; Sollbach, *Heimat Ade!*, 52 n. 180, citing report by the rector of a school from Hagen, 16 Sep. 1943, StadtA HA, 11319.

40 Sollbach, *Heimat Ade!*, 13 and 135 for Inge Reininghaus's account, 2 April 1997; Kundrus, *Kriegerfrauen*, 261 and 271; Stephenson '"Emancipation" and its problems', 358–60; Szepansky (ed.), *Blitzmädel, Heldenmutter, Kriegerwitwe*; Cologne Catholic Church visit to Niederdonau (summer 1944) and to Buchen (June 1945), in Kramer, *Volksgenossinnen an der Heimatfront*, 291 and 293–5; *MadR*, 5475–81 and 5907–14: 15 July 1943 and 21 Oct. 1943.

41 Kramer, *Volksgenossinnen an der Heimatfront*, 290–1, report of visit to women and children for the Rhineland, in Württemburg Oberland, 29 Oct. 1943 and Baden, report of 4 Aug. 1945 'Schwierigkeiten, Bitterkeiten, Lieblosigkeiten und Verständnislosigkeiten auf beiden Seiten auszuräumen.' Seelsorgehelferin, Odenwald, report of Feb. 1944. Brodie, 'For Christ and Germany', 244–76.

42 Hanna R. in Kramer, *Volksgenossinnen an der Heimatfront*, 303–4; Brodie, 'For Christ and Germany', 244–76.

43 *MadR*, 5720–4: 6 Sept. 1943; Kramer, *Volksgenossinnen an der Heimatfront*, 287–9; Stephenson, '"Emancipation" and its problems', 358–60.

44 Kramer, *Volksgenossinnen an der Heimatfront*, 288–9; Krause, *Flucht vor dem Bombenkrieg*, 128–30; Kreidler, *Die Eisenbahnen im Machtbereich der Achsenmächte*, 191–213.

45 Krause, *Flucht vor dem Bombenkrieg*, 117; *Stuttgarter NS-Kurier*, 22 Aug. 1944; Krause, *Flucht vor dem Bombenkrieg*, 118–21.

46 Kundrus, *Kriegerfrauen*, 245–321.

47 Kock, '*Der Führer sorgt für unsere Kinder . . .*', 218–19, 223–5, 242–4 and 255; Sollbach, *Heimat Ade!*, 11–12; *MadR*, 5827: 30 Sept. 1943; Christa G. Nauen, in Gröschner (ed.), *Ich schlug meiner Mutter die brennenden Funken*

ab, 353–4; numbers returning, Goebbels, *Tgb*, II/10, 506–19: 20 Dec. 1943.

48   *MadR*, 6029–31: 18 Nov. 1943; Sollbach, *Heimat Ade!*, 29.

49   Krause, *Flucht vor dem Bombenkrieg*, 125–6; Klee, *Im 'Luftschutzkeller des Reiches'*, 304; Kramer, *Volksgenossinnen an der Heimatfront*, 279 and 283.

50   Kramer, *Volksgenossinnen an der Heimatfront*, 273; Werner, *'Bleib übrig'*, 126–7, 198–9 and 268–74; Torrie, *'For their own Good'*, 94–127.

51   Krause, *Flucht vor dem Bombenkrieg*, 128–9: BA, R 22/2328, 'Bericht des Gauleiters Josef Grohé über die Luftangriffe der letzten Wochen'; Kramer, *Volksgenossinnen an der Heimatfront*, 273.

52   Kreidler, *Die Eisenbahnen im Machtbereich der Achsenmächte*, 316; Krause, *Flucht vor dem Bombenkrieg*, 132–4, 177–8.

53   'Aktuelle Fragen des Filmtheaterbesuchs', *Film-Kurier*, 25 July 1944, cited in Ross, *Media and the Making of Modern Germany*, 371.

54   Trümpi, *Politisierte Orchester*, 255–9. http://www.wienerphilharmoniker. at/new-years-concert/history: special historical commission of Fritz Trümpi, Oliver Rathkolb and Bernadette Mayrhofer appointed in 2013 by the Vienna Philharmonic to investigate the orchestra's history under the Third Reich.

55   De Boor, *Tagebuchblätter*, 179: 28 April 1944; Ross, *Media and the Making of Modern Germany*, 371–2; *MadR*, 5726–7: 9 Sept. 1943; Kundrus, 'Totale Unterhaltung?', 106–7.

56   *MadR*, 4766–7: 8 Feb. 1943; Strobl, *The Swastika and the Stage*, 212–15.

57   Kardorff, *Berliner Aufzeichnungen*, 183: 29 April 1944; Strobl, *The Swastika and the Stage*, 195–6.

58   Strobl, *The Swastika and the Stage*, 188–90; Kundrus, 'Totale Unterhaltung?', 147; Daiber, *Schaufenster der Diktatur*, 243.

59   Strobl, *The Swastika and the Stage*, 189–90.

60   Fritzsche, *Life and Death in the Third Reich*, 13–14.

61   Rilke, *Duineser Elegien*; Hoeniger, 'Symbolism and pattern in Rilke's Duino Elegies', 271–83; Koch, 'Rilke und Hölderlin', 91–102; Zeller and Brüggemann (eds), *Klassiker in finsteren Zeiten*, 2, 92–3: Georg Seidler had rearranged the text for performance, drawing on the two later and fragmentary versions.

62   Friedrich Hölderlin, 1798, set by Johannes Brahms (1833–97), 'Hyperions Schicksalslied', op. 54 (1868), published 1871; Trans. Emily Ezust as 'Hyperion's song of Fate' © 1995, (re)printed on this website with kind permission: http://www.recmusic.org/lieder/get_text.html?TextId=8134; Brahms, 'Hyperions Schicksalslied', op. 54; Zeller and Brüggemann (eds), *Klassiker in finsteren Zeiten*, 2, Marbach, 1983, 99: Günther Dahms to Wolfgang Hermann, 10 June 1943.

63   De Boor, *Tagebuchblätter*, 144: mid-June 1943; Kardorff, *Berliner Aufzeichnungen*, 186–7: 10 May 1944; Fritzsche, *Life and Death in the Third Reich*, 297.

64   Daughter in prison, de Boor, *Tagebuchblätter*, 164–6, 167, 170–3, 178–81, 151, 161, 160, 154, 158, 170, 189, 175, 159, 163, 175, 145, 192 and 167: 22 Dec. 1943–early Jan. 1944; 16–18 Jan., 20 Feb., 25–29 Feb., 26–28 April and 7–8 May 1944; 9–11 Aug., 13 Dec., 21 Nov., end Oct. 1943, 15–16 Feb., 20 Feb. and 14–19 July 1944; 2 April 1944 and 1 Nov. 1943; 18 Dec. 1943 and 19 Mar. 1944; 22 June 1943 and 7 Aug. 1944 (Jewish deportations); 8–15 Jan. 1944 (Jünger); Hoffmann, *Stauffenberg*, esp. chapters 2 and 8; Jens (ed.), *Hans Scholl, Sophie Scholl*, 251–3: Sophie Scholl to Fritz Hartnagel, 28 Oct. 1942.

65   Jünger, *Der Kampf als inneres Erlebnis*, rev. edn, 1933, 11 and 8; see also Weisbrod, 'Military violence and male fundamentalism', 69–94.

66   Reese, *Mir selber seltsam fremd*, 103.

67   Ibid., 135–6.

68   Ibid., 129–32.

69   Ibid., 147, 148–9; also 232–3.

70   Weisbrod, 'Military violence and male fundamentalism', 77; Stern, *Ernst Jünger*, 26; Reese, *Mir selber seltsam fremd*, 221 and 242–3; for a different translation, see Fritzsche, *Life and Death in the Third Reich*, 275.

71   Reese, *Mir selber seltsam fremd*, 209–10, 245, 217 and 247; Weisbrod, 'Military violence and male fundamentalism', 84.

72   See Klemperer, *To the Bitter End*, 289 and 291: 12 and 19 Mar. 1944, and his *The Language of the Third Reich*, 172–81; Stern, 'Antagonistic memories', in Passerini (ed.), *Memory and Totalitarianism*, 26; Schottländer, *Trotz allem ein Deutscher*, 48ff.

73   Kulka and Jäckel, *Die Juden in den geheimen NS-Stimmungsberichten*, #3582, NSDAP Ortsgruppe Nürnberg-Maxfeld, 9 April 1943; #3719, SD Außenstelle Würzburg III C 4, 8 May 1944; BA, R55, 571/46: Kurt L., 18 May 1944; R55, 571/145: 4 June 1944, Irma J.; BA, R55, 571/123–6, Georg R., 1 June 1944; BA, R55, 571/240: K. von N; Steinert, *Hitlers Krieg und die Deutschen*, 260–1.

13 Borrowed Time

1   Reese, *Mir selber seltsam fremd*, ed. Schmitz, 7, 9, 196, 211, 197.

2   Weinberg, *A World at Arms*, 667–8; Erickson, *The Road to Berlin*, 2, 225.

3   *MadR*, 6523: 11 May 1944; Danimann, *Flüsterwitze und Spottgedichte unterm Hakenkreuz*, 84–6.

4   *MadR*, 6419–22, 6511, 6521–5, 6535–7, 6551–3, 6563–4, 6571–2: 16 Mar., 4, 11, 18 and 25 May, 1 and 8 June 1944; Steinert, *Hitlers Krieg und die Deutschen*, 447–52.

5   *MadR*, 6481–8: 13 April 1944.

6   MfK–FA, 3.2002.0279, Kurt to Liselotte, 26 Nov. 1944; Liselotte to Kurt, 11 Nov. 1944; MfK–FA, 3.2002.0279, Liselotte Purper to Kurt Orgel, 31 Mar. 1944.

7   Kramer, *Volksgenossinnen an der Heimatfront*, 291, citing Cologne and Freiburg Church reports on evacuees; *MadR*, 6025–6 and 6481–8: 18 Nov. 1943 and 13 April 1944.

8   Hammer and Nieden, '*Sehr selten habe ich geweint*', 202–22: Heinz B. to Gisela, 27 Oct. 1943. Hammer and Nieden, '*Sehr selten habe ich geweint*', 205–6: Heinz B. to Gisela, 4 Jan. 1944.

9   MfK–FA, 3.2002.0279, Kurt Orgel to Liselotte Purper, 1 May 1944.

10   Inge Marszolek, '"Ich möchte Dich zu gern mal in Uniform sehen"', 56–8.

11   UV, SF/NL 75 II, Hans H. to Maria Kundera, 6 Feb. and 16 Jan. 1944.

12   UV, SF/NL 75 II, Maria Kundera to Hans H., 31 July 1944.

13   Ibid, Hans H. to Maria Kundera, 13 April 1944; Maria to Hans, 6 Aug. 1944; Heribert Artinger, 'Auswertung der Feldpostbriefe des Jahres 1944 von Hans H. an Maria Kundera sowie von Maria Kundera an Hans H.', University of Vienna, Geschichte, 2009, 9–10 and 18–19.

14   UV, SF/NL 75 II, Hans H. to Maria Kundera, 16 Jan., 23 July and 28 Mar. 1944; Hans H. to Maria Kundera, 7 and 28 Mar., 13 and 19 April, 31 Jan., 19 Mar., 30 and 31 May, 1, 2, 4, 5 and 7 June 1944.

15   Irrgang, *Leutnant der Wehrmacht*, 173: letter to family, n.d.; Gordon, 'Ist Gott Französisch?'; Torrie, '"Our rear area probably lived too well"'.

16   Reese, *Mir selber seltsam fremd*, 230.

17   Irrgang, *Leutnant der Wehrmacht*, 173: Stölten to parents, 17 May 1944.

18   Weinberg, *A World at Arms*, 676–89; Beevor, *D-Day: The Battle for Normandy*.

19   Hastings, *Overlord*; Forty, *Villers-Bocage*.

20   Irrgang, *Leutnant der Wehrmacht*, 178, n. 54: Wilhelm Stölten to Victor Meyer-Eckhardt, 9 July 1944.

21   Ibid., letter to family, 2 July 1944; Weinberg, *A World at Arms*, 682–95.

22   Ibid., 179–80: to parents, 8 July 1944.

23   Ibid., 180: to Dorothee Ehrensberger, 12 Aug. 1944.

24   Ibid., 180–3: to Dorothee Ehrensberger, n.d. (early–mid-Aug. 1944), 24 and 26 July 1944.

25   Ibid., 182–92.

26   Hölderlin, *Hyperion*, 185; Irrgang, *Leutnant der Wehrmacht*, 218: to Dorothee Ehrensberger, 12 Aug. 1944; Latzel, *Deutsche Soldaten*; Baird, *To Die for Germany*; Behrenbeck, *Der Kult um die toten Helden*.

27   Irrgang, *Leutnant der Wehrmacht*, 189.

28   Glantz and House, *When Titans Clashed*, 201–10; Grenkevich, *The Soviet Partisan Movement*, 257–62; Gerlach, *Kalkulierte Morde*, 1010–35 and 1085–9; Frieser, 'Zusammenbruch im Osten'; Weinberg, *A World at Arms*, 703–9.

29   Beevor and Vinogradova (eds), *A Writer at War*, 273.

30   Reese, *Mir selber seltsam fremd*, 249; losses, Kunz, *Wehrmacht und Niederlage*, 152–3; Overmans, *Deutsche militärische Verluste*, 277–9.

31   Woman soldier interviewed by Swetlana Alexijewitsch, 'Der Mensch zählt mehr als der Krieg', 45.

32   Borodziej, *The Warsaw Uprising*; Davies, *Rising '44*.

33   Hosenfeld, *'Ich versuche jeden zu retten'*, 822–4: letters to wife and children, 4 and 6 Aug. 1944.

34   Borodziej, *The Warsaw Uprising of 1944*, 79–82; Hosenfeld, *'Ich versuche jeden zu retten'*, 824: diary, 8 Aug. 1944.

35   Hosenfeld, *'Ich versuche jeden zu retten'*, 824–7: Hosenfeld letters and diary, 8–9 Aug. 1944.

36   Irrgang, *Leutnant der Wehrmacht*, 192 n. 109 and n. 204: Peter to Dorothee Ehrensberger, n.d. (late July 1944), 15 and 21 Aug. 1944; 'Gespräch', Le Mans, July 1944; ibid., 205: Stölten to parents, 7 Sept. 1944.

37   Ibid., 211–12: Stölten to father, 30 Aug. 1944.

38   Borodziej, *The Warsaw Uprising of 1944*, 78–80 and 97–8; Bishop, *SS: Hitler's Foreign Divisions*.

39   Irrgang, *Leutnant der Wehrmacht*, 210–14.

40   Ibid., 210: Stölten to Dorothee Ehrensberger, 28–29 Sept. 1944.

41   Hosenfeld, *'Ich versuche jeden zu retten'*, 824–34: Hosenfeld letters and diary, 8–12 and 23 Aug. 1944.

42   Irrgang, *Leutnant der Wehrmacht*, 207–9: Stölten to Dorothee Ehrensberger, 16 Sept. and 30 Aug. 1944; Satire, 2–3, and to family 1 Sept.

43   Borodziej, *The Warsaw Uprising of 1944*, 107–28; Davies, *Rising '44*, 400 and 427.

44   Hosenfeld, *'Ich versuche jeden zu retten'*, 856–7: 5 Oct. 1944.

45   Irrgang, *Leutnant der Wehrmacht*, 216–21 and 230: Peter Stölten to Dorothee Ehrensberger, 5 and 6 Oct. and 12 Aug. 1944; 18 Oct. 1944.

46   Hosenfeld, *'Ich versuche jeden zu retten'*, 862–3: 22 Oct. 1944.

47   Ibid., 849 and 856–73: 20 Sept., 5 Oct.–17 Nov. 1944; Szpilman, *The Pianist*, 177–82.

48   Weinberg, *A World at Arms*, 690–3; Beevor, *D-Day*.

49 UV, SF/NL 75 II, Hans H. to Maria Kundera, 16 Aug. 1944; Kuby, *Nur noch rauchende Trümmer*.

50 Kleindienst (ed.), *Sei tausendmal gegrüßt*: Guicking, diary extracts, 15–24 Aug. 1944.

51 Eisenhower, *Crusade in Europe*, 279; Weinberg, *A World at Arms*, 694–5.

52 Kleindienst (ed.), *Sei tausendmal gegrüßt*: Ernst Guicking, diary extracts, 26 Aug.–2 Sept. 1944.

53 Ibid., Ernst Guicking, diary extracts, 13 Sept. 1944.

54 Schumann et al., *Deutschland im Zweiten Weltkrieg*, 6, 105–12.

55 Kershaw, *The End*, 61–2 and 72–3: BA, R55/601, 104, Weekly propaganda report: 4 Sept. 1944.

56 Ibid., 62–74; *MadR*, 6697–8: 10 Aug. 1944; BA, R55/623, 56–9: Wochenübersicht über Zuschriften zum totalen Kriegseinsatz, 28 Aug. 1944.

57 Kershaw, *The End*, 69–70.

14 Digging In

1 Kershaw, *The End*, 88–90; Schumann et al., *Deutschland im Zweiten Weltkrieg*, 6, 236; Nolzen, 'Die NSDAP, der Krieg und die deutsche Gesellschaft', *DRZW*, 9/1 (2004), 182; Strobl, *The Swastika and the Stage*, 220–5.

2 Hubatsch (ed.), *Hitlers Weisungen*, 243–50: 8 Mar. 1944.

3 Kleindienst (ed.), *Sei tausendmal gegrüßt*: Irene to Ernst Guicking, 1 and 7 Sept. 1944.

4 Hoffmann, *The History of the German Resistance, 1933–1945*; Moorhouse, *Killing Hitler*; Ueberschär (ed.), *Der 20. Juli 1944*.

5 Kramarz, *Claus Graf Stauffenberg*, 201; Hoffmann, *Stauffenberg*, 243; Kershaw, *Hitler*, 2, 655–84.

6 Hitler, *Reden und Proklamationen*, 2127–9: 21 July 1944; *Manchester Guardian*, 21 July 1944.

7 Irrgang, *Leutnant der Wehrmacht*, 82: Wilhelm to Peter Stölten and Wilhelm Stölten, diary: 21 July 1944; Oberlandesgericht-Präsident Nürnberg, 1 Aug. 1944, in Steinert, *Hitlers Krieg und die Deutschen*, 477; SD report, 21 July 1944: *Spiegelbild einer Verschwörung*, 1–11: 21–24 July 1944.

8 Steinert, *Hitlers Krieg und die Deutschen*, 476–82; Kershaw, *The End*, 29–34; Breloer (ed.), *Mein Tagebuch*, 334; Feldpostprüfstelle of Panzer AOK. 3, 2 Sept. 1944, in Buchbender and Sterz (eds), *Das andere Gesicht des Krieges*, 20–3; BA, R55/601, 54–63 and 69–70, Propaganda Ministry

weekly reports, 24 July and 7 Aug. 1944; Gurfein and Janowitz, 'Trends in Wehrmacht morale', 81.

9   Steinert, *Hitlers Krieg und die Deutschen*, 482–3; Kershaw, *Hitler*, 2, 687–8; Ley, *Der Angriff*, 23 July 1944; Smelser, *Robert Ley*, 291; Oven, *Finale Furioso*, 505; Messerschmidt, 'Die Wehrmacht', in Volkmann (ed.), *Ende des Dritten Reiches – Ende des Zweiten Weltkrieges*, 240–1; Conze et al., *Das Amt und die Vergangenheit*, 305–9.

10   Kershaw, *The End*, 33–4 and 44–51; Clark, 'Johannes Blaskowitz', in Smelser and Syring (eds), *Die Militärelite des Dritten Reiches*, 28–49.

11   Lumans, *Latvia in World War II*, 252–8; Loeffel, 'Soldiers and terror', 514–30; Loeffel, *Family Punishment in Nazi Germany*.

12   Loeffel, 'Soldiers and terror'; IFZ-Archiv Munich, NOKW–535.

13   Kershaw, *The End*, 20–6 and 35–43.

14   Kunz, *Wehrmacht und Niederlage*, 156–89; female recruitment: Absolon, *Die Wehrmacht im Dritten Reich*, 6, 28; Morgan, *Weiblicher Arbeitsdienst*, 423; Nolzen, 'Die NSDAP, der Krieg und die deutsche Gesellschaft'; Kershaw, *The End*, 20–6 and 35–44; 1920s discussion, Mulligan, *The Creation of the Modern German Army*.

15   Yelton, *Hitler's Volkssturm*, 120–1, 105–18.

16   Maubach, 'Expansion weiblicher Hilfe', in Steinbacher (ed.), *Volksgenossinnen*, 93–111; Müller, *Der Bombenkrieg*, 140.

17   BA, NS 19/4015: Himmler to commanders of military districts and schools, 21 Sept. 1944, in Kunz, *Wehrmacht und Niederlage*, 167; Geyer, 'Endkampf 1918 and 1945', in Lüdtke and Weisbrod (eds), *No Man's Land of Violence*, 35–67.

18   Stehkämper in Steinhoff et al., *Voices from the Third Reich*, 362; BA, R55/601, 160: Propaganda report, 9 Oct. 1944; Steinert, *Hitlers Krieg und die Deutschen*, 506; Klönne, *Gegen den Strom*, 143–4; Beevor, *Berlin: The Downfall*, 181; also KA 1997, Werner K., '20 Monate Luftwaffenhelfer', 144–5 and 150: 21 and 30 Jan. 1945; similar transition in KA 920, Walter S., 'Mein Tagebuch', 15 Sept. and 3 Nov. 1944.

19   Orłowski and Schneider (eds), *'Erschießen will ich nicht!'*, 50, 318 and 321: 26 Oct. 1939, 6 Oct. and 6 Nov. 1944.

20   Irrgang, *Leutnant der Wehrmacht*, 233: Peter to Margarethe Stölten, 19 Nov., and to Dorothee Ehrensberger, 24 Nov. 1944.

21   BA, NS 19/4017, Heinrich Himmler, 3 Nov. 1944, cited in Kunz, *Wehrmacht und Niederlage*, 143; Lakowski, 'Der Zusammenbruch der deutschen Verteidigung zwischen Ostsee und Karpaten', 496–501; Noble, *Nazi Rule and the Soviet Offensive in Eastern Germany*, 152.

22   Weinberg, *A World at Arms*, 690–702; 760–3.

23   Yelton, *Hitler's Volkssturm*, 120–1; Müller, *Der letzte deutsche Krieg*, 285.

24   Zagovec, 'Gespräche mit der "Volksgemeinschaft"', 334–7.

25   Ibid., 347–9, and 289, citing Mann, *Der Wendepunkt*, 649; Kershaw, *The End*, 70–1; on Dicks, see Pick, *The Pursuit of the Nazi Mind*, 2012.

26   Overmans, *Deutsche militärische Verluste*, 238–43 and 277–83.

27   Kershaw, *The End*, 76–88.

28   Verdict, Duisburg Provincial Court, 14 June 1950 in *Justiz und NS-Verbrechen*, 6, no. 219; cited in Herbert, *Hitler's Foreign Workers*, 362; Kardorff, *Berliner Aufzeichnungen*, 264–5: 30 Nov. 1944.

29   MfK–FA, 3.2002.0279, Liselotte Purper, 'Berlin bleibt Berlin', 26 Sept. 1944; MfK–FA, 3.2002.0279, Liselotte to Kurt, 23 May 1944.

30   Joachim Fernau, 'Das Geheimnis der letzten Kriegsphase', *VB*, 30 Aug. 1944; Kardorff, *Berliner Aufzeichnungen*, 233: 5 Sept. 1944; Klemperer, *To the Bitter End*, 2, 337: 1 Sep. 1944.

31   MfK–FA, 3.2002.0279, Kurt Orgel to Liselotte Purper, 30 July and 30 Sept. 1944; Liselotte Purper to Kurt Orgel, 14 Oct. 1944.

32   Irrgang, *Leutnant der Wehrmacht*, 228–31: Peter Stölten to Dorothee Ehrensberger and to parents, 18, 20/23 and 25 Oct., 11 Nov. and 16 Sept. 1944.

33   Ibid., 235–6: Stölten, 19 Dec. 1944; 1 Jan. 1945; to Dorothee, 21/22 Dec. 1944; to Udo, 1 Jan. 1945.

34   Boor, *Tagebuchblätter*, 204–5, 202, and 208: 1 Nov., 29 and 14 Oct., 25 Nov. 1944.

35   Boor, *Tagebuchblätter*, 209 and 217: 25 Nov. and 28 Dec. 1944.

36   Kleindienst (ed.), *Sei tausendmal gegrüßt*: Irene to Ernst Guicking, 1 Aug. 1944; 7, 8 and 13 Dec. 1944.

37   Orłowski and Schneider (eds), *'Erschießen will ich nicht!'*, 327: 12 Dec. 1944, quoting letter from Gretel of 21 Nov. 1944; 328: 25 Dec. 1944.

38   MfK–FA, 3.2002.0279, Liselotte Purper to Kurt Orgel, 8 Dec. 1944.

39   Friedrich, *Der Brand*, 334–40.

40   Groehler, *Bombenkrieg gegen Deutschland*, 378–81.

41   Ibid., 316–20, for estimates of bombing dead, which are based on revising upwards the numbers reported immediately by the police in proportion to test cases. All statistics in these areas are tentative and still the subject of political controversy.

42   Steinert, *Hitlers Krieg und die Deutschen*, 524 and 526: Propaganda report, 21 Nov. 1944; Oberlandesgerichts-Präsident Düsseldorf, 29 Nov. 1944; Darmstadt, 1 Dec. 1944; Propaganda report, 5 Dec. 1944; Dabrowski, *Lippisch P13a and Experimental DM-1*; Birkenfeld, *Der synthetische Treibstoff*; Boog, 'Strategische Luftkrieg in Europa

und Reichsluftverteidigung'; Boog, *Die deutsche Luftwaffenführung 1935–1945*, 30.

43 Fisch, *Nemmersdorf, Oktober 1944*; Fisch, 'Nemmersdorf 1944', in Ueberschär (ed.), *Orte des Grauens*, 155–67; Fisch, 'Nemmersdorf 1944', 105–114.

44 Werner Kreipe, diary, 23 Oct. 1944, cited in Jung, *Die Ardennenoffensive 1944/45*, 227; *VB*, 1 Nov. 1944; *Die Deutsche Wochenschau*, Nr. 739, 2 Nov. 1944; Fisch, *Nemmersdorf*; Zeidler, *Kriegsende im Osten*, 150.

45 Kershaw, *The End*, 119, citing Reinhard, diary, 26 Oct. 1944; Steinert, *Hitlers Krieg und die Deutschen*, 523.

46 Kulka and Jäckel (eds), *Die Juden in den geheimen NS-Stimmungsberichten*, 546: SD Stuttgart, 6 Nov. 1944; Noakes (ed.), *Nazism*, 4, 652.

47 Semmler, *Goebbels*, 163–4, diary 2 Nov. 1944; Noakes (ed.), *Nazism*, 4, 496, 640 and 652, citing Stuttgart SD, 6 Nov. 1944; Wette et al. (eds), *Das letzte halbe Jahr*, 164: *Sondereinsatz Berlin*, 20–26 Nov. 1944.

48 Erickson, *Road to Berlin*, 238–9; Wiśniewska and Rajca, *Majdanek*; Noakes and Pridham (eds), *Nazism*, 3, 599–600; Bankier, *The Germans and the Final Solution*, 114.

49 Zeidler, *Kriegsende im Osten*, 139–40: Yuri Uspensky, 24 Jan. 1945.

50 Kardorff, *Berliner Aufzeichnungen*, 272: 27 Dec. 1944; Vrba and Wetzler report in Dawidowicz, *A Holocaust Reader*, 110–19.

51 Bankier, 'German public awareness of the final solution', in Cesarani (ed.), *The Final Solution*, 114, 215–27.

52 BA, R55/578, Bl 210, Hans Humel to Goebbels, 25 Oct. 1944; BA, R 55/577, 3 Dec. 1944: Parteigenosse, Dr A.D.B., Hamburg. Similar examples: BA, R55/577, 35–8, Friedrich Schauer, Rechtsanwalt am Landgericht, Freiburg im Breisgau, to Goebbels, 10 Nov. and 15 Dec. 1944; BA, R55/577, 89, Anon., 24 Nov. 1944 (also underlined in the Propaganda Ministry).

53 Steinert, *Hitlers Krieg und die Deutschen*, 511–27; Kunz, *Wehrmacht und Niederlage*, 250–3, for reports on military morale; Kleindienst (ed.), *Sei tausendmal gegrüßt*: Irene to Ernst Guicking, 15 and 17 Dec. 1944; Ernst to Irene, 29 Dec. 1944.

54 Kershaw, *The End*, 159; Goebbels, *Tgb*, II/14, 429, 433, 438–9, 445 and 450: 17–20 Dec. 1944; Oven, *Finale Furioso*, 526–9: 17 and 20 Dec. 1944; Steinert, *Hitlers Krieg und die Deutschen*, 527–31 and 575; Henke, *Die amerikanische Besetzung Deutschlands*, 316–17.

55 MfK–FA, 3.2002.0279, Kurt Orgel to Liselotte Purper: 18 Dec. 1944; Kleindienst (ed.), *Sei tausendmal gegrüßt*: Ernst to Irene Guicking, 21 Dec. 1944; Steinert, *Hitlers Krieg und die Deutschen*, 529–30.

56 Kershaw, *Hitler*, 2, 741–3; Weinberg, *A World at Arms*, 765–71.

57 Schumann et al., *Deutschland im Zweiten Weltkrieg*, 6, 133 and 137; Kunz, *Wehrmacht und Niederlage*, 71; Speer, *Erinnerungen*, 425; Kershaw, *The End*, 160.

58 Kershaw, *The End*, 128–39 and 155–61; Speer, *Erinnerungen*, 423; Schumann et al., *Deutschland im Zweiten Weltkrieg*, 6, 125.

59 Kershaw, *The End*, 159–60; Goebbels, *Tgb*, II/14, 486: 29 Dec. 1944; Wette et al. (eds), *Das letzte halbe Jahr*, 183–4: 18–24 Dec. 1944; Henke, *Die amerikanische Besetzung Deutschlands*, 316–17.

60 Clausewitz, *Historical and Political Writings*, 290; 1944 reading, Baldwin, 'Clausewitz in Nazi Germany', 10.

61 Hitler, *Reden und Proklamationen*, 2180–4: 31 Dec. 1944; Kershaw, *Hitler*, 2, 746; Oven, *Finale Furioso*, 537–8; Reisert, 'O Deutschland hoch in Ehren', song written by Ludwig Bauer (1859).

62 MfK–FA, 3.2002.0279, Kurt Orgel to Liselotte Purper, 1 Jan. 1945; Steinert, *Hitlers Krieg und die Deutschen*, 532–3.

63 Boor, *Tagebuchblätter*, 218.

64 Kleindienst (ed.), *Sei tausendmal gegrüßt*: Ernst to Irene Guicking, 22 Dec. 1944; diary, 26 and 31 Dec. 1945.

15 *Collapse*

1 Henke, *Die amerikanische Besetzung Deutschlands*; Zimmermann, 'Die Eroberung und Besetzung des deutschen Reiches', *DRZW*, 10/1 (2008), 277–435; Boog, 'Die Strategische Bomberoffensive der Alliierten'; Kunz, *Wehrmacht und Niederlage*; Kershaw, *Hitler*, 2, 768, 776 and 791–2; Trevor-Roper, *The Last Days of Hitler*, 87–9.

2 Overmans, *Deutsche militärische Verluste*, 238–43 and 279.

3 Hosenfeld, 'Ich versuche jeden zu retten', 885–8: 26, 27 and 30 Dec. 1944 and 7 Jan. 1945.

4 Military accounts of campaign: Lakowski, 'Der Zusammenbruch der deutschen Verteidigung'; Erickson, *The Road to Berlin*, 450, 457–8, 462, 471–2; Glantz and House, *When Titans Clashed*, 241–7; Beevor, *Berlin*, 11–23; Hosenfeld, 'Ich versuche jeden zu retten', 108–11; 887–8: 7 and 12 Jan. 1945; Szpilman, *The Pianist*, 183–7.

5 Strzelecki, *Endphase des KL Auschwitz*, 141–218.

6 Gève, *Youth in Chains*, 190–1.

7 KA 359, Jürgen Illmer, b. 1935, memoir; Gève, *Youth in Chains*, 190–1; Strzelecki, *Endphase des KL Auschwitz*, 144–7 and 169–70.

8 Davies and Moorehouse, *Microcosm*, 15–29; *Schlesische Tageszeitung*, 22 Jan. 1945.

9   Leonie Biallas in Jacobs, *Freiwild*, 15–35; Biallas, 'Komm, Frau, raboti'.

10 Irrgang, *Leutnant der Wehrmacht*, 235–7; to Dorothee, 23 Dec. 1944.

11 Glantz and House, *When Titans Clashed*, 247–8; Beevor, *Berlin*, 24–6; Erickson, *The Road to Berlin*, 463–70.

12 Irrgang, *Leutnant der Wehrmacht*, 238–41.

13 Lakowski, 'Der Zusammenbruch der deutschen Verteidigung', 538–42.

14 Schieder (ed.), *The Expulsion of the German Population*, 135–43: doc. 23, Lore Ehrich: 1946–7.

15 Erickson, *The Road to Berlin*, 463–70; Schieder (ed.), *The Expulsion of the German Population*, 33.

16 MfK–FA, 3.2002.0279, Kurt Orgel to Liselotte Purper, 21 and 22 Jan. 1945.

17 MfK–FA, 3.2002.0279, Kurt Orgel to Liselotte Purper, 12, 13 and 14 Feb. 1945; Liselotte Purper to Kurt Orgel, 22 Feb. 1945.

18 MfK–FA, 3.2002.0279, Liselotte Purper to Kurt Orgel, 13 and 28 Nov. 1944.

19 Kardorff, *Berliner Aufzeichnungen*, 287: 3 Feb. 1945; Görtemaker, *Ein deutsches Leben*, 201–10; *MadR*, 6740: end of Mar. 1945; Werner, 'Bleib übrig', 341; Wette et al. (eds), *Das letzte halbe Jahr*, 236, 254, 259, 264–5.

20 Taylor, *Dresden*; Bergander, *Dresden im Luftkrieg*, 148–95, 208–9, 247–74 and 290–2; Müller et al. (eds), *Die Zerstörung Dresdens am 13./15. Februar 1945*; Klemperer, *To the Bitter End*, 387–96: 13–24 Feb. 1945; RA, Anon., Burg Gymnasium UII/522, 2.

21 Boor, *Tagebuchblätter*, 228–30 and 235: 17–25 Feb., 2 and 11 Mar. 1945; Associated Press dispatch from Stockholm, reprinted as 'Berlin, Nerves Racked By Air Raids, Fears Russian Army Most', *Oakland Tribune*, 23 Feb. 1945.

22 MfK–FA, 3.2002.7209, Erna Paulus to her sister Martha Roether, 24/25 and 26 Feb. 1945; Friedrich, *Der Brand*, 109–16.

23 Taylor, *Dresden*, 427–8.

24 MfK–FA, 3.2002.7209, Erna Paulus to her daughters, 27 Mar. 1945.

25 MfK–FA, 3.2002.7209, Katharina Wuster to Erna Paulus, 15 Mar. 1945; Wette, *Das letzte halbe Jahr*, 332, 142; also 172 and 209.

26 *Titanic*, dir. Werner Klingler and Herbert Selpin, 1943; Strobl, *The Germanic Isle*, 150–2.

27 *Kolberg*, dir. Veit Harlan, 1945; Welch, *Propaganda and the German Cinema*, 221–37; Noakes (ed.), *Nazism*, 4, 494.

28 *Ohm Krüger*, Hinkel for RMVP, 29 Jan 1945, cited in Drewniak, *Der deutsche Film*, 340; 'Der Tod von Dresden: Ein Leuchtzeichen des Widerstands', *Das Reich*, 4 Mar. 1945; Taylor, *Dresden*, 412–26; Boor, *Tagebuchblätter*, 237: 19–21 Mar. 1945; MfK–FA, 3.2002.7209, Käthe Wurster to Martha Roether and Erna Paulus, 15 Mar. 1945.

29   Evans, *Telling Lies about Hitler*, 170–87.

30   Bergander, *Dresden im Luftkrieg*, 224–6; Evans, *Telling Lies about Hitler*, chapter 5; Taylor, *Dresden*, 412–26 and 478–86.

31   Taylor, *Dresden*, 412–19 and 429–31.

32   Kleindienst (ed.), *Sei tausendmal gegrüßt*: Irene to Ernst Guicking: 20 Jan., 10 and 12 Feb. 1945; Ernst to Irene, 19 Feb. 1945.

33   Ibid., Irene to Ernst Guicking: 12 Feb. 1945; Goebbels, 'Ein Volk in Verteidigungsstellung (In der härtesten Probe)', *Das Reich*, 11 Feb. 1945.

34   For this and the following see Henke, *Die amerikanische Besetzung Deutschlands*; Zimmermann, 'Die Eroberung und Besetzung des deutschen Reiches'; MacDonald, *United States Army in World War II*, 116–32.

35   Noakes, *Nazism*, 4, 654; Henke, *Die amerikanische Besetzung Deutschlands*, 172 and 841.

36   Steinert, *Hitlers Krieg und die Deutschen*, 558–60 and 564–6; Gellately, *Backing Hitler*, 230; Kershaw, *Hitler*, 2, 778; Goebbels, *Tgb*, II/15, 471: 11 Mar. 1945.

37   Goebbels, *Tgb*, II/15, 405: 3 Mar. 1945; Kershaw, *The End*, 262–4; Loeffel, 'Soldiers and terror', 526: IfZ-Archiv, NOKW–535; Henke, *Die amerikanische Besetzung Deutschlands*, 844–6.

38   Grimm, 'Lynchmorde an alliierten Fliegern', in Süß (ed.), *Deutschland im Luftkrieg*, 71–84; Mallmann, '"Volksjustiz gegen anglo-amerikanische Mörder"', in Gottwaldt et al. (eds), *NS-Gewaltherrschaft*, 202–13; Strobl, *Bomben auf Oberdonau*, 231–311.

39   Steinert, *Hitlers Krieg und die Deutschen*, 541–3 and 558–60; Zagovec, 'Gespräche mit der "Volksgemeinschaft"', 319–20, citing *DAZ*, 12 Jan. 1945; Gellately, *Backing Hitler*, 230; Kershaw, *The End*, 268–72.

40   Steinert, *Hitlers Krieg und die Deutschen*, 557; Klemperer, *To the Bitter End*, 407–8: 1 Mar. 1945; Goebbels, 'Deutschlands Kraft im Daseinskampf – Der Lagebericht von Dr Goebbels', *Hamburger Zeitung*, 1 Mar. 1945.

41   Goebbels, *Tgb*, II/15, 422: 5 Mar. 1945; Kershaw, *The End*, 254–5; Henke, *Die amerikanische Besetzung Deutschlands*, 343–64 and 377–90.

42   Kershaw, *The End*, 268–9.

43   Ibid., 288–91; Kershaw, *Hitler*, 2, 781; Domarus (ed.), *Hitler*, 2203–6: 24 Feb. 1945; *MadR*, 6733–4: 28 Mar. 1945.

44   BA, R55, 577, 221–237: letters from Christian Meyer, A. Müller, Dr Franz Orthner and others: 23–28 Jan. 1945.

45   Kleindienst (ed.), *Sei tausendmal gegrüßt*: Ernst to Irene Guicking, 24 Feb. and 9 Mar., 18 and 21 Feb. 1945.

46   Goebbels, *Tgb*, II/15, 25 Mar. 1945; Wantzen, *Das Leben im Krieg*, 1378 and

1403: 9 and 24 Mar. 1945; Kleindienst (ed.), *Sei tausendmal gegrüßt*: Irene to Ernst Guicking, 24 Mar. 1945.

47 Boor, *Tagebuchblätter*, 237 and 239–40: 22 and 27 Mar. 1945.

48 Ibid., 241: 28 Mar. 1945.

49 Kleindienst (ed.), *Sei tausendmal gegrüßt*: Ernst to Irene Guicking, 3 and 4 April 1945.

50 Henke, *Die amerikanische Besetzung Deutschlands*, 399–400; Gruchmann, *Der Zweite Weltkrieg*, 436–43.

51 Steinert, *Hitlers Krieg und die Deutschen*, 564–6: report to Propaganda Ministry, 21 Mar. 1945.

52 Steinert, *Hitlers Krieg und die Deutschen*, 567, and Werner, *Bleib übrig*, 356–8.

53 Herbert, *Hitler's Foreign Workers*, 369–72.

54 Roseman, *The Past in Hiding*, 384–9.

55 Herbert, 'Von Auschwitz nach Essen'.

56 Blatman, *The Death Marches*; Neander, *Das Konzentrationslager 'Mittelbau'*, 466–77.

57 Blatman, *The Death Marches*; Strzelecki, *Endphase des KL Auschwitz*; Strebel, *Celle April 1945 Revisited*.

58 Herbert, *Hitler's Foreign Workers*, 373–6.

59 Ibid., 363; *Justiz und NS-Verbrechen*, 7, no. 235.

60 Orłowski and Schneider (eds), *'Erschießen will ich nicht!'*, 347–8: 18 April 1945.

61 Ibid., 334 and 344–7: 18 Feb., 5, 10 and 15 April 1945.

62 MfK–FA, 3.2002.7209, Erna Paulus to Elfriede and Irmgard, 27 Mar. 1945, and to Martha Roether, May 1945.

63 KA 53, Jürgen H., b. July 1929, 29 Mar.–19 May 1945.

64 Roseman, *The Past in Hiding*, 391–3.

16 *Finale*

1 Goebbels, *Tgb*, II/15, 692: 9 Apr. 1945; Erickson, *The Road to Berlin*, 563–77; Lakowski, 'Der Zusammenbruch der deutschen Verteidigung', 608–33; Glantz and House, *When Titans Clashed*, 256–63; Beevor, *Berlin*, 206.

2 Fritzsch, *Nürnberg im Krieg*; Karl Kunze, *Kriegsende in Franken und der Kampf um Nürnberg im April 1945*.

3 Longerich, *Heinrich Himmler. Biographie*, 742–8; Padfield, *Himmler*, 565–6 and 578–89; Fleischhauer, *Die Chance des Sonderfriedens*, 58–61 and 268–75; Kershaw, *The End*, 281–9 and 336–7; Geyer, 'Endkampf 1918 and 1945',

in Lüdtke and Weisbrod (eds), *No Man's Land of Violence*, 35–67; Bessel, 'The shock of violence in 1945', in Lüdtke and Weisbrod (eds), *No Man's Land of Violence*, 69–99.

4   Gleiss, *Breslauer Apokalypse 1945*, 3, 651 and 910; 4, 651 and 1113–14; Davies and Moorehouse, *Microcosm*, 26–9.

5   Wette et al. (eds), *Das letzte halbe Jahr*, 259 and 271–9; Steinert, *Hitlers Krieg und die Deutschen*, 552, citing report to the Propaganda Ministry, 21 Feb. 1945; Messerschmidt and Wüllner, *Die Wehrmachtjustiz im Dienste des Nationalsozialismus*, 86.

6   KA 4709/1 and 2: KA 4709/1, Agnes S., diary, 'Lüneburger Heide 1945', 7–9 Feb. and 27 Mar.–8 April 1945; Klaus to Agnes S., 1 Mar. 1945; *MadR*, 6737: end Mar. 1945.

7   KA 4709/1, Agnes S., diary, 'Lüneburger Heide 1945', 16–30 April 1945.

8   Orłowski and Schneider (eds), *'Erschießen will ich nicht!'*: 10 and 12 April.

9   Klemperer, *To the Bitter End*, 396–421: 15 Feb.–1 April 1945.

10   Ibid., 421–2: 2 April 1945.

11   Ibid., 425: 4–5 April 1945.

12   Ibid., 426–31: 15 April 1945.

13   Ibid., 532–8: 15 April 1945.

14   Ibid., 538–41: 20–21 April 1945; Krone, 'Plauen 1945 bis 1949 16.

15   Kershaw, *Hitler*, 2, 791–2; Trevor-Roper, *The Last Days of Hitler*, 87–9; Steinert, *Hitlers Krieg und die Deutschen*, 570–1 and 578; Wette et al. (eds), *Das letzte halbe Jahr*, 334–8: 'Sondereinsatz Berlin' report, 10 April 1945.

16   Lakowski, 'Der Zusammenbruch der deutschen Verteidigung', 633–49; Glantz and House, *When Titans Clashed*, 263–6; Beevor, *Berlin*, 216–59.

17   KA 3697, Hertha von Gebhardt, diary, 20 April 1945.

18   Ibid., 23–24 April 1945.

19   Kershaw, *The End*, 325–6; Troll, 'Aktionen zur Kriegsbeendigung im Frühjahr 1945', in Broszat et al. (eds), *Bayern in der NS-Zeit*, 4, Munich, 1981, 650–4; Förschler, *Stuttgart 1945*, 8–19; Stephenson, *Hitler's Home Front*, 323–35.

20   Loeffel, 'Soldiers and terror', 528–9; Noakes, *Nazism*, 4, 657–8.

21   Klemperer, *To the Bitter End*, 442–3: 21–22 April 1945.

22   Kershaw, *The End*, 3–5 and 342; Klemperer, *To the Bitter End*, 442–4 and 447: 21–23 and 27 April 1945.

23   KA 3697, Gebhardt, diary, 25–26 April 1945; Beevor, *Berlin*, 283–4.

24   KA 3697, Gebhardt, diary, 27 April 1945; Yelton, *Hitler's Volkssturm*, 126–7; looting, Kuby, *The Russians and Berlin*, 1945, 223.

25   KA 3697, Gebhardt, diary, 27 April 1945; Le Tissier, *Battle of Berlin 1945*, 170–1 and 196.

26 VB, Munich edn, 20, 24 and 25 April 1945; Bessel, *Germany 1945*, 120; Troll, 'Aktionen zur Kriegsbeendigung im Frühjahr 1945', 660–71; Henke, *Die amerikanische Besetzung Deutschlands*, 854–61; Kershaw, *The End*, 343–5.

27 Marcuse, *Legacies of Dachau*, 50–2; Bessel, *Germany 1945*, 161–5.

28 Gröschner, *Ich schlug meiner Mutter die Brennenden Funken ab*, 242–6: R., 6. Klasse Volksschule; Wolfgang S., 6. Klasse; Walter B., 8. Klasse.

29 Naimark, *The Russians in Germany*, 69–140; Petö, 'Memory and the narrative of rape in Budapest and Vienna in 1945', in Bessel and Schumann (eds), *Life after Death*, 129–48; Bandhauer-Schöffmann and Hornung, 'Vom "Dritten Reich" zur Zweiten Republik', in Good et al. (eds), *Frauen in Österreich*, 232–3; Sander and Johr (eds), *BeFreier und Befreite*, 48–51; Mark, 'Remembering rape', 133–61; Kardorff, *Berliner Aufzeichnungen*, 312–14: 23 Sept. 1945; Boveri, *Tage des Überlebens*, 119: 6 May 1945.

30 Sander and Johr (eds), *BeFreier und Befreite*, 25–7; Anon., *Eine Frau in Berlin. Tagebuchaufzeichnungen*, 113 and 220.

31 KA 3697, Hertha von Gebhardt, diary, 27 and 28 Apr. 1945; Hoffmann, 'Besiegte, Besatzer, Beobachter', in Fulda et al. (eds), *Demokratie im Schatten der Gewalt*, 44; Naimark, *The Russians in Germany*, 69–140; Petö, 'Memory and the narrative of rape in Budapest and Vienna in 1945', 129–48.

32 Gröschner, *Ich schlug meiner Mutter die Brennenden Funken ab*, 355: interview with Christa J., b. 1931, Göhrener Str 3; RA, Luisenschule Essen, Anon., UI/ no no., 3–4; DLA, Hermine D., b. 28 Aug. 1931 Hundsheim, nr Krems, 'Auch deine Oma war ein Kind', MS, n.d., 42.

33 Köpp, *Warum war ich bloß ein Mädchen?*, 137–8.

34 Klemperer, *To the Bitter End*, 448–9 and 452: 28–9 April and 3 May 1945.

35 Bessel, *Germany 1945*, 127–31.

36 Gleiss, *Breslauer Apokalypse*, 5, 233.

37 Orłowski and Schneider (eds), *'Erschießen will ich nicht!'*, 351–2: 2 May 1945.

38 Ibid., 351–3: 2–6 May 1945; 338: 17 Mar. 1945; Stargardt, 'Rumors of revenge in the Second World War', in Davis et al. (eds), *Alltag, Erfahrung, Eigensinn*, 373–88.

39 Klemperer, *To the Bitter End*, 450–4: 2–4 May 1945.

40 *Die Wehrmachtberichte 1939–1945*, 3, 569; cited in Bessel, *Germany 1945*, 133.

41 KA 4709/1, Agnes S., diary, 'Lüneburger Heide 1945', 9–10 May 1945.

42 Jacobs, *Freiwild*, 35–8.

43 Anneliese H. in Kuby, *The Russians and Berlin*, 226; Hoffmann, 'Besiegte, Besatzer, Beobachter', 32–3 and 44–5, citing unpublished diaries of

Höcker and Grossman; KA 3697, Hertha von Gebhardt, diary, 15 May 1945.

44 KA 3697, Hertha von Gebhardt, diary, 30 April–9 June 1945.

45 Klemperer, *To the Bitter End*, 467; 459–68: 15–21 May 1945.

Epilogue: *Crossing the Abyss*

1 KA 2035, Wilhelm K., b. 1929, Diary for 23 Mar. 1942–29 May 1947: 16 May 1945.

2 *MadR*, 6738: end Mar. 1945.

3 Hammer and Nieden, *'Sehr selten habe ich geweint'*, 333: Liselotte G., diary, 29 April 1945.

4 Bankier, 'German public awareness of the final solution', in Cesarani (ed.), *The Final Solution*, 216, citing US Army, Psychological warfare estimate, 13 Oct. 1944, National Archives, Washington DC, RG 226 Entry 16, File 118485.

5 Hoffmann, 'Besiegte, Besatzer, Beobachter', 36–7, citing Kasack, *Dreizehn Wochen*, 225; and Irmela D., 'Tagebuch aus der Russenzeit' (Berliner Geschichtswerkstatt).

6 Kardorff, *Berliner Aufzeichnungen*, 306: 12 April 1945; Hoffmann, 'Besiegte, Besatzer, Beobachter', 25.

7 Longerich, *'Davon haben wir nichts gewußt!'*, 204: Göring, 4 Oct. 1943.

8 Service, *Germans to Poles*; Naimark, *The Russians in Germany*; Douglas, *Orderly and Humane*; Leonie Biallas in Jacobs, *Freiwild*, 45–7.

9 Bundesministerium für Vertriebene, *Dokumentation der Vertreibung*, 1, 199–200 and 205–6; and Moeller, *War Stories*, 81; KA 3666/1, Gisela G., diary, 26 April, 12, 26 and 27 May and 6–27 June 1945; Evans, *Rituals of Retribution*, 750–5; Jacobmeyer, *Vom Zwangsarbeiter zum heimatlosen Ausländer*, 212–14, 217, 211 and 224–31; Gross, *Fear*; Königseder and Wetzel, *Lebensmut im Wartesaal*, 25, 42 and 47–53; Shephard, *The Long Road Home*.

10 YIVO Archives, Leo W. Schwartz Papers, 87, 'Displaced Persons, 1945–1946: Office of the Chief Historian European Command', 61–2; Königseder and Wetzel, *Lebensmut im Wartesaal*, 138; Jacobmeyer, *Vom Zwangsarbeiter zum heimatlosen Ausländer*, 193–4.

11 Meyer and Schulze, '"Als wir wieder zusammen waren, ging der Krieg im Kleinen weiter"', in Niethammer and Plato (eds), *'Wir kriegen jetzt andere Zeiten'*, [305–26,] 315–19; DLA, Annelies Gorizhan, b. 25 May 1931, 'Vater, Mutter und ich', MS, 71; KA 4622, Laudan, 'Gefährdete Spiele', 34; Bessel, *Germany 1945*, chapters 8 and 9.

12   Schmitz and Haunfelder (eds), *Humanität und Diplomatie*, 182; Roseman, *Recasting the Ruhr, 1945–1958*; Herbert, *Hitler's Foreign Workers*, 378–80; Herbert, 'Apartheid nebenan', in Niethammer (ed.), *'Die Jahre weiss man nicht, wo man die heute hinsetzen soll'*, 258–62.

13   Bessel, *Germany 1945*, 273–5; Bader, *Soziologie der deutschen Nachkriegskriminalität*, 59–60.

14   Gregor, '"Is he still alive, or long since dead?"', *German History*, 21/ 2 (2003), 183; Black, *Death in Berlin*, 163–4.

15   MfK–FA, 3.2002.7209, Lt Heinz Wagener to Erna Paulus, 29 June 1944, and to Ernst Arnold Paulus, 16 Dec. 1943; Erna Paulus to Maria Roeterh, May 1945; Ernst Arnold Paulus to the Abteilung für Kriegsgefangene bei Amt der Etappe der Besatzungstruppe in Deutschland, Berlin Karlshort, 26 Jan. 1946, to the Gesellschaft vom Russischen Roten Kreuz und Halbmond, Moskau, n.d.; letters from Hans Casper, 8 and 30 Nov., 6 Dec. 1948 and 16 Jan. 1949; from Bishop Dibelius, 12 Nov. 1952; from Suchdienst des Deutschen Roten Kreuzes, 3 Sept. 1976.

16   MfK–FA, 3.2002.0306, Hildegard P., diary, 1 July and 1 Aug. 1945.

17   Gregor, '"Is he still alive, or long since dead?"', 190 and 186–91; also Lehmann, *Gefangenschaft und Heimkehr*, 115–17; Moeller, *War Stories*, chapter 4; Kaminsky (ed.), *Heimkehr 1948*.

18   Biess, 'Survivors of totalitarianism', in Schissler (ed.), *The Miracle Years*, 57–82, and 63 for letter by Frau R.

19   Overmans, *Deutsche militärische Verluste*, 286, table 65.

20   Orłowski and Schneider (eds), *'Erschießen will ich nicht!'*, 360–1.

21   Biess, 'Survivors of totalitarianism', 59–61; Herzog, 'Desperately seeking normality', in Bessel and Schumann (eds), *Life after Death*, 177–8; Goltermann, *Die Gesellschaft der Überlebenden*, 90–1.

22   Goltermann, *Die Gesellschaft der Überlebenden*, 55–7.

23   Vogel, 'Wilm Hosenfeld', in Hosenfeld, *'Ich versuche jeden zu retten'*, 84–5, 118–20 and 143–4.

24   Vogel, 'Wilm Hosenfeld', in Hosenfeld, *'Ich versuche jeden zu retten'*, 111–46.

25   Moeller, *War Stories*, 44; Hilger, *Deutsche Kriegsgefangene in der Sojetunion*, 137; Overmans, *Deutsche militärische Verluste*, 288–9; Streit, *Keine Kameraden*; Biess, *Homecomings*, 2–5.

26   Overmans, *Deutsche militärische Verluste*, 238–43, 279–83 and 300–1; 'Kriegsgefangene und Wehrmachtvermißte aus Hessen. Vorläufige Ergebnis der amtlichen Registrierung vom 20.–30. Juni 1947', in *Staat und Wirtschaft in Hessen. Statistische Mitteilungen*, 2 (1947), 4, 110–12; Müller-Hillebrand, *Das Heer: Zweifrontenkrieg*, 3, 263; Smith, *Die 'vermißte Million'*, 62 ff.; Böhme, *Gesucht wird . . .*, 115 and 234–7.

27   Statistisches Bundesamt, *Die deutschen Vertreibungsverluste*, 15, 34 and 46; Overmans, *Deutsche militärische Verluste*, 298–9; Groehler, *Bombenkrieg gegen Deutschland*, 316–20: Groehler assumed that police estimates under-reported the dead from Dresden and other raids by 40–50 per cent, which may not be correct, and had to extrapolate his statistics from March to April because of the breakdown in police reporting.

28   Moeller, *War Stories*, chapter 3, esp. 72–81 and 155–65; Beer, 'Im Spannungsfeld von Politik und Zeitgeschichte', *Vierteljahreshefte für Zeitgeschichte*, 49 (1998), 345–89; Knoch, *Die Tat als Bild*, 314–23; Biess, 'Survivors of totalitarianism'.

29   Hammer and Nieden, '*Sehr selten habe ich geweint*', 166–7, letter of a 30-year-old officer's wife, Ingeborg T.: 20 Nov. 1945.

30   Stasiewski and Volk (eds), *Akten deutschen Bischöfe*, 6, 506; Brodie, 'For Christ and Germany', 322–5: Frings, pastoral letter, 15 Mar. 1946, and to International War Crimes Tribunal at Nuremberg, 4 July 1945; Wantzen, *Das Leben im Krieg*, 1639: 16 Mar. 1946; KA 37, Hildegard Wagener-Villa, 15 Oct. 1946; KA, 1946 (Z 80 86), 70; AEK, Gen. II 23.23a, 6, 5.

31   Löffler (ed.), *Galen: Akten, Briefe und Predigten*, 2, 1152, 1231 and 1326; Mosse, *Fallen Soldiers*, 212.

32   *The task of the churches in Germany: Being a report from a delegation of British Churchmen after a visit to the British Zone October 16th–30th, 1946, Presented to the Control Office for Germany and Austria*, London, 1947, 3; Frings, *Für die Menschen bestellt*, 50; Brodie, 'For Christ and Germany', 325–6; Brown-Fleming, *The Holocaust and the Catholic Conscience*, 91 and 124; Frings, Westminster Cathedral, 29 Sept. 1946.

33   Hetzer, '*Deutsche Stunde*', 225–34; Althaus, 'Schuld', *Prisma*, 1/2 (1946), 7–8.

34   Althaus, *Gesetz und Evangelium*, 56–7.

35   Lau (ed.), *Luther-Jahrbuch*, Jg. 25 (1958), *Festgabe für Paul Althaus*; Hetzer, '*Deutsche Stunde*', 17–19 and 220–44; Vollnhals, *Evangelische Kirche und Entnazifizierung 1945–1949*; Ericksen, *Theologians under Hitler*; Hamm, 'Schuld und Verstrickung der Kirche', in Stegemann (ed.), *Kirche und Nationalsozialismus*, 13–49; Beyschlag, 'In Sachen Althaus/ Elert'.

36   Hetzer, '*Deutsche Stunde*', 224–7 and 27; Bentley, *Martin Niemöller*, 177; Hockenos, *A Church Divided*, 75–90; Lehmann, 'Religious socialism, peace, and pacifism', in Chickering and Förster (eds), *The Shadows of Total War*, 85–96; Huber, 'Die Kirche vor der "Judenfrage"', in Rentdorff and Stegemann (eds), *Auschwitz – Krise der christlichen Theologie*, 60–81;

Fenwick, 'Religion in the wake of "total war"', DPhil. thesis, University of Oxford, 2011.

37   Niethammer (ed.), *'Die Jahre weiss man nicht, wo man die heute hinsetzen soll'*; Niethammer, *'Hinterher merkt man, dass es richtig war, dass es schiefgegangen ist'*; Niethammer (ed.), *'Wir kriegen jetzt andere Zeiten'*.

38   Roseman, *The Past in Hiding*, 393–420.

39   Süß, *Death from the Skies*, 292–3; Klessmann, *Die doppelte Staatsgründung*, 372–4: doc. 25, 'Bericht des amerikanischen Geheimdienstes über die Einstellung der deutschen Bevölkerung in der US-Zone', 12 Aug. 1945; Merritt and Merritt (eds), *Public Opinion in Semisovereign Germany*, 9; also see Stern, *Whitewashing of the Yellow Badge*, 352, 367 and 382; Goschler (ed.), *Wiedergutmachung*, 257–85; Hockerts, 'Integration der Gesellschaft'; Hughes, *Shouldering the Burdens of Defeat*.

40   Merritt and Merritt (eds), *Public Opinion in Occupied Germany*, 32–3.

41   Ebert, *Feldpostbriefe aus Stalingrad*, 351–5; Margalit, 'Dresden and Hamburg', in Helmut Schmitz (ed.), *A Nation of Victims?*, 125–40; Margalit, *Guilt, Suffering and Memory*; 152; *Dresden*, dir. Richard Groschopp/DEFA, Sept. 1946; Biess, *Homecomings*, 49 and 61–2.

42   Black, *Death in Berlin*, 162 and 167; McLellan, *Antifascism and Memory in East Germany*.

43   Neugebauer, *Opfer oder Täter*.

44   Biess, *Homecomings*, 49 and 61–2; Margalit, 'Dresden and Hamburg'.

45   Frei, *Adenauer's Germany and the Nazi Past*, 48; Frei (ed.), *Karrieren im Zwielicht*; Roseman, *The Past in Hiding*, 466–72; Margalit, *Germany and its Gypsies*; Knesebeck, *The Roma Struggle for Compensation in Post-war Germany*; JZD, Josef Rimpl: Sozialversichungsanstalt Chemnitz to Frieda Rimpl, 19 Aug. and 9 Nov. 1950.

46   McDougall, *Youth Politics in East Germany*, 3–33; Geyer, 'Cold war angst', in Schissler (ed.), *The Miracle Years*, 376–408; Nehring, *The Politics of Security*, 37–77.

47   Ebert (ed.), *Feldpostbriefe aus Stalingrad*, 349 and 362–8; Moeller, 'The politics of the past in the 1950s', in Niven Frei (ed.), *Germans as Victims*, 38.

48   Böll, 'Wanderer kommst Du nach Spa . . .', in Böll, *Werke*, 194–202; Reid, 'Heinrich Böll, "Wanderer, kommst du nach Spa . . ."', in Werner Bellmann (ed.), *Klassische deutsche Kurzgeschichten. Interpretationen*, Stuttgart, 2004, 96–106.

49   DHM, Liselotte Purper: Kriegsversehrter, sog. Ohnhänder, bei Rehabilitationsmaßnahmen im Oskar-Helene-Heim, Berlin 1946; Friedrich, *Krieg dem Kriege*, 187.

50   Kleindienst (ed.), *Sei tausendmal gegrüßt . . .*: Siemsen, 'Biographie',
      'Feldpostbriefe Ernst und Irene Guicking'; Janet Heidschmidt, 'Das
      Zeitzeugeninterview als Erweiterung der Quelle Feldpostbrief am
      Beispiel des Briefwechsels zwischen Ernst und Irene Guicking 1937 bis
      1945', 66 and 98.

Bibliography

PRINTED PRIMARY

Althaus, Paul, 'Pazifismus und Christentum: Eine kritische Studie', in *Neue Kirchliche Zeitschrift*, 30 (1919), 429–78

Althaus, Paul, *Die deutsche Stunde der Kirche*, 3rd edn, Göttingen, 1934

Althaus, Paul, *Gesetz und Evangelium: Predigten über die zehn Gebote*, Gütersloh, 1947

Andreas Friedrich, Ruth, *Der Schattenmann: Tagebuchaufzeichnungen 1938–1945*, Frankfurt am Main, 1983

Anon., *Eine Frau in Berlin: Tagebuchaufzeichnungen*, Geneva and Frankfurt am Main, 1959

Auswärtiges Amt, 8. *Weissbuch: Dokumente über die Alleinschuld Englands am Bombenkrieg gegen die Zivilbevölkerung*, Berlin, 1943

Behnken, Klaus, *Deutschlandberichte der Sozialdemokratischen Partei Deutschlands (Sopade) 1934–1940*, Frankfurt am Main, 1980

Beutler, Ernst, *Von deutscher Baukunst: Goethes Hymnus auf Erwin von Steinbach, seine Entstehung und Wirkung*, Munich, 1943

Boberach, Heinz (ed.), *Berichte des SD und der Gestapo über Kirchen und Kirchenvolk in Deutschland 1934–1944*, Mainz, 1971

Boberach, Heinz (ed.), *Meldungen aus dem Reich: Die geheimen Lageberichte des Sicherheitsdienstes des SS 1938–1945*, 1–17, Berlin, 1984

Bock, Fedor von, *Zwischen Pflicht und Verweigerung: Das Kriegstagebuch*, Munich, 1995

Boelcke, Willi A. (ed.), *Wollt ihr den totalen Krieg? Die geheimen Goebbels-Konferenzen, 1939–1943*, Stuttgart, 1969

Böll, Heinrich, *Briefe aus dem Krieg*, 1, Munich, 2003

Boor, Lisa de, *Tagebuchblätter aus den Jahren 1938–1945*, Munich, 1963

Boveri, Margret, *Tage des Überlebens: Berlin 1945*, Munich, 1968

Breloer, Heinrich (ed.), *Mein Tagebuch: Geschichten vom Überleben 1939–1947*, Cologne, 1984

Busse, Hermann, *Das Elsaß: Jahresband Oberrheinische Heimat*, Freiburg, 1940

Clausewitz, Carl von, *Historical and Political Writings*, Peter Paret and Daniel Moran (eds), Princeton, NJ, 1992

Die verlorene Insel: das Gesicht des heutigen England, Berlin, 1941

Dürkefälden, Karl, *'Schreiben wie es wirklich war!' Aufzeichnungen Karl Dürkefäldens aus den Jahren 1933–1945*, Herbert and Sibylle Obenaus (eds), Hanover, 1985

Ebert, Jens (ed.), *Feldpostbriefe aus Stalingrad, November 1942 bis Januar 1943*, Göttingen, 2003

Ebert, Jens (ed.), *Im Funkwagen der Wehrmacht durch Europa: Balkan, Ukraine, Stalingrad: Feldpostbriefe des Gefreiten Wilhelm Moldenhauer 1940–1943*, Berlin, 2008

Eiber, Ludwig (ed.), *'". . . Ein bisschen die Wahrheit": Briefe eines Bremer Kaufmanns von seinem Einsatz beim Polizeibataillon 105 in der Sowjetunion 1941'*, 1999: *Zeitschrift für Sozialgeschichte des 20. und 21. Jahrhunderte*, I/91, 58–83

Frank, Hans, *Das Diensttagebuch des deutschen Generalgouvernors in Polen 1939–1945*, Stuttgart, 1975

Gelfand, Wladimir, *Deutschland-Tagebuch, 1945–1946: Aufzeichnungen eines Rotarmisten*, Berlin, 2005

Goebbels, Joseph, *Goebbels Reden 1932–1945*, Helmut Heiber (ed.), Bindlach, 1991

Goebbels, Joseph, *Die Tagebücher von Joseph Goebbels*, Elke Fröhlich/Institut für Zeitgeschichte, Munich (eds), Munich, 1987–2008

Goedecke, Heinz and Wilhelm Krug, *Wir beginnen das Wunschkonzert*, Berlin, 1940

Hahn, Lili, *Bis alles in Scherben fällt: Tagebuchblätter 1933–45*, Hamburg, 2007

Hammer, Ingrid and Susanne zur Nieden (eds), *'Sehr selten habe ich geweint': Briefe und Tagebücher aus dem Zweiten Weltkrieg von Menschen aus Berlin*, Zurich, 1992

Hassell, Ulrich von, *The von Hassell Diaries*, New York/London, 1947

Haydn, Ludwig, *Meter, immer nur Meter! Das Tagebuch eines Daheimgebliebenen*, Vienna, 1946

Hilberg, Raul, Stanislaw Staron and Josef Kermisz (eds), *The Warsaw Diary of Adam Czerniakow*, Chicago, 1999

Himmler, Heinrich, *Der Dienstkalender Heinrich Himmlers 1941/42*, Peter Witte (ed.), Hamburg, 1999

Himmler, Heinrich, *Die Geheimreden 1933 bis 1945 und andere Ansprachen*, Bradley F. Smith and Agnes F. Peterson (eds), Frankfurt am Main, 1974

Hitler, Adolf, *Reden und Proklamationen, 1932–1945*, 1–2, Max Domarus (ed.), Neustadt an der Aisch, 1962–3

Hitler, Adolf, *'Rede vor der deutschen Presse'*, Wilhelm Treue (ed.), *VfZ*, 2 (1958), 181–91

Hlond, Cardinal (ed.), *The Persecution of the Catholic Church in German-occupied Poland*, London, 1941

Hohenstein, Alexander, *Wartheländisches Tagebuch aus den Jahren 1941/42*, Stuttgart, 1961

Hölderlin, Friedrich, *Hyperion oder Der Eremit in Griechenland*, Frankfurt am Main, 1979

Hosenfeld, Wilm, *'Ich versuche jeden zu retten': Das Leben eines deutschen Offiziers in Briefen und Tagebüchern*, Thomas Vogel (ed.), Munich, 2004

Hubatsch, Walter (ed.), *Hitlers Weisungen für die Kriegführung 1939–1945: Dokumente des Oberkommandos der Wehrmacht*, Munich, 1965

Hürter, Johannes (ed.), *Ein deutscher General an der Ostfront: Die Briefe und Tagebücher des Gotthard Heinrici 1941/42*, Erfurt, 2001

Irrgang, Astrid, *Leutnant der Wehrmacht: Peter Stölten in seinen Feldpostbriefen: Vom richtigen Leben im Falschen*, Rombach, 2007

Jarausch, Konrad H. and Klaus Arnold (eds), *'Das stille Sterben . . .' Feldpostbriefe von Konrad Jarausch aus Polen und Russland 1939–1942*, Paderborn, 2008

Jochmann, Werner (ed.), *Monologe im Führer–Hauptquartier 1941–1944: Die Aufzeichnungen Heinrich Heims*, Munich, 2000

Jünger, Ernst, *Gärten und Straßen*, Berlin, 1942

Kasack, Hermann, *Dreizehn Wochen: Tage- und Nachtblätter: Aufzeichnungen aus dem Jahr 1945 über das Kriegsende in Potsdam*, Berlin, 1996

Katsh, Abraham, *The Diary of Chaim A. Kaplan*, New York, 1965

Kleindienst, Jürgen (ed.), *Sei tausendmal gegrüßt: Briefwechsel Irene und Ernst Guicking 1937–1945*, Berlin, 2001

Klemperer, Victor, *I Shall Bear Witness: The Diaries of Victor Klemperer*, 1, 1933–1941, London, 1999

Klemperer, Victor, *To the Bitter End: The Diaries of Victor Klemperer*, 2, 1942–45, London, 1999

Klepper, Jochen (ed.), *In Tormentis Pinxit: Briefe und Bilder des Soldatenkönigs*, Stuttgart, 1938

Klepper, Jochen, *Der Vater: Der Roman des Soldatenkönigs*, Stuttgart, 1937

Klepper, Jochen, *Kyrie: Geistliche Lieder*, Berlin, 1939

Klepper, Jochen, *Unter dem Schatten deiner Flügel: Aus den Tagebüchern der Jahre 1932–1942*, Stuttgart, 1955

Klukowski, Zygmunt, *Diary from the Years of Occupation, 1939–44*, Andrew Klukowski and Helen Klukowski May (eds), Urbana, Il., 1993

Kuby, Erich, *Nur noch rauchende Trümmer: Das Ende der Festung Brest: Tagebuch des Soldaten Erich Kuby*, Hamburg, 1959

Kuropka, Joachim (ed.), *Meldungen aus Münster 1924–1944: Geheime und vertrauliche Berichte von Polizei, Gestapo, NSDAP und ihren Gliederungen, staatlicher Verwaltung, Gerichtsbarkeit und Wehrmacht über die politische und gesellschaftliche Situation in Münster*, Regensburg, 1992

Löffler, Peter (ed.), *Bischof Clemens August Graf von Galen: Akten, Briefe und Predigten 1933–1946*, 1–2, Mainz, 1988

Nadler, Fritz, *Eine Stadt im Schatten Streichers: Bisher unveröffentlichte Tagebuchblätter, Dokumente und Bilder vom Kriegsjahr 1943*, Nuremberg, 1969

Orłowski, Hubert and Thomas F. Schneider (eds), *'Erschießen will ich nicht!' Als Offizier und Christ im Totalen Krieg: Das Kriegstagebuch des Dr August Töpperwien, 3. September 1939 bis 6. Mai 1945*, Düsseldorf, 2006

Redemann, Karl (ed.), *Zwischen Front und Heimat: Der Briefwechsel des münsterischen Ehepaares Agnes und Albert Neuhaus 1940–1944*, Münster, 1996

Reese, Willy Peter, *Mir selber seltsam fremd: Russland 1941–44*, Stefan Schmitz (ed.), Berlin, 2004

Ribbentrop, Joachim von, *Zwischen Moskau und London: Erinnerungen und letzte Aufzeichnungen*, Annelies von Ribbentrop (ed.), Leoni am Starnberger See, 1954

Rilke, Rainer Maria, *Duineser Elegien*, Leipzig, 1923

Schieder, Theodor (ed.), *The Expulsion of the German Population from the Territories East of the Oder–Neisse Line*, Bonn, 1956

Shirer, William, *Berlin Diary: The Journal of a Foreign Correspondent*, London, 1941

Stasiewski, Bernhard and Ludwig Volk (eds), *Akten deutschen Bischöfe über die Lage der Kirche 1933–1945*, 6, Mainz, 1985

Statistisches Jahrbuch für das Deutsche Reich 1924–5, 44, Berlin, 1925

Studnitz, Hans-Georg von, *While Berlin Burns: The Diary of Hans-Georg von Studnitz 1943–45*, London, 1963

Wantzen, Paulheinz, *Das Leben im Krieg 1939–1946: Ein Tagebuch: Aufgezeichnet in der damaligen Gegenwart*, Bad Homburg, 2000

Die Wehrmachtberichte 1939–1945, 1–3, Munich, 1985

Wolff-Mönckeberg, Mathilde, *Briefe, die sie nicht erreichten: Briefe einer Mutter an ihre fernen Kinder in den Jahren 1940–1946*, Hamburg, 1980

Wrobel, Hans (ed.), *Strafjustiz im totalen Krieg: Aus den Akten des Sondergerichts Bremen 1940 bis 1945*, 1, Bremen, 1991

Zacharias-Langhans, Heinrich, *Hoffen auf den kommenden Christus: 20 Predigten 1927–1965*, Heinrich Laible (ed.), Hamburg, 1983

PRINTED SECONDARY

Abelshauser, Werner, 'Rüstungsschmiede der Nation? Der Kruppkonzern im Dritten Reich und in der Nachkriegszeit 1933 bis 1951', in Lothar Gall (ed.), *Krupp im 20. Jahrhundert: Die Geschichte des Unternehmens vom Ersten Weltkrieg bis zur Gründung der Stiftung*, Berlin, 2002, 267–472

Abrams, Lynn, *The Orphan Country*, Edinburgh, 1998

Absolon, Rudolf, *Die Wehrmacht im Dritten Reich: Aufbau, Gliederung, Recht, Verwaltung*, Boppard, 1995

Adam, Christian, *Lesen unter Hitler: Autoren, Bestseller, Leser im Dritten Reich*, Berlin, 2010

Adler, Hans Günther, *Theresienstadt, 1941–1945: Das Antlitz einer Zwangsgemeinschaft*, Tübingen, 1960

Adolph, Walter, *Kardinal Preysing und zwei Diktaturen: Sein Widerstand gegen die totalitäre Macht*, Berlin, 1971

Alexijewitsch, Swetlana, 'Der Mensch zählt mehr als der Krieg', Deutsch-Russisches Museum Berlin-Karlshorst (ed.), *Mascha + Nina + Katjuscha: Frauen in der Roten Armee, 1941–1945*, Berlin, 2003

Aly, Götz, *'Final Solution': Nazi Population Policy and the Murder of the European Jews*, London, 1999

Aly, Götz, 'Die Deportation der Juden von Rhodos nach Auschwitz', *Mittelweg 36*, 12 (2003), 79–88

Aly, Götz, *Hitlers Volksstaat: Raub, Rassenkrieg und nationaler Sozialismus*, Frankfurt am Main, 2005

Aly, Götz and Susanne Heim, *Architects of Annihilation: Auschwitz and the Logic of Destruction*, London, 2002

Aly, Götz, *Die Belasteten: 'Euthanasie' 1939–1945: Eine Gesellschaftsgeschichte*, Frankfurt am Main, 2013

Arad, Yitzhak, *Belzec, Sobibor, Treblinka: The Operation Reinhard Death Camps*, Bloomington, 1987

Arbeitsgruppe Pädagogisches Museum (ed.), *Heil Hitler, Herr Lehrer: Volksschule 1933–1945: Das Beispiel Berlin*, Hamburg, 1983

Arbeitsgruppe zur Erforschung der Geschichte der Karl-Bonhoeffer-Nervenklinik (ed.), *Totgeschwiegen 1933–1945: Zur Geschichte der Wittenauer Heilstätten, seit 1957 Karl-Bonhoeffer-Nervenklinik*, Berlin, 1989

Arnold, Klaus Jochen, 'Die Eroberung und Behandlung der Stadt Kiew durch die Wehrmacht im September 1941', *Militärgeschichtliche Mitteilungen*, 58/1, 59 (1999), 23–63

Arnold, Jörg, '"Once upon a time there was a lovely town . . .": The Allied air war, urban reconstruction and nostalgia in Kassel (1943–2000)', *German History*, 29/3 (2011), 445–69

Arnold, Jörg, Dietmar Süß and Malte Thiessen (eds), *Luftkrieg: Erinnerungen in Deutschland und Europa*, Göttingen, 2009

Ausländer, Fietje, '"Zwölf Jahre Zuchthaus! Abzusitzen nach Kriegsende!" Zur Topographie des Strafgefangenenwesens der Deutschen Wehrmacht', in Norbert Haase and Gerhard Paul (eds), *Die anderen Soldaten: Wehrkraftzersetzung, Gehorsamsverweigerung und Fahnenflucht im Zweiten Weltkrieg*, Frankfurt am Main, 1995, 50–65

Ayass, Wolfgang, *Das Arbeitshaus Breitenau: Bettler, Landstreicher, Prostituierte, Zuhälter und Fürsorgeempfänger in der Korrektions- und Landarmenanstalt Breitenau (1874–1949)*, Kassel, 1992

Bader, Karl S., *Soziologie der deutschen Nachkriegskriminalität*, Tübingen, 1949

Baird, Jay W., 'The Myth of Stalingrad', *Journal of Contemporary History*, 4 (1969), 187–204

Baird, Jay W., *To Die for Germany: Heroes in the Nazi Pantheon*, Bloomington, 1992

Bajohr, Frank, *'Aryanisation' in Hamburg: The Economic Exclusion of the Jews and the Confiscation of their Property in Nazi Germany*, Oxford, 2002

Bajohr, Frank and Dieter Pohl, *Der Holocaust als offenes Geheimnis: Die Deutschen, die NS-Führung und die Alliierten*, Munich, 2006

Bajohr, Frank and Michael Wildt (eds), *Volksgemeinschaft: Neue Forschungen zur Gesellschaft des Nationalsozialismus*, Frankfurt am Main, 2009

Bajohr, Stefan, *Die Hälfte der Fabrik: Geschichte der Frauenarbeit in Deutschland 1914 bis 1945*, Marburg, 1979

Baldoli, Claudia, 'Spring 1943: The FIAT strikes and the collapse of the Italian home front', *History Workshop Journal*, 72 (2011), 181–9

Baldoli, Claudia and Marco Fincardi, 'Italian society under Anglo-American bombs: Propaganda, experience and Legend, 1940–1945', *Historical Journal* 52: 4 (2009), 1017–38

Baldoli, Claudia and Andrew Knapp, *Forgotten Blitzes: France and Italy under Allied Bombs, 1940–1945*, London, 2011

Baldoli, Claudia, Andrew Knapp and Richard Overy (eds), *Bombing, States and Peoples in Western Europe 1940–1945*, London, 2011

Baldwin, P.M., 'Clausewitz in Nazi Germany', *Journal of Contemporary History*, 16 (1981), 5–26

Bandhauer-Schöffmann, Irene and Ela Hornung, 'Vom "Dritten Reich" zur Zweiten Republik: Frauen im Wien der Nachkriegszeit', in David F. Good, Margarete Grandner and Mary Jo Maynes (eds), *Frauen in Österreich: Beiträge zu ihrer Situation im 19. und 20. Jahrhundert*, Vienna, 1994, 225–46

Bankier, David, *The Germans and the Final Solution: Public Opinion under Nazism*, Oxford, 1992

Bankier, David, 'German Public Awareness of the Final Solution', in David Cesarani (ed.), *The Final Solution: Origins and Implementation*, London, 1994, 215–27

Bartov, Omer, *The Eastern Front, 1941–45: German Troops and the Barbarisation of Warfare*, Basingstoke, 1985

Bartov, Omer, *Hitler's Army: Soldiers, Nazis, and War in the Third Reich*, Oxford, 1991

Bathrick, David, 'Making a national family with the radio: The Nazi *Wunschkonzert*', *Modernism/Modernity*, 4/1 (1997), 115–27

Bauer, Maja, *Alltag im 2. Weltkrieg*, Berlin, 1980

Bauer, Theresia, *Nationalsozialistische Agrarpolitik und bäuerliches Verhalten im Zweiten Weltkrieg: Eine Regionalstudie zur ländlichen Gesellschaft in Bayern*, Frankfurt am Main, 1996

Baumann, Ursula, 'Suizid im "Dritten Reich" – Facetten eines Themas', in Michael Grüttner, Rüdiger Hachtmann and Heinz-Gerhard Haupt (eds), *Geschichte und Emanzipation: Festschrift für Reinhard Rürup*, Frankfurt am Main, 1999, 482–516

Baumgart, Winfried, 'Zur Ansprache Hitlers vor den Führern der Wehrmacht am 22. August 1939', *VfZ*, 16 (1968), 120–49

Beauvoir, Simone de, *La Force de l'âge*, Paris, 1960

Beck, Gad, *An Underground Life: Memoirs of a Gay Jew in Nazi Berlin*, Milwaukee, 2000

Becker, Franziska, *Gewalt und Gedächtnis: Erinnerungen an die nationalsozialistische Verfolgung einer jüdischen Landgemeinde*, Göttingen, 1994

Becker, Jörg, *Elisabeth Noelle-Neumann: Demoskopin zwischen NS-Ideologie und Konservatismus*, Paderborn, 2013

Beer, Matthias, 'Im Spannungsfeld von Politik und Zeitgeschichte: Das Grossforschungsprojekt "Dokumentation der Vertreibung der Deutschen aus Ost–Mitteleuropa"', *Vierteljahrshefte für Zeitgeschichte*, 49 (1998), 345–89

Beevor, Antony, *Stalingrad*, London, 1998

Beevor, Antony, *Berlin: The Downfall 1945*, London, 2002

Beevor, Antony, *D-Day: The Battle for Normandy*, London, 2009

Beevor, Antony and Luba Vinogradova (eds), *A Writer at War: Vasily Grossman with the Red Army*, Pimlico, 2006

Behrenbeck, Sabine, *Der Kult um die toten Helden: Nationalsozialistische Mythen, Riten und Symbole 1923 bis 1945*, Vierow bei Greifswald, 1996

Bellmann, Werner (ed.), *Klassische deutsche Kurzgeschichten: Interpretationen*, Stuttgart, 2004

Bentley, James, *Martin Niemöller, 1892–1984*, Oxford, 1984

Benz, Wolfgang, 'Judenvernichtung aus Notwehr? Die Legenden um Theodore N. Kaufman', *Vierteljahrshefte für Zeitgeschichte*, 29/4 (1981), 615–30

Benz, Wolfgang (ed.), *Wie wurde man Parteigenosse? Die NSDAP und ihre Mitglieder*, Frankfurt am Main, 2009

Benzenhöfer, Udo, *'Kinderfachabteilungen' und 'NS-Kindereuthanasie'*, Wetzlar, 2000

Bergander, Götz, *Dresden im Luftkrieg: Vorgeschichte – Zerstörung – Folgen*, Cologne, 1977

Bergen, Doris L., *Twisted Cross: The German Christian Movement in the Third Reich*, Chapel Hill, 1996

Bergen, Doris L. (ed.), *The Sword of the Lord: Military Chaplains from the First to the Twenty-first Century*, Notre Dame, 2004

Bergen, Doris L., 'Instrumentalization of "Volksdeutschen" in German propaganda in 1939: Replacing/erasing Poles, Jews and other victims', *German Studies Review*, 31/2 (2008), 447–70

Berger, Andrea and Thomas Oelschläger, '"Ich habe eines natürlichen Todes

sterben lassen": Das Krankenhaus im Kalmenhof und die Praxis der national-
sozialistischen Vernichtungsprogramme', in Christian Schrapper and
Dieter Sengling (eds), *Die Idee der Bildbarkeit: 100 Jahre sozialpädagogische
Praxis in der Heilerziehungsanstalt Kalmenhof*, Weinheim, 1988, 269–336

Berkhoff, Karel, *Harvest of Despair: Life and Death in Ukraine under Nazi Rule*,
Cambridge, Mass., 2004

Berth, Christiane, *Biografien und Netzwerke im Kaffeehandel zwischen Deutschland
und Zentralamerika 1920–1959*, Hamburg, 2014

Bessel, Richard, 'The Shock of Violence in 1945 and its Aftermath in
Germany', in Alf Lüdtke and Bernd Weisbrod (eds), *No Man's Land of
Violence*, 69–99

Bessel, Richard, *Germany 1945*, London/New York, 2009

Bessel, Richard and Claudia B. Haake (eds), *Removing Peoples: Forced Removal
in the Modern World*, Oxford, 2009

Bessel, Richard and Dirk Schumann (eds), *Life after Death: Approaches to a Cultural
and Social History of Europe during the 1940s and 1950s*, Cambridge, 2003

Betts, Paul and Greg Eghigian (eds), *Pain and Prosperity: Reconsidering
Twentieth-Century German History*, Stanford, Cal., 2003

Beyschlag, Karlmann, 'In Sachen Althaus/Elert: Einspruch gegen Berndt
Hamm', in *Homiletisch-liturgisches Korrespondenzblatt*, 8 (1990/91), 153–72

Biallas, Leonie, 'Komm, Frau, raboti': Ich war Kriegsbeute, Hürth, 2004

Biernacki, Stanisław, Czesław Madajczyk and Blanka Meissner, *Generalny plan
wschodni: zbiór dokumentów*, Warsaw, 1990

Biess, Frank, 'Survivors of Totalitarianism: Returning POWs and the
Reconstruction of Masculine Citizenship in West Germany, 1945–1955', in
Hanna Schissler (ed.), *The Miracle Years: A Cultural History of West Germany,
1949–1968*, Princeton, NJ, 2001, 57–82

Biess, Frank, *Homecomings: Returning POWs and the Legacies of Defeat in Postwar
Germany*, Princeton, 2006

Birkenfeld, Wolfgang, *Der synthetische Treibstoff 1933–1945: Ein Beitrag zur
nationalsozialistischen Wirtschafts- und Rüstungspolitik*, Göttingen, 1964

Blaazer, David, 'Finance and the end of appeasement: The Bank of England,
the National Government and the Czech gold', *Journal of Contemporary
History*, 40/1 (2005), 22–56

Black, Monica, *Death in Berlin: From Weimar to Divided Germany*, Cambridge,
2010

Blank, Ralf, 'Kriegsalltag und Luftkrieg an der "Heimatfront"', *DRZW*, 9/1
(2004), 357–461

Blank, Ralf, *Ruhrschlacht: Das Ruhrgebiet im Kriegsjahr 1943*, Essen, 2013

Blet, Pierre, *Pius XII and the Second World War: According to the Archives of the
Vatican*, New York, 1999

Bobet, Jean, *Le vélo à l'heure allemande*, Paris, 2007

Bock, Gisela, *Zwangssterilisation im Nationalsozialismus: Studien zur Rassenpolitik und Frauenpolitik*, Opladen, 1986

Boddenberg, Werner, *Die Kriegsgefangenenpost deutscher Soldaten in sowjetischem Gewahrsam und die Post von ihren Angehörigen während des II. Weltkrieges*, Berlin, 1985

Bode, Sabine, *Die vergessene Generation: Die Kriegskinder brechen ihr Schweigen*, Stuttgart, 2004

Böhler, Jochen, *Auftakt zum Vernichtungskrieg: Die Wehrmacht in Polen 1939*, Frankfurt/Main, 2006

Böhme, Klaus and Uwe Lohalm (eds), *Wege in den Tod: Hamburgs Anstalt Langenborn und die Euthanasie in der Zeit des Nationalsozialismus*, Hamburg, 1993

Böhme, Kurt W., *Gesucht wird . . . Das dramatische Geschichte des Suchdienstes*, Munich, 1965

Bohn, Robert, *Reichskommissariat Norwegen: 'Nationalsozialistische Neuordnung' und Kriegswirtschaft*, Munich, 2000

Boll, Bernd, '". . . das gesunde Volksempfinden auf das Gröbste verletzt": Die Offenburger Strafjustiz und der "verbotene Umgang mit Kriegs- gefangenen" während des 2. Weltkriegs', *Die Ortenau*, 71 (1991), 645–78

Böll, Heinrich, *Brief an einen jungen Katholiken*, Cologne/Berlin, 1961

Böll, Heinrich, 'Wanderer kommst Du nach Spa . . .', in Heinrich Böll, *Werke: Romane und Erzählungen*, 1, 1947–1951, Cologne, 1977, 194–202

Boltanski, Christian and Bernhard Jussen (eds), *Signal*, Göttingen, 2004

Boog, Horst, *Die deutsche Luftwaffenführung 1935–1945*, Stuttgart, 1982

Boog, Horst, 'Strategischer Luftkrieg in Europa und Reichsluftverteidigung 1943–1944', *DRZW*, 7 (2001), 3–418

Boog, Horst, 'Die strategische Bomberoffensive der Alliierten gegen Deutschland und die Reichsluftverteidigung in der Schlußphase des Krieges', *DRZW*, 10/1 (2008), 777–885

Borodziej, Włodzimierz, *The Warsaw Uprising of 1944*, Madison, Wis., 2006

Brajović-Djuro, Petar, *Yugoslavia in the Second World War*, Belgrade, 1977

Bramsted, Ernest K., *Goebbels and National Socialist Propaganda, 1925–1945*, East Lansing, 1965

Brandt, Karl, *Management of Agriculture and Food in the German-Occupied and Other Areas of Fortress Europe: A Study in Military Government*, Stanford, Cal., 1953

Brantzen, Klaus, *Pater Franz Reinisch – sein Lebensbild: Ein Mann steht zu seinem Gewissen*, Neuwied, 1993

Brodie, Thomas, 'For Christ and Germany: German Catholicism and the Second World War', D.Phil. thesis, Oxford, 2013

Broszat, Martin, *Nationalsozialistische Polenpolitik 1939–1945*, Stuttgart, 1961

Broszat, Martin, 'Resistenz und Widerstand: Eine Zwischenbilanz des Forschungsprojekts', in Martin Broszat, Elke Fröhlich and Atina Grossmann (eds), *Bayern in der NS-Zeit*, 4, Munich, 1981, 691–709

Broszat, Martin et al. (eds), *Bayern in der NS-Zeit*, 1–6, Munich, 1977–1983

Broszat, Martin, Klaus-Dietmar Henke and Hans Woller (eds), *Von Stalingrad zur Währungsreform: Zur Sozialgeschichte des Umbruchs in Deutschland*, Munich, 1988

Brown-Fleming, Suzanne, *The Holocaust and the Catholic Conscience: Cardinal Aloisius Muench and the Guilt Question in Germany*, Notre Dame, Ind., 2006

Browning, Christopher, *The Origins of the Final Solution: The Evolution of Nazi Jewish Policy, September 1939–March 1942*, London, 2005

Brunswig, Hans, *Feuersturm über Hamburg: Die Luftangriffe über Hamburg im 2. Weltkrieg und ihre Folgen*, Stuttgart, 2003

Buchbender, Ortwin and Reinhold Sterz (eds), *Das andere Gesicht des Krieges: Deutsche Feldpostbriefe 1939–1945*, Munich, 1983

Bundesministerium für Vertriebene, Flüchtlinge und Kriegsgeschädigte (ed.), *Dokumente deutscher Kriegsschäden: Evakuierte, Kriegssachgeschädigte, Währungsgeschädigte: Die geschichtliche und rechtliche Entwicklung*, 1–5, Bonn, 1958–64

Bundesministerium für Vertriebene, Flüchtlinge und Kriegsgeschädigte (ed.), *Die Vertreibung der deutschen Bevölkerung aus den Gebieten östlich der Oder–Neisse*, 1–3, (reprinted) Augsburg, 1993

Burleigh, Michael, *Death and Deliverance: 'Euthanasia' in Germany, 1900–1945*, Cambridge, 1994

Bussmann, Walter, 'Zur Entstehung und Überlieferung der Hossbach Niederschrift', *VfZ*, 16 (1968), 373–84

Büttner, Ursula, '"Gomorrha" und die Folgen des Bombenkriegs', in Forschungsstelle für Zeitgeschichte in Hamburg (ed.), *Hamburg im 'Dritten Reich'*, Göttingen, 2005, 612–32

Carlton, David, *Churchill and the Soviet Union*, Manchester, 2000

Carter, Erica, *Dietrich's Ghosts: The Sublime and the Beautiful in Third Reich Film*, London, 2004

Ceretti, Adolfo, *Come pensa il tribunale per i minorenni: una ricerca sul giudicato penale a Milano dal 1934 al 1990*, Milan, 1996

Cesarani, David (ed.), *The Final Solution: Origins and Implementation*, London, 1994

Cesarani, David, *Eichmann: His Life, Crimes and Legacy*, London, 2004

Chiari, Bernhard, *Alltag hinter der Front: Besatzung, Kollaboration und Widerstand in Weißrußland 1941–1944*, Düsseldorf, 1998

Chickering, Roger and Stig Förster (eds), *The Shadows of Total War: Europe, East Asia, and the United States, 1919–1939*, New York, 2003

Chu, Winson, *The German Minority in Interwar Poland*, Cambridge, 2012

Clark, Christopher, 'Johannes Blaskowitz: Der christliche General', in Ronald

Smelser and Enrico Syring (eds), *Die Militärelite des dritten Reiches*, Berlin, 1995, 28–50

Clark, Christopher, *The Politics of Conversion: Missionary Protestantism and the Jews in Prussia 1728–1941*, Oxford, 1995

Cointet, Michèle, *L'Eglise sous Vichy, 1940–1945*, Paris, 1998

Coldrey, Barry, *Child Migration under the Auspices of Dr Barnardo's Homes, the Fairbridge Society and the Lady Northcote Trust*, Thornbury, 1999

Collingham, Lizzie, *The Taste of War: World War Two and the Battle for Food*, London, 2011

Confino, Alon, *Foundational Pasts: The Holocaust as Historical Understanding*, Cambridge, 2012

Confino, Alon, Paul Betts and Dirk Schumann (eds), *Between Mass Death and Individual Loss: The Place of the Dead in Twentieth-century Germany*, New York, 2008

Conze, Eckart, Norbert Frei, Peter Hayes and Moshe Zimmermann, *Das Amt und die Vergangenheit: Deutsche Diplomaten im Dritten Reich und in der Bundesrepublik*, Munich, 2010

Corni, Gustavo and Horst Gies, *Brot – Butter – Kanonen: Die Ernährungswirtschaft in Deutschland under der Diktatur Hitlers*, Berlin, 1997

Cox, Mary, 'Hunger games: Or how the Allied blockade in the First World War deprived German children of nutrition, and Allied food aid subsequently saved them', *Economic History Review*, Sept. 2014: doi: 10.1111/ehr.12070

Daiber, Hans, *Schaufenster der Diktatur: Theater im Machtbereich*, Stuttgart, 1995

Dallin, Alexander, *German Rule in Russia, 1941–1945: A Study of Occupation Policies*, 2nd rev. ed., Boulder, Col., 1981

Daniel, Ute, *The War from Within: German Working-class Women in the First World War*, Oxford, 1997

Daniel, Ute (ed.), *Augenzeugen: Kriegsberichterstattung vom 18. bis zum 21. Jahrhundert*, Göttingen, 2006

Danimann, Franz, *Flüsterwitze und Spottgedichte unterm Hakenkreuz*, Vienna, 1983

Datner, Szymon, 'Crimes committed by the Wehrmacht during the September Campaign and the period of military government (1 Sept. 1939–25 Oct. 1939)', *Polish Western Affairs*, 3 (1962), 294–328

Davies, Norman, *Rising '44: 'The Battle for Warsaw'*, London, 2004

Davies, Norman and Roger Moorhouse, *Microcosm: Portrait of a Central European City*, London, 2002

Davies, R.W. and Steve Wheatcroft, *The Years of Hunger: Soviet Agriculture, 1931–1933*, Basingstoke, 2004

Davies, R.W., Oleg Khlevnyuk and Steve Wheatcroft, *The Years of Progress: The Soviet Economy, 1934–1936*, Basingstoke, 2014

Deák, István, Jan Gross and Tony Judt (eds), *The Politics of Retribution in Europe: World War II and its Aftermath*, Princeton, NJ, 2000

Dean, Martin, *Collaboration in the Holocaust: Crimes of the Local Police in Belorussia and Ukraine, 1941–44*, Basingstoke and London, 2000

Defalque, R.J. and A.J. Wright, 'Methamphetamine for Hitler's Germany, 1937 to 1945', *Bulletin of Anesthesia History*, 29/2 (April 2011), 21–4

Dennler, Wilhelm *Die böhmische Passion*, Freiburg im Breisgau, 1953

Dettmar, Ute, 'Der Kampf gegen "Schmutz und Schund"', in Joachim Hopster (ed.), *Die Kinder- und Jugendliteratur in der Zeit der Weimarer Republik*, Frankfurt am Main, 2012, 565–586

Dickinson, Edward, *The Politics of German Child Welfare from the Empire to the Federal Republic*, Cambridge, Mass., 1996

Dieckman, Christoph, 'The War and the Killing of the Lithuanian Jews', in Ulrich Herbert (ed.), *National Socialist Extermination Policies*, New York/ Oxford, 2000, 240–75

Diedrich, Torsten, *Paulus: Das Trauma von Stalingrad: Eine Biographie*, Paderborn, 2008

Diercks, Herbert (ed.), *Verschleppt nach Deutschland! Jugendliche Häftlinge des KZ Neuengamme aus der Sowjetunion erinnern sich*, Bremen, 2000

Diller, Ansgar, *Rundfunkpolitik im Dritten Reich*, Munich, 1980

Doenecke, Justus and Mark Stoler, *Debating Franklin D. Roosevelt's Foreign Policies, 1933–1945*, Oxford, 2005

Dörner, Bernward, *'Heimtücke': Das Gesetz als Waffe: Kontrolle, Abschreckung und Verfolgung in Deutschland 1933–1945*, Paderborn, 1985

Dörr, Margarete, *'Wer die Zeit nicht miterlebt hat . . .': Frauenerfahrungen im Zweiten Weltkrieg und in den Jahren danach*, 1–3, Frankfurt am Main, 1998

Douglas, Ray, *Orderly and Humane: The Expulsion of the Germans after the Second World War*, New Haven, 2012

Dov Kulka, Otto and Eberhard Jäckel (eds), *Die Juden in den geheimen NS-Stimmungsberichten 1933–1945*, Düsseldorf, 2004

Drewniak, Bogusław, *Der deutsche Film 1938–1945*, Düsseldorf, 1987

Dröge, Franz, *Der zerredete Widerstand: Soziologie und Publizistik des Gerüchts im 2. Weltkrieg*, Düsseldorf, 1970

Drolshagen, Ebba, *Der freundliche Feind: Wehrmachtssoldaten im besetzten Europa*, Munich, 2009

Dunae, Patrick, 'Gender, Generations and Social Class: The Fairbridge Society and British Child Migration to Canada, 1930–1960', in Jon Lawrence and Pat Starkey (eds), *Child Welfare and Social Action: International Perspectives*, Liverpool, 2001, 82–100

Dülmen, Richard van, *Theatre of Horror: Crime and Punishment in early modern Germany*, Oxford, 1990

Düringer, Hermann and Jochen-Christoph Kaiser (eds), *Kirchliches Leben im Zweiten Weltkrieg*, Frankfurt am Main, 2005

Ebert, Jens, *Stalingrad: Eine deutsche Legende*, Reinbek, 1992

Eckel, Jan, *Hans Rothfels*, Göttingen, 2005

Emmerich, Norbert, 'Die Wittenauer Heilstätten 1933–1945', in Arbeitsgruppe zur Erforschung der Geschichte der Karl-Bonhoeffer-Nervenklinik (ed.), *Totgeschwiegen 1933–1945: Zur Geschichte der Wittenauer Heilstätten, seit 1957 Karl-Bonhoeffer-Nervenklinik*, Berlin, 1989, 185–9

Endlich, Stefanie, Monica Geyler-von Bernus and Beate Rossié (eds), *Christenkreuz und Hakenkreuz: Kirchenbau und sakrale Kunst im Nationalsozialismus*, Berlin, 2008

Engel, Gerhard, *Heeresadjutant bei Hitler 1938–1943*, Stuttgart, 1974

Epstein, Catherine, *Model Nazi: Arthur Greiser and the Occupation of Western Poland*, Oxford, 2010

Ericksen, Robert, *Theologians under Hitler: Gerhard Kittel, Paul Althaus, and Emanuel Hirsch*, New Haven, 1985

Erickson, John, *The Road to Berlin: Stalin's War with Germany*, 2, London, 1983

Ericsson, Kjersti and Eva Simonsen (eds), *Children of World War II*, Oxford, 2005

Evans, Jennifer V., *Life among the Ruins: Cityscape and Sexuality in Cold War Berlin*, Basingstoke, 2011

Evans, Richard J., *Rituals of Retribution: Capital Punishment in Germany, 1600–1987*, Oxford, 1996

Evans, Richard J., *Telling Lies about Hitler: The Holocaust, History and the David Irving Trial*, London, 2002

Evans, Richard J., *The Coming of the Third Reich*, London, 2003

Evans, Richard J., *The Third Reich in Power, 1933–1939*, London, 2005

Evans, Richard J., *The Third Reich at War, 1939–1945*, London, 2008

Faulstich, Heinz, 'Die Zahl der "Euthanasie"-Opfer', in Andreas Frewer and Clemens Eickhoff (eds), *'Euthanasie' und aktuelle Sterbehilfe-Debatte*, Frankfurt am Main, 2000, 218–32

Faulstich, Heinz, *Von der Irrenfürsorge zur 'Euthanasie': Geschichte der badischen Psychiatrie bis 1945*, Freiburg, 1993

Feingold, Henry L., *The Politics of Rescue: The Roosevelt Administration and the Holocaust, 1938–1945*, New Brunswick, NJ, 1970

Fenwick, Luke, 'Religion in the Wake of "Total War": Protestant and Catholic Communities in Thuringia and Saxony-Anhalt, 1945–9', D.Phil. thesis, Oxford, 2011

Fieberg, Gerhard, Ralph Angermund and Gertrud Sahler (eds), *Im Namen des deutschen Volkes: Justiz und Nationalsozialismus*, Cologne, 1989

Fisch, Bernhard, *Nemmersdorf, Oktober 1944: Was in Ostpreußen tatsächlich geschah*, Berlin, 1997

Fisch, Bernhard, 'Nemmersdorf 1944', in Gerd R. Ueberschär (ed.), *Orte des Grauens: Verbrechen im Zweiten Weltkrieg*, Darmstadt, 2003, 155–67

Fisch, Bernhard, 'Nemmersdorf 1944 – ein bisher unbekanntes zeitnahes Zeugnis', *Zeitschrift für Ostmitteleuropa-Forschung*, 56/1 (2007), 105–14

Fishman, Sarah, *The Battle for Children: World War II Youth Crime, and Juvenile Justice in Twentieth-century France*, Cambridge, Mass., 2002

Fleischhauer, Ingeborg, *Die Chance des Sonderfriedens: Deutsch-sowjetische Geheimgespräche 1941–1945*, Berlin, 1986

Fleming, Nicholas, *August 1939: The Last Days of Peace*, London, 1979

Forsbach, Ralf, *Die medizinische Fakultät der Universität Bonn im 'Dritten Reich'*, Munich, 2006

Förschler, Andreas, *Stuttgart 1945: Kriegsende und Neubeginn*, Gudensberg-Gleichen, 2004

Forschungsstelle für Zeitgeschichte in Hamburg (ed.), *Hamburg im 'Dritten Reich'*, Göttingen, 2005

Förster, Jürgen, 'Hitler turns East: German War Policy in 1940 and 1941', in Bernd Wegner (ed.), *From Peace to War: Germany, Soviet Russia and the World, 1939–1941*, Oxford, 1997, 115–33

Forstman, Jack, *Christian Faith in Dark Times: Theological Conflicts in the Shadow of Hitler*, Louisville, 1992

Forty, George, *Villers-Bocage*, Stroud, 2004

Fox, Frank, 'Jewish victims of the Katyn Massacre', *East European Jewish Affairs*, 23: 1 (1993), 49–55

Fox, Jo, *Film Propaganda in Britain and Nazi Germany: World War II Cinema*, Oxford, 2007

Franks, Norman, *The Air Battle of Dunkirk*, London, 1983

Frei, Norbert (ed.), *Medizin und Gesundheitspolitik in der NS-Zeit*, Munich, 1991

Frei, Norbert, *National Socialist Rule in Germany: The Führer State, 1933–1945*, Oxford, 1993

Frei, Norbert (ed.), *Karrieren im Zwielicht: Hitlers Eliten nach 1945*, Frankfurt am Main, 2001

Frei, Norbert, *Adenauer's Germany and the Nazi Past: The Politics of Amnesty and Integration*, New York, 2002

Frei, Norbert and Johannes Schmitz (eds), *Journalismus im Dritten Reich*, Munich, 1989

Frei, Norbert, Sybille Steinbacher and Bernd Wagner (eds), *Ausbeutung, Vernichtung, Öffentlichkeit*, Munich, 2000

Frewer, Andreas and Clemens Eickhoff (eds), *'Euthanasie' und aktuelle Sterbehilfe-Debatte*, Frankfurt am Main, 2000

Friedländer, Saul, *Kurt Gerstein: The Ambiguity of Good*, New York, 1969

Friedländer, Saul, *Nazi Germany and the Jews*, 1, *The Years of Persecution, 1933–39*, London, 1997

Friedländer, Saul, *The Years of Extermination: Nazi Germany and the Jews, 1939–1945*, 2, London, 2007

Friedrich, Ernst, *Krieg dem Kriege*, Munich, 2004

Friedrich, Jörg, '"Die Wohnungsschlüssel sind beim Hausverwalter abzugeben": Die Ausschlachtung der jüdischen Hinterlassenschaft', in Jörg Wollenberg (ed.), *'Niemand war dabei und keiner hat's gewußt': Die deutsche Öffentlichkeit und die Judenverfolgung 1933–1945*, Munich, 1989, 188–203

Friedrich, Jörg, *Der Brand: Deutschland im Bombenkrieg 1940–1945*, Munich, 2002

Frieser, Karl-Heinz, 'Zusammenbruch im Osten', *DRZW*, 8 (2007), 493–678

Frieser, Karl-Heinz, *The Blitzkrieg Legend: The 1940 Campaign in the West*, Annapolis, 2005

Frings, Josef Kardinal, *Für die Menschen bestellt*, Cologne, 1973

Fritzsch, Robert, *Nürnberg im Krieg*, Düsseldorf, 1984

Fritzsche, Peter, 'Volkstümliche Erinnerung und deutsche Identität nach dem Zweiten Weltkrieg', in Konrad Jarausch and Martin Sabrow (eds), *Verletztes Gedächtnis: Erinnerungskultur und Zeitgeschichte im Konflikt*, Frankfurt am Main, 2002, 75–97

Fritzsche, Peter, *Life and Death in the Third Reich*, Cambridge, Mass., 2008

Fuchs, Stephan, *'Vom Segen des Krieges': Katholische Gebildete im ersten Weltkrieg: Eine Studie zur Kriegsdeutung im akademischen Katholizismus*, Stuttgart, 2004

Gailus, Manfred, 'Keine gute Performance', in Manfred Gailus and Armin Nolzen (eds), *Zerstrittene 'Volksgemeinschaft': Glaube, Konfession und Religion im Nationalsozialismus*, Göttingen, 2011, 96–121

Gailus, Manfred, *Protestantismus und Nationalsozialismus: Studien zur nationalsozialistischen Durchdringung des protestantischen Sozialmilieus in Berlin*, Cologne, 2001

Gailus, Manfred and Hartmut Lehmann (eds), *Nationalprotestantische Mentalitäten*, Göttingen, 2005

Gailus, Manfred and Armin Nolzen (eds), *Zerstrittene 'Volksgemeinschaft': Glaube, Konfession und Religion im Nationalsozialismus*, Göttingen, 2011

Gall, Lothar (ed.), *Krupp im 20. Jahrhundert: Die Geschichte des Unternehmens vom Ersten Weltkrieg bis zur Gründung der Stiftung*, Berlin, 2002

Ganzenmüller, Jörg, *Das belagerte Leningrad 1941–1944: Die Stadt in den Strategien von Angreifern und Verteidigern*, Paderborn, 2006

Garbe, Detlef, *Between Resistance and Martyrdom: Jehovah's Witnesses in the Third Reich*, Madison, Wis., 2008

Gardner, W.J.R., *The Evacuation from Dunkirk: 'Operation Dynamo', 26 May–4 June 1940*, London, 1949

Gassert, Philipp and Alan E. Steinweis (eds), *Coping with the Nazi Past: West German Debates on Nazism and Generational Conflict, 1955–1975*, New York, 2006

Gehrke, Hans-Joachim, 'Die Thermopylenrede Hermann Görings zur Kapitulation Stalingrads: Antike Geschichtsbilder im Wandel von Heroenkult zum Europadiskurs', in Bernd Martin (ed.), *Der Zweite Weltkrieg in historischen Reflexionen*, Freiburg, 2006, 13–29

Gellately, Robert, *The Gestapo and German Society: Enforcing Racial Policy, 1933–1945*, Oxford, 1990

Gellately, Robert, *Backing Hitler: Consent and Coercion in Nazi Germany*, Oxford, 2001

Gepp, Thomas (ed.), *Essen im Luftkrieg*, Essen, 2000

Gerlach, Christian, *Krieg, Ernährung, Völkermord: Forschungen zur deutschen Vernichtungspolitik im zweiten Weltkrieg*, Hamburg, 1998

Gerlach, Christian, *Kalkulierte Morde: Die deutsche Wirtschafts- und Vernichtungspolitik in Weissrussland 1941 bis 1944*, Hamburg, 1999

Gerlach, Wolfgang, *And the Witnesses were Silent: The Confessing Church and the Persecution of the Jews*, Lincoln, Nebr., 2000

Gerwarth, Robert, *Hitler's Hangman: The Life of Heydrich*, New Haven, 2011

Gève, Thomas, *Youth in Chains*, Jerusalem, 1981

Geyer, Michael, 'Cold War Angst: The Case of West German Opposition to Rearmament and Nuclear Weapons', in Hanna Schissler (ed.), *The Miracle Years: A Cultural History of West Germany, 1949–1968*, Princeton, 2001, 376–408

Geyer, Michael, 'Endkampf 1918 and 1945: German Nationalism, Annihilation and Self-destruction', in Alf Lüdtke and Bernd Weisbrod (eds), *No Man's Land of Violence: Extreme Wars in the 20th Century*, Göttingen, 2006, 35–67

Gilbert, Martin, *The Holocaust: The Jewish Tragedy*, London, 1986

Gildea, Robert, *Marianne in Chains: Daily Life in the Heart of France during the German Occupation*, London, 2002

Gildea, Robert, Oliver Wieviorka and Anette Warring (eds), *Surviving Hitler and Mussolini: Daily Life in Occupied Europe*, Oxford, 2006

Gillingham, J.R., *Industry and Politics in the Third Reich: Ruhr Coal, Hitler and Europe*, London, 1985

Giziowski, Richard J., *The Enigma of General Blaskowitz*, London, 1997

Glantz, David, *Barbarossa Derailed: The Battle for Smolensk, 10 July–10 September 1941*, Solihull, 2010

Glantz, David, *When Titans Clashed: How the Red Army Stopped Hitler*, Lawrence, Kan., 1995

Gleiss, Horst, *Breslauer Apokalypse 1945*, 3, Wedel, 1986

Godau-Schüttke, Klaus-Detlev, *Ich habe nur dem Recht gedient: Die 'Renazifizierung' der schleswig-holsteinischen Justiz nach 1945*, Baden-Baden, 1993

Goeschel, Christian, *Suicide in Nazi Germany*, Oxford, 2009

Goltermann, Svenja, *Die Gesellschaft der Überlebenden: Deutsche Kriegsheimkehrer und ihre Gewalterfahrungen im Zweiten Weltkrieg*, Munich, 2009

Goltz, Anna von der, *Hindenburg: Power, Myth, and the Rise of the Nazis*, Oxford, 2009

Gordon, Bertram, 'Ist Gott französisch? Germans, tourism and occupied France 1940–1944', *Modern and Contemporary France*, 4/3 (1996), 287–98

Gordon, Sarah, *Hitler, Germans and the 'Jewish Question'*, Princeton, 1984

Görtemaker, Heike, *Ein deutsches Leben: Die Geschichte der Margret Boveri 1900–1975*, Munich, 2005

Goschler, Constantin (ed.), *Wiedergutmachung: Westdeutschland und die Verfolgten des Nationalsozialismus (1950–1954)*, Munich, 1992

Gottwaldt, Alfred, Norbert Kampe and Peter Klein (eds), *NS-Gewaltherrschaft: Beiträge zur historischen Forschung und juristischen Aufarbeitung*, Berlin, 2005

Graser, Gerhard, *Zwischen Kattegat und Kaukasus: Weg und Kämpfe der 198. Infanterie-Division 1939–1945*, Tübingen, 1961

Grass, Günter, *Im Krebsgang*, Göttingen, 2002

Gregor, Neil, '"Is he still alive, or long since dead?": Loss, absence and remembrance in Nuremberg, 1945–1956', *German History*, 21/2 (2003), 183–202

Grenkevich, Leonid D., *The Soviet Partisan Movement, 1941–1944: A Critical Historiographical Analysis*, London, 1999

Gribaudi, Gabriella, *Guerra totale: Tra bombe alleate e violenze naziste: Napoli e il fronte meridionale 1940–1944*, Turin, 2005

Griech-Polelle, Beth A., *Bishop von Galen: German Catholicism and National Socialism*, New York, 2002

Grimm, Barbara, 'Lynchmorde an alliierten Fliegern im Zweiten Weltkrieg', in Dietmar Süß (ed.), *Deutschland im Luftkrieg: Geschichte und Erinnerung*, Munich, 2007, 71–84

Groehler, Olaf, *Bombenkrieg gegen Deutschland*, Berlin, 1990

Gröschner, Annett (ed.), *'Ich schlug meiner Mutter die brennenden Funken ab': Berliner Schulaufsätze aus dem Jahr 1946*, Berlin, 1996

Gross, Jan, 'A Tangled Web: Confronting Stereotypes concerning Relations between Poles, Germans, Jews, and Communists', in István Deák, Jan Gross, and Tony Judt (eds), *The Politics of Retribution in Europe: World War II and its Aftermath*, Princeton, NJ, 2000, 74–129

Gross, Jan, *Fear: Anti-Semitism in Poland after Auschwitz: An Essay in Historical Interpretation*, Princeton, NJ, 2006

Grossjohann, Georg, *Five Years, Four Fronts: A German Officer's World War II Combat Memoir*, New York, 2005

Grossman, Wassili Semjonowitsch, and Ilja Ehrenburg (eds), *Das Schwarzbuch: Der Genozid an den sowjetischen Juden*, Reinbek bei Hamburg, 1994

Grossman, Vasily, *A Writer at War: Vasily Grossman with the Red Army, 1941–1945*, Antony Beevor and Luba Vinogradova (eds), London, 2005

Gruchmann, Lothar (ed.), *Autobiographie eines Attentäters: Aussage zum Sprengstoffanschlag im Bürgerbräukeller, München am 8. November 1939*, Stuttgart, 1970

Gruchmann, Lothar, *Justiz im Dritten Reich: Anpassung und Unterwerfung in der Ära Gürtner*, Munich, 1990

Gruchmann, Lothar, 'Korruption im Dritten Reich: Zur "Lebensmittelversorgung der NS-Führerschaft"', *VfZ*, 42 (1994), 571–93

Gruner, Wolf, *Widerstand in der Rosenstrasse: Die Fabrik-Aktion und die Verfolgung der 'Mischehen' 1943*, Frankfurt am Main, 2005

Grüttner, Michael, Rüdiger Hachtmann and Heinz-Gerhardt Haupt (eds), *Geschichte und Emanzipation: Festschrift für Reinhard Rürup*, Frankfurt am Main/New York, 1999

Guderian, Heinz, *Erinnerungen eines Soldaten*, Heidelberg, 1951

Gurfein, M.J. and Morris Janowitz, 'Trends in Wehrmacht morale', *Public Opinion Quarterly*, Spring 1946, 78–84

Gutteridge, Richard, *Open Thy Mouth for the Dumb! The German Evangelical Church and the Jews, 1879–1950*, Oxford, 1976

Haag, Anna, *Das Glück zu leben*, Stuttgart, 1967

Haase, Norbert and Gerhard Paul (eds), *Die anderen Soldaten: Wehrkraftzersetzung, Gehorsamsverweigerung und Fahnenflucht im Zweiten Weltkrieg*, Frankfurt am Main, 1995

Haebich, Anna, 'Between knowing and not knowing: Public knowledge of the stolen generations', *Aborginal History*, 25 (2001), 70–90

Hahnke, Heinz, *Luftkrieg und Zivilbevölkerung*, Frankurt, 1991

Haller, Uli, *Lieutenant General Karl Strecker: The Life and Thought of a German Military Man*, Westport, Conn., 1994

Hamm, Berndt, 'Schuld und Verstrickung der Kirche', in Wolfgang Stegemann (ed.), *Kirche und Nationalsozialismus*, Stuttgart, 1992, 13–49

Hämmerle, Christa, Oswald Überegger and Birgitta Bader Zaar (eds), *Gender and the First World War*, Basingstoke, 2014

Hansch-Singh, Annegret, *Rassismus und Fremdarbeitereinsatz im Zweiten Weltkrieg*, Berlin, 1991

Hansen, Eckhard, *Wohlfahrtspolititk im NS-Staat: Motivationen, Konflikte und Machtstrukturen im 'Sozialismus der Tat' des Dritten Reiches*, Augsburg, 1991

Hansen, Lulu Anne '"Youth off the Rails": Teenage Girls and German Soldiers – A Case Study in Occupied Denmark, 1940–1945', in Dagmar Herzog (ed.), *Brutality and Desire: War and Sexuality in Europe's Twentieth Century*, Basingstoke, 2009, 135–67

Harig, Ludwig, *Weh dem, der aus der Reihe tanzt*, Frankfurt am Main, 1993

Harris, Victoria, *Selling Sex in the Reich: Prostitutes in German Society, 1914–1945*, Oxford, 2010

Harten, Hans-Christian, *De-Kulturation und Germanisierung: Die nationalsozialistische Rassen- und Erziehungspolitik in Polen 1939–1945*, Frankfurt am Main, 1996

Hartmann, Christian, *Halder: Generalstabschef Hitlers 1938–1942*, Paderborn, 1991

Hartmann, Christian, *Wehrmacht im Ostkrieg: Front und militärisches Hinterland 1941–42*, Munich, 2009

Hartmann, Christian and Johannes Hürter, *Die letzten 100 Tage des Zweiten Weltkrieges*, Munich, 2005

Hartmann, Christian, Johannes Hürter and Ulrike Jureit (eds), *Verbrechen der Wehrmacht: Bilanz einer Debatte*, Munich, 2005

Hartmann, Grethe, *The Girls they Left Behind*, Copenhagen, 1946

Harvey, Elizabeth, *Youth and the Welfare State in Weimar Germany*, Oxford, 1993

Harvey, Elizabeth, *Women and the Nazi East: Agents and Witnesses of Germanization*, New Haven and London, 2003

Harvey, Elizabeth, '"Ich war überall": Die NS-Propagandaphotographin Liselotte Purper', in Sybille Steinbacher (ed.), *Volksgenossinnen: Frauen in der NS-Volksgemeinschaft*, Constance, 2007, 138–53

Harvey, Elizabeth, 'Seeing the World: Photography, Photojournalism and Visual Pleasure in the Third Reich', in Pamela Swett, Corey Ross and Fabrice d'Almeida (eds), *Pleasure and Power in Nazi Germany*, Basingstoke, 2011, 177–204

Haskins, Victoria and Margaret Jacobs, 'Stolen Generations and Vanishing Indians: The Removal of Indigenous Children as a Weapon of War in the United States and Australia, 1870–1940', in James Alan Marten (ed.), *Children and War: A Historical Anthology*, New York and London, 2002, 227–41

Hastings, Max, *Bomber Command*, Basingstoke, 2010

Hastings, Max, *Overlord: D-Day and the Battle for Normandy 1944*, London, 1984

Hauschild-Thiessen, Renate (ed.), *Die Hamburger Katastrophe vom Sommer 1943 in Augenzeugenberichten*, Hamburg, 1993

Havemann, Nils, *Fußball unterm Hakenkreuz: Der DFB zwischen Sport, Politik und Kommerz*, Bonn, 2005

Hayward, Joel, 'Too little too late: An analysis of Hitler's failure in 1942 to damage Soviet oil production', *Journal of Strategic Studies*, 18/4 (1995), 769–94

Heer, Hannes and Klaus Naumann (eds), *Vernichtungskrieg: Verbrechen der Wehrmacht 1941–1944*, Hamburg, 1995

Heidschmidt, Janet, 'Das Zeitzeugeninterview als Erweiterung der Quelle Feldpostbrief am Beispiel des Briefwechsels zwischen Ernst und Irene Guicking 1937 bis 1945', Diplomarbeit, Fachhochschule Potsdam, 2003

Heineman, Elizabeth, *What Difference Does a Husband Make? Women and Marital Status in Nazi and Postwar Germany*, Berkeley, 1999

Henke, Klaus-Dieter, *Die amerikanische Besetzung Deutschlands*, Munich, 1995

Hensle, Michael, *Rundfunkverbrechen: Das Hören von 'Feindsendern' im Nationalsozialismus*, Berlin, 2003

Herbert, Ulrich, 'Apartheid nebenan', in Lutz Niethammer (ed.), *'Die Jahre weiss man nicht, wo man die heute hinsetzen soll': Faschismuserfahrungen im Ruhrgebiet*, Berlin, 1983, 233–66

Herbert, Ulrich, *Best: Biographische Studien über Radikalismus, Weltanschauung und Vernuft, 1903–1989*, Bonn, 1996

Herbert, Ulrich, *Hitler's Foreign Workers: Enforced Foreign Labor in Germany under the Third Reich*, Cambridge, 1997

Herbert, Ulrich (ed.), *National Socialist Extermination Policies*, New York/Oxford, 2000

Herbert, Ulrich, 'Echoes of the *Volksgemeinschaft*', in Martina Steber and Bernhard Gotto (eds), *Visions of Community in Nazi Germany: Social Engineering and Private Lives*, Oxford, 2014, 60–72

Hermle, Siegfried, 'Die Bischöfe und die Schicksale "nichtarischer" Christen', in Manfred Gailus and Hartmut Lehmann (eds), *Nationalprotestantische Mentalitäten*, Göttingen, 2005, 263–306

Herrberger, Marcus (ed.), *Denn es steht geschrieben: 'Du sollst nicht töten!' Die Verfolgung religiöser Kriegsdienstverweigerer unter dem NS-Regime mit besonderer Berücksichtigung der Zeugen Jehovas (1939–1945)*, Vienna, 2005

Herzog, Dagmar, 'Desperately Seeking Normality: Sex and Marriage in the Wake of the War', in Richard Bessel and Dirk Schumann (eds), *Life after Death: Approaches to a Cultural and Social History of Europe during the 1940s and 1950s*, Cambridge, 2003, 161–92

Herzog, Dagmar, *Sex after Fascism: Memory and Morality in Twentieth-century Germany*, Princeton, 2005

Herzog, Dagmar (ed.), *Brutality and Desire: War and Sexuality in Europe's Twentieth Century*, Basingstoke, 2009

Hetzer, Tanja, '*Deutsche Stunde': Volksgemeinschaft und Antisemitismus in der politischen Theologie bei Paul Althaus*, Munich, 2009

Hilberg, Raul (ed.), *Documents of Destruction: Germany and Jewry, 1933–1945*, Chicago, 1971

Hilberg, Raul, *Die Vernichtung der europäischen Juden: Die Gesamtgeschichte des Holocaust*, Berlin, 1982

Hilberg, Raul, *Sonderzüge nach Auschwitz*, Mainz, 1981

Hilberg, Raul, *The Destruction of the European Jews*, London, 1961

Hilger, Andreas, *Deutsche Kriegsgefangene in der Sowjetunion: Kriegsgefangenenpolitik, Lageralltag und Erinnerung*, Essen, 2000

Hillgruber, Andreas, *Hitler, König Carol und Marschall Antonescu: Die deutsch-rumänischen Beziehungen 1938–1944*, Wiesbaden, 1953

Hillgruber, Andreas, *Hitlers Strategie: Politik und Kriegsführung 1940–1941*, Frankfurt am Main, 1965

Hillgruber, Andreas (ed.), *Staatsmänner und Diplomaten bei Hitler: Vertrauliche Aufzeichnungen über Unterredungen mit Vertretern des Auslandes*, 1–2., Frankfurt am Main, 1967/1970

Hillgruber, Andreas, *Zweierlei Untergang: Die Zerschlagung des Deutschen Reiches und das Ende des europäischen Judentums*, Berlin, 1986

Hionidou, Violetta, *Famine and Death in Occupied Greece, 1941–1944*, Cambridge, 2006

Hippel, Wolfgang von (ed.), *Freiheit, Gleichheit, Brüderlichkeit? Die französische Revolution im deutschen Urteil von 1789 bis 1945*, Munich, 1989

Hirschfeld, Gerhard (ed.), *Nazi Rule and Dutch Collaboration*, Oxford, 1988

Hoch, Anton, 'Der Luftangriff auf Freiburg am 10. Mai 1940', *VfZ*, 4 (1956), 115–44

Hochhuth, Rolf, *Eine Liebe in Deutschland*, Reinbek, 1978

Hockenos, Matthew, *A Church Divided: German Protestants Confront the Nazi Past*, Bloomington, Ind., 2004

Hockerts, Hans Günther, 'Integration der Gesellschaft: Gründungskrise und Sozialpolitik in der frühen Bundesrepublik', *Zeitschrift für Sozialreform*, 32 (1986), 25–41

Hoeniger, David, 'Symbolism and Pattern in Rilke's Duino Elegies', *German Life and Letters*, 3/4 (July 1950), 271–83

Hoffmann, Joachim, *Die Ostlegionen 1941–1943: Turkotataren, Kaukasier und Wolgafinnen im deutschen Heer*, Freiburg, 1976

Hoffmann, Kay, 'Der Mythos der perfekten Propaganda: Zur Kriegsberichterstattung der Wochenschau im Zweiten Weltkrieg', in Ute Daniel (ed.), *Augenzeugen: Kriegsberichterstattung vom 18. bis zum 21. Jahrhundert*, Göttingen, 2006, 169–192

Hoffmann, Peter, *The History of the German Resistance, 1933–1945*, Montreal, 1996

Hoffmann, Peter, *Stauffenberg: A Family History, 1905–1944*, McGill, 2003

Hoffmann, Stefan-Ludwig, 'Besiegte, Besatzer, Beobachter: Das Kriegsende im Tagebuch', in Daniel Fulda, Dagmar Herzog, Stefan-Ludwig Hoffmann and Till van Rahden (eds), *Demokratie im Schatten der Gewalt: Geschichten des Privaten im deutschen Nachkrieg*, Göttingen, 2010, 25–55

Hohkamp, Michaela and Claudia Ulbrich (eds), *Der Staatsbürger als Spitzel: Denunziation während des 18. und 19. Jahrhunderts aus europäischer Perspektive*, Leipzig, 2001

Hooton, E.R., *Luftwaffe at War*, Hersham, 2007

Hopster, Joachim (ed.), *Die Kinder- und Jugendliteratur in der Zeit der Weimarer Republik*, Frankfurt am Main, 2012

Hrabar, Roman, Zofia Tokarz and Jacek Wilczur, *Kinder im Krieg – Krieg gegen Kinder: Die Geschichte der polnischen Kinder 1939–1945*, Hamburg, 1981

Huber, Heinz and Artur Müller (eds), *Das Dritte Reich: Seine Geschichte in Texten, Bildern und Dokumenten*, Munich, 1964

Huber, Wolfgang, 'Die Kirche vor der "Judenfrage"', in Rolf Rentdorff and Ekkehard Stegemann (eds), *Auschwitz – Krise der christlichen Theologie*, Munich, 1980, 60–81

Hughes, Michael, *Shouldering the Burdens of Defeat: West Germany and the Reconstruction of Social Justice*, Chapel Hill, NC, 1999

Humburg, Martin, 'Feldpostbriefe aus dem Zweiten Weltkrieg: Zur möglichen Bedeutung im aktuellen Meinungsstreit unter besonderer Berücksichtigung des Themas "Antisemitismus"', *Militärgeschichtliche Mitteilungen*, 58 (1999), 321–43

Humburg, Martin, 'Siegeshoffnungen und "Herbstkrise" im Jahre 1941: Anmerkungen zu Feldpostbriefen aus der Sowjetunion', *Werkstattgeschichte*, 8 (1999), 25–40

Hummel, Karl-Joseph and Christoph Kösters (eds), *Kirchen im Krieg: Europa 1939–1945*, Paderborn, 2007

Hürter, Johannes, *Hitlers Heerführer: Die deutschen Oberbefehlshaber im Krieg gegen die Sowjetunion, 1941/42*, Munich, 2006

Jackson, Julian, *France: The Dark Years, 1940–1944*, Oxford, 2001

Jackson, Julian, *The Fall of France: The Nazi Invasion of 1940*, Oxford, 2004

Jacobmeyer, Wolfgang, *Vom Zwangsarbeiter zum heimatlosen Ausländer: Die Displaced Persons in Westdeutschland 1945–1951*, Göttingen, 1985

Jacobs, Ingeborg, *Freiwild: Das Schicksal deutscher Frauen 1945*, Berlin, 2009

Jacobsen, Hans-Adolf and Werner Jochmann (eds), *Ausgewählte Dokumente zur Geschichte des Nationalsozialismus 1933 bis 1945*, 2, Bielefeld, 1961

Jansen, Christian and Arno Weckbecker, *Der 'Volksdeutsche Selbstschutz' in Polen 1939/40*, Munich, 1992

Jarausch, Konrad and Martin Sabrow (eds), *Verletztes Gedächtnis: Erinnerungskultur und Zeitgeschichte im Konflikt*, Frankfurt am Main, 2002

Jarausch, Konrad H. and Michael Geyer, *Shattered Past: Reconstructing German Histories*, Princeton, 2003

Jatrzębski, Włodzimierz, *Der Bromberger Blutsonntag: Legende und Wirklichkeit*, Poznań, 1990

Jentsch, Werner, *Christliche Stimmen zur Wehrdienstfrage*, Kassel, 1952

Joel, Tony, *The Dresden Firebombing: Memory and the Politics of Commemorating Destruction*, London, 2013

Johe, Werner, 'Strategisches Kalkül und Wirklichkeit: Das "Unternehmen Gomorrha": Die Großangriffe der RAF gegen Hamburg im Sommer 1943', in Klaus-Jürgen Müller and David Dilks (eds), *Großbritannien und der deutsche Widerstand 1933–1944*, Paderborn, 1994, 217–27

Johnson, Eric, *The Nazi Terror: Gestapo, Jews and Ordinary Germans*, London, 1999

Jones, Michael, *Leningrad: State of Siege*, London, 2008

Jung, Hermann, *Die Ardennenoffensive 1944/45*, Göttingen, 1971

Jureit, Ulrike, 'Zwischen Ehe und Männerbund: Emotionale und sexuelle Beziehungsmuster im Zweiten Weltkrieg', *Werkstattgeschichte*, 22, 61–73

Justiz und NS-Verbrechen: Sammlung deutscher Strafurteile wegen nationalsozialistischer Tötungsverbrechen 1945–1966, Amsterdam, 1968–81

Justizbehörde Hamburg and Helge Grabitz (ed.), 'Von Gewohnheitsverbrechern, Volksschädlingen und Asozialen': Hamburger Justizurteile im Nationalsozialismus, Hamburg, 1995

Kaienburg, Hermann, Die Wirtschaft der SS, Berlin, 2003

Kalmbach, Peter, Wehrmachtjustiz, Berlin, 2012

Kaminski, Uwe, Zwangssterilisation und 'Euthanasie' im Rheinland: Evangelische Erziehungsanstalten sowie Heil- und Pflegeanstalten 1933–1945, Cologne, 1995

Kaminsky, Annette (ed.), Heimkehr 1948: Geschichte und Schicksale deutscher Kriegsgefangener, Munich, 1998

Kaplan, Marion, Between Dignity and Despair: Jewish Life in Nazi Germay, Oxford, 1998

Kardorff, Ursula von, Berliner Aufzeichnungen 1942 bis 1945, Peter Hartl (ed.), Munich, 1994

Kaspi, André, Les Juifs pendant l'occupation, Paris, 1991

Kater, Michael, The Nazi Party: A Social Profile of Members and Leaders, 1919–1945, Cambridge, Mass., 1983

Kay, Alex J., Exploitation, Resettlement, Mass Murder: Political and Economic Planning for German Occupation Policy in the Soviet Union, 1940–1941, New York/Oxford, 2006

Kedward, H.R., Resistance in Vichy France, Oxford, 1978

Keil, Wilhelm, Erlebnisse eines Sozialdemokraten, 1–2, Stuttgart, 1947

Kershaw, Ian, Popular Opinion and Political Dissent in the Third Reich: Bavaria, 1933–1945, Oxford, 1983

Kershaw, Ian, 'German Popular Opinion and the "Jewish Question": Some Further Reflections', in Arnold Paucker (ed.), Die Juden im nationalsozialistischen Deutschland, Tübingen, 1986, 365–86

Kershaw, Ian, The 'Hitler Myth': Image and Reality in the Third Reich, Oxford, 1989

Kershaw, Ian, Hitler, 1–2, London, 1998/2000

Kershaw, Ian, The End: Hitler's Germany, 1944–45, London, 2011

Kershaw, Ian and Moshe Lewin (eds), Stalinism and Nazism: Dictatorships in Comparison, Cambridge, 1997

Kershaw, Robert, War without Garlands: Operation Barbarossa, 1941/42, Shepperton, 2000

Kettenacker, Lothar (ed.), Ein Volk von Opfern? Die neue Debatte um den Bombenkrieg 1940–45, Berlin, 2003

Kirchner, Klaus, Flugblattpropaganda im 2. Weltkrieg, Munich, 1972

Klarsfeld, Serge, Vichy – Auschwitz: Die 'Endlösung der Judenfrage' in Frankreich, Darmstadt, 2007

Klausch, Hans-Peter, '"Erziehungsmänner" und "Wehrunwürdige": Die Sonder- und Bewährungseinheiten der Wehrmacht', in Norbert Haase and Gerhard Paul (eds), Die anderen Soldaten: Wehrkraftzersetzung, Gehorsamsverweigerung und Fahnenflucht im Zweiten Weltkrieg, Frankfurt am Main, 1995, 66–82

Klee, Ernst (ed.), *Dokumente zur 'Euthanasie'*, Frankfurt am Main, 1985

Klee, Ernst, *Was sie taten – was sie wurden: Ärzte, Juristen und andere Beteiligte am Kranken- oder Judenmord*, Frankfurt am Main, 1986

Klee, Ernst, *Die SA Jesu Christi: Die Kirchen im Banne Hitlers*, Frankfurt am Main, 1989

Klee, Ernst, Willi Dressen and Volker Riess (eds), *'The Good Old Days': The Holocaust as Seen by its Perpetrators and Bystanders*, Old Saybrook, 1991

Klee, Katja, *Im 'Luftschutzkeller des Reiches': Evakuierte in Bayern 1939–1953: Politik, soziale Lage, Erfahrungen*, Munich, 1999

Klemperer, Victor, *The Language of the Third Reich: LTI – Lingua Tertii Imperii: A Philologist's Notebook*, London, 2000

Klönne, Arno, *Gegen den Strom: Bericht über den Jugendwiderstand im Dritten Reich*, Frankfurt am Main, 1958

Knesebeck, Julia von dem, *The Roma Struggle for Compensation in Post-war Germany*, Hatfield, 2011

Knoch, Habbo, *Die Tat as Bild: Fotografien des Holocaust in der deutschen Erinnerungskultur*, Hamburg, 2001

Knoll, Harald, Peter Ruggenthaler and Barbara Stelzl-Marx, 'Zwangsarbeit bei der Lapp-Finze AG', in Stefan Karner, Peter Ruggenthaler and Barbara Stelzl-Marx (eds), *NS-Zwangsarbeit in der Rüstungsindustrie: Die Lapp-Finze AG in Karlsdorf bei Graz 1939 bis 1945*, Graz, 2004, 103-78

Koch, Hans-Jörg, *Das Wunschkonzert im NS–Rundfunk*, Cologne, 2003

Koch, Magnus, *Fahnenfluchten: Deserteure der Wehrmacht im Zweiten Weltkrieg – Lebenswege und Entscheidungen*, Paderborn, 2008

Koch, Manfred, 'Rilke und Hölderlin – Hermeneutik des Leids', *Blätter der Rilke-Gesellschaft*, 22 (1999), 91–102

Kock, Gerhard, *'Der Führer sorgt für unsere Kinder . . .' Die Kinderlandverschickung im Zweiten Weltkrieg*, Paderborn, 1997

Kollmeier, Kathrin, *Ordnung und Ausgrenzung: Die Disziplinarpolitik der Hitler-Jugend*, Göttingen, 2007

Königseder, Angelika and Juliane Wetzel, *Lebensmut im Wartesaal: Die jüdischen DPs (Displaced Persons) im Nachkriegsdeutschland*, Frankfurt am Main, 1994

Körner, Hans-Michael, 'Katholische Kirche und polnische Zwangsarbeiter 1939–1945', *Historisches Jahrbuch*, 1 (1992), 128–42

Kramarz, Joachim, *Claus Graf Stauffenberg, 15. November 1907–20. Juli 1944: Das Leben eines Offiziers*, Frankfurt am Main, 1965

Kramer, Alan and John Horne, *German Atrocities, 1914: A History of Denial*, New Haven, 2001

Kramer, Nicole, 'Mobilisierung für die "Heimatfront": Frauen im zivilen Luftschutz', in Sybille Steinbacher (ed.), *Volksgenossinnen: Frauen in der NS-Volksgemeinschaft*, Göttingen, 2007, 69–92

Kramer, Nicole, *Volksgenossinnen an der Heimatfront: Mobilisierung, Verhalten, Erinnerung*, Göttingen, 2011

Krause, Michael, *Flucht vor dem Bombenkrieg: 'Umquartierungen' im Zweiten Weltkrieg und die Wiedereingliederung der Evakuierten in Deutschland 1943–1963*, Düsseldorf, 1997

Krausnick, Helmut, Hans Buchheim, Martin Broszat, and Hans-Adolf Jacobsen (eds), *Anatomy of the SS State*, London, 1968

Krausnick, Helmut, and Hans-Heinrich Wilhelm, *Die Truppe des Weltanschauungskrieges: Die Einsatzgruppen der Sicherheitspolizei und des SD 1938–1942*, Stuttgart, 1981

Kreidler, Eugen, *Die Eisenbahnen im Machtbereich der Achsenmächte während des Zweiten Weltkrieges: Einsatz und Leistung für die Wehrmacht und Kriegswirtschaft*, Göttingen, 1975

'Kriegsgefangene und Wehrmachtsvermißte aus Hessen: Vorläufiges Ergebnis der amtlichen Registrierung vom 20.–30. Juni 1947', in *Staat und Wirtschaft in Hessen: Statistische Mitteilungen*, 2 (1947), 4, 110–112

Kris, Ernst and Hans Speier (eds), *German Radio Propaganda: Report on Home Broadcasts during the War*, London/New York, 1944

Krone, Andreas, 'Plauen 1945 bis 1949 – vom Dritten Reich zum Sozialismus', PhD diss., Technische Universität Chemnitz, 2001

Krüger, Norbert, 'Die Bombenangriffe auf das Ruhrgebiet', in Ulrich Borsdorf and Mathilde Jamin (eds), *Überleben im Krieg: Kriegserfahrungen in einer Industrieregion 1939–45*, Reinbek, 1989, 88–100

Krzoska, Markus, 'Der "Bromberger Blutsonntag" 1939: Kontroversen und Forschungsergebnisse', *VfZ*, 60/2 (2012), 237–48

Kuby, Erich, *The Russians and Berlin, 1945*, London, 1968

Kühl, Stefan, *The Nazi Connection: Eugenics, American Racism and German National Socialism*, New York, 1994

Kühne, Thomas, *Kameradschaft: Die Soldaten des nationalsozialistischen Krieges und das 20. Jahrhundert*, Göttingen, 2006

Kundrus, Birthe, and Patricia Szobar, 'Forbidden company: Romantic relationships between Germans and foreigners, 1939 to 1945', *Journal of the History of Sexuality*, 11/1–2 (Jan/April 2002), 201–22

Kundrus, Birthe, 'Totale Unterhaltung? Die kulturelle Kriegführung 1939 bis 1945 in Film, Rundfunk und Theater', *DRZW*, 9/2 (2005), 93–158

Kundrus, Birthe, *Kriegerfrauen: Familienpolitik und Geschlechterverhältnisse im Ersten und Zweiten Weltkrieg*, Hamburg, 1995

Kunz, Andreas, *Wehrmacht und Niederlage: Die bewaffnete Macht in der Endphase der nationalsozialistischen Herrschaft, 1944 bis 1945*, Munich, 2005

Kunz, Norbert, *Die Krim unter deutscher Herrschaft*, Darmstadt, 2005

Kunze, Karl, *Kriegsende in Franken und der Kampf um Nürnberg im April 1945*, Nuremberg, 1995

Kwiet, Konrad, 'The ultimate refuge: Suicide in the Jewish community under the Nazis', *Leo Baeck Institute Year Book*, XXIX, 1984, 173–98

Kwiet, Konrad and Helmut Eschwege, *Selbstverwaltung und Widerstand: Deutsche Juden im Kampf um Existenz und Menschenwürde 1939–1945*, Hamburg, 1984

Lacey, Kate, *Feminine Frequencies: Gender, German Radio, and the Public Sphere, 1923–1945*, Ann Arbor, 1996

Lagrou, Pieter, *The Legacy of Nazi Occupation in Western Europe: Patriotic Memory and National Recovery*, Cambridge, 1999

Lagrou, Pieter, 'The Nationalization of Victimhood: Selective Violence and National Grief in Western Europe, 1940–1960', in Richard Bessel and Dirk Schumann (eds), *Life after Death: Approaches to a Cultural and Social History of Europe during the 1940s and 1950s*, Cambridge, 2003, 243–58

Lakowski, Richard, 'Der Zusammenbruch der deutschen Verteidigung zwischen Ostsee und Karpaten', *DRZW*, 10/1 (2004), 461–679

Landeswohlfahrtsverband Hessen and Bettina Winter (eds), '*Verlegt nach Hadamar': Die Geschichte einer NS-'Euthanasie'-Anstalt*, Kassel, 1994

Lange, Herta and Benedikt Burkard (eds), '*Abends wenn wir essen fehlt uns immer einer': Kinder schreiben an die Väter 1939–1945*, Hamburg, 2000

Latour, Conrad, 'Goebbels' "Außerordentliche Rundfunkmaßnahmen" 1939–42', *VfZ*, 11/4 (1963), 418–55

Latzel, Klaus, 'Tourismus und Gewalt: Kriegswahrnehmung in Feldpostbriefen', in Hannes Heer and Klaus Neumann (eds), *Vernichtungskrieg: Verbrechen der Wehrmacht 1941–1944*, Hamburg, 1995, 447–59

Latzel, Klaus, *Deutsche Soldaten – nationalsozialistischer Krieg? Kriegserlebnis, Kriegserfahrung 1939–1945*, Paderborn, 2000

Lauber, Heinz, *Judenpogrom: 'Reichskristallnacht' November 1938 in Grossdeutschland*, Gerlingen, 1981

Lawrence, Jon and Pat Starkey (eds), *Child Welfare and Social Action: International Perspectives*, Liverpool, 2001

Lee Smith, Arthur, *Die 'vermißte Million': Zum Schicksal deutscher Kriegsgefangener nach dem zweiten Weltkrieg*, Munich, 1992

Lehmann, Hartmut, 'Religious Socialism, Peace, and Pacifism: The Case of Paul Tillich', in Roger Chickering and Stig Förster (eds), *The Shadows of Total War: Europe, East Asia, and the United States, 1919–1939*, New York, 2003, 85–9

Lepre, George, *Himmler's Bosnian Divison: The Waffen-SS Handshar Division 1943–1944*, Atglen, Pa., 1997

Lichtenstein, Heiner, 'Pünktlich an der Rampe: Der Horizont des deutschen Eisenbahners', in Jörg Wollenberg (ed.), '*Niemand war dabei und keiner hat's gewußt': Die deutsche Öffentlichkeit und die Judenverfolgung 1933–1945*, Munich, 1989, 204–44

Lichti, James Irvin, *Houses on the Sand? Pacifist Denominations in Nazi Germany*, New York, 2008

Lilienthal, Georg, *Der 'Lebensborn e.V.': Ein Instrument nationalsozialistischer Rassenpolitik*, Frankfurt am Main, 1993

Lipp, Anne, *Meinungslenkung im Krieg: Kriegserfahrung deutscher Soldaten und ihre Deutung 1914–1918*, Göttingen, 2003

Loeffel, Robert, 'Soldiers and terror: Re–evaluating the complicity of the Wehrmacht in Nazi Germany', *German History* 27/4 (2009), 514–30

Loeffel, Robert, *Family Punishment in Nazi Germany: Sippenhaft, Terror and Myth*, Basingstoke, 2012

Löffler, Klara, *Aufgehoben: Soldatenbriefe aus dem zweiten Weltkrieg: Eine Studie zur subjektiven Wirklichkeit des Krieges*, Bamberg, 1992

Longerich, Peter, *Politik der Vernichtung: Eine Gesamtdarstellung der national-sozialistischen Judenverfolgung*, Munich, 1998

Longerich, Peter, *'Davon haben wir nichts gewusst!': Die Deutschen und die Judenverfolgung 1933–1945*, Berlin, 2006

Longerich, Peter, *Holocaust: The Nazi Persecution and Murder of the Jews*, Oxford, 2010

Lorenz, Hilke, *Kriegskinder: Das Schicksal einer Generation Kinder*, Munich, 2003

Lowe, Keith, *Inferno: The Devastation of Hamburg, 1943*, London, 2007

Lower, Wendy, *Hitler's Furies: German Women in the Nazi Killing Fields*, London, 2013

Lubbeck, Wilhelm, *At Leningrad's Gates: The Combat Memoirs of a Soldier with Army Group North*, Philadelphia, 2006

Lüdtke, Alf, 'Denuziation – Politik aus Liebe?', in Michaela Hohkamp and Claudia Ulbrich (eds), *Der Staatsbürger als Spitzel: Denunziation während des 18. und 19. Jahrhunderts aus europäischer Perspektive*, Leipzig, 2001, 397–407

Lüdtke, Alf and Bernd Weisbrod (eds), *No Man's Land of Violence: Extreme Wars in the 20th Century*, Göttingen, 2006

Lukas, Richard C., *Did the Children Cry? Hitler's War against Jewish and Polish Children, 1939–1945*, New York, 1994

Lumans, Valdis, *Latvia in World War II*, New York, 2006

Luther-Jahrbuch: Organ der internationalen Lutherforschung: Festgabe für Paul Althaus, 25 (1958), Franz Lau (ed.) for the Luther–Gesellschaft, Göttingen

Lutz, Petr 'Eine "reichlich einsichtslose Tochter": Die Angehörigen einer in Hadamar ermorderten Patientin', in Uta George et al. (eds), *Hadamar: Heilstätte, Tötungsanstalt, Therapiezentrum*, Marburg, 2006, 293–304

Maas, Michael, *Freizeitgestaltung und kulturelles Leben in Nürnberg 1930–1945: Eine Studie zu Alltag und Herrschaftsausübung im Nationalsozialismus*, Nuremberg, 1994

MacDonald, Charles B., *United States Army in World War II: European Theater of Operations: The Last Offensive*, Washington, DC, 1973

McDougall, Alan, *Youth Politics in East Germany: The Free German Youth Movement, 1946–1968*, Oxford, 2004

McLellan, Josie, *Antifascism and Memory in East Germany: Remembering the International Brigades, 1945–1989*, Oxford, 2004

Madajczyk, Czesław, 'Introduction to General Plan East', *Polish Western Affairs*, 3/2 (1962), 391–442

Madajczyk, Czesław, *Die Okkupationspolitik Nazideutschlands in Polen 1939–1945*, Cologne, 1988

Mahood, Linda, *Policing Gender, Class and Family: Britain, 1850–1940*, London, 1995

Maislinger, Andreas, 'Der Fall Franz Jägerstätter', Dokumentationsarchiv des österreichischen Widerstandes, *Jahrbuch*, 1991, 20–31

Mallmann, Klaus-Michael, '"Volksjustiz gegen anglo-amerikanische Mörder": Die Massaker an westalliierten Fliegern und Fallschirmspringern 1944/45', in Alfred Gottwaldt, Norbert Kampe and Peter Klein (eds), *NS-Gewaltherrschaft: Beiträge zur historischen Forschung und juristischen Aufarbeitung*, Berlin, 2005, 202–13

Mallmann, Klaus–Michael, Jochen Böhler and Jürgen Matthäus (eds), *Einsatzgruppen in Polen*, Darmstadt, 2008

Mallmann, Klaus-Michael, and Bogdan Musial (eds), *Genesis des Genozids – Polen 1939–1941*, Darmstadt, 2004

Mann, Klaus, *Der Wendepunkt: Ein Lebensbericht*, Hamburg, 2001

Manoschek, Walter (ed.), *'Es gibt nur eines für das Judentum: Vernichtung': Das Judenbild in deutschen Soldatenbriefen 1939–1944*, Hamburg, 1995

Marcuse, Harold, *Legacies of Dachau: The Uses and Abuses of a Concentration Camp, 1933–2001*, Cambridge, 2001

Margalit, Gilad, *Germany and its Gypsies: A Post-Auschwitz Ordeal*, Madison, Wis., 2002

Margalit, Gilad, 'Dresden and Hamburg: Official Memory and Commemoration of the Victims of Allied Air Raids in the Two Germanies', in Helmut Schmitz (ed.), *A Nation of Victims? Representations of German Wartime Suffering from 1945 to the Present*, Amsterdam, 2007, 125–40

Margalit, Gilad, *Guilt, Suffering and Memory: Germany Remembers its Dead of World War II*, Bloomington, Ind., 2010

Mark, James, 'Remembering rape: Divided social memory and the Red Army in Hungary 1944–1945', *Past and Present*, 188 (2005), 133–61

Marszolek, Inge, '"Ich möchte Dich zu gern mal in Uniform sehen": Geschlechterkonstruktionen in Feldpostbriefen', *Werkstatt-Geschichte*, 22 (1999), 41–59

Marten, James Alan (ed.), *Children and War: A Historical Anthology*, New York and London, 2002

Martens, Erika, *Zum Beispiel Das Reich: Zur Phänomenologie der Presse im totalitären Regime*, Cologne, 1972

Martin, Bernd, *Friedensinitiativen und Machtpolitik im Zweiten Weltkrieg 1939–1943*, Düsseldorf, 1974

Martin, Bernd (ed.), *Der Zweite Weltkrieg in historischen Reflexionen*, Freiburg, 2006

Marxen, Klaus, *Das Volk und sein Gerichtshof*, Frankfurt am Main, 1994

Mason, Tim, *Arbeiterklasse und Volksgemeinschaft: Dokumente und Materialien zur deutschen Arbeiterpolitik 1936–1939*, Opladen, 1975

Mason, Tim, *Social Policy in the Third Reich*, Jane Caplan (ed.), Oxford, 1993

Matzerath, Horst (ed.), '. . . *Vergessen kann man die Zeit nicht, das ist nicht möglich . . .' Kölner erinnern sich an die Jahre 1929–1945*, Cologne, 1985

Maubach, Franka, 'Expansion weiblicher Hilfe: Zur Erfahrungsgeschichte von Frauen im Kriegsdienst', in Sybille Steinbacher (ed.), *Volksgenossinnen: Frauen in der NS-Volksgemeinschaft*, Göttingen, 2007, 93–111

Maubach, Franka, *Die Stellung halten: Kriegserfahrungen und Lebensgeschichten von Wehrmachthelferinnen*, Göttingen, 2009

Mausbach, Hans and Barbara Bromberger, 'Kinder als Opfer der NS-Medizin, unter besonderer Berücksichtigung der Kinderfachabteilungen in der Psychiatrie', in Christina Vanja and Martin Vogt (eds), *Euthanasie in Hadamar: Die nationalsozialistische Vernichtungspolitik in hessischen Anstalten*, Kassel, 1991, 145–56

Mazower, Mark, *Inside Hitler's Greece: The Experience of Occupation, 1941–44*, New Haven, 1993

Mazower, Mark, *Salonica, City of Ghosts: Christians, Muslims and Jews, 1430–1950*, London, 2005

Mazower, Mark, *Hitler's Empire: Nazi Rule in Occupied Europe*, London, 2008

Mechler, Wolf-Dieter, *Kriegsalltag an der 'Heimatfront': Das Sondergericht Hannover im Einsatz gegen 'Rundfunkverbrecher', 'Schwarzschlachter', 'Volksschädlinge' und andere 'Straftäter' 1939 bis 1945*, Hanover, 1997

Meinen, Insa, *Wehrmacht und Prostitution im besetzten Frankreich*, Bremen, 2002

Mennel, Robert, *Thorns and Thistles: Juvenile Delinquents in the United States, 1825–1940*, Hanover, NH, 1973

Merritt, Anna and Richard Merritt (eds), *Public Opinion in Occupied Germany: The OMGUS Surveys, 1945–1949*, Urbana, Ill., 1970

Merritt, Anna and Richard Merritt (eds), *Public Opinion in Semisovereign Germany: The HICOG Surveys, 1949–1955*, Urbana, Ill., 1980

Mertens, Annette, *Himmlers Klostersturm: Der Angriff auf katholische Einrichtungen im Zweiten Weltkrieg und die Wiedergutmachung nach 1945*, Paderborn, 2006

Mertens, Annette, 'NS-Kirchenpolitik im Krieg: Der Klostersturm und die Fremdnutzung katholischer Einrichtungen', in Karl-Joseph Hummel and Christoph Kösters (eds), *Kirchen im Krieg: Europa 1939–1945*, Paderborn, 2007, 245–64

Messerschmidt, Manfred, 'Die Wehrmacht: Vom Realitätsverlust zum Selbstbetrug', in Hans–Erich Volkmann (ed.), *Ende des Dritten Reiches – Ende des Zweiten Weltkrieges*, Munich, 1995, 223–57

Messerschmidt, Manfred, *Wehrmachtjustiz 1933–1945*, Paderborn, 2005

Messerschmidt, Manfred and Fritz Wüllner, *Die Wehrmachtjustiz im Dienste des Nationalsozialismus – Zerstörung einer Legende*, Baden-Baden, 1987

Meyer, Sibylle and Eva Schulze, '"Als wir wieder zusammen waren, ging der Krieg im Kleinen weiter": Frauen, Männer und Familien im Berlin der vierziger Jahre', in Lutz Niethammer and Alexander von Plato (eds), *'Wir kriegen jetzt andere Zeiten': Auf der Suche nach der Erfahrung des Volkes in nachfaschistischen Ländern*, Bonn, 1985, 305–26

Michel, Henri, *Paris allemand*, Paris, 1981

Middlebrook, Martin, *The Battle of Hamburg: Allied Bomber Forces against a German City in 1943*, London, 1980

Middlebrook, Martin, *The Berlin Raids: RAF Bomber Command Winter, 1943–44*, London, 1988

Moeller, Robert, *War Stories: The Search for a Usable Past in the Federal Republic of Germany*, Berkeley, 2001

Moeller, Robert, 'The Politics of the Past in the 1950s: Rhetorics of Vicitimisation in East and West Germany', in Bill Niven (ed.), *Germans as Victims: Remembering the Past in Contemporary Germany*, Basingstoke, 2006, 26–42

Moorhouse, Roger, *Killing Hitler*, London, 2006

Moorhouse, Roger, *Berlin at War: Life and Death in Hitler's Capital, 1939–45*, London, 2010

Morgan, Dagmar, *Weiblicher Arbeitsdienst in Deutschland*, Mainz, 1978

Motadel, David, *Islam and Nazi Germany's War*, Cambridge, Mass., 2014

Mühlen, Patrick, *Zwischen Hakenkreuz und Sowjetstern: Der Nationalismus der sowjetischen Orientvölker im Zweiten Weltkrieg*, Düsseldorf, 1971

Mühlhäuser, Regina, *Eroberungen: Sexuelle Gewalttaten und intime Beziehungen deutscher Soldaten in der Sowjetunion 1941*, Hamburg, 2010

Müller, Klaus-Jürgen and David Dilks (eds), *Großbritannien und der deutsche Widerstand 1933–1944*, Paderborn, 1994

Müller, Rolf-Dieter, *Der letzte deutsche Krieg*, Stuttgart, 2005

Müller, Rolf-Dieter, *An der Seite der Wehrmacht: Hitlers ausländische Helfer beim 'Kreuzzug gegen den Bolschewismus' 1941–1945*, Berlin, 2007

Müller, Rolf-Dieter, Nicole Schönherr and Thomas Widera (eds), *Die Zerstörung Dresdens am 13./15. Februar 1945: Gutachten und Ergebnisse der Dresdner Historikerkommission zur Ermittlung der Opferzahlen*, Dresden, 2010

Müller, Rolf-Dieter and Hans-Erich Volkmann (eds), *Hitlers Wehrmacht: Mythos und Realität*, Munich, 1999

Müller-Hillebrand, Burkhart, *Das Heer: Zweifrontenkrieg, 1–3*, Darmstadt, 1969

Mulligan, William, *The Creation of the Modern German Army: General Walther Reinhardt and the Weimar Republic, 1914–1930*, New York, 2004

Naimark, Norman, *The Russians in Germany: A History of the Soviet Zone of Occupation, 1945–1949*, Cambridge, Mass., 1995

Neander, Joachim, 'Seife aus Judenfett: Zur Wirkungsgeschichte einer zeit-genössischen Sage', *Fabula: Zeitschrift für Erzählforschung*, 46 (2005), 241–56

Nehring, Holger, *The Politics of Security: British and West German Protest Movements and the Early Cold War 1945–1970*, Oxford, 2013

Neugebauer, Wolfgang, *Opfer oder Täter*, Vienna, 1994

Neulen, Hans Werner, *An deutscher Seite: Internationale Freiwillige von Wehrmacht und Waffen-SS*, Munich, 1992

Neumann, Joachim, *Die 4. Panzerdivision 1938–1943: Bericht und Betrachtung zu zwei Blitzfeldzügen und zwei Jahren Krieg in Rußland*, Bonn, 1989

Nienhaus, Ursula, 'Hitlers willige Komplizinnen: Weibliche Polizei im Nationalsozialismus 1937 bis 1945', in Michael Grüttner, Rüdiger Hachtmann and Heinz-Gerhardt Haupt (eds), *Geschichte und Emanzipation: Festschrift für Reinhard Rürup*, Frankfurt am Main / New York, 1999, 517–39

Niethammer, Lutz (ed.), *'Die Jahre weiss man nicht, wo man die heute hinsetzen soll': Faschismuserfahrungen im Ruhrgebiet*, Berlin, 1983

Niethammer, Lutz, *'Hinterher merkt man, dass es richtig war, dass es schief-gegangen ist': Nachkriegserfahrungen im Ruhrgebiet*, Berlin, 1983

Niethammer, Lutz (ed.), *'Wir kriegen jetzt andere Zeiten': Auf der Suche nach der Erfahrung des Volkes in nachfaschistischen Ländern*, Berlin, 1985

Niewyk, Donald (ed.), *Fresh Wounds: Early Narratives of Holocaust Survival*, Chapel Hill, 1998

Nissen, Morgens, 'Danish Food Production in the German War Economy', in Frank Trentmann and Flemming Just (eds), *Food and Conflict in Europe in the Age of the Two World Wars*, Basingstoke, 2006, 172–92

Niven, Bill (ed.), *Germans as Victims: Remembering the Past in Contemporary Germany*, Basingstoke, 2013, 2006

Noakes, Jeremy (ed.), *Nazism: A Documentary Reader*, 1–4, Exeter, 1998

Noakes, Jeremy and Geoffrey Pridham (eds), *Nazism: A Documentary Reader*, 1–3, Exeter, 1983–1997

Noble, Alastair, *Nazi Rule and the Soviet Offensive in Eastern Germany, 1944–1945: The Darkest Hour*, Portland, Oreg., 2009

Noelle-Neumann, Elisabeth, 'The spiral of silence: A theory of public opinion', *Journal of Communication*, 24/2 (1974), 43–51

Nolte, Ernst, *Der europäische Bürgerkrieg 1917–1945: Nationalsozialismus und Bolschewismus*, Berlin, 1987

Nolzen, Armin, 'Die NSDAP, der Krieg und die deutsche Gesellschaft', *DRZW*, 9/1 (2004), 99–193

Nowak, Kurt, *'Euthanasie' und Sterilisierung im 'Dritten Reich'*, Göttingen, 1984

Nowak, Kurt, 'Widerstand, Zustimmung, Hinnahme: Das Verhalten der

Bevölkerung zur "Euthanasie"', in Norbert Frei (ed.), *Medizin und Gesundheitspolitik in der NS-Zeit*, Munich, 1991, 235–51

Offer, Avner, *The First World War: An Agrarian Interpretation*, Oxford, 1989

Orth, Karin, *Das System der nationalsozialistischen Konzentrationslager: Eine politische Organisationsgeschichte*, Hamburg, 1999

Osborn, Patrick, *Operation Pike: Britain versus the Soviet Union, 1939–1941*, Westport, Conn., 2000

Oswald, Rudolf, *'Fußball-Volksgemeinschaft': Ideologie, Politik und Fanatismus im deutschen Fußball 1919–1964*, Frankfurt am Main, 2008

Otto, Renate, 'Die Heilerziehungs- und Pflegeanstalt Scheuern', in Klaus Böhme and Uwe Lohalm (eds), *Wege in den Tod: Hamburgs Anstalt Langenborn und die Euthanasie in der Zeit des Nationalsozialismus*, Hamburg, 1993, 320–33

Oven, Wilfred von, *Finale Furioso: Mit Goebbels bis zum Ende*, Tübingen, 1974

Overmans, Rüdiger, *Deutsche militärische Verluste im zweiten Weltkrieg*, Munich, 1999

Overy, Richard, *Goering: The 'Iron Man'*, London, 1984

Overy, Richard, *Why the Allies Won*, London, 1995

Overy, Richard, *Russia's War*, London, 1998

Overy, Richard, *The Bombing War: Europe 1939–45*, London, 2013

Padfield, Peter, *Himmler: Reichsführer SS*, London, 1990

Pahl, Magnus, *Fremde Heere Ost: Hitlers militärische Feindaufklärung*, Munich, 2012

Paucker, Arnold (ed.), *Die Juden im nationalsozialistischen Deutschland*, Tübingen, 1986

Paulsson, Gunnar S., *Secret City: The Hidden Jews of Warsaw, 1940–1945*, New Haven and London, 2002

Peter, Karl Heinrich (ed.), *Spiegelbild einer Verschwörung: Die Kaltenbrunner-Berichte an Bormann und Hitler über das Attentat vom 20. Juli 1944: Geheime Dokumente aus dem ehemaligen Reichssicherheitshauptamt*, Stuttgart, 1961

Petö, Andrea, 'Memory and the Narrative of Rape in Budapest and Vienna in 1945', in Richard Bessel and Dirk Schumann (eds), *Life after Death: Approaches to a Cultural and Social History of Europe during the 1940s and 1950s*, Cambridge, 2003, 129–48

Peukert, Detlev, *Inside Nazi Germany: Conformity, Opposition and Racism in Everyday Life*, Harmondsworth, 1982

Phayer, Michael, *The Catholic Church and the Holocaust, 1930–1965*, Bloomington, Ind., 2000

Pick, Daniel, *The Pursuit of the Nazi Mind: Hitler, Hess and the Analysts*, Oxford, 2012

Plato, Alexander von, Almut Leh and Christoph Thonfeld (eds), *Hitlers Sklaven: Lebensgeschichtliche Analysen zur Zwangsarbeit im internationalen Vergleich*, Vienna/Cologne, 2008

Pohl, Dieter, *Von der 'Judenpolitik' zum Judenmord: Der Distrikt Lublin des Generalgouvernements 1939–1944*, Frankfurt am Main, 1993

Pohl, Dieter, *Nationalsozialistische Judenverfolgung in Ostgalizien 1941–1944: Organisation und Durchführung eines staatlichen Massenverbrechens*, Munich, 1996

Pohl, Dieter, *Die Herrschaft der Wehrmacht: Deutsche Militärbesatzung und einheimische Bevölkerung in der Sowjetunion 1941–1944*, Munich, 2008

Pospieszalski, Karol Marian, 'Nazi attacks on German property: The Reichsführer's plan of summer 1939', *Polish Western Affairs*, 24/1 (1983), 98–137

Powell, Anton and Stephen Hodkinson (eds), *Sparta beyond the Mirage*, London, 2002

Przyrembel, Alexandra, *'Rassenschande': Reinheitsmythos und Vernichtungslegitimation im Nationalsozialismus*, Göttingen, 2003

Quinkert, Babette, *Propaganda und Terror in Weißrußland 1941–1944: Die deutsche 'geistige' Kriegführung gegen Zivilbevölkerung und Partisanen*, Paderborn, 2009

Raschhofer, Hermann, *Der Fall Oberländer: Eine vergleichende Rechtsanalyse der Verfahren in Pankow und Bonn*, Tübingen, 1962

Rebenich, Stefan, 'From Thermopylae to Stalingrad: The Myth of Sparta in German Historiography', in Anton Powell and Stephen Hodkinson (eds), *Sparta beyond the Mirage*, London, 2002, 323–49

Reid, J. H., 'Heinrich Böll, "Wanderer, kommst du nach Spa . . .'", in Werner Bellmann (ed.), *Klassische deutsche Kurzgeschichten: Interpretationen*, Stuttgart, 2004, 96–106

Reifahrth, Dieter and Viktoria Schmidt-Linsenhoff, 'Die Kamera der Täter', in Hannes Heer and Klaus Naumann (eds), *Vernichtungskrieg: Verbrechen der Wehrmacht 1941–1944*, Hamburg, 1995, 475–503

Reimann, Aribert, *Der große Krieg der Sprachen: Untersuchungen zur historischen Semantik in Deutschland und England zur Zeit des Ersten Weltkrieges*, Essen, 2000

Reinhardt, Klaus, *Moscow – the Turning Point: The Failure of Hitler's Strategy in the Winter of 1941–42*, Oxford, 1992

Reisert, Karl, *O Deutschland hoch in Ehren – das deutsche Trutzlied: Sein Dichter und Komponist, seine Entstehung und Überlieferung*, Würzburg, 1917

Rentdorff, Rolf and Ekkehard Stegemann (eds), *Auschwitz – Krise der christlichen Theologie*, Munich, 1980

Richarz, Bernhard, *Heilen, Pflegen, Töten: Zur Alltagsgeschichte einer Heil- und Pflegeanstalt bis zum Ende des Nationalsozialismus*, Göttingen, 1987

Richie, Alexandra, *Faust's Metropolis: A History of Berlin*, New York, 1998

Riding, Alan, *And the Show Went On: Cultural Life in Nazi-occupied Paris*, London, 2011

Riedesser, Peter and Axel Verderber, 'Maschinengewehre hinter der Front': Zur Geschichte der deutschen Militärpsychologie, Frankfurt am Main, 1996

Rieß, Volker, 'Zentrale und dezentrale Radikalisierung: Die Tötungen "unwerten Lebens" in den annektierten west- und nordpolnischen Gebieten 1939–1941', in Klaus-Michael Mallmann and Bogdan Musial (eds), Genesis den Genozids – Polen 1939–1941, Darmstadt, 2004, 127–44

Roer, Dorothee and Dieter Henkel (eds), Psychiatrie im Faschismus: Die Anstalt Hadamar 1933–1945, Bonn, 1986

Rohde, Horst, 'Hitlers erster "Blitzkrieg" und seine Auswirkungen auf Nordosteuropa', DRZW, 2 (1979), 79–159

Rohland, Walter, Bewegte Zeiten: Erinnerungen eines Eisenhüttenmannes, Stuttgart, 1978

Röhm, Eberhard, Sterben für den Frieden: Spurensicherung: Hermann Stöhr (1898–1940) und die ökumenische Friedensbewegung, Stuttgart, 1980

Römer, Felix, Der Kommissarbefehl: Wehrmacht und NS-Verbrechen an der Ostfront 1941/42, Paderborn, 2008

Roseman, Mark, Recasting the Ruhr, 1945–1958: Manpower, Economic Recovery and Labour Relations, New York, 1992

Roseman, Mark, The Past in Hiding, London, 2000

Roseman, Mark, The Villa, the Lake, the Meeting: Wannsee and the Final Solution, London, 2003

Roseman, Mark, 'Gerettete Geschichte: Der Bund, Gemeinschaft für sozialistisches Leben im Dritten Reich', Mittelweg 36, 16/1 (2007), 100–21

Rosenstrauch, Hazel (ed.), Aus Nachbarn wurden Juden: Ausgrenzung und Selbstbehauptung 1933–1942, Berlin, 1988

Ross, Corey, Media and the Making of Modern Germany: Mass Communications, Society and Politics from the Empire to the Third Reich, Oxford, 2008

Rossino, Alexander, Hitler Strikes Poland: Blitzkrieg, Ideology and Atrocity, Lawrence, Kans., 2003

Rössler, Mechtild and Sabine Schleiermacher (eds), Der Generalplan Ost: Hauptlinien der nationalsozialistischen Planungs- und Vernichtungspolitik, Berlin, 1993

Rost, Karl Ludwig, Sterilisation und Euthanasie im Film des 'Dritten Reiches': Nationalsozialistische Propaganda in ihrer Beziehung zu rassenhygienischen Massnahmen des NS-Staates, Husum, 1987

Rubinstein, William D., The Myth of Rescue, London, 1997

Runzheimer, Jürgen, 'Der Überfall auf den Sender Gleiwitz im Jahre 1939', VfZ, 10 (1964), 408–26

Rüther, Martin (ed.), KLV: erweiterte Kinderlandverschickung 1940–1945, Cologne, 2000 [electronic resource only]

Rüther, Martin, Köln im Zweiten Weltkrieg: Alltag und Erfahrungen zwischen 1939 und 1945, Cologne, 2005

Rutz, Rainer, *Signal: Eine deutsche Auslandsillustrierte als Propagandainstrument im Zweiten Weltkrieg*, Essen, 2007

Sachse, Carola, *Siemens, der Nationalsozialismus und die moderne Familie: Eine Untersuchung zur sozialen Rationalisierung in Deutschland im 20. Jahrhundert*, Hamburg, 1990

Sander, Elke and Barbara Johr (eds), *BeFreier und Befreite: Krieg, Vergewaltigungen, Kinder*, Munich, 1992

Sandner, Peter, *Verwaltung des Krankenmordes: Der Bezirksverband Nassau im Nationalsozialismus*, Giessen, 2003

Sandkühler, Thomas, *'Endlösung' in Galizien: Der Judenmord in Ostpolen und die Rettungsinitiativen von Berthold Beitz 1941–1944*, Bonn, 1996

Sauer, Ernst, *Grundlehre des Völkerrechts*, Cologne, 1955

Scheck, Rafael, *Hitler's African Victims: The German Army Massacres of Black French Soldiers in 1940*, Cambridge, 2006

Schiller, Kay, *Gelehrte Gegenwelten: Über humanistische Leitbilder im 20. Jahrhundert*, Frankfurt am Main, 2000

Schissler, Hanna (ed.), *The Miracle Years: A Cultural History of West Germany, 1949–1968*, Princeton, NJ, 2001

Schlüter, Holger, *Die Urteilspraxis des Volksgerichtshofs*, Berlin, 1995

Schmidt, Gerhard, *Selektion in der Heilanstalt 1939–1945*, Frankfurt am Main, 1983

Schmidt, Paul, *Statist auf diplomatischer Bühne*, Bonn, 1953

Schmidt, Ulf, 'Reassessing the beginning of the "Euthanasia" programme', *German History*, 17/4 (1999), 543–550

Schmitz, Helmut (ed.), *A Nation of Victims? Representations of German Wartime Suffering from 1945 to the Present*, Amsterdam, 2007

Schmitz, Markus and Bernd Haunfelder (eds), *Humanität und Diplomatie: Die Schweiz in Köln 1940–1949*, Münster, 2001

Schmuhl, Hans-Walter, *Rassenhygiene, Nationalsozialismus, Euthanasie: Von der Verhütung zur Vernichtung 'lebensunwerten Lebens' 1890–1945*, Göttingen, 1987

Schneider, Karl, *Zwischen allen Stühlen: Der Bremer Kaufmann Hans Hespe im Reserve-Polizeibataillon 105*, Bremen, 2007

Schneider, Karl, *'Auswärts eingesetzt': Bremer Polizeibataillone und der Holocaust*, Essen, 2011

Schneider, Michael, *Unterm Hakenkreuz: Arbeiter und Arbeiterbewegung 1933 bis 1939*, Bonn, 1999

Schneider, Tobias, 'Bestseller im Dritten Reich', *VfZ*, 52/1 (2004), 77–98

Scholl, Inge, *Die weiße Rose*, Frankfurt am Main, 1952

Scholz, Susanne and Reinhard Singer, 'Die Kinder in Hadamar', in Dorothee Roer and Dieter Henkel (eds), *Psychiatrie im Faschismus: Die Anstalt Hadamar 1933–1945*, Bonn, 1986, 214–36

Schön, Hein, *Pommern auf der Flucht 1945: Rettung über die Ostsee aus den*

Pommernhäfen Rügenwalde, Stolpmünde, Kolberg, Stettin, Swinemünde, Greifswald, Stralsund und Saßnitz, Berlin, 2013

Schottländer, Rudolf, *Trotz allem ein Deutscher*, Freiburg, 1986

Schrapper, Christian and Dieter Sengling (eds), *Die Idee der Bildbarkeit: 100 Jahre sozialpädagogische Praxis in der Heilerziehungsanstalt Kalmenhof*, Weinheim, 1988

Schreiber, Gerhard, *Die italienischen Militärinternierten im deutschen Machtbereich 1943–1945: Verraten – verachtet – vergessen*, Munich, 1990

Schröder, Hans Joachim, *Die gestohlenen Jahre: Erzählgeschichten und Geschichtserzählung im Interview: Der Zweite Weltkrieg aus der Sicht ehemaliger Mannschaftssoldaten*, Tübingen, 1992

Schubert, Jochen, *Heinrich Böll: Schriftsteller*, Duisburg, 2007

Schuhmacher, Jacques, 'Nazi Germany and the Morality of War', D.Phil. thesis, Oxford, 2015 (in preparation)

Schüler, Klaus, *Logistik im Rußlandfeldzug: Die Rolle der Eisenbahn bei Planung, Vorbereitung und Durchführung des deutschen Angriffes auf die Sowjetunion bis zur Krise vor Moskau im Winter 1941–42*, Frankfurt am Main, 1987

Schulte, Jan, *Zwangsarbeit und Vernichtung: Das Wirtschaftsimperium der SS*, Paderborn, 2001

Schultheis, Herbert, *Juden in Mainfranken 1933–1945*, Bad Neustadt, 1980

Schulz, Hermann, Hartmut Radebold and Jürgen Reulecke, *Söhne ohne Väter: Erfahrungen der Kriegsgeneration*, Berlin, 2004

Schüssler, Werner, *Paul Tillich*, Münster, 1997

Schwartz, Paula, 'The politics of food and gender in occupied Paris', *Modern and Contemporary France*, 7/1 (1999), 35–45

Schumann, Wolfgang and Olaf Groehler with assistance of Wolfgang Bleyer (eds), *Deutschland im Zweiten Weltkrieg, 6, Die Zerschlagung des Hitlerfaschismus und die Befreiung des deutschen Volkes (Juni 1944 bis zum 8. Mai 1945)*, Berlin, 1985

Sefton Delmer, Denis, *Black Boomerang: An Autobiography*, 2, London, 1962

Seitz, Hanns, *Verlorene Jahre*, Lübeck, 1974

Service, Hugo, *Germans to Poles: Communism, Nationalism and Ethnic Cleansing after the Second World War*, Cambridge, 2013

Seydelmann, Gertrud, *Gefährdete Balance: Ein Leben in Hamburg 1936–1945*, Hamburg, 1996

Shephard, Ben, *War of Nerves: Soldiers and Psychiatrists, 1914–1994*, London, 2000

Shephard, Ben, *The Long Road Home: The Aftermath of the Second World War*, London, 2010

Shils, Edward and Morris Janowitz, 'Cohesion and disintegration in the Wehrmacht in World War II', *Public Opinion Quarterly*, 12/2 (1948), 280–315

Shirer, William, *This is Berlin: A Narrative History*, London, 1999

Sick, Dorothea, 'Euthanasie' im Nationalsozialismus am Beispiel des Kalmenhofs in Idstein im Taunus, Frankfurt am Main, 1983

Sielemann, Jürgen (ed.), Hamburger jüdische Opfer des Nationalsozialismus, Hamburg, 1995

Smelser, Ronald, Robert Ley: Hitler's Labor Front Leader, Oxford/NY, 1988

Smith Serrano, Andrew, German Propaganda in Military Decline 1943–1945, Edinburgh, 1999

Sollbach, Gerhard, Heimat Ade! Kinderlandverschickung in Hagen 1941–1945, Hagen, 1998

Sontheimer, Kurt, Antidemokratisches Denken in der Weimarer Republik: Die politischen Ideen des deutschen Nationalismus zwischen 1918 und 1933, Munich, 1994

Speer, Albert, Spandau: The Secret Diaries, New York, 1976

Spoerer, Mark, Zwangsarbeit unter dem Hakenkreuz: Ausländische Zivilarbeiter, Kriegsgefangene und Häftlinge im Deutschen Reich und im besetzten Europa 1938–1945, Stuttgart/Munich, 2001

Stahel, David, Operation Typhoon: Hitler's March on Moscow, October 1941, Cambridge, 2013

Stargardt, Nicholas, The German Idea of Militarism: Radical and Socialist Critics, 1866–1914, Cambridge, 1994

Stargardt, Nicholas, Witnesses of War: Children's Lives under the Nazis, London, 2005

Stargardt, Nicholas, 'Speaking in Public about the Murder of the Jews: What Did the Holocaust Mean to the Germans?', in Christian Wiese and Paul Betts (eds), Years of Persecution, Years of Extermination: Saul Friedländer and the Future of Holocaust Studies, London, 2010, 133–55

Stargardt, Nicholas, 'The troubled patriot: German Innerlichkeit in World War II', German History, 28/3 (2010), 326–42

Stargardt, Nicholas, 'Beyond "consent" or "terror": Wartime crises in Nazi Germany,' History Workshop Journal, 72 (2011), 190–204

Statistisches Bundesamt, Die deutschen Vertreibungsverluste, Wiesbaden, 1958,

Stayer, James M., Martin Luther, German Saviour: German Evangelical Theological Factions and the Interpretation of Luther, 1917–1933, Montreal, 2000

Steber, Martina, Ethnische Gewissheiten: Die Ordnung des Regionalen im bayerischen Schwaben vom Kaiserreich bis zum NS-Regime, Göttingen, 2010

Steber, Martina and Bernhard Gotto (eds), Visions of Community in Nazi Germany: Social Engineering and Private Lives, Oxford, 2014

Stegemann, Wolfgang (ed.), Kirche und Nationalsozialismus, Stuttgart, 1992

Steinbacher, Sibylle, 'Musterstadt' Auschwitz: Germanisierungspolitik und Judenmord in Ostoberschlesien, Munich, 2000

Steinbacher, Sybille (ed.), Volksgenossinnen: Frauen in der NS-Volksgemeinschaft, Göttingen, 2007

Steinert, Marlis, *Hitlers Krieg und die Deutschen: Stimmung und Haltung der deutschen Bevölkerung im Zweiten Weltkrieg*, Düsseldorf, 1970

Steinhoff, Johannes, Peter Pechel and Dennis Showalter, *Voices from the Third Reich: An Oral History*, London, 1991

Stelzl-Marx, Barbara (ed.), *Unter den Verschollenen: Erinnerungen von Dmitrij Čirov an das Kriegsgefangenenlager Krems-Gneixendorf 1941 bis 1945*, Waidhofen/Thaya, 2003

Stelzl-Marx, Barbara, *Zwischen Fiktion und Zeitzeugenschaft: Amerikanische und sowjetische Kriegsgefangene im Stalag XVIIB Krems-Gneixendorf*, Tübingen, 2003

Stephenson, Jill, '"Emancipation" and its problems: War and society in Württemberg, 1939–45', *European History Quarterly*, 17 (1987), 345–65

Stephenson, Jill, *Hitler's Home Front: Württemberg under the Nazis*, London, 2006

Stern, Frank, 'Antagonistic Memories', in Luisa Passerini (ed.), *Memory and Totalitarianism: International Yearbook of Oral History*, Oxford, 1992, 21–43

Stern, Frank, *The Whitewashing of the Yellow Badge: Antisemitism and Philosemitism in Postwar Germany*, Oxford, 1992

Stoltzfuss, Nathan, *Resistance of the Heart: Intermarriage and the Rosenstrasse Protest in Nazi Germany*, New York, 1996

Stone, Dan, *Histories of the Holocaust*, Oxford, 2010

Strachan, Hew, 'Clausewitz and the Dialectics of War', in Hew Strachan and Andreas Herberg-Rothe (eds), *Clausewitz in the Twenty-first Century*, Oxford, 2007, 14–44

Strachan, Hew and Andreas Herberg-Rothe (eds), *Clausewitz in the Twenty-first Century*, Oxford, 2007

Strauss, Herbert, 'Jewish emigration from Germany, Part I', *Leo Baeck Institute Year Book*, 25 (1980), 313–61

Strebel, Berhard, *Celle April 1945 Revisited*, Bielefeld, 2008

Streit, Christian, *Keine Kameraden: Die Wehrmacht und die sowjetischen Kriegsgefangenen 1941–1945*, Stuttgart, 1978

Strobl, Gerwin, *The Germanic Isle: Nazi Perceptions of Britain*, Cambridge, 2000

Strobl, Gerwin, *The Swastika and the Stage: German Theatre and Society, 1933–1945*, Cambridge, 2007

Strobl, Gerwin, *Bomben auf Oberdonau: Luftkrieg und Lynchmorde an alliierten Fliegern im 'Heimatgau des Führers'*, Linz, 2014

Strzelecki, Andrzej, *Endphase des KL Auschwitz: Evakuierung, Liquidierung und Befreiung des Lagers*, Oświęcim-Brzezinka, 1995

Süß, Dietmar (ed.), *Deutschland im Luftkrieg: Geschichte und Erinnerung*, Munich, 2007

Süß, Dietmar, *Death from the Skies: How the British and Germans Survived Bombing in World War II*, Oxford, 2014

Süß, Winfried, Der 'Volkskörper' im Krieg: Gesundheitspolitik, Gesundheitsver-
hältnisse und Krankenmord im nationalsozialistischen Deutschland 1939–1945,
Munich, 2003

Süß, Winfried, 'Antagonistische Kooperationen: Katholische Kirche und
nationalsozialistische Gesundheitspolitik', in Karl-Josef Hummel and
Christoph Kösters (eds), Kirchen im Krieg 1939–1945, Paderborn, 2007, 317–41

Sywottek, Jutta, Mobilmachung für den totalen Krieg: Die propagandistische Vorbereitung der deutschen Bevölkerung auf den Zweiten Weltkrieg, Opladen, 1976

Szarota, Tomasz, Warschau unter dem Hakenkreuz: Leben und Alltag im besetzten
Warschau, 1.10.1939 bis 31.7.1944, Paderborn, 1985

Szepansky, Gerda (ed.), Blitzmädel, Heldenmutter, Kriegerwitwe: Frauenleben im
Zweiten Weltkrieg, Frankfurt am Main, 1986

Szodrzynski, Joachim, 'Die "Heimatfront" zwischen Stalingrad und
Kriegsende', in Forschungsstelle für Zeitgeschichte in Hamburg (ed.),
Hamburg im 'Dritten Reich', Göttingen, 2005, 633–85

The Task of the Churches in Germany: Being a Report from a Delegation of British
Churchmen after a Visit to the British Zone October 16th–30th, 1946, Presented
to the Control Office for Germany and Austria, London, 1947

Taylor, Frederick, Dresden: Tuesday, 13 February 1945, London, 2004

Tessin, Georg, Verbände und Truppen der deutschen Wehrmacht und Waffen SS im
Zweiten Weltkrieg 1939–1945, 2, Die Landstreitkräfte, Osnabrück, 1973

Thalmann, Rita, Jochen Klepper: Ein Leben zwischen Idyllen und Katastrophen,
Gütersloh, 1997

Theweleit, Klaus, Male Fantasies, 1–2, Cambridge, 1987/1989

Thießen, Malte, Eingebrannt ins Gedächtnis: Hamburgs Gedenken an Luftkrieg
und Kriegsende 1943 bis 2005, Munich, 2007

Thomas, Martin, 'After Mers-el-Kébir: The armed neutrality of the Vichy
French Navy, 1940–43', English Historical Review, 112/447 (1997), 643–70

Tooze, Adam, The Wages of Destruction: The Making and Breaking of the Nazi
Economy, London, 2006

Toppe, Andreas, Militär und Kriegsvölkerrecht: Rechtsnorm, Fachdiskurs und
Kriegspraxis in Deutschland 1899–1940, Munich, 2008

Torrie, Julia, 'For Their Own Good': Civilian Evacuations in Germany and France,
1939–1945, New York/Oxford, 2010

Torrie, Julia, '"Our rear area probably lived too well": Tourism and the
German occupation of France, 1940–1944', Journal of Tourism History, 3/3
(Nov. 2011), 309–30

Trapp, Joachim, Kölner Schulen in der NS-Zeit, Cologne, 1994

Trevor-Roper, Hugh (ed.), Hitler's Table Talk, 1941–1944, London, 1953

Trevor-Roper, Hugh, The Last Days of Hitler, London, 1995

Trimmel, Gerald, Heimkehr: Strategien eines nationalsozialistischen Films,
Vienna, 1998

Troll, Hildebrand, 'Aktionen zur Kriegsbeendigung im Frühjahr 1945', in Martin Broszat, Elke Fröhlich and Anton Grossmann (eds), *Bayern in der NS-Zeit*, 4, Munich, 1981, 645–90

Trümpi, Fritz, *Politisierte Orchester: Die Wiener Philharmoniker und das Berliner Philharmonische Orchester im Nationalsozialismus*, Vienna, 2011

Ueberschär, Gerd R. (ed.), *Der 20. Juli 1944: Bewertung und Rezeption des deutschen Widerstandes gegen das NS-Regime*, Cologne, 1994

Ueberschär, Gerd R. (ed.), *Orte des Grauens: Verbrechen im Zweiten Weltkrieg*, Darmstadt, 2003

Ueberschär, Gerd R. and Lev A. Bezymenskij (eds), *Der deutsche Angriff auf die Sowjetunion 1941: Die Kontroverse um die Präventivkriegsthese*, Darmstadt, 1998

Ueberschär, Gerd R. and Wolfram Wette (eds), *Der deutsche Überfall auf die Sowjetunion: 'Unternehmen Barbarossa' 1941*, Frankfurt am Main, 1991

Umbreit, Hans, *Deutsche Militärverwaltung 1938/39: Die militärische Besetzung der Tschechoslowakei und Polens*, Stuttgart, 1977

United States Strategic Bombing Survey, 1, *The Effects of Strategic Bombing on German Morale*, Washington DC, 1947

Usbourne, Cornelie, *The Politics of the Body in Weimar Germany*, New York, 1992

Vaizey, Hester, *Surviving Hitler's War: Family Life in Germany, 1939–48*, Basingstoke, 2010

Vanja, Christina and Martin Vogt (eds), *Euthanasie in Hadamar: Die national-sozialistische Vernichtungspolitik in hessischen Anstalten*, Kassel, 1991

Verhey, Jeffrey, *The Spirit of 1914: Militarism, Myth, and Mobilization in Germany*, Cambridge, 2000

Virgili, Fabrice, *Shorn Women: Gender and Punishment in Liberation France*, Oxford, 2002

Virgili, Fabrice, *Naître ennemi: Les enfants de couples franco-allemands nés pendant la Seconde Guerre mondiale*, Paris, 2009

Vogel, Detlef and Wolfram Wette (eds), *Andere Helme – andere Menschen? Heimaterfahrung und Frontalltag im Zweiten Weltkrieg: Ein internationaler Vergleich*, Essen, 1995

Volkmann, Hans-Erich (ed.), *Ende des Dritten Reiches – Ende des Zweiten Weltkrieges*, Munich, 1995

Vollnhals, Clemens, *Evangelische Kirche und Entnazifizierung 1945–1949*, Munich, 1989

Wachsmann, Nikolaus, '"Annihilation through Labor": The killing of state prisoners in the Third Reich', *Journal of Modern History*, 71 (1999), 624–59

Wachsmann, Nikolaus, *Hitler's Prisons: Legal Terror in Nazi Germany*, New Haven, 2004

Wachsmann, Nikolaus and Jane Caplan (eds), *Concentration Camps in Nazi Germany: The New Histories*, London, 2010

Wagner, Bernd, 'Gerüchte, Wissen, Verdrängung: Die IG Auschwitz und das Vernichtungslager Birkenau', in Norbert Frei, Sybille Steinbacher and Bernd Wagner (eds), *Ausbeutung, Vernichtung, Öffentlichkeit*, Munich, 2000, 231–48

Wagner, Bernd, *IG Auschwitz: Zwangsarbeit und Vernichtung von Häftlingen des Lagers Monowitz 1941–1945*, Munich, 2000

Wagner, Patrick, *Volksgemeinschaft ohne Verbrecher: Konzeption und Praxis der Kriminalpolizei in der Zeit der Weimarer Republik und des Nationalsozialismus*, Hamburg, 1996

Wagner, Ray (ed), *The Soviet Air Force in World War II*, Newton Abbot, 1974

Waite, Robert G., 'Teenage sexuality in Nazi Germany', *Journal of the History of Sexuality*, 8/3 (Jan. 1998), 434–76

Wallach, Jehuda, *The Dogma of the Battle of Annihilation: The Theories of Clausewitz and Schlieffen and their Impact on the German Conduct of Two World Wars*, Westport, Conn., 1986

Walser Smith, Helmut, *The Butcher's Tale: Murder and Anti-Semitism in a German Town*, New York, 2002

Warring, Anette, *Tyskerpiger: Under besoettelse og retsopgør*, Copenhagen, 1994

Wecht, Martin, *Jochen Klepper: Ein Christlicher Schriftsteller im jüdischen Schicksal*, Düsseldorf, 1998

Wegner, Bernd, 'Hitlers "zweiter Feldzug"', *DRZW*, 6 (1990), 761–815

Wegner, Bernd, 'Hitlers Strategie zwischen Pearl Harbor und Stalingrad', *DRZW*, 6 (1990), 97–126

Wegner, Bernd (ed.), *From Peace to War: Germany, Soviet Russia and the World, 1939–1941*, Oxford, 1997

Weinberg, Gerhard L., *A World at Arms: A Global History of World War II*, Cambridge, 1994

Weindling, Paul, *Health, Race, and German Politics between National Unification and Nazism, 1870–1945*, Cambridge, 1989

Welch, David, *Propaganda and the German Cinema, 1933–1945*, Oxford, 1983

Welch, Steven R., '"Harsh but just"? German military justice in the Second World War: A comparative study of the court-martialling of German and US deserters', *German History*, 17/3 (1999), 369–89

Werner, Wolfgang Franz, *'Bleib übrig': Deutsche Arbeiter in der nationalsozialistischen Kriegswirtschaft*, Düsseldorf, 1983

Westenrieder, Norbert, *Deutsche Frauen und Mädchen! Vom Alltagsleben 1933–1945*, Düsseldorf, 1984

Wette, Wolfram, 'Die propagandistische Begleitmusik zum deutschen Überfall auf die Sowjetunion am 22. Juni 1941', in Gerd R. Ueberschär and Wolfram Wette (eds), *Der deutsche Überfall auf die Sowjetunion: 'Unternehmen Barbarossa' 1941*, Frankfurt am Main, 1991, 45–66

Wette, Wolfram, 'Massensterben als "Heldenepos": Stalingrad in der NS-Propaganda', in Wolfram Wette and Gerd R. Ueberschär (eds), *Stalingrad: Mythos und Wirklichkeit einer Schlacht*, Frankfurt am Main, 1992, 43–60

Wette, Wolfram, Ricarda Bremer and Detlef Vogel (eds), *Das letzte halbe Jahr: Stimmungsberichte der Wehrmachtpropaganda 1944/45*, Essen, 2001

Wierling, Dorothee, '"Kriegskinder": Westdeutsch, bürgerlich, männlich?', in Lu Seegers and Jürgen Reulecke (eds), *Die 'Generation der Kriegskinder': Historische Hintergründe und Deutungen*, Giessen, 2009, 141–55

Wiese, Christian and Paul Betts (eds), *Years of Persecution, Years of Extermination: Saul Friedländer and the Future of Holocaust Studies*, London, 2010

Wildt, Michael, 'Gewalt gegen Juden in Deutschland 1933 bis 1939', *Werkstatt Geschichte*, 18 (1997), 59–80

Wildt, Michael, *Generation des Unbedingten: Das Führerkorps des Reichsicherheitshauptamtes*, Hamburg, 2002

Wildt, Michael, *Volksgemeinschaft als Selbstermächtigung: Gewalt gegen Juden in der deutschen Provinz 1919–1939*, Hamburg, 2007

Wildt, Michael, 'Volksgemeinschaft: A Modern Perspective on National Socialist Society', in Martina Steber and Bernhard Gotto (eds), *Visions of Community in Nazi Germany: Social Engineering and Private Lives*, Oxford, 2014, 43–59

Wilhelm, Hans-Heinrich, *Rassenpolitik und Kriegsführung*, Passau, 1991

Williams, Thomas, 'Remaking the Franco-German Borderlands: Historical claims and commemorative practices in the Upper Rhine, 1940–49', D.Phil. thesis, Oxford, 2010

Winkler, Dörte, 'Frauenarbeit versus Frauenideologie: Probleme der weiblichen Erwerbstätigkeit in Deutschland 1930–1945', *Archiv für Sozialgeschichte* 17 (1977), 99–126

Winter Jay and Jean-Louis Robert (eds), *Capital Cities at War: Paris, London, Berlin 1914–1919*, Cambridge, 1997

Wiśniewska, Anna and Czesław Rajca, *Majdanek: The Concentration Camp of Lublin*, Lublin, 1997

Wöhlert, Meike, *Der politische Witz in der NS-Zeit am Beispiel ausgesuchter SD-Berichte und Gestapo-Akten*, Frankfurt, 1997

Wohlfuss, Joshua, *Memorial Book of Rawa Ruska*, Tel Aviv, 1973

Wolf, Gerhard, *Ideologie und Herrschaftsrationalität: Nationalsozialistische Germanisierungspolitik in Polen*, Hamburg, 2012

Wolf, Gerhard, 'Exporting *Volksgemeinschaft*: The *Deutsche Volksliste* in Annexed Upper Silesia', in Martina Steber and Bernhard Gotto (eds), *Visions of Community in Nazi Germany: Social Engineering and Private Lives*, Oxford, 2014, 129–45

Wolters, Rita, *Verrat für die Volksgemeinschaft: Denunziantinnen im Dritten Reich*, Pfaffenweiler, 1996

Yelton, David K., *Hitler's Volkssturm: The Nazi Militia and the Fall of Germany,* *1944–1945,* Lawrence, Kan., 2002

Zagovec, Rafael A., 'Gespräche mit der "Volksgemeinschaft": Die deutsche Kriegsgesellschaft im Spiegel westallierter Frontverhöre', *DRZW,* 9/2 (2005), 289–381

Zahn, Gordon, *German Catholics and Hitler's Wars: A Study in Social Control,* London/New York, 1963

Zayas, Alfred Maurice de, *Die Wehrmacht-Untersuchungsstelle: Unveröffentliche Akten über alliierte Völkerrechtsverletzungen im Zweiten Weltkrieg,* Berlin, 1979

Zeidler, Manfred, *Kriegsende im Osten: Die Rote Armee und die Besetzung Deutschlands östlich von Oder und Neiße 1944/45,* Munich, 1996

Zeller, Bernhard and Friedrich Brüggemann (eds), *Klassiker in finsteren Zeiten* *1933–1945: Eine Ausstellung des Deutschen Literaturarchivs im Schiller-Nationalmuseum, Marbach am Neckar,* 2, Marbach, 1983

Ziemann, Benjamin, 'Fluchten aus dem Konsens zum Durchhalten: Ergebnisse, Probleme und Perspektiven der Erforschung soldatischer Verweigerungsformen in der Wehrmacht 1939–1945', in Rolf-Dieter Müller and Hans-Erich Volkmann (eds), *Hitlers Wehrmacht: Mythos und Realität,* Munich, 1999, 589–613

Ziemann, Benjamin, *Gewalt im Ersten Weltkrieg: Töten – überleben – verweigern,* Essen, 2013

Zierenberg, Malte, *Stadt der Schieber: Der Berliner Schwarzmarkt 1939–1950,* Göttingen, 2008

Zimmermann, John, 'Die Eroberung und Besetzung des deutschen Reiches', *DRZW,* 10/1 (2008), 277–435

Index